THE DOCTORS' BIG BLACK BAG
OF CURES AND REMEDIES

Bottom Line Books
www.BottomLineSecrets.com

Contents

Preface

We are proud to bring you *The Doctors' Big Black Bag of Cures and Remedies,* with the latest low-cost discoveries, best treatments and safest solutions to your health concerns in today's economy.

When you choose a Bottom Line Book, you are turning to a stellar group of experts in a wide range of specialties—medical doctors, naturopathic doctors, alternative practitioners, nutrition experts, research scientists, consumer-health advocates, exercise physiologists, mental-health professionals and health-conscious chefs.

We go to great lengths to interview the foremost health experts. Whether it's cancer prevention, new heart therapies, breakthrough arthritis treatments or cutting-edge nutritional advice, our editors talk to the people who are creating the true innovations in health care.

How do we find all these top-notch medical professionals? Over the past 20 years, we have built a network of literally thousands of leading physicians in both alternative and conventional medicine. They are affiliated with the premier medical institutions throughout the world. We read the important medical journals and follow the latest research that is reported at medical conferences. And we regularly talk to our advisers in major teaching hospitals, private practices and government health agencies.

The Doctors' Big Black Bag of Cures and Remedies is a result of our ongoing research and contact with these experts, including their latest findings and advice. We hope that you will enjoy the presentation and glean new and helpful information about the health topics that concern you and your family.

As a reader of a Bottom Line Book, please be assured that you are receiving reliable and well-researched information from a trusted source. But, please use prudence in health matters. Always speak to your medical practitioner before taking any vitamins, supplements or over-the-counter medication…changing your diet…or beginning an exercise program. If you experience side effects from any regimen, contact your doctor immediately.

1

Natural Remedies

Natural Anxiety Soothers

Mark Blumenthal, founder and executive director of the American Botanical Council has a number of expert suggestions for natural products that are soothing, relaxing and helpful in overcoming anxiety symptoms. Some have even been found to help improve sleep and relieve stress and jitters.

TO HELP YOU RELAX

•**Theanine** is an amino acid found in green tea. A study measured the brain activity of volunteers after a single 200 mg dose of theanine. Researchers reported that the supplement helped generate alpha brain waves, which are usually considered to be associated with relaxation. Theanine (also known as L-theanine) is available in natural food stores.

•**GABA** (*gamma-aminobutyric acid*) is among the most important neurotransmitters in the brain, involved in relaxation and inhibition. In fact many of the pharmaceutical drugs used for treating anxiety, including Valium, act by enhancing the effects of GABA. Some research suggests that as a supplement, GABA works better when combined with other ingredients like theanine. If you can find the two together in a supplement, it makes sense to take them that way.

•**Lemon balm** (a plant, *Melissa officinalis*, in the mint family) is another mild sedative. A recent study of 24 healthy volunteers published in *Phytotherapy Research* found that a single dose of 600 mg of a product combining valerian (*Valeriana officinalis*) and lemon balm reduced reported anxiety.

•**Kava** is from a plant called *Piper methysticum*. Despite controversy associated with its use long-term, kava has a long history as an herbal medicine to relieve anxiety, stress and insomnia. A recent review of randomized clinical trials on herbal remedies that relieve anxiety published in *Phytomedicine* found evidence "beyond reasonable doubt" for kava's effectiveness

Mark Blumenthal is the founder and executive director of the American Botanical Council and the editor of the publication *HerbalGram*. *www.herbalgram.org*.

in the treatment of anxiety. "It relaxes skeletal muscles without causing drowsiness, so you can become physically relaxed but remain mentally sharp within just 15 minutes of taking a product containing kava," Blumenthal says. The recommended kava products are 70% standardized extract, sold in 100 mg doses, thus containing 70 mg of kavalactones (it will say so on the label).

Caution: Don't take kava with alcohol or drugs that have an adverse effect on the liver (e.g., *acetaminophen*, or Tylenol). Also, kava has been associated with some liver problems. It is not considered safe for breastfeeding women, pregnant women or people with a history of liver disease. Consult your doctor before considering kava for long-term use.

•**Lavender** is associated with relaxation, often used as aromatherapy in spas and as an ingredient in supposedly soothing lotions and teas. Just breathing the aroma of natural lavender oil—in a spray or infuser, or as a massage oil—has a mild relaxing effect.

NATURAL SLEEP AIDS

While the above products can help ease tensions during the day, sometimes you need some additional help at night. According to Blumenthal, these sleep inducers may work as well as the popular pharmaceutical drugs, but without their adverse side effects…

•**Valerian** is a natural sleep aid and daytime sedative, that contrary to the popular myth, is not related to the pharmaceutical drug Valium. Small doses of valerian can be used for calming during the day and higher doses as a sleep aid about a half hour before bedtime. Valerian can be taken in combination with lemon balm or other mildly sedative herbs (e.g., chamomile, hops, etc.), which makes it an even more powerful sleep aid.

•**Hops** (*Humulus lupulus*) can also be helpful. Yes, this is the same ingredient used in making beer—it is a gentle sedative that promotes relaxation and is available in pills, as well as in tincture and bulk flower form in health food stores. According to Blumenthal, it can be taken together with valerian.

HELP YOUR DOCTOR HELP YOU

As a general precaution, do not take any of these products while pregnant or breastfeeding.

While all are available at health food stores and on-line, it is important to take them only under the supervision of a trained practitioner. If anxiety and/or insomnia are more than an occasional problem, you may need to take a broader look at your life and make some changes— whether it's delegating responsibilities at home to family members or professionals, or shifting job obligations or saying "no" to some committees. Anxiety is a message that something's not right. Natural or pharmaceutical, nothing will solve such problems except solving the problem itself.

Important: You can't take care of everyone if you don't take care of yourself.

Ginkgo May Help Alleviate Anxiety

Mark A. Stengler, ND, naturopathic physician in private practice, La Jolla, California…adjunct associate clinical professor at the National College of Natural Medicine, Portland, Oregon…author of many books, including *The Natural Physician's Healing Therapies* and coauthor of *Prescription for Natural Cures* (both from Bottom Line Books)…and author of the *Bottom Line/Natural Healing* newsletter.

G inkgo is one of the best-selling supplements in the US right now, thanks to its long history of healing uses. As with many ancient remedies, modern science is now catching up with traditional applications and verifying their efficacy. Current evidence supports the use of ginkgo in the treatment of dementia disorders such as Alzheimer's disease, intermittent claudication (painful legs from clogged arteries) and cerebral insufficiency (decreased blood flow to the brain, also from clogged arteries). Recent research demonstrates that ginkgo may also be helpful in relieving anxiety.

RESEARCH CONFIRMS GINKGO HELPS

Scientists in a German trial looked at 107 people with two kinds of anxiety disorders (generalized anxiety disorder or adjustment disorder with anxious mood, which is the diagnosis for having a hard time dealing with change). Participants were randomly given 480 milligrams (mg) of standardized ginkgo extract…240 mg of standardized ginkgo extract…or a placebo. Before the trial, all scored about the same on a standard measurement of anxiety (approximately 30 points on the Hamilton Rating Scale for Anxiety). After four weeks, those taking the high dose of ginkgo experienced a nearly 50% drop in anxiety (14.3 points)…the lower dose was associated with a decrease of 12.1 points…and the placebo resulted in a 7.8 point decline.

This is a relatively new use for ginkgo and one worthy of consideration, says Mark Stengler, ND, author of *Bottom Line/Natural Healing* newsletter and *The Natural Physician's Healing Therapies*. He believes ginkgo might be especially helpful for people with mild to moderate anxiety, particularly when it is accompanied by memory problems. The mechanism by which ginkgo relieves anxiety is unknown, but Dr. Stengler speculates that it may work by reducing blood levels of the stress hormone cortisol or by enhancing brain neurotransmitter levels.

NOT FOR EVERYONE

While ginkgo is generally safe and can be extremely beneficial, it is best used under the care of a trained professional. Possible side effects may include dizziness, digestive upset, headaches, palpitations, diarrhea or skin rash— and these are more likely to be seen in people taking pharmaceutical drugs including cardiac meds, as well as those with chronic health problems such as IBS or allergies. Even more important, there have been reports of spontaneous internal bleeding with ginkgo.

Note: If you suffer from a bleeding disorder or take blood-thinning drugs such as *warfarin* (Coumadin), aspirin and other NSAIDs, antiplatelet drugs, other prescription drugs or supplements, be sure to consult a qualified health care professional before taking ginkgo. If you're clear to take ginkgo, the prescription of choice is generally a leaf extract product in tincture or capsule form (such as one manufactured by Herb Pharm or Eclectic Institute's fresh freeze-dried extract tablets or capsules).

Echinacea Works, As We've Been Saying All Along

Craig I. Coleman, PharmD, assistant professor of pharmacy practice, University of Connecticut School of Pharmacy, Storrs, Connecticut.

A recent analysis of echinacea studies has concluded that this popular botanical medicine significantly reduces the risk you'll catch a cold and also can cut a cold's duration. Yet it wasn't too long ago that a *New England Journal of Medicine* study stated just the opposite, calling the effects of echinacea not clinically significant in fighting colds. So which report should you trust?

According to Craig I. Coleman, PharmD, assistant professor of pharmacy practice at the University of Connecticut, who helped conduct this latest echinacea research, there are many possible reasons why one individual study might have found this treatment ineffective. For example, there are different types of echinacea, different dosages, different frequencies of dosage, etc. In the case of the *New England Journal of Medicine* study, Dr. Coleman points out that a less effective species of echinacea was used (*Echinacea angustifolia* rather than *Echinacea purpurea*), and at a dosage that was only one third of what was recommended. Moreover, only one of the more than 200 viruses that cause cold symptoms was tested.

THE POTENT PURPLE CONEFLOWER

To learn the truth about echinacea, Dr. Coleman and his colleagues combined data from 14 previous clinical trials involving nearly 3,000 people. Since many studies include less than 100 participants, he notes that the much larger meta-analysis packs more statistical power and is also likely to uncover effects of a treatment that might not have shown up in smaller studies. For the greatest accuracy, researchers also chose only randomized, placebo-controlled and peer reviewed trials—the ones most likely to yield reliable results.

The results were impressive. *Researchers found that…*

•**Echinacea reduces the chance of catching a cold by approximately 58%** when taken prior to or right at the first hint of a cold.

•**If you already have a cold,** taking echinacea can shorten the duration of it by almost a day and a half.

POWERFUL COLD PREVENTION AND TREATMENT

"The take-home message from our study is that echinacea does indeed have powerful cold prevention and treatment benefits," says Dr. Coleman. Yet with more than 800 echinacea products on the market today, he believes more research is needed to determine the best product preparation and proper dosage. Our medical expert, Andrew L. Rubman, ND, says his two favorite echinacea products are by Herb Pharm and Eclectic Institute. For best results, try taking echinacea at the first sign of a cold.

Natural Virus Killers Ease Flu Suffering

Jamison Starbuck, ND, a naturopathic physician practicing in Missoula, Montana. She is a past president of the American Association of Naturopathic Physicians.

Problems associated with the flu vaccine seem to appear annually. Sometimes there's not much that can be done to prevent getting sick, so the challenge is getting through it with as little misery as possible. For information on how to treat the miserable symptoms produced by viruses so your body can heal faster, we called Jamison Starbuck, ND, a naturopathic physician practicing in Missoula, Montana.

Viruses are the tiniest life form in existence—smaller, even, than a single cell. However their impact is huge as they are responsible for various infectious illnesses or diseases, from the common cold to chicken pox to much deadlier ones including HIV.

Natural medications are great at helping the body gear up to fight viruses, says Dr. Starbuck. They work by revving up the white blood cells of the immune system to target the bad guys causing the symptoms, boosting antibody production to encourage it to stop replicating. And, like pharmaceuticals, natural medicines can ease symptoms.

IMMUNE BOOSTING

Echinacea is high on Dr. Starbuck's list for treating viruses. This common immune booster comes in tea, capsules and tincture. Dr. Starbuck recommends the tincture because it is generally more potent and has superior bioavailability. (Test the tincture for freshness by putting a drop on your tongue—it should create a slightly numbing feel. If not, get another bottle. A good choice is Eclectic Institute's Specific Echinacea.)

Dr. Starbuck most often prescribes echinacea tincture to be taken by her patients at the first sign of sickness as follows: Place about 30 drops into an ounce of water...take every four hours away from meals. It's a good idea to drink additional water as well.

More: Dr. Starbuck often uses echinacea in combination with other herbs, too. She advises *Ligusticum porteri* (also named Osha root) to soothe congested tissue and stimulate circulation, again usually prescribing its tincture form. You can find "do it yourself" anti-viral herbal formulas prepared with one or several immune-strengthening herbs in natural stores such as Whole Foods Market. Dr. Starbuck likes the herbal mix Throat Mist for sore throats by Wise Woman Herbals (*www.wisewomanherbals.com*). Take these herbs at the first sign of sickness. The sooner you catch the virus, the easier it is to fight back—as always, under the oversight of a physician trained in natural healing.

VITAMIN POWER

Vitamin C does more than any other vitamin to boost immune function. Vitamin A is helpful in moistening mucus membranes in the upper respiratory tract.

Note: Too much vitamin A can be toxic. Dr. Starbuck advises her patients to get beta-carotene, the water soluble, precursor molecule of vitamin A, by eating foods that are high in it rather than taking vitamin A in supplement form. One way is to drink fresh carrot juice (two ounces, twice a day), or blend it with fresh orange juice for a combined A/C hit. Oranges, tangerines and, in fact, orange-colored produce of any kind (including pumpkin and sweet potatoes) are helpful. You can continue vitamin therapy for two to three weeks.

MANAGING FEVER

Fever is the body's natural weapon for killing viruses, so it's best to let it do its work. However, if a fever becomes too uncomfortable for you or your child (adults get fevers far less often) or if it is sudden, higher than is typical for you when you get sick or causes bright red cheeks, it may require treatment. Be sure to alert your physician to the fever, as an intense one may require suppression and even hospitalization. Dr. Starbuck says that she often prescribes just one dose of the homeopathic substance Belladonna—typically two pellets of 30C strength—which frequently takes care of a high fever. However, for fevers that are low grade, persistent and dragging you down, she may prescribe the homeopathic substance Gelsemium sempervirens, also 30C strength, two pellets at one time.

KEEPING SYMPTOMS AT BAY

For a runny nose and cold, Dr. Starbuck prescribes ginger or usnea, herbs that dry out the mucus and provide antiseptic properties. *She also directs her patients as follows...*

Vaporizing or steam will help thin out mucus and keep it flowing—use a humidifier or simply a bowl or pan of just-boiled water to which you can add one or two drops of eucalyptus or lavender essential oil or several peppermint tea bags. Drape a towel over your head and stand over the water, to breathe in its steam, taking care to avoid burning, of course. For patients suffering from a sore throat that feels hot and dry, Dr. Starbuck prescribes slippery elm, licorice or marshmallow root—all moistening herbs. A cool mist humidifier can also help.

Also: Saline solutions, including nasal sprays, can help break up mucus. For a more exotic approach, Dr. Starbuck often prescribes treatment with the neti pot, used in the practice of ancient ayurvedic medicine. When Mehmet Oz, MD, discussed how to use one on *The Oprah Winfrey Show* last year, these were boosted nearly into the "trendy" category as the must-have saline irrigation system. The neti pot resembles a teapot to be filled with four ounces of saline solution and poured into one nostril, thereby forcing mucus out of the other. Dr. Starbuck often directs her patients to add a quarter teaspoon of combined echinacea and eyebright tincture to the saline packet mix.

GENERAL RULES

When fighting a virus, it is good to give your digestive tract a break. Avoid proteins and fats—which are hard to digest, as well as dairy products—which create mucus. Warm up by eating hot foods—preferably soups, steamed vegetables and the like and, of course, drink lots of fluids. Get plenty of sleep and don't forego exercise, says Dr. Starbuck. Though a hard workout will only stress your already overstressed body, do get outside twice a day for a 15-minute relaxed walk in sunlight and fresh air.

You can protect others from your virus by washing your hands throughout the day and always after you blow your nose. Don't go to work when you are feeling sick since you'll expose your colleagues and prolong your misery. Dr. Starbuck points out that illness will disappear faster if you take care of yourself. Instead of being sick a week or longer, you can feel better in three to five days with rest and proper natural care.

More from Jamison Starbuck...

Treating Seasonal Allergies Naturally

Actifed, Benadryl, Claritin...you could make an alphabet book with the names of allergy medications drugstores sell to soothe seasonal symptoms. But all have side effects that can be as annoying as the sniffles and sneezes they treat. So, why not review some natural therapies for treating allergy symptoms?

Caution: As regular readers have heard before, using "natural" treatments for anything—allergies included—doesn't make this a do-it-yourself solution. Natural doesn't automatically mean safe and dosages must be adjusted to your individual needs by your own naturopathic physician. For broad advice on this topic we asked Jamison Starbuck, ND. She practices natural and holistic medicine in Missoula, Montana, is a past president of the American Association of Naturopathic Physicians, and has lots of helpful suggestions to discuss with your own doctor.

SOME TREATMENTS THAT HELP

Dr. Starbuck recommends assorted supplements to quell her patients' symptoms…

•**Quercetin.** Abundant in apples, citrus fruits, raspberries, black and green tea, grapes and red wine, this bioflavonoid has the capacity to strengthen the capillaries in the upper respiratory tract to make them less reactive to the airborne particles, including pollens or spores from grasses, weeds, trees and ragweed that trigger many allergic symptoms. Quercetin's anti-inflammatory capacity is especially helpful because some people prone to allergies simply have highly reactive mucus membranes, meaning they have a low tolerance for irritation. "Quercetin supports the immune system at the same time it helps to decrease inflammation," explains Dr. Starbuck. "Patients have told me that using quercetin alone has made a huge difference in their symptoms and suffering."

Note: This super bioflavonoid is inexpensive and available in capsule form at health food stores. Remember that quercetin may interact with certain drugs. Check with your doctor.

•**Vitamin C.** The anti-inflammatory and free-radical-quenching capacities of vitamin C decrease the release of histamines, which our bodies generate to manage allergic insults like pollen.

Important: Dr. Starbuck cautions that at higher dosages of this super-power vitamin, some people may notice a loosening of the bowels—if you're among them, ask your doctor to cut you back to a lower dose.

GARDEN VARIETY TREATMENTS

•**Stinging nettle.** This flowering plant is gaining popularity in its freeze-dried form as being moderately effective in soothing allergy symptoms. There's not much research supporting this—a study from the National College of Natural Medicine in Portland indicated it might have a mild helpful effect—but stinging nettle has a long history in traditional medicine as treatment for allergies, among other conditions. The fact that it also has an anti-inflammatory effect leads many practitioners to prescribe stinging nettle as part of a total natural treatment for allergies. It's most

effective if taken at the first sign of symptoms, says Dr. Starbuck, who has used it for years and finds it helps her patients.

Caution: If you are taking blood thinners like Coumadin or if you have diabetes, stinging nettle should be used very carefully. A small percentage of people are allergic, so if stinging nettle makes you feel worse, talk to your doctor. You can be tested for a nettle allergy. Pregnant women should avoid it.

•**Eyebright (Euphrasia).** This herb has been used as a compress to treat eye infections and irritation for hundreds of years. Dr. Starbuck points out that it's also effective when taken orally in a tincture for treatment of inflammation of nasal mucus membranes and sinuses.

AND NOW TO THE KITCHEN

•**Food allergies.** Though seasonal allergies and food allergies seem to be distinctly different entities, Dr. Starbuck explains that it is important to realize that they're not unrelated. "Seasonal allergies are definitely aggravated by food allergies and sensitivities," she says. Allergy sufferers should be aware that problem foods can amplify seasonal allergies so you should try eliminating the usual offenders, at least temporarily. "Dairy, wheat, corn and soy are all mucus-producing foods," she adds. They can make seasonal allergies like hay fever worse—avoiding them can make a big difference. Also avoid foods that contain mold (such as blue cheese) since these, too, can trigger allergy symptoms.

•**Chamomile tea.** This sleepy-time favorite soothes mucus-membrane activity, which will help allergy victims feel more comfortable.

Note: Chamomile tea can cause allergic reactions in those allergic to ragweed.

•**Decongestant snack.** Finally, Dr. Starbuck offers her own recipe for a homemade decongestant snack. Mix water and organic honey together (in a 50-50 mix), bring it to a simmer. Add to this the peels of organic grapefruit, lemons and oranges. These, she says, "are absolutely loaded with bioavailable quercetin and other bioflavonoids." Leave to simmer for 20 minutes. Once they've cooled, the peels are sweet, soft, and beyond delicious—keep them in the fridge for a healthy treat. The remaining liquid can be reheated and enjoyed as a beverage.

Natural Mood Elevators

Mark Blumenthal, founder and executive director of the American Botanical Council and editor of the publication *HerbalGram*.

Eric Yarnell, ND, president of the Botanical Medicine Academy and is ND clinical supervisor at Bastyr Center for Natural Health, both in Seattle, WA. He is coauthor of *Clinical Botanical Medicine*. Mary Ann Liebert.

Ads for antidepressants make it seem as though the most logical solution for a case of the blues is to seek a prescription. Pharmaceutical drugs may be helpful—even necessary—for people with severe depression, but for others, there are natural solutions that may work even better, with less risk of adverse side effects. Dietary supplements and lifestyle changes can be used to naturally lift your spirits.

NATURE CAN HEAL

"I think that a lot of our modern-day fatigue and depression has to do with the fact that we're totally separated from nature," suggests Eric Yarnell, ND, president of the Botanical Medicine Academy and coauthor of *Clinical Botanical Medicine*. "People don't eat well, they watch huge amounts of television and don't spend much time relating to people or the outdoors." He believes that eating plenty of whole, unprocessed foods and getting regular exercise are the first steps to take in attempting to boost your mood and energy level. "I tell people to turn off their televisions," he adds, noting that replacing TV with even 15 minutes of daily outdoor activity and sunlight will help, as will getting enough sleep.

According to Jonny Bowden, CNS, author of *The Most Effective Natural Cures on Earth*, many foods that are commonly thought to give us energy actually don't. "Foods that are processed and contain lots of sugar or white flour raise blood sugar temporarily, which feels good, but then set us up for a crash of energy and mood," he says. "Foods higher in protein (like grass-fed beef, chicken or fish) and higher in healthy fats (like nuts) will raise and sustain energy better."

But it is, as always, a matter of balance. Our medical expert, Andrew L. Rubman, ND, points out that an extreme low-carb diet can actually kick off fatigue: "Often, if people go overboard on an Atkins-esque high-protein regimen, they end up feeling lethargic, which in turn affects mood."

SUPPLEMENTS THAT HELP

Eating whole foods with little or no added sugar, exercising (even a bit) and getting some moderate sun exposure are all highly effective ways to beat the blues and lift the spirits. Some people, however, still feel like there are times when they need a more controllable lift—and for them, Dr. Yarnell says there are natural supplements that really do help. Research supports three, in particular—St. John's wort (*Hypericum perforatum*), Golden Root (*Rhodiola rosea*) and eleuthero (*Eleutherococcus senticosus*).

ST. JOHN'S WORT

A meta-analysis published in the *British Medical Journal* reviewed 23 trials on St. John's wort involving more than 1,700 patients, with researchers reporting it was more effective than a placebo at treating mild to moderately severe cases of depression. "The evidence is very strong that St. John's wort is an effective natural antidepressant for people whose depression is mild," says Mark Blumenthal, founder and executive director of the nonprofit American Botanical Council. This distinction is an important one, he notes—recalling how the reputation of St. John's wort was sullied by a study published in the *Journal of the American Medical Association* that called it ineffective. Blumenthal explains that this particular study had examined a group of patients that included those already unresponsive to treatment with a conventional antidepressant drug, so their depression was quite severe.

Caution: Those with severe depression should seek medical advice to ensure proper treatment and monitoring. "St. John's wort interacts with a whole suite of conventional pharmaceutical drugs," cautions Blumenthal, "so you must check with your health care provider about any possible interactions before taking it." Your prescriber will quite likely recommend preparations standardized to contain 0.3% hypericin, a naturally occurring compound in St. John's wort to which manufacturers standardize their extracts for quality control purposes. And, if you are scheduled to have elective surgery, make sure you discontinue this supplement ahead of time.

RHODIOLA ROSEA/GOLDENROOT

In Europe, *Rhodiola rosea* or *R. rosea*, the best known and most studied of different species of Rhodiola (also called goldenroot), has a long history of being used to treat chronic fatigue, especially in Sweden and Russia. One interesting study tested the effect of 170 mg of *R. rosea* root extract on 56 physicians who were on stressful night-call duty. *R. rosea* brought about a statistically significant reduction in general fatigue for the first two weeks—but the positive effect seemed to fade by six weeks, suggesting it might be a good short-term solution that is helpful for acute stressful conditions but not for chronic stress. An experienced naturopath can provide advice on what's the best dosage in your case.

As for depression, a recent clinical trial found that *R. rosea* can also work as an antidepressant and mood elevator. In this Swedish study, *R. rosea* extract was found to not only help reduce symptoms of depression in patients with mild to moderate depression, but also to enhance their cognitive and sexual function, as well as their mental and physical performance under stress.

ELEUTHERO

There is some debate about eleuthero, also known as Siberian ginseng (although it is no longer marketed under that name in the US). Blumenthal is not enthusiastic about eleuthero, calling it "not great" for fatigue, but Dr. Yarnell believes it's effective, doesn't have significant adverse effects and works "to balance people's systems." One clinical study evaluated 96 adults who had complained of fatigue for at least six months. They were given four capsules per day of eleuthero. While some reported their fatigue lessened considerably, the results were not statistically significant…though two sub-groups in the population—those with longstanding fatigue and those with less severe fatigue—experienced some effect from the treatment after two months.

ASK YOUR DOCTOR

Natural supplements aren't necessarily risk-free and so it is vitally important to seek supervision by a physician experienced in their use —good advice for addressing moods or physical ailments. You may find these products can be very beneficial and produce less adverse effects than pharmaceutical ones…but use them responsibly.

Aromatherapy Helps Heal Cancer Patients

Cherie Perez, RN, quality assurance specialist in the department of GU Medical Oncology at M.D. Anderson Cancer Center in Houston.

Like so many New Age practices and beliefs, aromatherapy has ancient roots. The use of essential oils to affect mood and well-being can be found far back in Egyptian, Greek and Roman history. In fact, when the three kings of biblical fame brought gifts, including gold, to baby Jesus, their other highly prized offerings were frankincense and myrrh …resins from these herbs are still in use today. While scientific evidence about aromatherapy is scant, its long-standing role in spirituality and healing, along with strong anecdotal support of its modern-day benefits, gives essential oils an important role as a complementary alternative medicine therapy.

Cherie Perez, RN, quality assurance specialist in the department of GU Medical Oncology at M.D. Anderson Cancer Center in Houston, is a strong proponent of aromatherapy, including as an adjunct for cancer treatment. She teaches monthly classes for patients on the topic. Used properly, Perez says essential oils can indirectly help bolster immune function in cancer patients, strengthening their ability to fight back against the disease by helping to ease pain, depression, sleeplessness and stress. The oils can also help relieve anxiety and improve memory—both frequent problems for people in cancer treatment as well as those who are healthy. Furthermore, aromatherapy offers patients an opportunity to take time for themselves and enjoy a mental and emotional break from their world of medicines and doctors.

ESSENTIALS ABOUT ESSENTIAL OILS

Some of the most popular essential oils include rosemary, eucalyptus, lavender and chamomile. They have various scents such as floral, minty, citrus and masculine—and Perez advises using the ones you like best among the choices indicated for a specific treatment, since more than one oil may address the same problem. She explains that the limbic system, which the sense of smell triggers, is the emotional seat of the brain, which is the reason why people often respond strongly to certain scents—positively or negatively. Lavender, for example, might bring back warm memories of a trip to Provence, or sour thoughts about a dour relative who wore it as a fragrance.

BEST PRACTICES

All oils are highly concentrated distillations of plant parts, including the flowers, leaves, branches and roots. Because they are so potent (hundreds of times more concentrated than the culinary fresh or dried herb or herbal teas, and therefore easy to overdose on) they should be used only under the supervision of a knowledgeable practitioner, such as a naturopathic physician, registered nurse, massage therapist, clinical herbalist or aromatherapist. Essential oils can be inhaled (safest with a simple diffuser), enjoyed in your bath or massaged onto your skin (but never directly in their undiluted form…because they can cause a rash or burning sensation).

Oils may come already diluted, and will say so on the ingredient label, but you can also dilute a pure oil yourself. Add three drops of an essential oil to a half tablespoon of scentless organic vegetable oil (such as sunflower or safflower) or to an unscented body lotion. People with sensitive skin should do a skin test before topical use. How much to dilute an oil depends on the type of oil and your skin's sensitivity. Thyme, for example, is quite irritating to some people, so it should be used more sparingly and with caution, whereas lavender is nonirritating to nearly everyone, says Perez. Citrus oils may cause sensitivity to sunlight, so avoid skin application if you are going to be in the sun. Because they're so pretty and fragrant and highly toxic if ingested, they should be kept where children cannot reach them.

MENU OF OPTIONS

Here's a list of popular oils that address some common problems, as well as those common among people in treatment for cancer…

• **Lavender.** Great as a general relaxant, it also treats migraines and relieves stress. It is excellent for insomnia resulting from cancer treatment.

• **Rosemary.** For muscle pain, low blood pressure (do not use if you have uncontrolled or high blood pressure) and cold feet and hands. Rosemary aids a loss of appetite.

• **Spearmint.** Used to ease nausea and to help digestion. Also can help ease gas and other treatment-related digestive problems.

• **Eucalyptus or peppermint.** For rubbing on sore muscles. Eucalyptus may also help joints, including arthritic ones. Eucalyptus may increase the absorption of certain cancer drugs that are applied topically, so use caution and try a patch test first, avoiding application to the same area as the cancer drug.

• **Pink grapefruit or juniper berry.** Used with massage to encourage lymphatic drainage of toxins and waste. Pink grapefruit is one of Perez's favorites for cancer patients, as she believes it helps energize them and raise their spirits. This and all citrus-type oils should be avoided during chemo and radiation—and should not be used until speaking with your doctor.

• **Lemongrass, tea tree and orange.** Mix together into two cups of Epsom salts. Use five drops of each oil—a total of 15 drops—for a soothing bath (use one-half cup per bath).

Helpful: Aromatherapy has become so popular that essential oils are now widely available, including in health food stores and supermarkets. However, Perez advises that it is far better to purchase them from a shop with a staff knowledgeable in aromatherapy. Oils should come in dark blue or brown glass containers, which prevent light or heat damage. Avoid bottles with rubber droppers—the rubber breaks down and contaminates the oil. Finally, the label should feature both the common and the botanical name of the oil (for example, Peppermint/Mentha piperita).

If you would like to learn more about how to incorporate aromatherapy in your life, Perez recommends *The Complete Book of Essential Oils &*

Aromatherapy, by Valerie Ann Worwood (New World Library), which she says is both thorough and easily understood. Again, as in the case with skin sensitivities, people with asthma or allergies need to avoid things that might trigger an attack—for example, chamomile is in the ragweed family.

Important: People who want to try inhalation aromatherapy should use only a few drops (two to three) of essential oils in a basin of water or diffuser, or on a napkin. And—always consult with your doctor before using aromatherapy or any complementary therapy.

Fish Oil Helps Post–Heart Attack

Laurence S. Sperling, MD, associate professor of medicine at Emory University School of Medicine, and founder and director of Preventive Cardiology at the Emory Clinic, Atlanta, Georgia.

In Europe, it's considered routine for a doctor to prescribe fish oil—which contains omega-3 fatty acids—usually in addition to other medical interventions to increase the odds of survival after someone suffers a heart attack. In contrast, most Americans who have heart attacks are treated primarily with expensive drugs and invasive procedures. An increasing number of cardiologists in this country now agree it may be time to more aggressively add safe, effective and inexpensive fish oils to the standard mix of post-heart attack treatments.

For expert advice, we asked Laurence S. Sperling, MD, associate professor of medicine at Emory University School of Medicine and director of Preventive Cardiology at the Emory Clinic in Atlanta, Georgia. "Not only do I agree with this approach," says Dr. Sperling, "the American Heart Association (AHA) recommends omega-3 fatty acids from fish for those without coronary heart disease (CHD)…and that those with CHD consume it preferably from fish, or through supplements under doctor supervision." Doctor-supervised supplementation is recommended for those with high triglycerides.

A SAFE, LOW-TECH APPROACH

The AHA confirms that consuming fatty fish (such as salmon, herring, trout and sardines) or fish oil supplements has been shown to reduce coronary heart disease mortality in those with coronary disease. *Omega-3s work by…*

•**Reducing inflammation.**

•**Decreasing stickiness of blood platelets** that can lead to the clots that cause heart attacks and strokes.

•**Slowing the growth of atherosclerotic plaque**—the deposits in the arteries.

•**Decreasing triglyceride levels.**

The AHA suggests that people with no known coronary heart disease should eat fish at least twice a week to reduce cardiovascular risk, and advises people who have existing heart disease to have one gram of fish oil daily containing the omega-3 fatty acids eicosapentaenoic acid (EPA) and docosahexaenoic acid (DHA) or consume fish with 1 g of EPA and DHA. Omega-3 activity varies widely across species and location of the fish (the colder the water the fish lives in, the higher the concentration of omega-3 in its tissues). For example, 2 to 4½ oz. of salmon contains 1 g of EPA and DHA…1½ to 2 oz. of herring contains 1 g…and 3 to 3½ oz. of trout contains 1 g. But some deep water fish are contaminated with toxins such as mercury, PCBs and dioxins. For information on the toxin levels of specific fish, go to *www.oceansalive.org.*

Note: According to the FDA, up to 3 grams a day of EPA or DHA from fish oil is generally recognized as safe. Fish oil supplements are largely free of toxins, since the oil is processed to remove them.

WHAT TO LOOK FOR IN A SUPPLEMENT

Fortunately, it's not necessary to buy the most expensive supplement to get a quality fish oil. Look for supplements that contain both EPA and DHA (such as Nordic Naturals and Pharmax products)…are molecularly distilled (so they are generally contaminant-free)…are encapsulated under nitrogen—which makes for a less fishy aroma and taste than when manufactured with oxygen…are highly concentrated—so you can take fewer capsules…and are verified by the United States Pharmacopeia (USP), which sets quality standards for pharmaceuticals and dietary supplements.

Of course, as with any dietary supplement, you must check with your doctor before adding fish oil to your health regimen—especially if you have other chronic diseases and/or are taking medication. That said, fish oil can be a safe, effective, inexpensive and low-tech addition to the expensive, invasive and high-tech approach commonly used to heal heart attack patients in this country.

B Vitamins Get A+ Results for MS

Shinjiro Kaneko, MD, PhD, research fellow at Children's Hospital, Boston.

Allen C. Bowling, MD, PhD, medical director of the Multiple Sclerosis Service and director of The Complementary and Alternative Medicine Service at the Colorado Neurological Institute. He is author of *Complementary and Alternative Medicine and Multiple Sclerosis*. Demos Medical Publishing.

An astounding 400,000 Americans have multiple sclerosis, and the classic profile can appear daunting. Typically, it strikes people between the ages of 20 and 50, and two-thirds of them are women. Most MS patients are Caucasian of northern European descent, and having a sibling with MS greatly increases the risk for developing it. After an initial struggle, most MS patients are able to return to regular activities—except for the days when fatigue interferes. There isn't much conventional doctors can offer for treatment to ease symptoms and stall the disease, and what drugs are available come with difficult side effects, such as fever, chills, muscle aches and fatigue. But hope—in the form of an everyday vitamin—may be in the offing for the many who have MS.

WHAT IS MS?

The complexity of MS has puzzled scientists for decades. Given that mostly women are affected, do hormones play a role? There is surely a genetic connection, but what? Scientists concur that MS is an inflammatory disease of the central nervous system (brain and spinal cord). It causes lesions to develop, apparently at random, on various spots on the nerve fibers (called axons). These lesions degenerate the myelin—material that coats and insulates nerves—damaging the ability of the axons to do their job, which is to transmit communication signals to and from the brain to nerves in the spinal column and elsewhere.

Because lesions can develop on axons anywhere in the central nervous system, they can affect a variety of signals…consequently MS has a wide and lengthy list of possible symptoms. These include fatigue, visual impairment, difficulty walking, spasticity, emotional and cognitive changes, pain and digestive problems. For most patients MS disease progression is slow, and their symptoms come and go (a pattern that vividly illustrates the concept of good days and bad), but about one-third of patients eventually need a wheelchair.

HOPEFUL FINDINGS

Until the early '90s there was no treatment for MS, but now there are several drugs that help reduce inflammation or preserve myelin in the early phase of the disease. However, these come with serious side effects and none have been successful in stopping the degeneration of axons that occurs in the later disease phase, which causes the greatest disability. Adding to frustration in the last few years, there were several promising medications that ultimately failed to deliver. All this makes a recent study on a common and inexpensive substance (that's unlikely to cause side effects) particularly exciting. Scientists at Children's Hospital Boston, affiliated with Harvard Medical School, have been working with a form of vitamin B-3 (commonly known as niacin) that seems not only to fight inflammation and stop myelin loss, but also appears to halt axon degeneration.

A BRIEF BACKGROUND

A coenzyme named *nicotinamide adenine dinucleotide* (NAD) is present in every cell. It is used by the body to produce energy. The precursor of NAD is nicotinamide, which is a form of vitamin B-3 closely related to niacin.

For the latest studies, scientists bred mice to have an MS-like disease. When the researchers administered nicotinamide to the mice, it increased NAD levels in their nervous systems, delaying the onset of neurological disability. The more NAD the mice had when symptoms developed, the less neurological damage they suffered. Conversely, the mice with the least NAD had the most neurological damage. Furthermore, the scientists found strong evidence that nicotinamide protected against damage to the axons in the later chronic disease stage as well.

THERE'S MORE TO LEARN

According to Shinjiro Kaneko, MD, PhD, a research fellow at Children's Hospital and lead author of the mice studies, this research is an extension of some they had done in the lab in vitro with the same results. Although B-3 (niacin) is often used by people who are trying to reduce high cholesterol levels, Dr. Kaneko says that this is the first study that researches how B-3 might be used in treating MS. The obvious question is whether B-3 should now be taken by all MS patients, but Dr. Kaneko explains that the doses they administered to the mice in their studies were substantially higher than people normally take. Until clinical trials have been done to investigate further, it is too early to make that suggestion.

Allen C. Bowling, MD, PhD, medical director of the Multiple Sclerosis Service at the Colorado Neurological Institute, agrees with Dr. Kaneko that, based on these studies, it is too early to recommend B-3 to MS patients. He adds that studies on other substances have seemed promising, and turned out not to be, so we need to wait and see about B-3.

However, our medical expert, Andrew L. Rubman, ND, says that a standard B complex vitamin regimen may be a useful intervention, under proper medical supervision. "A whole body approach that complements the additional B vitamins with diet, lifestyle and additional supplementation support will typically produce a much greater chance of success," he points out. "Giving an intervention of high levels of B-3 without substantive support from a broad-spectrum B supplement will not produce impressive outcomes."

Stay tuned: While further research projects need to be done, at the moment, it is promising enough that we can expect more good news coming out soon.

Asian Herb May Fight Urinary Infections

Soman N. Abraham, PhD, professor, department of pathology, Duke University Medical Center, Durham, North Carolina.

With their typical symptoms such as burning urination, a frequent urge to urinate and a general feeling of being unwell, urinary tract infections (UTIs) are an especially unpleasant problem for women. An estimated one in five women develop a UTI at some point during their lifetime and—even worse—many go on to have infection after infection, for UTIs are notoriously stubborn and often difficult to completely eliminate.

While many women rely on cranberry juice to avoid or ease their UTIs, there is another herbal remedy that might turn out to be even more effective—the Asian herb forskolin, an extract from the Indian coleus plant. Researchers at Duke University in Durham, North Carolina, have found that this herbal extract, which is commonly found in weight loss aids or bodybuilding products, may also help flush harmful bacteria from the bladder lining. Forskolin has a long history of medicinal use in Asia for ailments such as painful urination.

FLUSHING OUT HIDDEN BACTERIA

Nearly eight out of 10 uncomplicated UTIs are caused by *Escherichia coli*—better known as *E. coli*—bacteria. Even when you take antibiotics, UTIs often hang on or return, and as many as one in five women experience another infection, with some women getting three or more in one year. Why? According to Duke University Medical Center professor and study author Soman N. Abraham, PhD, many *E. coli* and other disease-causing pathogens avoid elimination from antibiotics by "hiding" within the cells of the bladder mucosa.

Dr. Abraham and his colleagues tested the effects of forskolin alone in reducing urinary tract infections in experimental mice. They discovered that the extract appeared to flush out more than 75% of hidden *E. coli* in mice bladders. Once flushed out of cells, these pathogens can be eliminated in the urine and/or readily killed by antibiotics.

DON'T TRY
THIS AT HOME

Although forskolin is a common herbal extract that can be purchased over-the-counter at health food stores, it hasn't been studied for efficacy for UTIs in humans. Forskolin has other effects on the body as well. It is a potent anticoagulant and reduces of intraocular pressure and blood pressure in some. Research is ongoing at Duke, and only time will tell if forskolin will come to play a role in eradicating UTIs. Until we know for sure, Dr. Abraham does not advise using it for urinary tract infections.

New, Natural Fix for Canker Sores

Jeff Haley, the inventor of CankerMelts, founder and chief scientist, OraHealth Corporation, the company that makes CankerMelts, based in Bellevue, Washington.

Michael D. Martin, DMD, MA, MSD, MPH, PhD, professor of oral medicine, University of Washington, Seattle, Washington.

How miserable a malady makes you is not always commensurate with how serious it is. The common belief regarding canker sores is that nothing but time heals them. The traditional painkillers and mouth-numbing agents like *benzocaine* (Anbesol) help symptoms a bit, but not for long. Now there's an all-natural remedy that's getting good reviews called CankerMelts. Based on traditional herbal medicine, CankerMelts are a patented, dissolving oral patch made from licorice root, among other ingredients. To learn more about this product, we consulted Jeff Haley, its inventor, and Michael D. Martin, DMD, MA,

MSD, MPH, PhD, the investigator who ran a clinical trial of CankerMelts at the University of Washington.

Unless they become infected, canker sores are not dangerous…but they really, really hurt. These shallow, painful mouth ulcers typically appear on the inside of your lips or cheeks, the base of your gums or under your tongue, as opposed to fever blisters, which are outside on your lips or at the corners of your mouth. Some believe canker sores have a genetic basis in that they can run in the family, but they're not contagious. Although anyone can develop them, they appear in women more than men, and in teens and young adults more than older adults. The cause isn't known but canker sores often arise during periods of stress and around the menses. They also may be triggered by poor nutrition and food allergies.

ABOUT CANKERMELTS

CankerMelts provide short-term relief within minutes by coating the sore with collagen. *Glycyrrhiza* extract, derived from licorice root, provides medium-term relief with its anti-inflammatory action, says Haley, noting that previous canker sore treatments such as benzocaine merely numb the area temporarily. Also, the older topical ointments are messy and may sting when applied.

Dr. Martin explains that licorice root contains natural anti-inflammatory properties. This itself, applied directly, may do the trick, even without the other ingredients. Collagen makes up the structure of the cells that line the mouth—and also sticks very well to itself, helping the CankerMelts disc to stick in place. As collagen molecules are released from the disc, they provide a soothing coating to the ulcer. This, along with other active ingredients such as flavonoids, accounts for the pain-relieving and healing qualities of CankerMelts.

TESTING HOW CANKERMELTS WORK

The University of Washington trial included 46 chronic canker sore sufferers who currently had an active sore. Half the participants applied CankerMelts, adhering the discs on or near the canker sores for, on average, eight hours daily. The other half used no canker sore treatment. At the first visit just prior to beginning treatment and then two, three and seven days afterward, the researchers asked both groups to rate their pain and also checked and photographed the sores. After three days, 81% of the group that used CankerMelts reported they no longer had pain, double the number in the no treatment group. After seven days, treated ulcers shrank by 90%, while the non-treated ulcers had grown larger.

As with most treatments, the earlier applied, the faster the relief. Haley claims that Canker-Melts can "stop a canker sore dead in its tracks" if used early enough, preventing pain and inflammation altogether. But even with larger sores that require multiple discs to treat, significant pain relief comes almost immediately and healing is accelerated. They are relatively inexpensive (about $8 for 12 discs, which should be enough to cope with an average sore). They are available at drugstores such as Rite Aid and natural food stores.

Helpful: Our medical expert, Andrew L. Rubman, ND, advises to make sure you are getting plenty of antioxidants—zinc and essential fatty acids (EFAs), in particular. These not only help healing but may also discourage canker sores from developing.

Homeopathic First Aid

Mark A. Stengler, ND, naturopathic physician in private practice, La Jolla, California…adjunct associate clinical professor at the National College of Natural Medicine, Portland, Oregon…author of many books, including *The Natural Physician's Healing Therapies* and coauthor of *Prescription for Natural Cures* (both from Bottom Line Books)…and author of the *Bottom Line/Natural Healing* newsletter.

Homeopathic medicine draws on exactly the same principles as vaccines and allergy treatments, though it is usually considered "alternative." All three are based on the principle that "like cures like," where exposure to a small amount of a substance, disease or allergen provokes a reaction in the patient that then serves to protect against it.

This concept is at the core of homeopathy, a medical tradition growing increasingly popular.

THE BASIC PRINCIPLE: LIKE CURES LIKE

In homeopathy, pain or symptoms of an illness are understood to be how the body tries to heal itself. This approach to medicine seeks in the short term to stimulate—not discourage—natural healing mechanisms, such as fever and inflammation. Using the "law of similars," the tiny remedy pellets incite many of the symptoms that characterize the illness the body is battling in order to stimulate the healing process. This is very different from conventional medicine, which instead acts to suppress symptoms.

Homeopathic remedies are made from plants, minerals and animal products. The usual homeopathic dosage is two pellets of a 12C or 30C potency ("C" potency is a 1/100 dilution) two to four times a day—but it's important to carefully follow package directions or the dosing instructions of a trained homeopath. Remedies are dissolved under the tongue. Avoid touching the pills with your hands, since contact with dirt or oil on the skin may deactivate the material—instead try pouring them into the plastic lid of the container and from there, into your mouth.

Note: Once symptoms begin to respond, stop taking the remedy and see if an improvement settles in. If some symptoms remain, you may then clear them altogether by taking the remedy a little longer. For acute attacks look for improvement within minutes to an hour…for chronic disease it may take one to two weeks to notice improvement.

DR. STENGLER'S FAVORITE REMEDIES

One big supporter of homeopathy is Mark Stengler, ND, author of *Bottom Line Natural Healing* newsletter and *The Natural Physician's Healing Therapies*. He regularly talks about the value of these remedies in his practice. *Here are some of his favorites…*

•**Apis—for skin reactions.** Derived from the venom of the honeybee, Dr. Stengler prescribes Apis for stinging, burning, swelling and itching. It may be useful for bee stings, arthritis, urinary tract infections, herpes, sore throat, hives and other allergic reactions. This is an example of how a remedy can sometimes work for disparate ailments, since similar biochemical processes are at root.

Note: Apis does not replace conventional medical treatment for severe allergic reactions.

●**Arnica—for bruises and muscle aches.** If Dr. Stengler had to choose just one homeopathic medicine to use, it would be Arnica. This anti-inflammatory preparation made from the mountain daisy is excellent at soothing bruises, aches, pains, swelling and other physical trauma. It also may provide relief for muscle soreness, such as from exercise. A recent study showed that Arnica helps recovery from plastic surgery. Arnica is also available as a topical cream or gel.

●**Cantharis—for burns.** This preparation from the blister beetle is used for burns and urinary tract infections. The beetle contains the chemical cantharidin, which when concentrated causes blisters and skin inflammation. Based on the homeopathic principle of "like cures like," cantharis is ideal for most burns.

●**Gelsemium—for the flu.** A classic flu remedy that was used to reduce duration and soothe symptoms during the devastating 1918 flu epidemic, Gelsemium is particularly beneficial for flu sufferers who experience fatigue, lethargy and shakiness. Dr. Stengler also prescribes it more generally for fatigue and headaches.

●**Ignatia amara—for anxiety.** Dr. Stengler frequently prescribes this medicine to relieve emotional distress and anxiety. In his opinion, many stressed-out type A's would benefit from taking Ignatia amara…in addition to trying other stress management techniques such as prayer, exercise and deep breathing. It may be especially helpful taken daily during stressful periods such as a divorce or the loss of a loved one. While it does not take away all of the emotional pain, it can reduce the intensity.

●**Nux vomica—for nausea and heartburn.** Derived from an East Indian plant we call Quaker's buttons, Nux vomica is most commonly used for stomach cramps, nausea and heartburn. Many people also find it helpful for anxiety, irritability, and as a hangover remedy.

●**Rhus toxicodendron—for poison ivy.** Rhus toxicodendron, often shortened to Rhus tox, consists of the homeopathic dilution of poison ivy, which with direct contact causes a blistering rash. Again recalling the principle of "like cures like," the salve form is one of the best skin remedies for poison ivy. You can also use it for arthritis, back strain and cold sores.

●**Sulphur—for skin ailments.** Dr. Stengler considers this one of the most profound and long-lasting of all homeopathic remedies. He prescribes it for rashes, eczema and psoriasis. Additionally, sulphur can be taken for digestive disturbances, insomnia and headaches.

FINDING A HOMEOPATHIC PHYSICIAN

Remedies are economically priced, readily available at health food stores and drugstores and—because they have few side effects—lend themselves easily to self-care for uncomplicated problems such as muscle soreness or a stomachache. For overall guidance and to treat more complex health problems—and most especially if you are pregnant or suffer from a chronic medical problem such as diabetes or heart disease—it's best to consult a medical practitioner trained in homeopathy. Homeopathic physicians carefully calibrate treatment to suit each individual, taking into account not only symptoms but also a person's emotional state, lifestyle and other factors.

info To learn more about homeopathy or locate a practitioner, visit the Web sites for the American Association of Naturopathic Physicians at *www.naturopathic.org* or the National Center for Homeopathy at *www.nationalcenter forhomeopathy.org.*

Eucalyptus Oil for Winter Discomfort

David Winston, RH, AHG, herbalist and ethnobotanist, author, *Adaptogens: Herbs for Strength, Stamina and Stress Relief.* Healing Arts.

Eucalyptus has a clean, fresh, invigorating smell and offers relief for assorted common ailments. This essential oil is a wintertime must-have to spray in the shower and inhale to treat symptoms of the common cold. It can also be used topically to provide relief for sore and stiff muscles, sprains and strains, and can be soothing when applied to the temples for tension headaches. Simply put a drop of diluted eucalyptus oil on your temples and massage lightly.

For advice on how to use eucalyptus oil safely and effectively, we asked herbalist and ethnobotanist David Winston, RH, AHG, author of several books on herbals including *Adaptogens: Herbs for Strength, Stamina and Stress Relief.*

CLEARS THINGS OUT

According to Winston, two of the best ways to use eucalyptus oil are topically and in boiling water to form an inhalant, to break up chest and head congestion. To clear out congestion, drip a few drops of the essential oil into about an inch of boiling water and make a steam tent over your head with a towel. Or, you can buy vaporizers made to be used with essential oils as an alternative for inhalation. There's also the old cure-all Mom used to rub onto your throat and chest to relieve cough and congestion—Vicks VapoRub, which contains lots of eucalyptus oil. Another idea is to make tea with eucalyptus leaves. Drink four ounces, three times daily.

Topically eucalyptus can be used to ease muscle aches and pains, sprains and strains. Put two or three drops of the pure essential oil in eight ounces of olive or sesame oil—this is great as massage oil, in addition to being an effective topical analgesic. You might notice when you first apply it that the oil feels warm and then a cool sensation kicks in—that is part of the oil's ability to down-regulate the sensation of pain, says Winston.

LOTS OF USES

Also try swishing a few drops of the oil in your mouthwash to ease bad breath or periodontal disease. Because eucalyptus is antibacterial, anti-fungal and anti-inflammatory, it not only helps to mask the odor or discomfort, but also helps cure the core problem. Again, be sure to use only very diluted oil for this. Pastilles with eucalyptus oil as an ingredient can be an effective antidote to bad breath or a sore throat. Winston likes Olbas pastilles. For liquid body soap that has natural antibacterial properties, try Dr. Bronner's Magic Soaps with eucalyptus oil.

Important: There are, of course, some precautions. Herbalists don't recommend eucalyptus for those with inflammatory or gastrointestinal diseases, kidney problems or liver disease because it can exacerbate symptoms—though some experienced naturopathic physicians might use it for these problems. Most eucalyptus preparations are too strong for the tender skin of children under age four—and be sure never to allow eucalyptus oil near their faces or noses either. Eucalyptus, like most therapeutic agents, can interact with some medications, herbal and dietary supplements so it's safest to use only after consultation with a doctor.

Healthful Use for Honey

Arne Simon, MD, pediatric oncologist and infectious disease specialist, University of Bonn, Germany.

Honey—it's great on toast and to sweeten tea. But to treat wounds? Yes, is the enthusiastic answer from physicians at the University of Bonn Children's Hospital in Germany, who have been using honey to treat wounds in pediatric cancer patients.

Wound healing is especially difficult for people of any age undergoing cancer treatment—because as the therapies slow the growth of or kill malignant cells, they also inhibit development of healthy tissue components that help heal wounds. The German pediatric oncologists have described their experience using honey to help heal their patients' wounds as "astonishing." In addition to faster healing, the honey also reduces the unpleasant odor of wounds, and renders the dressings easier and less painful to remove, which is of utmost importance in children. While their study was on cancer patients, it has broader implications for wound healing of all kinds. According to Arne Simon, MD, a pediatrician at the University of Bonn, who has led the group of physicians compiling and documenting Medihoney results, it has been shown to have antibacterial activity against nearly all clinically relevant bacterial causes of wound infection.

NOT LIKE A "SPOONFUL OF SUGAR"

Unfortunately, honey used for medical purposes is not what you'll find in your cupboard, and its healing properties are different than those of household honey. Household honey may contain bacterial spores and may therefore do more harm than good in wound care. The honey used in the research is a special blend that comes in two formulations called Medihoney Antibacterial Medical Honey and Medihoney Wound Gel, which were developed several years ago by an Australian company also named Medihoney, which was acquired by the New Zealand health-care company Comvita, and has since joined forces with Derma Sciences to market the wound-healing product in the U.S. It is irradiated to destroy bacterial spores at the end of the manufacturing process without negative impact on other ingredients and wound care properties.

What are additional differences? When making any kind of honey, bees add an enzyme (*glucose-oxidase*) that triggers constant formation of hydrogen peroxide, a natural antimicrobial substance. But, depending on their own diets, they produce different varieties of the sweet syrup with varying amounts of hydrogen peroxide. Medihoney is a blend of two types of honey—one of which forms an unusually large amount of hydrogen peroxide…and another called "leptospermum" honey (after a tree of that name found in New Zealand and Australia), which has a strong antibacterial effect. The practice of using Medihoney products to treat wounds is spreading rapidly throughout Europe and Australia, including in hospitals—and the product received FDA approval in the U.S.

Caution: As Medihoney's healing properties are strictly local, Dr. Simon warns that adjuvant systemic antibiotics have to be considered in patients with compromised immunity or additional risk factors for severe systemic infection. Patients who have chronic complicated wounds or severe immunodeficiency should use Medihoney only under the supervision of a wound care specialist.

It has few side effects, says Dr. Simon, who notes that about 5% of adults experience transient pain after administration, and about 2% of people develop local skin reactions (eczema) at the site of application. Both may be reasons to discontinue treatment with medical honey. Consequently, Dr. Simon advises putting Medihoney first on just a small area to test for a reaction.

WHERE TO FIND US?

Currently, Medihoney is used in the Middle East battlefields for wound care by United States Army physicians. Medihoney wound dressings and wound paste with medical-grade honey are available at amazon.com.

info For more information, contact Derma Sciences at (800) 445-7627, or go to *www.medihoney.com.*

2

Healthy Food Cures

Most Powerful Produce Choices

We know that we're supposed to eat plenty of fruits and vegetables to get our daily dose of antioxidants—those plant-based compounds that help bolster immunity and slow the aging process. But a surprising study by US Department of Agriculture (USDA) nutritionists reveals that the foods we thought were great sources—such as strawberries and spinach—are actually not at the top of the list. The most powerful produce? Small red beans, also known as Mexican red beans.

"We were surprised to find that these beans were the number one source," says lead study author Ronald Prior, PhD, research chemist and licensed nutritionist at Arkansas Children's Nutrition Center. "We had expected berries to be the best source."

The researchers used a technique called *oxygen radical absorbance capacity* (ORAC) to test the antioxidant power of more than 100 different kinds of fruits, vegetables, nuts and spices. His team's findings appeared in the *Journal of Agricultural and Food Chemistry.*

There were definitely some surprises on the list. Artichokes came in at number seven, prunes at number nine, pecans at number 14 and—Atkins diet enthusiasts, brace yourselves—russet potatoes at number 17. Other high-ranking nuts were walnuts and hazelnuts.

Although spices are generally consumed in small amounts, many are rich in antioxidants. Ground cloves, ground cinnamon and oregano were highest among those studied.

Official standings…

1. Small red beans (dried), also known as Mexican red beans

2. Blueberries (wild)

3. Red kidney beans

4. Pinto beans

Ronald Prior, PhD, research chemist, licensed nutritionist, USDA Agricultural Research Service, Arkansas Children's Nutrition Center, Little Rock, Arkansas.

5. **Blueberries (cultivated)**

6. **Cranberries**

7. **Artichokes (cooked)**

8. **Blackberries**

9. **Prunes**

10. **Raspberries**

11. **Strawberries**

12. **Red Delicious apples**

13. **Granny Smith apples**

14. **Pecans**

15. **Cherries**

16. **Black plums**

17. **Russet potatoes (cooked)**

18. **Black beans (dried)**

19. **Red plums**

20. **Gala apples**

Although this list is a helpful guide, it doesn't mean you should consume bowls of beans and blueberries at the expense of other produce. Dr. Prior advises eating five to nine servings a day of a variety of fruits and vegetables—and also getting your daily dose of other important nutrients. For example, spinach, which didn't even make the top 20, is a disease-fighting powerhouse, rich in iron, magnesium, folate, calcium and vitamins A, C and E.

Remember that produce is often most potent when eaten fresh, rather than frozen, canned or processed with sugars or other additives (so eating lots of apple pie this weekend isn't healthful).

Exception: Cooked tomatoes are more nutritious than raw. Cooking tomatoes breaks down much of the resilient fibrous structure that can impede the digestion of its antioxidants.

The bottom line? Eat your fruits and vegctables to maximize your health, which is exactly what your mother has been saying all along.

Fight Cancer by Eating Fruits and Veggies

The late Jane Higdon, PhD, research associate, Linus Pauling Institute, Oregon State University, Corvallis, Oregon, and coauthor of *An Evidence-Based Approach to Vitamins and Minerals.* Thieme Medical.

Food as "medicine"—what a concept! Entries on the "food-is-good-for-you" list include apples and cruciferous vegetables such as broccoli, brussels sprouts, cauliflower, cabbage, bok choy and kale. According to several new studies (as well as some older ones), these foods are particularly helpful in fighting certain types of cancer.

AN APPLE A DAY

Did you know that apples—those delicious, versatile, beautiful fruits—are actually natural-born cancer cell killers and more, too? Researchers at the French National Institute for Health and Medical Research in Strasbourg exposed cancer cells to apple antioxidants. They discovered that one type of antioxidant that is prominent in apples, *procyanidins*, was particularly effective in triggering cancer cell deaths. The French team then did a second-stage study for which they exposed laboratory rats to colon-cancer–causing substances and then fed one of two groups of rats the apple procyanidins for six weeks. The rats that fed on the antioxidant developed half as many precancerous lesions as the group on regular feed.

An earlier cell culture study at Cornell University also demonstrated that apple extract inhibited colon cancer cells, but this study reports that the effectiveness seems to come from not just one, but from all antioxidants contained in apples, especially those that are in the skin. A recent Cornell review of the literature on apple research showed that apples are also protective against several other types of cancer, as well as cardiovascular disease and asthma.

VEGGIES, TOO

One of the most recent studies on the curative effects of foods involved cruciferous vegetables. Researchers at the Mayo Clinic compared diets of 450 men and women, ages 20 to 74, who had non-Hodgkin's lymphoma (NHL) with the diets of a group of healthy people. The study found that the cancer-free group ate a diet rich in green, leafy vegetables and vegetables from the cruciferous group.

When a research team from the Harvard School of Public Health did an earlier survey of the 88,410 women in the ongoing Nurses' Health Study, they found that the women who ate more fruits and vegetables generally had a lower risk for NHL, and that those who ate at least five servings of cruciferous vegetables a week reduced the risk for NHL by a full 33%.

FUTURE RESEARCH

We consulted the late nutritionist Jane Higdon, PhD, research associate at the Linus Pauling Institute in Corvallis, Oregon, where she studied the function and role of vitamins, minerals and phytochemicals in human health. Dr. Higdon agreed that science is constantly fine-tuning conclusions about specific groups of foods and nutrients that affect health, and she said that we can expect to see more of this in the future. She added that scientists are finding cruciferous vegetables especially intriguing because they are rich in certain phytochemicals that seem to increase the activity of enzymes that detoxify the body.

As for apples, they indeed contain many nutrients, fiber and flavonoids, but a major reason they are the focus of so much research is that they are a common food that many people eat, and so make for easier studying. But, she qualified this by pointing out that cancer is not just one disease but rather a number of different ones with a common thread. Given this, it makes sense that some foods will affect certain types of cancers and not others. Whether certain varieties of apples pack a more potent punch than others remains to be seen.

Dr. Higdon was very quick to approve of eating apples and cruciferous vegetables, but she was cautious about jumping on the research-results bandwagon, based on studies thus far. She basically dismissed all cell culture studies because she said that they are far removed from what actually happens in the human body.

Reason: As the body metabolizes nutrients, it dilutes the concentration of a flavonoid, making it not at all akin to what researchers put into cancer cells in the lab.

Complicating the picture further is the fact that there are a number of genotypes among people, and individual response to some nutrients and plant chemicals is dependent on a person's genotype. It's impossible at this time to identify the different genotypes that make up a study group, but it is important to remember that any study is going to contain and reflect a broad variety of genotypes, and that is going to have some impact on the results, she said. Just to muddy the research waters further, a recent analysis of the ongoing Nurses' Health Study indicates that fruits and vegetables are helpful for preventing cardiac disease, but apparently *not* cancer.

THE DOCTOR'S ADVICE

With all of this in mind, Dr. Higdon's advice was as follows: Eat lots of fruits and vegetables because we *know* they are good for you. Include well-washed apples and their skin, which contains a healthy dose of flavonoids, and load your plate with cruciferous vegetables because they seem to be associated with decreased risk for some cancers. But avoid isolated plant chemicals such as the apple extracts that are cropping up in the marketplace now. It's a reminder, once again, that there are many nutrients and chemicals in foods and, most likely, they act in a synergistic manner. If you want to be sure that you're getting all the health benefits, eat fruits and vegetables whole—lots of them and often.

New Research: Eat Your Broccoli

Keith W. Singletary, PhD, professor of foods and nutrition, University of Illinois at Urbana-Champaign.

Broccoli is already known to be a power-house vegetable—its high levels of anti-oxidants even help fight cancer. Now scientists studying breast cancer have found that broccoli's (and other cruciferous vegetables') star antioxidant, *sulforaphane*, prevents cancerous cells from dividing and growing. That could be very important news for the 216,000 American women who develop the disease each year, many of whom rely on powerful drugs to fight cancer growth.

To find out more, we spoke with researcher Keith W. Singletary, PhD, professor of foods and nutrition at the University of Illinois at Urbana-Champaign. Dr. Singletary and his team exposed human breast cancer cells to sulforaphane, and found that this compound disrupts the activity of cell components involved in chromosome separation and cell division. In this way, he explained, sulforaphane blocks the multiplication process and signals cancer cells to die.

While more research needs to be done to determine how sulforaphane can best fight breast cancer, the study's findings may help in being able to develop new cancer prevention and treatment strategies, says Dr. Singletary. It has been reported that sulforaphane can suppress the proliferation of other cancers, such as colon cancer. It is not known yet whether it will have the same effect in other cancers as it did in the breast cancer cell studies.

IS THERE A SULFORAPHANE SUPPLEMENT?

Get your nutrients from whole foods, Dr. Singletary urges. "There's a wide variety of phytochemicals along with nutrients in vegetables." In addition to sulforaphane, a serving of broccoli, cauliflower or other crucifer is loaded with a bounty of disease-fighting nutrients, including vitamin C, beta-carotene, quercetin, indoles, glutathione and lutein, plus fiber, calcium and folate. "When contained in vegetables or fruits, these compounds are in proportions that seem to be most beneficial and safest for us to consume," Dr. Singletary says. "We don't know yet whether isolating these compounds provides a benefit or a risk. High amounts of one chemical can almost be like a drug."

DON'T LIKE BROCCOLI?

You can also get sulforaphane from cabbage, cauliflower, Brussels sprouts, bok choy, watercress and kale. Cooking may diminish some nutrients, but most health experts don't insist that you become a "raw foodie" quite yet. Have the vegetables any way that will entice you to eat them—raw, steamed or lightly boiled.

Dr. Singletary recommends that for optimal health, increase your consumption of vegetables and aim for a variety in your diet that includes cruciferous vegetables.

Fruits and Veggies Can Improve Your Bones

Katherine L. Tucker, PhD, professor, Friedman School of Nutrition Science and Policy, and director, Nutritional Epidemiology Program, Tufts University, Boston.
Andrew L. Rubman, ND, director, Southbury Clinic for Traditional Medicines, Southbury, Connecticut.

Thinning bones, stooped shoulders and hip fractures—it's a dreadful scenario for old age and one that has turned multitudes of people into regular consumers of calcium supplements and dairy products. But many people are overlooking another critical component of long-term bone health. Several new studies—a large one of teenage girls in Northern Ireland and an even larger study of adult American men and women—demonstrated that a diet full of fruits and vegetables is crucial for bone mineral density.

THE SCIENCE OF BONES

The author of the American study is Katherine L. Tucker, PhD, professor of nutrition and director of nutritional epidemiology at Tufts University. According to Dr. Tucker, many people don't realize that bone is complex living tissue that is constantly being broken down and rebuilt (called "remodeling"). After a rapid rate of bone remodeling in the growing-up years, bones stabilize until about age 40, at which time they begin to break down faster than they rebuild—a process that menopause accelerates in women. Fruits and vegetables support the continuation of bone rebuilding throughout our lives because, among other things, they supply phytochemicals, minerals (in particular, potassium and magnesium) and vitamin K (from green leafy vegetables), which bone needs to activate its protein.

PRODUCE PROTECTS

But there is yet another reason that fruits and vegetables are critical for bone health. According to our medical expert, Andrew L. Rubman, ND, eating habits, coupled with poor food and beverage choices, such as high-phosphate carbonated beverages (soda), can create compounds called metabolic acids that may accelerate bone loss. (Excess phosphates can appear as phosphoric acid that in turn leaches minerals from bone and other tissues.) Fruits and vegetables in sufficient quantities can neutralize this acid and keep bones from harm. This is of special concern because of popular high-protein diets that do not allow for sufficient portions of fruits and vegetables.

Overall, Dr. Tucker says that the most important thing you can do to keep your bones strong is provide a healthy long-term environment by eating five or more fruits and vegetables a day, getting enough calcium and exercising regularly.

Lower Your Risk of Rheumatoid Arthritis

Dorothy Pattison, PhD, RD, arthritis research campaign epidemiology unit, University of Manchester, England.

Did you know that vitamin C not only eases the common cold, it may also help prevent rheumatoid arthritis (RA)? A recent British study found that people who consumed more fruits and vegetables were less likely to develop this crippling autoimmune disease, which is characterized by joint inflammation, destruction and deformity.

ABOUT THE RESEARCH

The study was based on data collected in a cancer survey of 23,000 men and women in the United Kingdom, where the participants recorded what they ate each week. Researchers discovered that people who ate the fewest fruits and vegetables were more likely to develop

inflammation in the joints than those who consumed the most.

Because the study was a review of survey data, it did not test specifically for cause and effect of vitamin C and RA. However, the data shows a definite correlation between the two.

Vitamin C appeared to be the measured nutrient most responsible for this protective effect. Those with the lowest intake of vitamin C were three times more at risk than those with the highest intakes.

According to study coauthor Dorothy Pattison, PhD, RD, of the University of Manchester in England, vitamin C…

• **Acts as a powerful antioxidant that "mops up" the free radicals** that are produced during inflammation and joint damage.

• **Protects against infections that may trigger joint inflammation.**

• **Plays a vital role in the formation of collagen,** which is necessary for joint health.

FRUITS, VEGGIES OR SUPPLEMENTS?

When it comes to vitamin C, all sources are not created equal.

Dr. Pattison notes that the British study only reviewed data that reported on the consumption of fresh fruits and vegetables.

In addition, a recent study at Duke University suggested that the long-term use of vitamin C supplements might aggravate osteoarthritis (the more common wear-and-tear arthritis associated with aging). Researchers don't know exactly why, but the suggestion is that it has something to do with supplements versus fresh fruits and vegetables.

The good news is that you can easily get much of the vitamin C you need just by following the seven-to-nine servings recommendation. Dr. Pattison adds that fresh fruits appear to have a stronger protective effect than vegetables, so be sure to consume three or four servings of fresh fruit daily.

info For a list of the vitamin C content of fruits, go to *www.naturalhub.com* and click on the link under the heading "fruit."

Foods That Cure

Cass Ingram, DO, author of *Eat Right 4 Your Metabolic Type* and *The Cure Is in The Cupboard* (both by Knowledge House), and 13 other books.

Andrew L. Rubman, ND, director, Southbury Clinic for Traditional Medicines, Southbury, Connecticut.

Thanks to tremendous advances in modern medicine, we are all trained to think that when we have a symptom, we take a pill. According to Cass Ingram, DO, author of numerous books including *Eat Right 4 Your Metabolic Type* and *The Cure Is in the Cupboard*, the problem is that we've become so enamored of manufactured pharmaceuticals that we have forgotten that the original and safest medicines are actually food.

We had the chance to talk to Dr. Ingram about some of his favorite remedies from the refrigerator (or pantry). Some surprised us… and perhaps they will surprise you.

ALMONDS: THE IDEAL SNACK

These nuts give you energy during the day and help you sleep soundly at night, says Dr. Ingram. When you can't keep your eyes open at the office, grab a handful of salted almonds. Their winning combination of vitamins, minerals, protein and healthy fats imparts immediate energy. At night, the calcium and magnesium in almonds act as a natural sedative, and since they contain *salicylic acid* (which is essentially natural aspirin), versatile almonds can also help control headache pain.

GUACAMOLE FOR HEART AND SKIN HEALTH

Avocado's essential fatty acids and vitamin E make guacamole a top food for the heart.

Here is something you may not know: Your skin can benefit from a regular serving of guacamole, too. Natural oils in avocados perk up a poor complexion, make brittle nails strong again and improve dry skin.

Try: Dr. Ingram advises people with severe hair loss to eat three avocados daily, because they contain special oils that aid in the regeneration of hair follicles, stimulating the growth of new hair.

IMPROVE LIVER FUNCTION WITH A BOWL OF BORSCHT

Our livers are under siege, says Dr. Ingram. Every day, they are bombarded with toxins—from car exhaust fumes to secondhand smoke. To improve liver function, try beets.

The deep purple color of these root vegetables comes from a flavonoid called *betanin*, the active ingredient of which is betaine. This chemical is similar in structure to the nutrient choline, which studies have linked with the production of healthy liver and blood cells.

For best results, use fresh beets and cook them with their greens intact. If you boil beets, do not throw out the water. Most of the nutrients are found in the juice, so drink it right away or save it and add to soup.

Soups are perhaps the ideal way to serve beets, says Dr. Ingram. Beet soup is known as borscht, and it is often served with high butter-fat sour creams—an excellent combination, since fat helps extract the valuable pigment from beets and accelerates its absorption into the blood.

CURE STOMACH ULCERS WITH CABBAGE JUICE

Research dating back to Stanford University in the 1950s demonstrates that cabbage juice heals stomach ulcers. While it's still not exactly clear why this happens, Dr. Ingram notes that raw cabbage is packed with vitamin C, bioflavonoids, folic acid, amino acids and vitamin K.

To make cabbage juice, thoroughly wash several heads of raw organic green cabbage, chop them into thick slices and run through the juicer. To heal stomach ulcers, drink one liter of cabbage juice daily for two weeks. Juicing removes the fiber and essentially eliminates digestive side effects, such as discomfort, gas and bloating.

Our medical expert, Andrew L. Rubman, ND, adds that if you don't have a juicer, sauerkraut (or fermented cabbage) has also been found to be helpful in healing stomach ulcers.

HORSERADISH FOR WATER RETENTION

If you suffer from water retention, Dr. Ingram says to grate one tablespoon of fresh horseradish, crush with a mortar and pestle and mix with one tablespoon of apple cider vinegar. Add to a pint of boiling water, cover and steep for four hours. Strain pulp and drink.

RELIEVE CONSTIPATION WITH CHERRY TOMATOES

Cherry tomatoes contain more fiber than regular tomatoes, and improve digestion and bowel function.

Sun-ripened cherry tomatoes are also an excellent source of vitamin C and bioflavonoids. Never refrigerate tomatoes, as it inhibits ripening and damages their skin. Organically grown tomatoes are even better.

A TURNIP A DAY

Colds, flu, sinusitis and bronchitis can be signs of nutritional deficiencies. A turnip a day may be the answer, because these root vegetables are rich sources of selenium, sulfur, vitamin C and riboflavin. Dr. Ingram advises replacing potatoes with turnips in soups, stir-fry dishes and casseroles.

Also: Turnips are an excellent source of curcumin, also found in the cooking spice turmeric, which can help protect against neurodegenerative disorders, such as Alzheimer's disease.

GO FOR VINEGAR

Vinegar may just be the perfect food, says Dr. Ingram. A natural antibiotic, it stimulates the immune system and inhibits the growth of microbes. Vinegar is also an excellent source of acetic acid, which stimulates digestion. To help avoid food poisoning, Dr. Ingram recommends that you consume it with every restaurant meal, especially when you travel abroad. Add a splash of vinegar to salads or soups, or pour it over meat or fish dishes.

For arthritis, mix together one tablespoon each of honey and vinegar in a shot glass and drink it down twice a day.

Among the best varieties of vinegar are those made from grapes or apple cider. Dr. Ingram's personal favorite is dark balsamic vinegar, which is exceptionally rich in health-enhancing chemicals, such as bioflavonoids.

Food has always been medicine, says Dr. Ingram. While we may have temporarily lost sight of this fact, the cures for many common ailments are as close as your local supermarket.

Bananas Are Power-Packed

Suzanne Havala Hobbs, DrPh, MS, RD, clinical assistant professor and director, doctoral program in health leadership, School of Public Health, department of health policy and administration, University of North Carolina at Chapel Hill. Dr. Havala Hobbs is author of many books on nutrition, including *Vegetarian Cooking for Dummies*. For Dummies.

Bananas are not only good fruits to eat after heavy exercise due to their potassium content and ease of digestion, but their potassium can also reduce your risk for high blood pressure and stroke as well as strengthen your immune system.

According to Suzanne Havala Hobbs, DrPh, MS, RD, clinical assistant professor at the School of Public Health at the University of North Carolina at Chapel Hill, while many think bananas are just baby's first fruit, they are also a convenient source of nutrition. People with diabetes should keep in mind that bananas are high in sugar, so they should consult their physicians about how many are safe to eat.

Among the health benefits of bananas...

• **Potassium powerhouse.** One banana provides over 400 milligrams of potassium, or 11% of your daily quota. Taking in a sufficient amount of this nutrient is vital to maintaining a healthy heart and blood vessels. Not getting enough potassium can contribute to high blood pressure and increased risk for stroke. Additionally, many pharmaceuticals used to treat these conditions deplete potassium, so eating bananas can help replenish adequate levels.

• **Energizer.** On your next visit to the gym, instead of reaching for a power drink or energy bar, choose a natural and less-expensive alternative. Bananas provide a quick and efficient pick-me-up to replace the important vitamins and minerals you lose during a strenuous workout. In addition, their potassium is essential for building muscles.

• **Rich source of vitamin C.** This vital nutrient helps the body heal and defends against infection, and also aids in the absorption of iron, the synthesis of connective tissue and the formation of blood.

• **Immunity booster.** The vitamin B-6 in bananas gives your immunity a boost. One banana contains approximately 30% of your daily requirement of B-6, which helps synthesize antibodies in the immune system. This nutrient is also vital to protein metabolism, red blood cell formation and proper functioning of the central nervous system.

• **Fiber-filled.** One banana meets 16% of your daily fiber need. Like many other fruits and vegetables, fiber-rich bananas can help maintain or restore normal bowel function.

• **Easy on digestion.** Bananas are so easy on the tummy that even very young children, the elderly and those convalescing from illness find them easy to eat.

• **Diet-friendly.** Rich in nutrients and fat free, bananas are an excellent choice when you are trying to shed excess pounds. While the simple sugar in bananas has earned them a bad rap from popular low-carb diet plans, Dr. Havala Hobbs dismisses this notion as having no merit.

So go ahead and reach for a healthy and satisfying snack. Munch on a banana to help meet your daily requirement of five fresh fruits and vegetables. Eat it plain, with yogurt or blended into a delicious and nutritious smoothie.

The "Dirt" on Foreign Fruits

Ronald H. Schmidt, PhD, food science professor, University of Florida, Gainesville, and coauthor of *Food Safety Handbook*. Wiley.

Years back, there was a true season for summer fruits and vegetables. Now, due to miracles of modern trade and agricultural science, fruits and vegetables are available virtually all year long.

Locally grown produce is always best, but as the summer ends and the winter comes, our markets replace most local and domestic produce with foreign-grown foods.

Problem: The US Food and Drug Administration (FDA) has limited resources for inspecting foreign-grown foods, and there have been disturbing headlines in years past about the safety of food from less-developed countries. So…what to do? Go without? Or eat the imports?

Ronald H. Schmidt, PhD, food science professor at the University of Florida in Gainesville, is on the front line of professionals who watch over our food supply. His answers to our questions were surprisingly reassuring.

Dr. Schmidt reports that because of those headline events in the past, the countries that supply us with produce year-round have become extremely sensitive to safety issues. They simply cannot afford to alienate the American market by careless handling of produce.

Additionally, the companies that import foreign produce have tightened quality controls to help ensure safety. Perhaps the most stringent watchdogs are the produce buyers for large US stores and supermarket chains. Dr. Schmidt says that the buyers who work for the supermarkets show up regularly in foreign fields to be sure that workers are following best practice rules.

THE SAFETY GUIDELINES

The US Department of Agriculture has established standardized rules for safety through a formal system known as Good Agricultural Practices (GAPs), which is based at Cornell University where the guidelines were developed.

This addresses the three red-flag areas: The workers' hygienic practices…how water is used for irrigation and cleaning…and the proper use of fertilizers to avoid fecal contamination. Although GAPs is voluntary and is intended for domestic farms, Dr. Schmidt says that buyers are insisting that foreign producers also follow it. Indeed, consumers can ask at their own markets if the produce there meets GAPs' standards, he says. Other protective systems often used are the Hazard Analysis and Critical Control Point (HACCP) and the outreach efforts of a joint FDA-University of Maryland program called the Joint Institute for Food Safety and Applied Nutrition (JIFSAN).

SAFETY ENDS AT HOME

Knowing that these systems are in place eases anxiety to a great degree, but there remains the possibility of oversight and accidents. We wanted to know what consumers should be aware of as they shop for and prepare produce.

Dr. Schmidt reminds people to think about how food grows and respond accordingly.

Example: Melons grow on the ground, which means the rinds are apt to have—at the very least—some dirt on them. There is the remote possibility that the dirt could carry traces of fecal matter (from organic fertilizer) or pesticides. Always rinse a melon very well under running water (soap is not necessary, he says). Use a clean, freshly washed knife to cut into it to avoid cross contamination, and serve it on a plate that has not been in contact with the unwashed rind.

The other issue with produce from the ground has to do with "downed" crops. Those that grow above ground but are harvested after falling have dirt on them and are not fully cleaned. Downed apples, contaminated with a virulent strain of *E. coli* and the parasite *Cryptosporidium* and processed into an unpasteurized product, caused the contamination problem in apple juice a number of years ago. As a result, producers today no longer use downed apples for juice, nor do they produce unpasteurized juice.

Interestingly, Dr. Schmidt says that although grapes are sprayed and always require thorough rinsing before eating, they almost never carry any bacterial contamination. (The news of contaminated grapes from Chile in 1989 turned into a catastrophe for the grape producers and workers. Eventually it was discovered that the furor was over grapes in Philadelphia that were likely tampered with here in the US.) Blueberries are also generally free of contaminants, which, he says, is odd because they are hard to wash. Peeled fruit is safe as long as you handle it correctly, including washing your own hands after rinsing the fruit when necessary. He says that he has not heard of any contamination problems with banana peels.

BEWARE OF SPROUTS

Sprouts of any sort are the food that causes Dr. Schmidt particular concern. He explains that to germinate the sprout requires a wet environment that *salmonella* can actually grow in. The presence of salmonella requires chlorine to remove it, and even then it is almost impossible to do so successfully. People who are immunosuppressed should definitely avoid sprouts of any kind and even healthy people might be wise to forego commercially grown products, he says.

Another problem for immunosuppressed people could be raspberries. Because of their rough surface, if the parasite *Cyclospora* gets in them, it is nearly impossible to get out. Nevertheless, he does not advise healthy people to avoid the pleasure of this delectable and healthy berry.

SAFETY FIRST

No matter where the produce comes from, Dr. Schmidt says the most important step is for people to adopt their own best safety practices. Rinse everything, including prewashed, precut salad greens and garnishes, under running water. Regularly wash your hands, utensils and cutting boards in warm, soapy water to avoid any cross-contamination. With improved safety standards in the US and abroad and good practices in your own home, nature's bounty can indeed be enjoyed long after the lazy days of summer are over.

The Amazing Kiwi Cure

There's new evidence that eating kiwifruit can help prevent a heart attack.

In a recent study, people who ate two to three kiwifruits daily for 28 days reduced their platelet aggregation response (potential for blood clot formation) by 18% and their blood triglyceride (fat) levels by 15% compared with people who ate no kiwifruit.

The fruit is rich in polyphenols (antioxidant plant chemicals), vitamins C and E, magnesium, potassium and copper, all of which protect the blood vessels and heart. Kiwifruits are available in grocery stores year-round and can be peeled, sliced and added to green or fruit salads.

Asim K. Duttaroy, PhD, professor of nutritional medicine, department of nutrition, University of Oslo, Norway.

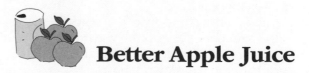

Better Apple Juice

In a new study, researchers measured levels of *polyphenols*—antioxidants thought to protect against cancer and heart disease—in pasteurized apple juice that was either clear or cloudy. They found that cloudy apple juice, which contains more pulp, had up to four times more polyphenols than the clear variety.

Theory: The manufacturing process used to make clear apple juice reduces polyphenol levels. It is important to choose pasteurized apple juice to ensure that the product does not contain bacteria.

Jan Oszmianski, PhD, professor and head, department of fruit, vegetable and cereal technology, Wroclaw Environmental and Life Science University, Poland.

Eat Nuts for Health

Pecans, almonds and walnuts protect the heart. Pecans and walnuts are high in a form of vitamin E called *gamma tocopherol* …almonds are high in *alpha-tocopherol*. These powerful antioxidants help reduce risk of hardening of the arteries and heart disease. They also lower total and LDL (bad) cholesterol and raise HDL (good) cholesterol.

Try to eat a moderate-sized handful of nuts every day.

Ella Haddad, DrPH, associate professor, department of nutrition, School of Public Health, Loma Linda University, Loma Linda, California, and leader of a study published in *Nutrition Research*.

Spice Up Your Memory

Nader G. Abraham, PhD, professor of pharmacology, New York Medical College, Valhalla, New York.

We now have another good reason to like Indian food. Not only do those spices taste good, they may just help ward off Alzheimer's disease.

In studies conducted jointly at three centers in Italy and New York Medical College in Valhalla, New York, researchers found that the Indian spice *curry* enhances the enzyme activity that has a protective effect on the brain. These findings were presented at the American Physiological Society's annual scientific conference.

ABOUT THE STUDY

According to researcher Nader G. Abraham, PhD, professor of pharmacology at New York Medical College, *curcumin*—a chemical compound that imparts the distinctive yellow color to the curry spice turmeric is the key ingredient. This substance is naturally rich in phenols, potent antioxidants that protect cells from free-radical damage.

Current theories of aging focus on free radicals as the primary culprits in brain aging processes and neurodegenerative diseases, such as Alzheimer's.

Curcumin triggers the production of an enzyme known as hemeoxygenase-1 (HO-1) says Dr. Abraham. He explains that this enzyme protects against oxidative distress and also appears to exhibit an anti-inflammatory effect. In the study, researchers exposed rats' brain cells to various concentrations of curcumin. After each treatment, they analyzed the cells and found that cells exposed to curcumin were associated with increased HO-1 activity.

Dr. Abraham adds that the antioxidant and anti-inflammatory benefits of curcumin are not limited to the brain. Having more HO-1 in your system can also offer protection against cardiovascular disease, high blood pressure and diabetes.

SPICE UP YOUR LIFE

While these results are encouraging, further laboratory research is needed to determine if curcumin can be used to prevent neurodegenerative conditions in human beings.

In the meantime, the next time you dine out, consider an Indian restaurant. Eating Indian food once a week will help you increase HO-1 in your system, says Dr. Abraham.

He also recommends keeping a jar of curry on hand, and adding a teaspoon or two to vegetable or meat dishes.

Cereal Killers

Udo Erasmus, PhD, developer of the "right fat, carb-conscious diet" and author of *Fats That Heal, Fats That Kill.* Alive Books. *www.udoerasmus.com.*

It's just like your mother always told you—breakfast is the most important meal of the day. The catch is that it has to be the *right* breakfast.

According to Udo Erasmus, PhD, developer of the "right fat, carb-conscious diet," most people believe that cereal is a healthy choice for breakfast, but there's a problem—most are packed with sugar, salt and refined white flour. In fact, according to a front page article in the *New York Times*, cereal is the "in" food for teens and college students—many of them eating it for breakfast, lunch and dinner.

SEPARATING THE WHEAT FROM THE CHAFF

The majority of cereals are fundamentally fuel without food, cautions Dr. Erasmus. Their empty carbohydrates lead to a fleeting sugar rush, which is soon followed by a plunge in energy that leaves you tired, irritable, hungry and craving something sweet. Any carbohydrates that you don't burn up, you will put on as fat.

This is not to say, of course, that cereals are universally bad. The eminent consumer advocate group Center for Science in the Public Interest recommends whole-grain cereals with no added sugars, and advises consumers to read labels carefully. According to the American Heart Association, eating whole-grain cereal every day is associated with a 15% reduction in risk for insulin resistance syndrome, a metabolic disorder that puts you at greater risk for developing diabetes and heart disease.

Note: The American Heart Association defines whole-grain cereals as those that list a whole grain or bran first in the ingredients list, or those that contain a whole grain and at least two grams of fiber per serving.

The problem is that these are not the cereals that most of us eat, and they are certainly not the ones that are being offered at "cereal bars" on college campuses, nor are they the ones your child sees advertised on Saturday morning TV and clamors for in the cereal aisle.

AN INDUSTRY-DRIVEN TREND

The thing to keep in mind is that the custom of eating cereal for breakfast is driven by marketers and the powerful food industry, and not by health concerns, observes Dr. Erasmus. Breakfast cereals are veiled in a healthy glow due to their claims of being low-fat and enriched with vitamins. *However, a daily bowl of corn flakes, cocoa cereal or crispy rice cereal—sugary cereals made with white flour—can...*

• **Inflate insulin levels,** which increases the risk for diabetes.

• **Boost the level of body fats called triglycerides,** raising the risk for heart disease.

• **Increase the risk for obesity.** The more empty carbohydrates you consume, the more insulin you produce and the more fat you store.

And to make matters worse, many of the unhealthiest cereals are specifically marketed toward children. Dr. Erasmus worries that eating them for breakfast every morning may set up a child for failure. Sugary cereals can lead to hyperactivity. The next thing you know, the teacher is complaining that a child has a bad attitude and needs counseling—when all he/she really needs is a healthier breakfast. Some children who simply suffer from poor diets end up receiving medication to calm them down.

START THE DAY OFF RIGHT

In other countries around the world, cereal is not necessarily the breakfast of choice. When you suggest eating salad for breakfast to an American, observes Dr. Erasmus, he'll look at you as if you're crazy. But this is a common option in Scandinavian countries. In Asia, a traditional breakfast consists of steamed vegetables and a bit of healthy protein such as tofu or fish.

Dr. Erasmus believes that it's time Americans got back on track to start the day with a healthy breakfast. *Helpful strategies...*

• **If you opt for cereal,** choose whole-grain alternatives that are the highest in fiber and lowest in sugar, such as bran flakes, shredded wheat, muesli and oatmeal. Have a bowlful with low-fat milk and toss in your own fresh blueberries or sliced strawberries or bananas.

• **Check the ingredients list on cereal boxes.** Sugars go by such monikers as corn sweetener, dextrose, fructose, high-fructose corn syrup, malt, honey, molasses and sucrose. But once you swallow them, as far as your body is concerned, they're all sugar.

• **Think outside the cereal box.** Once a week, choose a Scandinavian- or Asian-style breakfast—or have dinner for breakfast.

• **Stock your refrigerator with fresh fruits and veggies.** A tasty morning choice is a slice of whole-grain toast and a cup of nonfat yogurt with fresh fruit. (Steer clear of yogurt brands that take the fat out and replace it with loads of sugar.)

• **If you want to grab a healthy breakfast on the run,** you're better off with an apple or orange than a breakfast bar. To add some protein to the mix, you can also take a hard-boiled egg or a natural peanut butter sandwich on whole-grain bread with you.

Remember: Breakfast is a great way to start the day—but make sure it's a healthy one!

info For more information, contact the American Heart Association at *www.american heart.org* or the Center for Science in the Public Interest at *www.cspinet.org*.

Soy—A Little Goes A Long Way

Michael Janson, MD, author of *Dr. Janson's New Vitamin Revolution.* Avery. *www.drjanson.com.*

Soy has been one mainstay of supposedly healthy diets for years, but it has lately come under fire. We spoke with Michael Janson, MD, one of the many health and nutrition professionals who support soy as a healthful food.

A BRIEF REVIEW

Those who criticize soy are concerned primarily with the fact that it is rich in *isoflavones.* Isoflavones are *phytoestrogens,* or plant-based estrogens. Soy's two most common isoflavones are *genistein* and *daidzein.* With 25% of all US babies drinking soy formula, critics worry

that the isoflavones in the formula can cause a disruption of masculine development in boys… and cause girls to begin sexual development at a younger age.

Dr. Janson is adamant that plant estrogens are not the equivalent of female estrogen hormones and are therefore not dangerous. Neither of these phytoestrogens has an active hormonal effect and at most seems to block estrogen receptors. He points out that there is no evidence that any of the feared consequences have occurred and refers to a *Journal of the American Medical Association* study published in 2001 that researched 811 adults who drank either cow's milk or soy formula as infants. It found that more than 25 years later, the two groups were essentially indistinguishable in their history of sexual development and related problems.

Can soy formula cause *hypospadias* (a male genitalia birth defect, in which the urethra opens in the wrong place), as one study in England has suggested? Dr. Janson responds that the numbers of babies in the study actually affected was so small that the study is simply not conclusive and shows no specific association with soy.

THYROID CONNECTION?

The other major concern of those who are anti-soy is that isoflavones can cause thyroid problems, especially *hypothyroidism*, or an underactive thyroid gland. Dr. Janson acknowledges that animal studies have shown evidence of this, and he agrees that soy might exacerbate hypothyroidism. But he explains that animals do not often function the way humans do, so comparing species to species is not necessarily helpful.

For example, a cat study did reveal potential thyroid problems with soy consumption, but cats lack certain enzymes that humans have. The result is that soy affects felines differently than humans.

Furthermore, he says, a potentially significant cause of thyroid problems is a lack of iodine in the diet—not an abundance of soy. Researchers have found that various estrogen species have the capacity to block thyroid hormone receptors, and some surmise that this may actually be what causes the problem.

This is also the observation of one of the nation's top soy researchers, Daniel Doerge, PhD, at the Division of Biochemical Toxicology at the National Center for Toxicological Research. In 1999, Dr. Doerge and a colleague wrote a letter of protest concerning the US Food and Drug Administration's agreement to allow health claims on soy products.

In his later research, Dr. Doerge concluded that soy alone does not affect thyroid function. It appears that other factors, in particular iodine deficiency, must be present.

SORTING IT OUT

Does soy help or hurt? Surprisingly, there is some accord from both camps.

When it comes to soy, moderation is the key—as it is for most things in life. This is definitely not a case of "if a little is good, a lot is better." Dr. Janson suggests that soy be eaten as part of a good diet, not its centerpiece.

While a number of large studies have shown that soy has considerable health benefits, including protection from cardiovascular problems and possibly protection from breast and prostate cancer, you can get these benefits from eating a wide variety of healthful foods—whole grains, fruits, vegetables and fish—as well.

As for babies ingesting all that soy in their formula, Dr. Janson absolutely agrees with soy foes that breast milk is by far the best food for babies. For mothers who can't breast-feed, though, he sees no reason not to use soy if the situation calls for avoiding cow's milk formula.

People who suffer from hypothyroidism but want to include soy in their diets should talk to their doctors before doing so.

Another recommendation is to get soy from foods only, not from supplements. There is general agreement among experts that you shouldn't take soy supplements until more research has been done on soy.

Finally, Dr. Janson and others tell us to avoid highly processed soy foods, such as power bars and shakes. Tasty as they might be, Dr. Janson explains that highly processed foods have unpredictable effects. Tofu, being minimally processed, is fine.

Once again, the key is moderation. In moderation, you can get the benefits of soy without its potential risks.

Asian Delicacy Blocks Blood Clots

Mark Messina, PhD, adjunct associate professor of nutrition, Loma Linda University, California.

Some say it's an acquired taste, but natto, a Japanese delicacy for more than 1,000 years, is finally catching on in the United States. Its pungent scent and slimy, stringlike consistency may never make this fermented soybean food the cross-cultural menu star that sushi is, but natto's health benefits may move even timid souls to give it a try.

Soybeans are boiled and then fermented to make natto, and researchers say that two enzymes formed during this process—*pyrazine* and *nattokinase*—offer powerful protection against blood clots, including those that lead to heart attack, stroke and deep vein thrombosis. Pyrazine helps prevent blood clots from forming, while nattokinase actually dissolves clots. Some doctors think these enzymes may be apt stand-ins for drugs such as *warfarin* (Coumadin), a blood thinner, or *thrombolytics*, which are administered shortly after the onset of stroke or heart attack to break up clots and let blood flow. A few experts suggest eating natto on Sunday evening, since many heart attacks and strokes occur on Monday morning.

BEST WAYS TO EAT NATTO

In Japan, aficionados often eat natto, seasoned with soy sauce and spicy mustard, on top of rice for breakfast, but natto also appears in sushi, atop noodles and in other hot dishes. If you're thinking of trying natto for clot-busting purposes, make it raw. Nattokinase appears to lose its effectiveness when heated.

You can purchase natto in any store that sells Japanese foods, or you can buy the extract over the Internet and in some health-food stores.

HOW ABOUT OTHER SOY SOURCES?

Although you won't find clot-dissolving nattokinase in other soy foods, many health experts, including those at the American Heart Association, praise soy's ability to lower cholesterol and fight cardiovascular disease. Unfermented foods, such as tofu, soy milk and soy nuts, are also good sources of protein, but some health experts stress that fermented soy foods, such as natto, miso and tempeh, are much safer and healthier alternatives, claiming that fermentation blocks soy components that can interfere with protein digestion and mineral absorption.

SOY SAFETY

Meanwhile, the debate continues over whether soy adversely affects thyroid function, promotes dementia, increases breast cancer risk in women at high risk for this disease or increases the risk of developing a secondary tumor in breast cancer survivors. However, according to Mark Messina, PhD, adjunct associate professor of nutrition at Loma Linda University in California, and one of the top soy researchers, the clinical data clearly show that soy foods do not negatively impact thyroid function in men or women, and several studies published within the past three years offer hope that soy improves several aspects of cognitive function in postmenopausal women.

With regard to breast cancer, although the evidence is not definitive, Dr. Messina thinks that most of the studies published within the past two years suggest that soy does not pose any risk to high-risk women or breast cancer survivors. As a general recommendation, he encourages the consumption of two to three servings of soy foods daily. Consult with your doctor and discuss what is best for you.

Who should avoid natto? Those taking warfarin or any blood-thinning medication, or those who suffer from bleeding disorders or peptic ulcers. You also should avoid natto if you have had a recent ischemic stroke, neurosurgery or other major trauma.

For everyone else, it's nice to know about another natural tool in the heart health tool chest.

Is More Fat Healthier?

Udo Erasmus, PhD, developer of the "right fat, carb-conscious diet" and author of *Fats That Heal, Fats That Kill.* Alive Books. *www.udoerasmus.com.*

What could be more healthful than a big green salad topped with nonfat dressing? Surprisingly, the answer is… that same salad but with *full-fat* dressing.

Wendy White, PhD, an associate professor of food science and human nutrition at Iowa State University, ran a small study in which three groups of men and women ate three meals of salads comprised of spinach, romaine lettuce, cherry tomatoes and carrots. The groups took turns eating their salads with Italian dressing containing no fat…six grams (g) of fat…or 28g of fat. White took blood samples each hour for 11 hours following the salad eating and then had them analyzed.

The result: Those who ate the full-fat salads were winners, with the greatest absorption of the important nutrients lycopene and alpha- and beta-carotene, while the fat-free salad eaters absorbed only small amounts of these nutrients.

WHAT'S GOING ON HERE?

To understand the results of the study, we spoke with Udo Erasmus, PhD, author of *Fats That Heal, Fats That Kill.* He explains that because vegetables are so low in fat, adding fat to them will greatly enhance absorption of any oil-soluble nutrients they contain. Oil-soluble nutrients include vitamins A, D, E and K, carotene, lycopene and lutein, several other antioxidants and phytonutrients.

But, says Dr. Erasmus, that doesn't mean you can grab any bottle of blue cheese or Russian dressing off grocery store shelves and treat yourself to better health. Commercial oils are subject to corrosive processing that turns them toxic and damages many of the beneficial nutrients. The only commercial oil he advocates is extra virgin olive oil, which contains a small amount of the essential omega-6 fatty acids, but is woefully inadequate in equally essential omega-3s. He recommends consuming one tablespoon of undamaged oil rich in omega-3 and omega-6 essential fatty acids (2:1 ratio) per 50 pounds of body weight each day in winter and a little less in summer. This would account for the major part of fat consumption in a healthy diet.

One more note from Dr. Erasmus: He cautions against frying or sautéing in oil—poach, boil, steam or pressure-cook all foods instead. Frying, he says, turns oil toxic and increases its potential to cause inflammation in the body. Enjoy the oil's flavor and nutritional benefits by adding it after the food is cooked.

No Free Pass

Naomi Fisher, MD, assistant professor of medicine, Harvard Medical School, Boston.

Fans of dark chocolate thought that they were given a free pass several years ago when research indicated that dark chocolate contains health-giving antioxidants. For many people, the news made an occasional Godiva treat a guilt-free indulgence. But a new study raises a red flag in front of the chocolate lover, since most processed chocolates have "the good stuff" processed out.

LATEST STUDY

In this study, 27 people of varying ages who had no health issues, such as high blood pressure or high cholesterol levels, drank a special cocoa over a period of one month. Results showed that the cocoa seemed to improve the endothelial lining of the arteries and help open the vessels.

According to Naomi Fisher, MD, assistant professor of medicine at Harvard Medical School in Boston, and lead researcher of the study, the researchers believe it is the presence of a subclass of flavonoids called *flavonols*—specifically the molecules *catechin* and *epicatechin* in cocoa—that improve arterial condition. She notes that the molecules exist in many foods, but they are especially dense in cocoa. Interestingly, researchers saw results in all subjects—but it was particularly evident in the older ones. Furthermore, the improvement continued even after the digestion and elimination of the antioxidant-containing cocoa—sometimes 12 hours to 15 hours later.

The problem is that the cocoa in the study is not the cocoa available in grocery stores. Almost no chocolate or cocoa on the market today contains flavonols because of processing. Dr. Fisher says that a process called "dutching" mellows the flavor of cocoa by removing its bitter taste, but unfortunately the antioxidants go with it.

However, all is not lost. If the ingredient list on a dark chocolate includes *cocoa*, the flavonols may remain. This is the case with the dark chocolate at some of the larger health-food markets, such as Whole Foods Market and Trader Joe's. If there is no "cocoa" on the label, there are definitely no flavonols. And, while most baking cocoa has been dutched, some of the high-end brands have not.

Research continues as to how to prolong the cocoa effect on arteries. If the good news continues, you can be sure major food processors will figure out how to make flavonol-rich cocoa and dark chocolate available to American consumers.

The Magic of Green Tea

Lester A. Mitscher, PhD, distinguished professor of medicinal chemistry, University of Kansas, Lawrence. Dr. Mitscher won the American Chemical Society's lifetime achievement award for his work with teas and antibiotic resistance. He is coauthor of *The Green Tea Book: China's Fountain of Youth*. Avery.

Green tea has been promoted as having great health benefits. We decided to find out more by talking to Lester A. Mitscher, PhD, coauthor of *The Green Tea Book: China's Fountain of Youth*.

Green tea's health benefits were first touted by a Chinese emperor more than 4,000 years ago. Since then, these benefits have been scientifically validated. Green tea can help ward off many types of cancer, fight heart disease and colds and even prevent cavities.

WHY TEA HELPS

Green and black teas are made from the leaves of the *Camellia sinensis* plant. The leaves contain *catechins*, antioxidants that block the action of free radicals (harmful molecules).

The most powerful catechin is *epigallocatechin gallate* (EGCG). A study conducted at the University of Shizuoka in Japan showed that the antioxidant power of EGCG in green tea was 200 times stronger than that of vitamin E, another antioxidant.

Green tea is made from fresh, young leaves, which are steamed immediately to preserve the catechins and then dried.

SPECIFIC BENEFITS OF GREEN TEA

The health benefits are astonishing. *Catechins in tea...*

• **Reduce risk for certain types of cancer,** including cancers of the lung, breast and digestive tract. In a University of Minnesota study of more than 35,000 women, those who drank two or more cups of green or black tea daily over an eight-year period had a 10% lower risk of developing any cancer than those who seldom drank tea.

• **Curb risk of heart disease** by blocking the formation of plaque in the coronary arteries. A four-year study conducted at Harvard Medical School showed that participants who drank 14 cups or more of green or black tea weekly had a 44% lower death rate after a heart attack than people who didn't drink tea.

• **Fight colds and other illnesses.** Tea keeps free radicals from undermining the immune system. Researchers at Toyama Medical and Pharmaceutical University in Japan confirmed reports that catechins in green tea extract inhibit the growth of the influenza virus. Scientists at the State University of New York Health Science Center, University Hospital in Syracuse, New York, reviewed the literature and concluded that green tea enhances immunity.

• **Build bone density.** One study of more than 1,000 participants showed that drinking two or more cups of tea a day for at least six years strengthened bone density.

• **Prevent cavities** by blocking the growth of Streptococcus mutans, bacterium associated with dental plaque.

• **Aid digestion** by fostering the growth of beneficial bacteria in the intestines.

HOW MUCH TEA?

Aim for four cups of green tea daily—the health benefits build up over time. Expensive green teas may taste better, but they don't necessarily provide more health benefits.

Brew tea for three minutes to ensure the release of antioxidants. Longer steeping only produces more tannins, which taste bitter.

Iced tea yields the same benefits, but antioxidants degrade with time, so drink the tea soon after brewing.

Green tea contains less caffeine than coffee —up to 30 milligrams (mg) per cup, while one cup of coffee has 160 mg. People who are sensitive to caffeine may prefer decaffeinated tea. The process that removes caffeine from tea does not interfere with its health benefits.

Alternative: Try caffeine-free green tea capsules, available at health-food stores. Look for a brand that is organic, free of preservatives and has an expiration date to ensure freshness. The usual dosage is two 250-mg capsules daily.

A Honey of a Health Food!

Heidrun B. Gross, PhD, department of nutrition, University of California, Davis.

The average American enjoys a whopping 20 teaspoons of sugar each day. News from the University of California, Davis, is that there may be a way to turn bad to good by using honey instead. Honey raises the level of the immune-enhancing, disease-fighting antioxidants in the blood, says researcher Heidrun B. Gross, PhD.

ABOUT THE STUDY

Researchers gave 25 subjects approximately four tablespoons of dark buckwheat honey daily for 29 days. They were free to eat the honey in most forms. The exceptions were baked or dissolved in tea, since researchers believed that heat would destroy the honey's active constituents. Most of the subjects simply spooned the honey straight out of the jar into their mouths. Others spread it on toast, combined it with peanut butter and bananas or added it to milkshakes.

Dr. Gross explains that honey contains a large percentage of *polyphenols,* a type of antioxidant known to be important in the prevention of cardiovascular disease and cancer. Fruits, vegetables, seeds and tea are also rich in polyphenols.

The participants in the study were divided into two groups that received honey containing different amounts of polyphenols. At regular intervals following honey consumption, the subjects were given blood tests. The results showed a direct link between the type of honey consumption and the level of polyphenolic antioxidants in blood plasma. No participants experienced uncomfortable side effects, such as intestinal problems.

SWEETER THAN SUGAR

Bottom line: With its ability to increase the body's defense system against oxidative stress, honey can be part of a healthy, balanced diet. Dr. Gross recommends that when possible, you substitute honey for sugar and other sweeteners that do not provide immune-boosting antioxidants. Because honey is sweeter than sugar, you can use even a little less. Simply use it to taste, she advises.

A few words of caution: All honey is not created equal. Dr. Gross notes that dark honey contains more antioxidants than the light variety. Additionally, for those who are diabetic or sensitive to sugar, honey is not a "free pass." Since honey contains fructose and sucrose, regular intake increases the conversion of fructose to glucose in the liver, which makes consuming honey no better than consuming table sugar.

Never give honey to babies 12 months old or younger. It is associated with infant botulism, a rare but potentially life-threatening form of food poisoning in this age group.

New Ways to Fuel Your Brain

Antonio J. Convit, MD, medical director, Center for Brain Health, NYU School of Medicine, New York City.

Memory glitches—forgotten names, fuzzy details—are often assumed to be part of aging. But several years ago, researchers at the Center for Brain Health at NYU School of Medicine did a study showing that being insulin resistant, or prediabetic (having higher-than-normal blood glucose levels but not high enough to be classified as diabetic), as some 40 million Americans now are, plays an important role in the brain's ability to function in certain areas, including learning and some kinds of memory. Even better is the fact that by addressing insulin resistance, damage can be reversed.

ORIGINAL FINDINGS

The original research studied 30 people—with less-than-healthy habits—between the ages of 53 and 89 who were insulin-resistant but not diabetic. (Insulin is the hormone that regulates blood sugar or glucose, sending it to the tissue cells, among other things.) After giving the subjects glucose intravenously, the researchers administered cognitive function tests and did magnetic resonance imaging (MRI) brain scans.

Result: Subjects with the poorest glucose test results—that is, the glucose lingered in their blood rather than going to the tissues as it would normally—also had the lowest scores in the cognitive tests. Furthermore, the hippocampus, that part of the brain that is key for recent learning and memory, was smaller than normal.

We spoke with Antonio J. Convit, MD, medical director of the Center for Brain Health at NYU School of Medicine in New York City and head of the study, about this work and the follow-up research now going on. He says that while it's been known for some time that diabetes predisposes people to memory problems, his study was the first to provide evidence of a relationship between prediabetes and the brain. Assuming an adequate supply, glucose is the only fuel the brain uses—unlike other parts of the body, which need many additional nutrients. When the study put the hippocampus to work performing cognitive tests, it needed extra fuel or glucose. However, the subjects' insulin resistance prevented proper transportation of glucose to the brain and so deprived the hippocampus of the fuel it needed to do its work well. (Interestingly, in this study, the hippocampus was the only part of the brain affected by the lack of glucose.)

RESEARCH UNDER WAY

Dr. Convit is continuing his study by following a number of the original subjects to evaluate how lifestyle change affects glucose and memory function. Thus far, the evidence is anecdotal and it is too early for the long-range analysis, but Dr. Convit happily shares what he has found out to date. He says he gave these people what he calls his wrath-of-God speech concerning the health risks they were incurring. Following this wake-up call, a number of them corrected their harmful habits. Those who lost the excess weight and started exercising regularly are having what he terms vastly different results in their tests. They are no longer prediabetic…and their memories have improved, as have their other physical markers, such as cholesterol levels.

On the other hand, the subjects who failed to improve their diet and exercise regimen are getting worse in the same areas, he says.

THE MESSAGE IS CLEAR

Dr. Convit says the take-home message now is absolutely unambiguous. If you want your brain to work well, eat a diet that contributes to weight control and good health, and *exercise regularly*.

EXERCISE!

In fact, exercise is turning out to be a much more critical element than previously thought for contributing to both strong brain and insulin functions. In a study with mice, researchers were able to stimulate the essential neurological factors that help create new brain cells. They did this by getting the mice to exercise regularly, and although this was a study involving mice, Dr. Convit says there is no reason to think that it wouldn't be applicable to humans.

Exercise also helps regulate glucose because it increases insulin sensitivity. This is particularly true of any exercise that increases muscle mass, including Pilates and strength or weight training. Dr. Convit says that the best exercise package of all is to do both weight-resistant work and aerobic activities—and you don't need to do massive amounts. Thirty minutes a day of brisk walking most days will do. At the very least, regular walks, adding steps into your day and climbing stairs whenever possible is sufficient if that is all you can manage.

Dr. Convit also urges anyone who might be prediabetic to be tested. The test is not difficult, but it does take time. You start with a fasting glucose test (a blood test first thing in the morning before eating) and then you drink a high-glucose liquid. Two hours later, you will have another blood test that will show how effective your insulin is in getting glucose into the tissues. Symptoms of prediabetes include elevated blood pressure, large waist circumference (35 inches or more for women, 40 inches or more

for men), elevated triglycerides, a low HDL (the "good" cholesterol) count (below 41mg/dl) and an elevated blood sugar level. If you have three or more of these symptoms, you are considered likely to be prediabetic.

WORD TO THE WISE

We all think that our nutrition is complete when we leave the table—but that is just the start of the feeding process. We must put the right foods into a well-functioning body. Exercise is step one…followed closely by proper nutrition and assistance in getting a prediabetic condition under control.

Tempting Fate— Diabetes Dangers

Claresa Levetan, MD, endocrinologist, Lankenau Hospital, Wynnewood, Pennsylvania, and associate editor, *Diabetes Forecast*. ADA.

The threat of diabetes looms over our overweight nation, but many people think that if they fall victim, they'll just watch what they eat and take insulin if necessary. No big deal, right? *Wrong!*

Study after study is showing that having diabetes is a big deal—the latest ones show that it's even worse than most doctors previously thought.

An article in *Harvard Heart Letter* reports that heart attacks and strokes are four times more common among people with diabetes, that these episodes occur earlier in life and that they are more likely to be fatal than in people who do not have the disease.

We spoke with Claresa Levetan, MD, about this sobering finding. Dr. Levetan is an endocrinologist on the staff of Lankenau Hospital in Wynnewood, Pennsylvania, and in the forefront of diabetes care as an associate editor of *Diabetes Forecast*, the publication of the American Diabetes Association. She adds yet another fact to this troubling situation: People with diabetes who have never had a heart attack are as likely to have one as a nondiabetic patient who has just had an attack.

DIABETIC CONNECTION

Diabetes is a complex disease, says Dr. Levetan, and it is about much more than insulin response, diet and exercise. For some reason, in people with diabetes, the LDL cholesterol (the kind that causes problems) is denser and more dangerous than the light fluffy LDL found in nondiabetics. Dr. Levetan adds that even if total cholesterol isn't high in diabetics, because of the type of LDL they have, patients are more apt to have plaque, and it is more likely to break off and cause clots.

THE ABCs OF PREVENTION

Dr. Levetan has advice for those who already have diabetes. She says to be rigorous about following what's called the "ABC program." Every three months, have your **A**1C test (an indicator of how well your diabetes is being controlled)…keep your **B**lood pressure under 120/80mg/dL…and keep LDL **C**holesterol levels under 100. To reach these levels, she has her patients adopt a healthy eating and exercise regimen. If that does not bring the problem in line, she prescribes medication, including statins for cholesterol control. This is a case where the risk for heart problems outweighs the risk from taking statins.

For those who are not diabetic, Dr. Levetan has strong words of advice—do whatever you must to avoid getting diabetes. This includes keeping to a diet of nutrient-rich foods and exercising regularly. Our medical expert, Andrew L. Rubman, ND, says that dietary supplements that include chromium can help gain better control of glucose metabolism.

Those who are age 30 or older (now the recommended age for screening) with a family history of diabetes should have a fasting glucose test (a simple blood test taken before eating in the morning). This test will determine if you fall into the prediabetic category (blood glucose of 100 to 126). If you do, be sure to talk to your doctor *immediately* about gaining control.

Harvard Study: Magnesium Lowers Diabetes Risk

Jerry L. Nadler, MD, professor of medicine, and chief, division of endocrinology and metabolism, University of Virginia Health System, Charlottesville.

Andrew L. Rubman, ND, director, Southbury Clinic for Traditional Medicines, Southbury, Connecticut.

Over the years, scientists have discovered that a healthy diet is instrumental in preventing a number of diseases. Most recently, two large Harvard studies demonstrated that a diet rich in magnesium may help prevent type 2 diabetes.

Often associated with obesity, this condition —characterized by the body's inability to make efficient use of glucose—is associated with a number of potentially deadly complications, including heart disease, kidney failure, blindness and neuropathy (nerve damage).

With type 2 diabetes on the rise, the chance that simple dietary changes can prevent it is significant. To learn more about diabetes and magnesium, we contacted Jerry L. Nadler, MD, professor of medicine and chief of the division of endocrinology and metabolism at the University of Virginia Health System. Dr. Nadler wrote the editorial that accompanied the two studies in *Diabetes Care*.

ABOUT THE STUDIES

In the first study, researchers at the Harvard School of Public Health evaluated the diets of more than 85,000 women and 42,000 men. Looking at data accumulated over 18 years for the women and over 12 years for the men, they found that those who consumed the most magnesium through foods—such as leafy green vegetables and whole grains—were least likely to develop type 2 diabetes. Fewer than 5% of the participants took magnesium supplements.

A second study examined the diets of nearly 40,000 women. Harvard researchers at Brigham and Women's Hospital in Boston found that even among overweight women, those who ate plenty of magnesium-rich foods were 22% less likely to develop type 2 diabetes.

VEGETABLES, NUTS AND WHOLE GRAINS

The recommended dietary intake (RDI) for magnesium is 400 milligrams (mg). Whole grains, leafy green vegetables, avocados and nuts are the best sources. Dr. Nadler says that if you don't get enough magnesium in your diet, magnesium supplements should be considered.

Other good sources for magnesium include tofu, pumpkin seeds, dried beans (legumes), blackstrap molasses, cereal, bananas and wheat, oat and soy flour. That said, it would take very large quantities of food to ingest the suggested 400 mg of magnesium daily.

A MINERAL SUPPLEMENT

Our medical expert, Andrew L. Rubman, ND, recommends his favorite calcium/magnesium supplement, Butyrex, from T.E. Neesby, available on-line and at health-food stores. Talk to your health-care professional about what is right for you.

In the meantime, enjoy the guacamole.

info For more prevention advice, including a diabetes risk test, visit the American Diabetes Association at *www.diabetes.org*.

Tomato Juice Prevents Blood Clots

Manohar Garg, PhD, associate professor, nutrition and dietetics, University of Newcastle, Australia.

Here's a good reason to add tomato juice to your grocery list—especially if you or a loved one is fighting type 2 diabetes. According to researchers from the University of Newcastle in Australia, tomato juice has a blood-thinning effect in people who have the disease. That means it reduces the tendency of blood platelets to clump together and form clots that can lead to strokes, heart attacks as well as life-threatening conditions such as deep vein thrombosis (DVT)—a common problem for people who have diabetes.

THE FINDINGS

DVT occurs when a blood clot forms in a vein deep in the body, usually in a leg or hip vein. A clot that breaks off and travels to your lungs can cause death.

The researchers gave 250 milliliters (about one cup) a day of tomato juice or a tomato-flavored drink to 20 people with type 2 diabetes. Study participants had no history of clotting problems and took no aspirin or other medication that might affect clotting.

Blood samples collected at the beginning and at the end of the three-week study showed that the juice drinkers had significantly less platelet aggregation, which can result in clots that block blood flow through vessels to the brain or heart.

ADDITIONAL SOURCES

We contacted study coauthor Manohar Garg, PhD, associate professor of nutrition and dietetics, who told us that it's not yet understood how tomato juice reduces the ability of platelets to bind together. A tomato component named P3, found in the yellow, jelly-like fluid around the seeds, might be responsible.

According to Dr. Garg, this component appears both water-soluble and heat stable, so if you're not fond of tomato juice, don't worry, you're likely to get similar benefits from fresh tomatoes and processed tomato products such as canned or bottled tomato sauce.

TOMATOES FOR HEALTH

These findings may be welcome news to the rising number of Americans (about 24 million) with type 2 diabetes, who have an increased risk for cardiovascular problems from clotting. Smokers, long-distance travelers at risk for DVT and people genetically predisposed to forming blood clots may also benefit from adding tomato products to their diets. Plus, a nice tomato sauce is a lot tastier than current clot-preventing drugs, such as aspirin or blood-thinners.

About one cup of tomato juice per day offers the anticlotting benefit, Dr. Garg says. But more studies are needed to confirm the benefit from other tomato products and to determine how much we need to eat to get the same effect.

3

Nutritional Cures

Healthy Power of the Mediterranean Diet

Mediterranean cuisine is fabulous, full of richly colored, heart-healthy vegetables, fruits, whole grains, fish and poultry and, of course, plenty of olive oil.

Fascinating: In spite of the liberal use of oil and grains, researchers have found that people who eat a Mediterranean diet have vastly lower rates of heart disease than people in many other parts of the world. Harvard published a study in the mid-1990s about this effect among Greeks. *The New England Journal of Medicine* published a study that reiterated the power of this diet for advancing good health.

LATEST STUDY RESULTS

Dimitrios Trichopoulos, MD, PhD, from the Harvard School of Public Health, worked with a group of Greek scientists from the University of Athens Medical School to investigate the impact of the diet. For the study, 22,000 Greek men and women, ages 20 to 86, recorded what they ate each day over a four-year period. The investigators then rated the responses on a scale of zero through 10 based on how closely the participants stayed with the tenets of the diet, with 10 being the best. They discovered that following the diet not only lowered the risk of death by heart disease or stroke, but that for every two-point increase achieved in the rating scale, there was a 25% drop in mortality risk. A separate but similar American study showed that the diet also helps reduce the risk of gallstones by nearly 20%.

DIET DETAILS

Unlike the detailed approach of many weight-loss plans, this diet has no particular structure. *Instead, it includes...*

- **Lots of fruits and vegetables.**
- **Plenty of whole-grain products.**
- **Some beans, legumes and nuts.**

Eric B. Rimm, ScD, associate professor of epidemiology and nutrition, Harvard School of Public Health, Boston.

•A moderate amount of fish and poultry.

•Limited amounts of lean meats, dairy and alcohol.

That looseness makes it easy to fool yourself into thinking you are following it, but the key to success is not tucking it in between helpings of ice cream and chips. To discuss how careful people need to be and where their weak points are, we called Eric B. Rimm, ScD, associate professor of epidemiology and nutrition at the Harvard School of Public Health in Boston. Dr. Rimm has studied the diet extensively and coauthored an editorial in the *Journal of the American Medical Association* concerning it.

THE REAL DEAL

Dr. Rimm offers the following strategies for sticking with a true Mediterranean diet…

•Make sure your whole grains are really whole grains. In addition to their nutritive value, whole grains slow the digestion of other foods and leave you feeling full for a longer period of time. This lowers the "net carb" effect. He urges people to select the least processed whole-grain foods—even if a food is technically a whole grain, commercial preparation pulverizes the grain, reducing its healthfulness. Don't be fooled by packaging ploys. Bread must have the word "whole" in the first or second ingredient listed on the package to qualify as truly whole wheat.

•Variety of grains. Sure, images of those fabulous fresh breads make you think that it is a mainstay of those who partake of a Mediterranean diet, but in fact they eat a variety of delicious and nutritious grains. Brown rice also counts, as do a number of other grain products, including oats (especially steel-cut oats) and barley.

•Lots of produce. The Greeks typically eat nearly a pound of vegetables a day—twice the amount Americans eat. No need to be shy with your produce.

•Plenty of protein. Dr. Rimm advises having a good protein source on a daily basis, be it fish, poultry or eggs. Plant protein, in the form of beans and nuts, is also good.

•Counting calories. Portion control is always important—even when it comes to olive oil. Although this Mediterranean diet features up to 40% of calories from fat, this is from all sources, including fish, poultry and dairy, as well as from monounsaturated oils—canola, soy and especially olive oil. "Super-sizing" your portions definitely is not the way to go. Eat moderate amounts at all times.

•Active lifestyle. Another critical aspect of the true Mediterranean diet is actually their way of life. Exercise is as much a part of the diet, Dr. Rimm says, as olive oil. These people work hard physically each day, unlike many Americans, who live a more sedentary life. According to Dr. Rimm, it is mandatory to get at least 30 minutes of brisk exercise every day, most days of the week.

As for the gelato and other goodies from the region—Dr. Rimm says to limit these "extra" foods to occasional treats. These foods—including red meat—are tolerable only about once a week. Even then, he says, think small, not bingeing on three scoops of ice cream. He also advises moderation in dairy products. The diet includes dairy but doesn't emphasize it. Stick with low-fat products when possible and limit portions.

CULTURAL SATURATION

Dr. Rimm is one of the first professionals to acknowledge that changing the way you eat, fully and forever, is a major challenge. He suggests approaching it in two ways. First, make the decision and set it as a goal. Then transition slowly. Over whatever period of time you are comfortable with, slide the right foods into your eating regimen and the wrong ones out. Review where you are at six months and perhaps at a year, and see what changes you may need to make. Eventually, he says, you'll look forward to eating the Mediterranean diet foods because they taste wonderful and make you feel even better. *Mangia.*

The Only Diet That Works

Eric Yarnell, ND, president of the Botanical Medicine Academy and is an ND clinical supervisor at Bastyr Center for Natural Health, both in Seattle. He is coauthor of *Clinical Botanical Medicine*. Mary Ann Liebert.

The weight reduction list goes on and on—Atkins Diet…high-carbohydrate diet…Weight Watchers…Jenny Craig…South Beach Diet. People swear by the one on which they just had recent success—and then, usually, the weight returns and they are dismayed. In the end, there's really only one diet that works—eat less and exercise more.

To learn about dieting and weight loss, we spoke with Eric Yarnell, ND, RH, a core faculty member at Bastyr University in Kenmore, Washington, and president of the Botanical Medicine Academy in Seattle. The most important step to take, according to Dr. Yarnell, is to make the commitment to lose weight. Once you do, you must work with your health-care professional to develop a diet plan that you can realistically live with and follow—one that is also effective and practical.

THE LOW-FAT CRAZE

For the last 20 years, Americans have been on the low-fat bandwagon. In order to lose weight, we were instructed by the medical establishment—starting with the surgeon general on down—to cut the fat out of our diets. *That* certainly didn't work, as obesity and diabetes soon rose to epidemic proportions in the US.

The whole concept of "fat is bad" was very short-sighted, says Dr. Yarnell. It failed to take into account that there are healthy fats that our bodies require for normal function. Moreover, people have to eat *something*, and so they switched from high-fat foods to low-fat products packed with white flour, sugar and calories…and people continued to gain weight. Dr. Yarnell stresses that calories do matter, and people seem to have lost sight of this.

THE LOW-CARB CRAZE

Low-carb diets, from Atkins to South Beach, once assumed center stage. These popular plans allow fats and proteins, while severely limiting carbohydrates—pasta, white rice, white bread and sugar. Dr. Yarnell points out that in controlled studies, low-carb diets don't fare any better than other diet plans. In the long run, there is no difference in weight loss. He adds that a key reason any diet may work is that, when followed correctly, you consume fewer calories.

The bottom line is that elements of each of these approaches make sense—or have worked. Yes, it is good to limit your intake of the saturated fats in meat and dairy products, the trans fats in processed and fast foods, and refined carbohydrates in white flour and sugar. All of these contribute to higher rates of cardiovascular disease, obesity and diabetes. But don't throw out the baby with the bathwater—there are also plenty of healthy fats (in salmon, tuna, olive oil, sesame seeds, etc.) and healthy carbs (in vegetables and whole grains).

According to Dr. Yarnell, the key to any successful weight-loss plan is to eat a variety of whole foods and expend more calories than you take in. How can you do this? Simple—Eat less and exercise more!

TAKE SMALL STEPS

Dr. Yarnell acknowledges that it is very difficult for people to change their diets and lifestyles, so he encourages patients to start out by taking small steps. Walk before you run…limit a food before excluding it. *Other smart strategies…*

• **Cook for yourself,** and incorporate more nutrient-rich whole foods into your diet. Fast foods and processed products are packed with trans fats, empty carbohydrates and calories. Don't have time? Make double or triple batches when you cook, then freeze them. When it's mealtime, simply thaw and heat.

• **Eat more vegetables.** Not only are veggies packed with vitamins and minerals that benefit your overall health, they also fill you up so you are not as tempted to reach out for the troublesome foods.

• **Pay close attention to portion size** when you dine out. Most restaurant meals are far larger than necessary. Leave something on your plate, or take a doggie bag home.

• **Keep sweets and junk food out of the house.** Spare yourself the temptation of eating them by not buying them in the first place. But what about your children and spouse? They aren't on the diet? They also don't need to over-indulge in these empty calories, but you can buy one or two items that are for them—things that you don't like and would not be tempted to snack on.

•**If you've been inactive,** keep in mind that even a modest amount of exercise—such as walking for 20 to 30 minutes three or four times a week—is beneficial. As time goes on, you can gradually build up to 45- and then 60-minute walks. At a minimum, take the steps instead of the elevator…park at the far end of the parking lot instead of the first spot. Every extra step is extra calories expended.

•**Get your family and friends on board.** For dinner tonight, serve the whole family a meal based on vegetables, whole grains and small amounts of lean protein. Tomorrow morning, buddy up with a friend and take a brisk walk around the park.

Ultimately, losing weight is not a function of fad diets, crash diets or the diet du jour. Sustained weight loss requires a commitment to a complete lifestyle change, says Dr. Yarnell. If you start out by taking small steps, you'll eventually get there—and stay there.

Eat Less—Live Longer

John O. Holloszy, MD, professor of medicine, Washington University in St. Louis, School of Medicine.

Eat less and virtually every health-screenable measure in your body will improve. This not-so-surprising statement is based on the stunning results of a recent study from Washington University in St. Louis, School of Medicine, which measured the impact of lower-calorie diets on health risks.

In this pilot study, 18 people, ages 35 to 82 (average age of 50) ate 1,100 to 1,950 calories a day, depending on size and gender, for three to 15 years. (The average American diet is made up of 1,975 to 3,550 calories per day.) The test group was compared with 18 age- and gender-matched people who followed typical Western eating patterns.

Even though the test group was very small, the results were astonishing. The calorie-restricted group had total and LDL cholesterol levels comparable to the lowest 10% of the population in their age groups. Their HDL levels were in the 85th to 90th percentile for middle-aged men…and their triglyceride levels were lower than 95% of Americans who are still in their 20s. Blood pressure in this group averaged 100/60—what you'd expect to see in 10-year-olds—and glucose and insulin levels were also very low.

Additional health indicators: The restricted group's body mass index, body fat mass, C-reactive protein levels (a measure of inflammation in the body) and the thickness of the carotid artery that runs from the heart to the brain were all significantly better than in the comparison group.

According to the study's coauthor, John O. Holloszy, MD, professor of medicine at Washington University in St. Louis, School of Medicine, the good health of the study group goes beyond reduced calories. In order for them to stay within rigid caloric guidelines, the test group ate only nutrient-dense foods. Their diet was high in protein—26% versus 18% in the comparison group. The 28% fats in the lean group's diet (compared with 32% in the other group) were exclusively healthy fats, such as olive oil.

Furthermore, the lean group's carbohydrates, making up 46% of their diet (versus 50% in the other group), included lots of vegetables, some fruits and whole-grain foods. They ate no sweets or other refined, processed carbs.

WHAT DOES THIS MEAN FOR ME?

Although most people are not interested in severe calorie restriction, there are lessons to be learned from this group. How can you achieve the same benefits? Do what the test group did. In particular, cut out the junk (save the sweets for truly special occasions)…increase your fruit and vegetable consumption…and increase the percentage of high-quality protein in your diet. Dr. Holloszy advises one gram of protein per kilogram (kg) of body weight (2.2kg make up one pound). Best sources of protein? Lean meats, fish and poultry, skim milk and whey protein.

Secrets to Lasting Weight Loss

John P. Foreyt, PhD, professor, Department of Psychiatry and Behavioral Sciences, Baylor College of Medicine in Houston and coauthor of *Lifestyle Obesity Management*. Wiley-Blackwell. Dr. Foreyt acted as a member of the National Task Force on the Prevention and Treatment of Obesity, sponsored by the National Institutes of Health, which addressed concerns about the health effects of weight cycling.

James O. Hill, PhD, director, Center for Human Nutrition, University of Colorado, an adviser on obesity to the National Institutes of Health, a cofounder of the National Weight Control Registry, cofounder of the national health initiative America on the Move and coauthor of *The Step Diet Book: Count Steps, Not Calories, to Lose Weight and Keep It Off Forever*. Workman.

S ome people believe that it's not obesity that puts people's health at risk so much as yo-yo dieting—the repeated loss and regain of body weight.

Not so, says John P. Foreyt, PhD, professor of psychiatry and behavioral sciences at Baylor College of Medicine in Houston and a member of the National Institutes of Health panel on weight loss and management, including "weight cycling" (the medical term for yo-yo dieting). He points out that there are so many benefits to weight loss—even if you regain the pounds—that you should never see this as a reason not to lose weight. Even a modest weight loss can reduce the risk of very serious obesity-related health problems, such as high blood pressure, heart disease, stroke, diabetes, cancer, arthritis and gallbladder disease.

Still, many dieters say that losing weight is not nearly as hard as keeping it off.

THE SECRETS TO LASTING WEIGHT LOSS

To get the lowdown on lasting weight loss, we consulted James O. Hill, PhD, cofounder of the National Weight Control Registry, which tracks more than 5,000 people who have lost at least 30 pounds and kept them off for more than a year.

He explained that the four primary weight-loss maintenance strategies reported by all successful Weight Control Registry participants…

•**They engage in at least one hour of physical activity every day.** Walking is the most popular exercise, but many of the long-term losers have added another sport or activity (such as swimming or bicycling). Consistent physical activity is the best predictor of long-term success, observes Dr. Hill.

•**They weigh themselves regularly (at least once a week).** This way, once a person finds the pounds beginning to creep back on, he/she can quickly take action and cut back on calories or spend a few more minutes working it off on the treadmill.

•**They eat breakfast every day.** Research suggests that eating a healthy breakfast may help in managing hunger and consuming fewer total daily calories.

•**They follow a low-fat (24%), high-complex-carbohydrate diet.**

STEPS TO WEIGHT LOSS AND MAINTENANCE

After 25 years of helping people lose weight and sustain weight loss, Dr. Hill devised the Step Diet. In his program, he stresses that long-term lifestyle changes—not short-term fad diets—are the key to weight loss and maintenance. The Step Diet is about taking small steps that can be maintained forever.

Dr. Hill recommends the following…

•**Maintain the proper energy balance.** Dieters typically focus on either what foods to eat (or not to eat) or what exercise program to follow in order to lose weight. Dr. Hill stresses that what really matters is energy balance—how many calories you consume versus how many you burn. If you burn more than you eat, you will lose weight.

To shed pounds, he recommends simply reducing your daily food intake by 25%. Since most of us eat more than we need, this should not leave you feeling deprived. It's really just taking a step back to adequate portions, says Dr. Hill. Eat three-quarters of a sandwich for lunch or three-quarters of a chicken cutlet at dinner, and tuck away the rest for a snack the next day.

•**Small changes drive success.** Fad diets—such as low-carb, low-fat or cabbage soup—are doomed to failure. You may lose weight with them in the short-term, but few people can or even should follow these approaches indefinitely. Their common consequence is weight cycling—people lose weight, the weight comes back on, they lose it again, etc.

Instead, make smaller, incremental changes to your lifestyle over time.

• **Start with physical activity.** Your first small step is to walk more, and the key is counting steps. To start, wear a pedometer for seven days to measure your normal level of physical activity. You'll probably be surprised by how much you do or don't walk. Once you determine your baseline—how many steps you take a day—gradually build up to at least 2,000 more steps per day. Start by increasing daily steps by 500 each week. Most successful Weight Control Registry participants end up taking 12,000 steps a day—which equals six miles.

• **Anticipate success, but not instantly.** As you take small steps in changing how you eat and move, aim for long-term health gains rather than short-term weight loss. All this takes time, but it will be time well spent, says Dr. Hill.

• **The maintenance of weight loss is more important than the speed or amount of weight loss.** A healthy weight loss is one to two pounds per week, says Dr. Hill. Faster weight loss is typically followed by even faster weight regain. In order to keep pounds off, you must move more. Dr. Hill explains that your metabolism drops by eight calories per pound of weight loss. This means that the average person needs to take 160 to 200 more steps per day for every pound he loses. If you shed 10 pounds, you must take 2,000 more steps a day. Otherwise, your slowed metabolism will virtually guarantee that you will regain the lost weight.

Weight loss takes time, and maybe even more than one try before you succeed in keeping it off. Don't be discouraged. If you regain weight, pause to refocus, and then make long-term changes in your eating and exercise program. It is better to keep trying than to resign yourself to the risks of obesity.

info National Institute of Diabetes and Digestive and Kidney Diseases, National Institutes of Health, *www.niddk.nih.gov.*

The National Weight Control Registry, *www.lifespan.org/services/bmed/wt_loss/nwcr.*

Milk—A Magic Weight-Loss Potion?

Michael Zemel, PhD, director, Nutrition Institute, University of Tennessee, Knoxville.

We've all seen the advertisements that claim milk "does a body good." Now, numerous research studies give that phrase a whole new meaning. Apparently, drinking milk not only builds strong teeth and bones, it also helps weight loss, lowers body fat and increases the body's lean mass. A simple glass of milk instead of an hour at the gym—could this really be possible?

Of course, that's a stretch. No food, including milk, can eliminate the need for regular exercise. We spoke with Michael Zemel, PhD, director of the Nutrition Institute at the University of Tennessee in Knoxville, about these surprising findings.

Although Dr. Zemel describes the effect of dairy on weight and fat control as substantial, he quickly adds that calories are still the main determinant. Dairy is not a magic potion, but it can help. With a modest reduction in caloric intake, you can lose almost twice as much weight by including dairy in your diet than you would otherwise. Even if you do not restrict calories, dairy will help you lose 5% or more body fat and have a corresponding increase in lean mass.

HOW IT WORKS

Dr. Zemel explains the reason behind this. Too little calcium raises the level of a hormone called *calcitriol* in the body. This is bad news because calcitriol is part of what gets your body's machinery going to produce more fat, and it interferes with the fat-burning mechanism.

The result: You end up with bigger, fatter fat cells and reduced metabolic efficiency—in other words, fat burning slows. And there's more. Dr. Zemel and his research team recently discovered that calcitriol inhibits the progress of normal programmed cell death, meaning that without adequate calcium, your body hangs on longer to those bigger, older fat cells instead of efficiently sloughing them off.

HOW ABOUT SUPPLEMENTS?

Don't look to calcium supplements for help, says Dr. Zemel. Although some people feel that calcium supplements would be effective as well, Dr. Zemel says that his research has found dairy to be the real deal. The calcium in dairy works synergistically with other bioactive components of milk to achieve this impact on the regulation of fat. For instance, there are specific amino acids in dairy that regulate and stimulate muscle protein synthesis, and this contributes to increasing lean mass.

Furthermore, only three types of dairy products qualify to give this effect—milk, yogurt and hard cheese. You need three servings a day.

Serving size: Eight ounces of milk or yogurt or one-and-a-half ounces of cheese.

While both sheep's and goat's milk are rich in calcium, the extent to which the antiobesity-related bioactive compounds are found in these milks is not known. More research is needed.

Quick Fixes for Losing Weight

Allan Geliebter, PhD, research psychologist, New York Obesity Research Center, St. Luke's-Roosevelt Hospital, New York City.
Jana Klauer, MD, physician in private practice and a former research fellow, New York Obesity Research Center at St. Luke's–Roosevelt Hospital, New York City.

There are always times in your life when you'd like to shed a few extra pounds quickly, whether it is for an upcoming beach vacation or someone's wedding. Do any of the quick-fix pills, patches and whatnots that advertise "miracle weight loss" really work?

To get the lowdown, we called dieting expert Jana Klauer, MD, a former research fellow at the New York Obesity Research Center at St. Luke's–Roosevelt Hospital in New York City. Dr. Klauer, who has her master's degree in clinical nutrition, has a private weight-control practice.

THE PATCH?

Dr. Klauer gave a quick dismissal to the patch. She said to forget claims that by wearing it you'll get fat-burning and appetite-curbing compounds into your system 24 hours a day. As to the rainbow of over-the-counter pills on the market, she reports that there simply isn't any credible research to back up the extravagant promises.

THE PILL?

However, there is one type of pill—actually a chew—that, although Dr. Klauer does not usually recommend products, she feels might be useful for occasional short-term use called starch blockers, with names such as Starch Away and Carbo Grabber. They are based on extracts of white kidney beans. The idea is that you eat one shortly before you consume a meal containing starch, such as pasta or bread, and its ingredients bind to the carbs, ushering them directly out of your system without digestion. Several small studies show that the chew binds about 40% of the starch consumed. That's the good news.

The bad news: They can cause bloating, excess gas, diarrhea and abdominal pains. And besides the bean extract, the chews contain sugar, corn syrup and partially hydrogenated fats from coconut oil, none of which will do your health any good. If you are on medication for, say, diabetes, Dr. Klauer cautions that the starch blocker could interfere with it.

PRESCRIPTION DRUGS

We then spoke with Allan Geliebter, PhD, a research psychologist who also works at the New York Obesity Research Center at St. Luke's-Roosevelt Hospital, about prescription drugs. Dr. Geliebter says there are several that have been approved by the FDA that will help you lose weight—but he is reluctant about them for several reasons.

The stimulant drugs, such as *phentermine*, reduce appetite, but can also increase blood pressure. When you stop taking them, the weight comes right back on.

And Xenical, a medication that acts as a fat binder, creates tremendous abdominal discomfort and gas.

HEALTHIER SOLUTIONS

But do not despair—Dr. Klauer has easy tips for weight loss that go beyond pills…

• **Drink green tea.** Green tea is first on her list—she advises drinking three or four cups a day. Studies show that the *polyphenols* in it help people lose a pound or so a month in addition to loss through calorie control. Decaffeinated is fine, and although there are green tea supplements on the market, she says that it may be the brewing of the leaves that activate and release the polyphenols, thus creating the weight-loss effect.

• **Eat quality protein.** While Dr. Klauer is not an Atkins advocate, she does advise emphasizing quality protein in your diet with fish, omega-3 eggs, poultry and plant protein, such as legumes.

Be sure to start your day with a protein breakfast. Studies show that after having a protein breakfast, such as eggs and low-fat cheese, it is easier to eat less at subsequent meals and lose weight. Before lunch or dinner (or both), eat a large green salad with low-calorie dressing—olive oil is preferred. A Tufts University study divided overweight subjects into four groups. For two months, before lunch, each group ate a small salad or a large salad with low-calorie dressing, a small salad or a large one with fat-containing additions, such as cheese and bacon bits, and a high-fat dressing. The group that ate a large green salad with low-fat dressing lost the most weight. Dr. Klauer explains that salads are filling because of the many nutrients they provide, and so they diminish the desire for a bigger follow-up meal. The fully loaded salads ended up stimulating the subjects' desire for more food.

• **Get plenty of rest.** During sleep, levels of the hormone *leptin*, which helps regulate body weight, spike. This sends the message to your brain that your body has sufficient energy stores—so it is instrumental in keeping overall hunger properly regulated.

• **Don't eat after 9 pm.** It does not make any difference in how your body uses the calories, but late at night, people tend to give in to snack attacks.

• **Be aware of portion sizes.** Simply eating smaller amounts of the food you regularly consume will create weight loss.

• **Exercise.** While you have to burn 3,500 calories to lose one pound of fat, regular exercise will start to add up and help contribute to a slimmer you.

So—there are no quick fixes. Calories in, calories out. It seems to come back to that.

Three Steps to Conquering Illness

Andrew L. Rubman, ND, director, Southbury Clinic for Traditional Medicines, Southbury, Connecticut.

Wouldn't it be great if joint pain, chronic sinusitis or other conditions related to suppressed immune function could be dramatically reduced by removing three things from your diet?

It turns out that, for some people, dairy, wheat and sugar are extremely harsh on the body and are at the root of an array of illnesses and conditions related to suppressed immune function, including irritable bowel syndrome, urinary tract infection, upper-respiratory congestion, muscle fatigue and joint pain. The list may even include chronic degenerative and autoimmune diseases, such as rheumatoid arthritis and coronary vascular disease.

HOW DO DIETARY CHANGES HELP?

According to our medical expert, Andrew L. Rubman, ND, eliminating products made from dairy, wheat and sugar can fine-tune your digestion, lead to a rapid loss in size and weight (especially around the waist), give you more energy, improve sleep and boost your resistance to colds and allergies.

It's like shopping for gasoline at a more reputable station, says Dr. Rubman. When you put better fuel in your car, it sounds better, takes curves better and runs better overall. The same principle applies to the fuel you put in your body.

THE LOWDOWN ON DAIRY

Dr. Rubman believes that cow's milk is great for calves—but not for people. The problem is complex and involves nutrient ratios, allergenic proteins and processing difficulties.

If you want to use dairy products as a source of calcium and magnesium, consume a modest amount of cheese, advises Dr. Rubman. When possible, choose cheese that is made from goat's or sheep's milk, which is far less challenging to the digestive system.

THE TROUBLE WITH WHEAT

Gluten—a protein in wheat—damages the lining of the large intestine, which is a primary site of immune regulation. "Unbeknownst to many," says Dr. Rubman, "the intestinal tract is the major manager of overall well-being. Most people think of it primarily as a vehicle for excretion of waste, but it actually serves a multitude of functions, including hydration and electrolyte balancing. Damage to the intestinal tract increases your vulnerability to digestive disorders and autoimmune diseases. Although gluten is also found in other grains, wheat seems to be the big offender."

Foods likely to contain wheat gluten include bagels, bread, crackers, cereal, cake, cookies, pies, pasta, noodles, tortillas, etc. Read labels carefully. Wheat may be listed as wheat, wheat bran, wheat starch, durum flour, enriched flour, graham flour, hydrolyzed vegetable protein, malted cereal syrup, modified food starch, semolina or vegetable gum.

Instead, Dr. Rubman recommends foods such as whole-grain sprouted bread. This product slows down digestion, lessening the negative impact of gluten. Other safer and healthier alternatives include rice, arrowroot, buckwheat, rye, tapioca and soy flour. Soy flour breads are safe if added to the diet in moderation.

THE TRUTH ABOUT SUGAR

Since the body requires glucose to survive, why isn't eating sugar a good thing? The problem is that simple sugars can disrupt the immune system, explains Dr. Rubman.

A system for classifying carbohydrates—the glycemic index (GI)—measures how quickly blood sugar rises after eating foods that contain carbohydrates. Refined carbohydrates like white sugar (high-GI foods) cause a very rapid rise in blood sugar, which has been linked to an increased risk of diabetes and heart disease. The more quickly a carbohydrate is absorbed, the more destructive it is, says Dr. Rubman.

Good low-GI choices include legumes (such as lentils and beans), root vegetables (such as sweet potatoes and yams) and whole fruits.

GETTING STARTED ON A HEALTHIER DIET

To strengthen your immune system and improve your health overall, cut out the dairy, wheat and sugar (in that order), advises Dr. Rubman. Not ready to go cold turkey? Begin by limiting yourself to cheese (no milk, please!) and wheat twice a week. Then, consciously reduce your exposure to sugar as well.

Once you have successfully eliminated these dietary culprits, you'll find yourself feeling better, looking better, breathing better, sleeping better and more successfully fending off colds and allergies.

How can you tell that eliminating these foods works? Reintroduce them, suggests Dr. Rubman. Chances are that those same old health problems will come back to haunt you. But if you continue to watch what you consume, your health will keep improving.

info Harvard School of Public Health, *www.hsph.harvard.edu/nutritionsource.*

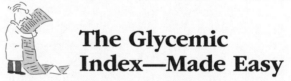

The Glycemic Index—Made Easy

The late Jane Higdon, PhD, former research associate, Linus Pauling Institute, Oregon State University, Corvallis, Oregon, and coauthor of *An Evidence-Based Approach to Vitamins and Minerals.* Thieme Medical.

Twenty-five years ago, the world had never heard of the glycemic index (GI) because it didn't exist. Nutritionists classified carbohydrates as either simple (sugars) or complex (starches) and that was that. Then, leading American nutritionist Phyllis A. Crapo, RD, proposed a "glycemic index" in her March/April 1984 paper published in *Nutrition Today.* She suggested that each carbohydrate food should have a number indicating the degree to which it causes blood sugar to rise.

While the GI is very helpful in understanding the "power" in your carbohydrates, it requires some basic education to fully understand and use properly.

GI BASICS

The GI is a measure of how fast and how high a carbohydrate food raises your blood sugar within two to three hours of consumption relative to the rate that pure glucose does. The GI is actually a numerical comparison with the glucose rate. For example, a food that raises blood sugar at the same rate that glucose does would have a GI of 100. By comparison, one that raises blood sugar one-half or 50% as fast and as high would have a GI of 50, and so on. *GI guidelines per portion of a single food are as follows...*

- **Low GI=0 to 54.**
- **Medium GI=55 to 69.**
- **High GI=70 or higher.**

The lower the better when it comes to GI.

The GI is important because the pancreas produces insulin in response to the level of blood glucose. When blood sugar rises quickly, insulin levels do as well, in order to store the excess glucose for later use. When insulin levels spike in this way, they also plummet quickly. This leads to swings in blood sugar levels, a sudden drop in energy and, often, renewed hunger. It also may, over time, increase the likelihood of reduced insulin sensitivity, a precursor to diabetes. The idea behind diets that focus on the GI is that eating low-GI foods stabilizes blood sugar, with the result that you experience greater, longer satiety and are less tempted to rummage around in the refrigerator.

THE NUMBERS BEHIND THE GI

According to the late Jane Higdon, PhD, former research associate at the Linus Pauling Institute at Oregon State University, most people miss a critical component of GI. It's based on portion sizes of any food that supplies 50 grams (g) of carbohydrates, because the glucose that foods are measured against contain 50g of carbohydrates and the measurement is gram-to-gram. For some foods (for example, fudge), that portion size is very small, while for others the portion size may be very large.

Case in point: Carrots. You may have heard that carrots have a very high GI—92 on some charts. But carrots are a low-carb food. To meet the 50g of carbohydrates that the GI measures would require eating 2.2 pounds of carrots!

HOW TO LOWER A FOOD'S GI

To make matters even more complex, there are other factors in addition to the number of carbs in a food that affect the GI. In particular, the GI is affected by anything that causes a food to be digested more slowly.

Properties that slow a food's digestion—and lower its GI—include fiber (unpeeled apples have a lower GI than peeled ones), and fat content. (You actually can lower the GI of popcorn by cooking it in vegetable oil rather than air popping it, because adding fat slows down digestion.) Another property is something she called "three-dimensionality." She said that this doesn't exactly describe fiber, but rather the chunkiness in refined foods—for example, the bits of grain that remain in coarsely processed flour. The degree of ripeness in the case of fruit also changes the GI (green bananas have a lower GI than ripe ones).

THE GLYCEMIC LOAD

To clarify the role of carbs in the diet, scientists built on the GI to create a second measure, the glycemic load (GL). Dr. Higdon explained that the GL is a better way to evaluate food because it shows the glucose response to a typical serving and it takes into account an entire meal.

To figure out the GL of foods, scientists came up with a somewhat complex mathematical equation. It is not necessary to know the equation, but it is important to remember that the GI of each food is completely different from the GL of the same food. *GL guidelines per portion of a single food are...*

- **Low GL=0 to 10.**
- **Medium GL=11 to 19.**
- **High GL=20 and higher.**

To put the GL into play, let's return to the example of the carrots. Although their GI is 92, their GL is a lowly 5, reflecting the actual glucose response to a typical serving.

THE GI AND GL IN USE

Whether you use GI or GL to monitor your consumption, keep in mind that the jury is still out on their effectiveness as diet tools. Studies show that people feel fuller after a low-GI meal, but there is no research yet that proves it is effective for long-term weight control. It can, however, be instrumental in keeping blood sugar stable. Of course, don't use the GI to determine all of your food choices. Total calories still count. Furthermore, some foods, such as brown rice with medium to high GI and GL, are nutritional bonanzas and should be part of a regular diet (brown rice has a GI of 55 and a GL of 18).

Dr. Higdon recommended using the information that both measures provide, with the goal of eating low-GL meals.

Example: If you want a baked potato (GI 85, GL 26), surround it with low GI/GL foods, such as a salad, vegetable and a protein, keeping the total GL of the meal low. Your GL daily intake should range from a low of 60 to a high of 180. You can lower the GI's impact of a carb if you eat protein first. GI is impacted by both gastric emptying time and speed of digestion in the intestines—and by adding the healthy fats, such as butter on popcorn, potatoes or pasta.

You can lower the ranking of pasta (which falls in the middle range of the GI) if you cook it al dente or mix whole-wheat pasta with regular pasta, and make a sauce with lots of vegetables and some protein. Eat plenty of low-GI foods, such as beans, legumes and fruits, throughout the day, and you'll easily keep within or even below the recommended daily GL of 100.

info To find out what the GI and GL of any carbohydrate is, click on "GI Database" at *www.glycemicindex.com.*

Carb-Conscious Beats Low-Carb Diet

Udo Erasmus, PhD, developer of the "right fat, carb-conscious diet" and author of *Fats That Heal, Fats That Kill*. Alive Books. *www.udoerasmus.com.*

There is no escaping it. Everywhere you go, someone is bound to rave about the pounds he/she just shed with a low-carbohydrate diet. Hundreds of new low-carb products line supermarket shelves. Meanwhile, the low-carb craze has many nutritionists wringing their hands and warning about the risks.

ALL CARBS ARE NOT CREATED EQUAL

Nutritionists fear that thousands of dieters are counting carbs but failing to distinguish between "good" carbs and "bad" carbs.

Think about it like this: A light beer (three net carbs, 95 calories) and a bag of low-carb chips (four net carbs, 90 calories) add up to fewer carbs than half a cup of black beans (12.9 net carbs, 114 calories), an apple (17.3 net carbs, 81 calories) or a sweet potato (19.2 net carbs, 95 calories).

Counting carbs is not the solution, emphasizes Udo Erasmus, PhD, developer of the "right fat, carb-conscious diet." A better approach is to be carb conscious rather than low carb. Your goal should be to eliminate the bad carbs from your diet, and to replace them with good carbs. But even good carbs will make you gain weight if you eat more than you burn. How much you burn depends on your level of physical activity. The more active you are, the more carbs you can burn, and therefore, the more carbs you can eat. Being overweight is your indicator that you are eating more than you burn, because what you don't burn is turned into fat in your body.

Hence the slogan: "When you eat carbs, either you burn them, or you wear them."

•**Eat more good carbs.** Healthy carbohydrates are found in whole grains, beans and vegetables. Because they contain fiber, good carbs break down slowly in your body, thus avoiding fattening sugar spikes and all the cravings that follow.

Unfortunately, because they are high in carbohydrates, whole grains and beans are very often banned in the early stages of the fad low-carb diet plans. Even fruits and vegetables can be limited. The foods people choose instead are invariably not healthy—a bacon cheeseburger is still a bacon cheeseburger, packed with calories and saturated fat, even if you eat it without the bun.

•**Eat fewer bad carbs.** When you consume bad carbs, such as cookies, sodas, potato chips or white bread, they are quickly broken down into glucose (blood sugar), which floods into the bloodstream. In response, your body produces insulin to allow glucose to enter cells for energy. If there is more glucose than the body requires to meet energy needs, the excess is used to make fat.

As Dr. Erasmus puts it, bad carbs are absorbed so rapidly that insulin turns on the fat production and turns off the fat burning. The rapid spike in blood sugar leads to a brief surge in energy, but when this sugar rush ends, you're left feeling tired, irritable, depressed and fidgety. This is when children lose their focus at school, or truck drivers doze and veer off the road. Even worse, the drop in energy leaves you craving something sweet to get your sugar back up—which starts the whole vicious cycle over again.

LOW-CARB LINGO: A TRANSLATION

Of course, it's not just about good carbs and bad carbs—the low-carb revolution has spawned a whole new lingo designed to create a halo of healthfulness around otherwise non-wholesome foods. What does it all mean? *Dr. Erasmus translates…*

• **What is a low-carb food?** You might think this is pretty basic, but the US Food and Drug Administration (FDA) has yet to agree on a legal definition. Until it comes to a decision, food manufacturers can get in trouble if they label their products low-carb, so they have come up with catchy phrases, such as "carb smart" and "carb fit" and "carb slim." Consumers should know that these are marketing tools and have no real meaning. You must read labels to learn carbohydrate, fat and calorie content. In addition, observes Dr. Erasmus, many manufacturers didn't change their products at all—they just added a new phrase to the labels.

• **What are "net carb" numbers?** Also known as impact carbs, these numbers are derived by subtracting fiber and sugar alcohol—carbohydrates with minimal impact on blood sugar levels—from the total carb count. It's very confusing and intended to make the carb numbers not look so bad for marketing purposes.

Best: Ignore net carb numbers.

• **What's in that low-carb candy bar?** It's still full of carbohydrates, including sugar alcohols, such as sorbitol, mannitol and maltitol, says Dr. Erasmus. Sugar alcohols are not calorie free, and they can cause cramps, bloating, gas and diarrhea.

LOW CARBS AT THE SUPERMARKET

Low-carb candy bars are only one of the many low-carb products that contain what Dr. Erasmus refers to as "the wide-ranging chemical garbage that food manufacturers feed you in place of whole, natural foods that keep you healthy." They're basically low-carb junk food.

When all is said and done, a calorie is still a calorie. If you eat low-carb foods that are high in calories, you're still going to gain weight.

THE RIGHT FAT, CARB-CONSCIOUS DIET

According to Dr. Erasmus, it's easy to follow a healthy carb-conscious diet. Steer clear of the bad carbs, ignore all these new, highly processed, low-carb junk foods and eat a variety of whole, natural, unprocessed foods, such as vegetables, fruits, lean proteins, nuts and legumes. In particular, he believes that green vegetables are the most important food on the planet. Remember that the more distant from the original food source the product is, the more stuff has been added that you probably don't need (in order to increase the manufacturer's profit, not your benefit).

And don't forget the fat—that is, the right fat. Dr. Erasmus recommends that you consume healthy fats, such as organic, unrefined seed oil blends. These provide the omega-3 fatty acids your body requires and, as an added benefit, they decrease your carb cravings.

In the long run, if embracing a carb-conscious lifestyle encourages you to give up white bread, candy and cookies, more power to you. But if you're cutting back on fruits, vegetables and whole grains and replacing them with animal fats or low-carb junk food, you're just trading one health challenge for another.

More Good News About Whole Grains

Elizabeth Lipski, PhD, CCN, author of *Digestive Wellness*. McGraw-Hill. *www.innovativehealing.com.*

Atkins fans would have us believe that all carbs are suspect. In fact, research has again proven the importance of complex carbohydrates—especially whole grains—as being a part of a healthy diet.

A number of large-scale studies have shown through the years that eating sufficient whole grains (with their high fiber content) can help reduce the risk of insulin resistance and diabetes, heart disease, perhaps cancer and definitely constipation. The power of whole grains was shown in an Australian retirement community that started a campaign to promote whole grains as the route to regularity. After four months, the sales of whole-grain bread were up 58% while laxative sales were down by 49%.

While we spoke to nutritionist Elizabeth Lipski, PhD, CCN, about this study, she added that grains are also an excellent source of micronutrients, including magnesium, folic acid and vitamin E, and of the potent antioxidants known as phytochemicals.

FOR THOSE
WITH DIGESTIVE TROUBLE

However, dieters aside, many people don't do well with grains for reasons having to do with assorted digestive disorders, such as celiac disease, Crohn's disease, ulcerative colitis and, sometimes, irritable bowel syndrome. Dr. Lipski suggests that people who are sensitive to the common whole grains of wheat, rye and barley should try brown rice, quinoa, millet, buckwheat, wild rice and amaranth. For many years, people thought that oats were on the never-eat list, but recent studies of celiac disease show that some people can tolerate oats after all.

READ THE LABEL

When you shop for whole-grain products, beware. Forget package labels that say multigrain, cracked wheat, oat bran and the like. Go straight to the list of ingredients. The first word should be "whole," followed by a grain.

Also, be aware that fiber content is not a reliable guide, in that it may reflect added processed fiber from other foods.

If you stop and think about how many times per day you eat processed wheat flour, you would be shocked. Adding a variety of whole grains to your diet is healthy, but it will also make for a far more interesting eating experience. Oh, and by the way…many of these whole grains are quite delicious, too.

What to Eat— Instead of Wheat

Judith Mabel, RD, PhD, nutritionist in private practice in Brookline, Massachusetts.

Long before there was a Dr. Atkins, there were multitudes of people avoiding wheat for reasons that had nothing to do with carbohydrate-phobia. Rather, they avoided wheat due to wheat sensitivity and celiac disease.

However, if you want to or must avoid wheat, its availability as "cheap filler" means it is virtually everywhere, and avoiding it is a very big challenge. It can even be hidden in products that are theoretically made from other types of grain.

Meanwhile, an important message that is lost in the low-carb craze is that whole grains are an important and nutritious part of our diets. They contain magnesium, vitamin E, some B vitamins and are an excellent source of fiber—something Americans don't consume enough of. The good news is that there are a number of delicious and nutritious non-wheat grains available.

WHOLE-GRAIN OPTIONS

To find other grains that best fit the bill and are tasty as well, we spoke with Brookline, Massachusetts, nutritionist Judith Mabel, RD, PhD. She treats many people who avoid wheat and says that even people who aren't wheat sensitive would do well to limit the amount of wheat they eat because of the gluten content. Gluten, the grain protein that gives dough its elasticity, is frequently the culprit behind wheat sensitivity. Many people may be wheat-gluten sensitive but not know it.

Dr. Mabel explains that gluten can trigger digestive problems, such as constipation, and endocrine problems. To underscore her point, she reminds people that when children make paste for gluing, it is composed of flour and water, which is not too different from the recipe for pasta and other wheat products. In addition to wheat, gluten is present in rye, barley, spelt, kamut, farina, triticale and, in the Western world, couscous. (In Africa, couscous is made with millet.)

INTRIGUING OPTIONS

Dr. Mabel recommends eating some form of whole grains as part of several meals each day. *Her favorites...*

● **Amaranth.** Tiny, pale-colored seeds with a peppery flavor, amaranth is rich in protein and calcium. It is delicious when added to bread and pudding.

● **Buckwheat.** Contrary to its name, buckwheat is not related to wheat. This grain (related to rhubarb) is useful as flour for preparing a variety of baked goods and pancakes. Kasha, the basis of many packaged cereals, is roasted buckwheat groats, which are the hulled grain. Read the label of cereals carefully—kasha is not "puffed wheat."

● **Millet.** If you've ever owned a bird, you probably fed it unhulled millet from the pet store. However, at your local health-food store, you'll find hulled millet, a mild-flavored grain that's meant for humans to eat. It is a tasty breakfast cereal addition.

● **Oats.** Although this cereal grain does not contain gluten, Dr. Mabel explains that celiac patients should avoid it anyway.

Reason: Mills often process both wheat and oats and the trace of wheat left over from milling can be enough to cause celiac distress. For those who do not have celiac disease, oats are a fine grain. They have a slightly sweet taste, and contain protein, calcium and potassium among other nutrients. The old standby oatmeal for breakfast is still a good choice.

● **Quinoa.** Pronounced *KEEN-wah*, this grain has a mild flavor and is slightly crunchy (rinse carefully before using to remove the bitter natural coating). Quinoa comes in several colors including yellow, red and black. Because it contains the amino acid lysine, it provides a more complete protein than many other grains. You can find quinoa pasta (along with assorted rice and potato pastas) at many health-food stores.

● **Teff.** Originating in Ethiopia, teff is the world's smallest grain—too small to process (parts can't be separated as they are in other grains), which means its nutrients are in place and it's a powerhouse with a nutrient profile similar to that of whole wheat but without its gluten. Teff, which has a slightly sweet, nutty flavor, comes in several colors, from white to reddish brown. In the US, teff is largely grown in the state of Idaho. You can find teff for sale on-line...and Whole Foods and other large, upscale markets may carry the grain as well.

READ THE LABELS

Even though the above grains are gluten free, Dr. Mabel cautions people to read the ingredient list on all cereals and other products made with these grains very carefully. Food producers sometimes add gluten-containing products, such as wheat germ, malt (from barley), hydrolyzed vegetable protein or TVP (textured vegetable protein) to the mix.

As stated earlier, everyone could benefit from reducing the wheat in their diets and rotating starches with other products, such as potatoes, rice and the more nutritious options listed above.

For instruction and inspiration about how to cook with these grains, Dr. Mabel says that there are many good cookbooks out there. You also can find a variety of recipes on the Web. In addition to cereals and breads, many of the grains are excellent additions to soups, stews and similar dishes.

 # Friendly Fats Your Body Needs

Udo Erasmus, PhD, developer of the "right fat, carb-conscious diet" and author of *Fats That Heal, Fats That Kill*. Alive Books. *www.udoerasmus.com*.

Andrew L. Rubman, ND, director, Southbury Clinic for Traditional Medicines, Southbury, Connecticut.

For the last two decades, it has been relentlessly drummed into our heads that in order to be healthy, we should eliminate fat from our diet.

With more Americans than ever overweight and diabetes at epidemic proportions, it's obvious that we still are not eating properly. According to Udo Erasmus, PhD, author of *Fats That Heal, Fats That Kill*, the message all along should have been to eat fats—just be sure they're the healthful ones.

AN OIL CHANGE

Dr. Erasmus points out that the health establishment's advice on avoiding fat overlooked one extremely important fact—fat is a vital nutrient, and the human body cannot survive without it. According to Dr. Erasmus, essential fatty acids are involved in virtually every body function. *They…*

• **Boost cardiovascular health** by normalizing blood pressure and cholesterol levels and making platelets less sticky.

• **Lower cancer risk.**

• **Aid in weight management** by shifting the body's metabolism from burning glucose to burning fats.

• **Make insulin-resistant people (those who are diabetic, obese, overweight) more insulin-sensitive.**

• **Increase energy and stamina.**

• **Elevate mood and lift depression.**

• **Improve brain function,** concentration, hyperactivity, stress management, learning and motor coordination.

• **Prevent leaky gut and other harmful digestive disturbances.**

• **Dampen overactive immune responses in autoimmune diseases.**

• **Decrease inflammation.**

• **Reduce symptoms of allergies.**

• **Speed the healing of injuries.**

• **Improve bone mineral retention,** which can help prevent osteoporosis.

• **Moisturize and protect skin.**

Of course, we're not talking about bacon or well-marbled steak. We're talking about healthy fats—the essential omega-3 and omega-6 fatty acids that come from plant foods, such as nuts and seeds, and from deepwater fish.

THE BAD FATS

Bad fats—in particular, trans fats, such as partially hydrogenated oils and overheated (fried) oils—are associated with increased premature deaths from heart disease, diabetes and cancer. Dr. Erasmus refers to these fats as "monkey wrenches" in the works of our bodies.

To reduce your risk for disease and improve your overall health, limit your consumption of the saturated fats in meat and dairy products, and—even more important—avoid trans fats found in most commercially produced breads, baked goods, crackers, pie dough, etc. If it says "partially hydrogenated," don't buy it.

Although they were originally conceived as an alternative to unhealthy saturated fats, it turns out that trans fats—which are in virtually all processed and fast foods—are even worse for you than saturated fats. They lead to disease and hasten death.

THE GOOD FATS—ESSENTIAL TO YOUR HEALTH

While omega-3 and omega-6 fatty acids are necessary for the health of every cell, tissue, gland and organ in your body, the body cannot produce them, so you must get them from foods or supplements. Dr. Erasmus believes the benefits of these fatty acids are legion, and that omega-3 fatty acids—flaxseed oil, walnut oil and fatty fish (salmon in particular)—can help combat cardiovascular disease, cancer and diabetes.

Dr. Erasmus notes that if you're not getting enough fatty acids, you can reverse all of the symptoms of deficiency and return to normal health. (Early signs of fatty-acid deficiency include dry skin and hair and low energy levels.) It is recommended that you get 15% to 30% of your daily calorie intake from good fats.

WHERE TO FIND GOOD FATS

Good sources of healthy fats include cold-water fish, such as salmon, mackerel, sardines and trout…nuts and seeds (flax, sesame, sunflower, etc.)…green vegetables…and oils carefully pressed from organically grown seeds and stored under protection from light, oxygen and heat.

You also can take supplements of fatty acids. Our medical expert, Andrew L. Rubman, ND, recommends a supplement with equal amounts of omega-3 and omega-6 oils derived from flax and borage seeds.

For optimal health, the choice is clear—don't be afraid to eat fats. Just say *no* to the processed junk foods and frozen prepared meals. For dinner tonight, treat yourself to poached salmon topped with sesame dressing. For lunch tomorrow, pass by the fast-food joint and try natural almond butter on whole-grain bread. You'll feel better and live longer.

Obesity Can Be Deadly

Jana Klauer, MD, physician in private practice and a former research fellow, New York Obesity Research Center at St. Luke's–Roosevelt Hospital, New York City.

Andrew L. Rubman, ND, director, Southbury Clinic for Traditional Medicines, Southbury, Connecticut.

There can be serious health consequences as a result of America's out-of-control eating habits.

Our bad food choices—french fries and other fast foods, snack foods and candy consumed while sitting in front of the television or computer screen—have caused 64% of us to be classified as overweight or obese.

Health-care professionals now consider a person to be overweight if he/she has a body mass index (BMI) of 25 or more, and as obese if one's BMI is 30 or more. (Learn more about BMI—and how to calculate your own—at *www.cdc.gov.*)

Aesthetics aside, there are huge health risks resulting from obesity. The Surgeon General's report "Overweight and Obesity: Health Consequences" opens with the fact that people with a BMI greater than 30 have a 50% to 100% increased risk of premature death from all causes, compared with people with a healthy weight. And that's just for starters.

Here are just some of the ways, according to the report, that excess weight impacts health…

• **High blood pressure is twice as common in overweight people.**

• **More than 80% of people with diabetes are overweight or obese.**

• **Extra weight is associated with an increased risk of colon, prostate, kidney and postmenopausal breast cancer.**

• **Sleep apnea (interrupted breathing while sleeping) is more common in obese people.**

• **Every two-pound gain in weight increases the risk of developing arthritis by 9% to 13%.**

• **Being overweight is associated with increased risk of gall bladder disease, incontinence, depression and a need for surgery.**

The list goes on, but the point is clear—being overweight is terrible for your health.

We wanted more information about obesity, so we called Jana Klauer, MD, a former research fellow at the New York Obesity Research Center at St. Luke's–Roosevelt Hospital Center. Dr. Klauer also has a master's degree in clinical nutrition and has a private practice in which she helps patients achieve healthy weight.

THE DIRECT IMPACT OF OBESITY

We asked Dr. Klauer to explain why obesity is so hard on the body. She reports that women who measure 35 inches or more at the waist and men who are 40 inches or more are more prone to have visceral fat, which is fat that surrounds the abdominal organs, including the liver and kidneys. This is a cardiovascular risk factor because this fat is metabolized by the liver, increasing cholesterol, insulin resistance and cardiovascular disease. Dr. Klauer says that insulin resistance is a serious prediabetic condition. It calls for lifestyle adjustment (diet and exercise) and, if necessary, medication to increase the cells' sensitivity to insulin. If insulin resistance does turn into type 2 diabetes, it can lead to impotence, kidney failure, limb amputation and even death. Diabetes also complicates other health problems a person may have.

As for subcutaneous fat, that which lies just under the skin, Dr. Klauer points out two serious complications from having too much. Excess weight affects breathing not only because it is harder to move a large body but because, in sleep, the weight rests on the lungs, making it more difficult to breathe. This may be one of the reasons why being overweight is associated with sleep apnea, in which the affected person wakes up frequently albeit briefly throughout the night.

MORE JOINT TROUBLE

Excess weight is also a strain on joints. Overweight people, she says, are more prone to develop osteoarthritis, especially in the knees, with rapid progression and deterioration. Studies show that levels of the hormone *leptin*—which is important in regulating body weight and metabolism but also is higher in obese people, contributes to the development of osteoarthritis. Many people seek joint-replacement surgery to remedy the wear and tear of osteoarthritis, but Dr. Klauer reports that excess weight makes the surgery more difficult to perform and causes the artificial joint to wear out more quickly.

THE CULPRITS OF EXCESS WEIGHT

Dr. Klauer points the finger at three culprits for the problem with weight in America—the snack-food industry, which is huge and advertises relentlessly…portion sizes that are so large that they should actually feed two people or more…and the fact that few people get enough physical activity.

Getting started on the road back to normal weight, says Dr. Klauer, is surprisingly simple. The absolute first thing you should do, even before you start to refashion your eating habits, is to take daily walks. She advises people to start with a commitment to walk for 30 minutes a day and build up to 45 and then 60 minutes a day. This burns calories and brings other health rewards—increased insulin sensitivity, a boon for those who are prediabetic or diabetic—and a significant decrease in visceral fat, according to recent studies in postmenopausal women.

Next step: According to our medical expert, Andrew L. Rubman, ND, you should work with your doctor in conjunction with a health-care provider who has a graduate education in clinical nutrition in order to develop a diet plan that is right for you. While it is tempting to simply buy the latest best-selling diet book, it is critical that your diet strategy be safe and provide the healthy, balanced nutrition specifically suited to your body needs.

Dr. Klauer has additional strategies to get you going on a weight-loss effort…

• **Fill your home with full-length mirrors** so that you can easily see if you are putting on any weight, and so that you can also applaud your progress as you lose it.

• **Read up on nutrition and portion sizes.** Dr. Klauer says that she is astonished by how little most people know about food even in this information-saturated society. When dining out, automatically cut portions in half and always leave something on your plate. Avoid buffets, but if you must go to one, decide ahead of time what you will eat and stick to it. If you use a small plate, you won't be as tempted to go overboard.

• **Enlist a walking buddy.** You're much more likely to stick to your commitment if you have a friend waiting on the corner to join you.

Don't think of your weight-management program as having to lose 30 or 50 or 100 pounds. Think of it as a series of individual choices. Take the stairs instead of the elevator. Have a salad and grilled chicken for dinner instead of pizza. Eat one cookie instead of two. Weight loss is a slow and arduous task. It took years to accumulate the weight, and it will take time to take it off. Monitor progress by observing the fit of your clothing and your body measurements. Often, fat and excess water is lost and replaced by muscle.

The effort will be well worth it. You will add years—and energy and vitality—to your life.

Breakthrough Research on Alzheimer's and Weight

William Thies, PhD, chief medical and scientific officer, Alzheimer's Association, Chicago, *www.alz.org*.

There has been an increasing amount of talk recently about the expansion of American waistlines and the increase in the number of people classified as "obese." And research is continually underscoring the fact that being overweight is a risk factor for many diseases. Unfortunately, a new study makes it look as if we may be adding another very tragic disease to the list—Alzheimer's.

THE STUDY

In the past, it was difficult to measure how body weight might relate to Alzheimer's disease (AD) because people who have the disease lose weight in its early stages. However, a long-range study done at Gothenburg University in Sweden tracked participants well before they got AD.

Researchers followed 392 adults from the ages of 70 until they reached 88. They found that women who were overweight at the age of 70, as determined by their body mass index (BMI), greatly increased their risk of developing AD in 10 to 18 years. The researchers say that men would probably show the same pattern, but so few overweight men live into their 80s that the number of them left in the study was too small to be significant. About 10% of all people over age 65 have AD, and about 50% of all people have it by the age of 85.

THE IMPLICATIONS

William Thies, PhD, is chief medical and scientific officer at the Alzheimer's Association in Chicago, which helped to fund the study. We talked with him about the implications of the research and what we can learn from it.

Dr. Thies observes that what is good for your heart is apparently good for helping prevent AD. He notes that it's well established that a high BMI is an underlying risk factor for cardiovascular problems, including high blood pressure, elevated cholesterol level and excess blood sugar. We now have considerable evidence that cardiovascular risk factors may also be risk factors for AD. The reason could be that cardiovascular disease affects blood flow to the brain, but it might also involve more intricate aspects of the body's functioning, says Dr. Thies. He reports that researchers think that there may be some relationship between AD and the body's biochemical response to fat, but we simply don't have enough evidence yet.

It's important to understand that the BMI associated with the eventual onset of AD is one that would make you considerably overweight. BMI is a measure of weight to height. If you have a BMI between 18.5 and 24.9, you are considered to be at a normal weight…if your BMI is from 25 to 29, you are overweight…and if your BMI is 30 or above, you fall into the obese category.

Women who had the highest risk factor for developing AD later in life had a BMI of more than 29 at age 70. This corresponds to a woman of 5 feet 4 inches weighing 170 pounds. The average BMI for women who did not develop the disease was 25, which would correspond to a 5-foot-4 inch woman weighing 145 pounds.

According to Dr. Thies, this is yet another indicator that there may be things you can do to avoid the tragedy of AD. People are now living longer than ever and can enjoy active lifestyles well into old age. He observes that there are many ways to anticipate the health risks that accompany old age, and there are also many ways to moderate those risks if you start now.

This study provides yet another reason to take control of body weight, activity level and dietary habits before tragedy strikes.

info To find out what your BMI is, go to the Centers for Disease Control and Prevention Web site at *www.cdc.gov*.

Best Foods for Snacking

The late Jane Higdon, PhD, research associate, Linus Pauling Institute, Oregon State University, Corvallis, Oregon, and coauthor of *An Evidence-Based Approach to Vitamins and Minerals*. Thieme Medical.

Elizabeth Lipski, PhD, CCN, author of *Digestive Wellness*. McGraw-Hill. *www.innovativehealing.com*.

Earl Mindell, PhD, RPh, professor emeritus of nutrition, Pacific Western University, coauthor of *Earl Mindell's New Vitamin Bible*. Grand Central.

Andrew L. Rubman, ND, director, Southbury Clinic for Traditional Medicines, Southbury, Connecticut.

Snacking is the great all-American pastime. Most of our tastiest snack foods are nutritionally bankrupt—and worse. Still, snacking in itself isn't unhealthy—it's what we snack on and how much we eat that creates the problems.

So for better health, we asked four nutrition experts to tell you about their favorite snacks. Our panel of nutritionists were Elizabeth Lipski, PhD, CCN, certified clinical nutritionist and author of *Digestive Wellness*…Earl Mindell, PhD, RPh, professor emeritus of nutrition, Pacific Western University, and coauthor of *Earl Mindell's New Vitamin Bible*…the late Jane Higdon, PhD, research associate at the Linus Pauling Institute at Oregon State University, and author of *An Evidence-Based Approach to Vitamins and Minerals*…and our medical expert, Andrew L. Rubman, ND.

EXPERTS' OPINIONS

There is debate between the experts about the need for snacking and the reasons that we all seem to get "snack attacks." Some feel that we actually need to eat five to six times per day for maximum health, while others feel that eating three well-balanced and properly digested meals maximizes the digestive tract's effectiveness and minimizes the need for snacking.

One thing is certain: We all snack. So, what are the best choices?

THE NO-NOS

As to appropriate snack choices, let's first address the no-no list, which includes most of what you find in the snack-food aisles. Here, all of our experts agree. Avoid any products that contain hydrogenated oils (also called trans-fatty acids), corn syrup, white sugar and white flour. In other words, avoid virtually all processed foods. Dr. Lipski also adds cottonseed oil to the list because there is heavy use of pesticides on cotton, and the oil has been associated with having an effect on hormones—folk medicine used cottonseed oil to cause miscarriages, she says.

Dr. Higdon pointed out yet another reason to avoid typical packaged snacks—most are often high on the glycemic index (GI), which causes a rapid blood sugar increase. That puts a demand on the pancreas to pump out insulin. Shortly after such an insulin spike, blood sugar plummets, backing the snacker into a nutritional and energy-deprived corner.

THE BEST OF THE BEST

It's not a big surprise to find that our nutrition experts agree on the award winners in the snack-food category—fruits, vegetables and unsalted raw nuts.

Fruits are fabulous, says Dr. Rubman, because in addition to the nutrients and satisfying taste, they are easily digested, requiring little stomach acid to do the job. When it comes to selecting produce for snacking, seek out a variety of colored fruits and vegetables—blueberries, yellow bananas and green snap peas. The different colors reflect the wide spectrum of cancer-fighting antioxidants that each of these foods contain.

As for nuts, Dr. Lipski points out that these are easy to carry and don't spoil quickly. (Nuts stored in your bag or your desk for several weeks will keep, she says.) Remember, though, that although nuts contain healthy unsaturated fats, they also have a significant number of calories—Dr. Higdon said that one ounce of nuts has at least 160 calories—so restrict yourself to a handful or so each day. As an alternative to raw nuts, Dr. Rubman suggests all-natural nut butters, including cashew or almond butters, in addition to the more traditional peanut butter.

SECOND TIER

After fresh produce and nuts, Dr. Mindell likes high-protein bars and shakes. He does, however, advise carefully checking the labels of bars to be sure that they are really protein-filled—and that they're not a sweet dressed up as a nutritious snack. Watch out for the carbohydrate and sugar levels of the protein bars.

For the shake, Dr. Mindell recommends mixing one from whey powder, available in health-food stores, while Dr. Rubman prefers protein powders made from "predigested" sources. Most of these medical protein powders are about 80% soy-based and 20% milk-based. Both agree that you should avoid premixed canned shakes since they are "junk."

POP IT

Popcorn was a favorite of Dr. Higdon's. Rather than putting salt and butter on it, she suggested spraying it with a little olive oil and then sprinkling it with favorite herbs or spices, perhaps oregano or thyme. Ironically, including oil with your popcorn is actually "less fattening" than air popped, due to the high GI of fat-free popcorn. She also treated herself to a bit of chocolate now and then, explaining that having a little is so satisfying that it kept her from eating a lot of something else.

COOL TREATS

During the summer, most of us like to treat ourselves to snacks that are chilled and cooling. That's not a problem, says Dr. Lipski, if we follow a few precautions. Don't kid yourself that frozen yogurt is good for you—it is, she points out, full of sugar and not a health food. However, Dr. Lipski admits to a weakness for ice cream—when she does give in to it, she is careful to choose only premium brands. Although they are high in calories, she recommends Häagen-Dazs, Ben

& Jerry's and Breyers ice cream, because these brands have few, if any, additives.

Other cool suggestions she makes are to keep homemade juice-based ice pops in the refrigerator and to try your hand at making an all-natural fruit sorbet.

Once you get into the habit of choosing healthy snacks, says Dr. Lipski, you'll find that it will change your approach to food. Your energy will become constant, and you'll no longer crave sugar and caffeine—which are, of course, instant but very short-lived energy boosters. You'll also find that you're not famished at dinnertime and reaching for high-fat, high-calorie temptations. Saying no will become a whole lot easier.

Sickeningly Sweet

Nancy Appleton, PhD, retired nutritional consultant and author of *Lick the Sugar Habit* (Avery) and *Stopping Inflammation* (Square One). Dr. Appleton's Internet site (*www.nancyappleton.com*) lists 146 ways sugar ruins your health.

Andrew L. Rubman, ND, director, Southbury Clinic for Traditional Medicines, Southbury, Connecticut.

A recent study challenges the impact of sugar on children's behavior, with experts suggesting that the sugar-hyperactivity link is just a myth. For anyone who has ever spoken to a teacher or witnessed a birthday party—before and after the cake was served—to say this report was surprising would be an understatement.

Nancy Appleton, PhD, a retired nutritional consultant and author of *Lick the Sugar Habit* and of *Stopping Inflammation*, explains that people metabolize sugar differently and every child is unique, so that not all children are impacted the same. Whether or not sugar lies at the root of behavioral problems, there is no question that it contributes to a host of other illnesses and conditions, such as autoimmune diseases, certain cancers, bowel problems, heart disease and liver dysfunction, to name just a few.

Many people are dangerously "addicted" to sugar, and the average American now consumes an astounding 150 pounds of sugar annually.

LEAKY GUT SYNDROME

There have been reports linking sugar to digestive challenges and an array of other ailments. Dr. Appleton concurs and views sugar as a primary contributor to leaky gut syndrome. Normally, the gut plays an important role in the immune system, transporting nutrients into the bloodstream and preventing foreign substances from infiltrating it. When excessive sugar intake disturbs the body's supply of minerals and the proper balance of intestinal flora normally present in the gut, the enzymes that facilitate digestion and protect the permeability of the intestinal wall no longer function as efficiently.

When this happens, large molecules of undigested food or bacteria penetrate the barrier of the intestinal wall and enter the bloodstream. The body sees these unfamiliar substances as foreign invaders, and the immune system shifts into a protective mode to fight back. It releases antibodies to repel the foreign substances, which trigger inflammatory reactions that can appear in various parts of the body.

How far-reaching is the impact? Inflammation in the lining of the gut can lead to colitis or Crohn's disease. If the antibodies attack the joints, it can result in arthritis. Inflammation in the lungs can cause asthma. The presence of foreign substances also imposes an additional burden on the liver, which plays a vital role in clearing toxins from the bloodstream.

HIGH-FRUCTOSE CORN SYRUP AND OBESITY

It's easy to know that sugar is in baked goods and candies. But, beware—sugar can masquerade in many forms, and food manufacturers have become very adept at disguising it. One particularly insidious form that sugar can take on is high-fructose corn syrup (HFCS).

According to research at Louisiana State University published in a recent issue of *The American Journal of Clinical Nutrition*, the increased use of HFCS in the US mirrors the rapid increase in obesity. Where's the connection between HFCS and obesity? HFCS "hides" on product labels because it does not have to be identified as sugar. And with the low-carb craze still ongoing, the use of HFCS is only likely to increase.

WHAT YOU CAN DO

While many sources of sugar are obvious (soft drinks, candy, ice cream, baked goods, etc.), others can be more subtle. Processed products from cereal to iced tea to ketchup to peanut butter to yogurt are hidden sources of sugar and often represent the real source of trouble for those trying to improve diet and nutrition.

To kick the sugar habit, Dr. Appleton says to…

• **Emphasize whole foods instead of processed ones in your diet.** Highly processed products are often packed with sugar, and eating them can trap you in a vicious cycle of energy surges and crashes.

• **Lay off the cookies, candy and cake.**

Most important: Stop drinking soft drinks. The US Department of Agriculture (USDA) recommends a maximum of six tablespoons of sugar a day for a person consuming a 1,600-calorie diet. One 12-ounce soft drink already contains three tablespoons, or half of your daily allotment.

• **Read food labels carefully, and learn to spot the jargon.** Other terms for sugar are corn sweetener, corn syrup, dextrose, fructose, fruit juice concentrate, glucose, high-fructose corn syrup, honey, lactose, malt or malt syrup, maltose, molasses and sucrose.

• **Steer clear of high consumption of mid-carb and low-carb products.** Many are sweetened with sugar alcohols (such as lactitol or sorbitol) instead of sugar. When eaten in large quantities, sugar alcohols cause digestive disturbances, such as gas, bloating and diarrhea. Pick your poison.

As to the issue of whether sugar contributes to attention-deficit/hyperactivity disorder (ADHD) in your child, it's very simple, says Dr. Appleton. For one week, remove all sugar from your child's diet. If his/her symptoms improve, sugar is the culprit. If not, sugar is not at the core of your child's behavioral issues. However, this does not mean that you should give your child free reign in the candy cupboard.

To help you and your family kick the sugar habit, follow a healthy diet rich in a variety of vegetables, fruits, whole grains, low-fat dairy products, fish and lean meats. Our medical expert, Andrew L. Rubman, ND, recommends that for the times when you "just gotta have something sweet," use products that are sweetened with fruit juice concentrates.

Do Diet Drinks Make You Fat?

Terry L. Davidson, PhD, professor, department of psychological sciences, Ingestive Behavior Research Center, Purdue University, West Lafayette, Indiana.

If that can of diet cola in the late afternoon spares you a few hundred calories that you would have gotten from a chocolate bar, it looks like you've come out ahead. But have you? Maybe not, say researchers from Purdue University. Sure, you saved some calories, but you might be throwing your body's ability to regulate calorie intake out of whack—and that could be the downfall of your diet in the long run.

It seems that human beings may have learned—or have been programmed to associate—food properties, such as sweetness, to predict the caloric content of the foods they eat, says Terry L. Davidson, PhD, a professor in the department of psychological sciences at the Ingestive Behavior Research Center at Purdue University in West Lafayette, Indiana, and coauthor of a recent study on sweetener use. When we eat "real foods," that ability helps us to quit eating before we've consumed more calories than we need. Products that use artificial sweeteners do not seem to trigger this mechanism.

If you regularly consume calorie-free sweet drinks, such as diet sodas, you might be less able to control your appetite later on.

THE STUDY

In Dr. Davidson's study, rats that were given a calorie-free, saccharin-sweetened drink for 10 days had a harder time controlling their appetites when exposed to a treat than rats fed a high-calorie sweet drink. "It seems possible that tastes and viscosity help animals and people anticipate the number of calories that are contained in a meal—a kind of early warning for the gastrointestinal tract," Dr. Davidson says.

If you're thinking that makes it better to grab a regular soda instead—you are wrong. A thin (low-viscosity), high-calorie beverage, such as juice, fruit drinks, "ades" and regular sodas, also may foil appetite control, says Dr. Davidson, who found in a second study that rats that ate a snack with a consistency similar to pudding were better able to regulate their calorie intake than rats that ate a snack with a consistency similar to milk, even though both snacks contained the same number of calories.

MORE DIET SODA, MORE OBESITY

Interestingly, the consumption of artificially sweetened drinks has increased during the very same period that more and more Americans have become overweight or obese. While the obesity epidemic has a number of causes, the increased use of sweeteners may be contributing factors, Dr. Davidson says.

Of course, the jury is out in general on the safety of most artificial sweeteners. Even if you haven't made up your mind on that issue, Dr. Davidson's research does make you wonder about whether that diet drink might be sabotaging your weight-control efforts in the long run.

The #1 Drug in America

Andrew L. Rubman, ND, director, Southbury Clinic for Traditional Medicines, Southbury, Connecticut.

With nearly 90% of Americans consuming caffeine daily, it's time to take a closer look at this drug.

Make no mistake about it—caffeine is a drug. According to our medical expert, Andrew L. Rubman, ND, caffeine has many profound effects on the human body…some helpful, others harmful.

WHAT'S GOOD ABOUT CAFFEINE

Besides the fact that it tastes and smells good, coffee—and its major component, caffeine—have a number of very positive effects…

• **Caffeine increases alertness and reaction time.** An occasional cup of coffee will leave you feeling cognitively empowered, reports Dr. Rubman.

• **Caffeinated beverages have a laxative effect.** An early morning cup of coffee will help move your bowels.

• **Caffeine affects how drugs work.** By stimulating enzymes in the liver, it lessens the side effects, and potentially increases the effectiveness of many pharmaceuticals. Caffeine is added to painkillers, such as Excedrin and Anacin, to enhance their function.

• **Caffeine can help reduce your risk of liver damage,** according to a recent study at the US National Institute of Diabetes and Digestive and Kidney Diseases. Researchers found that people at high risk due to factors such as alcoholism, hepatitis or obesity, reduced their risk by consuming caffeinated beverages. Dr. Rubman suggests that this is most likely because caffeine expedites the removal of toxic metabolites associated with these conditions from the liver.

WHAT'S BAD ABOUT CAFFEINE

The darker side of caffeine consumption…

• **Too much caffeine leaves you feeling restless and jittery.** It can cause nervousness, tremors, nausea, sleep disturbances and a racing heartbeat. What constitutes too much? That varies from person to person, says Dr. Rubman. Use common sense. If coffee or other caffeinated beverages make you nervous and hyper, you're drinking too many of them.

• **Regular coffee drinkers are more vulnerable to stress,** warns Dr. Rubman. People who suffer from anxiety, depression, panic disorder or premenstrual syndrome should be careful about caffeine consumption, as it can worsen symptoms.

• **Caffeine may cause elevated blood pressure and pulse rate.** If you have high blood pressure or an irregular heartbeat, ask your health-care provider what constitutes a safe level of caffeine consumption for you.

• **Because caffeine increases calcium mobilization from bone and other tissues,** calcium excretion in the urine and secretion into the gastrointestinal tract, bone-thinning disorders, such as osteopenia and osteoporosis, may be worsened in some people. Osteopenia is the milder version of bone loss that may precede osteoporosis.

• **Caffeine can be habituating.** Remember that it is a drug. Rapid withdrawal can result in symptoms, and in coffee's case—they are headache, restlessness and irritability.

HOW TO SAFELY CONSUME CAFFEINE

Dr. Rubman says…

• **Be consistently inconsistent.** Consume caffeine once a day in varied amounts and take the weekend off. He explains that like any drug or botanical, with overly frequent consumption, caffeine loses its effectiveness.

• **Enjoy your caffeine boost early in the day.** This will prevent it from disturbing your sleep cycle.

Also: Pregnant women should limit their consumption to one cup a day.

• **Consume caffeine apart from meals.** Caffeine halts carbohydrate digestion, which means that having a muffin with your morning cup of coffee can lead to flatulence later on in the day as the undigested muffin becomes fodder for the bacteria of the large intestine.

• **If you find that you're taking in too much caffeine, don't quit cold turkey.** This can lead to severe withdrawal headaches. Decrease your intake slowly but surely.

• **People under age 16 should not consume caffeine.** While the body is neurologically maturing and behaviors are still in flux, it is better to minimize drug use.

• **Coffee is not the only source of caffeine.** Many sodas, tea, iced tea and chocolate also contain varying amounts.

Moderation is the key, concludes Dr. Rubman. An occasional cup of coffee is a refreshing pick-me-up, but too much caffeine can lead to addiction and other health problems.

Be Safe from Mad Cow Disease

Robert B. Petersen, PhD, associate professor of pathology and neuroscience, Case Western Reserve University, Cleveland…consultant in genetics, National Prion Disease Pathology Surveillance Center…and chief scientific officer, Prion Developmental Laboratories, a company in Buffalo Grove, Illinois that has developed rapid testing for mad cow disease.

Until December 23, 2003, mad cow disease, or *bovine spongiform encephalopathy*, was something to worry about in other parts of the world. But the problem landed on our shores with the discovery of several infected cows in the state of Washington.

With other isolated cases occuring in Texas and Alabama, we investigated the disease—and what changes, if any, we should still be making to our eating habits.

We called Robert B. Petersen, PhD, an associate professor of pathology and neuroscience at Case Western Reserve University in Cleveland and chief scientific officer for Prion Developmental Laboratories in Buffalo Grove, Illinois, which is developing more rapid testing for mad cow disease.

WHAT IS MAD COW DISEASE?

Dr. Petersen explained that mad cow disease is one of several prion diseases. Prions are proteins normally found in mammals. As current thinking goes, when normal prions come in contact with abnormal misshapen prions, the normal prions can in some cases also become misshapen. The misshapen prions lead to degenerative changes, resulting in a disease of the nervous system that causes dementia and ultimately death. Humans who eat the nervous tissue of an animal with mad cow disease can develop what is called variant Creutzfeldt-Jakob disease (vCJD).

According to Dr. Petersen, no one in this country has developed vCJD other than a person who grew up in England in the early 1990s. Even so, he agrees that in spite of the small number of affected cows, mad cow is a real and serious disease, so it's prudent to take steps to be sure you won't become a victim. There are several ways to do this short of giving up beef entirely.

SAFETY STEPS

Dr. Petersen's first suggestion is one that the French government instituted—eliminate bone-in cuts, or meats still on the bone. The reason for this is that not just the cow's nervous system—but also its bone marrow and lymph nodes—harbor mad cow disease. When you cook meat that is on the bone, there is the possibility that marrow from the adjacent bone could contaminate the meat. To be safe, buy the steak or the roast, but remove the meat from the bone before you cook it.

As for hamburgers, there is no need to go without, says Dr. Petersen. Chopped meat can be dangerous only because you may not know what parts of the cow it comes from. Have a butcher grind it for you from a cut of meat, such as sirloin, that has nothing to do with the cow's nervous system and doesn't include any bone marrow.

GO ORGANIC

Organic beef producers have now jumped on the marketing bandwagon trumpeting messages that their products are safe. Dr. Petersen concurs that it's likely these animals are indeed protected. Cows get the disease by eating feed that contains remnants of animal carcasses, possibly including those that have prion disease. Because organically raised cows graze rather than being fed in feedlots, the odds of their encountering an infectious agent, he says, have been minimized. While some high-end markets are posting signs that assure you their beef is safe, Dr. Petersen is less confident about that. Unless it is organically produced beef, there is no reason to think that it is any safer.

Best bet: Japanese Kobe steak. In the US, we routinely test 450,000 cows a year—out of the nearly 40 million that go to slaughter each year. But the Japanese test each and every one of its cattle destined for slaughter. If you want steak from cattle that you know is disease-free, order Japanese Kobe steak. Although expensive, you can relax and enjoy your meal.

LOOKING AHEAD

Will there come a time when we can quit worrying about the possibility of mad cow disease in American beef? Dr. Petersen reports that the government is now looking at more efficient ways to test for the disease, but there is no way to know when and if one will be found and how long it would take to put it into use. The US government has had rigid standards for a number of years about what goes into cow feed to help prevent the possibility of mad cow disease, but it has been slow to find new ways to test quickly and efficiently for its presence in animals. In the meantime, he reminds us that the possibility of contracting vCJD is much lower than getting a disease such as Legionnaire's disease.

With safe choices, you can have your steak and enjoy it, too.

4

How to Stay in Great Shape

Get Moving, Get Healthy

Get enough exercise, and you'll reduce your breast cancer risk—that was the exciting conclusion that emerged from a substudy of the Women's Health Initiative report. Researchers analyzed data on 74,171 women ages 50 to 79 and discovered that the women who walked briskly for at least 1.25 to 2.5 hours a week had an 18% decreased risk of breast cancer. And, those who increased their rate of exercise lowered the risk even more.

Countless other studies also extol the virtues of exercise for health and weight loss. Some studies say to exercise for 30 minutes a day... others say to shoot for 60. The time commitment is clearly worth it. But it's tough to devote an hour a day to exercise when our schedules are already overburdened.

To get the inside story about how much exercise we really need, we called physical fitness expert Miriam E. Nelson, PhD, director of the

John Hancock Center for Physical Activity and Nutrition and associate professor of nutrition at the Friedman School of Nutrition Science and Policy at Tufts University.

EVERY LITTLE BIT HELPS

Dr. Nelson agrees that 60 minutes of exercise every day would be terrific, but she continues to support the Surgeon General's recommendation—30 minutes a day of moderate-level exercise most days of the week. And, she says, you can fill those 30 minutes with everyday activities that you do briskly—including walking to the car, climbing steps or even vacuuming your rugs with vigor.

However, that recommendation is only what's needed to get started. Dr. Nelson encourages people to bring themselves to that level and then "customize" exercise from there. To be aerobically fit, she says, you need to be sure

Miriam E. Nelson, PhD, director, John Hancock Center for Physical Activity and Nutrition and associate professor of nutrition, Friedman School of Nutrition Science and Policy, Tufts University, both in Boston. She is coauthor of *Strong Women Stay Young*. Bantam.

62

that the activity you perform gets your heart rate moderately high for 30 minutes at least three times a week. (You can determine the recommended target heart rate for your age and conditioning by going to the Web site of Changing Shape at *www.changingshape.com/resources/calculators/targetheartratecalculator.asp.*)

STRENGTH TRAINING, TOO

If you're approaching age 50 or are older, it's crucial to embrace strength training as part of your fitness regimen. The reason? People lose one-quarter to one-half pound of muscle every year starting in their mid-40s. That muscle is replaced by fat. The only way to avoid "muscle wasting," as it's termed, is through strength training with free weights, resistance equipment and resistance exercises, such as squats and lunges. (People with arthritis or who have had joint replacement surgery should not do squats.) Dr. Nelson recommends strength training sessions of 20 to 45 minutes, two or three times per week.

Important: Hire a trainer to work with you the first few times. Proper form is key in strength training.

BALANCE

Another critical area for older adults is balance training. Without it, you actually lose your ability to balance. According to Dr. Nelson, the neurological pathways controlling balance become duller and slower unless you strengthen them with exercise. Balance exercises are particularly easy to fit into your day. She recommends standing on one foot while you bend the other leg at the knee and gently swing it back and forth, thereby forcing your brain to constantly readjust. Do it while you watch TV or talk on the phone, but for safety's sake, be sure to have something secure nearby to grab if you start to wobble.

S-T-R-E-T-C-H-I-N-G

A fourth component of your workout regimen is stretching. It is important to keep your muscles flexible. Think about what happens to a rubber band that's left in a drawer—it dries out and gets brittle. That's just what happens to muscles that aren't stretched regularly. Dr. Nelson also recommends stretching for 10 minutes as the cooldown after exercising. Hold a stretch position for at least 30 seconds—never bounce. Bouncing can cause micro-tears in the muscles.

OTHER BENEFITS OF EXERCISE

Dr. Nelson also reminds older adults that exercise slows down or even prevents many diseases. Diseases that are dormant in the body, such as heart disease or type 2 diabetes, start to surface after about age 50. For many people, this is also the age at which they decide it's too late to get in shape anyway. But another study proves otherwise. A 10-year study published in *The Journal of the American Medical Association* followed 9,500 women age 65 and older and found that those who increased physical activity between the start of the study and its end had a 48% reduced risk of death compared with those who remained sedentary. The winning women, by the way, walked from 8.2 to 9.3 miles a week—just over a mile a day.

By combining aerobics, strength training, balance exercises and stretching into your workout routine, you will keep interested, have more fun and enjoy tremendous health benefits.

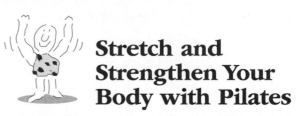

Stretch and Strengthen Your Body with Pilates

Kevin A. Bowen, owner and director of Pilates Miami.

Pilates has become popular among fitness enthusiasts. It promises to stretch, strengthen and balance the body. To become more educated about this exercise method, we called Kevin A. Bowen, owner and director of Pilates Miami, and past president of Pilates Method Alliance, an international, not-for-profit association in Florida that is dedicated to teaching Pilates and maintaining the highest of standards.

Surprisingly, given its recent surge in popularity, Pilates has been around for close to 85 years. Its founder, Joseph H. Pilates, opened the first Pilates studio in New York City in 1926. His exercise regimen is based on a unique system he had devised to rehabilitate English soldiers injured in

World War I. Until a decade ago, a lengthy legal battle over copyrights kept use of the name to a select few exercise methods. However, the courts finally overthrew the claim in 2000, thereby making the name widely available.

FUNCTIONAL FITNESS

The focus of the Pilates method is on creating "core" strength in the muscles in the trunk of the body. Pilates also improves flexibility, posture and body alignment, thereby complementing other physical endeavors, such as sports and dance. This is what Pilates referred to as creating "functional fitness," the kind that increases your pleasure in everything you do because you are comfortable in all of your movements.

Critical to Pilates effectiveness: You must perform the exercises precisely. This includes the angle at which you hold your body for an exercise, the muscles you tense and release, how you coordinate your breathing to the movements and the way you move your body through space. The reason such precision is necessary, says Bowen, is that by concentrating so totally on what you are doing with your body internally—your musculature and skeletal structure—you will develop correct external movement.

MACHINES OR MATS

There are actually two types of Pilates—one that uses machines, specially designed for Pilates and one that calls for exercises to be performed on the floor...known as mat Pilates. The five machines Joseph Pilates invented (with memorable names, such as the Reformer and the Cadillac) have pulleys and springs that the exerciser uses to stretch and strengthen. Learning to use the machines correctly takes close supervision. Bowen says that the machines in effect become your partner as you work on them because they are designed to assist you in your movements. He recommends that people who want to start Pilates and are out of shape, overweight or inflexible start on the machines rather than on the floor because they will find this approach a bit easier.

Mat Pilates is more popular today because it is more available—and less expensive since you do not need the space or investment for machines. Start with a good teacher, and then, if you choose, practice with a book or video. Although many people assume that mat Pilates is somehow less beneficial than machine work, Bowen says that is not true. In fact, Pilates devised the mat exercises early and wrote about them in his original book, *Pilates' Return to Life Through Contrology* (Presentation Dynamics).

Bowen says that the mat exercises are actually harder than the machines (though the machines offer more variation) because you are not assisted in your movement. If you never do anything other than mat Pilates, he says, you can rest assured that you are still getting an excellent Pilates workout.

How does Pilates compare with yoga? Yoga offers similar benefits in terms of stretching, but Pilates is more motion-oriented than the classical form of yoga.

THE REGIMEN

To gain the benefits of Pilates, Bowen recommends practicing it at least twice a week (in one-hour sessions). He says that if you are physically fit, Pilates can be performed throughout your life. In fact, one of the reasons Bowen was attracted to it was that some of the Pilates teachers he worked with had reached their 70s and 80s and were still going strong.

Many people wonder about combining Pilates with other fitness routines. In fact, it is important to include regular cardio workouts along with Pilates in your fitness program.

PICK THE RIGHT INSTRUCTOR

Selecting a teacher for Pilates can be tricky, says Bowen. There are group equipment classes at many health clubs today, called Reformer classes, but he stresses that it is a buyer beware situation. It is crucial to have good instruction for the machines—just as it is for the mat classes. This not only maximizes the benefits, but also avoids injury. Teacher certification is on the horizon. Until then, Bowen advises checking out an instructor's training and background. Ask questions, he says, about how he/she trained and for how long. He warns that many people complete a single weekend workshop and then teach, a situation he calls "absurd."

To be a competent instructor, one should have more than 200 hours of training. He points out that if an instructor is reluctant to discuss his background with you, it is likely that his training is insufficient. Well-trained instructors are excited about Pilates and, he says, eager to share information about it with others. The Web site for the Pilates Method Alliance (*www.pilates methodalliance.org*) maintains a list of member organizations that meet requirements for training instructors as well as a list of instructors who are qualified.

Easy Ways to Get Fit— While You Sit

Debbie Hollis, personal trainer, Saugatuck Rowing Club, Westport, Connecticut.

Believe it or not, you can get fit while you sit. If this sounds like a good idea, try perching yourself on a giant exercise ball at your desk.

Personal trainer Debbie Hollis, from the Saugatuck Rowing Club in Westport, Connecticut, says that many people are afraid that they'll be laughed at if they sit on an exercise ball, but the truth is that they'll get the last laugh. She says that sitting on an inflatable ball strengthens muscles, improves posture and balance, imparts energy and makes people feel better overall.

THE ADVANTAGES OF ACTIVE SITTING

• **While conventional desk chairs discourage movement,** exercise balls encourage "active sitting." According to Hollis, this means that you unconsciously adjust your position as you sit, and these movements strengthen and tone your center—your abdominals as well as your lower back.

• **Sitting on an exercise ball encourages good posture and balance.** In contrast, people tend to slump and slouch when seated at conventional desk chairs, causing the spine to remain in poor alignment for extended periods and placing pressure on the disks, muscles and ligaments that support it. Over time, this can lead to back damage and pain.

• **Sitting on an inflatable ball is more fun than sitting on a conventional chair.** The balls encourage slight bouncing movements that not only keep your muscles moving, but also keep you feeling more energetic and help keep

stress at bay. In contrast, slouching at a regular desk chair compresses the diaphragm, leading to shallow breathing, a slower metabolism and greater fatigue.

CHOOSING THE RIGHT EXERCISE BALL

Some people find slightly underinflated balls more comfortable for sitting, but Hollis prefers fully inflated balls. You get a better workout that way, she says. For most people, the 55- or 65-centimeter balls are best, but it does depend on a person's weight and height.

The best way to sit? According to Hollis, make sure that your feet are flat on the floor... your knees are level or slightly lower than your pelvis, creating a 90 degree or larger angle... and your pelvis, shoulders and ears are in a vertical line. Gym balls are sold in sporting-goods stores as well as on many Web sites.

Now go ahead and sit your way to fitness!

Exercise for Your Mind

Arthur F. Kramer, PhD, professor of neuroscience, University of Illinois at Urbana-Champaign, Illinois.

For years, there has been much anecdotal evidence about exercise "clearing your head." Now there's proof. In a startling study, researchers actually observed how aerobic exercise affects the brain itself—and the news is all good.

The research, which took place at the Beckman Institute at the University of Illinois at Urbana-Champaign, had the goal of discovering how exercise affects the aging brain. For the study, 41 participants ages 58 to 78 began a walking program. Over a three-month period, they gradually increased their effort until it became 45 minutes of walking, three times a week. A control group of people similar in age and health did toning and stretching, but no aerobic activity. The researchers studied participants' brain activity by measuring it with magnetic resonance imaging (MRI).

When we spoke with the study's principal investigator, Arthur F. Kramer, PhD, professor of neuroscience at the University of Illinois, he explained that his team has been studying exercise and the brain for more than 10 years and is now able to break down the results quite specifically regarding how it affects changes in the brain.

MENTAL IMPROVEMENT SHOWN

Dr. Kramer explained that participants who were part of the walking group showed increased activity and more intense blood flow in their frontal lobe, where the ability to multi-task and an array of memory functions reside. Furthermore, the "exercisers" accomplished attention-tasks faster than the other group. After three months, the active group had an 11% improvement on tasks that measured decision-making ability in a variety of everyday tasks. The control group's improvement was slight —just 2% in performance—and not statistically significant.

Dr. Kramer says that reaping the rewards of better thinking through fitness doesn't require marathon levels of exercise. Although the fit group walked farther and faster as the months went along, their exercise level never went beyond "moderate." His team is now investigating if increasing the amount of exercise would improve mental fitness even more.

Dr. Kramer is particularly excited that this study shows that our brains can continue to change as we age. He acknowledges that genetics plays an increasing role in brain function as people age, but his study demonstrated that even participants nearing age 80 can improve their brains. So, he says, there is no reason to believe that exercise wouldn't help those even much older.

Sleep Your Way To Better Health

Joyce A. Walsleben, PhD, a research associate professor of medicine and diplomate of the American Academy of Sleep Medicine, NYU Sleep Disorders Center, New York City, and coauthor of *A Woman's Guide to Sleep: Guaranteed Solutions for a Good Night's Rest*. Three Rivers.

The importance of a good night's sleep was detailed again in a report by CNN. It stated that sleep "gives the body time to rebuild damaged tissue and the brain time to replenish neurotransmitters, such as dopamine, which affect alertness. Poor sleep can cause fatigue, depression and poor concentration."

If sleep is so important, why does our culture celebrate the lack of it?

For starters, the critical restorative function of sleep is typically not taught in medical schools, notes Joyce A. Walsleben, PhD, a research associate professor of medicine at the Sleep Disorders Center at NYU School of Medicine in New York City. As a consequence, doctors, as well as their patients, are often in the dark as to its importance.

THREE-QUARTERS HAVE SLEEP PROBLEMS

Surveys show that 30% of the population have periodic insomnia, meaning that they have trouble drifting off or staying asleep all night, notes Walsleben, but three-quarters of all Americans are sleep deprived. "We try to cut it short Monday through Friday and make up for it on weekends," Dr. Walsleben explains, but the consequence is that we become less efficient as the workweek proceeds. Our reaction times are slower (a factor in many fatal accidents), our cognitive processes are fuzzier and—a telltale marker of inadequate rest—we get drowsy after lunch or fall asleep in front of the television right after eating dinner.

THE IMPACT ON YOUR HEALTH

Most people require at least seven to nine hours of sleep per night. Skimping on sleep can have a range of negative effects on overall health. If you get adequate sleep, your immune, neurological and hormonal systems may function more efficiently. You may also have a better chance of controlling mood disorders, such as depression, and possibly may even have an edge on controlling your weight.

We know that people feel that they don't have enough *time* to sleep.

But here's the deal: If you invest in your rest, you will actually get more done and *save* time because you will perform more efficiently with fewer mistakes. Research has repeatedly proven that test subjects who are well rested have better memory for detail, learn new material more quickly, make smarter decisions and perform at higher levels than those who aren't. Dr. Walsleben notes that in surveys of US Navy personnel, "people who were well rested got more promotions."

Because sleep plays a critical role in regulating neurochemicals, such as serotonin and epinephrine, sleep can sometimes even prove curative for depression and other mood disorders, says Dr. Walsleben.

A NATURAL IMMUNITY BOOSTER

Athletes know that a solid sleep assists in the rebuilding and repair of muscles and tissues to increase endurance and strength. But, less well known is that adequate "rack" time may help you fight off colds and flu by helping to restore and fortify germ-fighting cells and to help modulate the rhythm of secretion of certain inflammatory cytokines. This means that the sleep-deprived may have less-efficient immune systems, which repel germs and other challenges less efficiently than the immune systems of people who have had adequate rest.

UNEXPECTED DIETING TOOL

Sleeping can also help you lose weight, or stay at a stable weight. How? "We make less leptin, a substance that has complex functions, including satiety perception, when we don't sleep and wake up feeling starved because our brain has not had enough glucose fed to it during the night," Dr. Walsleben explains. This means that you are more likely to wake up craving donuts and sugary junk food because you want the instant energy they provide. Beyond that, you can make better food choices when your need for sleep is satiated.

In her book, Dr. Walsleben explains that even a single week of skimping on sleep can hinder the metabolism of glucose and change the body's reaction to insulin, which helps regulate blood sugar, lower thyroid stimulating hormones that are essential for a well-run metabolism and raise nighttime levels of cortisol. These effects might be linked to early onset type 2 diabetes or a worsening of its symptoms.

OTHER SLEEP BENEFITS

Other research indicates that inadequate slumber can actually be painful. In one study, the pain thresholds of women with arthritis and fibromyalgia were lower in those sleep-deprived than those who are solidly rested.

The research regarding the importance of sleep and fertility suggests that women who are trying to get pregnant may have more success if they—please excuse us—spend more time in bed.

It's no accident, says Dr. Walsleben, that many women fighting infertility finally find themselves pregnant after they've given up and gone on vacation. Everything in the body seems to work a little more efficiently when it's well rested.

Amazing…sleep offers us a place where we can actually get a lot done while doing "nothing." No more feeling guilty when you go to bed early. Instead, think of it as critical preparation for the next day's tasks.

Three Steps to a Sound Sleep

Robert E. Hales, MD, MBA, professor and chair, department of psychiatry, University of California, Davis School of Medicine. A past president of the Association for Academic Psychiatry, Dr. Hales has authored or edited 52 books, including *The Mind/Mood Pill Book*. Bantam.

Andrew L. Rubman, ND, director, Southbury Clinic for Traditional Medicines, Southbury, Connecticut.

If you're among the 40 million Americans who are troubled by insomnia, you probably already know about the importance of keeping regular bedtime and wake-up hours… avoiding late-afternoon or evening caffeine and alcohol…and forsaking reading and TV viewing while in bed.

While it is tempting to solve the problem with a pill, few over-the-counter (OTC) sedatives are of much benefit, and both OTC and prescription sleep aids can cause an array of serious and unpleasant side effects.

BEFORE TRYING SLEEP AIDS

Insomnia can occur for numerous reasons—lifestyle and dietary choices among them. Before heading for the medicine cabinet to solve your problem, it's important to consider your options. *Recently, we asked our medical expert, Andrew L. Rubman, ND, for his suggestions on decisions that can impact sleep…*

First, Dr. Rubman recommends that you find out if you are getting enough calcium in your diet. Calcium is important not only for strong teeth and bones, but also for many bodily functions, including handling stress. Inadequate levels of calcium and magnesium are associated with sleep difficulties. Your daily target for calcium consumption should be between 1,000 and 1,300 milligrams (mg), depending on your age and gender. To ensure adequate levels of calcium, Dr. Rubman recommends supplements.

His favorite: Butyrex, manufactured by T.E. Neesby Inc. of Fresno, California (800-633-7294).

In addition to calcium intake, your diet can have a great impact on sleep. *Specifically…*

- **Avoid caffeine and alcohol.**

- **Choose good evening snacks.** Bananas, dates, figs, nuts and nut butters, tuna, turkey, whole-grain crackers and yogurt are all good choices. These foods contain high levels of *tryptophan*, an amino acid that the brain uses to produce the neurotransmitter *serotonin*, which is responsible for normal sleep.

- **Avoid bad evening snacks.** Bacon, cheese, chocolate, eggplant, ham, potatoes, sauerkraut, sugar, sausage, spinach, tomatoes and wine are no-nos. All of these foods contain *tyramine*, which increases the release of the brain stimulant *norepinephrine*.

If these changes don't do the trick—or for those occasions when you can't get to sleep—herbal or prescription sleep aids often help you fall asleep faster and stay asleep longer. When used appropriately, they're quite safe.

Important: Before trying any sleep aid, you should be checked for the underlying cause of your sleeplessness, such as a prescribed medication, depression, anxiety or primary sleep disorder, such as obstructive sleep apnea, a potentially serious condition that causes a person to wake up repeatedly.

If you suffer from sleep apnea, *benzodiazepine* drugs or other sleep-inducing medications may interfere with your breathing, and this can be life threatening.

OCCASIONAL MILD INSOMNIA

Robert E. Hales, MD, MBA, professor and chair of the department of psychiatry at the University of California, Davis School of Medicine, advises using valerian…

This herbal remedy is often highly effective at curbing mild insomnia, which is defined as transient periods of disturbed sleep due to a major life event, such as a wedding, relocation or new job. Unlike sedative hypnotic agents, such as the benzodiazepine *temazepam* (Restoril), valerian does not cause morning-after drowsiness or stomach upset. It can, however, cause headaches and restlessness in some people.

Capsules and tea bags of valerian are sold in health food stores. Follow label directions carefully.

Caution: The US Food and Drug Administration does not regulate herbal remedies. It's best to stick with brands found effective by friends or recommended by your pharmacist or doctor. According to Dr. Rubman, it is best to try botanical medicines one at a time to assess their effectiveness. Often, just one capsule of a potent brand will provide the relief you seek. The premier manufacturer of valerian is the Eclectic Institute (800-332-4372, *www.eclecticherb.com*).

Lose Weight While You Sleep

Gary R. Hunter, PhD, metabolism researcher, University of Alabama at Birmingham.

Anyone who has watched television after 10 pm has seen ads for fat-burning potions that promise to melt off unwanted pounds while you watch TV, read a book or sleep. However, while you *know* that there is no magic potion to help you lose weight in the La-Z-Boy, there *are* steps that you can take to help your body burn more calories every day and lose weight faster—yes, even as you sleep.

The secret to better calorie burning is in raising your *resting energy expenditure*—your metabolism—the amount of calories you burn every moment as you live and breathe.

Sometime in our 30s, our metabolism starts slowing down at a rate of 5% every decade—a seemingly small decline, but one that can add up to more than 10 extra pounds' worth of calories a year if you're not careful.

Why the metabolism meltdown? Muscle loss. Muscle tissue burns about five times as many calories each day—even when you're not exercising—than fat tissue does. Unless you take action, by the time you're age 65 it's possible that you will replace half of your lean body mass with twice as much body fat.

MAKE SOME MUSCLE

"Resistance training probably is the best long-term method for increasing resting energy expenditure," says metabolism researcher Gary R. Hunter, PhD, of the University of Alabama at Birmingham. If you work every major muscle group twice a week, you can replace five to 10 years' worth of muscle loss in just a few months. That new lean muscle tissue will boost your resting metabolism. Plus you'll also burn about 200 calories by performing your strength training routine and your metabolism will stay revved up for about 48 hours afterward, says Dr. Hunter.

EAT TO LOSE

Exercise always works better if you eat right. *You can complement your calorie-burning efforts with these strategies...*

• **Eat breakfast.** According to a study by researchers at the George Washington University in Washington, DC, skipping breakfast can cause your resting metabolic rate to dip 5%. Eat a morning meal—oatmeal, yogurt and fruit provide a good protein-carbohydrate blend—and your metabolism will return to normal.

• **Get protein with every meal.** Protein not only makes you feel full faster than carbohydrates, but also takes more energy for your body to digest, so it gives you a slight metabolic boost.

Good sources: Fish, lean meats, poultry and legumes.

• **Eat frequent meals.** Whenever you deprive your body of food for too long, it goes into survival mode, slowing your metabolism and hording calories. Eat regular, healthy meals—along with one or two healthy snacks in between.

• **Drink plenty of water—and make it cold.** In a study from Germany, researchers reported that drinking water boosts your body's calorie burning rate by 30%. Ten minutes after 14 men

and women drank just over a pint of water, their metabolism sped up, and within 40 minutes, it reached a peak burning stage that lasted more than one hour. Since the metabolism spike is partly due to the body's efforts to warm the water you drink, cold water works best.

• **Drink green tea.** Researchers from Switzerland found that six out of 10 men who took a green tea supplement—the equivalent of one cup of green tea—three times a day with their meals burned about 80 more calories during the following 24 hours than those who took a caffeine pill or a dummy pill. They believe the tea's flavonoids enhance digestive efficacy.

Drink Up And Drown Dehydration Now!

Susan M. Kleiner, PhD, RD, owner, High Performance Nutrition, Mercer Island, Washington.

Andrew L. Rubman, ND, director, Southbury Clinic for Traditional Medicines, Southbury, Connecticut.

It can happen any time, not just in the summer. Suddenly you feel a little lousy—nothing serious—and then you realize you haven't drank much water all day. You drink some water and feel better quickly.

Most people are aware of the health dangers of severe dehydration, from cramps to exhaustion to life-threatening heat stroke. But what about chronic mild dehydration? This condition can sap your energy and make you feel light-headed, tired and irritable.

According to Susan M. Kleiner, PhD, RD, owner of High Performance Nutrition in Mercer Island, Washington, having a consistent 1% to 2% deficit of body weight (chronic mild dehydration) caused by fluid loss can have a negative impact on mental and physical performance, muscle growth and even long-term health.

Water makes up about 60% of the body weight of adults. All of the systems and processes of our bodies, from energy production to reproduction to muscle function to joint lubrication, are dependent on water for efficient operation.

EARLY SIGNS OF DEHYDRATION

Your best bet is to prevent dehydration from developing in the first place. Thirst is not the only symptom…nor is it always the earliest one. In fact, if you wait until you are thirsty before you drink, you already might be slightly dehydrated.

Early warning signs that Dr. Kleiner advises to watch out for include…

- **Fatigue.**
- **Loss of appetite.**
- **Flushed skin.**
- **Burning in stomach.**
- **Headache.**
- **Light-headedness.**
- **Dry mouth.**
- **Dry cough.**
- **Heat intolerance.**
- **Dark urine with a strong odor.**

These problems are caused by the failure to maintain your body's proper fluid balance.

DEVELOP A FLUID PLAN

Although the standard recommendation is to drink eight eight-ounce glasses daily, eight is not always enough, explains Dr. Kleiner. She recommends boosting this number to nine or even 11 glasses because every day you lose 10 to 12 cups of water that must be replaced to maintain a healthy fluid balance. For a more exact estimate of how much water your body requires, divide your weight in half. That number, in ounces, generally is considered your recommended daily water intake.

In Dr. Kleiner's opinion, it doesn't matter what kind of water you drink. The question is, which one will you drink more of? Tap or bottled? Still or sparkling? Since taste is the greatest reason people don't drink water, she advises you to choose whatever water you like.

Dr. Kleiner recommends that you develop a fluid plan, just like a food plan. *Some helpful strategies include…*

- **Drink a glass of water when you wake up,** and take frequent water breaks throughout the day.

- **Carry fluids with you.** Keep water bottles and pitchers handy at home and in the office.

- **Eat healthy,** fluid-filled foods, such as fruits and vegetables. With a diet that meets the five-a-day requirement, you can take in up to four cups of water from food alone.

- **Drink a variety of beverages,** such as fresh juices and herbal teas. You don't have to feel deprived. Other beverages count toward your daily requirement, too. However, avoid more than three caffeinated beverages per day as well as alcohol—both of which increase fluid loss.

- **Drink two cups of fluid two hours before exercise,** and four to six ounces every 15 to 20 minutes during exercise. When you exercise, your fluid requirements rise. For intense exercise or workouts that last more than one hour, Dr. Kleiner believes that carbohydrate-electrolyte sports drinks are best.

There are two caveats to keep in mind, however, with these drink-drink-drink recommendations. First, our medical expert, Andrew L. Rubman, ND, warns that too much liquid at mealtime dilutes the digestive enzymes, potentially leading to indigestion.

Better: Drink 30 minutes before a meal…or wait 60 minutes afterward. If you need liquid to help wash down your food, limit your consumption to a swallow when necessary.

Also, drinking this much water, particularly when coupled with exercise, is bound to deplete sodium levels. Although in some individuals, excess salt consumption may result in an increase in blood pressure, insufficient sodium is lethal. Don't restrict salt intake unnecessarily…and always pay attention to taste. Chances are that if your taste buds are asking for salt, you probably need it.

Water is a critical nutrient for growth, muscle development and health, so drink up.

Saline Solution

John McDougall, MD, director, the McDougall Program, McDougall Health Center, Santa Rosa, California, *www.drmcdougall.com*.

Andrew L. Rubman, ND, director, Southbury Clinic for Traditional Medicines, Southbury, Connecticut.

With all the press about what we should and should not eat, it's odd that we don't hear much about sodium.

In fact, it hardly made the news when the Institute of Medicine in Washington, DC, lowered its recommended daily consumption of sodium from 2.4 to 1.5 grams. (That's less than one teaspoon of table salt!) This inattention is particularly strange because almost all American adults have too much salt in their diets, and overconsumption of it is associated with high blood pressure, stroke and other health risks.

According to John McDougall, MD, director of the McDougall Program at the McDougall Health Center in Santa Rosa, California, the primary reason we consume so much salt today is that the food industry is loading many foods with it (as well as sugar—but that's a subject for another day). The taste buds for both salt and sugar are located on the front tip of the tongue, and we instinctively respond to those tastes with pleasure. Food manufacturers are catering to a taste that people are designed to crave.

DON'T BE FOOLED

Ironically, while the industry is allegedly laboring to become more health-friendly by curbing fat and carbohydrates, it is actually increasing sodium levels in some foods.

Example: Wendy's Ultimate Chicken Grill sandwich, which replaced the chain's previous grilled chicken sandwich, has less fat, but 1,000 milligrams of sodium, which is more than the earlier version. A spokesperson for the company explained this increase away by saying that consumers are looking for big taste, and that calls for salt.

Even salads aren't a guarantee against high amounts of sodium. Burger King's Tendergrill Salad has almost 1,450 mg of sodium.

SMART SALT STRATEGY

Our medical expert, Andrew L. Rubman, ND, reminds us that while there is an association between salt consumption and hypertension, there is not a causal relationship between them, and, more important, insufficient salt intake can create medical emergencies. Psychological and physical stress can each reduce the body's ability to recapture salt from the large intestine. He suggests having your doctor check your electrolytes when he/she does your yearly blood work.

To enjoy salt without overdoing it, Dr. McDougall has two pieces of advice. First, cook without salt whenever possible, and add it—in small amounts—to food once it's on the table. That way, the tip of the tongue is best able to respond to the salt because it is now on the surface of the food, not overwhelmed by other flavors. Second, eat whole foods rather than processed or prepared foods, which is where high quantities of sodium lurk.

Just following these two guidelines should bring your sodium intake well within healthful parameters.

Healing Wounds From the Inside Out

Alicia Capsey, ND, naturopathic physician in private practice at Whidbey Island Naturopathic, with offices in Oak Harbor and Greenbank, Washington. *www.whidbey naturopathic.com*.

Andrew L. Rubman, ND, director, Southbury Clinic for Traditional Medicines, Southbury, Connecticut.

Scrapes, cuts and bruises can happen to anyone at any time. Besides applying the usual antibiotic ointment and protective bandage, is there something we can do from the inside out on an ongoing basis to assist with wound healing?

We called Alicia Capsey, ND, a naturopathic physician in Oak Harbor and Greenbank, Washington. Since she practices in a deeply rural area where people do a lot of work outdoors, Dr. Capsey sees a good many patients with wounds and cuts—and more than a few, she told us, come in injured by kicks from their horses!

THE "INSIDE STORY"

According to Dr. Capsey, maximally effective wound healing does not begin after the wound occurs. It is a regular part of personal preventive health care to maximize your body's ability to quickly and efficiently rebuild injured connective tissue. What to do?

"You want to take substances on a regular basis that will help build the body's connective tissue and maintain blood vessel health," says Dr. Capsey. Specifically, she recommends the "big five" for building connective tissue—vitamin C with citrus bioflavonoids…*zinc*…copper…and the amino acids *lysine* and *proline*. She stresses that it is important to get vitamin C with citrus bioflavonoids. The label will say either "vitamin C with citrus bioflavonoids," or "vitamin C with rosehips." The citrus bioflavonoids help keep the "mesh" of the connective tissue in your body healthy and free from cell damage.

Our medical expert, Andrew L. Rubman, ND, suggests that eating sufficient amounts of animal protein will allow you to build up your stores of lysine and proline. He also cautions that amino acid supplements should not be taken without medical oversight. Talk to a trained professional to ensure that you set up a healthy protocol.

Dr. Capsey says that a high-quality multivitamin typically contains adequate levels of the "big five," though you may need to supplement the vitamin C/citrus bioflavonoids. Other vitamins that are important to connective tissue maintenance include vitamins A and E.

Dr. Capsey's favorite brands: Thorne, Tyler and PhytoPharmica.

An alternative to a multivitamin is an antioxidant formula that contains vitamins A, C, E and the trace minerals selenium and zinc, which Dr. Capsey calls "the ACEs plus zinc." This is a great synergistic antioxidant blend, she explains, that's available in health-food stores. The antioxidants will serve to protect against inflammatory and any other degenerative challenges that may arise from the injury.

Homeopathic defense: A high-quality multivitamin or antioxidant formula will be the basic foundation of a good tissue maintenance-and-repair protocol, but Dr. Capsey also rec-

ommends arnica, a homeopathic remedy that helps minimize bruising. Arnica may be used topically right after an accident.

Read This Before Taking a New Prescription

Derjung Mimi Tarn, MD, PhD, family physician and assistant clinical professor of family medicine, University of California, Los Angeles.

Nearly half of all Americans take one or more prescription drugs. You may assume that doctors would routinely explain the basics—what a drug does, how long to take it, etc. Don't count on it.

A recent study based on the audiotapes of 185 patient-doctor visits and published in *Archives of Internal Medicine* found that doctors do a poor job of explaining critical information related to medication.

Doctors discussed drug side effects in only 35% of cases…told patients how long to take a drug just 34% of the time…and were remiss in telling how many pills to take in 45% of the taped visits.

Prescription drug misuse accounts for thousands of deaths annually—and poor communication with doctors may be a contributing factor.

Patients can get some information from pharmacists, medication labels, package inserts and/or the Internet.* But doctors understand a patient's individual needs—and should know what other drugs a patient may be taking.

Before leaving your doctor's office, make sure that you understand…

- **Why the drug is being prescribed.**
- **The generic and brand names.**
- **How and when to take it.**
- **How long to take it.**
- **Whether it's likely to cause side effects or interact with other drugs.**

Don't settle for any less from your doctor!

*Consult the *Physicians' Desk Reference* Web site, *www.pdrhealth.com.*

How to Fight Calcification

Mark A. Stengler, ND, naturopathic physician in private practice, La Jolla, California…adjunct associate clinical professor at the National College of Natural Medicine, Portland, Oregon…author of many books, including *The Natural Physician's Healing Therapies* and coauthor of *Prescription for Natural Cures* (both from Bottom Line Books)…and author of the *Bottom Line/Natural Healing* newsletter.

We heard a story recently about a woman who underwent a breast biopsy for calcification and was told that she also had minor calcification in areas related to her heart. It made us wonder if there was a connection between different kinds of calcification, and if so, was it a problem? And what could be done about it?

To get some answers, we consulted Mark A. Stengler, ND, a naturopathic physician in private practice in La Jolla, California, and adjunct associate clinical professor at the National College of Natural Medicine in Portland, Oregon.

CALCIFICATION DEFINED

Calcification is the process by which calcium builds up in tissue, causing it to harden. This mineral is essential when it comes to building strong bones and teeth, and that's where 99% of calcium entering the body is deposited. The remaining 1% normally dissolves in the blood. When a disturbance—such as localized inflammation, infection or the effects of stress or poor diet—affects the balance between calcium and other minerals or hormones, it can be deposited in other areas of the body.

Dr. Stengler explains that calcification in these areas generally occurs as the body's response to tissue inflammation and injury in order to stabilize the injured site. He adds that although there may be calcification in different areas of the body, there is no connection. Even if you have gallstones or breast calcification, there is no need to worry about calcification leading to coronary artery disease.

Calcification is not necessarily a bad thing, observes Dr. Stengler. Very often, it is benign.

THE IMPACT ON CORONARY ARTERIES

Calcification of the coronary arteries is a recognized risk factor for heart attack and stroke. According to Dr. Stengler, this process occurs when calcium attaches to cholesterol deposits on the walls of arteries. Calcification causes these plaques to grow and become progressively harder and more brittle, and it can influence plaque rupture. This process of cholesterol deposit and subsequent calcification does not start unless inflammation damages the tissue.

Cardiologists use computed tomography (CT) scans to assess calcium buildup and cardiovascular risk. Dr. Stengler notes that calcification fits right in with the new theory of heart disease, which suggests that underlying inflammation is the true cause.

BREAST CALCIFICATION

Calcifications in the breast are common, and most are benign—but certain types can be associated with cancer. According to the American Cancer Society, women who have distinct patterns of calcifications are diagnosed with breast cancer two to three times more often than women with no calcifications. Problems most likely arise when calcifications are irregular, and when they are concentrated instead of being spread throughout the breast.

Mammograms or CT scans are necessary to assess calcifications, since they cannot be felt in physical exams.

HOW TO COMBAT CALCIFICATION

According to Dr. Stengler, there is not much in the way of studies on the treatment of calcification, since it is much easier to prevent than to treat. Prevention focuses on the reduction of underlying inflammation.

Helpful measures to control general inflammation and calcification include…

• **Eat plenty of fruits, vegetables, nuts and seeds,** which are rich in antioxidants that defend against the free-radical damage characteristic of inflammation. Some fruits and vegetables are also natural salicylates, which means they have an aspirin-like effect on inflammation. Pickles, plums, cherries, berries and dates are all good sources.

• **Eat a diet that has an alkalizing effect.** Dr. Stengler recommends one that decreases the likelihood that pro-inflammatory acidic residues may accumulate in tissues. Again, lots of veggies are important, especially green vegetables and super-green foods, such as chlorella, spirulina and wheatgrass. Avoid or reduce your intake of red meats and vegetable oils, as well as fried and fast foods, sugar and refined flours, which are acidic.

• **Vitamin K has been shown to help prevent calcification of the arteries and soft tissue,** according to Dr. Stengler. Dietary sources include cabbage, cauliflower, spinach and other green, leafy vegetables, whole-grain cereals and soybeans. Taking supplemental vitamin K may interfere with some prescription medications, so consult your health-care provider before taking it.

• **Magnesium supplements (up to 750 milligrams daily) help with calcification.** Reduce this dosage if loose stools develop. Always remember to take this mineral along with calcium, unless otherwise prescribed by your physician.

• **Physiotherapy, deep tissue massage and acupuncture can reduce inflammation** and calcium deposits in the case of joint calcification, notes Dr. Stengler.

• **Low-dose aspirin provides an effective defense against inflammation.**

The most serious calcification involves the coronary arteries. *To prevent coronary artery calcification, Dr. Stengler recommends that you...*

• **Achieve a healthy weight.**

• **Control related underlying health conditions,** especially high blood pressure and diabetes.

• **Engage in regular weight-bearing exercise.**

• **Refrain from smoking cigarettes,** cigars and pipes, and stay away from secondhand smoke and polluted areas.

• **Follow a healthy diet** that is low in trans-fatty acids, saturated fat and hydrogenated oils. Consume foods rich in omega-3 fatty acids (such as deepwater fish and flaxseeds) and take supplements.

info The American Cancer Society (ACS), *www.cancer.org.*

The American Heart Association (AHA), *www.americanheart.org.*

5

A Stress-Free Life

Ways to Fight Chronic Stress

Although life was hard in "the old days," the phrase "stressed out" did not exist. It wasn't until modern-day society—full of conveniences and 24/7 access to everything—that widespread chronic stress came into our world, and along with it an array of dangers to our health.

To learn more about the impact of chronic stress on our health and to find better ways to cope with it, we spoke with two experts—Joan Borysenko, PhD, cofounder and former director of the mind-body clinical programs at two Harvard Medical School teaching hospitals… and Elissa Epel, PhD, associate professor in the department of psychiatry at the University of California, San Francisco.

ACUTE OR CHRONIC STRESS?

There are two kinds of stress—acute and chronic. Short-term or acute stress occurs when you react to an immediate threat, such as when a car stops short in front of you in traffic.

In contrast, chronic stress is more akin to fighting rush hour traffic to and from work every morning and evening, day in, day out. It is a reaction to long-term problems, such as conflicts on the job, financial and health concerns, or family and relationship difficulties.

According to Dr. Borysenko, most people can handle the occasional stressful event. However, chronic stress takes a heavy toll on your emotional and your physical health. The consequences range from irritability, anxiety, anorexia and depression to lowered resistance to infection, diabetes, chest pain, irregular heart rhythm and even cardiac arrest.

Joan Borysenko, PhD, cofounder and former director, mind-body clinical programs at two Harvard Medical School teaching hospitals, now merged as the Beth Israel/Deaconess Medical Center in Boston. Dr. Borysenko is author or coauthor of over a dozen books, including *Inner Peace for Busy People* and *Inner Peace for Busy Women* (both published by Hay House). *www.joanborysenko.com.*

Elissa Epel, PhD, associate professor, department of psychiatry, University of California, San Francisco.

WHAT'S HAPPENING IN YOUR BODY?

When you are under stress, the hypothalamus in your brain sets off a chain reaction of events to stimulate your heart, lungs and other organs to fight or flee. The body releases hormones, such as corticotropin-releasing hormone (CRH), adrenocorticotropic hormone (ACTH) and glucocorticoids. In turn, your heart beats faster, your blood pressure rises, your breathing quickens and your liver pumps out more blood sugar to energize muscles and nerves.

Once the threat passes, your body can relax again and your organs return to normal. But if the threat never completely passes and stress becomes a chronic problem, there is a strain on your individual organs as well as your overall health.

WHAT IS YOUR STRESS QUOTIENT?

Stress is a very individual experience. A lot of it is perception. For example, some people don't mind sitting in traffic, while it makes others rage and curse and tear their hair out. The important thing is to identify the external events that trigger your stress, and devise ways to manage or avoid them, says Dr. Epel. She recommends listing your chronic stressors, rating them according to degree of stressfulness and then focusing on ways to change the most stressful situations.

For instance, if your stressful daily commute is getting to you, pop in a favorite CD or listen to a book-on-tape while you drive to and from work. Better yet, take the bus or train.

LIFE IS SO COMPLICATED

When your life becomes overcomplicated, take steps to simplify it. *Strategies our experts recommend for reducing and controlling stress…*

●**Separate large tasks into small ones,** says Dr. Borysenko. When your workload seems crushing, break it down into a list of smaller tasks that you can take on one at a time. Stay focused on the task at hand rather than getting overwhelmed by the many that follow.

●**Learn how to say no.** If you feel overwhelmed with personal or professional responsibilities, try to take a step back and think about which ones you can eliminate.

●**Take short breaks during work,** advises Dr. Epel. Get up from your desk and stretch, or use your lunch break to take a walk in the park.

●**Offset daily pressures with physical activity,** says Dr. Epel. A healthy lifestyle is your best defense against stress. In addition, follow a balanced diet, limit your intake of caffeine and alcohol and get sufficient sleep.

●**Share your feelings.** Instead of bottling them up, talk to a close friend or family member. Dr. Epel observes that lonely people suffer more from stress and poor health.

●**Try meditation.** Dr. Borysenko compares it with "mental martial arts," noting that meditation increases immune function, lessens anxiety and helps you enter into a more creative state of mind.

●**Center yourself each morning,** says Dr. Borysenko. Instead of jumping directly out of bed, think about what you are grateful for, or read something that inspires you to think about what is meaningful in life.

●**Dr. Borysenko emphasizes making peace of mind your first priority.** If you start to lose it, do something about it. Meditate, call a friend or take a 30-minute walk. You will restore your energy and equilibrium and afterward be able to work more creatively and effectively.

Different stress strategies will work for different people. Try several to figure out what works best for you. Most important is to do something—anything—to keep yourself from being stressed out.

Stay Cool— Stay Alive!

Willem J. Kop, PhD, associate professor of cardiology and director of the Behavioral Cardiology Program at the University of Maryland Medical Center, Baltimore.

We all know that strenuous physical exercise can lead to heart attack. A recent study indicates that mental stress, such as anger and frustration, can also provoke dangerously abnormal heartbeats that can lead to sudden cardiac death in vulnerable people. Given the level of day-to-day angst we all experience, this is frightening stuff.

According to lead author Willem J. Kop, PhD, an associate professor of cardiology at the University of Maryland Medical Center in Baltimore, this is the first study to show that extreme, acute mental stress, just like physical stress, is a serious risk factor for people who are prone to arrhythmias. The results were published in *Circulation: Journal of the American Heart Association.*

Note: Sudden cardiac death due to an irregular heartbeat is not the same as a heart attack, which is caused by a physical blockage of the arteries that supply blood to the heart.

THE RESEARCH

In normal people, heartbeats occur in a regular pattern, explains Dr. Kop. But in people who have life-threatening arrhythmias, heart rhythm disturbances can cause the heart to stop beating, or to stop contracting and pumping blood, resulting in sudden death. During this study, the goal was to compare beat-to-beat variations in heart rhythm when participants were under physical and mental stress.

The research involved 23 people with heart disease and implantable cardiac defibrillators (ICDs) and a control group of 17 people with no coronary artery disease. Heart medications were withheld for two days from most cardiac patients before starting. The average age was 62. Those with ICDs—built-in resuscitators that give the heart a jolt if it stops, shocking it back into a normal rhythm—were already at a higher-than-normal risk for sudden cardiac death.

On two alternate days, each group was exposed to mental or physical stress. *The tests in this study included...*

- **Mental stress.** Defined as anger recall and mental arithmetic, patients were first instructed to give a four-minute speech about a recent event that made them angry. Next, they were asked to solve math problems in their head (subtracting multiples of seven from four-digit numbers). While they did so, researchers deliberately interrupted them and told them to do better.

- **Physical stress.** Patients rode three to 15 minutes on a stationary bike until they were too tired to go on or until their heart rate reached the necessary peak level.

While the participants were under mental or physical stress, researchers used electrocardiograms (ECGs) to measure an abnormal heart rate pattern called *T-wave alternans* (TWA). An established marker of cardiac electrical instability, TWA has been used previously in exercise stress tests of heart attack survivors and people with ICDs. It measures tiny heartbeat irregularities that often precede potentially dangerous arrhythmias.

According to Dr. Kop, abnormal TWA patterns showed up much faster in people with ICDs than in those free of heart disease. Heartbeat irregularities also became apparent during the mental stress tests at a much lower heart rate than during the physical stress tests.

This demonstrates that electrical instability in the heart can be provoked by anger, frustration and stress, concludes Dr. Kop.

Interestingly, he adds, this electrical instability occurred at significantly lower heart rates with mental stress than with physical stress...

- It took a heart-rate increase of 53.7 beats per minute during exercise to cause irregularities.

- Irregularities occurred after an increase of only 9.7 beats per minute during anger recall, and after an increase of 14.3 beats per minute during mental math.

LOOKING TOWARD THE FUTURE

The next step is to figure out how to identify those at high risk for developing arrhythmias, says Dr. Kop, and examine whether we can predict future events.

According to Dr. Kop, mental stress often occurs more frequently than physical stress, and it is harder to control. Although researchers did not specifically examine this, the study suggests that people who are at high risk for heart irregularities may need to take steps to more effectively manage the stress in their lives, through regular exercise, meditation, progressive relaxation, deep breathing and yoga.

info For more heart-healthy information, visit the American Heart Association's Web site at *www.americanheart.org.*

Dissolve Tension With Yoga

Timothy McCall, MD, internist, medical editor of *Yoga Journal* and author of *Examining Your Doctor* (Citadel) and *Yoga as Medicine* (Bantam), *www.drmccall.com.*

With the fast-paced lifestyle everyone seems to be leading these days, it's hard to find the time to rest or relax. Busy schedules, family needs, work requirements, etc., make us push ourselves to go-go-go. Even if we can manage to get a good night's sleep, we sometimes still need to take a break from the many pressures of our lives.

If we don't allow ourselves to take a break, our bodies will probably start to tell us in no uncertain terms that they *need* to take a break. Maybe it's just a scratchy throat or the sniffles. Or, it might be back pain or stomach ailments—or worse.

LISTEN TO YOUR BODY

When your body sends you a signal, it's important to listen to it…or it may start talking "louder." Rather than ignoring the signals, consciously choose to take a break. Sometimes you simply need some time to yourself. Cancel that meeting or workout. Instead, curl up on the couch, and settle down with a bowl of steaming soup and a good book. Afterward, if you feel up to it, light your favorite scented candle, put on some quiet music and practice gentle stretches or yoga poses.

AN EASY YOGA MOVE TO RESTORE BALANCE AND ENERGY

According to Timothy McCall, MD, an internist, medical editor of *Yoga Journal* and author of *Yoga as Medicine*, yoga can be extremely beneficial when stress or illness threatens to overwhelm us, because it restores and energizes at the same time. In the frenetic culture we live in, no matter what the obstacle, the inclination is to fight through it…but don't. Instead, tune in to what you are feeling inside. Listen and respond to your own body.

Most important: Don't overdo.

One of Dr. McCall's favorite restorative yoga positions is "legs-up-the-wall." He *describes this pose as ideal to calm the nervous system, ease muscle fatigue and restore health…*

• **To begin, find a quiet space** and place a cylindrical yoga bolster or two very thick blankets folded into a rectangular shape a few inches from a wall.

• **Lie down on the floor,** with your hips elevated on the bolster or blankets, and prop your legs up against the wall so that you are in an "L" position.

• **Adjust your pose with your hips as close to the wall as is comfortable,** rest your arms above your head with your elbows bent or out to the sides and unclench your hands.

• **Once you are completely comfortable, close your eyes and exhale.** Mentally examine your body from head to toe, slowly and consciously dissolving the tension throughout. Be aware of your breath as it passes in and out of your body.

• **Rest in this position for as long as you feel comfortable,** then slowly open your eyes, straighten up and return to the "real world." According to Dr. McCall, when you surrender to the softness of this pose, you invite any residual knots of tension to dissolve, and it refreshes and renews, and may be beneficial to people who are exhausted, chronically ill or who have weakened immunity.

Whatever route you decide to take to relaxation and renewal, be it yoga, meditation or a cup of hot tea, make sure that you allow yourself the time to take a break. Sometimes it's all you need to accomplish your goals with even more strength and confidence.

Sit on Your Hands… And Other Instant Stress Relievers

Adair Wilson Heitmann, former director, Center for Creativity & Wellness, Fairfield, Connecticut.

One key to meeting the challenges of a busy life in the fast lane lies in being sure that the energy in your body is flowing smoothly. Adair Wilson Heitmann, former director of the Center for Creativity and Wellness in Fairfield, Connecticut, works with individuals to help them better manage their lives, including their stress levels. Heitmann explains that stress, whether it comes from ordinary life events or trauma, causes the body's chi energies (its principal energies) to become out of balance or even blocked rather than flowing smoothly as they should. She helps her clients keep their energy in check between appointments with some simple do-it-yourself techniques. We tried them. They're remarkably effective!

EXERCISE #1—
WRAP IT

To release tension, Heitmann advises a strategy that comes from the Japanese healing art called jin shin jyutsu, which is the basis of acupressure, acupuncture and massage techniques that use pressure points. While it's best to do this in a restful place where you can shut your eyes, it's not necessary. Heitmann says that you can do it any time you're feeling out of balance. It's especially good for nervous airplane travelers.

What you do: Wrap your entire right hand around your left thumb, as if your hand were a tortilla wrapping the thumb. Hold that for one to five minutes, and then alternate left hand on right thumb. Go through each of your fingers this way, always alternating hands. The energy flow through each of the fingers has a particular association—the thumb with worry…the index finger with fear…the middle finger with anger …the ring finger with grief…and the pinky with pretense. Although this method is excellent for releasing tension in general, if you are experiencing one of these aspects in particular, you can hold the corresponding digits of each hand, alternating style, to find relief.

EXERCISE #2—
SIT ON IT

Another tactic that will help you relieve stress is literally to sit on your hands. Place your hands palms down under your sitz bones (the ends of your pelvic bone that you can feel in your bottom) and hold this position for a few minutes. You'll find this helpful anytime, whether you are at your office or your dining room table. It takes just a few minutes to ease

your stress, but the longer you can sit on your hands, says Heitmann, the more grounded you'll feel.

OTHER IDEAS

While driving, you can relieve the stress that comes with it by making use of stop signs. When you come upon one, as you brake, exhale and say, "I breathe out peace."

While you are stopped, inhale and say, "I breathe in peace." You also can do this in traffic when there's no stop sign nearby just by chanting to your breathing.

Music is also an excellent stress soother, says Heitmann, whether through a CD or MP3 player in the car or headsets during a flight.

SMELL THE FLOWERS

Heitmann recommends another way to ease the stress that's involved with travel. Try using liquid flower essences for several days before you leave and during your trip. Two good ones to try are Bach Flower Rescue Remedy (*www.bachflower.com*) or Travel Ease (Alaskan Flower Essence Project, *www.alaskaessences.com*).

Caution: The flowers in Rescue Remedy are preserved in a brandy-type liquid, making it off-limits to alcoholics.

A TIME-PROVEN METHOD

The granddaddy tool of stress relief, though, says Heitmann, is meditation. While that isn't surprising, she has advice that pertains specifically to people in Western cultures. Because Westerners find it difficult simply to sit still, we benefit from having a number of types of meditation available, including those that engage the cognitive mind with chants or breathing routines. These make it easier to relax into deeper meditation. Heitmann finds that people do best trying out several different methods (which can be found in books or through local classes).

Start by fitting in just five minutes a day of meditation. Adopt the meditation schedule and technique that slips most efficiently into your typical day.

Whether it's meditation or some quick-fix tricks, getting your energy in check can make a big difference when it really counts. Ohmm.

Don't Worry...
Live Longer

Christopher M. Peterson, PhD, professor of clinical psychology, University of Michigan, Ann Arbor.

In the 1980s, a hit song by Bobby McFerrin urged us, "Don't worry, be happy." It was a catchy song, but it was overplayed and became a cliché very quickly. Now, however, recent studies are revealing that this message might just give you a longer and healthier life.

RECENT RESEARCH

To find out how being happy could make a difference, Dutch researchers from the Psychiatric Center GGZ Delfland gathered data from 941 men and women ages 65 to 85, who responded to 30 questions about their outlook on life and subjective feelings of well-being. Researchers then sorted participants into four groups, depending on their perceived levels of optimism. The research team followed the participants for just over nine years and then analyzed the results. Compared with the pessimists, the optimistic participants had a 55% lower risk for death from all causes and a 23% lower risk for cardiovascular death. This was independent of socio-demographic characteristics and cardiovascular risk factors, according to the study authors. This study bolsters an earlier Mayo Clinic study that followed 839 men and women for 30 years and showed that pessimists had a 19% increased risk for death when *actual* life span was put against *expected* life span.

EASIER SAID THAN DONE

Why isn't everyone happy? It makes you feel better—and now we know it's healthier. Easier said than done. Christopher M. Peterson, PhD, professor of psychology at the University of Michigan, has spent years studying optimism in general and how it relates to health and longevity specifically. We called him to discuss why optimism has such a profound impact and what people can do to bring their thinking into the "be happy" camp.

Dr. Peterson explained that optimism creates better health in a number of ways. Although many people do assume that cheerfulness boosts the immune system, he pointed out that most Westerners don't die of immune problems—they do, however, die of cardiovascular troubles. Optimists view life not as a hassle but as an adventure, as Dr. Peterson puts it, and they expect happy outcomes. This results in lower stress levels, a sure boost to cardiovascular health. Furthermore, happy people are popular, and it's well known that a vibrant social network is an asset to longevity. But Dr. Peterson feels that probably the most important reason optimists outlive pessimists is that they take good care of themselves. They do those things that contribute to long life because they think doing so will make a difference. And that, he says, defines optimism. Pessimists feel hopeless, not in control and have a "why bother" outlook. Optimists assume their actions will positively influence the future and they take steps to do so.

OPTIMIST OR PESSIMIST?

Interestingly, some people think of themselves as cheerful but are actually rather negative. We asked Dr. Peterson how people can tell if they fall on the optimist or pessimist side of the line. He said that the technique they use in their research to determine a person's mind-set is to ask them to imagine bad things happening —and how they would respond to them. Pessimists make small catastrophes of what are actually routine events...optimists brush off such events or view them as likely to have positive outcomes.

TURNING IT AROUND

So the next question is, how do you turn yourself from having a doomsday personality into one that has a sunnier outlook? Happily, Dr. Peterson says that this is totally possible to accomplish, although it's hardly as simple as "don't worry." He suggests that somewhat negative people surround themselves with optimists. A lot of personality traits are contagious, including optimism. By selecting cheerful people to be around, you'll find yourself starting to absorb their outlook on life.

For people who are extremely and chronically pessimistic, or even depressed, he recommends a cognitive therapy program for eight weeks, during which participants learn to recognize their automatic thought patterns. By taking notice of them, they can take steps to stop negative thoughts and perceptions of outside events. Eventually, he says, people get better at this, and if they are willing to work hard and stay mindful of their thought processes, they can unlearn pessimism and embrace a better viewpoint. He also urges everyone to practice gratitude on a daily basis. It's hard to have a gloomy world view, he notes, when you are counting your blessings.

We had one last question for Dr. Peterson. Do optimists, in their desire to see the world as a cheery place, tend to court denial as a way of getting there? He reported that there is no evidence that expecting good things relates to denial.

Example: If you are five feet tall and want to be a professional athlete, that could be a big stretch—but if your dream is to become a good jockey, why, it's not a stretch at all.

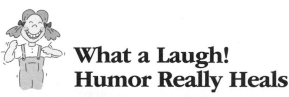

What a Laugh! Humor Really Heals

Allen Klein, MA ("The Jollytologist"), past president, Association for Applied and Therapeutic Humor and author of *The Healing Power of Humor*. Tarcher. Visit his Web site at *www.allenklein.com*.

When things are looking bleak for your health…at work…or in your personal life, it's difficult to see anything funny about anything. But there's a school of thought that says that's just what you should do—use humor to reduce stress and encourage physical and emotional wellness and healing.

To get the inside scoop on humor in healing, we spoke with Allen Klein, author of *The Healing Power of Humor*. Klein gives speeches and workshops around the world to teach people how to use humor to deal with changes, challenges and the not-so-funny stuff, from everyday trials to out-and-out tragedies.

MEDICAL FACT OR FICTION?

There are many theories to explain how humor can promote physical and emotional wellbeing. In a study by Lee Berk, DrPH, MPH, at Loma Linda University in California, the immune-suppressing hormone cortisol was found to be less prevalent in people's blood when they laughed. Another theory is that laughter triggers the secretion of pleasure-inducing endorphins, although this has never been proven.

While no one knows the precise connection between humor and healing, Klein points out that we do know that laughter…

• **Raises and then lowers our heart rate and blood pressure,** similar to aerobic exercise.

• **Relaxes our muscles.**

• **Oxygenates the blood,** so we think better after a laugh.

Of course, a lot of the evidence linking humor with healing and health is anecdotal. Klein advises that you ask yourself, *How do I feel when I laugh?* Chances are, you feel pretty good. Just as anger and hostility are bad for your heart and health, humor and laughter are good for you.

BE OPEN

"Humor is all around you," says Klein. "All you have to do is open your eyes and ears and look." He advises that you try to reframe challenging situations by using your "humor eyes." When you find humor in trying times, one of the first and foremost changes you experience is that you see your problems in a new light. Suddenly, you have a fresh perspective and may see new ways to deal with them.

Klein tells the story of a woman who was depressed and suicidal. Standing on a bridge, she was tempted to hurl herself off it, when suddenly she looked down at her new $150 shoes and said, "No way." This made her laugh, turn her back on the bridge and seek counseling.

SMALL DOSES

Humor can play a role in situations from the sublime to the ridiculous. In traffic jams, Klein blows bubbles out the window. While you may not want to carry your sense of humor this far, there are small steps you can take to start lightening up in your own everyday life. For example, keep a funny cartoon or photo on your desk at work. Or when the going gets tough, call an old friend or family member and make them tell you the childhood story that always makes you laugh.

Klein advises that you have a "humor mantra" on hand to repeat to yourself at stressful moments. *Make up your own or use one of his following suggestions…*

- **I have no time for a crisis, my schedule is very full.**

- **Oh, what an opportunity for growth and learning!**

- **I refuse to be intimidated by reality.**

- **Take it back. It's not what I ordered.**

- **I'd rather be _____ (dancing, skiing, jogging, etc.).**

- **Beam me up, Scotty.**

Research has shown that people who volunteer often live longer. Another important part of Klein's philosophy is sharing humor with others. When he sees a person in trouble, he tries to help. For example, when his plane was delayed for several hours, he gave the flight attendant one of his red clown noses (which you can usually buy at a costume or party-supply store) to wear. Next thing he knew, many of the aggravated passengers were smiling once again, and some of the uncomfortable tension drained out of the situation.

FILL YOUR WORLD WITH BRIGHT COLORS

According to Klein, your attitude is like a box of crayons that color the world. Constantly use gray colors, and your picture will always be dark and depressing. Use humor to add bright colors, and your picture begins to lighten up.

In his experience, humor has played a role in even the most difficult circumstances. Klein has worked with people with cancer, AIDS and Alzheimer's—among others—and all have found some humor to give them the courage to go on.

info The Association for Applied and Therapeutic Humor, *www.aath.org*.

Best Ways to Beat Winter Blues

Leo Galland, MD, director, Foundation for Integrated Medicine, New York City. His latest book is *The Fat Resistance Diet*. Broadway. Dr. Galland is a recipient of the Linus Pauling award.

Judith Mabel, RD, PhD, nutritionist, registered dietician, in private practice, Brookline, Massachusetts.

Robert E. Thayer, PhD, professor of psychology, California State University, Long Beach, and author, *Calm Energy*. Oxford University Press.

Whether you live in the snowbelt or not, the short winter days that follow all the holiday excitement can be just plain depressing. For information on ways to energize us in the bleak months, we called on Robert E. Thayer, PhD, who deals with related issues in his book *Calm Energy*. Dr. Thayer is a professor of psychology at California State University, Long Beach, and has done extensive research on how people can enhance their sense of well-being—even during winter's darkest and dullest days.

KEEP ON EXERCISING

For some people, maintaining a routine exercise program becomes too much of a chore in winter, so they avoid exercising. That, says Dr. Thayer, explains much of the lethargy and bad mood that descends during that time of year. Critical to avoiding the doldrums is to have high energy and lowered tension. Exercise directly impacts both, and all it takes is five to 10 minutes per day.

You can increase your energy and keep it revved for several hours through the simplest exercise of all—a five- to 10-minute brisk walk. Dr. Thayer's research has found this benefit to be very productive. In one study, he looked at the energy impact of walking versus eating a candy bar. Those who reached for candy to fuel them had an immediate rise in energy— but by the end of an hour, they had even *less* energy than before they ate the candy and felt significantly more tension. When tested after one hour, the walkers reported a substantial rise in energy and continued to feel more energetic for the following hour as well. According to Dr. Thayer, a 10-minute walk also gives you a cheerful outlook and clearer thinking.

A RAY OF SUNSHINE

An added benefit of a daily walk is the absorption of invigorating sunshine. Leo Galland, MD, director of the Foundation for Integrated Medicine in New York City, says, "Exposure of the unblocked eye to sunlight causes the pineal gland in the brain to make less melatonin. This hormone, which may cause symptoms of depression, is produced at increased levels in the dark." Even on a cloudy day, the sun's benefits will come through.

Note: People who have glaucoma or cataracts should avoid direct sunlight.

MORE EXERCISE, MORE ENERGY?

For some, five to 10 minutes is not quite enough to get them past the winter blues. Dr. Thayer suggests that by performing about 45 minutes of harder exercise, such as aerobic training, you will immediately reduce tension. Although your energy level will take longer to improve—you're likely to feel tired for about an hour after this kind of workout—it will surge shortly after that and stay high for a number of hours more. Dr. Thayer says that this type of exercise is the best antidote to negative moods, including anxiety and frustration, or what he describes as "tense tiredness."

SUNNY FOODS

Winter is notorious, of course, for changing food choices—somehow we tend to reach for rich comfort foods, such as macaroni and cheese or heavy desserts. Choosing foods that provide proper nutrition can help keep your energy up.

Nutritionist Judith Mabel, RD, PhD, says that the predictable craving for comfort food in winter makes stews, soups and root vegetables —carrots, sweet potatoes and the like—good choices. They are nutritious yet still fill that comfort need. However, because the body naturally slows a bit in winter, it's important to make your portions just a little smaller.

MORE HELPERS

For some, the use of a light box helps to ensure adequate levels of full-spectrum light exposure.

Easier than a light box is bringing the feeling of spring into your home with fresh-cut flowers. Treat yourself to some of your favorites and you'll soon be having thoughts of spring.

Shedding Light on Depression

Michael Terman, PhD, director, clinical chronobiology program, New York State Psychiatric Institute, and professor of clinical psychology, department of psychiatry, College of Physicians & Surgeons, Columbia University, both in New York City.

For some, the winter creates a severe and rather well-known clinical depression that's called seasonal affective disorder (SAD). But what about the rest of us, who just feel "blah" in the winter? How do we recapture some of the energy of summer?

To find out, we called Michael Terman, PhD, director of the winter depression program at the New York State Psychiatric Institute and professor of psychiatry at Columbia University, both in New York City. He says that SAD—which must, by definition, include having a major depressive episode in winter—affects over 5% of the American population. Statistics vary, but about 20% of us get what researchers call "winter doldrums." Symptoms of winter doldrums include increased intake of carbohydrates…difficulty waking up and longer sleep patterns…noticeable lethargy and being prone to fatigue, including a mid-afternoon slump. For most people, the onset is around Thanksgiving, though it can start as early as September or as late as January.

TREATING THE BLUES

The reason winter's darkness can be so upsetting is actually quite simple. Studies have shown that an early morning light signal is important for keeping the internal body clock in sync with local time. In vulnerable people, the lack of this light signal causes their bodily functions to drift, making them feel depressed or out of sorts. Although researchers haven't been able to identify the exact cause of SAD or the doldrums, they speculated that it has to do with melatonin, a hormone associated with sleep.

Indeed, researchers had long hoped that they could treat winter blues with melatonin, since one of its primary functions is to balance the body's daily rhythm. But Dr. Terman reports that a large clinical trial recently revealed some disappointing news—melatonin has no effect on this problem. The solution to date remains use of light therapy. This treatment involves sitting each morning at a specially designed light box that provides a simulated blast of morning light. This adjusts the internal clock and frees the user of SAD or winter doldrums.

WHAT ABOUT LIGHT THERAPY?

Light therapy has become so popular that we are now seeing ads for therapeutic light boxes. Dr. Terman cautions that many—perhaps most—of these advertised light boxes are ineffective. Even if you find a real light box, you may use it incorrectly, thereby negating the benefits of the therapy.

FIND YOUR RHYTHM

The first step to ensuring correct use of light therapy is identifying your own internal clock. People's internal clocks can vary markedly relative to external time. The pineal gland triggers an individual's circadian clock by releasing melatonin each evening—as early as 6:30 pm for some and in others as late as 1:30 am. Dr. Terman and his colleagues have made it possible for you to ascertain your own body clock quickly through a self-assessment questionnaire, available at the Center for Environmental Therapeutics Web site at *www.cet.org/en/index.html.* Click on "AutoPIDS" under the "Self-Assessment" menu.

Next, you'll need to obtain a light box, which should cost between $200 and $350. *Dr. Terman suggests six things to look for when purchasing a box...*

- **Testing in peer-reviewed clinical trials.**

- **10,000 lux of illumination.**

- **A smooth diffusing screen.** This prevents you from seeing the distinct contour of the lightbulbs and a filter that blocks ultraviolet rays.

- **White—not colored—light.**

- **The light should project downward** toward the eyes and at an angle.

- **The box should have a broad field of light** and be large enough that you can perform routine activities while remaining in the field. Acceptable activities are sedentary ones you can do while facing the light screen.

WHAT TO EXPECT

For most people, 30 minutes a day in front of a light box relieves symptoms. However, you'll need to experiment to determine the right amount of time for you. Signs that you are getting too much light include becoming fidgety, feeling queasy though not nauseous, having eye irritation and headaches. Dr. Terman advises people to wait until mild symptoms appear to start light therapy. After that, use the box daily for the several weeks it takes for the full effect of light to kick in. At that point, he says, it may be OK to skip a day here and there, though some people find they can't miss even one day.

Dr. Terman points out that winter doldrums and SAD are strictly related to the light that goes into the eyes, not the sun that reaches your skin. Getting sunlight on your body won't do a thing to relieve seasonal blues.

Remember when taking your morning anti-SAD light bath—either indoors or out—to remove contacts or glasses to get the "full bright effect." It's the light entering the eyes that helps.

And then, remember that spring and daylight savings time is just around the corner.

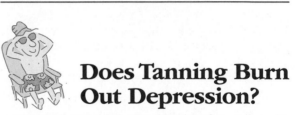

Does Tanning Burn Out Depression?

Norman E. Rosenthal, MD, clinical professor of psychiatry, Georgetown University, Washington, DC, and author of *Winter Blues.* Guilford.

For many warm-weather lovers, it's sad when the days get shorter and temperatures get colder. For those who suffer from seasonal affective disorder (SAD), a form of depression that is linked to less exposure to sunlight in winter months, the onset of winter truly is "sad." A common treatment for this problem is light therapy (phototherapy), which made us wonder if tanning beds might help. Could they?

No, according to Norman E. Rosenthal, MD, clinical professor of psychiatry at Georgetown University in Washington, DC. Tanning beds expose you to harmful ultraviolet (UV) rays, which increase the risk for skin cancer. Dr. Rosenthal points out that even if tanning beds do elevate mood (and this has yet to be properly studied and proven), the downsides far outweigh the benefits, and there are many more healthful options.

Symptoms of SAD include loss of energy, excessive sleep, carbohydrate cravings, weight gain, irritability, anxiety and trouble concentrating. These symptoms range in intensity from mild to disabling. The most challenging months are January and February, and younger people and women appear to be at the highest risk.

During his career as a National Institute of Mental Health researcher, Dr. Rosenthal pioneered the use of light in the treatment of SAD. For relief, he recommends getting more visible light into your environment—preferably natural light. Throw open the drapes, turn on the electric lights, book a trip to Florida and spend more time outdoors. In one study, researchers found that walking outside for one hour in the winter sunlight was as effective as two-and-a-half hours sitting under bright artificial light.

If these measures don't do the trick, another option is light therapy. This entails sitting in front of a specially designed light box for about 30 minutes a day during the winter (and fall, too, if it's necessary). Dr. Rosenthal reports that there have been no troublesome side effects from light therapy.

While it is tempting to believe that tanning booths could bring you the spirit of summer—it is better to catch the spirit with a walk in the sun.

info Mental Health America, *www.nmha.org.*

A Supplement to Ease Depression

Jonathan E. Alpert, MD, PhD, associate director, depression clinical and research program, Massachusetts General Hospital, Boston.

Major depression is still difficult to treat. Despite the wide array of antidepressant medications available today, finding the right medication is very much a hit-or-miss proposition. For a variety of reasons, some people never achieve total symptom relief with single-drug treatment and end up taking two or more drugs for long periods of time. Enter the dietary supplement SAMe (S-adenosyl-L-methionine, or Sammy).

Researchers at Massachusetts General Hospital in Boston recently reported that the effectiveness of antidepressive medications are often enhanced with the addition of SAMe. In an uncontrolled study of 30 people who struggled with depressive symptoms even while on antidepressants, half reported significant symptom improvement when they were given SAMe with their regular medication. Of these, 43% reported no depressive symptoms at all after six weeks of taking SAMe along with their prescribed antidepressant.

Jonathan E. Alpert, MD, PhD, lead researcher of the study, says symptom improvement was determined by looking at composite scores of three measures: The Hamilton Depression Rating Scale...the Montgomery-Asberg Depression Rating Scale...and Clinical Global Impressions. Although no qualitative symptom-by-symptom analysis was performed, Dr. Alpert's own clinical impression was that the greatest improvements were in patient motivation, interest and energy level.

The 30 patients in the trial were knowingly given 800 to 1,600 milligrams of SAMe daily, along with their current antidepressant medication. Study participants were taking either *venlafaxine* (Effexor) or one of the class of drugs known as selective serotonin reuptake inhibitors (SSRIs), including Prozac, Zoloft and Lexapro.

WHAT IS SAMe?

SAMe is not an herb or a hormone. It is a molecule that the human body manufactures from *methionine*, an amino acid that is commonly found in protein-rich foods.

How does SAMe improve mood? It is not known for sure, but researchers believe that SAMe enhances the action of various "mood-boosters" in the brain, such as *serotonin* and *dopamine*. Future research is required to learn more about the specific hows and whys of SAMe's impact.

ONGOING SAMe RESEARCH

Dr. Alpert continues working as a coinvestigator on trials that involve SAMe. One is a placebo-controlled study with 80 participants.

These subjects don't know if they are receiving SAMe or a placebo with their antidepressant. The larger number of participants and the creation of a control group allow a better examination of symptom-by-symptom results with both the antidepressant and the antidepressant-plus-SAMe groups, he explained.

The second trial examines SAMe as a single-agent treatment compared directly with an SSRI antidepressant and with a placebo. This trial elevates SAMe from adjunct status to a possible equal alternative to antidepressants.

Both SAMe studies are sponsored by the National Institutes of Health.

Can you try using SAMe today? In the study Dr. Albert conducted, the combination of SAMe with other antidepressants was well-tolerated. However, there have been previous reports of SAMe causing mania in predisposed individuals, such as those with bipolar disorders, and one report of SAMe causing a serotonin-overdrive state in an elderly patient also treated with an older tricyclic antidepressant (*clomipramine*). Also, people who take blood thinners should not take SAMe. Larger studies will shed more light on the actual risks associated with combining SAMe with conventional antidepressants. Talk to your doctor about whether or not it might be helpful for you…and take it only under his/her supervision.

SAMe has been reported effective with restoring arthritic joints and with chronic liver disease as well. However, the FDA has not extensively evaluated SAMe.

New Research on the Cause of Panic Disorder

Alexander Neumeister, MD, associate professor of psychiatry and director, molecular imaging program of the clinical neuroscience division, Yale University School of Medicine, West Haven, Connecticut.

For people suffering from panic disorder, life can be very frustrating. Their unexpected bouts of extreme anxiety create such symptoms as shortness of breath, agitation, dizziness, chills, sweating, heartburn, chest pain and a rapid heartbeat, all of which are often mistaken for heart attack and cost millions of dollars each year in visits to the emergency room. Now, it appears that there may be a chemical basis for this sometimes debilitating condition—low levels of serotonin.

Disruption of the effects of the neurotransmitter serotonin, an important brain chemical associated with mood regulation, has previously been linked with depression, obsessive-compulsive disorder and eating disorders. Now a study at the National Institute of Mental Health (NIMH) indicates that serotonin abnormalities may also contribute to panic disorder.

To learn more about the link between panic disorder and serotonin, we contacted lead author of the study, Alexander Neumeister, MD, Yale University School of Medicine in West Haven, Connecticut.

ABOUT THE STUDY

In the NIMH study, researchers used an imaging technique called positron emission tomography (PET) to visualize the brain chemistry of 16 people with panic disorder, seven of whom also suffered from depression. Patients were injected with a new tracer chemical called FCWAY, which allowed researchers to see Type 1A serotonin receptors (protein molecules on the surface of brain cells that regulate the use of serotonin).

When their brain chemistry images were compared with those of a group of 15 healthy controls, researchers discovered that people with panic disorder alone or panic disorder and depression had fewer type 1A serotonin receptors in three specific areas of the brain.

Evidence collected separately and from the study suggests no simple formula, such as "poor serotonin receptor function causes panic disorder or depression," says Dr. Neumeister. The causes are multifactorial, and although low levels of serotonin are a contributing factor, they may precipitate other disturbances in the brain, which may impact more directly on depression.

CORRECTING SEROTONIN IMBALANCES

According to Dr. Neumeister, the most effective suppressive treatment for panic disorder used by conventional physicians has been a combination of cognitive behavior therapy

(CBT) and antidepressants known as selective serotonin reuptake inhibitors (SSRIs), such as Prozac, Zoloft and others. These drugs work by modifying the brain's use of serotonin. The present recommendation is for patients to take SSRIs for approximately one year and then begin to taper off. However, this often results in an exacerbation of symptoms, says Dr. Neumeister, because while one year of drug therapy is good, it is probably not enough, so when you stop taking the drugs, the symptoms are apt to return. On the cognitive behavior side of treatment, one of the prestigious programs is actually a do-it-yourself program called "Attacking Anxiety & Depression" from the Midwest Center for Stress and Anxiety. Work closely with your medical professional to create a treatment program that is right for you.

While this study is limited in its scope and does not explain why serotonin function is lower in certain individuals, it does promise greater understanding of panic disorder for improved treatment in the future.

info Midwest Center for Stress and Anxiety, *www.stresscenter.com.*

National Institute of Mental Health (NIMH), *www.nimh.nih.gov.*

Volunteering Is Good For Your Health

Paul F. Whiteley, professor of government, University of Essex and director, Democracy and Participation Research Programme, Economic and Social Research Council (ESRC), both in England.

Natural tragedies often require volunteer aid on a scale beyond our imagination. One positive element, however, is that in the midst of terrible destruction, it is inspiring to see how the world can respond in a unified and generous way. Interestingly, even in the face of the horror, volunteers actually may be doing some good for themselves as well as others. According to a recent study by Great Britain's Economic and Social Research Council (ESRC), volunteering may benefit you as well as others.

ESRC researchers found that people who volunteer are happier and healthier. Not only that, communities with high rates of volunteerism have higher scholastic test scores and lower crime rates than their counterparts with fewer volunteers.

ABOUT THE RESEARCH

To learn more, we contacted Paul F. Whiteley, professor of government at the University of Essex, and director of the ESRC Democracy and Participation Research Programme, both in England. He told us that the study was a national probability sample survey that looked at organizational membership and informal volunteering in Britain. Professor Whiteley and his team examined a wide variety of voluntary activities, from participation in formal organizations to membership in informal groups, as well as volunteering that takes place outside groups altogether, such as helping elderly neighbors.

They found that British communities with high levels of volunteering activity experienced…

• **Improved educational performance.** Students received higher standardized test grades.

• **Lower crime.** There were fewer burglaries in communities of volunteers.

• **More satisfaction with their lives.** Communities that volunteered reported greater life satisfaction and happiness.

• **Better health overall.**

Interestingly, the study showed that the community benefits of volunteering were independent of wealth and social class. Professor Whiteley observes that even a relatively poor community that volunteers can perform better in terms of health, life satisfaction, crime and education than a relatively affluent community that does not.

HELP OTHERS TO HELP YOURSELF

According to Professor Whiteley, "The research has revealed an interesting link between helping others and enjoying a good quality of life. It seems that when we focus on the needs of others, we may also reap significant benefits ourselves."

There are many choices of how you can help others—locally, globally or wherever it happens to touch your heart. The more you give of yourself, the happier and healthier you will be. Organizations such as the Points of Light Institute and VolunteerMatch can help you find volunteer opportunities in your area.

info Economic & Social Research Council *www.esrc.ac.uk.*

Points of Light Institute (formerly the Points of Light & Hands On Network), *www.points oflight.org.*

VolunteerMatch, *www.volunteermatch.org.*

More Fun, Less Stress At Family Gatherings

Leonard Felder, PhD, psychologist in private practice in Los Angeles and expert in family conflict resolution. He is author of many books, including *When Difficult Relatives Happen to Good People.* Rodale.

Family get-togethers are often unsatisfying and difficult, rife with power struggles and nasty arguments. They can also be a lot of fun when you truly connect with people you care about. *Here's how to make holiday gatherings harmonious…*

SHORTEN THE DURATION

Shortening the party makes the most dramatic difference. The traditional seven-hour marathon—four hours of drinks and snacks, two hours of dinner, one hour of dessert and good-byes—is too much for most families.

ANTICIPATE TRIGGER POINTS

The majority of problems at family events occur at two crucial moments…

Arrival: You're greeted with insensitive comments, such as, "Did you put on weight?" or "I heard you lost your job."

After drinks, but before dinner: Hungry or intoxicated guests can sometimes provoke arguments by making hostile or challenging comments.

Don't let a comment or an argument ruin the holiday. Expect that someone will do or say something that will annoy you. Decide in advance how you will respond. *You can…*

●**Defuse the situation with humor.** If an insensitive comment is made about your weight, say, "I guess this side of the family is just feeding me too well!"

●**Ask for help.** "Not having a job is a bit stressful. I could use your support."

●**Acknowledge the comments without reacting to them.** Say, "Thanks for your input" or "I'm sorry you feel that way, but the holidays aren't an appropriate time for us to have this conversation."

●**Have an ally step in.** It can be a spouse, a friend or another relative—someone who is aware of how family events get to you. If the situation becomes intense, the ally can speak up on your behalf or go outside with you for a walk.

CREATE A DEEPER CONNECTION

A main reason why people feel so frustrated at family events is that they're often expected to do what more influential or opinionated members do.

Example: Your relatives spend Thanksgiving glued to the football games on TV—and you don't like sports.

What to do…

●**Spend time with one relative you really love and miss.** Volunteer to run an errand in the car with that person so you can talk privately. Achieving just one or two quality moments at a holiday event can balance negative ones.

●**Urge your host to set smaller tables for dinner and separate those known to argue.**

●**Ask an icebreaker question at dinner that focuses on the positive.** Let each person spend one minute answering.

Possible questions: What is your favorite family memory from past gatherings? What is your greatest hope for the coming year? Is there something that happened in the past year that you've struggled with and learned from?

6

Penny Cures

Buteyko Breathing Technique Can Improve Asthma

Breathing should be the most ordinary of physical tasks since we do it about 20,000 times each day. But for the many millions of Americans who have asthma and other breathing disorders, this ordinary act can be a challenge. Enter an effective natural breathing technique—the Buteyko Method.

Developed decades ago by a Russian doctor, Buteyko is popular among people with asthma in Australia, United Kingdom and Russia but has been virtually unknown in this country until recently. A study in the *Thorax* journal and another in *Journal of Asthma* found Buteyko can reduce reliance on bronchodilators and the need for corticosteroids in asthma patients.

BUTEYKO THEORY ON BREATHING

The basic theory underlying the Buteyko Method is that a dysfunctional breathing pattern evokes symptoms of asthma and is in fact one of the root causes of the constriction of the airways. Buteyko practitioners believe that many people with asthma actually over-breathe by taking in air too rapidly or through their mouth all the time, but only notice it when it becomes uncontrolled, during an attack. People with asthma typically breathe 12 to 14 liters of air per minute, compared with the normal intake of four to six liters. The body is designed to fully oxygenate itself via normal breathing—over-breathing (the same as hyperventilation) results in abnormally low levels of carbon dioxide (CO_2).

You may think of CO_2 as the "waste" exhaled from the lungs, but CO_2 is crucial for helping regulate many bodily functions including the blood pH, which affects release of oxygen into the tissues. In an attempt to reduce the

Carol Baglia, RRT, CBE, Correct Breathing Concepts, LLC, Cleveland, Ohio. *www.correctbreathing.com.*

89

intake of excess air from over-breathing and to preserve CO_2, the body narrows the airways and produces excess airway mucus, which, along with inflammation and swelling, is characteristic of asthma. In people with asthma, breathing stressors such as perfume, pollution or emotional upset may trigger even more rapid breathing or gasping for air, thus further decreasing CO_2.

BUTEYKO BASICS

We spoke with Carol Baglia, a registered respiratory therapist, certified in the Buteyko Breathing Method. The technique uses personal instruction and exercises to teach people with asthma a new way to breathe, thereby improving the balance between their oxygen and CO_2. Students learn to inhale and exhale through their nose only, because nasal breathing serves as a natural way to control the amount of air allowed in—Baglia calls this the "volume control." The measure of success for people learning Buteyko is a "control pause" (the amount of time you can comfortably hold your breath, starting at the end of a normal exhalation) of about one minute, says Baglia.

BUTEYKO HELPS OTHER BREATHING PROBLEMS TOO

The Buteyko Method also works well for many people who suffer from sleep apnea, chronic obstructive pulmonary disease (COPD), panic attacks and the many other conditions that can make it hard to breathe easily. People with sleep apnea over-breathe while asleep, causing CO_2 loss that soon overwhelms the body, which could be why sufferers stop breathing altogether—it's an attempt to regain balance. But having reached the opposite outer limit, the sleeper then gasps for air and another round of over-breathing and breath-holding begins. Baglia explains that in such cases the respiratory control center in the back of the brain has ceased to function properly and must be retrained. Rigorous practice of the Buteyko exercises over a period of weeks enables people to bring the control center back into proper functioning, and from then on they are able to breathe correctly in sleep as well as when awake.

Not only do the clinical trials of Buteyko show a vast reduction in asthma medication use

and symptoms, but also a significant improvement in quality of life and a sense of optimism about the future as people became less afraid of their asthma. While there are only a handful of Buteyko trainers in the US, training can be done over the phone—it does not require face-to-face interaction.

If you are interested in learning the method and don't have access to a trainer, it is possible to purchase a home-study kit on-line for under $100 that comes with personal e-mail and telephone support with a trainer who is certified in the technique (*www.buteykoworks.com*).

Try: While medical insurance won't cover this, people who have flexible spending accounts may be able to receive reimbursement for the purchase.

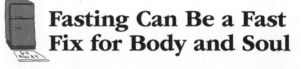

Fasting Can Be a Fast Fix for Body and Soul

Krista Varady, PhD, a research associate in the department of Nutritional Sciences and Toxicology, University of California at Berkeley.

Sonja Pettersen, NMD, a naturopathic physician and frequent Bottom Line contributor. She is based in Scottsdale, Arizona.

Elson M. Haas, MD, a specialist in family medicine, nutrition and detoxification and author of *The New Detox Diet*. Celestial Arts. Dr. Haas is founder and director of the Preventive Medical Center of Marin, an integrated health care facility in San Rafael, California.

Fasting to enhance your health is an ancient practice, supposedly recommended by Socrates, Plato and Hippocrates. Going without food for a prescribed period also has a rich spiritual tradition, while on a far less profound level assorted fasts or "detox programs" are popular in certain fashionable circles. Calorie restriction is a controversial issue. *Here's what we've learned…*

ENERGY THROUGH DETOXIFICATION

"Fasting is the single greatest healing therapy I know—with detoxification, it is the missing link in Western nutrition," says Elson Haas, MD, a specialist in family medicine, nutrition and detoxification. He is founder and director of the Preventive Medical Center of Marin, an integrated health care facility in San Rafael, California. Dr. Haas believes in the health benefits of fasting to help people feel more vital, creative and open to emotional and spiritual energies.

There are many types of diets, including the fast. Most stringent, according to Dr. Haas, is the "water fast," which is exactly what it sounds like: no food, no juice, nothing but water—and he doesn't recommend it. More than a day may in fact prove dangerous, though some spiritual disciplines continue to use it. Safer and more common is to diet by limiting yourself to the juices of fresh fruit and vegetables, as well as herbal teas, suggests Dr. Haas, noting this regimen has been popularized as calorie restriction and liquid-only diets. "Fresh juices are easily digested so the nutrients they supply are quickly absorbed," he explains. "This kind of fast stimulates the body to clear wastes. Juice fasting is safer than water fasting, since it supports the body nutritionally while cleansing."

MICE ON DETOX DIETS

Where previous animal studies have shown that calorie restriction boosts longevity, a recent series of research studies adds a bit of additional weight to the health claims by fasting advocates. Researchers at the University of California at Berkeley tested different kinds of fasts on mice, alternating between fast days and the non-fast ("feast") days, when they could eat however much they wanted. Lead researcher Krista Varady, PhD, tells us that certain fasting male mice showed reduced cell proliferation rates, including prostate cell proliferation, and reduced insulin-like growth factor IGF-1, which has been linked to various forms of cancer, including breast and prostate cancers.

There were four groups of mice, including a control group. One group was given nothing but water on alternate days...a second group got 50% of their normal caloric intake...and a third group ate 25% of their usual calories. The control group ate normally. Benefits correlated to fasting, with the most notably reduced cell proliferation rate seen in the most restricted—the water-fasters. But since all three test groups showed some reduction over four weeks, Dr. Varady concluded that "the research showed that you can consume about 25% of your food

on alternate days—about one meal a day—and still get some benefit."

FASTING MENUS

Dr. Varady's fasting mice did not eat any special food on their calorie-reduced days but humans on a "detox" program usually do—and should, Dr. Haas emphasizes. Like most other health professionals, Dr. Haas starts a detox plan by having his patients eliminate sugar, nicotine, alcohol, caffeine and chemicals (he calls it the "SNACC" program). After a week of this, he suggests following a simple diet consisting of one piece of fruit, one daily bowl (about a half-cup dry) of cooked whole grains (millet, brown rice, amaranth, quinoa or oatmeal), plus two to four heaping bowls of steamed vegetables eaten throughout the day—he calls this the "Detox Diet." "People who are fatigued or just feel they need protein can add three or four ounces of fish, poultry or beans without any reduction of benefits," he notes. This phase typically lasts a week or even two, and then people may slowly begin to add back more of their normal daily foods.

Other kinds of detox programs are variations of a juice fast, often involving a mix of vegetable juices and fruit juice smoothies, with optionally added protein powder. "Adding protein powder to your smoothies is especially important for those who don't want to lose weight, for athletes who don't want to lose muscle mass and for anyone with hypoglycemia or low blood sugar issues," Dr. Haas says.

Also: It's okay to use milk made from rice, almonds or oats as a base for your smoothie, instead of fruit juice. Dr. Haas' book, *The New Detox Diet* features a basic smoothie formula—one cup of liquid plus one cup of fresh or frozen fruit, plus whatever supplements you want or need to add, including ground flaxseed, wheat germ or fish oil. He often adds green powders with grasses and algae.

THIS JUST IN

Researchers examined the heart X-rays (called angiograms) of more than 4,000 male and female patients who participated in an eight-year study, called the Intermountain Heart Collaborative Study. They found that members of The Church of Jesus Christ of Latter-Day

Saints (Mormon faith) were significantly less likely to have coronary artery disease. Researchers have long known that Mormons are less likely to die of heart disease than the general population, but that's generally been attributed to the fact that they don't smoke. In this study, however, researchers controlled for the smoking factor and still found less coronary heart disease among Mormons. They devised a questionnaire to identify other healthy habits among the subjects and found that fasting was the strongest predictor of lower risk for heart disease. Mormons traditionally fast at least one day a month as part of their religion.

PROCEED WITH CAUTION

Fasting for the purpose of detoxifying is not without its risks—and should never be undertaken without medical supervision. This recommendation becomes all the more important as health challenges become more complex or profound. For instance, naturopathic physician Sonja Pettersen, NMD, advises that people who have been exposed to extremely toxic chemicals such as Agent Orange in the Vietnam War may encounter difficulties with stringent detoxification since toxins remain stored in fat until they are pulled out by such a program. "These should only be released under medical supervision," she warns. She also warns that fasting is not appropriate for people with insulin-dependent diabetes, since it is so critical to keep blood sugar even.

While maintaining that commercial detox products are profit-driven and of limited general value, our medical expert, Andrew L. Rubman, ND, agrees that "there are benefits of incorporating some principles of a restricted diet into your daily life." His opinion is that strict and structured regimens are usually unnecessary, since maintaining a healthy system is really as simple as merely cutting back on a regular basis. "Reducing your caloric intake every other day—or even for a week or so—may allow your body to unburden itself a bit," he says, adding that water-only and juice-only regimens should not be instituted unless medically necessary and supervised.

Because fasting, whether in the form of calorie restriction or for detoxifying, represents such a dramatic change from the way most of us eat, it can be a challenge.

Best advice: If you want to give it a go, try it for a day or so and work up to a longer period. "Detoxification can be intense, and it may temporarily increase symptoms of sickness for some people," notes Dr. Haas, "but it can also be immediately helpful and uplifting."

What to Eat So You Can Fall Asleep Fast

Chin Moi Chow, PhD, researcher, Delta Sleep Research Unit, and senior lecturer, discipline of exercise and sport science, The University of Sydney in Australia. Her coresearchers included Ahmad Afaghi and Helen O'Connor, PhD.

Don't you sometimes feel as if researchers spend a lot of time (and money) figuring out what everyone in the world already knows? For instance, eating carbohydrates at bedtime may make you sleepy. Isn't that why some moms treat their children to a snack of toast at bedtime? *It turns out that the relationship between carbs and sleep is a little more complicated—and interesting…*

SOME BACKGROUND

Researchers at The University of Sydney in Australia wanted to see if the glycemic index of a meal eaten before bed would have any effect on sleep. The glycemic index is a measure of how much your blood sugar goes up (and how quickly) after eating a particular food. Previous research has suggested that high-carb foods raise tryptophan, which then converts to serotonin and makes you sleepy.

Chin Moi Chow, PhD, and her colleagues hypothesized that a high glycemic index meal was going to be effective in inducing sleep. They believed it would directly impact the increase of tryptophan. To test this notion, she and her colleagues gave 12 healthy men three meals on three separate occasions. One meal was a high glycemic meal one hour before bed…one was a high glycemic meal four hours before bed…and the third was a low glycemic meal four hours before bedtime.

THE RESULTS

The researchers found that the men who ate the high glycemic meal four hours before bedtime fell asleep the fastest, in only nine minutes on average. The low-glycemic diners who ate at the same time took almost twice as long to fall asleep, while the men who had the high glycemic meal one hour before bed fell asleep a little sooner than the low carb diners (about 15 minutes). Though the research leaves some questions unanswered, and therefore should not be considered "conclusive," Dr. Chow sums up the findings, suggesting that "a high GI carb meal may help people with insomnia, both occasional and chronic."

THE CATCH

What is the wisdom in recommending high-carb meals at night, which increase insulin and may increase the amount of calories converted to fat? Dr. Chow cautions that it may not be appropriate for people who are obese or who have diabetes to use a high GI meal or snack to promote sleep, since these individuals are often advised to adopt a low glycemic eating plan." In addition, Dr. Chow qualifies that the men in the study were good sleepers, and the effect might be different with chronic insomniacs—another hypothesis she plans to pursue.

SOME ADVICE

"Getting a good night's sleep is about having good sleep habits," explains Dr. Chow. "That means regular bedtime and wake-up time and avoiding caffeine and alcohol before bedtime. If you struggle to fall asleep even after paying attention to those things, you can discuss with your doctor if a high GI evening meal might help you." For the record, the high GI meal Dr. Chow and her colleagues gave to subjects was a 767-Calorie (big "C" refers to kilocalories), very low-fat dinner of jasmine rice with just a little protein from vegetables.

Simple Strategies That Ease Neck Pain

Thomas H. Reece, DO, ND, one of only a few practitioners with dual degrees in Naturopathic and Osteopathic Medicine. Former medical director of the Southwest Naturopathic Medical Center in Scottsdale, Arizona, Dr. Reece now practices at Preventive Medical Center of Marin in California. He is a specialist in Osteopathic Manipulative Medicine. *www.elsonhaas.com/medcenter.html.*

Gerard Varlotta, DO, clinical associate professor in rehabilitation medicine at New York University, New York City.

Jeffrey Zimmerman, OMD, a Doctor of Oriental Medicine, acupuncturist and Qigong master based in Westport, Connecticut. *www.optimotion.net.*

Seven out of 10 Americans experience neck pain at some point in their lives, most especially as the years tick by—which may explain how the expression "pain in the neck" has worked its way into our vocabulary. Stretching and strengthening exercises have long been considered a must to keep the neck strong and healthy. A recent study in Denmark demonstrated this when researchers found that women with neck pain who practiced specific strength training (SST) exercises for the neck and shoulder muscles experienced substantial pain relief.

To get more details on possible cures for neck pain, we asked Gerard Varlotta, DO, clinical associate professor in rehabilitation medicine at New York University. Neck pain was common way before our modern passion for all things electronic—including telephones, BlackBerry devices and computers—but nowadays scrunching our necks to chat, hunching ourselves over a keyboard and spending long hours behind the wheel of a car are the major contributors, according to Dr. Varlotta.

Neck pain is usually triggered by repetitive use or habitually holding tension in the neck and shoulders, primarily from poor posture. Whatever its cause, there are assorted treatment options to consider.

SELF-CARE FOR NECK PAIN: EXERCISE AND MORE

There are many non-invasive options to pursue before considering more drastic treatment options for neck pain. *Many can even be done on your own…*

•**Stretching exercises.** Among Dr. Varlotta's favorite exercises are shoulder shrugs. With arms at your sides, breathe in slowly as you *shrug shoulders* up toward the ears, breathe out as you lower them to a relaxed position. This gentle, repetitive motion works the trapezius muscle in the back of the neck, relaxing this very common site of tension. Dr. Varlotta also recommends *head tilts* to relieve muscle spasms in the neck and increase range of motion. Just wrap your right arm around the left side of your head so your right hand is under your left ear. Gently stretch your head toward your right shoulder and count to 10. Repeat on the other side. Try to perform these exercises four to six times each during hourly work breaks.

•**Try the specific strength training exercises that worked so well for women in the Danish study.** These consist of five dumbbell exercises—the arm row, shoulder abduction, shoulder elevation, reverse flies and upright row—targeted toward strengthening the neck and shoulder muscles. Note, however, that in the study these exercises were performed under the close supervision of trainers. If you're interested in trying strengthening exercises, your best bet is to start by asking a trainer in your local gym or YMCA how to correctly perform them.

•**Take breaks hourly.** Long hours at the desk or computer can leave you achy and stiff. You may be reluctant to "waste" the time, but take several minutes once an hour to practice shrugs and head tilts, stretch the muscles and break up the tension. Also, change position frequently. These measures will pay off handsomely by preventing pain and disability over the long run.

•**Stand (and sit) up straight at all times.** Proper posture and alignment of the entire body is a must for ease and comfort in both the neck and back. Perhaps the best advice on how to attain this comes from Jeffrey Zimmerman, OMD, founder of Optimotion (*www.optimotion.net*) and a Qigong master...

Try: While sitting, create alignment from the base of your spine to the top of your head, with shoulders slightly back and the lower back slightly curved out. For standing, adjust this slightly, now picturing a straight line through your body, into the ground beneath your feet. Place your feet shoulder distance apart, bend knees slightly and find the place where you're neither leaning forward nor backward, but perfectly balanced, with head directly over your feet. If you are doing it correctly, you'll feel free of tension.

•**Examine your workspace.** Little tweaks can be significant in reducing neck strain and pain, says Dr. Varlotta. For example, make sure the computer monitor is at eye level...sit up straight with your feet resting comfortably flat on floor...use a desk with armrests that create an angle slightly greater than 90° for your arms.

•**Get a headset for your phone.** Crooking the phone between your ear and shoulder in order to talk hands-free is one of the worst things you can do to your neck.

•**Indulge in a self-massage.** You can give yourself a pretty good self-massage by putting two tennis balls in a long tube sock. Lie on your back on the floor, rolling these under your shoulder blades and upper back to massage the shoulder blades and break up muscle spasms in the upper back, which connects to the neck muscles, suggests Dr. Varlotta.

•**Relieve neck pain with heat and cold.** When your neck is sore, try a hot pack to soothe the pain—or for chronic or post-traumatic symptoms, alternating hot and cold packs can provide temporary relief. These are widely available in drugstores, or you can make your own. Simply wet a clean washcloth with moderately hot or cold water and wring it out. Wrap compresses around your neck to ease pain, loosen tight muscles, and increase blood and oxygen flow.

Note: Remember, moderation in all things. Make sure you don't go overboard either way on the temperature. Your ND or DO can evaluate your situation and prescribe a regimen specific for your needs.

LOOK INTO NATURAL MODALITIES

In addition, Thomas H. Reece, DO, ND, one of only a few practitioners with dual degrees in Naturopathic and Osteopathic Medicine, now a specialist in osteopathic manipulative medicine at the Preventive Medical Center of Marin, in California, offers insight into what are commonly termed "alternative" modalities. In his view, the treatment of neck pain depends on correctly identifying and addressing its cause, since there are different solutions for muscle pain versus pain from pinched nerves, disk injuries, worn disks or prior trauma.

Dr. Reece's treatment plan, depending on the underlying cause, might include a variety of hands-on osteopathic manipulation techniques to realign the spine, relieve pain, improve range of motion and restore normal structure and function. Osteopathic manipulation addresses the fact that an underlying muscle weakness may be the real cause of the problem, using manipulative techniques to strengthen the muscles so they will correctly hold the bone in place over the long term.

Trained as an acupuncturist in China, Dr. Reece finds that acupuncture can be helpful for neck pain. He also describes himself as a "quarterback" for his patients, referring them to other experts as needed—for example, licensed physical therapists, massage therapists, yoga instructors or teachers of the Alexander Technique or Feldenkrais Method (different systems to improve body awareness and movement). In cooperation with your primary health care provider, these experts can help you learn to tone and strengthen the muscles of the neck and back that support the body.

Important: If neck pain remains persistent, severe or if it gets worse, more extreme measures may be necessary. These can include anti-inflammatory drugs, injections of cortisone or lidocaine, or rarely surgery. See your health care provider for proper diagnosis and treatment.

 # Ten-Minute Stress Cure

Herbert Benson, MD. Dr. Benson is Director Emeritus of the Benson-Henry Institute for Mind/Body Medicine at Massachusetts General Hospital and Associate Professor of Medicine at Harvard Medical School. He is a pioneer in mind-body medicine whose books—including *The Relaxation Response* (Harper) and *The Harvard Medical School Guide to Lowering Your Blood Pressure* (McGraw-Hill)—have sold more than four million copies and have been translated into many languages.

Medical researchers are connecting more dots in their understanding of the insidious ways stress harms our health. No question it's important to learn all we can about this important topic, but do you ever wonder if we aren't chasing our own tails trying to find new solutions when simple ones are already known to be effective?

Consider the Relaxation Response, which has been around since the 1960s—and in fact has roots in virtually every religious tradition. Developed in 1968 by Harvard professor Herbert Benson, MD, this straightforward approach to stress relief has, 40 years later, amassed an impressive resume of research demonstrating its efficacy at improving a wide range of problems, from insomnia to high blood pressure to poor academic performance.

Widely recognized as one of the foremost researchers in the field of stress management, Dr. Benson is director emeritus of the Benson-Henry Institute for Mind Body Medicine at Massachusetts General Hospital. He confirms that "scores of diseases and conditions are either caused by or made worse by stress."

He adds that 60% to 90% of all doctor visits are for complaints related to or impacted by it, including anxiety, mild or moderate depression, anger, hostility, menopausal hot flashes, infertility, PMS, high blood pressure and heart attacks. To some extent, he says, "every one of those can be caused by stress or exacerbated by it."

TURNING THE HORMONES "OFF"

We now know that stress is more than just a mild feeling of being under the gun, but rather a complicated series of biochemical and hormonal processes in the body. Also known as the "fight or flight" response, the stress response activates stress hormones, including cortisol and adrenaline.

While cortisol has an important role in our health and is required for survival, research has demonstrated its ill effects, including (in the lab) that high levels cause shrinkage in a part of the brain called the hippocampus, central to memory and thinking. High levels of cortisol also contribute to accumulation of abdominal fat.

"The fact that for most of us these stress hormones are constantly in the 'on' position to varying degrees has significant health consequences," warns Dr. Benson.

The Relaxation Response is the exact opposite of the stress response. It mitigates the stress reaction by slowing metabolism, lowering heart rate and decreasing blood pressure. During the relaxation response, levels of nitric oxide, an important biochemical involved in circulation and the improvement of blood flow, are elevated. This calming biochemical response enables the muscles to relax and breathing to slow down to a more normal rate.

HOW DOES IT WORK?

The Relaxation Response is based on repetition of a simple word or phrase, just like prayer and other forms of meditation, Dr. Benson explains. "Prayer generally consists of repetitive words sometimes in a chant-like rhythm," he notes, and in fact his early research on the Relaxation Response used repetitive phrases like "Hail Mary, full of grace" for Roman Catholic research subjects, and "shalom" or "echat" for Jewish ones. Today research on the Relaxation Response typically uses the word "one" or "peace" to elicit the effect, which Dr. Benson finds useful for the widest variety of people.

Research on the short and long-term health benefits of the Relaxation Response is convincing. Published research going back to 1973 has demonstrated that use of the technique can lower blood pressure, anxiety, the symptoms and pain of headache and irritable bowel syndrome, the discomfort of PMS, as well as bring down stress hormone levels, improve insomnia and modify a number of risk factors for myocardial infarction (heart attacks).

More recently, educational research has demonstrated that incorporating use of the Relaxation Response into the school curriculum at the middle school, high school and college levels led to higher grade point averages, increased self-esteem, decreased psychological distress, better attendance and less aggression.

DO-IT-YOURSELF RELAXATION

The Relaxation Response has often been compared to Transcendental Meditation (TM), the technique taught by Maharishi Mahesh Yogi and popularized in this country by the Beatles in the mid-1960s.

However, it can cost thousands of dollars to learn TM from an authorized program, whereas the Relaxation Response can be mastered on your own, for free.

HOW TO ELICIT THE RELAXATION RESPONSE*

Set aside 10 to 20 minutes to try this technique once or twice daily, perhaps before breakfast and before dinner…

1. Sit quietly in a comfortable position.

2. Close your eyes.

3. Deeply relax all your muscles beginning at your feet and progressing up to your face. Keep them relaxed.

4. Breathe comfortably. Become aware of your breathing. As you breathe out, say the word, "ONE," silently to yourself. For example, breathe IN…OUT ("ONE"), IN…OUT ("ONE"), etc. Breathe easily and naturally.

5. Other thoughts will come to mind. This is normal and should be expected. When other thoughts occur, simply say "Oh, well" and return to repetition.

You may open your eyes to check the time, but don't use an alarm. When you finish, sit quietly for several minutes—first keeping your eyes closed, then slowly opening them. Wait a few minutes before standing.

Don't worry about whether you are "successful" in achieving a deep level of relaxation. Maintain a positive and passive attitude, permitting relaxation to occur at its own pace.

When distracting thoughts occur—and they will—don't be critical of yourself. Try instead to ignore them by not dwelling upon them, and just return to your breathing and repeating of the word "ONE."

Note: With practice, says Dr. Benson, this response will come with very little effort. He suggests practicing the technique once or twice a day, but also suggests not doing it within a couple of hours of eating, as the digestive process seems to interfere with eliciting the Relaxation Response.

*From "*The Relaxation Response*," used with permission from the author.

How to Heal, Energize, Relieve Stress

Ellen DiNucci, MA, Reiki practitioner and wellness and productivity consultant, Palo Alto, California. For more information on Reiki and energy healing in general, contact Ellen DiNucci at *ellen@ellendinucci.com* or visit her Web site at *www.ellendinucci.com*.

More and more alternative therapies are slowly making their way into mainstream medicine and conventional health care facilities. Reiki, an energy healing (EH) treatment that originated in Japan, is one of the EH treatments used in more than 50 US hospitals and clinics today. The word Reiki is composed of two Japanese words, Rei (universal spirit) and ki (life energy).

Ellen DiNucci, MA, a wellness and productivity consultant and Reiki practitioner in Palo Alto, California, regularly teaches "Energy Healing for Chronic Conditions and Stress" to the staff, faculty and community members at the Stanford Health Improvement Program. *Her thoughts on Reiki therapy…*

REIKI: A PRIMER

Reiki is similar to other EH techniques, such as Healing Touch and Therapeutic Touch. It is extremely versatile and practitioners claim that it may be used as an adjunct to standard medical care. The theory inherent in all touch therapies including Reiki, is that the practitioner affects a person's energy flow or energy field which in turn can improve both physical and emotional issues. As a stress-relaxation therapy, experts claim that it can promote a sense of well being on physical, emotional and spiritual levels. In addition, Reiki practitioners have had success with helping individuals decrease their perception of stress and related symptoms. In her own practice, DiNucci has worked with clients for stress, relationship and emotional issues, arthritis, sports injuries, pain, recuperation from illness, job burnout and spiritual matters.

There are few randomized, controlled studies on Reiki, acknowledges DiNucci. Articles reviewing the scientific research literature generally recommend larger, more rigorous and better-designed studies. Current Reiki studies—many funded by the National Institutes of Health's National Center for Complementary and Alternative Medicine—are focusing on Reiki's possible effects in managing the symptoms associated with prostate cancer, stress, fibromyalgia, advanced AIDS and neuropathy and cardiac function. Other EH studies examine its potential impact on pain and joint disorders.

HOW DOES REIKI WORK?

It is claimed that a Reiki practitioner acts as a conduit of universal life energy, directing it to others or to himself/herself, explains DiNucci. Universal life energy is referred to by different names in different cultures, but it is commonly known as *chi* and *ki*. This energy is believed to permeate the universe and surround and exist in all living things.

Reiki can be done for any length of time, with the practitioner's hands being either on or near a person to help focus and direct this energy throughout the body. A typical healing session runs about an hour. The client is fully clothed and usually lays on a massage table. Reiki can also be modified to be performed while the patient is seated, lying in bed or standing. It can even be practiced on unconscious recipients by a trained professional in a hospital.

Most practitioners use a common set of hand placements to transmit universal life energy. For example, hands may be placed palms down, with fingers extended, on a client's shoulder bones to stimulate the flow of universal life energy in his/her body. Each position is held two to five minutes.

Best: While Reiki and similar EH treatments and their safety have not been extensively studied, there appears to be little downside risk assuming you have a properly trained practitioner. *However, DiNucci notes that prior to receiving a Reiki treatment the practitioner should…*

• **Check first with the health care provider** for patients with serious psychiatric conditions.

• **Make sure individuals with any bone fractures** have already had their bones set by a physician.

Note: Reiki should be used only in conjunction with other health treatments—not as a replacement.

HOW TO FIND A REIKI PRACTITIONER

Reiki, unlike Healing Touch, does not have one organization that offers a standardized certification program. *DiNucci recommends seeking a Reiki practitioner through...*

- **A local clinic or hospital.** If they don't offer Reiki, they might maintain a list of local practitioners.
- **One's primary care physician.**
- **Word of mouth** from a trusted friend, colleague or relative.
- **Reiki associations** such as those listed below.

GET RELAXED, GET ENERGIZED

DiNucci's clients tell her that they feel simultaneously relaxed and energized after Reiki sessions, as though they've let go of emotional and mental baggage and physical symptoms of stress. By lightening their emotional or mental loads, recipients are free to let positive universal life energy flow through their bodies.

info The International Association of Reiki Professionals, *www.iarp.org.*

The International Center for Reiki Training, *www.reiki.org.*

The National Center for Complementary and Alternative Medicine, National Institutes of Health, *http://nccam.nih.gov/health/reiki/.*

Qigong Is a Gentle Yet Powerful Exercise

Jeffrey Zimmerman, OMD, once a classical musician and now a Doctor of Oriental Medicine, acupuncturist and Qigong master in Westport, Connecticut. *www.optimotion.net.*

For many years people went to the gym with visions of six-pack abs and toned thighs dancing in their heads. Plenty still chase those goals, but today many gym patrons are as apt to be chanting as panting. The widespread acceptance of yoga started people down the broader path of mind-body exercise, and now it's a busy path indeed. One previously obscure practice becoming quite popular is Qigong (pronounced chee-gung or chee kong). Perhaps the best living proof of Qigong's acceptance in the Western world is the fact that it cropped up on *The Oprah Winfrey Show* not long ago. However, like with the yoga and Pilates crazes, as popularity of Qigong has grown, so too have the variations, leading to potential confusion.

GENTLE BUT STRONG

Jeffrey Zimmerman, OMD, teaches Qigong as well as Tai Chi and Optimotion, a mind-body discipline he developed. Dr. Zimmerman explains that there are actually three types of Qigong—"health Qigong" describes the exercise discipline..."medical Qigong," which is a special type of massage that works on energy blockages...and a martial arts form of it. *While it won't build six-pack abs, health Qigong is said to do the following...*

- **Help cleanse the body of toxins.**
- **Restore energy.**
- **Reduce stress and anxiety.**
- **Promote healing.**
- **Integrate mind and body.**
- **Increase sense of balance.**

Some people scoff at the idea that the gentle movements of Qigong contribute to health, but the National Center for Complementary and Alternative Medicine of the National Institutes of Health has been impressed enough to sponsor several studies investigating Qigong's impact on the health of patients with heart disease, osteoarthritis and obesity. Other researchers have demonstrated that Qigong positively impacts balance (which can help prevent falling) and blood pressure.

HOW QIGONG WORKS

The "qi" in Qigong refers to the energy of the body, better known as chi. "Gong" means assiduous practice, and together they represent a way to harness your chi to help your body become soft, pliable and strong. As such, Dr. Zimmerman says Qigong is the underpinning of many other practices—he likens it to learning the notes and structure of music that enable you to play an instrument.

The practice of Qigong includes literally thousands of different forms and movements, including knee bends, hip twists and flowing arm motions that can be done while sitting, lying down, standing up or moving. To the untrained eye it looks similar to Tai Chi, a close relation. Breath is crucial to all postures and movements—the specialized breathing techniques merged with slow movement are what transport the chi into various organs and body parts. Dr. Zimmerman explains that along with increasing fluidity, Qigong creates a deep awareness of the body and its movements. You begin to focus on how you are distributing your weight, how you are balancing and your basic posture, which allows you to feel free and move easier.

THE CORE PRACTICE

Unique to Qigong is that it builds power through lack of tension, says Dr. Zimmerman—he says you can either have tension or you can have energy, but the two cannot co-exist. This is why he is greatly troubled by current hybrids like "power" Qigong, "fusion" Qigong and other versions that attempt to link modern Western physical fitness with this ancient Eastern practice. "These completely miss the point of Qigong," says Dr. Zimmerman in exasperation. "Qigong teaches fluidity, a concept that is totally opposite of the Western view of exercise. We Americans tend to go to the weak point and focus on ways to strengthen it. Qigong, on the other hand, educates and works with the entire body." Therefore, Dr. Zimmerman adds, learning Qigong can be a particular challenge for intellectually driven Westerners who "have to stop the brain from trying to take over in order to learn it," he explains.

TO FIND THE "REAL DEAL"

To find a class that is what Dr. Zimmerman calls "the real deal," he advises asking around to locate people who are knowledgeable about Qigong. Explore what kind of education the instructor has. Ask if he/she has a background in Chinese or Oriental medicine, how long they've been studying Qigong and who they've been studying with. He acknowledges it can be difficult to find a teacher qualified in the traditional form of Qigong, although more masters have emigrated from China in recent years.

Helpful: Take the time to observe a few classes with a particular instructor before making a commitment to it, though. Qigong should never be painful or tense, so if you see signs of those, keep looking. The teacher should move smoothly and gracefully, and be quick to help students get past their tension. Good teachers adapt Qigong's patterns to the needs of their students.

Taking a twice weekly class will put you on your way to learning this demanding art, says Dr. Zimmerman. And while it takes many years to master, even a shorter practice of Qigong will be beneficial for both a newfound physical freedom and to enhance your practice of Tai Chi, yoga and even other sports.

More from Jeffrey Zimmerman...

Healing Benefits of Medical Qigong

Medical Qigong is a traditional Chinese medical practice used to treat chronic illnesses, as well as physical and even emotional dysfunction. Just some of the reasons people seek out medical Qigong include the need for stress reduction, improved circulation, decreased chronic pain, better emotional balance and feelings of well-being, and a stronger sense of self-empowerment.

Jeffrey Zimmerman, OMD, Doctor of Oriental Medicine and a Qigong master, also practices medical Qigong. He has performed it on patients during open heart surgery to reduce their stress and afterward to improve surgical outcomes at the request of prominent cardiologist Mehmet Oz, MD, professor of surgery at New York-Presbyterian-Columbia University Medical Center in New York City. According to Dr. Zimmerman, it is so unobtrusive it can be practiced even in a busy OR. The practitioner doesn't even have to touch the patient, though he/she certainly can. The goal is redistribution and realignment of internal energy, the life force known as *qi* or *chi.*

Note: Chinese massage does involve being touched, and it is sometimes mistakenly referred to as medical Qigong.

THE MEDICAL QIGONG EXPERIENCE

In a routine session, which generally takes about 30 minutes to an hour, the client sits or lies down, fully clothed. The practitioner first takes the client's pulses in the Chinese fashion, using three fingers on each wrist, since each side of the body provides different messages about the energy of the individual.

When "listening" to the pulses, the Qigong practitioner is searching for signs and symptoms that could be associated with any number of organs and energy systems, to make a diagnosis of which ones are depleted and where balancing is necessary. Unlike Western medicine, which focuses on the "sick" organ or area of the body, Qigong is based on the interrelatedness of the entire system.

Example: Dr. Zimmerman often treats people with asthma. Instead of focusing on the lungs, he investigates the energy of the spleen too. If the spleen isn't doing its job well, phlegm becomes thick and gets into the lungs. Consequently, Dr. Zimmerman works with the energies of both organs to bring them back into proper balance. Indigestion is another problem that often brings people to see Dr. Zimmerman. For that he looks for excessive energy in the liver, which can cause stomach energy—normally downward-moving—to rise, resulting in heartburn. In surgery patients, since the experience is stressful to the entire body, Dr. Zimmerman works to support chi in the patient's kidneys (he calls them "the batteries of the body")...the liver, to keep blood flowing...and the lungs, to help with breathing. In fact, performing Qigong in the OR means he must go from system to system, switching gears as necessary in response to the patient's fluctuating needs.

THE ART IN QIGONG

Once the practitioner has a picture of where the client is energetically, he/she adjusts the chi by moving his/her hands a few inches or more above the client's body. Dr. Zimmerman explains that practitioners learn to feel the chi flow in and through their hands and eventually their whole body. "You coax it and listen to it," he says. "It becomes clear whether you need to soften the energy, make it fuller or maybe firmer. Eventually the practice becomes an artistic interpretation and experience." Medicine is both a science and an art. The effects of medical Qigong are sometimes subtle and may be difficult for the patient to feel, but they're real.

Surprising: Although most people who seek medical Qigong do so to address their physical health, some choose to see Dr. Zimmerman because they are unhappy with the direction of their life. By helping realign their energy circuits, Qigong creates greater connection between the body and brain, and this corrected energy flow helps people get in touch with their true selves. Some people go on to make changes, but others, says Dr. Zimmerman, simply learn to appreciate the life they have. "I am not in charge of that," he adds. "I listen to and help bring the body to its natural state, but the person's body and brain do the work."

FINDING A QIGONG PRACTITIONER

To find a qualified practitioner, ask at places where tai chi is taught or that feature the healing side of martial arts. Once you have located a potential practitioner, meet to see if you feel a positive connection. Be aware that some practitioners receive their medical Qigong training from a weekend course. Try to find someone who has more extensive training and experience. Costs vary from $50 an hour to hundreds, depending on the area of the country and the nature of the clientele. It may take two or three sessions to address a specific concern, though some people experience an immediate effect.

Note: If, after two to three sessions you feel like nothing happened, discuss it with your Qigong practitioner. He/she may not be the person you need or medical Qigong may not be the right healing modality for you. However, Dr. Zimmerman also has executive clients who come almost weekly because they find that Qigong helps them function at a higher level in business, as well as in their lives. Skeptics have often turned out to be his most committed clients.

Craniosacral Therapy Helps Chronic Pain

Thomas A. Kruzel, ND, who practices CST at the Rockwood Natural Medicine Clinic in Scottsdale, Arizona. He is the former vice president of clinical affairs and chief medical officer at the Southwest College of Naturopathic Medicine in Phoenix.

Can a gentle scalp massage really cure illnesses and injuries as diverse as carpal tunnel syndrome and Bell's palsy? How about healing long-ago trauma and emotional distress?

As a matter of fact, it can—if you put yourself in the hands of a trained and skilled craniosacral therapist. Of the many alternative therapies, craniosacral therapy (CST) is surely one of the most unusual.

WHAT IS CST?

CST is a variation of osteopathic and chiropractic medicine, where a therapist gently places his/her hands atop your skull and feels for the oscillation frequency—the small degree of movement that the skull bones naturally retain throughout life. This is a subtle motion of the membrane encasing the cerebrospinal fluid in the brain and spinal cord down to the sacrum, the bone at the bottom of the spine. The therapist gently manipulates the bones to bring them back into proper alignment.

It feels like a very gentle massage, but CST is a potent healing therapy for a wide variety of disorders, including chronic pain, headaches, carpal tunnel syndrome, fibromyalgia, learning disabilities, depression, post traumatic stress disorder, vertigo, whiplash injury, TMJ, herniated disc pain and musculoskeletal problems. While surprising and somewhat inexplicable, even many skeptics acknowledge that "sometimes it just works."

HOW CST WORKS

CST is based on research from the early part of the last century by osteopathic doctor William Garner Sutherland, DO. His work centered on the theory that the skull bones have a rhythm that he called the "breath of life" and others call "the vital force."

The theory now associated with CST, besides one of treating illness, is that physical or emotional trauma, even from birth, can cause a disturbance in this oscillation that can last for years. Cerebrospinal fluid affects nerves that control all tissues in the body, so any disruption can contribute to a wide range of problems. It's believed that restoring its natural flow enables the body to begin healing itself.

Here in the US, thousands of osteopathic doctors, naturopathic doctors, chiropractors and massage therapists are also CST practitioners. But you probably won't be surprised to learn that the medical world considers CST just this side of loony. Skeptics say its very basis is impossible because the skull bones fuse completely in childhood. CST practitioners respond that this is not so—the skull bones have motion throughout life. They say that even the elderly continue to respond well to CST.

AN EXPERT'S EXPLANATION

Thomas A. Kruzel, ND, practices CST at the Rockwood Natural Medicine Clinic in Scottsdale, Arizona. He is the former vice president of clinical affairs and chief medical officer at the Southwest College of Naturopathic Medicine in Phoenix. Dr. Kruzel likens the concept of opening up cerebrospinal fluid flow to the underlying principles of chiropractic in which "communication channels" are realigned throughout the body. CST does not itself heal problems—it releases inertia and congestion, thereby returning homeostasis and enhancing the body's ability to heal and regulate itself.

According to Dr. Kruzel, the hardest part of his CST training was learning to discern the motion in the skull, which he describes as something like an undulation. When a patient comes to see him, he places his hands on his/her head to get an exact sense of this person's motion. This gives him information he uses in clearing restrictions in the pumping of the fluid through the brain, into the spinal column and the emanating nerve roots. Sometimes he may also gently manipulate the lower part of the spine in an osteopathic fashion to restore tandem movement in the sacrum and the spine.

Benefits: Dr. Kruzel often uses CST to treat Bell's palsy. He says he can correct it very quickly if the patient comes in right after onset. He has used it for hypertension—he says it brings some patients' pressure back to normal. Some parents of newborns bring their baby for a treatment after the emotional and physical rigors of birth. Another frequent reason people come to him is after an athletic or other injury.

Example: One patient had been severely injured in a car accident the previous year. She had many broken bones and went through a year of physical rehab, but even after her physical injuries had healed she struggled with depression. When she came to Dr. Kruzel, he found that she had almost no cranial motion because the flow of the fluid had been truncated when her pelvis broke. He treated her regularly for a time and today she is doing very well physically and mentally.

WHAT WILL YOU FEEL?

Patients don't always feel the change as it is occurring, he says, but they often experience a kind of gastrointestinal release such as a gurgling in the bowels when the fluid is freed up. Constipated patients frequently find that their bowels begin moving again after a treatment. Dr. Kruzel says in older people CST helps reduce risk of stroke and of falling, and that for children it helps with ADD as well as learning disabilities and even possibly autism. Virtually all patients, adults and children alike, find the treatment to be extremely relaxing, he says.

Patients remain fully clothed for CST treatment. Sessions usually last 30 minutes to one hour. Patients may come only one or two times, or several times a week for a number of months. Elderly patients tend to check in for a session once every few months, says Dr. Kruzel. Costs vary by area of the country and many insurance plans cover the cost when treatment is from an osteopathic or naturopathic doctor.

FINDING A THERAPIST

The technique may seem simplistic, even magical—but craniosacral therapy is actually a precise skill a good therapist has trained long and hard to learn. You can find a CST practitioner near you by going to the site of osteopathic doctor John Upledger, DO, OMM, *www. upledger.com.* Dr. Upledger was instrumental in heightening awareness of CST in this country during the 1980s and today his institute trains many people in it. Another resource is the Craniosacral Therapy Association of North America, which provides CST standards.

Best: Since quality may vary widely in the absence of national standards, it's helpful to get a recommendation from someone you trust who has personal experience with a particular therapist.

The Magic of Your Touch

Tiffany Field, PhD, director of the Touch Research Institute at the University of Miami School of Medicine in Florida. She is author of *Touch*. MIT Press.

For centuries, mothers have instinctively known it works—pick up young children and they'll stop crying…gently rub babies' backs and it's off to dreamland they go. Now scientists are also coming to recognize the power of touch—and not just touch therapies such as reflexology, but simple acts such as giving a backrub, holding hands, sharing a hug or putting your arm around someone. With research demonstrating the healing power of touch, more hospitals are incorporating massage programs into care protocols for cancer and cardiovascular patients, among others.

Tiffany Field, PhD, director of the Touch Research Institute at the University of Miami School of Medicine, has studied the benefits of touch for many years. Her book, *Touch*, reviews medical and sociological research on the importance of touch to good health and also argues that the Western world, including the medical profession, has marginalized and minimized its importance. According to Dr. Field, many forms of touch can help reduce pain, anxiety, depression and aggressive behavior…promote immune function and healing…lower heart rate and blood pressure…and improve air flow in asthmatics. All this, and no drug side effects!

THE VITAL IMPORTANCE OF TOUCH

Previous research has suggested that touch deprivation leads to aggression and violent behavior in animals. Dr. Field's concern is that living in our largely touch-deprived Western society can have negative consequences. That concern led researchers at the Touch Research Institute to examine how touch is treated differently in two cities with very different cultures—Miami and Paris.

In one study, published in *Early Child Development and Care*, Dr. Field and her colleagues measured how much affectionate touch preschoolers received from their parents on playgrounds and also the children's level of aggressive behavior. In Paris, they found there was more touch toward peers and parents by children and less aggression. In a separate study, researchers also observed that French adolescents—raised with more affectionate touch—were more affectionate and less physically and verbally aggressive with one another than American adolescents. This association does not imply or prove causation, but does make a case for closer examination with further research.

REACH OUT AND TOUCH

Dr. Field observes that the benefits of touch seem to stem largely from its ability to reduce levels of cortisol, a stress hormone manufactured by the adrenal glands. This was measured in two dozen studies. She says that touching with moderate-pressure (a firm handshake) stimulates activity in the vagus nerve, one of the 12 cranial nerves in the brain, which in turn slows the heart and decreases the production of stress hormones including cortisol.

Other studies published from the Touch Research Institute, in peer-reviewed journals demonstrate that touch contributes to...

•**Decreased pain.** Children with mild to moderate juvenile rheumatoid arthritis who were given massages by their parents 15 minutes per day for one month experienced less anxiety and lower cortisol levels. Over a 30-day period, parents, kids and their physicians reported less pain overall in the children.

•**Enhanced immune function.** In studies, women with breast cancer and HIV patients showed a measurable increase in natural killer cells—part of a line of defense in the immune system against virus-infected cells and cancer cells—after massage. They also experienced less anxiety and depression.

•**Happier, healthier babies.** Preemies who were touched more while in the NICU gained more weight.

•**Less labor pain.** Women in labor who received a backrub the first 15 minutes of every hour of labor reported less pain and made fewer requests for pain medications. Their labor was also shorter, on average.

•**Enhanced alertness and performance.** Following massage, adults completed math problems in significantly less time and with fewer errors.

TOUCH IS MUTUALLY BENEFICIAL

Touching is good for the giver as well as the recipient, says Dr. Field. She cites a study in which 20 children with leukemia were given daily massages by their parents. After one month, the parents' depressed moods decreased, and the children's white blood cell and neutrophil counts increased. In another study of elderly volunteers who were trained to give massages to infants, Dr. Field found that after three weeks the seniors experienced improved mood with less anxiety or depression, decreased levels of stress hormones and had more social contacts and fewer doctor visits.

GET IN TOUCH

Touch comes more naturally to some people than others. You can make a conscious effort to bring more touch into your daily life—and more happiness to yourself and those around you. Give your kids hugs when they leave for school in the morning and when they come home. Hold your partner's hand when you take a walk, exchange back rubs and don't forget good-night kisses. Pet your dog or cat. Schedule a few sessions with a professional massage therapist and pay attention to what feels especially good—then try it at home on one another. Relax and enjoy.

 # Do-It-Yourself Facelift

Annelise Hagen, New York City yoga expert and author of *The Yoga Face: Eliminate Wrinkles with the Ultimate Natural Facelift.* Avery.

Yoga keeps the body and the mind young, but can it maintain and even restore youth to the face as well? Hearing her students complain about creeping wrinkles and sagging skin inspired New York City yoga expert and instructor Annelise Hagen to develop a class with poses that target facial aging. The results were so positive she wrote a book called *The Yoga Face: Eliminate Wrinkles with the Ultimate Natural Facelift.* This may sound like an out-of-the-ordinary yoga practice, but a relaxing facial workout can slow, even reverse, some of the effects of aging, says

Hagen. She believes that regularly practicing yoga strengthens and tones even the muscles in the face. Why use Botox, she asks, when you can erase years naturally—not to mention for free?

GETTING STARTED

"Facial yoga" (Hagen's term) involves not just the poses but also breathing exercises and mild inversion—but not headstands. Breathing exercises and inversions are relaxing, lower the heart rate, increase blood flow to the head and act as antidotes to stress. The inversions she recommends are simple ones, including *Forward Bends*, either from the waist or while sitting on the floor, and the classic *Downward-facing Dog* pose (bend from the waist making a V position, hands and feet on the floor with your arms and legs straight). Hold each pose for 10 to 30 seconds. Experienced yoga students should feel free to move on to more advanced inversion poses, including the *Supported Shoulder Stand* and *Plow*, which are also good for toning facial muscles.

BREATHE AWAY THE YEARS

Hagen recommends three breathing exercises to help oxygenate and relax the body and the face…

•**Alternate Nostril Breathing.** Block your right nostril with your thumb, then breathe through the left to a count of four…Next, switch sides to block your left nostril with your ring finger and exhale through the right to a count of eight. Pause, switch sides again and repeat, either eight or 16 times, on alternate sides.

•**Skull Brightener Breath.** This is a quick and intense cleansing breath that pumps the diaphragm muscles, stimulates the lungs, releases toxins and brings freshly oxygenized blood into the face. Start with a focus on your exhalation. Expel your breath vigorously through your nose, pumping your diaphragm as you exhale, allowing the in-breath to follow the out-breath automatically, which forces the release of air trapped in the respiratory tract. Do this about 45 times.

•**Breath Retention.** Begin this breathing exercise after your last skull brightener exhale. Draw your pelvic floor muscles in and up, then pull your navel in toward the spine. Consciously "lock" these muscles (this is called a bandha).

Now take a short, quick breath through your nose to the upper chamber of your chest and hold it, tucking your chin toward your sternum while keeping the back of your neck long. Hold the breath for as long as you can comfortably do so, then lift your chin, release the lower abdominal/pelvic muscular lock, and exhale slowly. Savor your next inhalation, and return to calming regular breath.

Benefits: These exercises send vital energy to your face and head, bringing a rosy glow and more efficient circulation to your facial skin.

FACIAL POSES RELAX AND REJUVENATE

Hagen also teaches yoga poses that target the most common trouble spots—the crease between the brows (furrows), crow's feet (eye lines), fine lines around the mouth, the nose-to-mouth fold (nasolabial folds) and sagging jaw lines and neck.* Hagen says it takes about two weeks of practice to master the poses, and after that you'll need just five or so minutes to complete the cycle. Or you can do them intermittently throughout the day if you prefer. *Prepare to laugh, she says—some of these look downright silly, at least when you start…*

•**Lion Face.** This targets laugh lines around the mouth. Clench hands into fists, close your eyes and tense your entire body, including your rear-end and face, squeezing hard as you pucker your lips and slowly inhale through your nose. Then exhale, open your eyes, hands and mouth wide, stick out your tongue and forcefully exhale saying "HAAAA." Do this three times—on the last one, to attain complete jaw relaxation, hold your tongue out for 60 seconds with your eyes opened as wide as possible.

•**Satchmo Pose.** It's aptly named because it employs the same small muscles inside the cheeks (the buccinators) that would be used to blow a trumpet. This is an anti-jowls exercise. Inhale through your nose and puff the air from one cheek to the other until you run out of breath…as you exhale blow out imaginary smoke rings. Repeat three times.

•**Kiss the Ceiling** helps firm the jawline and neck. Bring your chin up, gently tilting your head back, as if you are trying to kiss the

---

*For images and more information, visit Hagen's Web site, *www.yogaface.net.*

ceiling. Repeat this motion three times, once looking straight up...then looking to the left... then to the right. Repeat the cycle three times.

Note: The advanced version of this exercise is called *Baby Bird* and Hagen calls it a "real workout for the cheeks and jaw." When you tilt your chin up, push the tip of your tongue to the roof of your mouth, then smile and swallow, keeping your tongue in that position. Keep a glass of water handy—this exercise will dry your throat, she says.

Helpful: These exercises are effective and easy to do. Hagen's only caution is that while doing them, especially at first, you are likely to also scrunch other areas of your face. More wrinkling is definitely not what you want—to avoid that, do the exercises in front of a mirror, watching to see which muscles you squeeze and wrinkle up. Lightly press your hand or fingers on any involuntary wrinkling to smooth it all away.

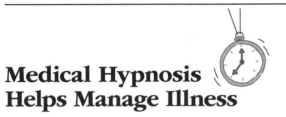

Medical Hypnosis Helps Manage Illness

James S. Gordon, MD, founder and director, The Center for Mind-Body Medicine in Washington, DC, clinical professor, Georgetown University School of Medicine, and former chairperson, White House Commission on Complementary and Alternative Medicine Policy.

Hypnosis used to be considered some kind of parlor trick to make people behave in bizarre ways. But, oh, how that's changed—nowadays people seek out hypnosis because they know it can help them with assorted health-related matters. Studies show that among other things, hypnosis is effective as a tool to reduce pain and manage anxiety, as well as a way to help people curb certain habits such as smoking and overeating. According to James S. Gordon, MD, founder and director of The Center for Mind-Body Medicine in Washington, DC, self-hypnosis can also help lower blood pressure, reduce stress and calm anxiety in fear-filled situations, including cancer treatment or surgery.

Dr. Gordon, who is also a clinical professor at Georgetown University School of Medicine in Washington, DC, and the former chairperson of the White House Commission on Complementary and Alternative Medicine Policy, explains that self-hypnosis is very similar to deep meditation. However, he distinguishes that it goes even further in giving the mind a way to directly affect the body. Hypnosis is successful because it teaches the parasympathetic nervous system—the one in charge of relaxation—to counteract the "fight or flight" responses of the sympathetic nervous system.

Note: Although a few people still worry that hypnosis opens the mind to outside influences and so can be dangerous, Dr. Gordon says that's not even possible. Under self-hypnosis your mind alone exercises control and what it achieves is completely up to you.

CLOSE YOUR EYES... INTRODUCTORY TECHNIQUES

Dr. Gordon says there are several simple ways to start the practice of self-hypnosis. The first one he teaches is particularly easy and is called "soft belly."

Here is how to do it: Sit in a relaxed position, eyes closed and begin to breathe slowly and deeply, in through the nose, out through the mouth. Then on the inhale, say to yourself "soft" and focus on making your belly soft (this will allow your breath to go even deeper and will be even more relaxing), and as you exhale say the word "belly." Repeat this as many times as you need to feel completely calm. The point is simply to relax you.

The next technique has a more scientific name, "autogenic training." Dr. Gordon says it's a great introduction to learning self-hypnosis. It consists of six verbal phrases, all of which give specific instructions to the body to produce physiological changes that induce relaxation. Again sit in a relaxed position, eyes closed and breathing deeply (in fact, "soft belly" is a good lead-in to this). Repeat each one of the six self-instructions six times before you move on to the next. (The first few times you can repeat them out loud, after that, you can simply and silently recite them to yourself.) *They are...*

•**"My arms and legs are heavy...I am at peace."** (This starts to bring the blood flow away from the body's core—where it heads when you're anxious or upset—and back into your limbs.)

•**"My arms and legs are warm…I am at peace."**

•**"My heartbeat is calm and regular…I am at peace."**

•**"My abdomen radiates warmth…I am at peace."**

•**"My forehead is cool…I am at peace."**

•**"My breathing is easy…I am at peace."**

Autogenic training can be used to quiet your mind anytime you feel yourself growing agitated. It can also be used to help break the cycle of longing for a cigarette or the urge to indulge in an eating binge. You could use autogenic phrases to help you achieve specific goals. Begin with the six phrases above, and then, for example, if you are having trouble falling asleep at night, add the phrase, "I am happily going to sleep…I am at peace."

A CALMING RETREAT

Everyone should have a "safe place" in their mind where they can find peace, says Dr. Gordon, and he suggests creating one right away. Having it already established allows you to retreat to your peaceful corner anytime you feel threatened, are ill or when you just need some comfort and a sense of being safe. This is a place you can conjure up in your mind using mental imagery. Some people base their retreat on a real place they know well, but others create one that is fictional and built entirely from fantasy. "Make experiencing the place as real as possible," suggests Dr. Gordon. "Picture what you are wearing and the smells of the place, its sounds, how it feels." You can choose whether you want to be alone there or with others—it's completely yours to fashion as you like.

Reason: This retreat is not just whimsical or even about the physiological relief you experience in its calm—it also brings a sense of control and hopefulness that is healing to people who are anxious, depressed or ill. Dr. Gordon suggests hospitalized patients may teach themselves to "retreat" this way when undergoing an uncomfortable procedure. Surgery patients can take themselves to their safe place on their way into the operating room and again when coming out of the anesthesia. Additionally, practicing this relaxation technique will help the healing process, he adds.

Here is how to go to your safe place: Start with a few minutes of "soft belly," which will put you into a relaxed state in which suggestions about your safe place will have maximum effect. Now imagine you are going to your safe place. Make yourself comfortable there, look around. What do you see? What do you hear? What do you feel and smell? Relax. Breathe deeply. Enjoy yourself. Know that you can return here whenever you like. After a while, perhaps five or 10 minutes, let your breathing deepen and become aware of yourself sitting in the room where you began this exercise. Remind yourself that you can breathe deeply and return to your special safe place any time you wish. Dr. Gordon says that soon you will be able to put yourself there after just a few deep breaths.

FOR MORE TECHNIQUES

These are just a few basic techniques of self-hypnosis. Many people find they are all they need, but more sophisticated ones are also available to help with such issues as stress relief. The Center has a "Best of Stress Management" kit, with 10 CDs, a DVD, workbook and an electronic biofeedback monitor, which costs $219. *www.cmbm.org/kit.*

7

Surprising Healers

Breakthrough! Supplement Works Better Than Statins

Statins, statins, statins. They seem to be *the* drug of the early 21st century—except for the "minor detail" that they may cause dangerous side effects.

In meeting with our medical expert, Andrew L. Rubman, ND, we learned about an all-natural option called *policosanol*. Some tests have shown it to be just as effective in lowering cholesterol as statins but without the risks and at a far lower cost. (How does one-tenth the cost sound?) Talk about a silver bullet.

WHAT IS POLICOSANOL AND WHAT DOES IT DO?

Policosanol is a long-chain alcohol that is derived either from beeswax or from sugar-cane wax. It has been shown in randomized, double-blind studies to significantly lower overall cholesterol levels, and raise HDL ("good") cholesterol levels while lowering LDL (bad) levels. It also reduces other cardiac risk factors, such as platelet clumping (blood clots), high blood pressure and atherosclerosis (hardening of the arteries caused by a buildup of plaque inside the artery walls)—all without the dangerous side effects of statins.

An article in the *American Heart Journal* reported that policosanol "lowers total cholesterol by 17% to 21% and LDL cholesterol by 21% to 29% and raises HDL cholesterol by 8% to 15%." This was at doses of 10 to 20 milligrams (mg) per day. The authors state that at higher doses, policosanol could be even more effective.

Finally, the authors concluded that "policosanol seems to be a very promising phytochemical

Samuel J. Mann, MD, hypertension specialist, associate attending physician, NewYork–Presbyterian Hospital–Weill Cornell Medical Center, New York City. He is author of *Healing Hypertension: A Revolutionary New Approach*. Wiley.

Andrew L. Rubman, ND, director, Southbury Clinic for Traditional Medicines, Southbury, Connecticut.

Louis E. Teichholz, MD, chief of cardiology and director of cardiac services, Hackensack University Medical Center, Hackensack, New Jersey.

alternative to classic lipid-lowering agents, such as the statins, and deserves further evaluation."

SO WHY ISN'T POLICOSANOL BEING PRESCRIBED IN AMERICA?

The answer seems to be *business as usual.* Policosanol was developed in Cuba and our country doesn't do business with that country. Sugarcane "waste products" such as policosanol are abundant and cheap. Yet the large drug companies, such as Pfizer, which makes the hugely profitable Lipitor, have a vested interest in policosanol not being available in America, particularly because it will be sold over-the-counter and at much lower prices.

Just how much cheaper is it? Approximately 10 cents per 10mg pill of policosanol compared with more than one dollar per pill for Lipitor, depending on the dose.

This isn't just whining. Associated Press news stories regarding the Food and Drug Administration's recommendations for expanded use of statins said, "Most of the heart disease experts who urged more people to take cholesterol-lowering drugs have made money from the companies selling those medicines."

WHERE CAN YOU GET POLICOSANOL?

In spite of its place of origin, policosanol is available at US health-food stores and on-line, although it is not recommended as a do-it-yourself supplement. Some doctors are prescribing it, including Samuel J. Mann, MD, a hypertension specialist and associate attending physician at NewYork–Presbyterian Hospital/ Weill Cornell Medical Center. Dr. Mann has prescribed policosanol to a handful of his patients with very good results.

"About 10% to 20% of people can't tolerate statins," he explains. He believes that policosanol is a very attractive alternative that deserves more study. Right now, there isn't enough long-term data to justify the use of policosanol as a first-line drug.

There is no evidence yet that it prevents further heart attacks—evidence that is abundant with statins. Until a study can prove that, statins will be the first choice for people at high risk.

Louis E. Teichholz, MD, chief of cardiology and director of cardiac services at Hackensack University Medical Center in Hackensack, New Jersey, says that his hospital is involved

in a randomized, double-blind, multicenter study to test the effectiveness of policosanol. The participants are tested for cholesterol levels and C-reactive protein levels (considered a predictive factor for heart attacks). The results will be available in five years.

WHAT TO DO

According to Dr. Mann, statin drugs have a proven record, tested over two decades, of lowering the risk for heart attack in people who are in danger. So far, he points out, policosanol has not shown that it can lower the incidence of heart attacks.

So, although policosanol has not yet had the extensive research that statins have had, it is well worth discussing with your doctor if he/she is concerned about your cholesterol levels.

Healing Magic Of Mushrooms

Mark Blumenthal, founder and executive director, American Botanical Council, Austin, Texas, and senior editor, *The ABC Clinical Guide to Herbs.* American Botanical Council.

Andrew L. Rubman, ND, director, Southbury Clinic for Traditional Medicines, Southbury, Connecticut.

Paul Stamets, director, Fungi Perfecti Laboratories, advisory board member, *International Journal of Medicinal Mushrooms,* and author, *MycoMedicinals: An Informational Treatise on Mushrooms.* MycoMedia.

When we think of mushrooms, we tend to think of those white and brown buttons that populate American produce aisles, but there are more than 14,000 known species that do much more than flavor chicken marsala.

Used for centuries in folk medicine throughout the world, mushrooms can help in the fight against a variety of serious diseases, including cancer, heart disease, diabetes, arthritis and hepatitis. They also can fight viral infections, such as AIDS, as well as bacterial and parasitic infections.

"Mushrooms are one of the most misunderstood, underappreciated and underutilized resources in natural medicine," claims Mark Blumenthal, the founder and executive director of the American Botanical Council. "In Western culture, they're viewed as either poisons or foods, but mushrooms have many health benefits, have no known side effects or drug interactions and don't cost much."

WHAT MAKES THEM SO EFFECTIVE?

The "magical" ingredients in mushrooms are complex sugar polymers called *polysaccharides*, especially *lentinan* and those known as the *beta-glucans*, which boost the immune system in various ways. You don't have to be sick to receive their health benefits. "People can use medicinal mushrooms proactively to help maintain optimal health and wellness," says Blumenthal.

Prevention is even more critical these days, with our bodies under unprecedented assault from environmental toxins, contends mycologist Paul Stamets, author of many books on mushrooms, including *MycoMedicinals: An Informational Treatise on Mushrooms.* "Although we may know how one dioxin or one pesticide or one heavy metal can harm human health, we have no clue as to the crossover effects of hundreds of these toxins," says Stamets, who serves on the advisory board of the *International Journal of Medicinal Mushrooms.* "That's why we need to support the immune system, and mushrooms can help."

TRY SOME!

Here are six of the best studied, most powerful healing mushrooms. You're free to eat all you like of them, but it's the concentrated extracts (in liquid or capsule form) that pack the biggest punch. Unless you are allergic to edible mushrooms, there are no substantive health concerns associated with trying these products.

Stamets also says your best bet is to take one to four capsules a day of a "combo supplement," which combines several different kinds of mushrooms. A number of excellent products are now available. According to our medical expert, Andrew L. Rubman, ND, those with the greatest clinical acceptance are produced by Fungi Perfecti LLC (*www.fungi.com*) and New Chapter (*www.newchapter.info*). Just make sure it's organic to avoid pesticides and heavy metals.

Should you choose to try them, you can sample a single mushroom preparation first, then look for a combination that has your favorites.

SHIITAKE (LENTINULA EDODES)

A large body of research suggests shiitake mushrooms, a popular ingredient in Chinese food, may be a potent weapon against tumors. Although its active ingredients don't attack cancer cells directly, they stimulate the body's immune response, prompting it to make more of the white blood cells that destroy malignant cells and boost resistance to bacteria and viruses. Research also shows shiitakes to be good for lowering blood pressure, reducing cholesterol, cleansing the liver and kidneys, and boosting energy. They're a good source of fiber as well as of vitamins A, B and C.

CORDYCEPS (CORDYCEPS SINENSIS)

Sometimes called "caterpillar fungus" because it grows on the bodies of moth larvae (but can also be cultivated on grain), this mushroom may not only fight tumors, stimulate immunity, reduce cholesterol and improve heart and lung function, but it's also known for increasing endurance and heightening sex drive. It made international news in 1993 when the coach of a Chinese women's running team that shattered nine world records partially credited the team's performance to cordyceps's energy and stamina-enhancing qualities.

REISHI (GANODERMA LUCIDUM)

Known in China as an "elixir of immortality," researchers have found this mushroom to enhance immunity, fight viruses, reduce cholesterol and help prevent fatigue. Like shiitakes, reishis are also known to combat cancer—by boosting the body's killer agents, *interleukin-1*, *interleukin-6* and *T-lymphocytes*. Because it also has anti-inflammatory effects, reishi mushrooms may be used to treat arthritis and possibly the brain swelling associated with Alzheimer's disease. Studies already compare the mushrooms favorably with the drug *prednisone*, which is often prescribed for arthritis.

MAITAKE (GRIFOLA FRONDOSA)

In addition to its antitumor and antiviral properties, maitake mushrooms show promise as a treatment for diabetes. They work by improving glucose metabolism in those with hypoglycemia and reducing blood sugar in diabetics. Maitake also may be the most potent immune-booster among the medicinal mushrooms because they have a high percentage of the complex sugar betaglucan and for their ability to reach and activate more immune cells. When eaten, maitakes are a good source of nutrients, including vitamins B-2, C and D, as well as niacin, magnesium, potassium, fiber and amino acids.

ENOKI (FLAMMULINA VELUTIPES)

This potent immune booster caught the attention of Western scientists when researchers from the National Cancer Institute of Tokyo discovered that families of enoki mushroom growers had a nearly one-third lower death rate from cancer than the rest of the community. Enoki mushrooms also contain compounds that have been shown to lower blood pressure. The Japanese have cooked with this delicately flavored mushroom for centuries.

LION'S MANE (HERICIUM ERINACEUS)

Legend has it that this mushroom, named for its long cascading tendrils, produces "nerves of steel and the memory of a lion," because it contains compounds called *erinacines* that may stimulate the growth of nerve cells. Studies suggest that increasing nerve cells may help reduce symptoms associated with Alzheimer's disease, Lou Gehrig's disease, multiple sclerosis and other nervous system disorders. Lion's mane is also used in traditional Chinese medicine to treat indigestion and other gastrointestinal disorders, including stomach ulcers and chronic gastritis.

 # When the Cure Is Worse Than The Disease

Christopher Hobbs, LAc, AHG, licensed acupuncturist, herbalist and botanist, Sutter Center for Integrative Health, Davis, California, and author, *Herbal Remedies for Dummies*. Wiley.

Some drugs can cause more trouble than the diseases they're meant to heal. This is often said about prednisone, the corticosteroid used to treat inflammatory ailments—such as arthritis, asthma, colitis and some cancers—and to prevent rejection of transplanted organs. Its nasty side effects—from a swollen "moon face" to increased infections—are legendary. But what

many people don't know is that there's a medicinal mushroom known as reishi (Ganoderma lucidum) that could, in some cases, do as good a job without wreaking havoc on the body.

A NATURAL CURE

Reishi, known in China as an "elixir of immortality," has been used for more than 3,000 years to rev up the immune system and heal chronic inflammatory conditions. Dozens of preliminary studies support its anti-inflammatory properties. One Chinese study found that of the more than 2,000 people with chronic bronchitis who took reishi syrup for two weeks, 60% to 90% said they felt better.

The best part? Its side effects are as minimal as those you might have from taking a placebo. "I can guarantee that the side effects, if any, will be less than one-quarter of those you might have with prednisone—and the cost is less than one-quarter that of a drug prescription," says herbalist and botanist Christopher Hobbs, LAc, AHG.

Hobbs, who has written many books on alternative therapies, including *Herbal Remedies for Dummies*, acknowledges that prednisone has its place. "For short-term life-threatening conditions, it may save your life," Hobbs says, noting that a friend recently benefited from the drug when he experienced a flare-up of irritable bowel syndrome. "But if you have an ongoing inflammatory condition, reishi may be the best first line of treatment."

YOUR BODY'S CHEMISTRY

Prednisone is a poor long-term solution because it stops inflammation by literally shutting down immune function—and an operational immune system is not something you want to live without for too long. "We need to be able to modulate inflammation because it allows immune cells to come in and fight infections as necessary," Hobbs says. "With prednisone, you're impacting the body's ability to do its job." The drug also causes severe water retention, affects your adrenal hormones, changes your insulin balance and can trigger insomnia, anxiety and depression.

Reishi, by contrast, works slowly *with* your immune system, to reduce abnormal inflammation. Reishi also has an antistress effect, earning it the nickname "calming the spirit."

If your doctor prescribes prednisone and it's not a life-threatening situation, you might discuss trying reishi first. It is available in health-food stores in powder form, as well as capsules and tablets.

Caution: Do not take immune-boosting supplements without the advice of your health-care professionals—preferably both a physician and a licensed oriental medical practitioner—if you suffer from rheumatoid arthritis, lupus or other autoimmune diseases. Reishi should also be used with caution in individuals who have a history of bleeding or those who are on anticoagulants.

Kitchen Cupboard Cure Helps Fight Infection

Cass Ingram, DO, author of *Eat Right 4 Your Metabolic Type* and *The Cure Is in the Cupboard* (both by Knowledge House), and many other books.

Americans spend billions of dollars each year on antibiotics to fight infection. Meanwhile, there are many very effective natural infection-fighting antiseptics that have been used for eons that are cheaper, less risky and more accessible than antibiotics. One of the best is oregano.

A MEDICINE CHEST IN A BOTTLE

According to Cass Ingram, DO (doctor of osteopathy), oil of oregano is one of nature's most powerful and versatile antiseptics. It contains hundreds of potentially healing compounds, including *phenols, terpenes* and *esters.* Phenols, such as carvacrol and thymol, are natural antiseptics…terpenes possess antiseptic, antiviral and anti-inflammatory qualities…and esters are antifungals.

In his opinion, this versatile herb can be used in the prevention or treatment of numerous ailments. It can be applied topically or taken orally depending on the ailment. Talk to a professional about taking it orally to ensure the proper dosing. Oregano is very potent and can be harmful if taken in excess. *Here are some of Dr. Ingram's favorite uses for oregano…*

ACNE

To prevent or control acne, apply a few drops of oil of oregano to liquid face soaps or cleansers, and use it to wash your face twice daily. You can also dab a small amount directly on pimples. An initial short-lived rash may result. If this persists for three or more days, discontinue.

ARTHRITIS

Oregano has anti-inflammatory as well as pain-relieving properties that make it an effective weapon against arthritis. Dr. Ingram notes that oil of oregano is often a safer alternative than drugs such as aspirin or ibuprofen. Rub it on painful areas in the morning and just before going to bed.

ATHLETE'S FOOT

Oil of oregano helps destroy the fungus responsible for this most common of all fungal infections. Apply the oil liberally to all affected regions, especially between the toes, two or three times a day. To prevent infection, apply to the feet after contact with shower floors in health clubs and hotels. If a rash lasting three days or more is produced by this therapy, discontinue use.

COLD SORES

These painful lesions are caused by a toxic event, such as stress, illness or food allergy, explains Dr. Ingram. When you sense the first tingling sign of a cold sore, dab the oil on directly.

TICK BITE

Oil of oregano can kill ticks on contact, says Dr. Ingram. If the tick is attached to your skin, saturate it and the bite site with oil.

PSORIASIS

Although conventional medical practitioners believe that psoriasis has no known cause or cure, Dr. Ingram says that this vexing skin disorder is largely due to fungal infection. The root of the problem may be a malfunction in the intestinal tract due to overconsumption of sugar. He recommends a diet rich in healthy proteins and fats, and oil of oregano taken under the tongue or in juice two to three times daily. Discuss internal use with a medical professional before using. Oil of oregano can also be used topically for psoriasis.

WOUNDS

According to Dr. Ingram, oil of oregano is a potent treatment for any superficial open wound. Apply oil to the wound and along the edges, and cover.

Conventional medical treatments, such as antibiotics, are typically overprescribed and may lead to superinfections. Think outside the box. Bacteria, viruses and fungi are no match for oregano, says Dr. Ingram. Oil of oregano is readily available at your health-food store, or you can purchase it from North American Herb & Spice (available from Internatural, 800-643-4221 or *www.internatural.com*). Oreganol P73 oil, the strongest formula, is available in a dropper bottle. Oregamax—the unprocessed raw, dried oregano leaf with garlic and onion powder in capsules—is a milder formulation.

Caution: As noted above, talk to a medical professional formally trained in botanical medicine about the appropriateness and dosing level for internal use of oregano.

The bottom line remains that wild oregano is an herb, so it is one of the safest supplements we know.

The Wonder from Down Under: Tea Tree Oil

Chanchal Cabrera, a medical herbalist practicing in Courtenay and Vancouver, British Columbia, *www.chanchalcabrera.com*.

Medical herbalist Chanchal Cabrera, who practices in British Columbia, never leaves home without her portable first-aid kit, which includes three essential oils—peppermint (for nausea or car sickness), lavender (for stress or headache relief) and tea tree (for minor cuts, scrapes and more).

Made from the leaves of the Australian tree *Melaleuca alternifolia*, tea tree oil is renowned for its strong antiseptic properties, but, Cabrera says, it has potent antibacterial, antifungal and antiviral activity as well. In an Australian study of tea tree's effectiveness against oral microorganisms, when used topically, it successfully reduced populations of bacteria, such as clostridium, Haemophilus and streptococcus. For best results, Cabrera recommends the pure,

organic and unadulterated essential oil, which has a refreshing scent reminiscent of eucalyptus.

HOW TO USE IT

Tea tree oil is a valuable ingredient in a number of natural shampoos, skin cleansers, creams, toothpastes, mouthwashes, deodorants and even household cleaning products. *Specific ways you can use it…*

• **For minor cuts,** scrapes and burns to promote healing, apply a drop of oil directly to the injury. Tea tree oil also protects the skin from radiation burns during cancer treatments. Expect some iodine-like burning associated with using tea tree oil. If in three days the burning associated with repeated applications persists, or the wound fails to look improved, discontinue its use. Tea tree is only for minor wounds. Major wounds require medical attention. People with sensitive skin or inflammatory conditions, such as eczema, should exercise caution when using tea tree oil.

• **On athlete's foot, use small amounts of undiluted tea tree oil,** at least once daily. Again, expect the burn and keep an eye on the tissue. These types of infections may take up to a month to respond.

• **At the first tingling signs of a cold sore,** apply a drop of tea tree oil.

• **To combat acne,** apply a drop directly to pimples. For best results, apply a warm washcloth to open pores first.

• **To take the sting out of insect bites,** use a cool tea tree compress.

• **For sore throat,** gargle with a diluted solution of tea tree oil. Start with a one in 10 dilution of oil to water and increase in strength to five in 10. Remember to shake well—after all, you are mixing "oil and water."

• **For dandruff control or to discourage lice infestation,** wash hair with a tea tree shampoo, or one "spiked" with the oil. The usual dilution is a one to eight concentration, depending on the oil strength and purity.

• **Tea tree oil can also play a role in pet care.** Instead of extremely toxic commercial treatments, use a flea repellent made with tea tree oil. Cabrera says that you can also put a drop of tea tree oil on your dog's collar or on its bedding. She notes that dogs usually don't mind the strong odor, but cats do.

Tea tree oil is an exceptionally safe and versatile remedy to keep on hand. You can often purchase a larger bottle on-line. Even with shipping costs, it can be cheaper in the long run than purchasing the tiny bottles in the health-food store or bath and beauty shops.

Epsom Salts Help More Than Your Feet

Annie B. Bond, author of *Clean & Green* (Ceres) and more recently in reprint paperback, *Home Enlightenment: Create a Nurturing, Healthy, and Toxin-Free Home* (Rodale), and former executive editor of the on-line environmental network, Care2.com.

Andrew L. Rubman, ND, director, Southbury Clinic for Traditional Medicines, Southbury, Connecticut.

Some things never go out of style. So it is with Epsom salts, an old-fashioned remedy dating back to Greek and Roman times that continues to have many healthful uses today. According to our medical expert, Andrew L. Rubman, ND, Epsom salts can reduce swelling, improve drainage and help get a sluggish system up and running again.

Environmental activist Annie B. Bond, former executive editor of the environmental network Care2.com, finds the salts particularly soothing and relaxing in the bath. Epsom salts, made from the mineral magnesium sulfate, are a natural sedative.

HOW TO USE EPSOM SALTS

Bond has a number of helpful tips for using Epsom salts…

• **To reduce the swelling of sprains and bruises** or just to enjoy an especially relaxing bath, add two cups of Epsom salts to a tub of warm water. Even better, also add several drops of lavender or neroli oil.

• **To soothe achy feet,** absorb their odors and soften rough skin, soak them in a pan of warm water with one-half cup of Epsom salts.

• **To wash your face,** combine one-half teaspoon of Epsom salts with your regular cleansing cream. Massage into skin and rinse thoroughly with cold water. This will help dry out oily skin and renew all skin types.

• **To exfoliate skin,** massage handfuls of Epsom salts into your wet skin when in the bath or shower. Start with the feet, and slowly work your way upward. Afterward, rinse thoroughly.

• **To make your own facial mask,** for normal to oily skin, combine one tablespoon of cognac, one egg, one-quarter cup of nonfat dry milk, the juice of one lemon and one-half teaspoon of Epsom salts. For normal to dry skin, mix one-quarter cup of grated carrot, one-and-one-half teaspoons of mayonnaise and one-half teaspoon of Epsom salts. Apply the mask to damp skin for approximately 10 minutes.

• **To reduce the swelling of minor insect bites,** apply a warm Epsom salt compress. Use Epsom salts with just enough water to make into a thin paste. Apply the paste to the bite, then cover with a washcloth saturated with water that is just short of scalding hot. Add more very hot water to the washcloth, covering the bite every few minutes to keep it very hot. Continue this for 10 minutes and repeat every hour.

Note: Be sure to remove the stinger, if present, before starting.

info To learn more about the many other uses for Epsom salts—from getting rid of blackheads to cleaning bathroom tiles to cultivating a healthier lawn—visit the Epsom Salt Council at *www.epsomsaltcouncil.org.*

You Can Ease Anxiety with Kava

Jamison Starbuck, ND, a naturopathic physician in family practice and a guest lecturer at the University of Montana, both in Missoula. She is past president of the American Association of Naturopathic Physicians.

Recently, there have been a lot of questions about the popular antianxiety herb kava. In 2002, the US Food and Drug

Administration (FDA) issued a warning about a possible association between kava and liver damage, and *Consumer Reports* included kava on its list of the so-called "dirty dozen" supplements. Kava has been banned in some countries, but it might be too soon to completely discount it.

According to Jamison Starbuck, ND, a naturopathic physician in family practice in Missoula, Montana, most negative incidents that concerned kava arose from incorrect manufacturing practices, and she stresses that there is nothing wrong with properly made kava products. Dr. Starbuck continues to carry kava in the pharmacy associated with her practice and recommends it to patients for anxiety or insomnia.

HOW KAVA IS USED

For hundreds of years, kava beverages made from *Piper methysticum* have been used ceremonially, socially and medicinally in the South Pacific islands, including Fiji, Samoa, Papua New Guinea and Tonga, and in Hawaii. They induce a sense of well-being, relaxation and, some say, euphoria.

With the boom in natural remedies, kava became the subject of many medical studies. In one study, it was shown to be as effective as the prescription drug *buspirone* (BuSpar) for generalized anxiety disorder. Another study suggested that kava may have an impact similar to benzodiazepine medications, such as *diazepam* (Valium). An added benefit is that kava causes fewer side effects than prescription antianxiety medications.

Dr. Starbuck recommends kava for...

•**Severe, consistent anxiety.** Take twice a day—once in the morning and again at bedtime. See a naturopathic doctor (ND) for exact dosage and directions. Dr. Starbuck emphasizes that kava is not for occasional bouts of anxiety, such as nervousness before a business meeting or presentation.

•**Sleep disorders.** Take once a day at bedtime. Dr. Starbuck often combines kava in capsules with other soothing and relaxing herbs, such as hops.

USE CAUTION

Kava may cause mild side effects, such as stomach upset, allergic rash or slight headache. With large and more frequent doses, there have been reports of liver toxicity. Dr. Starbuck advises against its use in anyone with a history of liver disease. It should also be used with caution in people taking medications that are toxic to the liver, which could include something as commonplace as chronically used NSAIDs (nonsteroidal anti-inflammatory drugs). There are more than 100 drug interactions, so you must exercise caution. Therefore, use kava primarily for infrequent symptoms, not prophylactically, and only under the guidance of an ND. Periodic monitoring may include checkups and blood tests. You should also always report any side effects promptly.

Although kava can be a very beneficial herb, there have been problems with commercial brands. To be on the safe side, Dr. Starbuck recommends that you get kava directly from a naturopathic physician, rather than picking up a bottle of capsules at your local pharmacy.

info To locate a naturopathic physician in your area, go to *www.naturopathic.org*.

Natural Sex Boosters

Chris D. Meletis, ND, executive director, the Institute for Healthy Aging (*www.theiha.org*). He is author of several books, including *Better Sex Naturally* (HarperResource), *Complete Guide to Safe Herbs* and *Instant Guide to Drug- Herb Interactions* (both DK publishing).

A recent study in *Urology* showed that men can reduce their risk of developing impotence by burning at least 200 calories a day through exercise. That's great...exercise wins again—over time. Now, what about dealing with the *immediate* problem?

We all know that Viagra has changed the sexual landscape, but it comes with a number of problems. Its side effects include headaches, indigestion, vision problems and diarrhea, not to mention the fact that it is expensive and requires a prescription.

Fortunately, according to Chris D. Meletis, ND, executive director of the Institute for Healthy Aging, there are a number of safe herbal and nonprescription remedies available for men and women to enhance their desire and performance.

Key: Using the right remedy for the problem.

ERECTILE DYSFUNCTION

More than half of men over age 40 have some degree of erectile failure, according to a recent study. The condition can be caused by a variety of health problems, such as poor circulation or nerve damage, so it is important to see your primary care physician for a diagnosis.

An erection depends on healthy blood flow to the penis. Clogged arteries reduce circulation, which compromises a man's ability to achieve an erection.

The herb ginkgo biloba dilates blood vessels, improving circulation and helping to restore the ability to achieve erection. In a recent study, 78% of men who had erectile dysfunction who took ginkgo biloba regained the ability to have erections.

Good news for women: Women who use ginkgo biloba may notice longer, more intense orgasms.

People most likely to benefit from ginkgo biloba have circulatory symptoms, such as dizziness, varicose veins, cold hands or feet or high blood pressure.

Typical use: 40 milligrams (mg), three times daily. Look for a formula containing 24% flavonglycosides, the active ingredient.

Ginkgo should not be taken by anyone who uses blood-thinning medication, such as *warfarin* (Coumadin)…aspirin…or antidepressants that are known as MAO-inhibitors…or anyone who has had a stroke or has a tendency to bleed or bruise easily. Consult your doctor.

INHIBITED SEXUAL DESIRE

Low libido can plague men and women. Fortunately, both sexes can benefit from ginseng. This herb energizes the body, helping it respond better to almost any health problem. It also boosts the production of sex hormones, such as testosterone in men and women, to enhance sexual response.

People likely to get the most benefit from ginseng have anxiety, blood sugar problems, fatigue, high levels of stress, menopausal symptoms or frequent infections, such as colds.

Typical use: Look for a product that contains *ginsenoside Rg1*, the active ingredient. Take 10 mg, twice daily.

Ginseng is a stimulant. It is not recommended for people with high blood pressure or anyone taking medication for diabetes, bipolar disorder or heart disease.

FOR WOMEN ONLY

Levels of hormones play a very crucial role in a woman's sexual health and emotional involvement during sex.

Too much estrogen can thin the vaginal walls, causing painful intercourse. Too little testosterone reduces your sex drive. Too little progesterone or too much prolactin can lead to anxiety and depression.

The following herbs* can help regulate female hormones…

•**Black cohosh** helps regulate hormones by controlling the secretions of the pituitary gland, which help balance estrogen and progesterone production. This can enhance a woman's interest in sex and help with vaginal lubrication.

Typical use: 500 mg, twice daily. Or, if you are using a standardized tablet, take 2 mg of *27-deoxyacteine*, the active ingredient.

•**Dong quai.** The herb *angelica sinensis* grows around the world but is most commonly known by its Chinese name, dong quai. It balances estrogen levels and can enhance sexual pleasure.

Typical use: 500 mg, twice daily.

Better yet: Consider taking a formula that combines black cohosh and dong quai, particularly if you have premenstrual syndrome (PMS) or are menopausal. Dong quai can increase energy and improve mood, while black cohosh helps reduce PMS symptoms, such as bloating, and menopausal symptoms, such as hot flashes.

DANGEROUS REMEDIES

Some "natural" aphrodisiacs can be dangerous. *Stay away from…*

•**Damiana.** Derived from the leaves of a shrub found in the southwestern US and Mexico, this herb has many possible side effects, including diarrhea, vomiting, heart palpitations and anxiety.

•**Spanish fly.** This beetle from southern Europe is pulverized and eaten. It contains the chemical *cantharidin*, which can damage your heart, kidneys, stomach and intestines—or even kill you.

*Pregnant or lactating women should not use these herbs.

More from Chris D. Meletis...

Four Ways to Calm Motion Sickness

Nothing kills a car trip or boating adventure faster than a bout of motion sickness. While both Dramamine and Bonine are effective over-the-counter drug options, there are a number of natural alternatives you can try. Some are more effective when taken before leaving the dock, while others can help after that queasy feeling sets in.

Caution: Both of these medications may affect your cognitive function and have other side effects. If you are on any medications, including supplements or botanicals, consult your doctor before taking them.

Important: If you do choose Dramamine or Bonine, take it before you get in the car or on the boat. If you wait until you start to feel sick, they won't help.

HOMEOPATHIC HELPER

One option is a homeopathic medicine that has the unfortunate name of *nux vomica*, commonly known as "poison nut." A standard adult dosage, taken before you leave the dock, is three to five tablets (24X or 12C strength)—but, as always, check with your doctor. Nux vomica can be found at health-food stores in the homeopathic section. Homeopaths swear it is both safe and effective in appropriate dosages.

GINGER ALE...GINGER AID

In ancient times, sailors from Asia used to chew ginger to prevent seasickness. Folklore, some might say.

But in the 1990s, a researcher at the American Phytotherapy Research Laboratory in Salt Lake City performed an experiment with 36 volunteers who tended to get motion sickness. He gave each participant either 940 milligrams (mg) of ginger powder or 100 mg of Dramamine before seating them in motorized chairs that were designed to simulate choppy seas. The participants were instructed to stop the chairs when they felt sick. Those who took the ginger powder lasted 57% longer than those who took Dramamine.

To keep things simple, try taking 1,000 mg of dried ginger 30 minutes before you set sail or get in the car. Those of us who are more unsteady can safely opt for 2,000 mg. Do not take dried ginger at all if you are pregnant.

If you find yourself queasy while in motion, try some ginger ale or gingerbread cookies. Or you can try candied ginger, which is widely available. Be sure to brush teeth and rinse well after this sweet treat.

ANOTHER FORM OF GINGER

Ajuron, an Ayurvedic ginger compound, can also alleviate nausea and vomiting associated with motion sickness. Look for ready-made stomach remedies containing ajuron at your health-food store. The advantage of ajuron over other ginger remedies? You don't need to take as large a dose. Follow package instructions.

MIND OVER MATTER

Even if your boat contains an assortment of motion sickness remedies, the most important elements are attitude and behavior. Keeping your mind on success and not focusing on any feelings of discomfort can be a huge help in overcoming the challenge of the sea.

And, while you're keeping your mind on success, be sure to keep your eyes on the horizon. If you must go below deck, keep your eyes focused outside—this will let your brain avoid the mixed signals that can lead to sickness.

Common "Scents" Healing

Alan R. Hirsch, MD, founder and neurological director, Smell & Taste Treatment and Research Foundation, Chicago, and author of *Life's a Smelling Success.* Authors of Unity.

Andrew L. Rubman, ND, director, Southbury Clinic for Traditional Medicines, Southbury, Connecticut.

Smell is a powerful sense that can have a strong effect on emotions. It was surprising to hear that it could also have medical implications.

To learn more about the power of smell, we spoke with Alan R. Hirsch, MD, founder and neurological director of the Smell & Taste Treatment and Research Foundation in Chicago. He told us that as more baby boomers face the vicissitudes of aging and push for approaches to wellness other than medication, aromatherapy—the art and science of using essential oils extracted from plants for health and healing—is likely to play an increasing role in health care.

BENEFITS WITH MINIMAL SIDE EFFECTS

The scents of fragrant essential oils offer a wide range of gentle, generally noninvasive health benefits. Lavender is a well-known soothing scent, but most people are not aware that vanilla also reduces stress. Additionally, citrus scents and jasmine purportedly increase energy…pungent eucalyptus can ease congestion…peppermint calms motion sickness… and sandalwood is traditionally used to focus thoughts during yoga and meditation.

Lesser known, observes Dr. Hirsch, are the benefits of the scent of green apple to reduce the duration and severity of migraines… and the combination aromas of lavender and pumpkin pie to increase penile blood flow.

In two studies, Dr. Hirsch demonstrated aromatherapy's effect on weight reduction through the inhalation of peppermint, banana or green apple and "olfactory nostalgia," the happiness of childhood evoked through remembered scents.

AROMATHERAPY FOR WEIGHT REDUCTION

With obesity rising to epidemic proportions, Dr. Hirsch finds it very curious that little research has focused on how the sense of smell affects weight. To assess the effect of aromas on weight control, he and his colleagues studied more than 3,000 overweight volunteers. The study was controlled. It was found that the more an individual liked a scent, the more effective it was in helping the participant to lose more weight.

Researchers gave the participants inhalers with aromatic ingredients—peppermint, banana or green apple—and instructed them to inhale three times in each nostril whenever they were hungry. They were told not to change their normal diet and exercise habits.

The amount of weight participants lost corresponded directly to how often they used their inhalers. The group that didn't do as well showed poor olfactory abilities, snacked more than five times a day and disliked chocolate.

At the end of the six-month study, the subjects whose test scores showed they had good olfactory abilities and who used their inhalers frequently ate two to four meals a day, and felt bad about overeating but did not feel bad about themselves…and they lost nearly five pounds per month. This suggests that inhaling aromas can play a part in weight loss.

REMEMBRANCE OF THINGS PAST

In times of stress and angst, sometimes a walk down memory lane can help ease one's way. For this, there is nothing quite so powerful as reminiscent scents of times gone by. In a survey conducted by Dr. Hirsch, the scent most commonly reported as evoking cherished childhood memories was that of freshly baked cookies, cake or bread. More than eight out of 10 participants experienced smell-induced nostalgia, and for the vast majority who reported having happy childhoods, this was a positive experience.

Interestingly, the one person in 12 who reported an unhappy childhood was also two times as likely to associate childhood with foul odors, such as body odor, bus fumes, mothballs, sewer gas, dog waste and the like.

In difficult times, notes Dr. Hirsch, we are more prone to idealize the past. This means that during periods of physical or emotional stress, which everyone is bound to encounter, it is soothing to capture remembered scents, such as Mom's baking or a summer afternoon at the beach.

Dr. Hirsch notes that the memory of childhood scents breaks down regionally. In the West, a common scent memory is that of barbecuing meat…in the East, it is the aroma of flowers…in the South, fresh air…and in the Midwest, farm animals.

LOOKING TOWARD THE FUTURE

Dr. Hirsch believes that the sense of smell is a great untapped resource. As noted above, aromatherapy can address a wide range of health issues, including arthritis, headache, menopause, weight loss and sexuality. Dr. Hirsch predicts that in the not too distant future we will all be turning to essential healing oils just as we would any other pharmaceutical.

Caution: According to our medical expert, Andrew L. Rubman, ND, the compounds in aromatherapy must be processed by the liver, so people on strong prescriptive regimens or with chronic diseases affecting liver function, including Epstein-Barr infections, should watch closely for side effects and consult a knowledgeable physician before self-medicating.

info Essential oils are widely available at quality health-food stores and often discounted on-line. Learn more about aromatherapy from Web sites such as the Smell & Taste Treatment and Research Foundation at *www.smellandtaste.org*...the National Association for Holistic Aromatherapy at *www.naha.org*... and the Pacific Institute of Aromatherapy at *www.pacificinstituteofaromatherapy.com*.

Scents That Can Energize

Mynou de Mey, director, the American Institute for Aromatherapy & Herbal Studies, Eldred, New York, *www.aromatherapyinst.com*.

We've all been hearing a lot about aromatherapy from our friends. They like it because the scent of lavender or tangerine helps them unwind after a busy day. We wondered if aromatherapy would help fire up a working mother early in the morning who didn't drink coffee at the start of a demanding day.

To find out, we called aromatherapy educator Mynou de Mey, director of the American Institute for Aromatherapy & Herbal Studies, in New York, and she answered our question with a resounding yes. In fact, the list of invigorating essences is substantial—basil, rosemary, eucalyptus, peppermint, spearmint, pine, grapefruit and aniseed. De Mey suggests experimenting to find out which ones work best for you.

She recommends using these in the morning. Put a few drops in the bath or at the bottom of the shower, so the steam releases the scent. Or put one drop on a cotton ball and inhale the scent. They work so well, she says, that using some of them too late in the day may leave you too energized to sleep.

BUY CAREFULLY

Many oils today are synthetic, not the authentic essential oils that really work, explains de Mey. *Before you purchase any products, here is how to tell if you're getting the real thing...*

• **Skip the oils sold at bath-product chain stores.** Buy instead from qualified people selling essential oils and herbal products (usually small companies). Always check the background of anyone selling essential oils.

• **Actual proof of authenticity should appear on the label.** An authentic oil's label will include the English and botanical names. A synthetic oil will not have a botanical name, since it is man-made. The label also should offer the name and location of the company selling the product.

HOW TO USE OILS

• **Dab one drop of diluted oil directly under your nose.**

• **Place a dish with three or four drops of oil nearby while you shower...**or put drops directly into your bathwater.

• **Place up to five drops in a diffuser** on your desk to energize yourself at work. Diffuse for no longer than 20 minutes.

Caution: It is especially important to dilute oils for use on the skin in fractionated coconut, sweet almond or grapeseed oil. The actual doses should be discussed with a qualified aromatherapist. Otherwise, people with sensitive skin may develop irritation, a rash or a burning sensation. Over time and with repeated use of undiluted oils, more serious problems may develop.

By the way, scented candles are not considered aromatherapy, as they are often made with synthetic scents.

Sweet Citrus Stomps Strep

Jaime De La Barrera, medical herbalist, Westcoast Reiki Centre, Vancouver, British Columbia. De La Barrera is the producer of the herbal educational Web site *www.infoherb.com*.

With infectious diseases and drug-resistant strains of bacteria on the rise, health-care providers are always on the lookout for new weapons to add to their germ-fighting arsenals. Enter grapefruit seed extract (GSE). It is a natural antimicrobial agent made from grapefruit seeds and pulp that fights *Streptococcus*, *Staphylococcus*, *Salmonella*, *E. coli*, *Candida*, herpes virus and more.

Numerous studies back up the effectiveness of the extract. For example, research at the University of Texas suggests that it has antibacterial characteristics comparable with those of proven topical antibiotics, such as Bactroban, Nystatin and Silvadene.

HOW TO USE GRAPEFRUIT SEED EXTRACT

GSE comes in a number of different forms—capsules, tablets and liquid concentrate. Medical herbalist Jaime De La Barrera, who practices in Vancouver, British Columbia, says that the liquid concentrate is his favorite formulation because it is so versatile. He cautions, however, that you should never use it at full strength—always dilute. Applying or ingesting too concentrated a solution can cause inflammation, indigestion or flatulence.

De La Barrera recommends GSE liquid concentrate as a...

• **Dental rinse.** For healthy gums and fresh breath, mix three drops with two or more ounces of water. Rinsing your mouth with a small amount of this mixture for 10 seconds once or twice daily can help to reduce plaque buildup.

• **Throat gargle.** For a sore throat, mix three drops with three or more ounces of water. Gargle as needed. It is not dangerous to swallow if it is properly diluted.

• **Vaginal rinse.** For yeast infections, mix five to 10 drops with six to eight ounces of water. Douche once daily for one week. If an irritation occurs, discontinue use immediately.

• **Facial cleanser.** For acne, moisten your face using warm or cool water, apply two to three drops of the liquid concentrate to wet fingertips and gently massage into affected areas. Rinse thoroughly with cool water and pat dry.

• **Wash or skin rinse.** For minor skin irritations, mix five to 10 drops with one tablespoon of water. Using a washcloth, apply gently to affected areas twice daily.

• **Cutting-board disinfectant.** Apply 10 to 20 drops of liquid concentrate to the cutting board and rub in with a wet sponge. Leave on for 30 minutes, then thoroughly rinse.

• **Fruit and vegetable wash.** Add 20 drops of liquid concentrate to a 32-ounce pump-spray bottle filled with water. Spritz on your produce, then rinse.

There are also many commercial products made from GSE, including skin cleansers, shower gels, deodorants, foot powders, ear drops and nasal sprays. Look for the liquid concentrate and other GSE products at quality health-food stores, or purchase on-line from NutriBiotic at *www.nutribiotic.com*. Compared with tea tree oil and oregano oil—two other antimicrobial options—GSE is generally safer for internal use than oregano oil...and all are fairly comparable for topical use. Pick your favorite scent.

Simple Steps to Stop Dizziness

Andrea Radtke, MD, researcher, Neurologische Klinik der Charité, Campus Virchow-Klinikum, Berlin, Germany.
Andrew L. Rubman, ND, director, Southbury Clinic for Traditional Medicines, Southbury, Connecticut.

Do you feel dizzy when you get out of bed in the morning? How about when you roll over in bed? You may have *benign paroxysmal positional vertigo* (BPPV). BPPV is a common type of vertigo, especially in older people.

It is sometimes called "top-shelf vertigo" because changes in head position, such as looking up and down, trigger dizziness. Caused by small stones, or crystals, of calcium carbonate in the inner ear, dizziness results when the moving stones stimulate inner ear nerves.

The good news is that BPPV can be treated successfully with a simple physical therapy regimen called the "Epley maneuver." It is the most widely used treatment for BPPV in the US. Until now, Epley had to be performed by a doctor or a physical therapist in a medical setting. However, a recent study published in *Neurology* compared the effects of two maneuvers, the Epley versus the Semont, when performed at home without medical supervision.

Results: Within one week, 95% of the patients who performed a modified Epley maneuver in their homes experienced no episodes of dizziness, compared with 58% of patients who performed the Semont maneuver.

DOING "THE EPLEY" YOURSELF

We spoke with Andrea Radtke, MD, lead researcher on the study regarding do-it-yourself Epley. The most important thing to know, says Dr. Radtke, is that the procedure needs to be done in different directions, depending on the ear from which the vertigo originates.

What to do…

• **You will need a clock** or a watch with a second hand.

• **Sit on your bed with a pillow behind you,** positioned so that it will be under your shoulders when you lie back.

If the vertigo originates in the left ear…

• **Turn your head 45 degrees to the left.**

• **Lie back quickly, placing shoulders on the pillow, neck extended.** In this position, the affected ear (the left) is facing the bed. Wait for 30 seconds.

• **Turn your head 90 degrees to the right** (without raising it) and wait for 30 seconds again.

• **Turn your body and head another 90 degrees to the right,** and wait for another 30 seconds.

• **Sit up without rolling back.**

If the vertigo originates in the right ear…

• **Turn your head 45 degrees to the right.**

• **Lie back quickly, placing shoulders on the pillow, neck extended.** In this position, the affected ear (the right) is facing the bed. Wait for 30 seconds.

• **Turn your head 90 degrees to the left** (without raising it) and wait for another 30 seconds.

• **Turn your body and head another 90 degrees to the left,** and wait for 30 seconds again.

• **Sit up without rolling back.**

This procedure should be performed three times a day and repeated daily until there are no symptoms of dizziness for at least 24 hours.

Researchers recommend self-administered Epley for patients who do not get relief after treatment from a doctor or therapist and for those who have a recurrence of vertigo—about one-third of patients have recurrences within a year of treatment…and half have recurrences within five years.

Although the study results indicate that performing Epley at home will most likely be successful in alleviating symptoms of BPPV, it is vitally important that you know the cause of your dizziness before trying it. See your physician for a diagnosis first.

We also asked our medical expert, Andrew L. Rubman, ND, if there is anything that can be done to avoid the calcium carbonate crystals from forming in the first place. He said that there are, indeed, some underlying causes, such as chronic inflammation and insufficient dietary calcium uptake and utilization, and that a naturopathic physician can help you address these issues.

Ancient Chinese Pain Cure

Roger Jahnke, OMD, doctor of acupuncture and traditional Chinese medicine…CEO and chief of staff, Health Action Clinic…and director, Institute of Integral Qigong and Tai Chi, Santa Barbara, California. He is also author of *The Healer Within* (HarperOne) and *The Healing Promise of Qi* (McGraw-Hill).

Qigong (Chi Kung) is an ancient Chinese practice that combines movement, meditation and breath regulation, and is often used to help manage chronic pain.

To learn more about qigong, we spoke with Roger Jahnke, OMD, doctor of acupuncture and traditional Chinese medicine…CEO and chief of staff of the Health Action Clinic…and director of the Institute of Integral Qigong and Tai Chi, in Santa Barbara, California.

ABOUT QI AND QIGONG

Qigong works by stimulating and balancing the flow of *qi*—the vital life energy that sustains health and calms the mind. However, Dr. Jahnke notes that qi really is much more than this. A major concept, and not easily translatable, he says that qi is the fundamental energy of the universe, an invisible feature of the world that is present everywhere.

The practice of qigong is intended to open the meridian system of energy pathways throughout the body, thereby preventing or treating disease, improving health and promoting longevity. Thrills and depression both strain the nervous system, explains Dr. Jahnke. Qigong takes you out of the distractions of life so that you can move to an inner focus on the present moment. It switches you from a state of doing to a state of being.

THE HEALTH BENEFITS

The regular practice of qigong may help resolve health problems including digestive disturbances, asthma, arthritis, insomnia, pain, depression and anxiety. In China, it is used as a cancer treatment. On a day-to-day basis, qigong can be practiced to counteract the health deficiencies created by the typical Western lifestyle of poor eating habits, little exercise, chronic stress and a polluted environment.

According to Dr. Jahnke, there have been many studies that demonstrate qigong's ability to alter the body's internal functioning, thus allowing healing to occur.

HOW TO PRACTICE QIGONG

Qigong is a very versatile practice that can exercise the mind, body and spirit, explains Dr. Jahnke. It ranges from simple calisthenic-like movements combined with breath coordination, to complex exercises through which a person intentionally modulates brain-wave frequency, heart rate and other organ functions.

Dr. Jahnke emphasizes that anyone, in any state of health and at any age, can benefit from qigong. Qigong can be performed standing up, sitting, walking or lying down. It is even gentle enough to be done in a hospital bed or in a wheelchair.

There are four main components of qigong…

• **Postural adjustments along with gentle movements.**

• **Purposeful, focused breathing.**

• **Self-applied massage.**

• **Meditation or deep relaxation.**

In practice, you can combine two, three or even four components at a time. Dr. Jahnke notes that you can also make up your own qigong routine, structuring your movements, postures and breathing to meet your personal needs, desires and limitations.

A QIGONG SAMPLER

A typical qigong exercise consists of controlled breathing and deep relaxation as you stand on your tiptoes and reach your arms upward. This can help prevent headache, constipation and insomnia by improving blood and lymphatic fluid circulation and modulating brain function.

A classic warm-up with a beneficial effect on the spine is called "Ringing the Gong." As you twist at the waist, your hands strike the body, stimulating the internal organs. Begin by standing with your feet spread out to shoulder width and rotate your torso. Upper-body movement should come from the waist, with the shoulders following the waist, and arms following the shoulders. Dangle your arms and swing, as you turn your head as far as it will comfortably go to look behind you while breathing fully. Now begin turning rhythmically from left to right, making hands comfortably strike the body with loose open hands or fists. As your hands hit your lower torso, they stimulate the kidneys, liver and spleen. However, use common sense and don't do it if it hurts.

Another early morning warm-up traditionally used by the martial-arts warriors to clear the gut and "stuck" emotions is "Warrior's Breath." Standing with knees slightly bent, breathe in deeply and raise the hands to heart level with palms facing out. Next, unbend the knees and raise the whole body slightly. Either right away or after briefly holding your breath, sink down while extending the palms out forcefully and exhaling sharply. Then drop the hands below the waist, breathe in and use the hands as if you were clearing cobwebs from the qi field in front of the body. At the top of the inhaled breath, when the hands again reach the level of the heart, repeat this Warrior's Breath sequence with a sharp exhalation. You can make a sound such as "ho" or "yah" as you exhale.

For those people who are physically unable to perform even these gentle movements, there is qigong meditation. In this practice, a person inhales and visualizes a concentration of qi in his/her abdominal area. Upon exhalation, the person visualizes these resources speeding out to circulate the healing energy throughout the entire body.

It is important to approach each practice with an intention to relax. According to Dr. Jahnke, you should direct your mind toward a state of quiet indifference. He also says to regulate your breath so that both the inhalation and exhalation are slow and deep, but not urgent or exaggerated. Above all, take it slow. Pushing yourself or trying too hard goes against the natural benefits of qigong.

GROWING AWARENESS AND AVAILABILITY

Through this ancient healing practice, individuals can learn to heal themselves and maintain health. Qigong classes are increasingly available around the country. Look for them in your area at local hospital wellness programs, YMCAs, health clubs, schools, adult education centers, community fitness programs and churches.

info A directory of qigong instructors can be found at the National Qigong (Chi Kung) Association's Web site, *www.nqa.org*.

To learn more about the benefits of qigong, visit Dr. Jahnke's Web sites at *www.feeltheqi.com* and *www.healerwithin.com*.

Healing Power Of Eastern Medicine

Raven Keyes, certified Reiki master, hypnotherapist and meditation teacher who conducts workshops on chakras at Equinox Fitness Clubs in New York City.

More and more people are making a connection between their health and the Eastern concept of spiritual and physical ("life force") energy. For those interested in this belief system, one of the core concepts is *chakras*. Chakras are energy centers in the body. Each one of the seven chakras represents a different aspect of life. According to Caroline Myss, PhD, in her book, *Anatomy of the Spirit* (Three Rivers Press), you can best understand and work with your chakras if you think about yourself as an energy being as well as a physical being.

UNDERSTANDING CHAKRAS

Many people believe that the chakras interact with both the endocrine and nervous systems, and that each one relates to a particular area of the body as well as to consciousness. The theory is that emotional issues manifest themselves physically in certain body zones—and conversely, that physical ailments can find their roots in emotional issues tied to the specific area in which the ailment is centered.

The value of understanding the chakras is that when you are experiencing stress in an area of your life, the corresponding chakra will reflect that energy block. Unless you address the problem and relieve the stress it is causing you, it can eventually translate into illness.

ENERGY HEALING BALANCES CHAKRAS

We spoke with Raven Keyes, a certified Reiki master, hypnotherapist and meditation teacher who has students throughout the world. Reiki is a form of energy healing that clears and balances the chakras as well as other energy points. Keyes has provided Reiki in the operating room at New York–Presbyterian Hospital—once to an open-heart patient of renowned cardiac surgeon Mehmet C. Oz, MD, and the second time to a double lung transplant patient. She says that part of achieving good health in all areas of life is becoming balanced—and that balancing your chakra energy centers each day is vital to bringing that about.

THE SEVEN CHAKRAS

There are seven chakras, structured to follow the path of human development and maturation, with the first associated in part with family and clan…and the last with spiritual connection. *Specifically…*

Chakra one: *Root chakra.* Located in the pelvic region, this chakra encompasses everything that is manifested in your life, the material world and the people around you, specifically your family and feelings of safety and security. Sometimes called the "tribal" chakra, it is associated with the adrenal glands, which are in charge of fight-or-flight responses. If you are out of balance, you act out of fear and can actually cause what you fear to come about, says Keyes. The emotional situations this chakra relates to are frustration and rage, as well as fear and depression. Physical ailments that can be manifested due to root chakra issues include lower back pain, sciatica, hemorrhoids, constipation, obesity and weight problems.

Chakra two: *Sacral chakra.* This is located several inches below the navel, the creative center, and relates to relationships in the outside world. Not surprisingly, the sacral chakra is associated with the sexual glands and organs and a willingness to experience emotions. When this chakra is out of balance, the result is despair or hopelessness and a general tendency toward overindulgence because of neediness. Physically, chakra two issues can be connected to fertility and gynecological problems, sexual potency, kidney problems and muscle cramps/spasms.

Chakra three: *Solar-plexus chakra.* Above the navel and below the sternum, this chakra represents the relationship to one's self and has to do with personal honor, self-esteem and perceptions of power, control and freedom. A problem that causes imbalance in the solar-plexus chakra results in feelings of weakness and loss, anxiety, guilt and doubt. The associated body part is the pancreas. Not surprisingly, chakra three issues can create problems in your midsection, including food allergies, digestive disorders, diabetes, gallstones, arthritis, ulcers, liver complaints and eating disorders.

Chakra four: *Heart chakra.* Located in the center of the chest, this is the "in-between" chakra. Those below it have to do with the earth and are primal. The ones above it are connected to more spiritual aspects of life. The heart chakra mixes the two and relates to love, compassion and forgiveness—of others and especially of self. Keyes says that healers work from the heart chakra because love is the greatest healing force there is. An imbalance will cause feelings of loss, grief, anguish, worthlessness and the like. Although a feeling might start in another chakra, such as in the solar plexus chakra, it can manifest itself here. The heart chakra relates to the thymus gland, a central part of the immune response, and could lead to physical challenges that include heart conditions, lung problems, asthma, allergies, fatigue, breast cancer, bronchitis and pneumonia.

Chakra five: *Throat chakra.* In the middle of the neck, this chakra has to do with expressing what you want and being able to put your own desires for yourself out into the universe. It also relates to intuition and being receptive to the abundance of the universe coming back to you. A problem in this chakra shows in feelings of repression, an inability to express oneself and lack of inspiration. The chakra's associated body part is the thyroid. Physically, chakra five problems can be felt as sore throats, loss of voice, thyroid problems, mouth ulcers, teeth and gum condition, headaches and ear infections.

Chakra six: *Brow chakra.* Also known as the third eye, this chakra is in the middle of your forehead between the brows. It represents wisdom and clairvoyance and the willingness to learn from others. An imbalance shows in obsession or even insanity. It is associated with the pituitary gland, the controller of the endocrine gland's functions, and is manifested in ailments that include learning difficulties, brain tumors, blindness and deafness.

Chakra seven: *Crown chakra.* The last chakra is at the top of the head, half in and half out of it, says Keyes. It connects the spiritual world with your spiritual center, and relates to the ability to trust life, values, ethics and courage and the ability to see the grander pattern of life. The physical association is with the pineal gland, which connects nervous system signals to the endocrine system. Unhealed issues in chakra seven can manifest as chronic exhaustion, depression and paralysis.

WORKING WITH THE CHAKRAS FOR HEALTH

By increasing your awareness of the spiritual-physical connection, you can identify the unresolved issues that could be creating health challenges for you. When illness strikes, reflect on any underlying emotional issues that may be showing themselves. Often by confronting the emotions, the physical challenges can ease.

On a daily basis, the goal is to have all seven chakras in alignment, generally done through balancing exercises. It is possible to align all seven chakras in one brief meditation or to address specific problems in a chakra through what Keyes refers to as "spot-check meditations." Doing these will go far in helping you achieve balance in your life on a routine basis, and it is that harmony of physical, emotional, mental and spiritual that comes together in glowing health.

The following article will explain Keyes' technique for balancing chakras.

More from Raven Keyes...

Using Meditation to Heal

In the previous article, *Healing Power of Eastern Medicine*, Reiki master Raven Keyes explained the Eastern concept of chakras, seven energy centers in the body that align from the pelvic floor to the top of the head. The chakras are associated with specific areas of physical well-being, human maturation and emotionality.

According to energy healers, chakra therapy—practicing techniques that keep the chakras in balance—is vital to achieving maximum good health. These beliefs and practices have been in existence for centuries.

Keyes told us about an easy meditation that connects the chakras and brings them into balance with one another. She explains that the chakras are closely related. Making something happen in one of the chakras requires the "participation" of multiple chakras. You may have a desire that is associated with the throat chakra, for instance, but to make it happen, the desire must move to your heart chakra to empower it with love, to the power chakra to gain force, and finally, to the root chakra where it will manifest in your life.

EASY TO DO

The meditations are based on each chakra's color and an associated sound that helps to balance the chakra. A meditation takes only about five minutes, and you can do it in bed each morning or evening, or seated at home or in the office.

Although they aren't high tech—and you will need to make some funny sounds—they are worth a try. The worst thing that can happen is that they won't work. The best thing that can happen is that they will help you feel better and perhaps even reduce or avoid the need for medication. *Here's what to do...*

• **In a relaxed position,** with eyes closed, breathe deeply and send the color *red* to your root chakra in the pelvic floor. (You might envision the color there, sense it, feel it or otherwise be aware of it.) Make the sound *laam* as you exhale each breath. Repeat five to 10 times, each time enlarging the circle of red until it reaches the next chakra.

• **Moving up to the sacral chakra,** breathe deeply as you send the color *orange* into the abdominal area. Make the sound ooo (as in *boo*) while you enlarge the orange ball to reach the next chakra.

• **For the solar-plexus chakra** that's between your navel and your chest bone, send the color *yellow* to the area, enlarging it with each breath you take and making a *rah* sound every time you exhale.

• **For the heart chakra** in the center of your chest, send and enlarge the color *green* to the area and exhale to the sound *ay* (as in *play*).

• **For the throat chakra** in the center of the neck, send and enlarge the color *sky blue* and exhale to the sound *eee*.

• **For the brow chakra** between the brows, send and enlarge the color *indigo* (dark bluish purple) and exhale to the sound *ohm*.

• **For the crown chakra** at the top of the head, send the color *violet* and exhale to the sound *eenngg*.

Did you notice? By completing the meditation you brought the colors of the rainbow to your chakra system.

You can also perform "spot-check meditations." If you are experiencing an upsetting feeling, target the associated chakra as described in the previous article and send its color to the area along with the chant. You will quickly restore the balance to your body and will feel more relaxed and peaceful.

There are dozens of other types of treatments that focus on chakras, but this is one that is easy and fun.

These balancing meditations are small acts you can do that will help you strengthen and take care of *yourself*, says Keyes. That, she adds, is key because having the self in order is what leads to all other good things.

Hypnosis—More Than Just Hype

Sebastian H. W. Schulz-Stübner, MD, PhD, former assistant professor of anesthesia at the University of Iowa's Roy J. and Lucille A. Carver College of Medicine, Iowa City, Iowa.

If you think pain is where the wound is, think again. In some instances, it is actually in your head—and medical hypnosis can help.

According to Sebastian H. W. Schulz-Stübner, MD, PhD, former assistant professor of anesthesia at the University of Iowa's Roy J. and Lucille A. Carver College of Medicine in Iowa City, it's time that the public overcomes the stereotype that hypnosis is simply grandstanding entertainment. Hypnosis is used today for a number of real medical challenges, including anxiety relief, smoking cessation and pain control.

A NATURAL PALLIATIVE FOR PAIN

Hypnosis can help relieve many types of pain—including chronic pain, cancer pain, headache and labor pain—by decreasing the intensity of the pain signal perceived by the brain, although the exact location where hypnosis interferes in the pain perception process is still unknown, explains Dr. Schulz-Stübner. It is most effective when used in combination with more standard modalities of pain relief, and in an individually modified manner. Studies show that when hypnosis is employed preceding invasive medical procedures, patients experience less pain and anxiety.

Dr. Schulz-Stübner would not use hypnosis to replace anesthesia, at least in a North American population, where we seem to hold stereotypes about hypnosis as entertainment. However, he notes that it is a good way to provide sedation as well as comfort while a regional block provides anesthesia for the part of the body the surgeon is operating on. Hypnosis can also make the placement of the blocks more comfortable.

HOW IT WORKS

Hypnosis usually begins with a concentration exercise and goes on to use body sensations and visualization. The imagery chosen can be highly individual, but common themes are nature and travel, family and home, and personal skills.

According to Dr. Schulz-Stübner, hypnosis does not work on everyone. On average, 60% of people can reach a deep level of hypnosis for pain control…20% reach a superficial level…and the remaining 20% reach an insufficient level—or none at all.

LOOKING TOWARD THE FUTURE

Dr. Schulz-Stübner observes that hypnosis is similar to meditation exercises. The goal is to eventually use this practice on your own. This is called self-hypnosis (or in Europe, autosuggestive training), and provides people with another valuable tool to control various types of pain, such as headache, chronic nerve or muscle pain, or cancer pain.

Hypnosis is more widely used in Europe, especially in psychotherapy, but also for sedation and relaxation purposes (for example, in dentists' offices). Here in the US, hypnosis is gradually gaining greater acceptance.

The National Center for Complementary and Alternative Medicine (NCCAM) has conducted a study to test the effectiveness of self-hypnotic relaxation to control the distress from minimally invasive surgical procedures. Analgesics and sedatives have limited effectiveness and serious side effects in these cases. The study was done at the Beth Israel Deaconess Medical Center in Boston. It was found that women who used self-hypnosis during a type of core needle breast biopsy experienced anxiety relief and reduced pain when compared with standard care.

Be certain that your hypnotist has special training and a thorough background in psychology or psychiatry.

info If you want to find out more about hypnosis for control of pain, visit NCCAM at *http://nccam.nih.gov*.

Hypnosis is not regulated in most states, so you must be careful in selecting a hypnotist. A good place to start is the American Society of Clinical Hypnosis at *www.asch.net*.

Natural Cures for Back Pain

Jamison Starbuck, ND, a naturopathic physician in family practice and a guest lecturer at the University of Montana, both in Missoula, Montana. She is past president of the American Association of Naturopathic Physicians.

Low back pain is a common complaint—especially after age 60, when one out of every two people is affected.

In a recent issue of *The Journal of the American Medical Association* (*JAMA*), new research concluded that back surgery and nonsurgical treatment provide similar relief for back pain in patients with lumbar disk herniation (protrusion of a disk out of the normal vertebral space).

Nonsurgical treatment, which helps heal back pain in part by improving circulation, is far less expensive than back surgery and avoids its risks, such as infection.* *Jamison Starbuck, ND, recommends…*

•**Walking.** Regular walking is by far the best medicine for back pain. Walking uphill is particularly useful because it strengthens muscles that support the low back. Start with very short distances (one-eighth of a block, or about 25 steps). It's fine to start walking at a slow pace. Just keep moving and do the distance three times a day, every day. Wear comfortable, supportive shoes, such as running shoes. Use a walking stick initially, if it helps. As soon as you are able to walk your starting distance without pain, increase the distance.

*Seek medical attention if your back pain is not improving or is getting worse or if you experience numbness in the legs or paralysis.

•**Deep breathing.** As you walk, take deep breaths to increase oxygen intake and help relax back muscles. Imagine your back muscles relaxing with each inhalation, strengthening and healing with each exhalation.

•**Thai massage.** This ancient, interactive type of massage—which involves "assisted" stretching, yoga, reflexology (massage of pressure points on the feet that correspond to other parts of the body) and acupressure (massage of points on the body that correspond to energy pathways known as "meridians")—reduces back pain. Thai massage increases muscle relaxation, mobility and overall energy. A 60-minute Thai massage, once a week for a month, can significantly improve back health. To locate a practitioner, consult Thai Healing Alliance International, *www.thaihealingalliance.com.*

•**Homeopathic remedies.** *Cuprum metallicum* and *Rhus toxicodendron,* both available at health-food stores, are most widely used for back pain. Cuprum is indicated when the pain is sharp, and the muscles are tight and in spasm. Rhus is useful for stiffness and soreness that improves when you limber up with movement. Take two pellets of the 30C potency of either remedy, under the tongue, two times a day for no more than two weeks.

•**Epsom salts.** Add two cups of Epsom salts to a tub of hot water and soak for 20 minutes. Epsom salts reduce back pain by relaxing your muscles. To supplement your pain relief, burn a lavender-scented candle in the bathroom. The aroma of lavender helps relax your body and your mind.

8

The Best Vitamins, Herbs And Supplements

Best Supplements to Take at Every Age

It seems that every day there is another article about the benefits—or lack thereof—of taking vitamin supplements. Attempting to wade through all of the choices of which brands and which supplements to take, and in what quantity, is enough to make you say, "Forget it," and not take any at all.

But many health-care experts feel that to ensure the best possible health throughout life, supplements—in combination with a good diet and plenty of exercise—are critical.

To simplify things, we called Jamison Starbuck, ND, a naturopathic physician in family practice in Missoula, Montana, and past president of the American Association of Naturopathic Physicians.

These are her recommendations—for a healthy individual who does not have special needs or an unusual family medical history—listed decade by decade...

TWENTIES

Dr. Starbuck says that since most people in their 20s are strong and vital, their goal should be to fortify themselves so as to sustain their vitality as much as possible throughout the many years to come.

Supplements to choose: Start with a high-quality daily multivitamin, to be taken throughout life. Young adults should also start taking 1,000 milligrams (mg) a day of vitamin C, which enhances immunity to fight off colds and more serious disorders. Dr. Starbuck says virtually any kind of vitamin C is fine. You may prefer to take your C in 500-mg doses twice a day because larger doses can cause loose stools.

Additionally, a good B-complex supplement is helpful for stressful situations, such as graduate school. It contains thiamine, riboflavin, niacin, B-12 and no more than 100 mg of B-6, plus

Jamison Starbuck, ND, a naturopathic physician in family practice and a guest lecturer at the University of Montana, both in Missoula. She is past president of the American Association of Naturopathic Physicians.

folate, which, though not a B, is often included in the supplement.

THIRTIES

In this decade, stress levels increase as people balance the demands of jobs and children. Increased stress requires additional support for your system.

Supplements to choose: In addition to the multivitamin and C, Dr. Starbuck suggests 400 international units (IU) daily of vitamin E to help handle stress and support the function of other antioxidants. Select one that is either a food-derived *multi-tocopherol E* or a combination of the *alpha-* and *gamma-tocopherols.*

Caution: More than 200 IUs of vitamin E may be dangerous for some people. Check with your doctor for the dosage that's right for you.

Also: Because stress is high for most thirty-somethings, Dr. Starbuck believes B complex should be a permanent addition to this balanced supplement list.

To help make the most of the limited hours spent sleeping, Dr. Starbuck advises 500 mg of calcium and 500 mg of magnesium daily. (These amounts may be in your multivitamin. If not, take them separately. The calcium/magnesium combination can be found in one supplement.)

Other tips for sleeping well: Take the B-complex in the morning and the calcium/magnesium just before bedtime.

Reminder: Dr. Starbuck says that although people may feel constantly in gear juggling the many facets of their lives, it doesn't count as real exercise. A structured exercise program is essential for its health and relaxation benefits.

FORTIES

Hormones begin to shift in this decade, especially for women, and life's daily demands are still high. *To accommodate the physical shifts in the body…*

Supplements to choose: Anyone not already taking omega-3 fatty acid supplementation should start now, says Dr. Starbuck, to enhance cardiovascular health, among other benefits. The omega-3 fatty acids to take are EPA (*eicosapentaenoic acid*) and DHA (*docosahexaenoic acid*) because the body cannot make these in sufficient quantities on its own. She advises

1,000 mg a day of EPA and 750 mg of DHA. Any high-quality omega-3 is fine.

Reminder: Choose a fish oil supplement (flaxseed oil has omega-3 but not DHA or EPA) that has been filtered or assayed for heavy metal to avoid high levels of mercury and *polychlorinated biphenyls* (PCBs), and one that is cold-processed, which will help prevent spoilage. Refrigerate capsules after opening the package and periodically do a "sniff" test. If they smell rancid (i.e., fishy), they should be discarded, says Dr. Starbuck.

The multivitamin/mineral for this age group should have up to 30 mg of zinc and 2 mg of copper, which are good for fighting inflammation, such as arthritis, and enhances the effects of over-the-counter painkillers, such as aspirin, Aleve and Motrin. Zinc and copper may actually decrease the need for NSAIDs (nonsteroidal anti-inflammatory drugs).

As women begin to experience perimenopausal symptoms: They may want to increase their intake of vitamin E to 800 IU. This will aid in the processing of estrogen in the body, an imbalance of which has been linked to these symptoms and even to reproductive cancers.

For the sleep disturbances that often start in these years, Dr. Starbuck likes Calms Forté (manufactured by Hyland's). This homeopathic preparation of minerals and homeopathic herbals includes valerian, hops and passionflower, and she says the formula is extremely safe. (Take two pellets at bedtime or when you awaken during the night.) As with all low-potency homeopathics, these should be taken only as needed rather than regularly.

FIFTIES

The needs in these years are similar to those in the 40s, but at this point, some people begin to experience problems with digestion and absorption of vitamins and minerals. Digestive secretions made in the stomach, gall bladder and pancreas decline with age.

Supplements to choose: According to Dr. Starbuck, people who experience these problems probably do not need digestive enzymes and should not take antacids. Instead, consider taking a little acid with meals, such as vinegar or lemon juice on salad, and having ginger or peppermint tea at the end of a meal.

An increase in calcium intake to 750–1,000 mg will help protect bones. If it causes constipation, go back to a smaller amount.

SIXTIES AND OVER

Other problems may surface in this decade, such as memory trouble, high blood pressure and cardiac issues.

Supplements to choose: In addition to your established protocol, add glucosamine for arthritis and joint pain. To maximize brain power, Dr. Starbuck has several suggestions —300 mg daily of a nutrient-derived tablet called *phosphatidylserine*. Taking 60 mg of ginkgo biloba a day may also improve memory, she says.

For those with a heart problem or a family history of heart disease, she advises adding 30 to 60 mg a day of coenzyme Q10. High blood pressure affects at least half the people of this age group. Because there is now evidence linking a lack of vitamin D with high blood pressure, she recommends taking up to 800 IUs of D every day. (But check to see what quantity you are already getting in your multiple before you increase it. Vitamin D can be dangerous in excess quantities.)

Check with your physician to see if your potassium levels (measured with conventional blood tests) are within the normal range. If you need to take this mineral, do so only under the direct supervision of your physician—excess consumption can be dangerous.

WHICH BRANDS?

In spite of all the bottles there are to choose from, it's important to select products that are of high quality, advises Dr. Starbuck. A naturopathic doctor can prescribe the pharmaceutical-quality supplements and most often will consult with your conventional treatment team.

Critical: If you take prescription medication, you must discuss all supplements you are taking or plan to take with your doctor.

The Buzz on "B" Vitamins

Michael Hirt, MD, medical director, the Center for Integrative Medicine at Encino-Tarzana Regional Medical Center and associate clinical professor, UCLA School of Medicine. *www.drhirt.com.*

Andrew L. Rubman, ND, director, Southbury Clinic for Traditional Medicines, Southbury, Connecticut.

The B-complex vitamins are a mystery to many people. They realize that these are important supplements, but are often unsure of which ones they should take, and in what amount.

To gain a clearer understanding of the Bs, we called Michael Hirt, MD, medical director of the Center for Integrative Medicine at Encino-Tarzana Regional Medical Center and assistant clinical professor at the UCLA School of Medicine.

Dr. Hirt told us immediately that he cannot think of a single person who wouldn't benefit from taking a B-complex supplement.

Reason: Certain Bs are difficult to get in sufficient quantity through diet alone, and the Bs are crucial for many health reasons.

BS DEFINED

When researchers first isolated the B nutrient from extracts of liver, rice and yeast, they assumed that it was just one vitamin. But later, they found that there actually were a number of vitamins and named them all as part of a B complex. *The complex includes…*

- **Thiamine (B-1)**
- **Riboflavin (B-2)**
- **Niacin (B-3)**
- **Pantothenic acid (B-5)**
- **Pyridoxine (B-6)**
- **Biotin**
- **Folic acid**
- **Cobalamin (B-12)**

The Bs are busy vitamins, playing a role in the health of both your immune and nervous systems, your eyes, mucous membranes, nerve sheaths, skin, gastrointestinal (GI) tract, the metabolism of food, the expression of DNA, hemoglobin synthesis and more. Three of the Bs —B-6, B-12 and folic acid—are the most vulnerable to problems or deficiencies.

•**B-6.** B-6 has become a popular way to relieve carpal tunnel syndrome as well as premenstrual symptoms. This vitamin is crucial for healthy immune function and helps maintain blood glucose in a normal range.

Warning: Taking too much B-6 is dangerous. Although it is water soluble, excessive amounts can saturate the tissues, leaving a residue that can result in nerve damage, which may be irreversible. The key to taking B-6 is never to take more than 100 milligrams (mg) a day, including that from all the supplements you are taking, such as your multivitamin, says Dr. Hirt. Some people were treating carpal tunnel and PMS with amounts of up to 200 mg daily—a dangerous practice.

Dr. Hirt has found that 100 mg a day of B-6 is helpful for carpal tunnel and may ease PMS. It is important to remember that when taking B-6, you must also take B-1 and B-2 because the body needs them to utilize B-6.

•**B-12.** Gross deficiency in B-12 can lead to anemia and can, over time, cause permanent damage in the central nervous system. Marginal deficiencies in challenged individuals lead to psychological, neurological and immunological vulnerabilities.

Certain groups, including people over age 50 who generally have reduced stomach acid, are more vulnerable to B-12 deficiency because B-12 requires adequate stomach acid to be absorbed by the body. In addition to older adults, people taking medications that lower stomach acid, or who have chronic GI problems, such as celiac disease or irritable bowl syndrome, may be functionally deficient in B-12. Strict vegetarians are also often deficient because B-12 is found mostly in meat and dairy products.

•**Folic acid.** Most women who have had children are aware of folate or folic acid because it is necessary to prevent neural tube defects in the developing fetus. In recent years, researchers have established an important link between coronary artery disease, stroke and thromboembolism and higher levels of the amino acid *homocysteine.* Taking folic acid can help combat higher levels of homocysteine, especially when taken in combination with B-6 and B-12.

GETTING YOUR BS

Foods that contain the B vitamins include meats, fish, poultry, rice, milk products, eggs, legumes, soybeans and green vegetables. Whole-grain products do as well—and most cereals today are fortified with B vitamins. Whenever you choose a supplement, Dr. Hirt suggests you take a complex containing B-6, B-12, B-1, B-2 and folate, and that it contains one to two times the recommended daily intake.

Our medical expert, Andrew L. Rubman, ND, suggests that the simplest strategy is a B-50 supplement, which is widely available. When taking all B vitamins, divide them into two doses daily. This is because serum levels tend to peak and drop after 15 hours to 18 hours. By using divided doses, the peaks overlap and a more constant supply to the tissue is maintained. Also, be sure to keep your B vitamins refrigerated, because it helps maintain the active levels of the pills or capsules.

What Happens When Beta-Carotene Backfires

The late Jane Higdon, PhD, research associate, specialist on nutrition, Linus Pauling Institute, Oregon State University, Corvallis, Oregon.

The bloom is off beta-carotene's rose. Before the late 1990s, many people considered beta-carotene, a relative of vitamin A, a sort of wonder supplement—an antioxidant that could help prevent cancer, particularly lung cancer, and possibly other diseases. However, recent research indicates that beta-carotene, like other supplements, can create problems when taken in excess.

Note: The combination formulas that include beta-carotene in modest doses have not been found to have negative effects.

THE STUDIES

Two large studies revealed that taking beta-carotene supplements actually *increased* the risk for lung cancer, especially in heavy smokers. (Current heart disease studies suggest that beta-carotene supplements may be similarly dangerous for the heart.) Participants in both studies took high-dose supplements of beta-carotene—seven times the amount available in a diet rich in beta-carotene foods. In the first study—which included nearly 30,000 male smokers in Finland—the group taking beta-carotene had an 18% higher incidence of lung cancer than those taking the placebo. In the second study—which included more than 18,000 men and women who were heavy smokers or who were exposed to asbestos—there was a 28% higher incidence of lung cancer among the group taking beta-carotene supplements. A third large study looked at 22,071 healthy male physicians with a very small smoking population (11%).

Its outcome: The supplements didn't hurt… but they didn't help either.

WHAT'S GOING ON?

Beta-carotene is one of hundreds of *carotenoids*, natural antioxidant compounds that give plants their many colors. Its particular colors are deep yellow, orange and dark green. The body converts beta-carotene to vitamin A, which is necessary for healthy eyes and skin, among other things.

But it appears that high doses of beta-carotene are metabolized in an oxygen-rich environment, such as the lungs, and become carcinogenic. Some experts also speculate that cigarette smoke puts so much demand on the antioxidant property of beta-carotene that it depletes it, thereby turning it into a pro-oxidant, which increases oxidation and releases free radicals. The late Jane Higdon, PhD, research associate at the Linus Pauling Institute at Oregon State University in Corvallis, Oregon, acknowledged that this is indeed what happens in a test tube, but it hadn't yet been confirmed that that's what occurs in the human body.

Dr. Higdon stated that even though the studies focused on the harmful effects of beta-carotene supplements on smokers, she advised everyone to avoid taking individual beta-carotene supplements.

She also suggested that everyone eat plenty of foods containing beta-carotene, such as carrots, squash, yams and spinach. The hundreds of antioxidants in plants seem to work in synergy with one another. By eating a variety of them, we are making sure that our bodies are getting the correct balance that they need.

Carrots, squash and spinach…what a perfect autumn palette.

Pump Up Your Heart With Vitamins

Louis E. Teichholz, MD, chief of cardiology and director of cardiac services, Hackensack University Medical Center, Hackensack, New Jersey.

News reports extolling the virtues of antioxidants and folic acid as being good for our hearts were recently so common, they were practically old hat. So it was quite a shock to read headlines that said these supplements don't help—and that one antioxidant in particular, beta-carotene, may actually hurt you.

THE REPORT

Reporters based their startling news on a study conducted by the US Preventive Services Task Force, a group of health experts that makes recommendations based on its evaluation of published research. The task force's purpose in this case was to determine whether taking vitamins A, C and E, beta-carotene and folic acid (alone, in combination or as part of a multivitamin) lowers people's chances of developing cardiovascular disease (CVD) and cancer. The conclusion led many reporters and even some doctors to believe that taking these supplements was worthless in terms of both CVD and cancer.

WHAT'S GOING ON?

We called CVD expert Louis E. Teichholz, MD, chief of cardiology and director of cardiac services at Hackensack University Medical Center in New Jersey and an advocate of integrated health measures, for an explanation of what is going on.

Dr. Teichholz immediately pointed out that many people are misinterpreting the report. It did not say that people should *avoid* vitamins A, C and E, folic acid and a multivitamin, as some headlines blared. The correct conclusion to draw

131

from the report is that based on the current research, the task force could not recommend one way or another whether it was helpful or not to take the vitamins and folic acid for the primary purpose of preventing CVD or cancer.

BETA-CAROTENE WARNING

The experts, however, did find sufficient research evidence to identify beta-carotene supplements as being potentially harmful, particularly in heavy smokers. And the task force did recommend against their use. This is particularly important for smokers because several high-quality studies suggest that taking beta-carotene by itself might increase the chance of developing lung cancer in smokers. Dr. Teichholz supports the task force on its beta-carotene position and advises his cardiac patients against using it as well.

DIGGING DEEPER

Why don't the studies show more support for the other supplements? Dr. Teichholz explains that current available research studied the effect of supplements on patients who had a heart attack or who died. The length of time that these end-stage patients took the supplements was relatively brief—no more than a few years. He goes on to say that the major effect of vitamins is not to prevent CVD but to help achieve wellness and slow the progression of disease in general. No one has looked at how effective vitamins are in doing this, and any study that does will have to take place over a much longer stretch of time.

Another problem, he says, is that most participants in the studies took the supplements in a combination form which included beta-carotene. He speculates that the presence of beta-carotene—which we now know to be potentially harmful for smokers—might have played a role in the outcome of studies.

OTHER VITAMIN CONSIDERATIONS FOR YOUR HEART

For the purpose of future studies in this area, Dr. Teichholz presents some intriguing possibilities. He points out that vitamin E comes in several forms, including *alpha-tocopherol* and *gamma-tocopherol*. All of the current studies used alpha-tocopherol rather than gamma-tocopherol, which is both an antioxidant and an anti-inflammatory.

Inflammation plays a role in CVD, says Dr. Teichholz, so he and other physicians who recommend vitamin E prescribe the mixed tocopherol (alpha, beta and gamma) forms of it. He would like to see studies that research the effectiveness of this mixed form of vitamin E.

TAKING ACTION

Dr. Teichholz remains a firm supporter of the use of C, E, folic acid and a multivitamin for cardiovascular health.

His advice: Take 500 milligrams of vitamin C together with 400 international units of vitamin E.* Vitamins E and C will work better when taken together because one is fat soluble and the other is water soluble, and they invigorate each other. He also advises patients to take 400 micrograms of folic acid in a high-quality multivitamin…to drink green tea…and to have a few glasses of red wine a week if they drink alcohol.

Dr. Teichholz cautions against taking megadoses of any vitamin because that could be harmful, and he does not recommend that his patients take vitamin A, citing that there is no data to support its use for cardiac purposes. Of course, you should discuss any supplements you take with your doctor.

Dr. Teichholz also notes that the task force emphasized that vitamins can never replace a healthy diet. He concurs with this statement and tells his patients, "Eat for health."

*More than 200 IUs of vitamin E may be dangerous for some people. Check with your doctor for the dosage that's right for you.

Most Important Nutrient For Great Health

Carol S. Johnston, PhD, RD, professor and chair, department of nutrition, Arizona State University East, Mesa, Arizona.

The boom in the uses of traditional medicine has made us familiar with all sorts of previously "obscure" vitamins, minerals and herbs, such as coenzyme Q10, L-carnitine, folic acid, selenium, echinacea, ginkgo biloba, glucosamine—the list goes on and on. Meanwhile, one of the best-researched, most fundamentally important nutrients other than water, salt and the carbs, proteins and fats necessary for life and good health is something that has been around for decades—vitamin C (ascorbic acid).

SUPER HEALING VITAMIN C

Fresh fruits and vegetables, such as oranges, grapefruit, cantaloupe, strawberries, broccoli and peppers, are packed with vitamin C, a powerful antioxidant essential for tissue growth and wound healing. The late Nobel Prize winner, Linus Pauling, PhD, recommended this miracle vitamin for everything from preventing the common cold to treating arthritis to fighting cancer, and believed that we get far too little of it in our regular diets.

Exciting research—a study of 4,740 people, conducted by researchers at the Johns Hopkins Bloomberg School of Public Health and published in the *Archives of Neurology*—even suggests that long-term supplementation with vitamins C and E may significantly reduce the risk for Alzheimer's disease.

Carol S. Johnston, PhD, RD, chair of the department of nutrition at Arizona State University East in Mesa, Arizona, agrees with Dr. Pauling, noting that 15% to 20% of Americans do not get sufficient amounts of vitamin C. She says that this deficiency can lead to fatigue and malaise, painful joints and poor wound healing.

WHAT IT DOES

•**Vitamin C is a strong immune system booster,** rich in antiviral and antibacterial properties. Although it has not been proven to prevent colds, vitamin C has been shown to reduce their severity and duration (by one day).

•**Vitamin C is required** for the synthesis of collagen, connective tissue protein that is crucial to the structure of skin, gums, arterial walls, bone, ligaments and tendons.

•**Vitamin C is good for your heart.** It can help reduce blood pressure, raise HDL (good) cholesterol and reduce oxidative stress to the arteries.

•**High levels of vitamin C** may lower the risk of cataracts, and reduce symptoms of Parkinson's disease and amyotrophic lateral sclerosis (ALS), also known as Lou Gehrig's disease.

•**Vitamin C is required** for the synthesis of carnitine, which allows fat to be utilized for energy.

HOW MUCH TO TAKE

The recommended daily intake for vitamin C is 75 milligrams (mg) a day for adult women and 90 mg a day for adult men. One eight-ounce glass of orange juice is all you need to meet this requirement. But, for maximum antioxidant benefit, Dr. Johnston recommends that you take a daily vitamin C supplement of 500 to 1,000 mg.

Large amounts of vitamin C can cause loose stools and diarrhea. However, Dr. Johnston notes that diarrhea is usually a problem only at very high doses of 3,000 to 4,000 mg a day—and even at these doses, it affects fewer than one in 10 people. The highest level that the government deems safe for the average American is 2,000 mg a day.

An apple a day may keep the doctor away, but an orange a day may prove to be even more beneficial to your health. Better yet, have both.

More from Carol S. Johnston...

"C-Sickness"—Danger of Low-Carb Craze

The newest danger of the low-carb craze? All-protein-all-the-time diets may be contributing to the revival of a disease of the ancient mariners—scurvy. A deficiency of vitamin C can lead to this fatigue-inducing disease, from which sailors once suffered after spending months at sea with no access to fresh fruits and vegetables.

AMERICANS SHORT ON VITAMIN C

The recommended daily intake for vitamin C is 75 milligrams (mg) a day for adult women, and 90 mg a day for adult men. However, according to one recent study at Arizona State University, nearly 15% of Americans do not take in these amounts (up from 5% in the 1970s).

We spoke with Carol S. Johnston, PhD, RD, professor in the department of nutrition at Arizona State University East in Mesa, Arizona. She attributes much of this problem to the processing of our food supply.

A case in point: Orange juice. OJ is the most commonly consumed vitamin C–rich food in the US, says Dr. Johnston. Beginning in the late 1980s, the industry increased production of refrigerated OJ and reduced production of

133

frozen concentrate. This switch reduced the vitamin C content of the juice by 40% to 50%. (Freezing preserves the vitamin C molecule much better than refrigeration temperatures.)

THE CONSEQUENCES OF VITAMIN C DEFICIENCY

Vitamin C is probably the most studied of all vitamins. According to Dr. Johnston, a deficiency of vitamin C can lead to scurvy symptoms, such as fatigue...limping, caused by muscle soreness...bleeding gums...and swollen extremities. To actually have overt symptoms of scurvy (such as an inability to walk normally) is unlikely, but the early signs of scurvy (general fatigue and poor exercise performance) are common in individuals with "biochemical" scurvy. You just feel kind of rotten, says Dr. Johnston. Vitamin C deficiency is diagnosed with a blood test.

Why such a big impact from just one vitamin? Dr. Johnston explains that vitamin C is needed to burn fat—the main fuel for exercising and daily living. In vitamin C deficiency, the inability to oxidize fat causes immense feelings of malaise and fatigue.

In addition, vitamin C is required for the synthesis of collagen, the connective tissue protein comprising 30% of body protein and essential to the structure of skin, gums, arterial walls, bones, ligaments and tendons. The absence of vitamin C from the diet leads to uncontrolled bleeding, joints that are painful and the inability of wounds to heal.

GOOD SOURCES OF VITAMIN C

With year-round fresh fruits and vegetables in abundance, it is easier than ever to get the recommended 75 to 90 mg of vitamin C each day. You just have to ignore the high-protein/low-carb craze in favor of healthy living.

Among her recommendations...

•**An eight-ounce glass of orange juice** contains approximately 50 to 90 mg of vitamin C, depending on whether it is packaged in a carton or made from frozen concentrate, respectively.

•**Eat five servings a day of a variety of fruits and vegetables.** Those highest in vitamin C include oranges, orange juice, potatoes, broccoli, cabbage, grapefruit, cantaloupe, strawberries, tomatoes and yellow and red peppers.

•**A daily multivitamin is a good idea** to ensure meeting the recommended daily intake for vitamin C as well as other nutrients that may be limited in poorly planned diets.

Some experts believe that vitamin C is probably the most important of all the vitamins. And many experts believe that the RDA for C should be much higher. Because scurvy is not on the current diagnostic radar, it's easy to mistake the symptoms, such as fatigue and exercise intolerance, for other disorders. First step, make sure your diet is in order.

Reduce the Risk Of Alzheimer's With Vitamins

William Thies, PhD, chief medical and scientific officer, Alzheimer's Association, Chicago. *www.alz.org.*

Until recently, it seemed that there wasn't really anything you could do to prevent Alzheimer's disease (AD) if you were fated to get it. Recent research is beginning to change that assumption, however. The latest studies are now pointing to relatively simple lifestyle changes you can make to protect yourself from the "unavoidable."

DYNAMIC DUO

One of the more recent of these studies, published in the *Archives of Neurology*, looks at the effect that taking vitamins C and E, in combination, might have on developing Alzheimer's. Researchers working at the Johns Hopkins University Bloomberg School of Public Health collected and assessed information about vitamin usage from 4,740 residents of Cache County, Utah, age 65 and over, from 1995 to 1997 and from 1998 to 2000.

Lead researcher Peter P. Zandi, PhD, says that the findings suggest, though can't prove, that vitamins E and C—when taken together—may offer protection against AD. Study participants who took individual E and C supplements in combination, with or without an additional multivitamin, had a 78% lower incidence of AD going into the study. About 64% lowered their own odds of developing it in the three-year follow-up period. The study also found that taking just E or just C alone or only a multivitamin or vitamin B-complex supplement did not offer a protective effect.

Dr. Zandi explains that the biological reason why E and C work so well in combination may be that E is a fat-soluble vitamin and C is water soluble. E remains in the body's fat tissue for some time, and its presence may "recharge" the ordinarily shorter-acting antioxidants of C so that they continue to function longer.

CAUTIOUS OPTIMISM

We talked with William Thies, PhD, the chief medical and scientific officer at the Alzheimer's Association in Chicago, about his response to the study. Dr. Thies is enthusiastic about the research but cautions that this study was not a classic double-blind one with a control group taking a placebo. Even so, he still feels that the data are promising.

Important: Vitamin E in particular may act as a blood thinner and be incompatible with some types of bleeding disorders or anticoagulant therapy. It may also be toxic in large doses. Before taking supplements, discuss these vitamins with your physician, especially if you are taking other mediations.

Are You Missing This Energy Booster?

Richard A. Anderson, PhD, director of the molecular and cellular pharmacology program at the University of Wisconsin–Madison.

Andrew L. Rubman, ND, director, Southbury Clinic for Traditional Medicines, Southbury, Connecticut.

If, like most people, you've been known to indulge in muffins, doughnuts and pasta and skimp on vegetables, you are probably running low on *chromium*, a trace mineral that helps the body manage carbohydrates and keep blood sugar levels in check. Apparently, 80% of us don't get our daily dose, which not only piles on the pounds and leaves us feeling sluggish, but also puts us at risk for insulin resistance, diabetes, high cholesterol, obesity and heart disease.

The main culprit? Our high-sugar, highly processed diets—they provide only small amounts of chromium.

Even worse: They can sap what stores we do have. "When you eat pastries, sodas or any sort of refined goods, your insulin goes up, the chromium in your body gets mobilized to help process it, and once it's mobilized, it gets lost in the urine," explains professor of pharmacology at the University of Wisconsin–Madison Richard A. Anderson, PhD. "You can eat a bad diet for a while with no problem, but after 20 or so years, you'll probably develop some degree of glucose intolerance, high blood sugar, high cholesterol, possibly obesity and any of the diseases that go along with that, including diabetes."

Unfortunately, because the symptoms of chromium deficiency are common to many ailments, it's tough to know whether a low supply of the mineral is to blame. The good news? It's virtually impossible to get too much. "Good chromium intake is like insurance because you never know when you'll need it," Dr. Anderson says. "If you improve your chromium supply, you may be able to improve your overall health."

Some surefire ways to stock up on this important, disease-fighting mineral…

• **Curb your simple carbs.** Cut back on high-sugar and refined foods—which include bread, pasta, bagels, crackers, white rice, cookies, candy and soda. They use up your body's supply of chromium and don't replenish it.

• **Have some beer and nuts.** Food is still the best and safest source of chromium. When possible, choose whole grains, ready-to-eat bran cereals, potatoes, seafood, green beans, green peppers, broccoli, spinach, prunes, apples, bananas, nuts, peanut butter and even beer. (Of course, don't try to get most of your chromium from beer, for obvious reasons.)

• **Pop a pill.** The recommended daily intake for chromium is 120 micrograms (mcg), however our medical expert, Andrew L. Rubman, ND, says we need much more to compensate for our poor diets. He says that most people would do well to take a supplement containing 200 mcg twice a day. Consult with your doctor.

Chromium Cuts Carb Cravings

John P. Docherty, MD, president and CEO, Comprehensive NeuroScience, Inc., White Plains, New York, and adjunct professor of psychiatry, Weill Medical College of Cornell University, New York City.

There is an interesting and often undiscussed phenomenon among depressed people—they eat a lot of carbohydrates. One theory is that it's the endorphins that are released by the consumption of carbohydrates that help people who are struggling with depression feel better.

However, eating carbohydrates sets up a different cycle of problems related to blood sugar swings. The answer might lie in your chromium levels. This mineral helps insulin work efficiently in the body. Now, a study suggests that the mineral, in the form of *chromium picolinate*, helps to control carbohydrate cravings in certain people who suffer from depression.

The research was sponsored by Nutrition 21, Inc., marketer of Chromax, a chromium picolinate product, but the lessons may apply to all chromium picolinate products. Findings were presented at the National Institute of Mental Health's annual new clinical drug evaluation unit conference.

ABOUT THE STUDY

According to lead researcher John P. Docherty, MD, the president and CEO of Comprehensive NeuroScience, Inc., in White Plains, New York, as well as adjunct professor of psychiatry at Weill Medical College of Cornell University, in New York City, researchers for the small double-blind, placebo-controlled clinical trial discovered that daily supplementation with Chromax brought about significant improvement in people who were both depressed and had carbohydrate cravings, as compared with a placebo.

Two-thirds of these participants were given supplements of chromium picolinate for eight weeks, and one-third received a placebo. Those with the highest levels of carbohydrate cravings experienced the greatest benefit from chromium supplementation. Carb cravings diminished, as did rejection sensitivity, which is an emotional vulnerability common in this type of depression. There were no significant drug-related side effects reported.

THE INSULIN CONNECTION

Many studies note that chromium supplementation can improve diabetes symptoms and the function of insulin and blood sugar. Dr. Docherty observes that there is a strong connection between depression and diabetes. He reported to us that diabetes predicts the onset of depression, and depression predicts the onset of diabetes. Depression is two times as common in diabetics than in the general population.

Chromium's role in insulin regulation may be the biological link between diabetes, carbohydrate cravings and atypical depression. Atypical depression is a common, but frequently undiagnosed, disorder that affects as many as one-third of depressed patients. It is characterized by carbohydrate cravings, weight gain and unexplained fatigue. If a person consumes excessive carbohydrates, more pressure is brought to bear on insulin regulation, and he/she faces a greater risk of diabetes. In theory, speculates Dr. Docherty, giving chromium to people who suffer from depression and related carbohydrate cravings may prevent them from developing diabetes.

It is important to note that while this study used Chromax, there are many forms of supplemental chromium picolinate that may provide similar results.

Further study is necessary to see whether this proves to be the case.

People who take prescription medication, such as antidepressants, should consult their physicians about any and all dietary supplements before taking them.

info To learn more, visit the Web site of Nutrition 21, Inc., *www.nutrition21.com.*

Best Way to Get Vitamin D

Laurie Tansman, MS, RD, clinical nutritionist, Mount Sinai Medical Center, New York City.

There's been a lot of talk about the virtues of vitamin D, including a recent study showing a possible link between it and the prevention of multiple sclerosis (MS).

Our bodies need vitamin D because it allows calcium to be absorbed into our tissues. Without the proper amount, osteoporosis will become a much bigger possibility, especially for older women. In children, vitamin D deficiency can produce rickets, a painful condition that causes bone deformity and even death.

That said, supplemental vitamin D in excess can be toxic. What is the optimal level of vitamin D and the best way to get it?

A LITTLE GOES A LONG WAY

Many people can get all the vitamin D they require just from being outdoors. Your body will produce its own vitamin D if you get enough sunshine. The National Institutes of Health recommends exposure to the sun for 10 to 15 minutes, three times weekly. Sunscreen that has a protection factor of more than eight does block vitamin D absorption, but not totally.

The US Food and Drug Administration's recommended allowance is 5 micrograms (mcg), or 200 international units (IU), daily for people under age 50...10 mcg (400 IU) daily for people ages 50 to 70...and 15 mcg (600 IU) daily for those over age 70.

However, if you are vitamin D deficient and taking supplements, it is important to proceed only under the guidance of a trained medical practitioner because excess amounts of vitamin D can cause high blood pressure, premature hardening of the arteries and kidney failure.

Bones may weaken and a calcium buildup in muscle and other soft tissue may occur. The Institute of Medicine considers the tolerable upper intake level (UL) for infants up to 12 months of age to be 25 mcg (1,000 IU) and 50 mcg (2,000 IU) for children, adults and pregnant and lactating women.

A daily intake above the UL increases the risk of adverse health effects and is not advised.

Eating a diet that contains a moderate amount of fortified dairy and breakfast cereals does not typically cause hypervitaminosis D—an excessive intake of vitamin D that can cause deposits of calcium in the kidney—because the body will regulate its own production of vitamin D in response to the amount consumed. Fish and oysters are also good sources of vitamin D.

TAKE SUPPLEMENTS CAUTIOUSLY

Those who take lots of calcium supplements that contain vitamin D may be at risk for excess vitamin D intake, according to Laurie Tansman, MS, RD, a clinical nutritionist at Mount Sinai Medical Center in New York City. Read the label of the calcium supplement bottle carefully to see if vitamin D is also present and be sure not to take more than the recommended daily dosage.

Bottom line: Our bodies need—and generally get—vitamin D every day. Take a brief 10- to 15-minute walk outside in the early morning. You'll clear your mind for the day, get your vitamin D and avoid the dangers of sunburn that you might get at midday.

Unsafe Supplements— Bitter Pills To Swallow

Andrew L. Rubman, ND, director, Southbury Clinic for Traditional Medicines, Southbury, Connecticut.

A list of the so-called "dirty dozen" supplements on the market—those that are most likely to lead to liver damage, heart attack, cancer and even death—was released by *Consumer Reports*. It seems to us that, in a sincere effort to protect consumers, magazine articles like these sometimes throw out the baby with the bathwater.

Are these supplements really that bad? To get the lowdown on them, we spoke with our medical expert, Andrew L. Rubman, ND.

FROM A NATUROPATHIC DOCTOR'S POINT OF VIEW

Dr. Rubman outlined two general observations below…

•**Media outlets** need to be aware that medical doctors are not good sources of information about botanicals since, generally speaking, they have not been trained in this area. A better strategy would be for the media to consult with medically trained naturopathic doctors (NDs), or other health-care professionals who have been educated in these areas.

•**Although supplements can be safe and effective,** many should not be sold over the counter (OTC), says Dr. Rubman. He points out that three out of four drugs are made from manipulated derivatives of botanicals. It follows then that most botanicals also work in a drug-like fashion. Consumers should not make the false assumption that just because herbs are "natural," they have no side effects or interactions and can be taken on a casual basis. What is the best way to safely and effectively take an herbal supplement?

The answer: Under the guidance of an expert, such as a medically trained ND.

ABOUT THE "DIRTY DOZEN"

Supplements to watch out for…

•**Androstenedione**—better known simply as "andro"—is sometimes recommended to address problems with skewed estrogen or testosterone levels. Andro is a member of a group of steroidal hormones that includes both estrogen and testosterone, which are available by prescription only. Like estrogen and progesterone, androstenedione can have serious side effects, such as increased cancer risk and a decrease in HDL (good) cholesterol. However, this precursor of testosterone is available on an OTC basis rather than by prescription. This has made androstenedione subject to abuse, says Dr. Rubman. He believes that more consistent governmental regulation of all steroidal hormones would be beneficial.

•**Aristolochic acid** is the only supplement described by *Consumer Reports* as "definitely hazardous." Dr. Rubman agrees. This supplement is a carcinogen and has, in the past, been associated with organ failure.

•**Chaparral** (a natural antibiotic and antioxidant), *germander* (a remedy for gout and a tonic for fevers) and *pennyroyal* (a natural stimulant) are difficult to use and should not be sold on an OTC basis, says Dr. Rubman. They should only be prescribed by a medically trained ND, he believes.

•**Glandular extracts.** *Consumer Reports* advises against the use of organ or glandular extracts because of the risk for mad cow disease. Dr. Rubman believes that this risk is small, but that people should always be cautious about using the tissue of another animal.

•**Scullcap.** Small amounts of the tranquilizing herb scullcap are reputed to have a useful sedative effect. However, since large amounts can cause liver damage, this is another herb that should only be used under the close supervision of an expert, says Dr. Rubman.

•**Yohimbe** is a natural aphrodisiac and is used in a similar fashion to the pharmaceutical drug Viagra (which is prescribed for erectile dysfunction). It also has the same potential side effects as Viagra, including blood pressure changes, heartbeat irregularities and heart attack.

Dr. Rubman wonders: If yohimbe is condemned because it has the same potential side effects as Viagra, why not condemn Viagra at the same time? That said, take yohimbe only under a doctor's guidance.

•**Bitter orange** is a stimulant that has suddenly attracted attention now that ephedra is off the market. *Consumer Reports* warns that it can be associated with such problems as high blood pressure and heart arrhythmias. Dr. Rubman notes that this association is much less clear with bitter orange than with ephedra.

•**Comfrey** has been prized since ancient times for its ability to heal wounds. This botanical contains *allantoin*, a chemical agent that promotes cell proliferation and is an active ingredient in a number of OTC and prescription skin medications. Many NDs believe that the controversy surrounding comfrey (side effects that include abnormal liver function and damage) has been overstated. Dr. Rubman has found that it is possible to design a comfrey extract that is safe, effective and does not cause liver damage. However, this type of extract is not readily available on a commercial basis, and patients would have to get it through their health-care provider.

•**Kava.** The traditional preparation of kava—a calming, antianxiety agent—is very different from the commercial preparations currently available, and far safer, says Dr. Rubman. He explains that traditionally, kava was soaked and heated gently. However, for economic reasons, herbal manufacturers now prepare kava remedies at high temperatures, and this causes the release of harmful constituents that do not appear in traditional remedies and that have been associated with abnormal liver function and damage.

•**Lobelia,** a time-honored lung tonic, was used by herbalists to treat tuberculosis outbreaks in the 19th century. When taken under the proper guidance of an ND, Dr. Rubman says that lobelia can be safely used to counter nicotine addiction.

The bottom line? Like drugs, dietary supplements can have extremely beneficial effects as well as side effects that range from unpleasant to unsafe. If you elect to take a botanical or other supplement—whether in place of or in addition to conventional medications—your best bet is to consult an experienced and knowledgeable practioner.

info You can find a naturopathic doctor in your area at *www.naturopathic.org.*

Choosing Herbs That Really Help

Francis Brinker, ND, clinical assistant professor, Program in Integrative Medicine, University of Arizona, and author of *Complex Herbs—Complete Medicines.* Eclectic Medical Publications.

Andrew L. Rubman, ND, director, Southbury Clinic for Traditional Medicines, Southbury, Connecticut.

Feeling down in the dumps? Perhaps you are considering ginseng. Or maybe St. John's wort can help you to cope. But what type of ginseng? And which formulation

of St. John's wort? How do you sort through the hundreds of products lining store shelves to locate the quality herbal medications you want and deserve? We spoke with Francis Brinker, ND, a clinical assistant professor with the Program in Integrative Medicine at the University of Arizona, regarding the critical factors to consider when purchasing herbal remedies.

START WITH HIGH-QUALITY HERBS

Not surprisingly, the best herbal remedies begin with the freshest, highest-quality herbs harvested at their peak. Dr. Brinker prefers organic herbs, not only because there are fewer concerns about toxic residues, but because they are grown in nutrient-rich soil, they absorb trace minerals from it and therefore provide greater healing benefits. Although the manufacturers are not legally required to list how herbs are grown, it is in their economic self-interest to note when remedies are made from organic or wild-crafted herbs (those picked in their natural habitats)—so look for this information on labels.

Excellent option: Remedies made from wild-crafted herbs. Of course, with wild-crafted herbs, there are ecological matters to consider. For example, because many plant communities in the wild are endangered, some herbalists recommend harvesting only cultivated sources of certain species, such as goldenseal.

Avoid: Dr. Brinker's least-favorite remedies are those made from chemically cultivated herbs. He warns that chemical pesticides, fungicides and fertilizers may wind up dispersed in the environment and in the herbal remedy you take.

SOME HERBAL MANUFACTURERS ARE MORE RELIABLE THAN OTHERS

Unfortunately, as herbal remedies continue to grow in popularity, a few unscrupulous manufacturers inevitably have paid more attention to profit margins than to product quality. In recent years, the news has been full of stories about adulterated products and herbal medications that don't contain the amounts of active ingredients stated on their labels.

Problems are common when it comes to the more popular herbs, says Dr. Brinker, for this is where the greatest profits lie. He looks forward to new government guidelines that would closely regulate herbal medications. The

US Food and Drug Administration (FDA) is in the process of improving regulations to ensure proper labeling and manufacture. Hopefully, these regulations will be in place within the next few years.

SMALLER IS BETTER

Dr. Brinker generally prefers products made by smaller companies run by naturopaths or herbalists rather than those made by giant pharmaceutical companies, which have now branched out from manufacturing drugs and vitamins to herbs as well. If you are uncertain which products might be preferable, consult with a local herbalist or naturopathic doctor.

Pharmaceutical companies manufacture herbal products through standardization. The resulting highly processed products end up more like medical drugs than whole herbs, observes Dr. Brinker. These standardized herbal "fractions" can be effective when limited to their established uses and are also usually safer than drugs. However, Dr. Brinker explains, sometimes the chemical to which they are standardized is not even appropriate—that is, it does not turn out to be one of the necessary active constituents.

DIFFERENT FORMULATIONS, DIFFERENT EFFECTS

A common mistake is assuming that different formulations of an herb have the same effect. As an example, Dr. Brinker cites the standardized extract of the entire aerial herb (the aboveground part) of St. John's wort. For years, this medication was standardized to *hypericin*, an active constituent that helps fight viruses but has very little impact on depression—the primary illness for which it is taken. To treat depression, you are much better off with a St. John's wort preparation made from the flowering tops of the herb, which are high in flavonoids and the major antidepressant active component hyperforin. And the oil extract should be used to treat sprains and bruises.

Whole herbs and traditional extracts made from whole herbs provide the most support for your overall health and well-being, stresses Dr. Brinker. Unlike the conventional drugs and standardized botanical preparations, whole herbs are not used simply to correct a pathological imbalance, but in a broader manner to create or maintain physiological balance. Using the whole herb is also less likely to cause adverse effects associated with stronger concentrations.

COST, CONVENIENCE AND COMPLIANCE: YOUR CHOICE

There are many considerations to take into account when purchasing and using an herbal medication. Organic herbs are best…but they are almost always more expensive. It may be preferable to prepare and sip a variety of healing herbal teas at least once each day…but it's simpler to take a capsule. On a practical level, if your child is coming down with a cold, it's easier to give him/her echinacea twice a day than six times a day…even though the smaller, more frequent doses are known to be more effective in treating the early stages of a cold.

The bottom line? To make sure that you are getting a top-quality herbal medication, do your homework, don't be afraid to ask questions in the herb store and buy products produced by reliable herbal manufacturers. Our medical expert, Andrew L. Rubman, ND, recommends several reputable companies, including the Eclectic Institute (*www.eclecticherb.com*)…Gaia Garden (*www.gaiagarden.com*)…and Herb Pharm (*www.herb-pharm.com*).

Armed with the best information available, and taking into account your own values, needs and pocketbook, you can make an informed decision about what is best for you and your family.

Delicious and Healthy Herbs You Can Grow

Leslie Gardner, MH, CSHS, instructor, herbology, California School of Herbal Studies, Forestville, California, and director, Sonoma County Herb Exchange, Sebastopol, California.

T his year, when it's time to plant your garden, why not consider including some herbs that might benefit your health, as well as add to the tastiness of your meals?

We consulted Leslie Gardner, a master herbalist, member of the American Herbalists Guild and director of the Sonoma County Herb

Exchange in Sebastopol, California, who came up with a list of herbs that fit the bill. None of them will replace medications and supplements, she says, but adding them to your recipes can enhance your general health.

Remember that even the most innocuous of herbs can impact the function of medication and supplements and that these helpful plants are best used intermittently. All of Gardner's recommendations are perennials except the fragrant basil plant. *At the top of her list...*

•**Peppermint.** Gardner says that this herb is excellent for promoting blood circulation or to take when you're not feeling well. You can either brew the leaves as a tea or use them as a beverage garnish. Even the smell stimulates taste buds and, of course, it is a wonderful digestive aid—one reason after-dinner mints are so popular. It's best to grow all mint plants, including peppermint, in their own containers because otherwise they will gradually take over the garden. When in the wild, peppermint grows in boggy wet areas. It doesn't need too much sun, but it does need plenty of water.

•**Basil.** Basil plants are annuals, but having to replant every year is worth it. Gardner says that the Greeks held basil in such high esteem that only the aristocracy was allowed to grow it and that its distinctive scent was associated with healing spirits. It is well known as a stomachic (meaning good for the stomach), she says, so make plenty of fresh pesto and add the leaves to your salads and other sauces.

•**Rosemary.** This plant has a long tradition as a healing herb. It is, says Gardner, quite medicinal and a powerful antioxidant as well as mood elevator. Brew it in a tea to pick up your spirits. Or use rosemary in oven-roasted potatoes. The fragrant pinelike needles of the rosemary bush will also increase circulation in the periphery of the body—the hands, feet and the brain. As Shakespeare wrote, "There's rosemary for remembrance."

•**Thyme and oregano.** Both of these herbs have antiviral and ample antioxidant properties and are digestive aids. They are also *carminative*, meaning that they help relieve flatulence. Thyme has the additional benefit of helping control the growth of yeast in the body. Use thyme

to flavor most meats, vegetables and sauces. It is particularly good in combination with rosemary and sage.

•**Garden sage.** Its botanical name is *salvia officinalis*—salvia means to heal and officinalis showed that it was officially sanctioned for use in doctors' offices. Sage is an antiseptic and an antifungal. It helps dry up secretions in the body, so if you are suffering from a cold, it might ease that stuffy nose. In the old days, sage was used to increase circulation and to help make people wise. Today it is best known for its tonic benefits.

•**Common fennel.** Although the word "fennel" might bring to mind the anise-flavored bulb popular in many Italian dishes, Gardner explains that the bulb is Florence fennel. Common fennel, she says, is a weed and has many seeds. Its seeds sweeten the breath, and are a carminative and a digestive aid. A brew of fennel tea is an effective way to increase mothers' milk. Common fennel seed is often offered in Indian restaurants, sometimes sugared and sometimes plain for its own sweet taste.

HOW TO GROW THEM

All of the plants listed here, except peppermint, grow in Mediterranean climates—lots of sun and not a lot of water. In fact, Gardner says most (except basil) do well in drought conditions, so let them dry out thoroughly before you water, and then give them a good dousing. Basil requires more frequent and less enthusiastic watering, however. Only peppermint and basil need fertilizing (organic), says Gardner, and none of them like rich soil, such as potting soils. She adds that they seem to prefer conditions that would stress many other plants. As a rule, herbs grow better in the ground than they do in containers, but if you have only containers available to you, be sure to use deep ones. The short root space of a window box or small pots will not produce large plants.

It's easiest to start your herb garden with flats of small plants available at the nursery rather than from seed. Wait until the last frost (admittedly a hard call) to put them in the ground. You can snip from your herb plants throughout the growing season. When the colder weather returns, cut your fennel, oregano and peppermint back to the ground, says Gardner. For the

141

bushy rosemary, sage and thyme plants, she recommends cutting them to the place where they begin to get woody, just where you can see a bit of green left. Your herbs will greet the return of many springs to come.

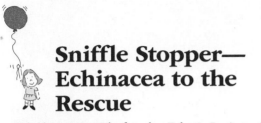

Sniffle Stopper— Echinacea to the Rescue

Ed Alstat, ND, RPh, founder, Eclectic Institute, Sandy, Oregon.

Carlo Calabrese, ND, MPH, research professor, National College of Naturopathic Medicine, and senior investigator at the Helfgott Research Institute, both in Portland, Oregon. He is also assistant clinical professor, Oregon Health & Science University, Portland.

Andrew L. Rubman, ND, director, Southbury Clinic for Traditional Medicines, Southbury, Connecticut.

In our data-driven world, we have become trained to accept as fact the results of scientific studies. That said, the media has a magical way of twisting the truth in order to create the most drama.

Example: The highly publicized research on *echinacea purpurea* and its ineffectiveness in treating upper respiratory illness in children (financed by the National Center for Complementary and Alternative Medicine, part of the National Institutes of Health). If we take the news at face value, we should all be throwing away our bottles of echinacea. However, there are several types of echinacea—they vary based on the material used to manufacture it—and the study tested only one type.

WHAT KIND WAS USED?

One of the researchers of a prior study conducted at Bastyr University, Carlo Calabrese, ND, MPH, and research professor at the National College of Naturopathic Medicine, explained that the echinacea used in the study was a type manufactured by Madaus Murdock Schwabe, better known as Nature's Way, that is "widely distributed internationally." However, the Madaus Murdock Schwabe product is made from the whole plant, which is generally thought by some to be less effective than versions developed from the root only. Additionally, this product is a glycerin-sweetened and spray-dried reconstituted powder, making it quite different from other more potent forms of echinacea.

NO TWO PRODUCTS ARE ALIKE

One authority on echinacea, Ed Alstat, ND, RPh, founder of Eclectic Institute, a manufacturer of organic botanical products, says that the published interpretation of the results is misleading. "There are easily more than 500 various forms of echinacea products on the market. Since many forms of processing are involved with various manufacturers, you can assume that no two products are the same," explains Dr. Alstat. "The press greatly errs when it assumes that every form of echinacea, whether fresh or dried, extracted with one or 100 chemicals, is the same." Comparing the material used for this study with a proper traditional extract of a potent echinacea cultivar is like comparing grapes to raisins, adds Dr. Alstat. Even the Bastyr researchers concluded that further studies were necessary, but using different echinacea formulations.

THE NEED FOR CONSISTENCY

The real lesson of the study is the reaffirmation of the critical need for creating standards in the supplement and herbal community. The alternative medicine community has long been criticized for a lack of manufacturing standards and the potential dangers that this creates. There are vast differences within botanical species and their extractions. The Bastyr study makes this fact very clear.

Self-defense: Be aware that all herbal offerings at health-food stores are not created equal. Talk to a naturopathic physician or trained herbologist about the best forms to take.

As for echinacea and colds, our medical expert, Andrew L. Rubman, ND, and Dr. Alstat agree. When it's taken at the onset of cold symptoms, echinacea has been proven time and again to reduce the impact of the illness. Echinacea has few side effects (a few people experience stomach upset of allergies). Take one dose—two 300-milligram tablets of dried root or one teaspoon (5 milliliters) of echinacea root tincture—three times every day. The fresh freeze-dried root in capsule form is the strongest and most complex reliable form.

Good News on Ginkgo Biloba

Ray Sahelian, MD, author of *Mind Boosters: A Guide to Natural Supplements That Enhance Your Mind, Memory, and Mood*. Griffin. *www.raysahelian.com*.

With the aging baby-boomer population, it is not surprising that there is endless reporting on aging and the memory problems it brings. But do any of us need a study to tell us that? Misplaced keys, forgotten names, words that suddenly slip from recall are daily reminders—and they make the concept of a memory booster mighty attractive. Perhaps it is time to review the herbal supplement ginkgo biloba again. It is supposedly great for the brain…and, in particular, one's memory.

To get up-to-date information on the herb, we called Ray Sahelian, MD, who specializes in natural supplements and is author of *Mind Boosters: A Guide to Natural Supplements That Enhance Your Mind, Memory, and Mood*. He reports that for years, Europeans have been prescribing ginkgo extracts to treat, among other things, age-related cognitive decline.

NOT FOR EVERYONE

Dr. Sahelian reports that about half of his patients who start taking ginkgo to sharpen their memory see improvement—the other half do not. He suggests that people give ginkgo a four-week trial. That amount of time, he says, will let you know if it is effective for you. Take ginkgo twice a day, in the morning and at lunch, in 40- to 60-milligram doses. Avoid taking it later in the day because it may increase alertness—not a good idea when you are trying to sleep.

THINNING BLOOD

Although ginkgo has few known side effects, it is a blood thinner. Dr. Sahelian says that anyone who is on medication for blood-thinning purposes, including aspirin, probably shouldn't take ginkgo. At the very least, he says, you *must*

discuss ginkgo with your doctor before taking it and notify doctors or dentists before undergoing any procedure that might cause bleeding. It should be discontinued at least 48 hours prior to a planned surgery.

This is also true for people who regularly take *ibuprofen* or other over-the-counter painkillers for arthritis or any other conditions. These painkillers are also blood thinners, as is vitamin E. And taking too many blood thinners can trigger internal bleeding and failure to clot when you need it. Use caution.

FOOD FOR THOUGHT

One of the reasons ginkgo seems to help memory, says Dr. Sahelian, is that some of its most active ingredients are flavonoids, the same antioxidant substances that are found in fruits and vegetables.

He explains that flavonoids help prevent "clumping" of red blood cells and platelets, thus clearing the way for more oxygen to reach the neurons in the brain.

If flavonoids are found in fruits and vegetables, is it possible that we can help our memory through food? Some experts believe that it can indeed help, but that you would have to consume one gram or more of food flavonoids a day for them to be effective. Information on this is somewhat limited because there are few research studies on the matter. Even so, experts say that eating six servings of fully ripe fruits and vegetables a day should probably supply the minimum of flavonoids that might help us remember where we put our keys.

Little-Known Herb Is a Wonder

Andrew L. Rubman, ND, director, Southbury Clinic for Traditional Medicines, Southbury, Connecticut.

The herb *glucomannan* is effective in treating the seemingly unrelated conditions of constipation, high cholesterol, hepatitis, headache and early stages of colitis. Are you familiar with it?

WHAT'S THAT?

Unlike some of the higher-profile herbs that we have come to know, such as ginseng or the wildly popular echinacea, glucomannan is relatively unknown to most Americans. But it is worth learning about, because glucomannan is a multitasking powerhouse with a wide range of uses.

GETTING TO KNOW GLUCOMANNAN

Glucomannan is a natural dietary fiber derived from the *konnyaku root*, a common plant found in Japan and other parts of Asia. In Japan, konnyaku root has been a staple of the traditional Japanese diet for more than 2,000 years, and is available in all supermarkets in Japan. Typically, konnyaku root is consumed as a fiber-rich vegetable about once a week by most people in that country. It is sold in blocks and can be cooked in stir-frys, or it may be ground into flour and made into noodles.

Our medical expert, Andrew L. Rubman, ND, prescribes glucomannan for a variety of conditions, ranging from constipation to headaches. He explains that glucomannan helps the body in one of its most necessary and often underrated functions—waste elimination.

This does not simply mean maintaining daily bowel movements, but, more important, helping the liver act as the end organ of excretion, as well. More often than not in our culture, due to the widespread consumption of prescription drugs and poor lifestyle choices, the gastrointestinal system becomes overburdened. Glucomannan helps eliminate the toxins throughout the body, particularly those that become unstable in the colon, which is why it helps even headaches. Glucomannan appears to be safe and free of side effects for most people.

THE MANY USES OF GLUCOMANNAN

Dr. Rubman has prescribed glucomannan for a wide range of ailments, including…

•**Hepatitis.** Glucomannan is extremely effective for problems that, directly or indirectly, involve the liver, or where the liver is part of the mechanism that needs to be treated, says Dr. Rubman. It helps the liver lessen the ill effects of the disease.

•**Constipation.** As a natural fiber, glucomannan is good for all types of bowel irregularity, including irritable bowel syndrome and the beginnings of colitis.

•**High cholesterol.** Dr. Rubman believes that as a dietary staple in Japan, konnyaku root might be one of the factors resulting in the typically low serum cholesterol levels (average 155 to 160) of the Japanese population.

•**Headaches.** A primary cause of headache is irregular digestion in the large intestine, says Dr. Rubman.

•**Polypharmacy.** Glucomannan helps decrease side effects of taking multiple drugs simultaneously, while potentially increasing the efficacy of drugs, says Dr. Rubman.

Note: It is important to take glucomannan separately from your medications so that it does not conflict with them.

Because competent gastrointestinal function is crucial to overall health, Dr. Rubman believes that most people would benefit from daily glucomannan supplement. He recommends taking one capsule with 10 ounces of water about 20 minutes to one-half hour before the largest meal of the day. (Glucomannan is available at health-food stores.)

Dr. Rubman advises that patients consult a naturopathic doctor to determine dosages for specific conditions. Be sure to advise your general practitioner if you take glucomannan, or any herb, regularly.

Herb Experts Recommend Milk Thistle

Mark Blumenthal, founder and executive director, American Botanical Council, Austin, Texas, and senior editor, *The ABC Clinical Guide to Herbs*. American Botanical Council.

James A. Duke, PhD, former chief, USDA Plant Laboratory, and author of *Dr. Duke's Essential Herbs: 13 Vital Herbs You Need to Disease-Proof Your Body, Boost Your Energy & Lengthen Your Life*. Rodale.

Milk thistle has been a staple in European medicine for more than 2,000 years to treat liver diseases, due to its ability to both protect the liver from damage and help stimulate production of new liver cells. To learn more about one of the classic "great herbs," we spoke with Mark Blumenthal, the founder and executive director of the American Botanical Council, and James A. Duke, PhD, author of *Dr. Duke's Essential Herbs*.

Here's a rundown on milk thistle's many liver-related uses...

•**In alcoholic liver diseases.** Milk thistle helps the liver regenerate and detoxify, explains Blumenthal, by stimulating RNA (a companion to DNA) synthesis in the liver and by coating the liver cells so that they are less susceptible to insult from foreign compounds.

•**In hepatitis.** Milk thistle is so effective in treating hepatitis that Dr. Duke says he would take it before he would take *interferon* for the disease. Blumenthal reports that he has taken milk thistle instead of getting a preventive hepatitis A shot before a trip to Africa.

Result: No hepatitis, although Blumenthal admits that preventive effects are difficult, if not impossible, to prove.

•**As an antioxidant.** Milk thistle is now a recognized antioxidant. According to Dr. Duke, *silymarin* (one of the active compounds in milk thistle) is 10 times more potent in antioxidative power than vitamin E.

•**In reducing hepatotoxic drug effects.** Milk thistle is of great benefit when taken with medications that are known to have toxic effects on the liver, such as Tylenol and some other over-the-counter (OTC) pain relievers. It helps the liver to process toxins produced by these drugs while not adversely influencing the medications' effectiveness.

•**Before and after drinking any alcohol.** Milk thistle is good to take before you drink alcohol as well as after, says Dr. Duke, because of its protective effect on the liver cells, and its regenerative activity.

Note: This should not, however, be an excuse to abuse alcohol.

Dosages: For all of the above conditions, patients are encouraged to seek out a health-care provider's assistance for milk thistle sources and dosage recommendations. The upper recommended dosage on the bottle (420 milligrams per day) is typical.

The only known and reported adverse side effect of milk thistle is that it may have a slight laxative effect. There are no known interactions with medications. Pregnant or nursing women may want to avoid it, however. As with all herbs, make sure your doctor is aware that you are taking milk thistle.

Olive Leaf Extract—Hype or Healthy?

David Winston, RH, registered herbalist and founding member of the American Herbalists Guild. He is coauthor of *Herbal Therapy & Supplements: A Scientific and Traditional Approach*. Lippincott.

There's always a lot of talk about what's hot and what's not in herbs. A certain buzz has surrounded olive leaf extract (*Olea europaea L.*), a plant remedy traditionally used for mild hypertension and currently touted for its abilities as a natural infection fighter. Sometimes, the buzz is just noise.

And so it is with olive leaf extract. According to David Winston, registered herbalist and founding member of the American Herbalists Guild, the hype about this herb's infection-fighting abilities is just marketing from self-interested supplement manufacturers. Winston has yet to see any convincing data in human or clinical studies that document its antiviral or antibacterial properties—though he acknowledges that it continues to have a role in helping with hypertension.

EVERYTHING BUT THE KITCHEN SINK

Curious, we looked up olive leaf extract on the Internet. *Sure enough, manufacturers claim that it may...*

•**Combat infections.**

•**Fight HIV, colds, flu, Epstein-Barr virus and more.**

•**Boost the immune system.**

•**Manage diabetes.**

•**Lower cholesterol.**

•**Lower blood pressure.**

According to Winston, the big problem with many dietary supplements is that manufacturers will typically make a wide variety of vague health promises about supplements with scant scientific evidence to back them up. As for the infection-fighting claims of olive leaf extract, he informed us that these are based on the extraction and testing of just one constituent—*oleuropein.*

Furthermore, there are plenty of herbs that possess well-documented infection-fighting abilities, such as garlic, sage, elderberry, thyme and honeysuckle—so there's no need to consider an unproven entry.

OLIVE LEAF EXTRACT
FOR MILD HYPERTENSION

According to Winston, olive leaf extract can be useful in its traditional role as a remedy for hypertension around the 140/95 level. It is commonly used in Europe for this purpose. Although olive leaf extract is a safe remedy, always inform your doctor about all dietary supplements that you take. Olive leaf extract may have a cumulative effect when taken with other blood pressure medication, causing blood pressure to fall *too* low.

Winston cautions that even mild high blood pressure can be a cause for concern, and you should not attempt to manage it yourself. See your medical doctor or naturopath for proper diagnosis and treatment.

9

How Safe Are Your Drugs?

Are Brand-Name Drugs Worth the Price?

There has been a lot of debate regarding ways to reduce prescription drug expenses. One method has been available in the US for years now—the use of generic versus brand-name drugs. Insurance companies claim that generics are just as effective as the brand-name versions. However, a recent study cautions that for some generic epilepsy drugs, this is not the case.

According to the Center for Drug Evaluation and Research (CDER) part of the US Food and Drug Administration (FDA), a generic drug is the same as a brand-name drug in dosage, safety, strength, how it is taken, quality, performance and intended use. It must meet certain criteria to be deemed "bioequivalent" to the brand-name drug.

However, Ilo E. Leppik, MD, clinical professor of pharmacy, adjunct professor of neurology at the University of Minnesota, and director of research at MINCEP, both in Minneapolis, warns

that this is an overly simplistic definition, and that the issues are not so black and white.

Case in point: The epilepsy drug *phenytoin* (Dilantin). When the state of Minnesota switched epilepsy patients on Medicaid from brand-name Dilantin to the generic version, patients experienced more seizures.

Although in most cases, less-expensive generic drugs are as safe and effective as their brand-name counterparts, Dr. Leppik believes that each generic substitution merits careful consideration by your physician.

GENERIC DRUGS: THE BASICS

New drugs are developed under patent protection. The patent protects the drug manufacturer's investment by giving the company the sole

---

Ilo E. Leppik, MD, clinical professor of pharmacy, and adjunct professor of neurology, University of Minnesota, and director of research at MINCEP, a national epilepsy center for children and adults, both in Minneapolis. Dr. Leppik is a past president of the American Epilepsy Society and a past chairman of the Professional Advisory Board of the Epilepsy Foundation of America.

right to market the drug while the patent is in effect. After the patent expires, other drug manufacturers can apply to the FDA to sell generic versions of the medicine. These are less costly to consumers (although Dr. Leppik points out that the price for generic drugs is not as discounted as in the past and the price gap is narrowing).

Even though the approval process for a generic drug is not as rigorous, the drug must still meet the same rigid standards as the original drug. *According to the FDA, it must...*

• **Contain the same active ingredients** (although inactive ingredients may vary).

• **Be identical in strength, dosage and the means of administration.**

• **Have the same use(s).**

• **Be bioequivalent.** It must act on the body with the same strength and similar bioavailablity as the same dosage of a given substance.

• **Meet the same requirements for identity, strength, purity and quality.**

• **Be manufactured under the same strict standards.**

THE DILANTIN SAGA

The FDA approved a generic form of Dilantin, namely *phenytoin*, in 1998. However, according to Dr. Leppik, Mylan Pharmaceuticals's testing did not meet the standards of clinical care on Dilantin testing protocol.

He explains that in the FDA research, generic phenytoin and brand-name Dilantin were bioequivalent when patients were fasting, but this does not accurately reflect how people live and take their medicines in the real world. Moreover, the study was done on volunteers not receiving phenytoin regularly, and they were given a single dose each—also conditions that are very different from what is seen in practice.

Generic phenytoin has been periodically substituted for Dilantin with extremely serious results. All epilepsy drugs have a very narrow therapeutic range, meaning that the dose at which the drug is effective and at which it becomes toxic are very close. Even a small dose or absorption change can have life-threatening implications for patients.

Dr. Leppik says the Dilantin saga unfolded like a detective story. It all started when formerly stable epilepsy patients suddenly began appearing at clinics and emergency rooms across Minnesota with unexpected seizures. Researchers knew that something was wrong, but they couldn't pinpoint the reason.

Dr. Leppik's team took a closer look at the eight patients at his clinic who had suddenly started having seizures. They examined their medical records from when they were taking Dilantin...when the state switched them to its generic equivalent without informing their physicians...and after Dr. Leppik and his colleagues switched them back to Dilantin.

Researchers discovered a 30% decrease of phenytoin in blood levels during the administration of the generic drug. It was this that brought on the increase in seizures, even though the prescribed dosages were the same.

Dr. Leppik contacted the Minnesota Department of Health and reported the situation. In response, the state changed the rule and put an end to automatic generic substitutions. However, he warns that the battle is not over—this type of switch has the potential to happen again at some point in a different state.

In the long run, this type of drug substitution is penny-wise and pound-foolish. Dr. Leppik notes that the cost savings from using generic phenytoin versus brand-name Dilantin for epilepsy is roughly just two cents per pill. When epilepsy goes uncontrolled and seizures result, this small savings is more than offset by the cost of emergency room visits and hospitalizations, not to mention accidents and injuries.

THE BOTTOM LINE

The story of Dilantin is a cautionary tale that demonstrates the importance of examining each medication individually. Naturally, you want the most effective drug at the best price, and it is a great idea to save money by using generics. But first discuss the possible health risks with your physician. If you decide to go with the generic version, make sure that your doctor approves.

Beware of Drug Bargains

Jack M. Rosenberg, PharmD, PhD, professor of pharmacy practice and pharmacology, International Drug Information Center, Long Island University, New York.

It is a painful reality in America—health care and prescription medications cost a bundle. And many Americans—especially seniors who take multiple medications—are tempted to buy cheap prescription medications in Canada or over the Internet. But are these drugs safe?

The answer depends upon the source of information. *Here's the background...*

THE OFFICIAL POINT OF VIEW

Under a law passed in 1987, it is generally illegal for anyone other than the manufacturer to import drugs into the US. The US Food and Drug Administration (FDA) warns that any imported medication may be outdated, contaminated, counterfeit or contain too much or too little of the active ingredient.

Not surprisingly, pharmaceutical companies agree with this official point of view. Ironically, however, the fact is that we already do import a huge quantity of drugs from other countries. While drug manufacturers publicly worry about the safety of the medications from abroad, they have quietly relocated many of their own factories to foreign countries to take advantage of cheaper labor costs.

The difference is that these plants are considered safe because they are inspected by the FDA.

PLAYING WITH FIRE

Although everyone agrees that what we want are safe drugs, problems arise because of the pharmaceutical industry's unbalanced pricing structure.

American consumers pay the world's highest prices for drugs, while price controls and shrewd bargaining compel manufacturers to sell the same drugs for far less money in foreign markets. This makes imported drugs a great bargain.

Unfortunately, when you buy imported drugs that have not been inspected by the FDA, you are playing with fire, says Dr. Jack M. Rosenberg,

PharmD, PhD, professor of pharmacy practice and pharmacology at the International Drug Information Center of Long Island University in New York. Ten percent of drugs worldwide are counterfeit, according to the World Health Organization. Without FDA inspection, there is usually no way to tell whether a drug is real or fake.

There is also no way to know how imported drugs have been stored. According to Dr. Rosenberg, in one sting operation, the FDA discovered that a Canadian supplier mistakenly shipped insulin, which requires refrigeration, at room temperature.

CONSUMERS SEEK A MORE ECONOMICAL ALTERNATIVE

Safe or not, legal or not, seniors in border states from Maine to Washington organize regular bus trips to Canada to purchase prescription medications. In only one trip, they collectively save thousands of dollars.

Moreover, American consumers tend to trust the safety of Canadian drugs, which are regulated much like the drugs in the US. (This is clearly not the case with all imported medications.)

In a trend that extends beyond individuals, several cities and states around the country have also expressed interest in buying drugs from abroad.

Dr. Rosenberg is sympathetic to seniors who are coping with the high cost of drugs but emphasizes that the answer is not to run to other countries.

However, if you are set on visiting a Canadian pharmacy, he recommends that you first check to see if it is accredited at *www.napra. org*, Canada's National Association of Pharmacy Regulatory Authorities.

EXERCISE CARE ON THE INTERNET

Another tempting alternative is shopping on the Internet.

Both domestic and imported drugs are available on-line. If you spend much time on the Web, chances are you are already bombarded with E-mail opportunities to buy prescription drugs.

On the Internet, it's "buyer beware." Although it's very tempting to buy a drug you're taking at a significant discount, you must be careful, advises Dr. Rosenberg.

Which sites are safe? *The FDA offers the following suggestions…*

●**Check with the National Association of Boards of Pharmacy** (*www.nabp.net*) or at the Verified Internet Pharmacy Practice Sites (VIPPS) (*vipps.nabp.net/verify.asp*) to determine whether the Web site is a licensed pharmacy in good standing.

●**Don't use sites that offer to prescribe a prescription drug for the first time** without verification that you have had a physical exam or that will sell a prescription drug without a prescription from a doctor.

●**Avoid sites that do not provide a US address and phone number** to contact if there is a problem.

●**Steer clear of foreign sites that advertise "new cures" or "amazing results"** and sites that claim the government or researchers have conspired to suppress a product.

SAFER ALTERNATIVES

Many states offer discounted-drug plans to seniors with limited incomes. Call your local office for the aging to inquire about your particular state's policies.

There are also options that guarantee health insurance to all children of low-income parents. Contact your local or state authorities for details.

Finally, if you are having difficulty with prescription bills, talk to your doctor. Most pharmaceutical companies offer discounts to those who can't otherwise afford their medications.

 US Food and Drug Administration, *www.fda.gov.*

The Worst Time of Month To Fill Prescriptions

Don't fill prescriptions at the beginning of the month. Deaths due to mistakes—the wrong drug, the wrong dose—tend to rise by as much as 25% at the start of any month.

Theory: This is probably due to a surge in orders received by pharmacies when government assistance payments are made to seniors and Medicaid patients.

Self-defense: Review your prescriptions with your doctor—know drug names, dosages and purposes.

Also: At your drugstore, double-check the information with the pharmacist, including your name and address.

David P. Phillips, PhD, professor of sociology, University of California San Diego, La Jolla, and leader of a study of medication deaths, published in *Pharmacotherapy.*

Between the Lines: Understanding Clinical Trials

Timothy McCall, MD, internist, medical editor of *Yoga Journal* and author of *Examining Your Doctor* (Citadel) and *Yoga as Medicine* (Bantam), *www.drmccall.com.*

Many clinical drug trials go unseen by the public, and that can be harmful to the consumer.

Result: Favorable research results on a certain drug might be publicized while the more mixed results are swept under the carpet.

Example: Reportedly, drug manufacturer GlaxoSmithKline originally failed to publish negative results suggesting that the use of the antidepressant Paxil in children and teenagers might provoke suicidal thoughts.

To learn more about the ins and outs of clinical trials, we spoke with Timothy McCall, MD, an internist and the author of *Examining Your Doctor: A Patient's Guide to Avoiding Harmful Medical Care.* Dr. McCall says that under pressure, some of the pharmaceutical companies are beginning to release information on all the studies they are conducting, but so far, the information they are providing is incomplete.

WHAT YOU CAN DO NOW

In the meantime, current trial registries are maintained by a variety of institutions, such as the National Institutes of Health and the

National Cancer Institute. Listings vary. They include open trials, active ongoing studies and links to and summaries of completed trials.

Note: Although the current focus has centered on published research, the overall goal is to achieve more open disclosure of all studies, for consumers as well as for medical professionals.

HOW TO JUDGE A CLINICAL STUDY

The next step is to determine what the results mean. Dr. McCall observes that it is very difficult for a consumer to make judgments about a clinical trial from, say, an abstract on Medline. *When you visit Web sites and look at studies, he recommends that you ask the following critical questions...*

• **Was it a controlled study?** How many participants were involved? A large, double-blind, randomized, controlled study has the most validity. In this type of trial, neither the participant nor the investigator know who is receiving the placebo and who is receiving the active drug.

• **Were patients in the trial like you?** If the study looked at 65-year-old men and you are a 40-year-old woman, it may not have much relevance, says Dr. McCall.

• **Who paid for the study?** If it was the manufacturer of the drug that's being looked at, the information presented may well be accurate, but take it with a grain of salt.

• **Who conducted the study?** Are the scientists who carried out the research paid consultants to the pharmaceutical companies involved?

• **Where was it published?** Rigorous, peer-reviewed journals are the best. The prestigious "biggies"—such as the *Journal of the American Medical Association*, the *New England Journal of Medicine* and *The Lancet*—all undergo peer review. The easiest way to find out is to look on-line. These journals publish letters critiquing the study in subsequent issues and invite the authors of the studies to respond.

STAY INFORMED

Dr. McCall says to keep in mind that no studies are 100% definitive. Having as much information as possible about your condition and having a critical eye in reviewing that in-

formation will help you ask better questions and better evaluate your doctor's answers and actions.

Also: You can protect yourself by sticking with tried-and-true drugs, rather than what is new on the market.

A final reminder from Dr. McCall—in an ideal world, there would be an equal number of dollars distributed to clinical trials on all treatments. Unfortunately, reality doesn't work that way.

Since so much research is funded by pharmaceutical companies, alternative approaches, such as yoga, herbal remedies or acupuncture, are often shortchanged. However, do not rule them out—even if there isn't as much scientific backing—you may be missing the opportunity to try other valuable healing modalities.

info For more information on clinical trials, visit the National Institutes of Health registry at *www.clinicaltrials.gov.*

Search for more clinical trials via the National Cancer Institute, *www.cancer.gov.*

Cross-reference clinical trials with the US National Library of Medicine, *www.medlineplus.gov.*

The Link Between Drug And Insurance Companies

Charles B. Inlander, a consumer advocate and health-care consultant based in Fogelsville, Pennsylvania. He was founding president of People's Medical Society, a consumer advocacy group active in the 1980s and 1990s. He is the author of more than 20 books, including *Take This Book to the Hospital With You*. St. Martin's Press.

We recently read a story about a man who had filled his prescriptions for antacids and later received a coupon from his insurance company for an over-the-counter (OTC) acid blocker. The letter accompanying the coupon suggested that rather than pay for prescription medications, he try OTCs and save some money.

Was this just blatant collusion? How could he trust this kind of recommendation from his insurance company? What kind of money did it receive from the pharmaceutical company to mail out that coupon? Had his insurance company succumbed to a shrewd marketing proposal by a drug manufacturer? It seemed irresponsible to push medication in general, let alone one, such as an acid blocker, that can have serious side effects.

To gain more perspective on this situation, we called Charles B. Inlander, consumer advocate and health-care consultant. To our surprise, he did not think the coupon was such a bad idea.

Inlander notes that OTC medicines are generally safer than prescription medications, if you use them according to the label instructions. Everything consumers need to know—such as warnings about possible side effects, drug interactions, etc.—is right there on the package label or insert. This is not the case with prescription medications.

Although he could not swear to it, Inlander didn't believe money changed hands between the pharmaceutical and insurance companies. Perhaps it did not—however the letter did mention that Procter & Gamble was "sponsoring this communication."

DOCTORS WOOED BY DRUG COMPANIES

Inlander says that *doctors* are the ones to watch out for. Pharmaceutical company representatives have been known to go to doctors' offices not only with free samples, but also dangling attractive perks, such as invitations to deluxe all-expense-paid conferences at ski lodges and Caribbean islands. Facing increased scrutiny from federal prosecutors, the drug industry only recently agreed to end the most blatant forms of these abuses.

How do you know if a drug offered by free sample or coupon is the best drug for you? You don't, says Inlander.

The bottom line is that you need to exercise caution when taking any drug. You have to act as your own health-care advocate.

Best: Do your homework—learn as much as you can about any medication that is prescribed or recommended for you, and don't be afraid to ask questions.

More from Charles B. Inlander...

Is Drug Advertising Safe for Consumers?

Are you aware that the fastest-growing group of men who take drugs for erectile dysfunction (ED) is between the ages of 18 and 45? It is not because this group is suddenly impotent. Rather, drug manufacturers are pumping millions of dollars into advertising their products directly to the consumer.

In the case of ED drugs that were once directed toward Bob Dole and his contemporaries, however, a much broader and much younger male audience is now the target for what many suspect is primarily recreational use. The advertising efforts are working.

DIRECT-TO-CONSUMER ADVERTISING: A GOOD IDEA?

The biggest question about such direct-to-consumer advertising is whether it is educating consumers or, rather, encouraging consumers to use pills and other prescription medications instead of more healthful techniques to solve their problems.

Pharmaceutical companies say that these ED drug ads have motivated men who were undertreated for some conditions, such as diabetes, to see their physicians, and that's a good thing. Diabetes impairs circulation, which can lead to ED. Of course, you also need to consider that the drug company stands to profit handsomely when patients take drugs they wouldn't otherwise take.

Critics reply, saying that direct-to-consumer ads are designed simply to sell more pills. They are concerned that when drugs are developed for a particular condition, manufacturers market the *condition* rather than the medication.

Using the traditional marketing strategies of sex and fear, opponents say that pharmaceutical firms are creating illness where it didn't exist and leading consumers to think that there is a magic pill for every ailment (real or imaginary). Down in the dumps? How about a Zoloft? Did you sneeze? Have a Claritin. Overindulge at the dinner table this evening? If you don't take this little purple pill, you'll get heartburn.

We teamed up with the Web site Vote.com to pose the question, "Should Congress ban drug advertising?" Most voters agreed with critics that direct-to-consumer advertising was not a good idea. *Of the 29,323 people who voted...*

• **19,080, or 65%, said yes.** Drug advertising drives up the cost of medications, and the decision about what to prescribe is better left to the doctors.

• **10,243, or 35%, said no.** Patients have a right to educate themselves about drugs and to ask doctors about them.

MORE INSIDIOUS: DRUG ADVERTISING TO DOCTORS

Charles B. Inlander, consumer advocate and health-care consultant, weighs in with the "no" camp. He believes that banning direct-to-consumer advertising means withholding valuable information from the public.

Inlander notes that many doctors originally opposed direct-to-consumer advertising because it put patients on an equal footing with them in terms of drug awareness. On the downside, he acknowledges that pharmaceutical companies tend to advertise more expensive products, and he'd like to see broader advertising of a wider selection of medications at all price levels.

Inlander is much more concerned about pharmaceutical companies marketing directly to the doctors. He notes that drug manufacturers spend three times more money on advertising to physicians than to the public, and that this practice can result in serious conflicts of interest.

For example, Pfizer paid a $430 million fine because drug representatives illegally promoted Neurontin to doctors for nonapproved uses to increase sales. The partial-seizure drug was illegally promoted for off-label uses such as pain syndromes and diabetic neuropathy.

Kickbacks to physicians come in many shapes and sizes, from golf outings to free tickets to ball games to lavish dinners. In one of the more extreme examples of what could be considered direct-to-doctor advertising, Schering-Plough sent unsolicited $10,000 stipends to physicians to encourage them to prescribe its hepatitis C drug and participate in clinical trials that turned out to be thinly veiled marketing initiatives. This dubious tactic triggered the scrutiny of federal prosecutors.

CHANGE IS IN THE AIR

The good news is that several states are cracking down on how pharmaceutical giants advertise their medicines (not just pills) to doctors and the public. In recent years, federal prosecutors and state attorneys general have taken a number of the big drug companies to court, accusing them of illicit marketing programs that cost the government billions of dollars in drug benefit payments.

AstraZeneca and TAP Pharmaceutical Products have both pleaded guilty to criminal charges of fraud for encouraging doctors to bill the government for drugs that the companies provided for free, and paid millions of dollars in fines. Other drug companies are setting aside funds to cover present or anticipated legal problems.

Consumer groups are also taking pharmaceutical companies to task. When heart disease experts made an announcement in July 2004 urging more people to take cholesterol-lowering statin drugs, the Center for Science in the Public Interest harshly criticized them for failing to reveal potential conflicts of interest.

Six of the nine experts who composed the new cholesterol guidelines—which would add seven million more Americans to the 36 million who are presently encouraged to take cholesterol-lowering drugs—had financial ties to the makers of statins, whose profits could soar as a result of their recommendation.

WHAT YOU CAN DO NOW

In the meantime, between biased ads and doctors who themselves may be influenced by pharmaceutical companies, what's a consumer to do?

Stay informed, says Inlander. Visit reputable Web sites, such as the US National Library of Medicine, *www.nlm.nih.gov*, the National Institutes of Health at *www.medlineplus.gov* (click on "Drugs & Supplements"), and the US Food and Drug Administration at *www.fda.gov*. These will help you keep up on the latest research on your medical condition and the drugs you can take for it.

Helpful...

• **Speak up at your doctor's office.**

153

- **Feel free to get second opinions.**
- **Ask your pharmacist questions.**
- **Keep in mind that you know your body best** and are the best advocate for your own health.

Remember: Sometimes, believe it or not, you may not even need a pill to fix your illness. Sometimes drugs for one condition can create or exacerbate other conditions, and some conditions are the direct result of diet and lifestyle choices.

Best: Look at the entire situation. Make the appropriate lifestyle changes that you know are simply unhealthy (e.g., smoking, poor eating habits). Then, as Inlander said, make informed decisions along with your health-care team.

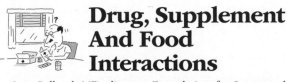

Drug, Supplement And Food Interactions

Leo Galland, MD, director, Foundation for Integrated Medicine, New York City. He is author of *The Fat Resistance Diet*. Broadway. Dr. Galland is a recipient of the Linus Pauling award. *www.fatresistancediet.com.*

There have been a lot of headlines about the risk of combining drugs with dietary supplements and *nutraceuticals* (fortified food products, such as calcium-enriched orange juice). According to Leo Galland, MD, director of the Foundation for Integrated Medicine in New York City, there are both positive and negative interactions among drugs, dietary supplements and some foods.

Dr. Galland is also director of Applied Nutrition, a firm that manufactures Medical Foods products and develops software for nutritional analysis and the study of drug-supplement interactions. Among the many dietary supplements that interact with medications are capsicum, co-enzyme Q10, dong quai, echinacea, garlic, ginger, ginkgo biloba, ginseng, kava and melatonin.

In our conversation with Dr. Galland, he illustrated the highly complicated nature of interactions by describing in great detail those of two popular supplements—the mineral calcium and the herb St. John's wort.

CALCIUM INTERACTIONS

Dr. Galland warns that when you take drugs such as corticosteroids (to treat inflammation) and anticonvulsants (prescribed for epilepsy, anxiety, depression and chronic pain), you face a greater risk for bone fractures and the bone-thinning disorder osteoporosis. To prevent these problems, he recommends that you take calcium, a mineral which is essential for strong, healthy bones and teeth. He observes that while it is possible to take in enough calcium through diet alone, most Americans fail to do so.

On the other hand, combining calcium with certain other drugs—for example, the blood pressure medication *atenolol* or the antibiotic *tetracycline*—impairs the absorption and therefore the effectiveness of the medication. Dr. Galland explains that calcium binds with them in the intestine to form an unabsorbable chemical complex. To prevent this from occurring, he advises that you separate the time you take these medications from calcium supplements by at least two hours.

In addition, he points out that the same issue arises with magnesium, iron and zinc—minerals that are chemically similar to calcium. It would be wise to follow the same precautions with these minerals and the medications with which they interact, such as atenolol and tetracycline. Take them at least two hours apart. This advice also applies to nutraceuticals such as calcium-enriched orange juice.

Common calcium interactions…

- **Antibiotics.** Calcium will interfere with the absorption of quinolone antibiotics, such as *ciprofloxacin*. When antibiotics are not fully absorbed, even a complete course may fail to completely eradicate bacteria. This can result in the development of even more destructive drug-resistant bacteria.

Best: As above, be sure to separate doses of certain antibiotics and calcium by at least two hours. Alternatively, since most antibiotics are prescribed for about 10 days, unless there is some compelling reason for taking calcium, Dr. Galland suggests that you simply stop using it while taking the antibiotic.

- **Anticonvulsants.** These drugs, which are prescribed for epilepsy, anxiety, depression and chronic pain, are associated with an increased risk for bone problems, such as osteoporosis.

Best: Dr. Galland recommends taking calcium and vitamin D supplements when on anticonvulsants.

• **Atenolol.** If you take this blood pressure medication too close to a calcium supplement, atenolol may form an unabsorbable complex with the mineral and therefore be less effective in controlling hypertension.

Best: Take atenolol at least two hours before or after a calcium supplement.

• **Corticosteroids.** Similar to anticonvulsants, these drugs—used for inflammatory conditions, such as asthma, allergies and colitis—increase your risk for bone fractures and osteoporosis.

Best: If you must take them, also take calcium and vitamin D supplements.

• **Oral diabetes drugs.** *Metformin* and other oral diabetes preparations that contain metformin induce a deficiency of vitamin B-12.

Best: This can be prevented if the drugs are taken together with B-12 supplements.

• **Thyroid hormones.** Calcium interferes with the absorption of thyroid hormones, and should be taken at a different time of day.

Best: For most consistent absorption, Dr. Galland recommends that you take thyroid hormones first thing in the morning. Keep medication by your bedside and take it as soon as you wake up. Then don't eat or drink anything else for one hour (or at least two hours in the case of food products enriched with calcium).

ST. JOHN'S WORT INTERACTIONS

According to Dr. Galland, this herb, which is used to treat depression, has the potential to impact virtually any medicine that you take. Chemical compounds in St. John's wort alter the activity of enzymes that are involved in metabolizing (breaking down) drugs in the intestinal tract and liver. In speeding up the pace at which your body metabolizes drugs, it can dilute their effects.

While the standard admonition is to simply avoid taking it with drugs because of the high rate of interactions, Dr. Galland notes that the most important thing is to inform your health-care provider that you are taking St. John's wort so that he/she can adjust your medication accordingly, and then maintain consistency.

Note: Problems develop primarily when you suddenly start or suddenly stop taking St. John's wort or when you change your dosage.

For example, say that your health-care provider gives you a prescription for *warfarin* to prevent blood clots. St. John's wort increases the rate at which warfarin is broken down in the body—which increases the dose you would need of warfarin. If you suddenly begin taking St. John's wort or increase your dosage, you will be at an increased risk for blood clotting. On the other hand, if you suddenly stop taking St. John's wort or reduce your dosage, you face an increased risk for bleeding.

Note: Other drugs that interact with this herb include birth control pills, antidepressants, *digoxin* and other heart medications, protease inhibitors for HIV, immunosuppressant drugs to prevent rejection of organ transplants, *tamoxifen* used in the treatment of breast cancer and the anti-asthma medicine *theophylline*.

COMMUNICATION IS KEY

Interactions between drugs and dietary supplements are more common than you think. It's a good idea to talk to your health-care provider about all the supplements you take (or are thinking about taking). In some cases, supplements can be very beneficial. In others, they are not appropriate and may even cause harm.

Caution: Deadly Drug Interactions

Timothy McCall, MD, internist, medical editor of *Yoga Journal* and author of *Examining Your Doctor* (Citadel) and *Yoga as Medicine* (Bantam), *www.drmccall.com.*

It's great to have experts in individual medical specialties, but if you rely solely on specialists for your care, you could run into problems. When a patient goes to an array of doctors, he/she may get different medications from each, and neither physician may be aware of what the other is doing. Worse, patients may combine these medications with herbal formulas and supplements and then end up sicker than before.

Why? Because no one doctor is taking a look at the big picture when it comes to the patient's overall drug intake.

For example, did you know that…

• **The impotence drug Viagra** can cause a deadly drop in blood pressure in men who use *nitroglycerin* or other nitrate-containing heart medications?

• **Certain antidepressants (MAO inhibitors)** can cause dangerous *increases* in blood pressure when combined with tyramine-rich foods—including aged cheeses, avocados and sour cream?

• **Taking both the herb ginkgo and a blood thinner,** such as aspirin or *warfarin* (Coumadin), can cause hemorrhage?

• **Grapefruit juice can heighten the effects of a number of drugs,** leading to dangerous conditions? Blood-pressure drugs, cholesterol-lowering statins and certain antidepressants can be affected.

As more dietary supplements and other over-the-counter (OTC) products hit the shelves, the number of possible adverse interactions continues to grow.

"It's a whole new ball game," says Timothy McCall, MD, an internist, medical editor of *Yoga Journal* and author of *Examining Your Doctor: A Patient's Guide to Avoiding Harmful Medical Care.*

His prescription for winning this life-or-death game…

• **Take the fewest drugs at the lowest provided doses.** Remember that even the most innocent substances, such as vitamin C and aspirin, can affect the way your body reacts to prescription medications.

Helpful: Lifestyle changes can reduce the need for medication. The right diet, exercise and relaxation techniques, such as yoga and meditation, can help cut the use of antidepressants, blood pressure medications and other popular drugs.

• **Keep a current list of all the medications you use.** Do this even if you do not take them on a regular basis. Include both prescrip-

tion and OTC drugs, herbal remedies, vitamins, etc. Show the list to every doctor you see.

Although physicians and pharmacists can tell you about some drug interactions, no one is aware of all the risks. Interactions with new medications may not be known until years after the drugs have been introduced.

According to Dr. McCall, the individual responses to a particular drug are highly variable. A substance that exerts a powerful effect on one person may hardly be noticed by another. Often, older people are especially sensitive to a drug's effect.

Self-defense: When you start taking a new drug or supplement, be aware of how your body is responding. Consult your physician if you develop any problems—and bring along that list of medications, just in case.

info For more information, visit the Institute for Safe Medication Practices Web site at *www.ismp.org.*

Thousands of Medical Testing Errors Each Year

Charles B. Inlander, a consumer advocate and health-care consultant based in Fogelsville, Pennsylvania. He was founding president of People's Medical Society, a consumer advocacy group active in the 1980s and 1990s. He is the author of more than 20 books, including *Take This Book to the Hospital With You.* St. Martin's Press.

Every year, as many as 98,000 hospital patients die as a result of medical errors. This means that there are more deaths caused by preventable medical errors than by motor vehicle accidents, breast cancer or AIDS.

One of the areas in which errors commonly occur is medical testing. Results are routinely misinterpreted, mixed up, handed out to the wrong people or not handed out at all. Some of these errors are benign while other mistakes are life-threatening.

According to Charles B. Inlander, consumer advocate and health-care consultant, there are specific steps you can take to minimize the risk for medical testing errors…

•**Learn all you can about the test.** To prevent confusion and misunderstandings, prepare beforehand by asking your health-care provider these questions...

•How should I prepare for the test?

•Exactly what does the test consist of?

•How long will the test take?

•Will there be any pain or discomfort?

•What should I expect afterward?

Seek out any available written information, and visit reliable Web sites, such as the US National Library of Medicine and the National Institutes of Health's MedlinePlus (*www.medline plus. gov*) to learn more about testing.

•**What are the risks?** Ask whether a test will pose any risks, and if so, what they are. For instance, in younger women with dense breast tissue, the benefits of mammography are uncertain and the repeated exposure to radiation may pose unnecessary health risks.

•**More is not necessarily better.** Always ask why a suggested test is needed and how it will help you. In some cases, you might be better off without it.

For example, certain types of screening tests—such as those for prostate cancer—have both benefits and limitations, and people should learn about these before making their decisions.

•**Is this the best available test?** Do not be afraid to ask questions and express concerns. Find out whether better screening tests are available but not recommended because of cost considerations.

One case in point is screening for colon cancer. Insurance is more apt to cover sigmoidoscopy (an examination of the lower colon with a flexible tube) than colonoscopy (a similar, but more extensive examination of the entire colon). If you are at particular risk, consider asking your health-care provider to perform the more extensive test, even if you have to pay for it out of your own pocket.

•**Choose the testing facility with care.** Inlander notes that a common problem is the misreading of test results, such as those for magnetic resonance imaging (MRI) scans, mammograms or X-rays. Often, the doctor simply reviews them too fast.

If you have a choice, your best bet is to get tested at a facility where the staff has experience. Research shows that results are more accurate at facilities where experienced radiologists, pathologists and other medical personnel perform the procedure and interpret the results.

One study showed that physicians who annually performed 100 or more colposcopies (a test performed as a follow-up to an abnormal Pap smear) obtained more accurate results than those who did the procedure less often.

•**Share your medical history.** Do not assume that everyone has all the information they need about you. Make sure that the testing facility is aware of any allergies or any pre-existing conditions that you have.

For example, some people may be allergic to latex gloves. For your own safety, your health-care provider should know about any conditions that you have, including diabetes, high blood pressure or asthma, before performing a test. Be sure to double check with the person giving the test that he/she is aware of your special needs.

Also inform the testing facility of all prescription and over-the-counter (OTC) medications you take as well as dietary supplements, such as vitamins and herbs. For example, to reduce the risk for bleeding, surgeons advise their patients to avoid taking aspirin or dietary supplements that reduce clotting (such as ginkgo biloba) for a week or more before an invasive or surgical procedure.

The same advice applies if you are having an invasive test, such as a biopsy or colonoscopy. However, new research shows that people with known heart disease should not stop taking aspirin abruptly.

•**Bring a family member or friend along.** Ask your spouse, a sibling or a friend to be there with you and act as your advocate. Undergoing a test can be a stressful experience, and having an extra set of eyes and ears can be an excellent insurance policy.

GET THE RESULTS

Don't assume that no news is good news. Ask beforehand when and how you will get test results, and don't take for granted that all is well if you don't receive them. Call for results a week or two after having a test, and ask your health-care provider what the results mean for your future care.

If your test results are abnormal, Inlander recommends that you sit down with your health-care provider and discuss all the available options. For example, an abnormal mammogram can be followed up with an additional mammogram or an ultrasound. Explore the merits of each test to determine which is best for you.

• **Beware of inaccurate results.** A major problem, says Inlander, is that test results are often inaccurate. According to a study at the Boston University School of Public Health, nearly one in four women who regularly have mammograms will have at least one false-positive result—and false-positives can lead to anxiety and unnecessary interventions. On the other hand, a false-negative leads to a false sense of security, and a person may miss out on the opportunity for early intervention and treatment.

• **Double-check the results.** If you suspect something is wrong, get it double-checked, says Inlander. He emphasizes that you have the legal right to copies of all your medical records and X-rays.

When in doubt, have the results sent to another lab for verification or have another health-care provider review your X-rays. If there is still uncertainty, have the test repeated.

• **Get a second opinion.** About ten years ago, Inlander himself received a PSA (prostate-specific antigen) test result that was unusually high—a possible sign of prostate cancer. Because he was tested regularly and always had negative results, had no family history of prostate cancer and led a healthy lifestyle (good diet, regular exercise, no smoking), he was suspicious of the results and looked further into the matter. As it turned out, his test results had been mixed up with those of another man.

Whenever you get suspicious results, whether they seem like a false-positive or a false-negative, get a second opinion, stresses Inlander. Don't put yourself through an invasive procedure, such as a biopsy, until you are absolutely certain that it is necessary. Nor should you let something potentially wrong fester due to a false-negative.

• **Keep in mind that current knowledge is just that—current.** A good example of this is the chest X-ray. Beginning in the 1950s, doctors recommended chest X-rays. More recently, the Mayo Lung Project concluded that screening for lung cancer using chest X-rays does not save lives and it detects tumors that may not be life-threatening (which can lead to interventions that are not necessary).

• **Be your own watchdog.** Inlander notes that some people hold up a line in the supermarket when they are overcharged 50 cents… but these same people don't bother to double-check a mammogram or PSA test result that doesn't seem right. He stresses that you must act as your own health-care advocate.

By learning all you can about the tests you undergo and speaking up when you think there may be a problem, you stand the best chance of avoiding dangerous medical testing errors.

info Agency for Healthcare Research and Quality, *www.ahrq.gov.*

Institute of Medicine of the National Academies, *www.iom.edu.*

Americans Overmedicated: A Man-Made Epidemic

Jay S. Cohen, MD, adjunct associate professor of family and preventive medicine, University of California, San Diego. Dr. Cohen is author of *What You Must Know About Statin Drugs & Their Natural Alternatives* (Square One) and *Over Dose: The Case Against the Drug Companies* (Tarcher). Visit his Web site at *www.medicationsense.com.*

Andrew L. Rubman, ND, director, Southbury Clinic for Traditional Medicines, Southbury, Connecticut.

Are you tossing and turning at night? Try taking a sleeping pill. Nervous around other people? Try an antidepressant. Balding? Have trouble in the bedroom? There are pills for just about everything these days.

Americans are overmedicated, and as a consequence, we suffer millions of avoidable side effects. To make matters even worse, one of the most vulnerable segments of the population—senior citizens—are the most overmedicated of all. They bear the brunt of the majority of adverse reactions and dangerous drug interactions.

AN EPIDEMIC OF SIDE EFFECTS

To find out more about drugs and the elderly, we spoke with Jay S. Cohen, MD, adjunct associate professor of family and preventive medicine at the University of California in San Diego.

He told us that drug side effects lead to some 100,000 deaths each year in hospitals, making them one of the leading causes of death in the US. Once in the hospital, older people face the greatest risk of a serious medication-related death or side effect. Although people over age 60 represent less than 20% of the population, they account for an estimated 39% of hospitalizations and approximately 51% of deaths related to medication reactions.

DOSING DANGERS

In Dr. Cohen's view, dosage plays a major role in this problem. He points out that it is not medically rational to prescribe the same amount of medication to a young person the size of a professional football player as to a tiny 80-year-old grandmother—but that is what routinely happens.

In addition, seniors are repeatedly put on drugs that are sedating or cause dizziness. He also believes that doctors need to look at better alternatives.

RESEARCH SUPPORT

In a study conducted at Duke University, it was revealed that at least one in five older Americans take an inappropriately prescribed drug.

Researchers looked at the prescription drug use of more than 765,000 people age 65 and over who were enrolled in a major medication benefits plan. They compared their medication use to the Beers Criteria, a compilation of drugs that are associated with thinking and alertness problems and that likely lead to an increased risk of falls (a major health problem in the elderly that can result in broken hips, disability or even death).

An update of the Beers list, reflecting even more recent results, was then published in the *Archives of Internal Medicine*. Researchers found that 21% of seniors in the study filled a prescription for one drug of concern, and 4%

filled prescriptions for three or more of these flagged drugs.

The drugs of concern include mood-altering drugs, such as…

- *hydroxyzine* **(Atarax)**
- *amitriptyline* **(Elavil)**
- *flurazepam* **(Dalmane)**
- *chlordiazepoxide* **(Librium)**
- *diazepam* **(Valium)**
- *doxepin* **(Adapin and Sinequan)**

Also of concern are certain muscle relaxants including…

- *cyclobenzaprine* (Flexeril)
- *chlorzoxazone* (Paraflex and Parafon Forte)
- *methocarbamol* (Robaxin)
- *metaxalone* (Skelaxin)
- *carisoprodol* (Soma)

The most commonly prescribed drugs on the list were doxepin and amitriptyline.

WHY OLDER PEOPLE ARE MORE VULNERABLE

Given that there are many safer alternatives, observes Dr. Cohen, it is troubling that so many medicines are prescribed inappropriately for the elderly. *He explains that there are several reasons why seniors are especially prone to side effects…*

- **Older people typically process drugs more slowly than younger people.** This is a function of their diminished kidney and liver function, which causes blood concentrations of drugs to reach higher levels and take longer to be eliminated.

- **Most seniors have multiple illnesses.** According to Dr. Cohen, 78% take at least one prescription drug and 60% take at least one nonprescription medication. The average older person takes three drugs daily. This means a greater risk for side effects and drug interactions.

WHAT YOU CAN DO

- **Do your homework.** Learn all that you can about the condition you have, the medicine you take for it and the possible side effects (such as problems with thinking and alertness) and drug interactions. Ask your doctor and pharmacist questions, and carefully read the package inserts.

You can also learn more about medications at such Web sites as MedlinePlus (*http://medline plus.gov*), click on "Drugs and Supplements," and PDR Health (*www.pdrhealth.com*).

• **Stress to your physician that you want to stick to the lowest effective dosage of medication.** Older patients are hurt by the one-size-fits-all mentality of prescribing drugs says Dr. Cohen. Newly introduced medications are typically offered at identical doses for young and old, well and infirm, large and small. However, in many cases, lower doses of drugs are safer and still effective for older people.

• **Report all potential drug side effects to your physician, and insist that he/she take your concerns seriously.** A problem peculiar to older people is that their doctors frequently attribute side effects to illness or the effects of aging. If an older man feels that his focus is not what it once was or a senior woman thinks that her memory is vague or her balance is off, it is often attributed to old age.

In many instances, however, the problem could be remedied by adjusting the dosage of medication. If your physician doesn't want to consider this, Dr. Cohen recommends considering changing physicians.

• **All things being equal, ask for the drug with the longest track record for safety.** With the blizzard of drug ads being directed toward consumers and doctors alike, it's tempting to think that the newest drug on the market is the best one.

However, this is not always (or even usually) the case. Often, a medication that has been around longer is just as effective, safer, less expensive and perhaps most important, has the longest track record of experience for known side effects.

Well informed is well armed. Whatever your age, but especially if you are elderly, there are many steps that you can and should take to protect yourself from dangerous side effects and drug interactions. Our medical expert, Andrew L. Rubman, ND, notes that certain interventions, such as increases in B vitamins and fiber, can improve the function of your liver and digestive tract, thus reducing risk for some side effects.

Custom Prescriptions— Safer for You

L.D. King, executive director, International Academy of Compounding Pharmacists, Sugar Land, Texas.

A big challenge with the effectiveness of many drugs is getting the dosing right. The local pharmacy only stocks materials in specific doses that are designed for "adults." No one takes into account that a 5-foot, 3-inch tall woman weighing 118 pounds takes the same "adult" dose as a 6-foot tall, 200-pound man.

If you have ever struggled with getting the dosing right on your medication, you may want to talk to your doctor about getting your medication custom-compounded from a compounding pharmacist in order to meet your individual needs.

There are a number of reasons why physicians prescribe compounded drugs rather than standard-issue medications. In particular, compounding allows a pharmacist to alter a drug's dosage, to create a lozenge instead of a capsule, to prepare a medication without dyes or preservatives for allergic patients, to flavor pediatric medication or to prepare a drug that is too rare for a pharmaceutical house to bother with. Some medical and naturopathic doctors have pharmacists compound their particular pharmaceuticals to ensure high quality and to balance medical influences, such as nutrients, for a patient's particular problems.

THE INDUSTRY

Drug compounding today accounts for about 1% of the prescriptions in this country. That doesn't sound like much, but it adds up to more than 30 million prescriptions each year in the three-billion-plus market of prescriptions filled in the US annually.

Compounding pharmacies were in the news recently due to drug-compounding errors. Some patients suffered severe injuries, including blindness from eye drops…and others died due to infections from contaminated injected steroids. For the most part, the injuries and deaths have resulted from lack of sterility in drugs.

However, according to L.D. King, executive director of the International Academy of Compounding Pharmacists, the safety record for compounders is quite good given the huge number of prescriptions filled.

To address the recent problems, King says that the druggists who specialize in compounding receive the same education as a regular pharmacist and additional training in continuing medical education programs offered by nonprofit associations. The courses cover, in particular, basic and advanced techniques that ensure sterility. Compounding pharmacies are also subject to strict federal oversight similar to that of manufacturing facilities for major drug companies.

Additionally, King explained that the industry is taking all previous errors seriously to learn from them and to take steps to prevent any future mistakes. King reports that eight different pharmacy-related organizations have come together to form the Pharmacy Compounding Accreditation Board (PCAB). The purpose of the board is to develop standards based on the best practices and a program to accredit pharmacies that demonstrate adherence. Members of the board are at work on this now.

AVOIDING RISK

King notes that many drugs produced by compounding pharmacists are extremely low risk. These include topical gels and creams, such as ibuprofen cream that offers pain relief to arthritic patients whose stomach problems preclude taking painkillers, and oral medications such as syrups, tablets and capsules.

The highest-risk compounded medications are, as past problems would indicate, sterile products—in particular, drugs that are meant to be injected. Hospital pharmacies primarily are responsible for compounding these drugs, meaning that patients have no direct contact with pharmacists and so, frankly, no control.

Consumers do, however, have some input when purchasing directly from the compounding pharmacist. King advises consumers to ask at a compounding pharmacy if it is in compliance with the *USP*, chapter 797. (USP is United States Pharmacopeia, a nonprofit organization that establishes standards for drugs. Chapter 797 covers production of sterile products.) At that time, PCAB accreditation is your assurance of high drug-compounding standards and the guide for careful consumers.

A Doctor's Caution on Statins

Jay S. Cohen, MD, adjunct associate professor of family and preventive medicine, University of California, San Diego. Dr. Cohen is author of *What You Must Know About Statin Drugs & Their Natural Alternatives* (Square One) and *Over Dose: The Case Against the Drug Companies* (Tarcher). Visit his Web site at *www.medicationsense.com*.

If you believe the drug manufacturers, you might think that statins are the best thing since sliced bread. Recent studies suggest that not only do they reduce cholesterol, prevent heart disease and lower the risk for heart attack and stroke, they also might cut Alzheimer's risk…help prevent glaucoma… ease macular degeneration…and reduce the inflammation and scarring of the myelin sheath (a fatty covering that protects nerve fibers) and underlying nerves that are associated with multiple sclerosis. The response overall has been so positive that an over-the-counter version of one statin has already been made available in the United Kingdom.

Now, a study reports that people who take statins may experience another unexpected benefit—a reduced risk of developing colorectal cancer. Other research suggests that statins offer protection against prostate and kidney cancer, breast cancer and melanoma.

Should we all start popping statins?

DON'T LEAP TO CONCLUSIONS

The answer to that question is an emphatic no, according to Jay S. Cohen, MD, adjunct associate professor of family and preventive medicine at the University of California, San Diego. He told us that the side effects of statins are drastically underestimated by pharmaceutical companies.

Even the researchers who conducted the latest cancer study caution that it is too soon to leap to conclusions, noting that findings are preliminary and that statins have potentially serious side effects. Not only that, there are far less risky ways to prevent colorectal cancer, including healthy diet, regular exercise and screening tests for early detection.

TAKING A SECOND LOOK

Dr. Cohen is concerned that in the rush of enthusiasm for all things statin, we fail to fully take into account the impact of their side effects. While drug companies report that these affect only 1% to 2% of statin users, Dr. Cohen says that published data show that some 15% to 30% of people who take these drugs experience muscle pain, joint pain, abdominal discomfort or cognitive or memory problems.

About 60% of the people who are prescribed statins quit taking them, notes Dr. Cohen, often because of intolerable side effects. In other cases, even though the effects can be severe, statin users fail to make the connection and do not attribute them to statin use.

Unfortunately, doctors often make the same mistake. There are reports of people with statin-related confusion, altered mood, impaired memory or debilitating muscle pain, whose complaints are dismissed by their physicians because they failed to associate them with statin use. Or worse, additional drugs are prescribed to control these symptoms, which can lead to even more side effects.

Dr. Cohen notes that we also need to take a second look at why statins have become so popular. More and more scientists believe that inflammation is the key to understanding and controlling not only heart disease but all major age-related diseases as well. Statins have a positive impact on these diseases because they reduce inflammation. But, Dr. Cohen asks, why isn't anybody asking why we are so inflammation-prone in the first place?

He believes that drug companies should invest more of their research dollars into learning the answer to that question rather than spending hundreds of millions of dollars finding new ways to market best-selling drugs. For example, Dr. Cohen points out that Americans consume far too many omega-6 fatty acids and not nearly enough omega-3s, which creates an inflammatory climate in our bodies—yet this is not a profitable avenue of research for drug companies, and so it is neglected.

Ultimately, the answer is not a magic pill. A healthy lifestyle is your best and safest bet to prevent diseases that grow more common as we age.

info For more information, visit the American Cancer Society, *www.cancer.org.*

Assess your cancer risk and learn ways to lower it with the Harvard School of Public Health's Disease Risk Index at *www.diseaserisk index.harvard.edu/update.*

More from Jay S. Cohen...

Should Statin Drugs Be OTC?

Should the United States move cholesterol-lowering statin drugs from a prescription-only to an over-the-counter (OTC) status, like England has already done?

First up: *Simvastatin* (Zocor), at a daily dose of 10 milligrams (mg), half the standard prescription dosage.

Although the US Food and Drug Administration (FDA) turned down applications for OTC statins in the 1990s, their approval abroad has spurred pharmaceutical companies to renew efforts for OTC approval here in the US. But is this a good idea? With the many risks associated with taking statins, are they really something that you should self-prescribe? Or is this a self-serving move on the part of greedy drug manufacturers?

SIDE EFFECTS NOT UNCOMMON

To get some answers, we spoke with Jay S. Cohen, MD, adjunct associate professor of family and preventive medicine at the University of California in San Diego.

He told us that side effects from statins are not as uncommon as the pharmaceutical companies would have you believe. While manufacturers claim that side effects impact only 1% to 2% of statin takers, the data show that about 15% to 30% of statin users get muscle pain, joint pain, abdominal discomfort or cognitive or memory problems.

The higher the dose, the greater the risk of side effects. In some instances, these effects can be so severe that they are disabling, yet statins are often overlooked as the cause, says Dr. Cohen.

Although lower doses are safer, he warns that side effects can still happen. Moreover, making statins available OTC would significantly increase the number of people who take them, while decreasing medical monitoring for side effects.

THE CASE FOR STATINS

Statins already are best-selling drugs, netting their manufacturers billions of dollars in annual profits. Yet pharmaceutical companies contend that fewer than half of all Americans who could benefit from taking statins do so. They say that making these medicines available OTC will provide greater access and protect more Americans with mild to moderately elevated cholesterol levels from developing heart disease.

Critics counter that the economics motivate pharmaceutical manufacturers to make statins available OTC. With patents on several statins expiring in the next few years, OTC sales could keep the billions rolling into their coffers.

Many experts also remain unconvinced that everyone who has mildly elevated cholesterol needs to take a pill to lower it. Dr. Cohen recommends first trying dietary changes, such as eating less saturated fat and more fresh fruits and vegetables.

OTC SAFETY CONCERNS

According to Dr. Cohen, most OTC medications have an immediate, measurable effect. For example, an aspirin alleviates headache pain…an antihistamine controls sneezing and itchy, watery eyes.

Statins are different. They work by lowering the level of cholesterol in your body—an effect that you cannot see or monitor without a blood test.

Dr. Cohen is concerned that OTC access may encourage people to take statins without paying sufficient attention to side effects, such as muscle aches or joint pain. Even more serious are potentially life-threatening liver injury and toxicity—which, like cholesterol levels, cannot be seen and must be monitored carefully with blood tests.

If you're not medically trained, it is easy to overlook the significance of side effects, observes Dr. Cohen. For example, if a person experiences joint pain, he/she may not associate it with statins at all and may begin taking anti-inflammatory medications. This can lead to a cascade of even more damaging side effects, since anti-inflammatories such as ibuprofen are associated with an increased risk of gastrointestinal bleeding and liver damage.

DOSAGE MATTERS

The one-size-fits-all dosage of the OTC preparation is another cause for concern. The standard starting doses of statins are often double the amount that people need, says Dr. Cohen.

The higher the dosage, the greater the risk for side effects. However, if you need larger doses to sufficiently lower your LDL (the so-called "bad" cholesterol), you could not accomplish this by simply taking the OTC product.

Dr. Cohen adds that most people (even doctors) are unaware that lower dosages are sometimes sufficient…

Zocor	Daily Dosage	Average Reduction in LDL
Standard initial prescription dosage	20 mg	38%
Standard OTC dosage in England	10 mg	30%
An effective lower dosage for many people	5 mg	26%

Source: Chart is adapted from *What You Must Know About Statin Drugs & Their Natural Alternatives*, by Jay S. Cohen, MD (Square One).

LIFESTYLE CHANGES ARE KEY

Many people who have mildly to moderately elevated cholesterol levels may not even need statins, emphasizes Dr. Cohen. He notes that these drugs are very effective in lowering cholesterol in people with heart disease or at high risk of developing it—but most people do not fit in this category.

Will statins become available OTC in the US? Only time will tell.

In the meantime, keep in mind that these are serious drugs with potentially serious side effects. Use them only if you really need them, and under the supervision of your health-care provider. And before you resort to statins, consider simple solutions such as healthier eating, more regular exercise, maintaining a proper weight and refraining from smoking.

Antibiotics: Magic Bullets Or Boomerangs?

Leo Galland, MD, director, Foundation for Integrated Medicine, New York City. His latest book is *The Fat Resistance Diet*. Broadway. Dr. Galland is a recipient of the Linus Pauling award.

It is common knowledge now that the over-use of antibiotics is wreaking havoc on our future health by creating antibiotic-resistant strains of bacteria. But antibiotic use itself can also pose its own set of problems—we call it the "antibiotic cycle."

THE START OF THE CYCLE

Leo Galland, MD, director of the Foundation for Integrated Medicine in New York City, explains that the body contains hundreds of different types of friendly bacteria in addition to microbes. There are 100 trillion microbes in the digestive tract alone. All of these microbes, about 98% of which are bacteria, compete for space and nutrients. However, most of these bacteria actually serve a *positive* purpose in the body, helping to ward off disease and keep our systems in balance.

Antibiotics, or *antibacterials*, as Dr. Galland prefers to call them, are designed to suppress certain groups of bacteria in the body. For all their sophistication, none of the antibiotics can yet target just the "bad" bacteria. So, when you take an antibiotic, a lot of "good" bacteria is suppressed as well. And that's the problem.

The depopulation that results sets the stage for unfriendly bacteria—as well as yeast—to flourish in the competition for space and nutrients. In short, they overgrow and you may be left with a microbial imbalance. The effects of this on your body, says Dr. Galland, can be anything from trivial to devastating.

Think of your lawn—you aim to have a nice, green lawn without weeds and clover. However, given the opportunity, the hardier clover often overtakes the grass. Getting rid of the clover and returning your lawn to grass is incredibly challenging. So, too, with your body.

PLANTING THE SEEDS

With luck, the negative result of antibiotics is so slight that you might not notice a thing. For those who are not so lucky—due to repeated use, poor diet or other factors—the overgrowth of certain bacteria, especially those that produce toxins, can contribute to the development of colitis, diarrhea, bleeding and gut disorders such as irritable bowel syndrome (IBS). Without a proper bacterial balance, you may lose resistance and become more vulnerable to food poisoning, allergies and illnesses.

BROADENING THE SCOPE

According to Dr. Galland, the use of antibiotics creates a second imbalance problem in the body—yeast. Women know all too well about the vaginal yeast infections that can result from antibiotics, but antibiotics can also allow yeast to grow out of control and trigger infections in the mouth and esophagus in both men and women, a form of thrush we more typically associate with infants.

Thrush shows up as white patches that can be uncomfortable and interfere with taste. Thrush may also produce chest discomfort if the infection is in the esophagus.

Yeast infections can also develop in the lower bowel, causing anything from rectal itch to diarrhea. Left untreated, yeast overgrowth can lead to an array of illnesses.

BREAKING THE ANTIBIOTIC CYCLE

Fortunately, there is much you can do to treat these problems…or avoid them altogether. One possible way is with *probiotics*, says Dr. Galland. Probiotics are living organisms that you ingest. Although there are several groups of these, the most common is *Lactobacillus*, which includes the well-known probiotic acidophilus. As you may know, *acidophilus* is added to yogurt, but loading up on supermarket yogurts may not help because Lactobacillus survival rates depend on characteristics of the particular strain, individual components in the yogurt and temperature over time.

To more reliably counteract the effects of the antibiotics, Dr. Galland has patients take a combination of two products. First, when it comes to battling a yeast infection, Dr. Galland claims that "it's yeast against yeast." He recommends a yeast with the botanical name *Saccharomyces boulardii*, which is similar to, but distinct from, baker's or brewer's yeast. Europeans routinely treat food poisoning and travelers' and antibiotic-induced diarrhea with this yeast, which can be found in the French market under the name Ultra-Levure. You can find it in US health-food stores and in some pharmacies under the name Florastor.

Caution: Dr. Galland warns that those who are allergic to baker's or brewer's yeast should avoid Florastor.

Dr. Galland also recommends taking Lactobacillus in capsule form to add back the "good bacteria." He prefers Culturelle, which you can find at many health-food stores.

DOCTOR'S ORDERS

Dr. Galland's regimen to avoid getting either a yeast infection or the more common bacterial one is to take 250 milligrams (mg) of Florastor twice each day with food and at the same time you take your antibiotic. After you finish the antibiotics, switch to Culturelle (the probiotic), and take 100 mg a day for 30 days.

If you are allergic to Saccharomyces boulardii, take Culturelle twice a day while on the antibiotic and once a day for a month afterward. Remember, follow this advice only after checking with your physician to be sure that it is safe for you.

OTHER SURPRISES

When using antibiotics, patients could experience a number of side effects. According to Dr. Galland, it is important to watch for allergic symptoms—blisters, hives and swelling, as well as fever, headaches, diarrhea and skin rashes.

If a symptom emerges *after* you have started the antibiotic or the treatment recommended above, notify your doctor right away. Check with your doctor to see if you should avoid sunlight while on antibiotics, especially tetracycline or doxycycline drugs. And of course, always ask your doctor or pharmacist about possible drug interactions.

Dangerous Prescription Combinations

Jeffrey S. Borer, MD, Harriman professor of cardiovascular medicine, NewYork–Presbyterian Hospital/Weill Medical College of Cornell University, New York City.

Chances are excellent that at some time in your life—probably a number of times—you've been given the popular antibiotic *erythromycin*. This 60-year-old drug is effective in combating numerous infections and it does not carry the allergy risk that penicillin does.

A study published in the *New England Journal of Medicine* reports that when people take erythromycin in combination with certain other drugs, they might be dramatically increasing their risk for cardiac arrest.

The study, from the Vanderbilt University School of Medicine, reviewed medical records of 4,404 Medicaid patients from Tennessee with death attributed to cardiac arrest. After establishing the medications these patients were taking, researchers determined that erythromycin in combination with antihypertensive drugs, such as the calcium channel blockers *verapamil* and *diltiazem*, or antifungals, such as *ketoconazole, itraconazole* and *fluconazole*, increased the chances for sudden cardiac death fivefold. Three people died of sudden cardiac death, a small but statistically significant number, according to the study's lead author Wayne A. Ray, MD.

WHAT'S GOING ON?

The reason why erythromycin can potentially combine lethally with other drugs is not a mystery. Some drugs, newer ones in particular, slow the removal of erythromycin from the body. This increase in erythromycin levels can trigger an abnormal and potentially fatal heart rhythm. Incidentally, grapefruit juice can also block the body's metabolism of erythromycin and therefore should be avoided when taking the drug.

PERSPECTIVE ON THE STUDY

We spoke with cardiologist Jeffrey S. Borer, MD, Harriman professor of cardiovascular medicine at NewYork–Presbyterian Hospital/Weill

Medical College of Cornell University in New York City, about the study and his advice on the matter.

He agrees that this study provides important cautionary information about the drug, but he says that it's necessary to put the study in a broader context. The decision to prescribe any drug should always be based on the potential benefit versus the potential risk.

Doctors prescribe erythromycin in many instances because it is the best antibiotic to treat the infection. He explains that this study does not provide large enough numbers of patients affected or cover enough years to determine an accurate comparison among those taking the drugs in combination, those taking them singularly and those not taking them at all.

For example, Dr. Borer notes that the three patients who died combined erythromycin with calcium channel blockers for high blood pressure. But calcium channel blockers, he says, have been associated with cardiac risk and other problems in certain clinical settings, and they call for careful monitoring.

WHAT TO DO

What are we to make of this study? Dr. Borer emphasizes that this is an excellent opportunity to review the general use—or misuse—of erythromycin.

Doctors often prescribe erythromycin to treat nonspecific respiratory tract infections, which are rampant in the winter months. Current research shows that most of these infections are viral in nature, so antibiotics won't help them. Consequently, his first advice is to be sure you need to take a drug before you agree to it.

Always tell your doctor about all medications and drugs you are taking, including herbs and supplements, to avoid the danger of drug interactions. Furthermore, be sure to read all of the information that comes from the pharmaceutical company with medications. Dr. Borer says that these spell out whether or not a drug combines to inhibit the metabolism of other drugs. This is critical to know because anytime you inhibit the breakdown of a drug, its levels build up in your bloodstream, potentially into the toxic range.

People on calcium channel blockers should not take erythromycin at all, and those taking the other associated risk medications should discuss with their doctors alternatives to erythromycin.

Remember: All drugs are powerful—they must be to accomplish their job. But with their power comes potential risks, and it is something to always keep in mind. When you need them, drugs are a godsend—just be sure the necessity is there and that you take them wisely.

More Dangers Of Painkillers

Steven E. Nissen, MD, chairman, department of cardiovascular medicine, Cleveland Clinic, Cleveland, Ohio. Dr. Nissen is past president of the American College of Cardiology.

For people suffering from arthritis or headache pain, the solution used to seem relatively simple—take one or two aspirin, ibuprofen or other NSAID (nonsteroidal anti-inflammatory drug) as per label instructions and the pain will go away, or at least recede to a manageable level. However, that advice has become suspect in recent years. Ever since hidden cardiovascular risks forced the withdrawal of the NSAID *rofecoxib* (Vioxx) from the market because it was linked to increased risk of heart attack and stroke, all kinds of questions have arisen about the safety of NSAIDs.

UNDER A CLOUD

Recent criticism has been leveled at the popular over-the-counter pain reliever *naproxen* (brands such as Aleve and Naprosyn), which had been considered the safest cardiovascular choice among the NSAIDs. Steven E. Nissen, MD, chairman of the department of cardiovascular medicine at the Cleveland Clinic and a past-president of the American College of Cardiology, says that, in his opinion, the study criticizing naproxen was flawed, in that it was terminated early—but he does concur that this entire class of drugs is under something of a cloud, and agrees that people with cardiovascular problems should be very careful about taking any NSAID (as should people with a long list of other health problems, too, including digestive, liver and kidney disorders).

A FLAWED STUDY

The anticipated ADAPT (Alzheimer's Disease Anti-Inflammatory Prevention Trial) research study was designed to compare naproxen and *celecoxib* (Celebrex) in the prevention of Alzheimer's disease. However, the National Institutes of Health (NIH), in response to concerns from the ADAPT Steering Committee, halted the study prematurely (before a reliable conclusion about its potential for Alzheimer's could be made from the data) after Merck withdrew Vioxx and a second study showed increased risks with Celebrex. According to Dr. Nissen, the decision to stop the naproxen trial was made "in a panic" after the publicity about the risks of Vioxx and Celebrex. The details of the study were only recently published two years later.

According to Dr. Nissen, stopping the trial before its intended completion resulted in data that cannot be reliably interpreted—either relative to Alzheimer's disease or cardiac risks. He describes the warnings about naproxen as "the medical equivalent of yelling 'fire' in a crowded auditorium," and he believes the premature termination of the drug trial was not decided for scientific reasons.

TAKE ALL NSAIDS WITH CAUTION

It's important to understand that, to varying degrees, all NSAIDs have cardiovascular and gastrointestinal side effects. In various studies comparing naproxen with other NSAIDs, naproxen has often come out as least harmful to the heart—and one of the hardest on the stomach. Therefore, in the opinion of Dr. Nissen, naproxen is still the safest NSAID for a person with cardiovascular risk factors, although someone who has ulcers might be better off with other alternatives.

LOOK FOR ALTERNATIVES

That said, if you don't need a drug, don't take it, emphasizes Dr. Nissen. If you are experiencing such severe pain that you need to take something, take the lowest possible dose for the shortest possible period of time. For example, people with osteoarthritis have good days and bad days. They should take pain medication only when they are really suffering and need relief. If you have unrelenting chronic pain, such as from rheumatoid arthritis, and take pain relievers daily, ask your health-care provider to weigh the risks and benefits of the drugs, and discuss if a drug or non-pharmaceutical option —such as meditation, massage, Reiki or music —is a possibility for you.

10

Health Alerts

What's Behind the Rise in Health-Care Costs?

Health-care premiums are on the rise, outpacing wages and inflation. And, frighteningly, the spike in health-care costs is actually low compared with the fact that insurance costs have been averaging double or triple inflation for years. How did we get to this point and what can we do about it? Charles B. Inlander, founder of the People's Medical Society, offers an explanation and—even though this is a complicated situation with no easy solutions—a few coping tips to rein in runaway costs.

A HEALTH-CARE SYSTEM IN DISARRAY

The numbers are grim. The United States spends twice as much money per capita on medical care as any other industrialized country, yet we tend to have worse results with infant mortality, disease-free life expectancy, cancer rates, hospital infections, drug errors and many other health-care measurements. We spend more, and we get less. This is because of rampant waste and inefficiency in our health-care system, says Inlander.

According to a 2007 survey conducted by the Commonwealth Fund (*www.cmwf.org*), a private foundation that supports independent research on health-care issues, Americans are more than aware of the critical flaws in the system. Only four of ten adults said that they are confident in their ability to get safe, effective care. More than one third of underinsured respondents reported that they had received poorly coordinated, inefficient or unsafe care at some time during the past two years. This included unnecessary treatments, duplicate tests, drug or lab test errors and failure to provide test results or other important medical information.

Charles B. Inlander, a consumer advocate and health-care consultant based in Fogelsville, Pennsylvania. He was founding president of People's Medical Society, a consumer advocacy group active in the 1980s and 1990s. He is the author of more than 20 books, including *Take This Book to the Hospital With You*. St. Martin's Press.

THE NUMBER OF UNINSURED AMERICANS IS ALARMING

According to the survey by the Commonwealth Fund, the problem has been persistent. Employers have reacted to rocketing health-care costs by reducing or dropping health-care benefits for workers, adding to the growing ranks of the uninsured.

Statistics from the Census Bureau for the year 2008, the most recent available statistics, indicate that over 46 million Americans, or about 15% of the population, are uninsured. About 17% of adults under the age of 65 are not insured (Those over 65 are generally covered by Medicare.)

People without insurance are less likely to have a regular doctor or get important screening tests such as mammograms. According to the Institute of Medicine, approximately 18,000 Americans die prematurely each year because they have no health insurance. And a recent study estimates that as many as 45,000 U.S. deaths may be linked to lack of health insurance.

This is why Inlander feels we may eventually end up with national health insurance. But is national health insurance the solution? Would offloading the expense of medical care to the government address the inefficiencies in the system? Or would this just guarantee payment for them? Whatever the future holds, here's how to be proactive.

WHAT YOU CAN DO

While the politicians bicker about how to fix the rising health-care costs, there are steps that we can take as individuals to keep a lid on our own medical expenses. *Inlander recommends the following…*

•**Use generic prescription drugs.** Not only are generics equally as effective as brand-name drugs, they are often less expensive. Generics only become available after a brand-name drug loses its patent protection (after years on the market) and thus have a longer track record for safety as well.

•**Negotiate fees.** Don't assume you have to pay the posted fees. Many physicians will be flexible depending on your circumstances, and may waive fees for repeat visits. For example, if your physician tells you to come back in for a blood pressure check or to examine your child's ears after an infection, say you're not coming back if you get charged again.

•**Shop around for the most economical health-care plan** that fits the specific needs of your family. You can learn more about how to choose at Web sites such as the Agency for Healthcare Research and Quality's, *www.ahrq. gov,* and the Robert Wood Johnson Foundation's project at *www.covertheuninsured.org.*

Also: Our medical expert, Andrew L. Rubman, ND, recommends that his patients focus on another important aspect of "beating health-care costs"—staying healthy through a focus on creating wellness in their lives. Whereas the mainstream medical community is geared toward symptom suppression through pharmaceutical, holistic practitioners work with patients to maximize their body's function and help it avoid disease…and in turn this reduces unnecessary health-care costs. Whether or not your insurance company covers these visits, you may well find a better return on your investment with an alternative practitioner.

info The Center on Budget and Policy Priorities, *www.cbpp.org.*
The Commonwealth Fund, *www.cmwf.org.*

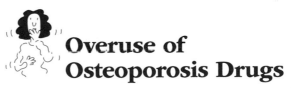

Overuse of Osteoporosis Drugs

Pablo Alonso-Coello, MD, family practitioner, Hospital de Sant Pau, Barcelona, Spain.

There was a time when osteoporosis was diagnosed only in frail, elderly people with brittle, easily broken bones. Then Big Pharma developed drugs to treat it and suddenly this so-called "disease" became much more common—and was seen to be endangering wide swaths of postmenopausal women. Over the years, the definition of osteoporosis has been broadened to include even more women and older men and greater awareness of osteopenia, a sort of "pre-osteoporosis" in which bone density is low but not so low as to constitute osteoporosis, was urged.

UNNECESSARY DRUGS WITH DANGEROUS SIDE EFFECTS?

Now it's hard to turn on the TV (or open a newspaper or go on-line) without being bombarded with ads for drugs not only for osteoporosis, but also encouraging women to proactively ask their doctors if they should take these drugs if they are "at risk," with hardly a mention of the very real side effects and dangers associated with them.

Caution: The US Food and Drug Administration (FDA) issued a drug alert in 2008 for bisphosphonates (a class of drugs that includes *alendronate* and *ibandronate*), warning that they can cause severe bone, muscle or joint pain. Other side effects of bisphosphonates include difficulty swallowing, esophageal problems, gastric ulcer and bone tissue death of the jaw. *Raloxifene* (Evista), another type of osteoporosis drug known as a selective estrogen receptor modulator or SERM, increases the risk of blood clots and stroke. Ironically, *alendronate* (Fosamax) has been linked to femur fractures.

MORE RISKS THAN BENEFITS FOR OSTEOPENIA

According to a recent report in the *British Medical Journal*, drug manufacturers regularly smudge the line between osteoporosis itself and osteopenia in order to sell more drugs. It's true that these drugs can successfully reduce the risk of fractures, at least in the short term, in people who actually have osteoporosis…and now that we're living longer lives, osteoporosis may become more common. But, says article coauthor Pablo Alonso-Coello, MD, a family practitioner affiliated with Hospital de Sant Pau in Barcelona, Spain, the benefits of osteoporosis drugs are exaggerated for people who just have osteopenia.

"This move to treat pre-osteoporosis raises serious questions about the benefit-risk ratio for low-risk individuals, and about the costs of medicalizing and potentially medicating an enormous group of healthy people," writes Dr. Alonso-Coello. Not coincidentally, using current medical criteria, nearly half of postmenopausal women could be said to have osteopenia,

which represents a huge and highly profitable potential new market for Big Pharma.

PLAYING WITH STATISTICS

Drug companies commonly cite several studies on four different osteoporosis drugs to demonstrate their benefits for women with osteopenia. In their research, Dr. Alonso-Coello and his colleagues found that the results of these studies were expressed in a way that suggested the benefits were greater than they really are. Statistics can tell almost any story you want, after all.

Example: Osteoporosis drugs are generally reported to reduce the risk of fracture by 50%…but it is important to look at "absolute" rather than "relative" risk. A woman with osteoporosis might reduce her absolute risk of a fracture from, say, 10% to 5% (which might be a clinically relevant benefit), while the risk for a person with osteopenia drops only from an already low 2% to 1% or even 1% to 0.5%. So calling it a 50% reduced risk in these cases distorts its clinical significance. He warns that many study authors were employees of, or otherwise connected with, drug companies, pointing to a conflict of interest.

TAKE STEPS TO PROMOTE BONE HEALTH

Don't be swayed by the advertising. There are a number of strategies you can follow to prevent fractures and keep your bones strong and healthy as you age—and they don't all involve taking drugs.

Among the non-pharmaceutical steps recommended by the National Osteoporosis Foundation to promote bone health…

•**Get adequate calcium and vitamin D.** Current daily guidelines for adults over 50 are 1,200 mg of calcium and 800 to 1,000 IU of vitamin D. D-3, or cholecalciferol, is the form of vitamin D best for bones. Taking a daily walk in the sunlight can also boost vitamin D levels.

•**Engage in regular weight-bearing exercise such as walking and dancing,** and resistance exercises such as using weight machines or resistance bands. Read more about safe exercises online at *www.nof.org*, and talk to your doctor before embarking on any exercise program.

•**Don't smoke at all and don't drink alcohol to excess.**

•**Consider having a bone mineral density test if there is indication you need one.** Dr. Alonso-Coello advises bone density testing not as a regular screening exam, but for women who have had a prior osteoporatic fracture or who have risk factors for a fracture (e.g., a family history of maternal fractures). Early menopause may be another risk factor.

Dr. Alonso-Coello recommends instituting these additional measures to prevent falls for older people…

•**Use a walker or cane as necessary.**

•**Wear supportive, low-heeled shoes.**

•**Install grab bars on bathroom walls near the tub, shower and toilet.**

•**Be sure your home is well lit.**

•**Keep rooms free of clutter.**

•**Be sure that all carpets have skid-proof backing.**

Important: Osteopenia is not osteoporosis, and using drugs for prevention is not the same as using drugs for treatment. If you consider taking any drug solely as a preventive treatment—especially if the treatment is long-term and has potentially serious side effects, as with osteoporosis drugs—Dr. Alonso-Coello strongly advises that you seek a second opinion. Be sure to talk with your family physician and research treatment options before making your decision. With so many ways to keep bones strong naturally, medication should only be considered as a last resort.

Generic Doesn't Always Mean Cheap

Larry D. Sasich, PharmD, MPH, assistant professor, department of pharmacy practice, Lake Erie College of Osteopathic Medicine (LECOM) School of Pharmacy, Erie, Pennsylvania.

It's commonly accepted consumer wisdom that generic drugs are cheaper than brand-name drugs, and by and large that's true.

But as it turns out, generics aren't always as inexpensive as many expect them to be, and it can be a challenge to get truly deep discounts on them. Costs vary wildly.

To learn more about the prices of generic drugs versus brand-name ones and for advice on how to purchase prescription medicines wisely, we asked Larry D. Sasich, PharmD, MPH, assistant professor in the department of pharmacy practice at Lake Erie College of Osteopathic Medicine (LECOM) School of Pharmacy in Erie, Pennsylvania.

WHY AREN'T GENERIC DRUGS CHEAPER?

A generic drug is the therapeutic equivalent and has the same active ingredients of a brand-name drug whose patent has expired. Once a brand-name drug's patent expires, other pharmaceutical companies are free to manufacture a drug with the same active ingredients and market it under a generic name.

The theory is the more competition, the cheaper the drug should be. However, especially when a generic drug first goes on the market, the price may not drop dramatically, because the initial manufacturer is legally entitled to an exclusivity period of about six months in which they alone can market the generic alternative.

HANGING ON TO PROFITS

When a drug goes off patent and becomes available generically, drug manufacturers typically scramble for new ways to shore up profit margins. One strategy is selling generics through their own subsidiaries. Another is tweaking molecules.

According to Dr. Sasich, it's a common practice for pharmaceutical firms to introduce "new, better" versions of blockbuster drugs as they near the end of the patent life. These slightly reformulated drugs, known as "me-too" drugs, are modified versions of the original medicine that are marketed as being even better. However, usually they really aren't.

Case in point: Nexium and Prilosec. *Esomeprazole magnesium* (Nexium) is basically a knock-off of *omeprazole* (Prilosec), says Dr. Sasich. Both heartburn medications are proton pump inhibitors (PPIs). When Prilosec went off patent and became available generically, its manufacturer introduced the supposedly improved drug, Nexium, and claimed it was metabolized more slowly and produced superior results in order to maintain its share of the hugely profitable PPI market.

However, most consumers are likely to find sufficient relief for occasional heartburn and indigestion with generic *omeprazole*. Also, *omeprazole* is available over-the-counter as Prilosec OTC, and is priced at a fraction of Nexium's cost.

PRACTICE MONEY-SAVING STRATEGIES

Remember that drug manufacturers and pharmacies are in business to make money, which sometimes means they will attempt to sell us expensive medicines with high profit margins—even when cheaper generics are available. *To get the safest, most effective drugs at the lowest possible prices, Dr. Sasich recommends the following strategies…*

•**Always ask your physician or pharmacist whether generic versions of your regimen are available.** In many cases, when a less expensive generic version of a drug is available, your insurance company will require this. By law generic drugs must meet the same quality standards as the brand-name ones they replicate.

•**If you are taking a brand-name drug, consider a switch to its generic version if one is available.** *Widely prescribed drugs that in recent years have become available in a generic form include…*

•Fexofenadine hydrochloride, the generic of the antihistamine Allegra.

•Meloxicam, the generic of Mobic, an arthritis pain medication.

•Pravastatin sodium, the generic of the cholesterol-lowering statin drug Pravachol.

•Sertraline hydrochloride, the generic of the antidepressant Zoloft.

•Simvastatin, the generic of the cholesterol-targeting statin drug Zocor.

•Venlafaxine hydrochloride, the generic of the antidepressant Effexor.

•Zolpidem tartrate, the generic of the sleep aid Ambien.

•**Shop around.** Especially if you're paying out-of-pocket, Dr. Sasich says it is worth shopping around for the best price.

Example: At wholesale or warehouse stores such as Costco and Sam's Club, you are apt to find huge discounts on generic prescription drugs. On Costco's Web site, *www.costco.com*, I found the brand-name statin Zocor (30 20-mg tablets) listed at $152.78, and its generic alternative *simvastatin* (also 30 20-mg tablets) for just $5.90. At Drugstore.com, their equivalents were priced at $149.97 and $27.99, respectively.

•**Beware of new drugs, which are usually more expensive**—and incidentally, not always as safe. Unless there is a compelling therapeutic reason, Dr. Sasich advises against taking a new drug until it has been on the market for a minimum of seven years, which is long enough to begin to see long-term side effects. All too often, as happened with *rofecoxib* (Vioxx) and *cisapride* (Propulsid), dangerous side effects of drugs emerge only after they have been on the market for months or years.

•**Visit Web sites to learn more about prescription drugs.** Many give information about drugs, including drug and price comparisons. *Among the most helpful…*

•*www.worstpills.org.* Brought to you by the Washington, DC-based watchdog group Public Citizen, this site offers information on drugs and their potential health dangers and legal issues.

•*www.CRBestBuyDrugs.org.* This Consumer Reports site compares and contrasts many drugs by category. Use it to see which prescription medicines might work best for you, so you can discuss alternatives with your doctor.

•*www.destinationrx.com.* Visit this site for specific price comparisons. For example, see if Drugstore.com is offering the same prescription you need for less than Costco.com. For additional on-line price comparisons from verified pharmacies, try *www.pharmacychecker.com*.

As you can see, there are lots of remedies for overcoming the rising costs of prescription and even non-prescription drugs, but usually it's up to you to take charge of getting the medicine you need at the best possible price. Keep your physician up to date on your research and questions, of course. And remember, the medicine you need to be healthy shouldn't come at the cost of your financial well-being.

Pharma Promotion To Doctors Greater Than Ever

Marcia Angell, MD, senior lecturer, department of social medicine, Harvard Medical School, Boston, Massachusetts, and author of *The Truth About the Drug Companies: How They Deceive Us and What to Do About It*. Random House. She is the former editor-in-chief of the *New England Journal of Medicine* and has been named one of *Time* magazine's 25 most influential Americans.

The book *The Truth About the Drug Companies: How They Deceive Us and What to Do About It* by Marcia Angell, MD, a senior lecturer at Harvard Medical School, caused a stir when she unmasked the level of influence pharmaceutical companies have over decisions and recommendations made by doctors. Sadly, the ruckus has calmed but nothing has changed. Medical consumers continue to be treated based on marketing messages rather than best medical practice.

Example: According to recent reports, pharmaceutical companies spend anywhere from $28 to $58 billion on promotional activities, and a report in the *Journal of the American Medical Association* recently disclosed that 90% of the money companies spend on marketing is directed toward physicians.

Also: Researchers at a scientific meeting of the American Academy of Family Physicians reported that doctors who hand out sample medications are also more likely to write prescriptions for them. A survey of physicians found that nearly all doctors say they accept free drug samples, free meals and free travel from pharmaceutical and medical device companies or other industry representatives. It's an issue getting more attention—and one consumers can impact by recognizing its roots.

NO SUCH THING AS A FREE LUNCH

Drug company representatives routinely bring meals and gifts to the staff at physicians' offices and also wine and dine the doctors themselves. The indoctrination begins as early as medical school, where drug reps connect with hungry, sleep-deprived residents and medical students by bringing them pizzas and colas—not to mention free medical equipment, like stethoscopes that cost as much as $250 and are emblazoned with the name of the sponsoring drug company.

Drug companies call these outreach efforts "education"—sponsoring dinners at fine restaurants and conferences in exotic locales such as Hawaii or Puerto Rico. Many physicians go along with this and even receive CME credits (Continuing Medical Education, often required for licensure and admitting privileges at hospitals) at these junkets.

Dr. Angell points out that drug company activities are not education. What they are is marketing. There is no such thing as unbiased education from drug companies.

WHAT YOU CAN DO

The bottom line is that the system should be changed, and laws should be enacted to bring a halt to these sorts of actions of pharmaceutical companies. Activists are working toward this goal, but why sit around waiting for it?

According to Dr. Angell, the important drugs don't need big marketing budgets—they sell. Most marketing, she says, is for "me-too" drugs (trivial variations to expand the market of a major drug—for instance, there are six statin drugs similar to Lipitor). She believes, therefore, that the economic impact of cutting out inappropriate marketing would be huge—roughly 30% of their revenues. *Strategies you can undertake on your own include...*

● **Always ask about cheaper or generic drugs.** As noted above, physicians are influenced by free samples of "new and better" drugs from pharmaceutical companies. But it may be safer in many cases and also far less expensive to stick with older drugs with a long-established track record, unless there is a compelling therapeutic reason to take a new and more expensive drug. And, while it may be convenient when your doctor hands you a freebie, be sure to ask if the free product is really the *right* product. If a prescription was written, would it be for this product in this dose?

● **Speak up at the doctor's office.** Dr. Angell says she'd raise an objection if she happened to be sitting in a doctor's office when a drug rep stopped by...and she urges us to do the same.

Try: Ask office staff how much time they give to the reps while their waiting room is filled and appointments run late. Share with them your concern that they are often being educated by recent college graduates with large expense accounts and no medical training. Ask what they're doing to keep themselves apprised of the latest medical breakthroughs not funded or sponsored by drug companies.

Note: Other warning signs of drug company influence to look for in medical offices—pens, prescription pads and other trinkets with telltale drug company logos. If you see these, express your concerns to your doctor. If a physician asks if you mind if a drug rep comes into the exam room with you, don't just object…get a new doctor.

Best: Concentrate on staying healthy. That way you will see your doctor less and take fewer drugs.

 # Making Medical Paperwork Easier

Nora Johnson, CCP (Certified Compliance Professional), medical advocate with her own company, Med-X, (Medical Expense Review & Recovery), in Caldwell, West Virginia, and director of education and compliance for Medical Billing Advocates of America, Salem, Virginia.

Medical bills are incredibly complicated and expensive—even for those with health insurance.

But here's what you may not know: Hospital bills aren't "unavoidable" in the same way as, say, taxes and death. The number at the bottom of the bill may not be the amount you have to pay at all. In fact, there are a number of things you can do to protect yourself from unfair medical charges, including working with a professional "medical billing advocate."

Nora Johnson, CCP (Certified Compliance Professional), a medical advocate with her own company, Med-X (Medical Expense Review & Recovery), and director of education and compliance for Medical Billing Advocates of America

has some answers. Though most of these strategies relate to those with health insurance, Johnson has plenty of advice for those uninsured as well.

BE SURE YOU GET WHAT YOU'RE INSURED FOR

Here's Johnson's first rule for those with health insurance: Know your policy. It's boring as anything, she admits, "so most people never bother to find out what their policy covers and—often even more important—what it doesn't include."

If you know in advance that a treatment or procedure you need is not covered, you can negotiate the price with the physician or facility beforehand, while you still have some room to do so. Most health-care policies exempt emergency room doctors and procedures from needing to be "in network." But emergency coverage is policy-specific.

Caution: Another common trap for the insured is inadvertently going "out of network," she says.

Example: Say you are having gallbladder removal, which is typically an elective surgical procedure. You've chosen a surgeon covered by your plan and he's chosen a team, including the anesthesiologist and pathologist, all of whom you assume are on the plan as well. That's not necessarily true, says Johnson. Often radiologists, anesthesiologists and pathologists are out of network or even do not participate with any insurance companies.

Best: Always confirm by calling your insurance company (the published list of participating providers may not be up to date) before a procedure and confirm with the physician. If a provider is not covered, you have the right to one who is.

Try: Ask for the names of participating providers in your area and request in writing that the hospital use one of them. If the hospital refuses, tell them you will sign an agreement for the provider(s) they want to use on condition those providers will accept the out-of-network fee from your insurance company as payment in full.

Helpful: As further protection, Johnson suggests noting on the back of the hospital admissions form that you are responsible only for participating providers' billing. On the same form there will be an item that says you will pay all "usual and customary charges." Cross that out, she says, inserting the words that you are responsible only for "fair and reasonable" charges for anything your insurance plan does not cover.

WHAT'S "FAIR AND REASONABLE"

This brings us to a brief discussion of what hospitals charge. They say they charge all patients the same rates, says Johnson, which is basically true—but what's also true is that not everyone has to pay the same fees. When negotiating for clients, she bases what they should pay on that same phrase mentioned above, "fair and reasonable," which is the reimbursement most commonly accepted by that hospital, usually from Medicare.

Rule of thumb: The hospital's billed charge is the gross charge and it is more than the hospital accepts from most other payers for the same service, she says.

DECIPHERING THE CHARGES

Further confusing matters, all medical billing is based on three coding systems—ICD-9-CM, CPT and HCPCS—used for reimbursement, and she estimates that about one-third of all billing errors result from incorrect coding, such as entering a code for a procedure you never had. While these codes aren't available to the public, you can and should request an itemized bill from your hospital, which includes explanations. Review it carefully, and if you're confused or see an error, ask for clarification from the hospital's billing office.

Note: Pay close attention to seemingly minor billing incidentals such as IV start kits (quoted cost, $57…real cost, 61 cents). Medicare does not allow independent charges for such incidentals, so it stands to reason that you should not have to pay them either.

Reason: Supplies are calculated into the room/unit/procedure charge. Therefore they are duplicates when billed again for a separate dollar amount.

TROUBLESHOOTING

Medical Billing Advocates of America say 90% of medical bills contain errors. If there are mistakes in your bill, Johnson says you should address them immediately.

If your insurance company refuses payment for something, figure out where it went wrong—perhaps the statement was miscoded or the doctor's office filed incorrect information. Talk to both the insurance company and the doctor's office to learn if there is an error, and then correct it.

Caution: People with high deductible policies have one more consideration—the hospital may charge its full (and inflated) fee up to that amount. Don't let them get away with that. Insist instead that fees against your deductible are the discounted rate (at least 35%)—not the full—charges.

EMERGENCY ROOMS CAN'T REQUIRE PAYMENT IN ADVANCE

Nearly all emergency rooms cannot, by law, withhold emergency medical treatment based on payment issues. The Emergency Medical Treatment and Active Labor Act requires all hospitals accepting Medicare to not withhold screening, stabilizing treatment or appropriate transfer of patients, regardless of whether patients are on Medicare or have no insurance or ability to pay.

Caution: Some hospitals will attempt to get a credit card number up front in order to ensure payment. If this happens, warns Johnson, ask that they put the demand for payment prior to rendering treatment in writing, specifying whatever the amount or percentage they are requesting. Simply say "I won't pay unless you put it in writing."

Reason: By asking for them to request payment in writing, you will find they quit bothering you for payment before service, since Federal law mandates that hospitals render emergency treatment that is medically necessary to save lives regardless of inability to pay. After that, if you feel you are being overcharged, you can get the official hospital policy about payment requirements in writing, which you can then take to an advocate for help in negotiating.

Also: Patients can inquire about "charity care," says Johnson. All hospitals that participate with Medicare have to provide a certain amount of charity care to patients who qualify. Get the charity care forms from the hospital, fill them out, make copies and return them directly to the hospital.

WHEN TO CALL IN BACK-UP ASSISTANCE

If you have been unsuccessful at resolving your billing problems or feel that the fees charged are truly unreasonable, it may be time to call in a professional advocate to help. These professionally certified and trained specialists will advocate on behalf of individuals to combat unreasonable or outrageous medical fees.

Reason: Although hiring an advocate to fight your battle might at first seem as though you are just adding another cost to already high expenses, in reality their training and negotiating savvy can actually reduce costs. The depth of their knowledge and experience with complex medical billing enables advocates to negotiate fair fees for virtually everything—including CAT scans and other imaging procedures, as well as hospital and doctor bills and fees. Johnson advises calling a medical billing advocate after you have reviewed an itemized bill yourself if you think it is not fair—say, $6,000 for two stitches in the emergency room.

Advocate fees vary. Johnson says they charge by the hour or a percentage of the money saved. They aim to be "reasonable" and always negotiate up front to spare you more stomach-turning surprises.

info To find a qualified advocate, you can go to the Medical Billing Advocates of America Web site *www.billadvocates.com*, or call 540-387-5870.

Are Specialty Cardiac Hospitals Better?

Peter Cram, MD, MBA, assistant professor of internal medicine, University of Iowa Hospitals & Clinics, Iowa City, Iowa.

There's a new trend in the delivery of medicine—specialty hospitals that focus on a single, lucrative area of care such as cardiology or orthopedics. The idea is that a more efficient and focused health-care model will enable physicians to deliver a higher standard of care that costs less. It has long been recognized that the higher volume of a particular surgery performed at a medical center—whether it's removing a gallbladder, opening a blocked artery or replacing a hip—the better outcome, on average. Using this rationale, specialty hospitals make sense, don't they?

Well, not really. Though the argument might be made for more quality control and cost-effective care, there are other factors that can influence outcome data—for instance, heart hospitals attract patients who are healthier and wealthier. So, it's hard to know definitively whether they achieve better results than hospitals where a comparable volume of similar procedures are performed.

Example: A recent study demonstrates that when a specialty heart hospital is opened in a neighborhood, suddenly more heart procedures—in one case a 42% higher rate of elective heart procedures—are performed.

AT THE HEART OF THE MATTER: POLITICS AND PROFITS

University of Iowa researcher Peter Cram, MD is involved in research on the impact of specialty hospitals on the delivery of care to financially vulnerable populations. He notes that specialty hospitals are usually for-profit facilities owned at least in part by doctors who refer their own patients to them. Most that have opened since 1990 are located in states lacking a "certificate of need" permit for the construction or expansion of health-care facilities (such as Texas, Arizona, California, Kansas, Louisiana, Oklahoma and South Dakota).

CLEAR CONFLICTS OF INTEREST

The conflicts of interest aren't hard to identify. Critics instantly pointed out that when doctors share in hospital ownership, they're more likely to refer patients for procedures there since financial incentives add to the medical considerations. This in and of itself could account for the significant rise in the volume of expensive and specialized procedures. Another problem is that these specialty facilities rapidly earned a reputation for "skimming" the healthier, better-insured patients, leaving the burden of caring for the sicker and uninsured on general hospitals.

Example: At the VA Health Services Research and Development Center of Excellence in Ann Arbor, Michigan, researchers examined the provision of heart care for Medicare beneficiaries 65 and older in various regions around the country. Their goal was to determine whether specialty heart hospitals were associated with an increase in volume of heart procedures to unblock clogged arteries—specifically, coronary artery bypass surgery (CABGs) and "percutaneous coronary interventions" (PCIs), which are less invasive artery-opening techniques, such as angioplasty and stenting.

Results: The researchers found that four years after the opening of a new heart hospital in a region, the rate of heart procedures performed in that area doubled when compared with those where no new specialty hospital opened or even where heart programs were opened at a general hospital. The numbers were more dramatic when it came to post-heart attack PCI procedures (emergency) versus non-emergency (elective) PCIs—in the latter, the medical benefits are less clear-cut. When a specialty heart hospital opened in a particular community, the rate of elective PCIs jumped by 42%. This was nearly twice the rate of growth for these procedures both in regions where a general hospital had recently added cardiac services (23%), and where no new cardiac care facilities had opened (24.8%). These results were published in the *Journal of the American Medical Association*.

Note: Sufficient concern on this topic once prompted the federal government to put a now defunct ban on opening new specialty hospitals and deny Medicare coverage at these facilities as well. Now a host of new specialty hospitals for cardiac care and orthopedic care are scheduled to open around the country, sparking renewed controversy and debate.

PUT YOUR HEART IN THE RIGHT HANDS: CHOOSING YOUR HOSPITAL

Whether you go to the hospital for a major or minor problem, you must ensure you are in the best hands possible. In Dr. Cram's opinion, that equals experience. Facilities performing the highest volume of the particular procedure you require—whether general or specialty hospitals—remain the safest and most effective choice.

Also: It's best to get a second opinion prior to undergoing such a procedure.

Note: Additionally, hospitals are required to be ever more transparent about reporting on quality—including medical errors, outcomes and more. Asking a physician you trust for advice always makes sense, but now you can also do your own research by going on-line to compare and contrast all types of hospitals in your area. *Good Web sites include...*

• *www.jointcommission.org.* To see how hospitals stack up against one another, visit the free Web site of the Joint Commission and click on "Quality Check."

• *www.leapfroggroup.org.* This not-for-profit, employer-based coalition tracks data on safety and quality practices at more than 1,300 hospitals around the country.

• *www.hospitalcompare.hhs.gov.* A Web site of the US Department of Health & Human Services, this resource contains free performance reports on thousands of hospitals.

Drugstore Medical Clinics Scorecard

Trisha Torrey, syndicated columnist for Syracuse, New York's *Post-Standard* and the *Knoxville News Sentinel's WELL Magazine.* She hosts SUNY Upstate Medical University's HealthLink On Air in upstate New York and is guide of the Patient Empowerment Forum at About.com. Visit her blog at *www.everypatientsadvocate.com.*

Americans spend double what residents of many other industrialized countries do on health-care. Yet, we still have a hard time getting appointments with our doctors, and so we often go without treatment for illnesses and injuries.

A new solution available in many states is retail-based medical clinics, making walk-in clinics even more convenient by locating them in drugstores, supermarkets and other convenient facilities. These may not be the solution to the health-care crisis at large—but walk-in clinics can fill a void by providing very basic care in a far more accessible way.

SO MUCH MORE CONVENIENT...

With the elite concierge medical practices on one end of the spectrum, these are at the other, with care that is down-to-earth and convenient to all. Medical professionals are on staff to treat simple-to-diagnose problems, such as a strep test for a sore throat or a case of poison ivy. They also offer flu shots. Some are operated by independent organizations or hospitals. And, of course, they offer convenient one-stop shopping in that you can even fill your prescription right there if medication is required.

It's all good for the consumer, but it is no surprise that some physicians are up in arms complaining how store-based and walk-in clinics pose a threat to patient safety, not to mention their own profit margins. So, what's a cautious consumer to do?

Patient advocate Trisha Torrey, About.com's expert on patient empowerment and a syndicated newspaper columnist explains that walk-in clinics offer real benefits for consumers—as long as they are used with appropriate caution.

EASY ACCESS, LOWER FEES

Many retail clinics are open on weekends, evenings and holidays. The average visit, including waiting time takes just 15 to 25 minutes, according to the Convenient Care Association, *www.ccaclinics.org*, an organization made up of walk-in clinics across the nation. This is quite a bargain in terms of time, especially when a two-hour wait is not an unusual experience nowadays—even with an appointment.

Torrey says prices are lower at walk-in clinics, and therefore it's not just time but also money you save by using walk-in clinics for medical care. This is especially important for people who are uninsured or under-insured and must pay out-of-pocket for their care.

Bonus: Many insurance plans allow treatment at retail clinics and, in fact, the CCA estimates that 70% of people who visit store-based clinics have health insurance and are using the clinics primarily for convenience. In those cases,

the same insurance co-payments apply as with doctors' offices.

Best: Insurance plans vary, so Torrey advises confirming your company's policy in advance.

Example: Some plans require you to call for preapproval if you go to any office other than your own provider (e.g., on a weekend). Otherwise, unless it is a bona fide emergency such as a car accident—not a Sunday morning sore throat—they won't cover it.

SAFETY CONCERNS PERSIST

Still it is valid to raise questions about safety. Some states require a physician on the premises at all times, while others merely mandate that one is on call. Among the concerns doctors list are no continuity of care, the lack of familiarity with patients' medical histories and "less-than-expert treatment" delivered by nurse practitioners and physician assistants, rather than primary care physicians—though in truth, these professionals often do the same work in private physician practices as well.

Note: Symptoms can be difficult to interpret, Torrey warns. A seemingly innocuous problem, like a bad cough, may be a sign of something more serious than a cold. While there's no guarantee your physician would diagnose this correctly either, the fact that he/she has more training and immediate access to your medical history makes it likelier a more complicated illness would be correctly identified and treated before serious problems arise.

The American Medical Association (AMA) is calling on state and federal governments to investigate how clinics are run and place regulations on what they do. A major reason for this is that many walk-in medical clinics are joint ventures with store-based pharmacies. This opens the door to a potential conflict of interest, since drugstores clearly stand to make money from the prescriptions written in their clinics.

THE DOS AND DON'TS OF DRUGSTORE CLINICS

Torrey's tips on how to use walk-in retail clinics safely and to your best advantage...

•**Don't go to a drugstore clinic for serious medical problems.** If you have chest pain or trouble breathing, for example, call 911. Likewise, walk-in clinics may not be a good idea for people with other health issues, like cancer or even diabetes. You may be better off seeing your primary care physician.

•**Research options in advance.** As noted above, depending on your particular state's regulations, you may be seen by a nurse practitioner, physician assistant or other "physician extender," says Torrey, while others have doctors in attendance at all times. It's a really good idea to call around before you need to visit such a clinic—so you know in advance where to go for the best care when you are sick.

•**Learn a clinic's policy on prescriptions.** Also best done in advance, Torrey recommends that you ask staff what they would do if you wanted to fill your prescription elsewhere. How they respond offers insight into how the clinic operates. If prescriptions written by their medical practitioners can only be filled within their facilities, you may want to seek medical care elsewhere.

•**Bring a list of all drugs and supplements you take and the dosages.** This is the single best way to avoid medical errors such as potentially dangerous drug interactions. Also, check beforehand whether you are up-to-date on immunizations, such as tetanus shots, as this can sometimes affect treatment.

•**Request copies of all medical records of your visit and make sure your regular physician receives these.** While many say they do this automatically, Torrey cautions that they don't always follow through.

Best: Use simple common sense. If you're in good health and have a minor medical issue, you may indeed find that walk-in medical clinics offer some advantages, including easy access, short waits and low prices. Those with chronic or serious health problems do better to seek conventional medical treatment. These walk-in clinics are best used for treating illness and aren't targeted to achieving wellness.

11

Doctors' Good Advice

Help Surgical Wounds Heal Better and Faster

 Are there any ways to help make your surgical wounds heal better and faster naturally? We asked Dr. Alicia Capsey, a naturopathic physician located in Oak Harbor and Greenbank, Washington, to find out.

TWO WEEKS BEFORE SURGERY

Avoid all blood thinners, including aspirin, garlic, ginseng (in excess) and large doses of vitamin E. Taking 100 to 200 international units (IU) of vitamin E or one capsule of ginseng is OK. Typically, physicians will advise stopping or cutting back on blood-thinning medications, such as *warfarin* (Coumadin), before surgery.

If you are not already taking a good-quality multivitamin, start taking one now. That will provide the basic building blocks for healthy skin production and wound healing. Check to make sure that the following supplements, in these dosages—or close to these dosages—are included in your multivitamin (they probably are). If not, you will need to purchase additional supplements.

•**Vitamin A.** 20,000 IU a day. However, Dr. Capsey warns that pregnant women should not take more than 10,000 IU, because the higher dosages can cause birth defects.

•**Zinc.** 30 to 50 milligrams (mg) a day, but take with food to avoid upset stomach.

•**Vitamin E.** 200 IU a day.

•**Copper.** 2 to 3 mg a day.

•**Vitamin C with citrus flavonoids.** 1 to 2 grams a day (for bowel tolerance) with 25 to 50 mg of citrus flavonoids.

Alternatively, take an antioxidant blend that includes vitamins A, C, E, selenium and zinc as your presurgery protocol to reduce inflammation.

Example: Carlson's ACES + Zn, two soft gels per day.

Alicia Capsey, ND, naturopathic physician in private practice at Whidbey Island Naturopathic, Oak Harbor and Greenbank, Washington.

FIVE DAYS BEFORE SURGERY

Dr. Capsey recommends two homeopathic treatments to minimize bruising and bleeding. Start five days before surgery and alternate one night of arnica with one night of phosphorus. Both treatments come as tiny pellets that you swallow. Follow directions on the packages for correct dosing.

● **Arnica.** You can take the homeopathic treatment arnica to minimize bruising.

● **Phosphorus.** In order to minimize bleeding, Dr. Capsey recommends phosphorus, especially if you tend to be a heavy bleeder.

TWO DAYS BEFORE SURGERY

Two days before surgery, take bromelain for just one day. This enzyme helps reduce inflammation. Pineapples are an excellent source of bromelain as a regular part of good nutrition, but for serious wound healing from surgery, you will need to take very high doses, so a bromelain supplement is the way to go. Take three capsules of 250 mg, three times a day in between meals.

Note: Be sure to stop the day before surgery, as bromelain can interfere with fibrin deposition, which is necessary to form clotting around the surgical site—and avoid for three days subsequent to surgery.

AFTER SURGERY

After the surgery is over, take arnica and phosphorus again, using the same dosing schedule as above, until bruising and bleeding are improved.

To help alleviate pain in the incision itself, take bellis perennis, another homeopathic remedy. The Boiron company is a good source for bellis perennis.

Also continue your multivitamin or antioxidant formula for a week or two following surgery, though ideally, these should become a part of your daily health-care routine.

Note: Review homeopathic dosing and protocol for both pre- and post-surgery with a professional specifically trained in it. You can locate someone in your area at *www.homeopathic.org.* Also, be sure to discuss all of Dr. Capsey's recommendations with your surgeon before embarking on them so that he/she is aware of them.

Keeping Minor Surgery Minor

Mark A. Stengler, ND, naturopathic physician in private practice, La Jolla, California...adjunct associate clinical professor at the National College of Natural Medicine, Portland, Oregon...author of many books, including *The Natural Physician's Healing Therapies* and coauthor of *Prescription for Natural Cures* (both from Bottom Line Books)...and author of the *Bottom Line/ Natural Healing* newsletter.

Many people are afraid to be admitted to the hospital—not because of their own health issues, but because of the health issues that may result from being in the hospital. We've all heard stories of people entering the hospital for a "minor" procedure only to suffer complications or even die. According to the Centers for Disease Control and Prevention (CDC), nearly two million Americans each year get an infection in the hospital and more than 90,000 die as a result.

AN INCREASE IN HOSPITAL-ACQUIRED INFECTIONS

Hospital-acquired infections are on the rise. These dangerous infections are difficult to cure, especially when they affect the elderly and those with compromised immune systems. CDC data indicate that more than 70% of the bacteria that cause hospital-acquired infections are resistant to at least one of the drugs most commonly used in treating them.

Antibiotic-resistant staph infections—most notably *methicillin-resistant staphylococcus aureus* (MRSA)—pose an especially grave threat. Even if you survive one, you're more likely to face a longer hospital stay and require treatment with second- or third-choice drugs that may be less effective or ineffective, more toxic and more expensive.

To learn how to stay healthy in the hospital, we consulted Mark A. Stengler, ND, a naturopathic physician in private practice in La Jolla, California, and adjunct associate clinical professor at the National College of Natural Medicine in Portland, Oregon.

WHERE DO HOSPITAL INFECTIONS COME FROM?

Hospital-acquired infections are usually related to a procedure or treatment performed to diagnose or treat a patient's illness or injury, says Dr. Stengler. Urinary tract infections are the most common. These typically occur *after* catheterization and are caused by invasion of bacteria from the skin into the bladder via the catheter. Pneumonia ranks as the second most common type of hospital-acquired infection, and Dr. Stengler warns that patients with poorly functioning immune systems or who are taking antibiotics are at risk for infection by a yeast called *Candida.*

The growing hospital infection problem is due primarily to the huge increase in antibiotic-resistant bacteria, says Dr. Stengler. In his estimation, 25% of all hospital-acquired infections could be prevented by health-care workers if they took proper precautions when caring for patients.

HOW TO PROTECT YOURSELF

If you are given the choice, says Dr. Stengler, opt for outpatient procedures performed by quality doctors. Hospitals, by their nature, are a breeding ground for pathogens because they are filled with sick people.

If you must enter the hospital, Dr. Stengler advises that whenever possible, you first give your immune system a boost. Optimally, begin the boosting regimen one week before entering any hospital and then continue during your hospital stay. *With your doctor's knowledge and permission, Dr. Stengler recommends...*

• **Vitamin C.** 1,000 milligrams (mg) twice daily. It should not be taken 24 hours before surgery, however, because it may interfere with anesthetics.

• **A multivitamin and mineral formula every day.**

• **A probiotic (good bacteria).** Five billion active organisms daily.

• **The herbs astragalus and echinacea.** Take 500 mg or 30 drops three times daily of each product, five days before and during hospitalization, and for two weeks following surgery. (Do not use these herbs in the case of organ transplants.)

More safety strategies include...

• **Whenever possible, check into a private room** in a well-designed hospital with good air quality and ventilation. (*See "Healthy Hospital Stays Start with the Right Room" on the following page.*)

• **Place your own air purifier in the room,** with the hospital's consent.

• **Ask family or friends to give their support and supervise your care** while you are in the hospital.

• **Keep a copy of your medical records on hand,** including a list of all the medications you take. Read the patient's bill of rights you receive when admitted, to be aware of who to contact if you have questions or concerns. *Also...*

• Hand washing. It is not groundbreaking news, but according to the CDC, hand washing is still the single most important procedure for preventing hospital-acquired infections. Make sure that health-care workers wash their hands before touching you for any reason.

• Regularly wash your own hands thoroughly, especially after you have used the bathroom.

• Ask friends and relatives not to visit if they are ill, and encourage them to frequently wash their hands if they do visit.

• **Inform your doctor that, whenever possible, you wish to avoid high-risk procedures, such as urinary catheterization.** If this is not advisable, catheters should be left in for as little time as possible, says Dr. Stengler.

• **Keep the skin around dressings, catheters and drainage tubes clean and dry.** If a dressing becomes loose or gets wet or a tube becomes loose or dislodged, promptly inform your nurse.

• **If you are diabetic, have your blood sugar properly monitored.** High blood sugar increases the risk for infection.

Most important, don't be afraid to speak up, express your concerns and ask questions. You know your body best and are the best advocate for your own health. If you're not up to the task, ask a family member or close friend to speak for you.

info Learn more by visiting the National Patient Safety Foundation's Web site, *www.npsf.org.* Centers for Disease Control and Prevention, *www.cdc.gov.*

Healthy Hospital Stays Start with the Right Room

Debra J. Levin, president, the Center for Health Design, Concord, California.

With medical mistakes and hospital-acquired infections among the leading causes of death in the US, the architectural details of a hospital are probably not your first priority. However, with four strains of superinfection bacteria accounting for the majority of hospital-acquired infections, it's important to know that a well-designed hospital can play an important role in preventing errors and infection and help you to get well, says Debra J. Levin, president of the Center for Health Design in Concord, California. This nonprofit organization advocates the use of evidence-based design to create hospitals that are not only nicer or fancier, but that focus on how the physical environment can play a role in healing.

ARCHITECTURE AND OUTCOME

Researchers at the Center for Health Design have uncovered more than 600 studies pointing to hospital characteristics that enhance patient safety, increase staff effectiveness, reduce stress and improve overall health-care quality and cost.

Among their findings…

• **Private rooms have numerous advantages over multi-bed rooms.** Use of them reduces the rate of hospital-acquired infections, cuts back on medical errors, lessens noise, improves patient confidentiality and privacy, increases social support from family and boosts patients' satisfaction with health care.

• **Noise is a major cause of stress,** awakenings and sleep loss in hospitals. In addition to private rooms, the Center for Health Design recommends the installation of sound-absorbing ceiling tile and flooring to control high noise levels.

• **It's beneficial to provide patients with distractions,** such as restorative and calming window views of nature and access to hospital gardens. Studies suggest that viewing nature reduces pain and stress.

• **Better lighting, especially more access to natural light,** can help shorten the length of hospital stays. Using light has been found to reduce depression in patients.

• **Air quality and ventilation play a key role** in controlling disease-causing pathogens and other contaminants. The Center for Health Design recommends air-quality control measures, such as the use of improved filters, notably high-efficiency particulate air (HEPA) models and special vigilance during periods of construction.

• **Many falls occur when patients try to get out of bed** unassisted or unobserved. Decentralized nursing stations placed in closer proximity to patients' rooms are associated with fewer injuries from falls. Proper design—such as toilet and bed height and placement of handrails—is also important for preventing falls.

To help make your hospital stay safer and shorter, consider the design when making your selection. Tour a hospital before you are admitted for a non-emergency procedure…and when choosing a doctor, take into account where he/she has admitting privileges.

Private In-Hospital Caregivers Result in Safer Stays

Charles B. Inlander, a consumer advocate and health-care consultant based in Fogelsville, Pennsylvania. He was founding president of People's Medical Society, a consumer health advocacy group active in the 1980s and 1990s. He is author of more than 20 books, including *Take This Book to the Hospital With You.* St. Martin's.

If you have a loved one who will be spending a few days in the hospital after undergoing a minor surgical procedure, why not hire a private caregiver to keep an eye on him/her as an added safety precaution? Not only is this great for the patient's care and comfort, but it's also beneficial for your peace of mind.

According to Charles B. Inlander, consumer advocate and health-care consultant, visiting hours are *suggested* by the hospital. A patient, however, has the right to have someone at the hospital with him 24 hours a day, even in the intensive care unit—in spite of the fact that there are more restrictions there, sometimes involving quarantine. He recommends that you exercise this right. If a family member is unable to be with you when you are hospitalized, hire a professional caregiver to help out.

Inlander says that this is especially important if the patient is frail and elderly, recovering from a stroke or surgery or otherwise has trouble attending to his own basic personal needs. With hospital staffing stretched, having a caregiver in attendance helps ensure that the patient is comfortable and his needs are met.

FINDING A CAREGIVER

How to find a good caregiver? If your loved one already has a home health aide that you like and trust, so much the better. You're all set. If not, ask your doctor, hospital social worker, county health department or area office on the aging to recommend a reputable health-care or nursing agency. You can also ask around.

Once you have located an agency, questions to ask include…

- **How long has the nursing or health-care agency been in existence?**
- **Is the agency licensed by the state?**
- **Are the caregivers bonded and insured?**
- **Can the agency provide references?**

In Inlander's opinion, you are better off with a caregiver who can assist with all basic needs—eating, washing, communication, getting to the bathroom and reducing the risk for falls—such as a home health aide. If possible, and depending on the patient's needs, consider hiring someone who has some medical understanding/training. Then he can also be on the lookout to ensure that the correct medications are given at the proper times in the proper amounts. With nearly 100,000 people dying each year from medical errors in hospitals, you simply cannot assume accuracy on the part of the hospital staff.

That said, Inlander cautions that the caregiver must function as *your* eyes and ears, not as a replacement for hospital staffing. The caregiver's job is to protect the patient, not to do the hospital's job. He should be careful not to put the patient in the middle of an uncomfortable—not to say potentially health-threatening—power

struggle that may interfere with the hospital's ability to deliver appropriate care to the patient. A private caregiver is merely a visitor and has no special privileges or rights. He can inform the staff that something is going wrong and, of course, call the family, but the caregiver has no standing in the hospital and therefore cannot interfere with the normal delivery of care.

COST OF HIRING A CAREGIVER

Depending on the qualifications of the caregiver you hire, Inlander says that you can expect the cost to be between $100 to $300 a day. That's a relatively small price to pay for the extra safety assurance and peace of mind.

More from Charles B. Inlander…

Choosing a Doctor— Does Age Matter?

An article published in the *British Medical Journal* revealed no significant difference between death rates from surgery performed by older versus younger heart surgeons. This raised the question about picking a new doctor—how does the wisdom of "old age" compare with the cutting-edge knowledge and training of youth? And what other factors should you take into account when choosing a new physician?

Here is more expert advice from consumer advocate Charles B. Inlander…

YOUNGER OR OLDER?

According to Inlander, there are two schools of thought on the issue of a physician's age. He said that it is indeed true that young doctors are exposed to the most up-to-date research and techniques, and that it's a mistake to equate youth with inexperience. For example, a young heart surgeon has gone through multiple years of medical school, internship and residency, and has already performed many procedures— but not as many as an experienced surgeon.

When is youth preferable in a doctor? Inlander observes that it took 20 years for lumpectomies to replace mastectomies as the treatment of choice in women who have breast cancer, even though the research showed that in most cases, lumpectomies were equally effective and far less traumatic.

Reason: Older surgeons were convinced that mastectomies were better, because that's what they learned in medical school. It took a whole generation of younger physicians to finally turn the tide.

When is age preferable in a physician? On the other side of the coin, older doctors have been around longer and seen more, and this may make them better diagnosticians. Inlander tells the story of a man who went to a young doctor complaining of severe pain that was traveling up his back. Back spasms were the diagnosis, but medication didn't help. Several days later, he visited an older doctor, who ordered a chest X-ray and discovered a potentially life-threatening blood clot in the man's lung. The blood thinner *warfarin* (Coumadin) was prescribed and all turned out well, but this diagnosis hadn't occurred to the younger physician.

FIND A PHYSICIAN WHO COMPLEMENTS YOU

More important than a doctor's age, notes Inlander, is whether he/she is a good match for your medical needs and your philosophy. He emphasizes that you are the central figure here, not the doctor. The doctor isn't going to change to suit you, but neither should you have to adjust your views to suit him.

To see whether a physician shares your outlook, Inlander recommends a "get-acquainted" visit. He says that most doctors offer these now, and even if you have to pay for it out of your own pocket, it is well worth the price.

Especially with managed care, a physician's time is at a premium, so you can't expect him to spend a great deal of time with you, even in this initial visit. Inlander says that the key is what happens during this time. He advises that you listen carefully to how a doctor puts you into the equation. Does he listen to you or lecture you? Are your concerns addressed? Does the doctor answer your questions or find it irritating that you ask them?

A get-acquainted visit is your opportunity to ask the doctor…

- **Are you board certified?** Inlander notes that being board certified is a good sign, although it is no guarantee of quality.

- **How much experience do you have treating people with medical concerns similar to mine?** Or how many times have you performed the procedure I need? The more experience, the better.

- **Do you see yourself as a partner and coach in your patients' care?** Or do you approach your practice in more of the doctor-knows-best style?

- **Do you focus on enhancing wellness in addition to curing disease?**

- **Are you open to complementary approaches?** What if I want to add a nutritionist, acupuncturist or naturopathic physician to my health-care team?

PRACTICAL FACTORS TO CONSIDER

Other practical questions to ask yourself when choosing a new doctor include…

- **What type of doctor do I need**—a primary care practitioner or a specialist?

- **Does the doctor speak my language?**

- **Is the practice conveniently located?**

- **Which health insurance plans does the doctor accept?**

- **What are my doctor's hospital affiliations?** Inlander says that this is crucial, since some hospitals have better track records than others.

- **Is this a group or solo practice?** If it is a group practice, do I get to see the doctor I want?

Call the office and ask questions about the doctor's education and training, how long a wait there is for an appointment, office hours and who will see you and answer your questions when the doctor is not available.

How the office staff answers your questions is another factor to take into account. Are they friendly and informative? Or are they frazzled and busy and anxious to get off the phone with you? If so, it's time to try another doctor at another office.

DO YOUR HOMEWORK

Before making a final decision, research your potential new doctor's credentials on Web sites, such as the American Medical Association (AMA) DoctorFinder at *www.ama-assn.org/aps/amahg.htm*. This Web site provides basic professional information on most licensed physicians in the United States.

When it comes time to choose a new doctor, the task may at first appear overwhelming, but if you do your homework and ask the right questions, you'll find a physician who will listen to you and provide the highest level of health care.

Overdoing Over-the-Counter Remedies

Marc K. Siegel, MD, clinical associate professor of medicine, New York University, New York City.

Sometimes we all do foolish things. For example, in spite of a number of news stories concerning the serious side effects associated with over-the-counter (OTC) pain relievers, such as aspirin, *ibuprofen* (Advil) and *acetaminophen* (Tylenol), a survey of 4,263 people by the National Consumers League showed that 44% of respondents admitted to exceeding the recommended dose of these drugs.

Even worse: Only 16% bothered to read the labels of these products carefully.

"As more and more drugs go over the counter, the implied message is, 'You don't need your doctor's guidance to take these things,'" says Marc K. Siegel, MD, clinical associate professor of medicine at New York University in New York City. "If you don't need a physician's guidance, people think they can use them liberally. People are actually surprised to learn that taking only five Advils a day is damaging to your liver and kidneys. And, they don't realize that 15,000 people each year die from aspirin complications."

PERSISTENT PAIN NEEDS PROFESSIONAL CARE

The real concern isn't over the occasional excess, says Dr. Siegel. "If you overdo it in the garden one Saturday and you take a little more than the label recommends, that isn't going to be a big issue. But repeated doses definitely can damage organs and lead to gastrointestinal bleeding."

If you have daily pain, you need to address the cause, not simply mask the symptoms, says Dr. Siegel. "There are other ways to address pain that can actually help you live without it," he says.

"It's not a coincidence that more people are misusing these drugs as the population becomes more sedentary and overweight," he says. "Excess pounds, even just 10 or 20, put greater amounts of pressure on the joints and connective tissues. Weight loss can relieve that pressure and lessen your pain." Also, by exercising properly, you loosen up your muscles and improve circulation, which means easier, less painful movement. "For chronic problems, such as back pain, physical therapy is often a good solution," he says.

If you have persistent pain that does not improve with exercise, weight loss and healthy living, you need to see your health-care provider, says Dr. Siegel. "He or she can help you safely manage—and hopefully reduce—your pain, which is better than self-diagnosis and potentially dangerous self-treatment any day."

Rub Out Germs With Sanitizing Gels

Michael D. Cirigliano, MD, associate professor of medicine, University of Pennsylvania School of Medicine, Philadelphia.

It's gaining widespread acceptance that the best way to keep germs from spreading in your house is to wash your hands—often—with anything *but* antibacterial soap. On the other hand, the water-free sanitizing gels have been shown in a recent study to be quite effective in protecting against respiratory infections and especially gastrointestinal illnesses.

We discussed this with internist Michael D. Cirigliano, MD, associate professor of medicine at the University of Pennsylvania School of Medicine in Philadelphia. He says that the reason the alcohol-based gels are so good is that while antibacterial soaps *reduce* the amount of bacteria on the skin, the gels actually *kill* the bacteria. Hospitals now use the sanitizing gels because of these germ-killing properties. Although you may think that the gels are harder on the skin, soap and water is a greater irritant.

OTHER CONSIDERATIONS

Of course, it's never quite that simple. Gels will not clean your hands of dirt and grime. If you've tackled the dusty garage, for instance, you'll need soap and water to clean the residue from your hands.

Additionally, Dr. Cirigliano has a more theoretical concern, although he hasn't found any evidence or case reports on the concept. Some people have expressed concern about using gel on toddlers' hands because it has an alcohol content and young children constantly put their hands in their mouths. The alcohol evaporates quickly when the standard amount of gel is used, but with children it could get tricky if they get their hands into their mouths before the gel evaporates. It doesn't mean you shouldn't use gel on them, but you should use caution when doing so.

Dr. Cirigliano suggests keeping gels handy on the road and in the home. Use often, especially after using the bathroom, and in the kitchen, where they are valuable as antimicrobial agents. However, he reminds parents not to forget to teach their kids proper hand-washing techniques (use soap, warm water and rub for about 20 seconds) and hygiene. Gels are very good, but you still need to know how to wash your hands.

Sweet Smells May Spell Danger

Jeffrey C. May, author of *My House Is Killing Me! The Home Guide for Families with Allergies and Asthma* (Johns Hopkins University), and principal, May Indoor Air Investigations LLC, Cambridge, Massachusetts.

Air fresheners can cause cancer. That was the conclusion many people might have drawn from a US Environmental Protection Agency study that was published in *Environmental Science & Technology*. The researchers first plugged in four electrical-outlet-powered air fresheners in a closed room. They then turned on an ozone generator to test how chemicals commonly used in air fresheners, such as pinene and limonene, react with ozone, which is produced at ground level when car exhaust emissions react with sunlight.

Result: Formaldehyde—which has been shown to bring on cancer in animals and may cause cancer in humans—as well as related compounds that may cause breathing problems were formed.

The Consumer Specialty Products Association (CSPA) was quick to put the kibosh on the media frenzy before it could get off the ground. A lengthy press release made it clear that the extreme and artificial conditions in which these products were tested "was not intended to represent consumer use of air fresheners, nor does it do so." When used according to label instructions in real-life situations, the products are completely safe, the CSPA concluded.

HOW SWEET IT ISN'T

The study may have set off a false alarm, but it also raised an important issue about the air quality in our homes and how quickly we are willing to compromise it to have the sweet-smelling houses the commercials claim we need. "People don't understand that all the fragrances and products we use in our homes create a chemical soup," says Jeffrey C. May, principal, May Indoor Air Investigations LLC in Cambridge, Massachusetts. "If you have asthma, allergies or are sensitive to chemicals, it can be a real health concern."

Even aromatic candles, like tea lights or the poured-wax jar varieties, have come under fire in recent years. "Those jar candles are enormous soot factories. Just look at how black the rims are," says May, who also does home inspections. "Millions of dollars have been spent repainting houses and redoing carpets to get rid of candle soot. It's an enormous problem."

Also on the offending list: Incense, which releases particulate matter as well as benzene and carbon monoxide, two dangerous gases, into the air…and spray fresheners, which experts argue expose your lungs to more unnecessary chemicals.

One solution is simply to live in a fragrance-free home. But pet owners, fish eaters and those with smelly shoes may argue otherwise. *Some natural alternatives for those who need to clear the air…*

• **Remove the moisture.** "Excess moisture encourages microbial growth and really makes a house smell bad," says May. "Keep your house clean and the relative humidity down and you won't need air fresheners."

• **Simmer some sweet stuff.** One safe way to make your house smell good enough to eat is the old real estate trick of simmering orange peels and warm spices, such as cinnamon or cloves, in a pot of water on the stove.

• **Burn beeswax.** If you're a candle junkie, burn beeswax. It's cleaner than those made with paraffin or petroleum products. In the Middle Ages, the Catholic church legislated the use of pure beeswax candles in churches because they didn't damage the interior and artwork. They're also naturally colored and scented.

A clean, welcoming home—yes. What you don't want is an artificially clean, welcoming home. The facade is not worth the price or the risk to your health.

Supplementing With Sunshine

Leo Galland, MD, director, Foundation for Integrated Medicine, New York City. He is author of *The Fat Resistance Diet*. Broadway. Dr. Galland is a recipient of the Linus Pauling award. *www.fatresistancediet.com*.

Andrew L. Rubman, ND, director, Southbury Clinic for Traditional Medicines, Southbury, Connecticut.

After a long, cold winter, many of us just can't wait for the nicer weather to bask in the sun—with the appropriate sunscreen and cover-ups, of course.

The rising rate of skin cancer has put using sunblock right up there with flossing your teeth when it comes to healthy habits. In 2008, it is estimated that there will be more than one million new cases of skin cancer—of which nearly 1,000 will be fatal. It is easy to understand why many people have become fearful of the sun's warmth and glow.

Believe it or not, though, some of us may not be getting enough sunshine.

"Sunshine is crucial for the production of vitamin D," explains Leo Galland, MD, director of the Foundation for Integrated Medicine in New York City. "Our bodies can't absorb calcium without the presence of vitamin D. When you don't obtain enough vitamin D, your bones become thin…they get brittle or soft…and children may get rickets.

"And," says Dr. Galland, "as we get older, our bodies have a harder time absorbing vitamin D so we need more of it."

LIMITED AVAILABILITY

While some foods are fortified with modest amounts of vitamin D, notably milk and some cereals, the only other food source is fatty fish—specifically salmon, mackerel and sardines. Vitamin D is also found in cod liver oil. You may be getting some vitamin D in your daily multivitamin as well.

While it is possible to get vitamin D in supplement form, our medical expert, Andrew L. Rubman, ND, is firmly against it. Why? Because it puts you at risk for vitamin D toxicity. Since vitamin D is fat soluble, the body does not rid itself of excessive amounts. Getting too much can cause nausea, vomiting, mental confusion, and heart rhythm and kidney problems—even kidney failure.

The federal government's Adequate Intake (AI) guideline for vitamin D starts at 5 micrograms (mcg), or 200 international units (IU), a day for individuals under age 50. The AI increases to 10 mcgs, or 400 IU, per day for people ages 51 to 70, and then to 15 mcgs a day, or 600 IU, for those over age 70. Dr. Rubman cautions that you should not exceed these guidelines except under medical supervision. It is highly unlikely that you could exceed these guidelines with just the foods you eat and a multivitamin a day.

The good news—your body can't overproduce vitamin D that is the direct result of sunshine. As your body produces more vitamin D from exposure to the sun, it slows production of additional vitamin D. Wearing sunscreen or sunblock will not appreciably affect your body's ability to produce vitamin D.

THE WARM GLOW

Besides helping us produce vital vitamin D, the sun also provides other benefits…

Dr. Galland points out that sunlight feels good, and it should. Exposure of the unblocked eye to sunlight causes the pineal gland in the brain to make less melatonin. "This hormone, which may cause symptoms of depression, is produced at increased levels in the dark," explains Dr. Galland.

The National Mental Health Association reports that when the days are shorter and darker, the production of melanin increases. Indirect sunlight exposure, even through cloud cover, is sufficient to counteract the effects of melatonin.

Direct exposure to sunshine also helps control skin rashes and infections, including yeast and fungi infections, according to Dr. Rubman. Sunscreen or sunblock will lessen but not stop this effect.

BUT STILL BE CAREFUL...

Despite all these findings, no one is advocating baking at the beach. *You should continue to take all the normal precautions when spending time in the sun...*

• **Avoid the strongest sun**—between the hours of 10 am and 4 pm.

• **Apply sunscreen 30 minutes prior to sun exposure.** Light-pigmented persons especially should apply a coating of at least SPF 15 sunblock every day—even on overcast and winter days.

• **Wear a hat**—so that even your scalp, back of the neck and ears are protected.

• **Get regular skin checks.** Have a dermatologist check your skin at least once a year for any signs of skin cancer...and check your own skin monthly.

• **Wear sunglasses**—with lenses that block UVA and UVB rays.

info For more lifesaving information, visit the Melanoma Oncology Web site, *www. dermoncology.com.*

It's Never Too Late to Quit

Truls Ostbye, MD, MPH, PhD, professor and vice-chair, department of community and family medicine, Duke University Medical Center, Durham, North Carolina.

Lifelong cigarette smokers die on average 10 years earlier than nonsmokers. However, a 50-year British medical study indicates that it is never too late to kick the habit. In fact, if you quit by age 35, you can *add* 10 years to your life!

To learn more about these latest findings on the benefits of quitting, we contacted Truls Ostbye, MD, PhD, professor and vice-chair in the department of community and family medicine at Duke University Medical Center in Durham, North Carolina. In a similar study at Duke, Dr. Ostbye found that people in their 50s who had quit smoking 15 years or more earlier had similar life expectancies, and they could expect to live healthy lives for the same number of years, as those who never smoked.

ADD YEARS TO YOUR LIFE

According to the British study, which tracked nearly 35,000 doctors from 1951 to 2001, 42% of those who start smoking at a young age die early (before age 70) from smoking-related diseases, such as lung cancer, heart disease, cancers of the mouth, throat and esophagus, and respiratory diseases including emphysema.

The good news? Researchers also found that...

• **If you quit smoking around age 40,** you can add nine years to your life.

• **Quitting at age 50** adds an additional six years to your life.

• **Even at age 60,** kicking the habit can add three years to your life.

These results were published in a recent issue of the *British Medical Journal.*

IT'S NEVER TOO LATE TO QUIT

As you grow older, the difference in years of healthy life between smokers and those who quit gets smaller—but Dr. Ostbye emphasizes that advantages do persist. Even in the oldest age group considered by Duke researchers—those ages 80 to 84—the difference was approximately one year.

Now for the hard part—how do you quit? Dr. Ostbye acknowledges the difficulties. For those who need encouragement, here it is—when you quit smoking, you gain years of healthy life to spend with your family and friends.

The sooner the better, but it's never too late.

Quit Smoking For Good

Deborah Hudson, registered respiratory therapist, program manager, Clarian Tobacco Control Center, Clarian Health, Indianapolis. *www.clarian.org*.

For most people giving up smoking is not a one-shot deal. Statistics show that it takes eight to 11 attempts. Deborah Hudson, a registered respiratory therapist and the program manager of Clarian Tobacco Control Center in Indianapolis, which offers a gamut of tobacco-related tools, including prevention and cessation techniques, explains that giving up tobacco is so hard because smoking is actually not one but three forms of addiction—physical, psychological and behavioral.

Although all smokers suffer from all three types of addiction, the intensity varies from person to person. Hudson says that it is important for people struggling to quit to understand this because it will give them insight into their particular challenge and how best to face it as they work through the cycle of quitting and then potentially relapsing.

ONE STEP BACK IS NOT DEFEAT

Smokers often consider a relapse as proof they can't quit and that they are failures. You can help a smoker see the bigger picture and thereby not succumb to the belief that he/she is helpless to overcome smoking. Give up your own feelings of disappointment and anger and instead look at his attempt as taking him further down the road to success, says Hudson.

Explore what it was that drove him to light up again. Was it a physical craving? The need to ease anxiety or tension? The enjoyment of how it makes him feel—at peace…soothed? His answers can show the way to the right tools to overcome it. For instance, someone who has a strong physical addiction may want to try the physical tools—nicotine patches, gums, etc.—because they help to ease physical cravings. Someone who is more psychologically attached may need individual counseling to help him through the emotional struggle. Someone with a strong behavioral addiction is likely to benefit from working together with a group.

Continue to offer your nonjudgmental support throughout the relapse period. And soon enough, many smokers decide to try quitting again. When that happens, you can help him identify and learn to avoid the triggers that set off the relapse. Develop new nonsmoking activities, such as going out to lunch, taking a walk or working out at the gym together. Practice your listening skills as he hashes out feelings and frustrations.

REAPING THE REWARDS

However difficult the process of giving up tobacco is, former smokers experience exciting and recognizable physical and psychological benefits. Enjoy with your loved one his feelings of euphoria for having taken action. Talk about the rewards of improved circulation and cardiac function, and celebrate as he witnesses himself develop better stamina, healthier breathing and a newly heightened sense of smell and taste.

More from Deborah Hudson…

Help Your Friends Kick the Habit

With all of the documented facts about how incredibly bad smoking is for your health, it baffles us that people continue to do it. Sure, the incidence of smoking is down substantially compared with 1964—but 47 million Americans continue to smoke.

For those of us who have a loved one who smokes, watching him/her light up day after day is frustrating and frightening. As much as you might want to shake him and throw out his cigarettes, pipes or cigars, taking a head-on approach is guaranteed to fail. To find out what does work, we spoke again with smoking cessation expert Deborah Hudson.

STEP ONE: THROUGH THE SMOKER'S EYES

Hudson points out that helping a loved one through the painful process of giving up tobacco requires great patience and understanding. First, look at why a tobacco addict clings so tightly to what he knows is a lethal habit. Simply put, smoking can be a source of great pleasure. Hudson explains that tobacco smoke chemically alters the body in many ways, but along with the terrible things it does, it changes six neurotransmitters in the brain to actually increase pleasure, enhance memory, reduce anxiety and tension, modulate mood and suppress appetite. Add to this the fact that for a smoker, having cigarettes at hand is akin to having a best friend to soothe you when you need it, to entertain you when you're bored and to give you extra time to ponder your response to a challenging person or situation. So it is really no wonder why smokers love smoking.

And the sobering realization that faces smokers grappling with their addiction is that giving up this extraordinarily satisfying habit can be and usually is excruciating—more difficult, in fact, than getting off cocaine or heroin, says Hudson. No, it's not a pretty picture. But then again, neither are the cancers, cardiovascular diseases and numerous other physical consequences of continuing to smoke.

Trying to shame or criticize a smoker or "force" him to give up the habit with rational explanations is the worst possible approach, says Hudson. Smokers view these kinds of maneuvers as attempts to wrestle control from them, and they respond by going on the defensive. In fact, Hudson likens them to teenagers when it comes to their attitudes toward smoking. Tell a smoker he "has" to quit and he'll end up puffing away *more* just to prove that he, not you, controls his life. And don't bother playing the how-inconsiderate-it-is-for-others card. Years of smoking dull a smoker's sense of smell and create greater tolerance for smoke-filled rooms, says Hudson. A smoker simply doesn't experience the unpleasantness of tobacco smoke to the extent that a nonsmoker does, and he is apt to wonder what all the fuss is about.

STEP TWO: STRIKE WHEN HE'S READY

At some point, though, most smokers try to quit or decide they are ready to do so. Only when that happens, says Hudson, is it possible for you to be genuinely helpful. As you prepare to take action, keep an empathetic and nonjudgmental attitude. View a smoker as separate from the habit—he is a person who is suffering from an addiction and what Hudson considers a chronic disease.

Once you know that a smoker is ready to quit, you can help in the following ways…

•**Share your concern** about the dangers of the habit.

•**Let the person know** that you are there to help him lick this.

•**Ask permission to do so.**

•**Don't tell the person what to do**—ask for suggestions about what you can do to help.

•**Ask if you can assist** in finding him a program or other tools that ease the process.

•**If you are a former smoker,** talk about what it was like for you to give it up.

•**Never nag.**

STEP THREE: SHARE THE EXPERIENCE

Have no illusions. However cheerful and pleasant a person is ordinarily, being in the throes of giving up smoking obliterates these traits. Expect the person to be outrageously cranky and suffer from a variety of physical and psychological symptoms, including headaches, nasal and chest congestion, inability to concentrate, nausea, constipation or diarrhea, forgetfulness, restlessness, anxiety, depression and aggressive behavior. While these symptoms will start to ease after about three days, it's just the beginning of a very long process.

Here are some ways that you can be a source of support as your ex-smoker endures the withdrawal period…

•**Provide plenty of fruits and vegetables** —fiber will help ease the gastrointestinal symptoms and healthful nutrients will make it easier to avoid fattening foods.

•**Offer to exercise with the ex-smoker.** Physical activity enhances mood, increases focus and is relaxing—all properties that nicotine was providing.

•**Help the former smoker find new ways to de-stress.** Deep breathing, a few minutes of meditation, going to the movies or going for a quiet stroll can help fill the spaces that smoking once did.

• **Remind the person that your support** is unswerving and show it with regular calls. Just be sure you don't come across as checking up.

• **Help the person avoid the situations that trigger his smoking**—socializing at a party, etc.

This will be a long and challenging process. The smoker may miss his cigarettes forever, but the benefits gained are well worth it in the end.

Learning to Deal With Alzheimer's

Joanne Koenig Coste, nationally recognized Alzheimer's expert and educator, and a patient advocate since 1973. She is author of *Learning to Speak Alzheimer's: A Groundbreaking Approach for Everyone Dealing with the Disease*. Houghton Mifflin.

In recent years, there have been many studies published regarding Alzheimer's disease. Some say that educated or slim people are less likely to get the mind-robbing ailment…others say that eating fish and nuts—or that ballroom dancing—may keep the memory intact. But what about those people who already have the disease—and their loved ones who struggle to care for them?

Joanne Koenig Coste, an Alzheimer's expert and educator, has written a book about a whole new way of dealing with the disease. *Learning to Speak Alzheimer's: A Groundbreaking Approach for Everyone Dealing with the Disease* grew out of her own experiences of caring for her husband, a successful advertising writer, who developed the illness in his 40s shortly after the birth of their fourth child.

Her novel approach involves approaching the world from the patient's point of view…

STRUCTURE FOR SUCCESS

Koenig Coste describes how five core tenets helped her family make the best of a very difficult situation, and how incorporating these principles into daily caregiving routines can turn a sense of crushing defeat into small victories…

• **Make the physical environment work.** People with Alzheimer's have problems with visual perception and distinguishing color, depth and contrast, says Koenig Coste. Simplifying home surroundings early on can make a huge difference by eliminating confusing choices. *Among her suggestions…*

• Clean out closets and eliminate clutter to simplify choices.

• Use bright lights to eliminate shadows, which can appear threatening to the patient.

• Create contrasts in color and avoid over-stimulating stripes and patterns. She describes how her husband wandered about the house until one of their kids placed a red pillow on the seat of an oak dining room chair, "so Daddy would have a soft place to sit." It turned out the bright red provided enough contrast against the hardwood floors for her husband to feel he could safely sit.

• Hang familiar family photos and mementos in the den or living room. Keep sounds from TVs and radios low.

• Use pictures or simple cue cards on kitchen cupboard doors so that the patient knows where to retrieve or place cups and dishes.

• Paint bathroom walls a deep or bright color to draw attention to the contrasting white toilet. Cover the mirror if the patient feels "invaded" by the "stranger" looking back.

• Leave a toothbrush that has toothpaste on it by the sink and put other items away. Schedule a shower when the patient is feeling "up"—first thing in the morning is often a good time.

• Be sure to keep utensils and condiment choices to a minimum. "Finger foods" are an excellent choice.

• Lay out clothes for the day, placing items to put on first (underwear, socks) on top of the pile.

• **Know that communication remains possible.** "People with Alzheimer's learn early on to pay attention to what our bodies are saying," says Koenig Coste.

• Speak slowly, using simple sentences.

• Communicate using gestures, body language, eyes and tone of voice when words begin to fail.

• **Focus on remaining skills.** If you can help the patient feel successful, even with the smallest tasks, everyone will feel better, says Koenig Coste.

- Assign a simple chore, such as folding laundry or drying dishes, even if it takes several hours to complete.

- Enlist the patient's help. One Alzheimer's patient in Koenig Coste's group was terribly upset by her daughter's decision to make the holiday strudel alone. "I could have rolled the dough. I could have chopped the apples," the woman lamented. "I'm still here. I'm not gone." Find out what's still there—and use it!

- **Live in the patient's world.** Seeing the world from the patient's perspective is at the core of Koenig Coste's approach.

- Stop questioning the patient. Resist the natural instinct to ask things like, "What did you have for lunch?" or "You remember what we did this morning, right?" It makes the patient feel tested—and sadder.

- Don't try to reason. Avoid statements like, "Don't go out in the rain without your raincoat, because you know you'll catch cold." Patients can't understand them.

- Avoid corrections. If a patient is reading a book upside down, fight the urge to turn it right side up. If the patient tells you it's 1973, join him/her there. Ask him what his favorite things about the year were.

- **Enrich the patient's life.**

- Create "successes," and praise often. Koenig Coste describes how her husband spent two hours at the kitchen sink studiously "cleaning" the nonstick surface off her favorite frying pan. When he was through, she and the kids applauded. The next morning, he was still smiling.

- Find humor whenever possible. One of her patients told a joke and got the group to laugh. "The best thing about having Alzheimer's," he continued, "is that I can tell the same joke next week!"

These tenets teach us to speak and understand Alzheimer's, Koenig Coste convincingly argues, and offer a win-win situation for patients and caregivers alike. Many more useful tips are discussed in her book. It is highly recommended for anyone touched by Alzheimer's—and sadly, that is more and more people every day.

info Fisher Center for Alzheimer's Research Foundation, *www.alzinfo.org*.
Alzheimer's Association, *www.alz.org*.

Soothing Secrets for Chapped Lips

Nicholas Lowe, MD, consultant dermatologist, Santa Monica, California, and London, England, and clinical professor of dermatology at UCLA School of Medicine, Los Angeles.
Andrew L. Rubman, ND, director, Southbury Clinic for Traditional Medicines, Southbury, Connecticut.

What do you get when you combine the cold of winter with the dryness from indoor heating systems?

Answer: Chapped lips.

SOLVING THE RIDDLE

We spoke with Nicholas Lowe, MD, a consultant dermatologist in Santa Monica, California, and London, England, and a clinical professor of dermatology at UCLA School of Medicine about the cause of chapped lips and the best ways to avoid getting them in the first place, or make them feel better.

He explained that central heating and low humidity are responsible for dry lips and skin in the winter months. However, even in the summer, low humidity and sun exposure can also lead to chapped lips, especially in the dry, desert-like climates.

According to Dr. Lowe, the single best remedy for cracked, chapped or burning lips is good old-fashioned lip balm. He recommends such products as natural beeswax, ChapStick, Blistex, NeoStrata and Vaseline. The secret is to reapply it regularly and frequently throughout the day and at bedtime to both protect and heal.

SELF-HELP FOR CHAPPED LIPS

Other strategies include…

- **Reapply lip balm after you eat or drink.** Find one that soothes as well as improves the condition of your lips. Your naturopathic physician can help you choose the best preparation for your particular problem.

- **Use a lip balm that contains a broad-spectrum sunscreen,** especially during the summer months.

- **Women should choose a creamy lipstick with a moisturizing base.** Use lip balm first, let it dry and then apply lipstick.

• **Avoid licking your lips.** Although this may provide temporary relief to dryness and discomfort, it will inevitably backfire. Saliva contains digestive enzymes that irritate rather than moisturize the lips.

• **Invest in a humidifier** to counteract dry air in the home.

• **Drink eight glasses of water** every day to moisturize from the inside out.

• **When flying long distances,** protect against dehydration by keeping lip balm and skin moisturizer handy. Also, drink plenty of water, and cut down on alcohol and caffeine.

According to our medical expert, Andrew L. Rubman, ND, *squalane*, a derivative of shark liver oil, is a wonderful natural moisturizer for your lips and other body parts. This material is used by major domestic and European cosmetic manufacturers and can be purchased in its pure form from The Chemistry Store (800-224-1430 or *www.chemistrystore.com*). He also suggests adding B-complex to your regimen to help heal chapped lips and cracking in the corners of the mouth. A 25-milligram multi-B vitamin taken twice a day usually does the trick, claims Dr. Rubman, who recommends taking these supplements at least twice a day because they only stay in the blood 15 hours or so.

NOT TO BE IGNORED

Don't simply ignore chapped lips and hope that they'll go away. If your lips become too dry and cracked, a virus can sneak in and cause painful cold sores (*herpes simplex*). In other cases, people develop allergies to ingredients in balm, lipstick or even toothpaste. *Candida* (yeast) infections or dermatitis can also cause such problems as chapped or cracked lips.

When chapped lips fail to respond to the simple remedies already mentioned, see your dermatologist. Dr. Lowe warns against self-treating with over-the-counter hydrocortisone creams or antibiotic ointments. Dr. Rubman points out that chronically dry lips may be an indication of deeper deficiencies or metabolic disorders. Consider seeking the advice of a naturopathic physician who works in conjunction with a dermatologist to get the best of both worlds.

Fortunately, in the vast majority of cases, liberal application of lip balm and other self-help measures are all that's necessary to keep your lips smooth and kissable throughout the cold and dry winter months.

Don't Drink the Water—on the Airplane!

The late Richard P. Maas, PhD, a founder and former codirector, Environmental Quality Institute, University of North Carolina, Asheville.

As if the long lines and security checks at airports weren't enough to drive you crazy, now there's something new to worry about during air travel—the safety of the drinking water on the plane itself.

According to a recent analysis by the Environmental Protection Agency (EPA) of the aircraft tank water used in the galleys and lavatories of 158 randomly selected aircraft, nearly one out of every eight passenger planes in the US carries water below federal standards for drinking.

Specific results were as follows…

• **The water supply on 20 planes tested positive for total coliform,** a group of closely related bacteria that are natural and common inhabitants of the human digestive tract. Although coliform bacteria are not likely to cause illness themselves, they are an indication that pathogens (disease-causing organisms) associated with intestinal illnesses may be contaminating the water supply.

• **The water on two of the 20 planes also tested positive for E. coli.** While most E. coli are harmless and in fact can be helpful in the large intestine, some strains cause diarrhea, cramps, nausea, headache or other symptoms.

WHAT YOU CAN DO

The late Richard P. Maas, PhD, former codirector of the Environmental Quality Institute at the University of North Carolina in Asheville, had recommended these simple steps that you can take to protect yourself…

• **Drink bottled water only.** Take a pass when the flight attendant comes around with a tray filled with glasses of tap water from the plane's galley.

• **Never drink water from the lavatory sinks in airplanes.**

• **Refrain from drinking coffee or tea that is not made with bottled water.** Although boiling water for one minute removes pathogens, according to the EPA the water used to prepare coffee and tea on planes may not reach sufficiently high temperatures.

• **Be especially vigilant on international carriers.** The EPA notes that these aircraft may board water from foreign sources that are not subject to EPA drinking water standards. Insist on bottled water during international travel, and order all beverages *without ice*.

The EPA plans more investigation to determine whether the bacteria comes from the original water supply, the tanker trucks that load the water on to planes or the airplanes themselves. In the meantime, it is better to be safe than sorry. Stick with bottled water when you fly.

info For more information, contact the US Environmental Protection Agency at *www.epa.gov.*

Avoid Germs at the Gym

Germs, including some potentially deadly antibiotic-resistant bugs, are often present at fitness clubs.

Self-defense: Minimize skin-to-equipment contact by keeping cuts clean and bandaged. Also, carry one towel for yourself and another to wipe down mats and other equipment before and after use. Use an alcohol-based hand sanitizer on your hands before and after your workout. And finally, wash your workout clothes after every use.

Charles P. Gerba, PhD, professor of microbiology, department of soil, water and environmental science, University of Arizona, Tucson.

12

Surprising Health Facts

Do Antioxidants Raise Your Cholesterol?

or a long time, we have believed that antioxidants are all good and that oxidants, also called free radicals, are all bad because they contribute to a wide range of internal problems, including major diseases. However, there is a connection between oxidants and diabetes—scientists are now discovering that the picture is much more complex and that oxidants do serve a purpose in the human body.

Scientists at the NYU School of Medicine have published a report on a study that demonstrates oxidants' role in keeping LDL ("bad") cholesterol at lower levels. Study leader Edward A. Fisher, MD, PhD, professor of cardiovascular medicine and cell biology at NYU, outlines the implications of his research.

THE SCIENCE BEHIND THE STUDY

To create LDL (low-density lipoprotein), the liver must have a protein called *Apo B-100*.

However, the presence of a type of oxidant called *lipid peroxide* reduces the availability of Apo B-100 to the liver. With less Apo B-100 available to it, the liver can produce only a limited amount of LDL. The fortunate result is that lower levels of LDL cholesterol venture into the bloodstream. Again, an oxidant acts as a signal, informing the liver to decrease LDL production.

THE RESEARCH

To determine how an antioxidant would affect this process, the investigators introduced a high level of vitamin E to the liver cells of mice. The vitamin E attached to the oxidant, which in turn left the liver free to create LDL.

Result: LDL blood levels rose. Even though this study was done on mice, Dr. Fisher says that it is in line with a previous heart study that proved human subjects taking antioxidants ended up with slightly *higher* LDL levels than those who were not taking them. Before

Edward A. Fisher, MD, MPH, PhD, Leon H. Charney professor of cardiovascular medicine and professor of pediatric and cell biology, NYU School of Medicine, New York City.

the study, Dr. Fisher and his colleagues described the presence of oxidants as "oxidative stress." Now they are considering calling it "oxidant signaling."

Although these studies support the idea of oxidants' usefulness, Dr. Fisher emphasizes that it's not yet time to sing their praises. He describes the value of oxidants in the body with the old real estate saying—location, location, location. In other words, the same oxidative reaction can be beneficial in one place but destructive in another.

For example, there was a large observational study conducted recently that showed a dramatic reduction in the onset of Alzheimer's disease for people who took vitamins E and C in tandem. But as we have just seen, vitamin E in the liver can allow for production of excess LDL. Our medical expert, Andrew L. Rubman, ND, observes that this study examined the effects of adding just vitamin E, rather than adding it as a component of broad-based antioxidant intervention. Balance is critical throughout the body.

WHAT SHOULD YOU DO ABOUT IT?

In the meantime, there are thousands, maybe millions, of people who include antioxidants in their diets and supplement with them. Dr. Fisher reports that although he can't make a correlation between the quantity of vitamin E they gave the mice in the study and the amount humans typically consume, he says that the quantity given to the mice was very high. Consequently, his concern centers on the megadoses of antioxidants that some people choose to take. His advice is to avoid such megadoses, but if your LDL levels are in the acceptable range (below 100 mg/dL for people who are not in the high-risk group for cardiac disease) and you're taking 200 international units (IU) of vitamin E each day, there's really no reason to stop. People who have higher LDL levels, however, should be sure to discuss these findings with their doctor to decide if an adjustment to their antioxidant intake should be made.

Bottom line: The vitamin E studies suggest using caution against excessive single antioxidant supplementation. They also illustrate why it's important to speak with a professional instead of self-medicating.

Simple Blood Test Cuts Antibiotic Use in Half

Beat Müller, MD, researcher, University Hospitals, Basel, Switzerland.

Doctors pen millions of useless and potentially dangerous antibiotic prescriptions for lower-respiratory infections, such as bronchitis and pneumonia, each year simply because they have no good way of discerning a bacterial infection—which benefits from antibiotic use—from one that is viral and unaffected by antibiotics.

That not only creates a problem of wasted dollars, it's also leading to a dangerous rise in antibiotic-resistant microorganisms. Now a simple solution in the form of a quick blood test that screens for viral versus bacterial infections has shown promising research results. If successful in the long term, it could potentially cut the number of antibiotic prescriptions in half without any ill consequences to sick patients.

THE TEST

In a Swiss study of 243 men and women with suspected lower respiratory infections who were admitted to a hospital, the researchers assigned half of the group to receive standard care. This was defined as relying on a doctor's diagnosis of symptoms to determine antibiotic use. The other half of the group was given the blood test to help determine if antibiotics were necessary.

In the end, antibiotic use in the blood-test group was 50% lower than that of the doctor's diagnosis-only group. What's more, the patient outcomes between the groups were the same —no one in the nonantibiotic group suffered for lack of medicine.

Currently, as much as 75% of all antibiotic doses are prescribed for acute respiratory-tract infections, despite the fact that most are caused by viruses.

The test used in this study works by screening for the hormone-related chemical *procalcitonin*, which may appear in the bloodstream in high amounts when a bacterial infection is present, and in low amounts during viral infections.

THE FUTURE FOR THIS TEST

"This test could be adapted to screen for all bacterial infections, including meningitis and sepsis," says study researcher Beat Müller, MD, of University Hospitals in Basel, Switzerland. But it will take time before such a test is widely available in the US, he says. Infectious disease specialists as well as the pharmaceutical companies need to support the fact that further study is necessary to determine the broad utility of the test.

Though it may be a few years before procalcitonin screening has scientific support and is widely accepted and used for diagnosis, the researchers remain optimistic that their findings will one day help significantly lower the use of inappropriate antibiotics and ultimately slow down the development of the antibiotic-resistant bacteria.

While the early tests are promising, remember that the "best offense is a good defense." With lifestyle modification, sensible eating and guidance on the use of immune-boosting supplementation, you may avoid the need for the test at all—let alone the antibiotics.

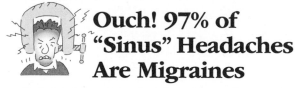

Ouch! 97% of "Sinus" Headaches Are Migraines

Mark W. Green, MD, clinical professor of neurology, Columbia University, and director of the Columbia University Headache Center, both in New York City.

Americans spend $2 billion annually on over-the-counter (OTC) medications for sinus headaches. Yet, according to a recent study that was conducted by the International Headache Society, 97% of people who believe they have sinus headaches are actually suffering from migraines. These people may be getting temporary relief from sinus medication, but they may be making their problems worse in the long run.

MYTH OF THE SINUS HEADACHE

To learn more about the myth of the sinus headache, we spoke with Mark W. Green, MD, clinical professor of neurology at Columbia University and director of the Columbia University Headache Center in New York City.

He explained that this lack of understanding can have serious consequences to your health. For instance, Dr. Green is concerned that people who wrongly believe they have sinus headaches mistreat themselves with pain relievers, decongestants, antihistamines and antibiotics. The longer you wait to treat migraines properly, he cautions, the tougher they are to control.

The concept of sinus problems as a cause of headache is deeply ingrained in the American psyche. Dr. Green speculates that this is at least partially because we are regularly bombarded with ads for sinus headache remedies. We've been sold a bill of goods by the pharmaceutical companies—all of those TV commercials about sinus headaches have convinced us that "everybody" has them. At least in this instance, Dr. Green notes that direct-to-consumer advertising by pharmaceutical companies is driving people to mistreatment.

There is scant scientific evidence to support any relationship between sinus problems and headaches. Far more commonly, the problem is a migraine that is accompanied by sinus symptoms, such as nasal congestion and facial pain.

Dr. Green explains how pain location, environmental factors and sinus symptoms can lead people to mistake migraines for sinus headaches…

- **Location.** Sinus pain does not necessarily mean that you have a sinus headache. A migraine is more frequently the cause of pain in the sinuses, forehead, cheeks and jaw.

- **Seasonal changes.** Sudden changes in the weather, pressure variations and seasonal exposure to allergens can trigger migraines. However, most people associate seasonal changes with allergies and related sinus problems.

- **Allergy and sinus symptoms.** Because a migraine is frequently accompanied by nasal symptoms, such as a runny nose, congestion, watery eyes and postnasal drip, it's easy to mistake it for a sinus headache. The sinus symptoms are the body's reaction to the migraine pain. If you have all of these symptoms and they do not resolve over time, you may in fact be suffering from migraine and not upper-respiratory infection, including sinus infection.

THE CONSEQUENCES OF MISTREATMENT

Migraine is a progressive disorder. When not appropriately diagnosed and treated, headache pathways become etched in the nervous system. Dr. Green warns that it is as if the brain becomes "hardwired" for headaches. Over time, headaches become more frequent.

Dr. Green's advice: Pay attention to the pain. If you can manage an occasional headache with an OTC painkiller, that's fine. But if you find yourself popping sinus headache remedies on a regular basis, see your doctor. These may provide temporary relief from the symptoms, but in the long run, repeated mistreatment will only cause migraines to grow worse since the root problem is not being properly treated.

An additional concern is that when you self-treat yourself with OTC medications, not only do you fail to address the underlying problem, you also expose yourself to unnecessary side effects. Antihistamines can make you drowsy… decongestants can cause nervousness, agitation, palpitations and sleeplessness…chronic use of nonsteroidal anti-inflammatory drugs (NSAIDs), such as *ibuprofen* (Motrin), can lead to gastrointestinal and liver damage…and it is wise to be careful with *acetaminophen* (Tylenol), which, when taken in large amounts, is a significant liver toxin.

Even worse, patients often demand antibiotics and doctors often prescribe them for alleged sinus headaches caused by supposed sinus infections. All this poses a serious public health problem, since the overuse or inappropriate use of antibiotics leads to more antibiotic-resistant bacteria and increasingly ineffective antibiotic treatment.

WHEN TO SEEK TREATMENT

When it comes to headache pain, don't try to tough it out. Don't say, "It's not too bad" or "I can tolerate the pain." Dr. Green recommends that you seek treatment sooner rather than later under the following circumstances…

●**If you experience chronic headaches** that are not manageable.

●**If you have progressive headaches.** For example, you used to have a headache every few months, and now you're experiencing them on a monthly basis.

●**If you experience what feels like a brand-new type of headache.**

●**If a headache is associated with weakness or numbness.**

The bottom line? Sinus headaches are relatively rare, and most people who self-diagnose sinus headaches actually have migraines. When in doubt, see your physician.

Effective treatments for migraine headaches are available—both pharmacological and non-pharmacological. When it comes to migraines, ignoring or mistreating them will not make them go away.

Old Water Rule Goes Down the Drain

Patrick J. Bird, PhD, former dean, College of Health & Human Performance, University of Florida, Gainesville.

Andrew L. Rubman, ND, director, Southbury Clinic for Traditional Medicines, Southbury, Connecticut.

Heinz Valtin, MD, kidney specialist and professor emeritus of physiology, Dartmouth Medical School, Hanover, New Hampshire.

Do you remember the old mantra, "Drink eight glasses of water a day?" Well, most experts no longer recommend this. Though that rule has been easy to remember, it has no basis in fact.

The real story: How much water a person needs varies greatly from individual to individual and situation to situation. Larger people need more than smaller people. Increased amounts are called for if you have been out in sunshine or performing heavy exercise. The eight-by-eight rule has been replaced by "drink when you are thirsty." What a wonderfully commonsensical rule!

Water needs don't have to be met by pure water. First of all, most people take in about four cups of water a day from food, depending on their vegetable and fruit intake. And just about any beverage—juice, milk, etc.—can hydrate the body.

It was commonly believed that drinks containing caffeine were diuretic—causing a net loss of fluids from the body. Not so for people who regularly drink coffee, tea or other caffeinated beverages, says physiologist and kidney specialist Heinz Valtin, MD. Although caffeine is a diuretic when used as a drug, it is not so when consumed as part of common drinks.

The only drinks shown to have a dehydrating effect are beverages with a high alcohol content. Gin-and-tonic lovers, beware!

Another cause of dehydration is certain medications, such as *furosemide* (Lasix) and other diuretics...*sertraline* (Zoloft) and some other antidepressants...various antihistamines...and many chemotherapy drugs. Check with your physician to see if any of your medications—prescription or over-the-counter—have this side effect.

Dehydration can be especially problematic for the elderly. Our medical expert, Andrew L. Rubman, ND, notes that the elderly are better off drinking outside of mealtimes because water can interfere with digestive processes.

WHEN WATER CAN KILL

Conventional wisdom says that long-distance athletes should gulp down as much water as possible to avoid dehydration. But too much water during strenuous activity can cause *hyponatremia*, a precipitous drop in sodium levels that may lead to seizures, respiratory failure and even death. Hyponatremia has been reported to affect almost 20% of marathoners.

Usually the fastest runners aren't in a race long enough to develop hyponatremia. Experts are more concerned about the slower and/or less-experienced athletes who are exerting themselves for more than four hours. The combination of heavy perspiration and excessive intake of water (without sodium) dilutes sodium levels in the bloodstream and may cause hyponatremia.

USA Track & Field (the national governing body for runners) issued fluid-replacement guidelines for long-distance runners. Its recommendation is to drink only when you feel thirsty—not to stay *ahead* of thirst. (Sports drinks that contain sodium and other electrolytes are preferred.)

Drinking when you feel thirsty is a lot easier to remember—and to follow—than the old eight-times-eight rule. Doing what your body tells you is often—*very* often—the best advice.

Fluoride: Friend or Foe?

Mike Coplan, a former engineering and environmental consultant to NASA, EPA and other governmental agencies. He is recognized in American Men of Science and holds 32 patents. He is based in Massachusetts.

The late Richard P. Maas, PhD, founder and former codirector, Environmental Quality Institute, University of North Carolina, Asheville.

Andrew L. Rubman, ND, director, Southbury Clinic for Traditional Medicines, Southbury, Connecticut.

The controversy over fluoridation of our water rages on. Fluoride is supposedly beneficial for dental health. However, research continues to demonstrate that it is harmful to our general health. Is it really worth the trade-off?

FLUORIDE AS FRIEND

The discovery of fluoride's ability to fight cavities and tooth decay began with experiments by Basil Bibby, MD, in the early 1940s at the Tufts Dental School in Boston. Dr. Bibby discovered that if a little bit of fluoride was put on a cotton swab and then applied to a decayed tooth, the tooth could be saved.

Fluoride halts tooth decay because it inhibits the growth of enzyme-causing bacteria. It also can remineralize tooth enamel. Fluoride's primary benefit comes through direct contact with the teeth. According to many scientists, topical application to the tooth is the *only* effective delivery path for fluoride's decay-fighting abilities.

Several studies support this view. In the largest dental survey ever conducted in the US, the National Institute of Dental and Craniofacial Research found virtually no differences in dental decay in children living in areas with fluoridated water versus unfluoridated water. Five peer-reviewed studies found that dental decay does not increase when communities stop fluoridating their water.

FLUORIDE AS FOE

Although the benefits of fluoride are primarily topical, its risks are primarily systemic (that is, resulting when fluoride is swallowed). A look at the medical literature revealed many study results suggesting negative health effects of fluoride.

A few examples…

• **A study published in *Behavioral Brain Research*** found that water with concentrations of one part per million fluoride (the standard amount in most communities that have fluoridated water supplies) facilitated the absorption of aluminum in the brains of rats, producing the type of brain formulations that are associated with Alzheimer's disease and other types of dementia.

• **Fluoride stimulates abnormal bone development,** according to clinical trials published in the *New England Journal of Medicine* and the *Journal of Bone and Mineral Research.* Researchers report that while high-dose fluoride treatment does increase bone mass, the newly formed bone is structurally unsound, causing increases in hip fractures. There are also concerns that even low doses of fluoride, taken over long periods of time, as would be the case in communities with fluoridated water, may also increase the rate of hip fracture. More than half of 19 recent studies found an association between low levels of fluoride in water and an increase in hip fracture.

• **Fluoridated water has been associated with elevated levels of lead** in children's blood, according to a study published in an issue of *NeuroToxicology.*

BIG BUSINESS AND POLITICS

Most of us have had fluoride in our drinking water for many years. Why? As early as the 1930s, the manufacturers of aluminum needed something to do with the sodium fluoride that was a by-product of the aluminum smelting process. When the industry became aware of Dr. Bibby's work at Tufts, a campaign was mounted to convince the American Dental Association to accept fluoride as a topical anticavity treatment so that it could be advocated as a value-added component of toothpaste. In 1950, the Public Health Service authorized the use of fluoride in water systems as a way to get fluoride to the general public as a tooth-decay preventive agent.

Mike Coplan, former consultant to the National Aeronautics and Space Administration (NASA), the US Environmental Protection Agency (EPA) and other government agencies, and a lifelong "student" of water fluoridation, says that during the 1960s and 1970s, heavy phosphate mining for fertilizers produced another type of fluoride as a by-product—fluorosilicic acid. This time, the industry got rid of the new type of fluoride by marketing it to municipalities as a less-expensive alternative to sodium fluoride, and most municipalities in the US bought it. However, as you will see below, if fluoride in the water was questionable before, recent changes in water-disinfection procedures have made it even more questionable now.

A FLUORIDE/LEAD STORY: THE SYNERGY FACTOR

Research involving fluoride in lead contamination of water was conducted by the late Richard P. Maas, PhD, former codirector of the Environmental Quality Institute at the University of North Carolina at Asheville. The results of his study provide some insight into the flouride/lead connection. The problem is not just the fluoride —it's the *combination* of the type of fluoride added to the water and the type of disinfecting agents used in the water.

Specifically, Dr. Maas found the highest levels of lead in the water in areas that combine chloramines, the agent now used to comply with EPA standards for lower levels of chlorine by-products in the water, with fluorosilicic acid.

Scary: 89% of communities fluoridate with the less expensive fluorosilicic acid versus the traditional sodium fluoride.

MINIMIZE EXPOSURE

To minimize your exposure to fluoride…

• **Use a reverse osmosis filter on your water tap.** The only filters that will reliably remove more than 90% of fluoride are those that use reverse osmosis technology, so be sure to ask. Prices range in the neighborhood of $200. Some pitcher filters may remove fluoride as well, but you must make sure that you change the cartridges frequently.

• **Use a water cooler/dispenser.** Water coolers typically hold five-gallon jugs of springwater. Coolers are more convenient than buying small bottles of water, and you can avoid maintaining a filter. Ask about the fluoride concentrations in the water you are buying. (Try to get water with less than 0.1 parts per million.) Prices for water coolers range from $100 to $800 and are often free with a delivery service…a five-gallon jug of water typically costs about $8.

• **Install a water distillation system on your water tap.** Water distillation will remove all fluoride. Prices vary widely according to size. Small units run about $200, while the larger ones can cost as much as $1,600 and up.

• **Cook with spring water.** If you don't install a distillation system on your tap water, consider cooking with bottled water as well. Heating does not remove fluoride from the water.

• **Use fluoridated toothpaste properly.** Believe the warning label when it says "do not swallow." Used properly, this is where the fluoride benefits do exist.

Even with these precautions, it is nearly impossible to completely avoid ingesting fluoride. Most prepared foods, including frozen foods, were probably manufactured with fluoridated water, says Coplan. Whenever possible, fresh foods are best.

A note of comfort for you: Our medical expert, Andrew L. Rubman, ND, says that we don't have to be obsessive about fluoride—it is a necessary nutrient in microscopic amounts. If we exclude it from our drinking water, we should be all right.

To find out the type of disinfectant and fluoridating agents being used in your community, call your local water company.

Delicious Cocoa Quiets Coughs

Peter J. Barnes, MD, professor, department of thoracic medicine, National Heart and Lung Institute, Imperial College School of Medicine, London.

There are some people who place foods such as ice cream and chocolate in a category all by themselves because, in spite of their nutritional challenges, they just make you feel so good. Now researchers in the United Kingdom have identified an ingredient in cocoa, theobromine, that proves it really can be good for you. In their study, theobromine was found to help stop persistent coughs.

While a cough is a common and protective reflex, persistent coughing is detrimental and can even prevent people from leading normal lives, says study coauthor Peter J. Barnes, MD, of the National Heart and Lung Institute at the Imperial College School of Medicine in London. Remedies that contain codeine are generally recognized as the most effective cough stoppers, but they have unpleasant side effects—such as drowsiness, dizziness and light-headedness—and long-term use may cause addiction. This means that there is a great need for safe and effective cough treatments.

MORE EFFECTIVE THAN CODEINE

In the small UK study, 10 healthy volunteers were first given a theobromine, codeine or placebo pill. Next, they were asked to inhale the extract of hot chili pepper (capsaicin). Dr. Barnes explains that capsaicin is commonly used in research to produce coughing and measure the effectiveness of cough medicines.

Researchers compared the levels of capsaicin it took to provoke coughing with each of the three pills. *They discovered that theobromine was more effective than either the placebo or codeine in suppressing coughs…*

• **When participants took theobromine,** the concentration of capsaicin required to provoke coughing was approximately one-third higher than in the placebo group.

• **Those given codeine required** only slightly higher amounts of capsaicin to produce a cough compared with a placebo.

SAFER THAN CODEINE

A major plus is that, unlike standard cough remedies, theobromine does not cause such side effects as drowsiness, dizziness and light-headedness. In contrast to codeine, which acts on specific areas of the brain and spinal cord, Dr. Barnes explains that theobromine appears to act outside the brain. Researchers believe that it works by calming down the nerves in the lungs that become activated by irritants, leading to coughing.

Although further research is needed, Dr. Barnes and his colleagues see theobromine as a novel and promising treatment that may someday lead to a new class of antitussive drugs, which suppress or relieve coughing. When you are home nursing a cough and cold, a steaming cup of hot chocolate may be more comforting than you realized. Just be sure that you use quality chocolate made from real cocoa. A semisweet or bittersweet chocolate contains between 15% and 35% cocoa solids. Super dark chocolates are 60% to 90% cocoa solids.

As for how much chocolate to eat, moderation in all things is best, so keep calories and sugar content in mind when eating chocolate.

Expert Prefers Milk "In the Raw"

Ron Schmid, ND, a naturopath and owner of the Ultra-Pure company, Watertown, Connecticut, and author of Traditional Foods Are Your Best Medicine: Improving Health and Longevity with Native Nutrition (Healing Arts) and The Untold Story of Milk (NewTrends), www.drrons.com.

Milk—it does a body good. That's what the National Dairy Council would have us believe. Meanwhile, we continue to read about the various dangers of dairy—that it may cause allergies…or it could have a negative impact on the immune system. What are we supposed to believe?

According to Ron Schmid, ND, a naturopath in private practice in Watertown, Connecticut, dairy products are both good and bad for our health.

AT ITS ROOT

Dr. Schmid is a staunch believer in the benefits of dairy products. In its raw (unprocessed) form and when it is from healthy, grass-fed cows, milk is loaded with calcium, of course, and many vitamins, including B and C. Even more important, he says, is that milk is full of enzymes, which the body needs for every chemical action and reaction. Every organ needs enzymes, and they play a crucial role in the proper function of the immune system.

In fact, Dr. Schmid says the raw milk that comes from grass-fed cows is so healthy that even patients who thought they were allergic or lactose intolerant had no problems digesting it. Furthermore, a study reported in *The Lancet* showed that children fed raw milk in their early years had an asthma rate of only 1%, compared with 11% in the group that drank processed milk…and a hay fever rate of 3%, compared with the processed milk group's rate of 13%.

The big catch here—and of course you knew there was one—is that you can't get milk's enzymes and most of its vitamins and minerals from the vast majority of dairy products available in this country. Dr. Schmid is adamantly opposed to the milk products that line our supermarket shelves.

MASS PRODUCTION STRIKES AGAIN

Dairy production has become a huge business that is dependent on mass production and pasteurization, which uses high temperatures to kill disease-causing bacteria. Where farmers once kept a few head of dairy cows munching on grass in the fields, dairy producers now jam many cows into a barn and feed them the high-grain, high-acid diet that produces the maximum amount of milk.

In addition, most cows today are so unhealthy that they live only three or four years, not the normal life span of 15. The diet for mass production, says Dr. Schmid, biochemically alters the cows' milk, and pasteurization wipes out virtually any nutritional value that is left.

So mass production and pasteurization are the primary reasons that milk can be bad for you. They contribute to the allergies and other conditions, such as gastrointestinal diseases, that have caused so many health-care professionals today to take an anti-milk stance.

Even more surprising is that commercially available "organic milk" is the worst offender of all, says Dr. Schmid, since it is *ultrapasteurized* (a high-heat process that sterilizes the milk, destroying its enzymes and many of its vitamins so that it can last for six months).

According to Dr. Schmid, however, pasteurization only became necessary about 100 years ago because of the pressure to produce large quantities of milk, especially for the burgeoning cities.

The resulting careless production allowed bacteria into the milk, causing tuberculosis and other diseases. Amazingly, while pasteurization made milk safe to drink, it also made it less healthful.

Controversy still runs high about the need to maintain pasteurization to protect consumers.

RAW LAW

Today, it is possible in 33 states to purchase raw milk on the farm where it is produced, reports Dr. Schmid. In three states—California, Connecticut and New Mexico—you can now find it in a few retail markets. Farmers may apply for a license to distribute milk this way, but very few do because qualifying is so difficult.

For those of us who can't keep a cow in our backyards, Dr. Schmid strongly believes that it is worth the effort to scout out a farmer who sells raw milk. He adds, however, that it is extremely important to check out the farmer's reputation to be sure he/she makes the good health of his cows a priority. Confirm that he feeds the cows grass and perhaps a small amount of grain and allows them to roam in the fields. Healthy cows, he reminds us, produce healthy milk.

If the farmer does not conform to these standards, it is possible for the raw milk to cause gastrointestinal problems, including salmonella food poisoning, a potential problem for people on antibiotics and possibly lethal for those who are immunosuppressed due to aging, chemotherapy or disease.

The Problem with Pasteurized Milk

Andrew L. Rubman, ND, director, Southbury Clinic for Traditional Medicines, Southbury, Connecticut.

Ron Schmid, ND, a naturopath and owner of the Ultra-Pure company, Watertown, Connecticut, and author of *Traditional Foods Are Your Best Medicine: Improving Health and Longevity with Native Nutrition* (Healing Arts) and *The Untold Story of Milk* (NewTrends), *www.drrons.com.*

In order to be fully knowledgeable about the health problems associated with mass-produced milk today, it is important to understand the two processes that are integral to milk production—pasteurization, which employs high heat to rid milk of certain bacteria, yeasts and molds…and homogenization, the process by which the fat molecules in milk are altered so that they stay evenly distributed throughout the liquid.

Dr. Schmid, ND, a naturopath in private private practice in Watertown, Connecticut, notes that today's mass-produced milk must be pasteurized to eliminate bacteria that can cause serious health risks, such as tuberculosis and gastrointestinal disease. Unfortunately, pasteurization also robs the milk of many enzymes and other health-giving properties.

HEATING UP

Enzymes are an integral part of every chemical action and reaction in the body. Our bodies have many enzymes, but as we age, their levels decrease. This makes us more susceptible to chronic degenerative diseases and speeds up the aging process.

We can get more enzymes from our diets, but we would have to eat uncooked animal foods and raw or lightly cooked grains, fruits and veggies to get the entire array. We all know it is best not to eat raw meat, poultry and fish due to health risks.

Raw milk, however, can be a great source of these enzymes—but pasteurization destroys them. In fact, the test for properly pasteurized milk is that it is enzyme free.

In addition, says Dr. Schmid, the heat of pasteurization alters the amino acids in milk, making it harder for the body to use the milk's protein. Pasteurization also lowers milk's vitamin C content by at least 50%…and destroys much of its vitamin A, B-12, B-6 and D. Finally, the heat process makes the minerals in milk—which include calcium, chlorine, magnesium and phosphorus—less available.

Pasteurized milk, denuded of its enzymes and other benefits, is more difficult to digest, according to Dr. Schmid. The result? Pasteurization, combined with the poor quality of grain-fed cows' milk, contributes to the allergies and other diseases that so many health-care professionals are concerned about today.

OBSOLETE REASONING?

Fifty-plus years ago, milk went into open vats that were susceptible to bacteria from a variety of life-threatening diseases, including tuberculosis. Hence, the need for the pasteurizing process.

Today, however, milk is protected with sanitary production measures enforced by state governments. While both raw and pasteurized milk have caused salmonella outbreaks, the largest outbreak by far—milk produced in Illinois in 1985 infected more than 18,000 people in five states with salmonella and resulted in 16 deaths—was caused by pasteurized milk, notes Dr. Schmid.

In spite of modern precautions, pasteurized milk can still be contaminated during or after pasteurization. Ironically, pasteurization completely destroys the very organisms—the enzymes and natural bacteria—that could protect milk from invading pathogenic bacteria, says Dr. Schmid.

HOMOGENIZATION DANGERS, TOO?

The case against homogenization is not as clear, but its implications are still disturbing. Dr. Schmid is quick to acknowledge that he presents this not as a fact, however, but as a theory based on his knowledge and experience.

He explains that research conducted by Kurt Oster, MD, former chief of cardiology at Park City Hospital in Bridgeport, Connecticut, indicates that homogenization is a primary cause of heart disease.

According to Dr. Oster, the homogenization process breaks down fat into tiny particles so that it won't separate in milk. This extends the shelf life of a carton of milk—an obvious plus for milk producers and distributors. Dr. Oster's research indicates that homogenization allows a substance in fat called *xanthine oxidase* (XO) to pass through the walls of the intestines into the circulatory system, where it can trigger arterial problems that lead to heart attacks.

While Dr. Schmid feels that the XO theory is probably valid, it remains only a theory until it is confirmed by further investigation. However, he observes that in some countries where milk is not homogenized—and France is a leading example—there are far fewer heart attacks.

TO DRINK OR NOT TO DRINK?

Dr. Schmid is a strong advocate of healthy raw milk. The operative words, though, are healthy and raw. He is the first to point out that in order to be good for you, raw milk must come from healthy grass-fed cows that roam freely in fields.

Dr. Schmid even advises against the supposedly healthier "organic milk," since it is ultra-pasteurized—effectively sterilized—to attain a six-month shelf life.

If you can't find healthy raw milk or don't live in one of the 35 states that allow the sale of on-farm raw milk, he says, there is no one-size-fits-all advice about consuming dairy products. He suggests that you educate yourself further and discuss your individual situation with a naturopathic physician.

If you can't find raw milk and decide to forgo regular milk, make sure that your intake of calcium and enzymes is adequate. Consider a calcium/magnesium supplement that mimics the form in which these minerals are found in mother's milk and healthy raw milk. One such supplement recommended by our medical expert, Andrew L. Rubman, ND, is Butyrex, offered by T. E. Neesby in Fresno, California (800-633-7294).

Can Cleaning Make You Sick?

Scott T. Weiss, MD, professor of medicine, Harvard Medical School, and associate physician, Brigham and Women's Hospital, both in Boston.

Americans are admittedly, even proudly, obsessed with cleanliness. We like bathing daily, use antibacterial soap to wash our hands and scour our homes with just about every germ-fighting product we can find.

By and large, living the clean life is good. Thanks primarily to improved personal hygiene and public sanitation, coupled with medical advances, such as the introduction of antibiotics and vaccinations, infectious diseases that once wreaked havoc on our health have now been largely vanquished.

But it turns out that there might also be a downside to all this cleanliness and "germphobia." In recent years, there has been a virtual epidemic in allergic diseases (sinusitis, asthma, etc.) and autoimmune diseases (multiple sclerosis, rheumatoid arthritis and type 1 diabetes). These diseases are most common in the affluent, Western, industrialized societies, particularly the US.

THE HYGIENE HYPOTHESIS

One theory that has been proposed to explain this phenomenon is the "hygiene hypothesis." According to Scott T. Weiss, MD, professor of medicine at Harvard Medical School and associate physician at Brigham and Women's Hospital, both in Boston, the idea is that exposure early in life to microbes, such as bacteria and viruses, strengthens the developing immune system. As increased sanitation and cleaner lifestyles have reduced this exposure, the number of allergic and autoimmune diseases has risen.

STUDIES SUPPORT THE HYGIENE HYPOTHESIS

The hygiene hypothesis was first put forth by epidemiologist E.P. Strachen in the late 1980s, when he noticed that older children were typically more likely to suffer from hay fever than their younger siblings.

Today, the results of a number of epidemiological studies support this theory, including...

•**Children in large families**—especially the younger siblings of brothers—have fewer allergies than children in small families. Researchers speculate that as older children carry germs into the home, younger siblings' exposure to them builds immunity and provides protection from developing allergies.

•**Children from small families** who attend day care before age one are less likely to develop allergies.

•**Children who receive oral antibiotics** before age two are more likely to develop allergies. This is because the antibiotics that fight infection also kill beneficial bacteria that normally colonize the gastrointestinal tract. These harmless bacteria are important to normal immune system development early in life.

•**Hay fever is less common in children who live on farms.** This is thought to be due to their exposure to endotoxins—substances in certain bacteria that are most common in soil, the feces of farm animals and house dust.

•**Without stimulation early in life, the immune system may grow confused** and strike out inappropriately. For example, now that intestinal parasites have been largely eliminated by modern sanitation, the immune system sometimes turns on itself and attacks the lining of the intestines, leading to inflammatory bowel disease. At the University of Iowa, mice deliberately infected with parasitic worms called helminths were protected from inflammatory bowel disease. Now, several human patients have also been treated—successfully—with a drink laced with eggs from a harmless pig whipworm.

WHAT YOU CAN DO

Eating dirt or moving to a farm are at best theoretical rather than practical clinical recommendations, observes Dr. Weiss in an editorial published in the *New England Journal of Medicine*. However, he adds that a number of environmental factors are known to be associated with a lower incidence of allergic disease in early life. *These factors include...*

•**Having a dog or other pet in the home.**

•**Attending day care in the first year of life.**

•**Lactobacillus ruminus supplements.** Of course, be sure to consult your health-care professional before giving any supplement to a young child.

SCIENTIFIC RESEARCH CONTINUES

Inspired by studies that support the hygiene hypothesis, researchers are working to create vaccines that imitate the immune effects of the microbes that cleanliness has brushed aside. The goal of these vaccines is to strengthen the body's immune defenses.

Scientists are also continuing to look at probiotics—living cultures of beneficial bacteria, such as *lactobacillus*. Probiotics would ideally replace the beneficial bacteria that we have inadvertently suppressed or eliminated in our quest for cleanliness. The more-recent investigations have included prebiotics (substances and organisms which contribute to the colonization of the "friendly flora") and a more in-depth study of the evolution of a healthy microbial environment in newborns.

It seems that these particular factors may be among the most important influences in protecting us from infections and limiting the severity and duration of them if they take hold.

LET THEM MAKE MUD PIES

Don't abandon the basic principles of good hygiene, but let your child play in the backyard and make all the messy mud pies he/she wants. And when you give him a bath afterward, plain old soap and water will suffice.

Surprising Places Where Germs Grow

Charles P. Gerba, PhD, professor of environmental microbiology, University of Arizona, Tucson.

Germs don't always turn up where you expect them. For instance, which do you think is more contaminated—the toilet seat or your kitchen sink? The doorknob of a public restroom or the buttons on an ATM?

In a recent nationwide telephone survey, most people opted for the toilet seat and public restroom over the kitchen sink and the ATM. Not so, says Charles P. Gerba, PhD, professor of environmental microbiology at the University of Arizona in Tucson. Germs lurk in some surprising places.

THE PROBLEM: A FALSE SENSE OF SECURITY

The common lack of knowledge about where germs are found constitutes a significant health problem, says Dr. Gerba, because it gives people a false sense of security.

His studies have unearthed some surprising discoveries...

•**Germs love moisture,** and the kitchen sink is just about the germiest place in the house. It's more contaminated than the toilet bowl.

•**Busy ATMs are home to even more germs** than public restroom doorknobs.

•**Phone receivers are the most contaminated** surfaces found in the workplace. Computer keyboards as well as elevator buttons are also germ havens.

•**Outdoor portable toilets are cleaner** than public picnic tables.

•**Playground equipment** is the most germ-laden outdoor item.

THE SOLUTION: GOOD HYGIENE

It's a popular misconception that coughs and sneezes are the culprits in spreading microbes. In fact, 80% of infections are spread through hand contact. According to the Centers for Disease Control and Prevention, simple hand washing is one of the most effective ways to kill off germs. Yet Dr. Gerba points out that most of Americans admit that they don't clean their hands often enough. Only 17% report that they wash after shaking hands, while 51% say that they wash their hands after coughing or sneezing.

What to do? Among Dr. Gerba's solutions...

•**Practice proper hygiene** by frequently washing your hands with soap and water and by using an alcohol-based hand sanitizer, such as Purell.

•**Use disinfecting wipes** to clean highly contaminated surfaces, such as desktops, phones and copy machines.

•**Always cover public picnic tables** with a clean tablecloth.

•**Make sure that children wash their hands** after coming back from the playground, and don't permit them to munch on snacks while swinging on the monkey bars.

Good for Your Body, Good for Your Brain

Hugh Hendrie, MB, ChB, DSc, professor of psychiatry and codirector, Center for Alzheimer's Disease and Related Neuropsychiatric Disorders, Indiana University School of Medicine, Indianapolis.

The fear of dementia has always been a particularly gloomy one because it appeared to be a question of fate—you either develop it or you don't. But science is slowly discovering that the risk of developing Alzheimer's disease (AD) and other forms of dementia is much more complex than bad genes or bad luck. In study after study, it's becoming clear that AD and other forms of dementia are associated with specific health factors. Having this information—and acting on it now—may make it possible to protect yourself from developing dementia down the road.

The most important conclusion in studies thus far is that the risk factors for cardiac disease—obesity, high blood pressure, high levels of LDL (bad) cholesterol—are coming up as risk factors for AD as well. In other words, what's bad for your heart is also bad for your brain. *Several new studies add to that information and then some...*

RECENT STUDIES

One study from Harvard analyzed data from the 39,000 women who make up the ongoing Women's Health Study. The study looked for a possible link between the women's cholesterol levels and cognitive decline that took place more than 10 years later. Researchers discovered that having a high HDL (good) cholesterol level was protective. For example, the women who had high HDL readings between 60 and 75 showed a 50% reduction risk for AD compared with those whose HDL levels were lower. The average level for men is 45...women, 55. Low is considered to be 35 or less.

The subsequent study, though, was a twist on most of the previous AD research. Ara S. Khachaturian, PhD, of Johns Hopkins University School of Medicine, analyzed data on memory and aging that was collected over three years from 3,300 participants, all over the age of 65. What emerged was that users of high blood pressure medication (antihypertensives) had a 36% or better risk reduction for AD, and that those on certain potassium-sparing diuretics had a 75% risk reduction! This study underscored previous studies that also showed a link between taking antihypertensives and a reduced AD risk, but it was the first to focus on the effects of diuretics in particular.

DETAILS ON THE
BLOOD PRESSURE CONNECTIONS

We wanted to better understand the current research, especially the Johns Hopkins study concerning antihypertensives, so we called leading international AD researcher Hugh Hendrie, MB, ChB, DSc, at the Center for Alzheimer's Disease and Related Neuropsychiatric Disorders at the Indiana University School of Medicine in Indianapolis. Dr. Hendrie says that this study adds to the growing evidence that high blood pressure is

likely a risk factor for AD. It also shows that antihypertensive medications may play two roles—they help correct hypertension and they seem to do something to prevent brain disease.

However, Dr. Hendrie is cautious about the above finding concerning diuretics. He says that the decreased risk of developing dementia might actually reflect a link to use of diuretics.

Dr. Hendrie goes on to say that all studies thus far, including these, are far too preliminary to explain why such diseases as high blood pressure and diabetes (also known to be a risk) have a role in the development of AD. The picture, he says, is undoubtedly complicated.

A MESSAGE IN THE MIDST

However, if Dr. Hendrie is cautious about the preliminary state of current research, he feels strongly that there is a message in it—quite simply, that it's vital to pay attention to your numbers (your blood pressure reading, your cholesterol levels and your blood glucose levels) to reduce your risk of brain disease. Furthermore, Dr. Hendrie emphasizes that it is never too early to start. Most people assume that dementia is a disease of old age and so there is no reason to worry about it when you're younger. But action is in order starting in middle age or even before. The earlier years, he says, may be when the seeds of dementia are sown. As evidence, he points to the Honolulu heart study that spanned from 1965 to 1998. It showed that the plaques and tangles of AD in its late-in-life victims related to hypertension they developed in midlife, typically around age 50.

So, for the sake of your brain, it's never too early to start paying close attention to your health—and, says Dr. Hendrie, it's never too late for healthy habits, no matter how old you are.

"Miracle" Pills Help Strokes and More

Andrew L. Rubman, ND, director, Southbury Clinic for Traditional Medicines, Southbury, Connecticut.

We have been hearing reports about "miracle" brain medication *piracetam* (Nootropil) that have proven helpful for some after having a stroke. Patients have recounted that it has helped their focus and memory and that it has even boosted their creativity. Although there currently is no approved version by the US Food and Drug Administration (FDA), it has been on the market in Europe for 40 years, with no serious adverse reports, and it is readily available on-line from pharmacies in other countries.

IMPROVED COMMUNICATION WITHIN THE BRAIN

To learn more about this magic brain pill, we spoke with our medical expert, Andrew L. Rubman, ND. He explained that piracetam seems to increase the flow of information through an area of the brain called the *corpus callosum*, the structure connecting the two cerebral hemispheres. Increased traffic literally improves communication between the hemispheres, enhancing right and left brain integrative function.

This allows the uninjured areas in one hemisphere of the brain to assume partial duty for the same areas in the other hemisphere that had sustained damage.

According to Dr. Rubman, this more efficient information flow is associated with improved coordination of literal and symbolic storage, integration of sensory input and retrieved memory, potentially facilitating creative thought, rich recall and photographic memory. In other countries, piracetam is used to treat such conditions as stroke, dyslexia, senile dementia and alcoholism.

WHAT IS PIRACETAM?

Piracetam is a derivative of GABA, an inhibitory neurotransmitter of the central nervous system. While based in nature, it is created by science. The material, however, most closely resembles the amino acid *Pyroglutamate*. The safety and efficacy of piracetam has been studied formally since the mid-1970s and reported in peer-reviewed literature.

TREATMENT IS SHORT AND SWEET

The usual dose of piracetam is up to 800 milligrams once or twice a day. Take pills in between meals with a fruit snack. A great advantage, says Dr. Rubman, is that you don't have to take piracetam for the rest of your life. Once the effect takes hold, and the neuronal pathways have been facilitated, your brain "remembers" it.

He recommends that you take piracetam for one month…and then for seven to 10 consecutive days per month for several months as a booster. Some patients, however, benefit from one dose every three or four days on an ongoing basis.

You can stop taking it once you and your health-care provider determine that its effects have taken hold. There are no known drug interactions, but it should be used under the supervision of a doctor.

It is conceivable that some people might find piracetam a little disruptive at first, says Dr. Rubman. There have been reports that a few individuals think that it is overstimulating. But, he adds, it just requires a little getting used to.

To be on the safe side, take piracetam only under the supervision of a health-care provider who is familiar with its use.

Healing Power Of Pets

Karen Allen, PhD, research scientist, School of Public Health, State University of New York, Buffalo.

Bernie S. Siegel, MD, founder, Exceptional Cancer Patients (ECaP), *ecap-online.org*. He is an author, lecturer and advocate for cancer patients and the chronically ill.

In a television interview, Bernie S. Siegel, MD, founder of Exceptional Cancer Patients (ECaP), an advocacy organization for people facing cancer as well as other chronic illnesses, discussed the effects of pets on heart attack victims in Australia. After one year, 6% of the patients who owned a dog had died, compared with a 25% mortality rate in those who did not own a dog. This seemed to be a pretty remarkable statistic, especially after he said that someone in Australia calculated that if everyone in Australia were given a dog, it would save $145 million per year in health-care costs.

For years, we've all heard about the therapeutic effects of pets in healing depression and in stress reduction. We decided to look at some of the scientific data on how pets affect us. We called Karen Allen, PhD, a research scientist at the School of Public Health at the State University of New York at Buffalo. Dr. Allen's work focuses on the effects of pets on human stress reactions.

PEOPLE OR PETS— WHICH ARE BETTER FOR STRESS?

Dr. Allen has conducted several studies that address such intriguing questions as…

• **Which is better—to have your best friend or your pet present in stressful situations?**

• **Which is better—to have your spouse or your pet present in stressful situations?**

• **How do pets affect blood pressure** (a common measure of stress response) in people who are already taking blood pressure lowering medication?

• **Can newly acquired pets affect stress?**

In one study, Dr. Allen looked at women performing mental arithmetic problems alone… then with their best female friends present…and finally, with their dogs present. Interestingly, with the friends present, the subjects experienced large increases in blood pressure (compared with when they worked on their own). However, when the dogs were present, insignificant increases—or none at all—occurred in blood pressure.

"One study participant suggested that we compare the effect of her dog's presence with the effect of her husband's presence," recalled Dr. Allen. She and her colleagues laughed at the idea at first but then decided to test it out. In this study, in addition to performing mental arithmetic, participants were asked to hold their hands under cold water and endure it to test both their "active coping" and "passive coping" responses.

Once again, and in both active and passive coping trials, participants experienced dramatic stress responses in the presence of another person versus only slight increases in blood pressure in the presence of a pet. The consistent results led Dr. Allen to conclude that pets are clearly a preferred source of social support.

An interesting result of the study was that when the pets and the spouses were both present, the effect of the dogs cancelled out the stress that the presence of spouses generated.

PET/PEOPLE PREFERENCE?

One valid criticism Dr. Allen encountered was the notion that the pets really had produced no effect at all. Pet owners generally are healthier, happier and better adjusted than those who do not own pets—therefore, their blood pressure is less likely to rise under stress.

To test whether a pet would affect people who did not previously own one, Dr. Allen designed a study in which half of the participants were randomly selected to adopt a cat or dog from an animal shelter. The study participants, all stockbrokers who lived alone, described their work as extremely stressful. In addition, they all exhibited high blood pressure (greater than 160/100)…and they were all scheduled to begin drug therapy with lisinopril, a medication that successfully reduces resting blood pressure.

Once again, participants performed mental arithmetic as the stress provoker, but in addition, they were asked to give speeches to imaginary clients whose money they had lost. As predicted, lisinopril lowered the resting blood pressure of all participants. However, while doing the mental arithmetic or giving the speeches, the pet-owning participants' blood pressure increased by less than half of their petless counterparts.

HOW DOES THIS HAPPEN?

Dr. Siegel has seen firsthand the extraordinary effects animals can have. "People's physiology, their body chemistry, literally changes when pets are around," he says. Levels of the stress hormone cortisol go down, immune function improves and, perhaps more significantly, serotonin and oxytocin levels increase. These are the same hormones that become elevated in a woman after giving birth, which promote bonding with the new baby.

But why do these chemical changes occur? Dr. Siegel believes that the bottom line is the unconditional acceptance and connection that animals will consistently provide. In addition, he notes, the responsibility of pet ownership can give one's life meaning, especially in the absence of other close relationships. "I've worked with cancer patients who literally could not die because they had dogs and cats who had to be taken care of," Siegel says. "These people hung on to life until they were sure that their pets would be provided for."

Dr. Siegel explains that an important reason why we feel a close connection to our pets is that they can be incredibly intuitive. Often, if a person is sick in bed, a dog comes and sits beside him/her, whereas if he is just taking a nap, the dog does not show the same level of concern and interest. Animals respond to feelings, to what is really going on with their owners.

"Animals have an incredible ability to be completely there and completely devoted," Dr. Siegel says. "How many of us can say that we are totally devoted to someone else's well-being? Animals are, and we respond positively to that."

Can Dogs Really Smell Cancer?

Caroline M. Willis, PhD, director of academic research, department of dermatology, Amersham Hospital, Buckinghamshire, England.

A Border collie/Doberman mix sniffs at a mole on his owner's leg so persistently that the woman consults her doctor, who diagnoses and successfully treats her early-stage melanoma. A Labrador named Parker nudges his owner's thigh so frequently that the man sees his doctor for what he thinks is eczema, only to learn it is cancer.

We read about these tales in tabloid magazines, but now there is scientific evidence to support what we dog lovers have known in our hearts all along—your dog *is* your best friend. In a small study reported in the *British Medical Journal*, dogs actually detected cancer through their sense of smell.

THE WET NOSE KNOWS

At the Amersham Hospital in Buckinghamshire, England, director of academic research, department of dermatology, Caroline M. Willis, PhD, and her colleagues trained six dogs of various breeds and ages for about seven months to detect bladder cancer in people's urine. Tumors produce volatile organic compounds, some of which are likely to have distinctive odors. These may be detected by dogs, who have an exceptional sense of smell. Researchers used urine from bladder-cancer patients, from healthy people and from patients who had non-cancerous diseases to train the dogs to distinguish those with bladder cancer. The dogs were trained to identify the sample with bladder cancer by lying down next to it. In their final exam, the dogs scored 41%, correctly recognizing the samples in 22 out of 54 instances. Their success rate was significant, as untrained dogs might be expected to identify only 14% by chance alone.

According to Dr. Willis, the cocker spaniels were the most successful detectives, which is consistent with the fact that this breed is widely used in uncovering drugs and explosives. But she adds that the little papillon also did reasonably well, suggesting that different types of dogs may have this capability if properly trained.

One of the most intriguing findings was that every dog identified one particular urine sample as cancerous, even though researchers originally believed it to be cancer free. When the volunteer was tested, the diagnosis was cancer of a similar type, but it was located in the kidney rather than the bladder.

THE FUTURE

The researchers plan to train more dogs to help identify markers for other types of cancer, especially skin cancer. In addition, they are seeking to chemically identify the odor of bladder cancer, and hope that this will lead to the development of an instrumental screening method for this disease.

PAY ATTENTION TO YOUR PUP

Every owner knows how sensitive his/her best friend is. Dogs are in tune with their owners. When we're on top of the world, they are with us, romping and playing. When we're under the weather, they're gentle and caring.

Still, dogs are never going to replace blood tests, magnetic resonance imaging (MRI) and computer tomography (CT) scans and all the other high-tech cancer-screening alternatives we have at our fingertips today. So what can we learn from this study?

Pay attention. If your pooch acts strangely, don't casually dismiss his behavior. He may be trying to tell you something very important about your health.

Does Country Living Pack on the Pounds?

Nico P. Pronk, PhD, vice president and senior research investigator, HealthPartners' Center for Health Promotion, Minneapolis.

Many people move to the suburbs for the fresh air and better quality of life. How ironic that a report shows that residents in sprawling urban county suburbs are fatter and have higher blood pressure than those in dense urban areas.

The study, *Relationship Between Urban Sprawl and Physical Activity, Obesity, and Morbidity*, from the advocacy group Smart Growth America, measured the degree of sprawl in 448 urban-area counties. Those that had the greatest sprawl earned the lowest numerical ranking on a sprawl index. Researchers then evaluated and compared health characteristics, including weight and hypertension, of more than 200,000 people living in all study counties.

Results: For each 50-point increase (the measure of increased density) on the sprawl index, county residents weighed one pound less. It doesn't sound like much, but wait. Residents in the county with the greatest sprawl—Geauga County outside of Cleveland—were likely to weigh six-plus pounds more than people living in the densest urban one, New York County (Manhattan). Incidence of high blood pressure among New Yorkers was still slightly less frequent than among residents living in the most sprawling counties, in spite of the city's fast pace.

Nico P. Pronk, PhD, vice president and a senior research investigator for the health system HealthPartners' Center for Health Promotion in Minneapolis, has been closely involved in this research. We called him to discuss his suggestions for automobile-bound Americans to get more exercise.

Dr. Pronk says that a key discovery in the report is that people who exercise regularly but live in sprawling counties are still heavier than their counterparts in dense counties. The difference is that New Yorkers, for example, walk a great deal in their daily life, simply to get from place to place, and suburbanites *drive everywhere*. He and other researchers realized that a good solution would be to get people to increase the number of steps they take routinely. And *voilà*—the birth of HealthPartners' well-known 10,000 Steps program.

10,000 STEPS

Participants in the 10,000 Steps Program are encouraged to take 10,000 steps every day—about five miles. Don't despair. Even nonwalkers take about 4,000 steps (approximately two miles) each day just going about the office, their homes and to and from their cars. You just need to increase your activity somewhat to meet the goal. There are many ways to do this, and you've heard them before—park farther out in the lot…take the stairs…walk the long way up the hall at the office, etc.

Dr. Pronk recommends that you track your steps each day with a pedometer (you can buy one for about $15). HealthPartners offers a Web site at which people can sign up for a one-year program (*Cost:* $20 for HealthPartner members, $30 for others).

info Go to *www.10k-steps.com* for more information—and get moving.

Buckle Up for Family Safety

Peter Cummings, MD, MPH, professor of epidemiology, School of Public Health and Community Medicine, Harborview Injury Prevention and Research Center, University of Washington, Seattle.

The argument for wearing seat belts has traditionally revolved around saving oneself. Now research shows that buckling up may actually help you save the lives of your passengers as well.

To investigate what dangers unrestrained passengers pose to each other—and, in particular, to fellow passengers wearing seat belts —researchers from the Harborview Injury Prevention and Research Center in Seattle studied more than 70,000 motor vehicle crash reports over a 12-year span. They found that during an accident, unrestrained occupants raise the risk of death for others in the same vehicle by up to 22%, mainly by colliding with them upon impact. The risk of crash-related deaths was lowest when all of the occupants in a vehicle were wearing seat belts, including car-seat restraints for young children and babies.

"We already knew from prior studies that wearing a seat belt reduces your risk of fatal injury by about 60%," says lead investigator Peter Cummings, MD, MPH, professor of epidemiology at the University of Washington in Seattle. "Now we've found that it is also important to make sure that other people in your car wear their seat belts as well."

Though the back seat is generally safer than the front, it's equally important to wear your restraints here, say the researchers. Rear-seat occupants could prevent about one in six deaths of front-seat passengers by wearing their seat belts.

"It's such a simple thing to do. Our goal is not just for everyone to buckle up when they get in a car but to insist that all other passengers do so as well," says Dr. Cummings.

Important: Remember to reposition items on the car floor, in the trunk or in an otherwise protected location. Just as on an airplane during take-off or landing, the last thing you want is a book or toy to become a projectile and cause distraction or injury.

13

Not-So-Common Ailments

10 Ways to Fight Constant Fatigue

You think you eat pretty well, try to exercise, get sufficient sleep on most nights and know you're not sick, but you're still tired every day. What can you do to perk yourself up?

According to Jamison Starbuck, ND, a naturopathic physician in family practice and a lecturer at the University of Montana, both based in Missoula, nine out of 10 people expend their energy in unhealthy ways. Fatigue is a sign that it's time for a self-examination.

THE NATUROPATHIC POINT OF VIEW

According to Dr. Starbuck, we are all designed to have enough energy for our day-to-day lives. However, the problem is that many people are out of shape, eat poorly or make poor lifestyle choices. Then they complain of being exhausted and want to boost their energy through artificial methods that can include sports drinks and energy bars.

Dr. Starbuck is not a fan of energy-boosting products and does not believe that these are the answer. Although just a little bit of caffeine now and then is fine, keeping yourself going with multiple coffees or caffeinated colas is ignoring the underlying issue. What you must do is look at how you care for yourself and use your energy.

When a patient complains of fatigue, Dr. Starbuck performs a physical and a blood test to check for serious health problems. She also takes the time to inquire about her patient's daily life—what's going on with his family? His work? How is his diet? Is he getting enough exercise? Maybe he thinks he's exercising well, but is he overdoing it? Is he under stress? How is he managing that stress?

Alan R. Hirsch, MD, director, Smell & Taste Treatment and Research Foundation, Chicago, and author of *Life's a Smelling Success*. Authors of Unity.

Jamison Starbuck, ND, a naturopathic physician practicing in Missoula, Montana. She is a past president of the American Association of Naturopathic Physicians.

214

Steps that Dr. Starbuck recommends to counter fatigue...

• **Reflect on your life.** She advises keeping a journal to learn more about how you expend your energy now and to make certain that you expend it in positive ways in the future.

• **Replenish your energy with "good" rest.** In most cases, observes Dr. Starbuck, people who are overtired are really struggling with a lack of restorative downtime. This isn't just sleep—though you should aim to get seven to nine hours per night, depending on your age and physical condition. Sometimes you just need to "take a break" from your list of to-dos and do nothing.

• **Manage stress.** Explore new ways that will help to restore your energy, such as meditation and yoga.

• **Watch your diet.** Eating sugary processed junk foods is a recipe for short bursts of energy followed by longer periods of lethargy and food cravings. Instead, fill your plate with whole foods, such as nutrient-rich fruits and vegetables, and healthy sources of protein, such as fish, soy and hormone-free chicken.

• **Engage in regular exercise.** However, don't push too hard, especially if you're out of shape. When in doubt, see an exercise specialist for advice and guidance.

• **Take dietary supplements.** During short periods of stress, Dr. Starbuck recommends B-complex vitamins and astragalus, an immune-enhancing Chinese herb. Go with the dosage recommended on the label. She also suggests adaptogenic herbs, such as licorice and Siberian ginseng, in moderation.

Caution: If you have high blood pressure, these herbs generally are not recommended.

• **If fatigue lasts for six weeks, see a naturopathic doctor (ND) for an assessment.** In some cases, this is a symptom of a more serious psychological or physical disorder. Your ND will address the issue in a holistic way.

THE POWER OF SMELL

As Dr. Starbuck points out, it's not always necessary—or desirable—to take an energy-boosting product or even a supplement. An increasingly popular alternative to counter simple fatigue is aromatherapy, the art and science of using essential oils extracted from plants for health and healing. You can harness this energizing power by using scented candles or putting a few drops of essential oil on a lightbulb or in your bathwater.

For recommendations on energizing scents, we spoke with Alan R. Hirsch, MD, the director of the Smell & Taste Treatment and Research Foundation in Chicago. He is a strong proponent of using aromatherapy to boost energy in a safe and natural way.

His recommendations...

• **Jasmine.** A classic remedy for fatigue, diffusing its scent into the air around you can be uplifting.

• **Essential oils with a strong trigeminal component,** such as citrus, peppermint and menthol. (The trigeminal nerve delivers sensory stimuli to the brain from the face, teeth and tongue. It is the irritant nerve that makes you cry when you cut onions.) These act as a stimulating wake-up call. Essential oils are widely available at quality health-food stores and on-line.

• **Aromas that you associate with alertness**—for example, your morning coffee or grapefruit juice—can help you perk up at any time of day. In a Pavlovian conditioning response, scent becomes associated with a particular situation or environment.

According to the general "affective theory of aromas," Dr. Hirsch says that any odor that you like—whether the scent of an ocean breeze or of fresh bread baking—can make you happy, and when you're happy, you're more alert and productive. You focus better, learn better and exercise better.

info To learn more about aromatherapy, visit these Web sites...

Smell & Taste Treatment and Research Foundation, *www.smellandtaste.org.*

National Association for Holistic Aromatherapy, *www.naha.org.*

Pacific Institute of Aromatherapy, *www.pacific instituteofaromatherapy.com.*

The Mystery of Fibromyalgia

Timothy McCall, MD, internist, medical editor of *Yoga Journal* and author of *Examining Your Doctor* (Citadel) and *Yoga as Medicine* (Bantam), *www.drmccall.com.*

You ache all over, and your energy level is nonexistent. You just can't get a good night's sleep, you can't concentrate, and to top it all off, you're frustrated because your doctor doesn't take any of this very seriously.

Sound familiar? Symptoms such as unexplained fatigue and body pain are typical of *fibromyalgia syndrome* (FMS), a condition that affects millions of Americans, over 90% of them women. Unfortunately for these women, fibromyalgia gets little respect. Sufferers are viewed as not really being sick. But, as sufferers of this condition know all too well—there is something real going on.

According to Timothy McCall, MD, an internist, medical editor of *Yoga Journal,* and author of *Examining Your Doctor,* fibromyalgia is a very real medical condition. Unfortunately, there is no clinical test for FMS, and many doctors are not educated to know what to do for people who suffer from it.

The good news is that FMS can be managed successfully. It's a matter of finding an appropriate doctor to get the correct diagnosis and identifying the right combination of treatment modalities that work for you.

DO YOU HAVE FMS?

In 1990, the American College of Rheumatology (ACR) identified specific criteria for the diagnosis of fibromyalgia. If a person has at least 11 of 18 specific areas of the body that are painful under pressure and has experienced widespread pain for at least three months and does not have another condition that explains the same symptoms, he/she meets the criteria for FMS.

Dr. McCall explains that FMS symptoms tend to wax and wane over time. They may develop after a period of stress, lack of sleep or unusually heavy physical activity, and then subside. *Symptoms vary from person to person and may include...*

- **Widespread musculoskeletal pain** and multiple tender points.
- **Severe fatigue.**
- **Sleep disturbances.**
- **Stiffness upon waking.**
- **Irritable bowel syndrome** (constipation, diarrhea, abdominal pain and bloating).
- **Chronic headache and facial pain.**
- **Heightened sensitivity to bright lights,** noise and odors.
- **Depression and anxiety.**
- **Numbness or tingling.**
- **Memory and concentration difficulties.**
- **Painful menstruation** or pelvic pain.
- **Dry eyes, skin and mouth.**

WHAT CAUSES FMS?

No one knows the exact cause. There may be a connection with sleep disturbances, but on the other hand, it is unclear whether these are a cause or an effect of fibromyalgia. *The ACR has identified several associated factors that contribute to the development or perpetuation of this condition...*

- **Stress.**
- **Immune or endocrine abnormalities.**
- **Biochemical abnormalities** in the central nervous system.

Dr. McCall adds that studies have found that FMS sufferers have greater levels in their spinal fluid of *substance P,* a neurotransmitter associated with pain. This causes them to perceive the symptoms of pain at a lower level than people with normal levels of this chemical. However, testing for substance P in the spinal fluid is a research tool and not yet used in clinical practice.

DIAGNOSIS AND TREATMENT

Even with the ACR's designated criteria, diagnosis can be tricky, since fibromyalgia mimics the symptoms of other conditions, such as chronic fatigue syndrome and chronic sinusitis. Dr. McCall believes that FMS is generally underdiagnosed. He says that the key is to find a physician who has expertise in the field.

Certainly, you are more likely to get good care from a doctor who not only believes that fibromyalgia exists, but who also has experience in treating it. Beware of any doctors who patronize you and do not believe you're sick, advises Dr. McCall.

When it comes to treatment, there is no magic combination that works for everyone. Whatever you think may work—as long as it's safe—is worth a shot, says Dr. McCall.

Treatment options include…

●**Pain relievers, antidepressants and muscle relaxants.** While the drugs wont cure the condition, many people find they reduce symptoms.

●**Try yoga.**

●**Engage in regular mild exercise to relieve body aches and pains.** Dr. McCall says various mind-body modalities, such as yoga, meditation and tai chi can be useful. Walking and swimming are good options too.

The cumulative impact of steady practice is best, explains Dr. McCall. He says you'll get more of a benefit if you do 15 minutes of yoga daily instead of attending a one-and-a-half hour class each week.

●**Practice good sleep habits.** Go to bed and get up at the same time every day, and limit daytime napping. Sleep difficulties, fatigue and exhaustion are all characteristics of FMS, so maintaining a good balance of rest and exercise is essential.

●**Pace yourself.** Dr. McCall warns that on your good days, you may be tempted to overdo it physically…but don't! Doing too much can end up backfiring, triggering an exacerbation of symptoms.

●**Reduce stress.** Choose your favorite stress-management technique. A simple meditation technique is to choose a quiet space, close your eyes and follow your breath or repeat a mantra. People often give up on meditation too easily, says Dr. McCall, but he encourages everyone to persevere. It can be transformative.

●**Join a fibromyalgia support group.** People with FMS tend to feel isolated. To find like-minded people, visit the Fibromyalgia Network Web site at *www.fmnetnews.com.* They also have an informative journal.

●**Educate yourself.** The more you learn about your condition, the more control you will have over it. (See the informative Internet sites listed at the end of this article.)

●**Maintain a healthy lifestyle.** Follow a balanced diet…get an appropriate balance of rest and exercise…don't smoke…and limit your intake of caffeine.

●**Other alternatives** can include cognitive-behavioral therapy, physical therapy, tender-point injections (injections to break up painful, hardened knots in muscles), bodywork, traditional Chinese medicine, acupuncture and chiropractic care.

Dr. McCall's personal favorite treatments for addressing fibromyalgia are yoga and meditation. He notes that fibromyalgia is a disempowering condition, and these are strategies that can help you seize control of your health. In the long run, you may have to experiment a bit, mixing and matching the various modalities, but be patient—while there is no cure, there are steps you can take to improve your health and reduce symptoms while living with FMS.

info The American College of Rheumatology, *www.rheumatology.org.*

Arthritis Foundation, *www.arthritis.org.*

Fibromyalgia Network, *www.fmnetnews.com.*

Natural Relief for Fibromyalgia Sufferers

Ray Sahelian, MD, physician in private practice in Los Angeles, California, and author of numerous books, including Mind Boosting Secrets *(Bottom Line Books). To learn more about Dr. Sahelian's work, visit his Web site at* www.raysahelian.com.

Fibromyalgia is a very serious condition that can significantly impact the quality of life for millions of sufferers due to the fatigue and body pain associated with the disease. What can you do from the inside out to help case the pain and perhaps overcome the condition?

To learn about natural approaches to relieving the symptoms of fibromyalgia, we spoke with Ray Sahelian, MD, a physician in private practice in Los Angeles and author of numerous books, including *Mind Boosting Secrets*.

Unfortunately, no one knows exactly what causes fibromyalgia, and there is no one magic pill you can take to cure it. According to Dr. Sahelian, your best bet is to mix and match a variety of approaches to control your symptoms. An empathetic health-care practitioner with experience in treating fibromyalgia can help you sort through the many conventional and natural treatment alternatives to determine the combination that will work best for you.

HELP FROM THE INSIDE

• **Supplementation.** A number of the herbal and mineral supplements can be helpful for fibromyalgia sufferers. Talk to a trained health-care provider about what might be best for you. *Options include...*

• Coenzyme Q10 (CoQ10). This popular supplement increases energy levels, enhances the immune system and provides disease-fighting antioxidant activity. Although CoQ10 is available in a variety of dosages, Dr. Sahelian says that high dosages may not be necessary. Except for temporary treatment of medical conditions, he generally recommends 50 to 100 milligrams (mg) daily.

• Ginkgo biloba. Ginkgo extract is widely used in Europe for such conditions as memory and concentration problems, confusion, depression, anxiety and headache. In an open, uncontrolled study, volunteers with fibromyalgia were given both 200 mg of CoQ10 and 200 mg of ginkgo biloba extract daily for 84 days. The individual effects are not clear, but the volunteers recorded progressive improvement on quality-of-life questionnaires. At the close of the study, 64% reported that they felt better. These research results appeared in the March-April 2002 issue of the *Journal of International Medical Research. Note*: Do not take ginkgo if you have a bleeding disorder, plan to undergo surgery or are taking blood-thinning drugs such as *warfarin* (Coumadin).

• Fish oil capsules. If you do not regularly include enough cold-water fish, such as salmon and halibut, in your diet, Dr. Sahelian recommends three to five fish oil capsules a day or one teaspoon of flaxseed oil per day. Fish and fish oil are excellent sources of omega-3 fatty acids, which

provide fluidity to cell membranes and improve communication between brain cells.

• SAMe. This natural antidepressant can lift mood within hours in some individuals, says Dr. Sahelian. The daily dose is best kept to below 200 mg, preferably half a tablet (100 mg). It is always best to take the lowest possible effective dose. According to Dr. Sahelian, SAMe has a stimulating nature, and even 200 mg daily can be a lot for some people. Possible side effects at high doses include anxiety, restlessness, headache and insomnia. Take SAMe in the morning a few minutes before breakfast.

• L-tryptophan. Sleep difficulties and frequent waking are a common problem for people with fibromyalgia. This amino acid is a precursor of the neurotransmitter serotonin, which plays a role in how your brain regulates sleep, mood and behavior. Take one 500-mg capsule of L-tryptophan in the evening on an empty stomach an hour or two before sleep.

• B-complex vitamins and L-carnitine to help boost flagging energy levels...and calcium/magnesium, melatonin or 5-HTP to help you get a good night's sleep. At a minimum, you should consider a daily multivitamin and mineral supplement.

• **Check for food allergies.** Dr. Sahelian cites a study in which 17 people with fibromyalgia eliminated foods such as corn, wheat, dairy, citrus and sugar from their diets. After two weeks, nearly half reported a significant reduction in pain. Most also noted relief from headache, fatigue, bloating and breathing difficulties. When foods were reintroduced, some participants once again experienced pain, headache and gastrointestinal distress.

HELP FROM THE OUTSIDE

In addition to diet changes and supplements, Dr. Sahelian is a big believer in the value of lifestyle changes for fibromyalgia. *Specifically, he suggests...*

• **Keep moving.** Although this is not likely to be your first inclination when you are feeling achy and tired, Dr. Sahelian emphasizes that exercise is more effective than medication in easing symptoms. Consistent, gentle, low-impact activity such as walking is best for relieving pain and stiffness. Avoid the temptation to do too much, which can end up making you feel worse. In particular, Dr. Sahelian recommends yoga.

•**Try acupuncture.** In 1997, a National Institutes of Health panel determined that this ancient Chinese practice may provide relief from pain associated with fibromyalgia.

•**Use muscular manipulation.** Some fibromyalgia sufferers can obtain relief through treatments including chiropractic...osteopathy ...massage, such as lymphatic drainage (a technique that drains excess fluid from the tissues throughout the body) and Swedish techniques ...or physical therapy.

•**Get focused.** Hypnosis, a focused state of concentration, is another alternative for pain relief. Varieties include self-hypnosis (in which you repeat a positive statement or mantra over and over) and guided imagery (in which you create relaxing images in your mind). Other relaxation methods include biofeedback, meditation and deep breathing exercises.

•**Change your ways.** Stress can aggravate symptoms of fibromyalgia. Consider cognitive-behavioral therapy or other stress-management techniques to gain control of the stressors in your life.

TRIED AND TRUE

Before taking any supplement, always check with your health-care provider. Remember, no supplement replaces a healthy lifestyle.

To cope best with fibromyalgia, the tried-and-true advice still holds: Follow a balanced diet, get a good balance of rest and exercise, practice effective stress-management techniques and avoid unhealthy habits, such as smoking, drinking and excessive caffeine intake.

There may be no cure for the moment, but there are plenty of steps you can take to control symptoms and live a full life with fibromyalgia.

info American College of Rheumatology, *www.rheumatology.org.*

Arthritis Foundation, *www.arthritis.org.*

Fibromyalgia Network, *www.fmnetnews.com.*

The National Certification Commission for Acupuncture and Oriental Medicine, (NCCAOM), *www.nccaom.org.*

The National Fibromyalgia Association, *www.fmaware.org.*

Amazing Link Between Sinusitis, Fatigue and Fibromyalgia

Alexander C. Chester, MD, general internist and clinical professor of medicine, Georgetown University Medical Center, Washington, DC.

Andrew L. Rubman, ND, director, Southbury Clinic for Traditional Medicines, Southbury, Connecticut.

Although the causes of chronic fatigue syndrome and fibromyalgia continue to confound scientists, research suggests that they both may be linked to sinus problems.

FAMILIAR AND FRUSTRATING SYMPTOMS

According to the author of the study, Alexander C. Chester, MD, general internist and clinical professor of medicine at Georgetown University Medical Center in Washington, DC, unexplained fatigue and body pain are familiar and frustrating symptoms that are often seen by internists.

These vague symptoms are typical of many different diseases, including chronic fatigue syndrome, fibromyalgia and chronic sinusitis.

But Dr. Chester found that when he treated sinusitis symptoms, fatigue and body pain were often relieved as well. This intrigued him and led him to investigate further.

ABOUT THE STUDY

To get to the bottom of the mystery, Dr. Chester interviewed 297 patients, men and women age 40 or younger, in the course of general medical exams.

He inquired about fatigue, body pain and the other symptoms consistent with a sinus infection (such as heavy-headedness, frontal headache and marked facial pressure).

Here are the results, which were reported in the *Archives of Internal Medicine...*

•**Sixty-five patients noted unexplained chronic fatigue (UCF).**

•**Thirty-three patients had unexplained chronic muscle, joint or abdominal pain for more than a month.**

•**Twenty-six suffered both unexplained chronic fatigue and body pain.**

• **Sinus symptoms were nine times more common** in people complaining of unexplained fatigue and six times more common in those with unexplained chronic pain.

MAKING THE CONNECTION

Unfortunately, there is no easy way to know if you have chronic sinusitis, chronic fatigue syndrome or fibromyalgia. All three conditions defy easy clinical diagnosis.

If a person goes to a general practitioner and complains of fatigue or body pain, the first thing that pops into the doctor's mind is not going to be chronic sinusitis, observes Dr. Chester.

The study suggests that a patient who has symptoms such as fatigue or body pain may be suffering from chronic sinusitis, however, and this is a diagnosis that the doctor should at least be considering.

According to Andrew L. Rubman, ND, our medical expert, these complaints also can be symptoms of a systemic immune problem. Ignoring the root causes could leave underlying conditions untreated.

THE BEST DEFENSE

Should you suffer from chronic fatigue or chronic pain, talk to your doctor about investigating further, and consider consulting a naturopathic physician as a member of your treatment team to look for patterns in the symptoms.

In the meantime, you can strengthen your immune system and your resistance to all of these illnesses by following a healthy diet…getting a good balance of exercise and rest…and avoiding negative lifestyle habits, such as a high alcohol intake and smoking.

info National Institute of Allergy and Infectious Diseases, *www.niaid.nih.gov.*

Overwhelmed? Exhausted? You Could Have Adrenal Fatigue

James L. Wilson, DC, ND, PhD, one of the founders of the Canadian College of Naturopathic Medicine and the author of *Adrenal Fatigue: The 21st Century Stress Syndrome.* Smart.

Do you ever feel overwhelmed by stress? Are you exhausted for no reason? Do you have to drag yourself out of bed in the morning? Do you depend on coffee, sodas and candy bars to keep going?

If so—like eight out of 10 Americans—you may be suffering from some form of adrenal fatigue (which is also known as hypoadrenia or hypoadrenalism).

According to James L. Wilson, DC, ND, PhD, one of the founders of the Canadian College of Naturopathic Medicine and author of *Adrenal Fatigue: The 21st Century Stress Syndrome*, adrenal fatigue is a common disorder that is largely ignored by the medical community, which dismisses it as "just another health fad." This is unfortunate, because there's hope out there for all of us who have over-stressed our systems.

ADRENAL FATIGUE: A PRIMER

Adrenal fatigue is a decrease in the ability of the adrenal glands to carry out their normal functions, explains Dr. Wilson. These glands are designed to mobilize the body's fight-or-flight response to physical or emotional stress through hormones that help regulate energy.

If they fail to respond or do not do so adequately, you may be experiencing adrenal gland fatigue. The two adrenal glands rest over the kidneys. Their primary responsibility is to govern the body's adaptation to stress of any kind.

Adrenal fatigue can occur in people of either gender and any age as a stand-alone syndrome, or it may accompany another chronic health problem, such as alcoholism, allergies, mild depression, type 2 diabetes, chronic fatigue, fibromyalgia, chronic hepatitis, hypoglycemia, heart disease, difficult menopause, premenstrual syndrome, rheumatoid arthritis, chronic or recurrent respiratory infections or obesity. It may also develop as a result of taking corticosteroids.

How do you know if it's adrenal fatigue as opposed to some other illness? *According to Dr. Wilson, you may be suffering from adrenal fatigue if you experience one or more of the following signs or symptoms...*

• **Unexplained fatigue,** especially during the morning.

• **Trouble getting up in the morning** even when you go to sleep at a reasonable hour.

• **Feeling run-down or overwhelmed.**

• **Low blood pressure.**

• **Decreased sex drive.**

• **Immune weakness,** or an inability to bounce back from stress or illness.

• **Craving for salty or sweet snacks.**

• **Low energy in the afternoon.**

• **Feeling best after 6 pm** or after your evening meal.

• **Mild depression.**

These are only some of the many symptoms of adrenal fatigue, and most of them can also be associated with other health conditions. The best way to diagnose adrenal fatigue is to order a simple, noninvasive saliva cortisol hormone test that measures stress hormone levels in the saliva. You can order this test yourself from several testing labs without a physician's requisition. Search on the Internet for "saliva hormone tests."

Once the diagnosis is made, Dr. Wilson says that most people can recover using the suggestions below. He emphasizes that recovery usually does not require prescription drugs. However, if you are in doubt, or if you have an especially complicated case, locate a healthcare provider to work with who has a lot of experience with adrenal fatigue.

If you do have adrenal fatigue, it must be attended to, otherwise the circumstances can get even worse. Stress will become increasingly hard to cope with. If you get a cold or flu, it may be harder than usual to shake. You may become even more tired or fatigued...your memory may be less reliable...and your ability to concentrate may decline.

In addition, your patience may reach a new low...your endurance will be even lower...and you will feel like you are falling behind and less able to catch up at work. This can lead to more stress and often to negative outcomes, such as excess alcohol consumption, driving yourself with caffeine, overeating or filling up on sugary junk foods.

THE ROAD TO RECOVERY

How can a person conquer adrenal fatigue? There are several components to recovery, says Dr. Wilson, including a commitment to lifestyle changes in diet, exercise and stress management, as well as regular use of a variety of dietary supplements. *He recommends the following strategies...*

• **Eat fresh good-quality whole foods.** By the time you enter a state of adrenal fatigue, your body has already depleted its supply of stored nutrients. Dr. Wilson stresses that food is the beginning and the sustaining element of adrenal recovery. Combine healthy fats, protein and unrefined, starchy carbohydrates at each meal and snack. If you have salt cravings and do not have high blood pressure (most people with adrenal fatigue have low blood pressure), it's fine to salt your food. Chew every bite at least 30 times for maximum digestion.

• ***When* you eat is nearly as important as what you eat.** Dr. Wilson explains that the adrenal hormone cortisol helps keep blood sugar at adequate levels to meet energy needs. When adrenal glands are fatigued, cortisol, and consequently, blood sugar levels, drop. *To defeat this pattern, he advises that you eat...*

• Breakfast before 10 am.

• Lunch between 11 am and 11:30 am.

• A nutritious afternoon snack between 2 pm and 3 pm.

• Dinner around 5 pm or 6 pm.

• A small, high quality snack shortly before your bedtime.

• **Avoid foods that provide quick energy at the expense of the adrenal glands.** These include sugar and white-flour products, coffee, black tea, cola and other caffeinated beverages. Also avoid deep-fried foods, fast foods and foods with hydrogenated oils (trans fats).

• **Eliminate foods to which you are sensitive, allergic or addicted.** If you're not sure what these are, keep a food-reaction diary or see your health-care professional for simple blood tests to identify allergens. According to Dr. Wilson, the most common food allergens are milk, wheat, corn, soy, chocolate, peanuts, tomatoes and beef. A comprehensive list of foods containing common allergens can be found at *www.adrenalfatigue.org.*

•**Get regular physical exercise.** When you're tired and stressed, exercise may be the last thing that appeals to you. Yet exercise is known to decrease depression, a common accompaniment of adrenal fatigue.

Dr. Wilson recommends any exercise that you really enjoy. It doesn't matter what, just do *something.* As a general guideline, he advises that it is important not to overexercise. If you feel worse after your workout or the next morning, decrease the length or intensity of your workout.

Also: Increase your exercise program gradually, so you do not tax your adrenals. Easy does it—building slowly usually produces better long-term results.

•**Practice stress-management techniques.** Dr. Wilson advises progressive relaxation, such as belly breathing, exercise, rest and laughter. He also suggests spending less time with "energy-robbing people," those who sap your energy instead of making you feel better about yourself. Spend your time with those who give you energy and make you feel good.

•**Get a good night's sleep.** According to Dr. Wilson, although often underrated, sleep is just as important an element of a healthy lifestyle as diet, exercise and stress management. Try to get to bed before 10 pm each night.

•**Avoid all environmental toxins.** Try to breathe fresh, clean air. Exposure to polluted air and airborne chemicals—including perfumes, colognes and hair sprays to which you are sensitive—can increase adrenal fatigue. If you live or work in an environment that contains toxins, Dr. Wilson recommends doing whatever you can to avoid exposure.

Also: Take extra antioxidants, including dietary supplements that support liver detoxification, such as milk thistle and burdock, daily (two to four capsules) for two to three months.

This will help rid the body of built-up environmental toxins.

•**Have your teeth checked.** Unresolved dental problems, such as periodontitis and decay, are common but unrecognized sources of stress and adrenal fatigue.

•**Take dietary supplements.** *These are usually essential to recovery…*

•Vitamin C/magnesium/pantothenic acid. To avoid low energy at 3 or 4 pm, Dr. Wilson recommends 1,000 milligrams (mg) of vitamin C complex with 200 mg of magnesium and pantothenic acid, along with a small snack at 2 pm every day. Average total daily doses should be 2,000 to 4,000 mg vitamin C…400 mg magnesium…and 1,500 mg pantothenic acid.

•Other recommended supplements include safe doses of vitamin E, the B vitamins, calcium, selenium, chromium, fiber and herbs, such as licorice, ashwagandha, ginseng and ginger. In some cases, replacement hormones (natural cortisol, DHEA, progesterone or pregnenolone) are also necessary. It is best to consult with a trained health practitioner who is familiar with the successful treatment of adrenal fatigue to develop the appropriate regimen.

It's not easy to conquer adrenal fatigue, and Dr. Wilson acknowledges that the road to recovery often presents challenges. But to rediscover your health and vitality, it's worth it.

info To find a naturopathic physician in your area, check out *www.naturopathic.org.*

Dietary supplements that Dr. Wilson specifically designed for adrenal fatigue are available at *www.adrenalfatigue.org.*

Is Your Immune System Triggering Disease?

Leo Galland, MD, director, Foundation for Integrated Medicine, New York City. He is author of *The Fat Resistance Diet*. Broadway. Dr. Galland is a recipient of the Linus Pauling award. *www.fatresistancediet.com.*

Burn yourself? Trip and scrape a knee? Catch a cold? In a rapid-fire defensive response to injury, your body is primed to kick instantly into action, releasing a cascade of chemical messengers called *cytokines* to overcome foreign invaders, such as bacteria and viruses, and heal your body.

Leo Galland, MD, director of the Foundation for Integrated Medicine in New York City, explains that this complex series of chemical and physiological reactions plays an important role in the recovery from injury and protection from infection. However, he adds, more and more research indicates that in many instances, the defense response spirals out of control, causing inflammation and triggering disease. New research is finding inflammation implicated in an array of diseases from heart disease to cancer to Alzheimer's.

A NEW VIEW OF HEART DISEASE

For years, cardiovascular disease was seen as a plumbing problem. Over time, fatty deposits composed of LDL, the "bad" cholesterol, built up in arteries and eventually clogged them—much like sludge builds up and clogs the pipes underneath your sink. When the artery opening became blocked and no blood could pass through, the person then suffered a heart attack.

More recently, doctors have come to realize that while cholesterol is a significant factor in heart disease, it is by no means the only one—and may not even be the most important. The new thinking is that inflammation of the arteries plays a major role in heart disease, says Dr. Galland. This may solve the mystery of why half of heart attack victims have normal (or even low) cholesterol.

When excess fat in the blood builds up as plaque within heart vessel walls, an inflammation alarm is triggered, causing immune cells known as *monocytes* to rush in and attach to the plaque. The monocytes soon develop into *macrophages,* which begin devouring the fatty plaque. This immune activity causes the liver to release *C-reactive protein* (CRP), which joins in the attack on the growing plaque. Plaque becomes increasingly unstable and eventually can rupture, leading to a heart attack.

A RISK FACTOR FOR CANCER

When a person has inflammatory bowel disease, he/she is at an increased risk for colon cancer. Other causes of inflammation that can lead to cancer include viral infections (such as hepatitis)...chronic heartburn (where the esophagus is continually assaulted with stomach acid)...and exposure to asbestos, air pollution or cigarette smoke, which causes irritation and leads to inflammation. The longer the inflammation persists, the higher the risk for cancer.

The theory is that the body's immune system produces agents that cause normal cells to become cancerous. Macrophages and other inflammatory cells produce free radicals, highly reactive substances that damage other cells. This can lead to a genetic mutation that enables the damaged cells to continue growing and dividing. To the immune system, this damage appears like a wound that requires fixing. Immune cells rush in, bringing along with them growth factors and other proteins—but instead of healing a wound, they end up feeding an abnormal growth.

INFLAMMATION AND ALZHEIMER'S DISEASE

Studies also indicate that inflammation plays a role in age-related illnesses such as Alzheimer's disease. At the University of California in San Francisco, researchers studied the blood samples of more than 3,000 seniors for three known markers of inflammation—interleukin-6 (IL-6), CRP and tumor necrosis factor. They repeated the same tests two years later. At both times, participants were also administered a battery of cognitive function tests.

Researchers found that seniors who had the highest levels of inflammation (those whose blood levels of IL-6 and CRP were in the upper one-third) had substantially more cognitive decline than those with blood levels in the lowest one-third. These results were published in the journal *Neurology*.

HOW TO CONTROL INFLAMMATION

The diseases we've looked at here are just the tip of the iceberg. Chronic inflammation has long been known to play a role in such inflammatory diseases as arthritis, asthma, allergies, skin diseases and assorted autoimmune diseases. Dr. Galland notes that low-grade inflammation has also been associated with obesity, type 2 diabetes and high blood pressure.

The following strategies can help to reduce your risk for inflammation-related problems…

• **One of the best weapons against inflammation is low-dose aspirin, says Dr.** Galland. Aspirin, or salicylic acid, reduces blood clotting, turns off the genes that promote inflammation and inhibits the manufacture of inflammatory hormones called *prostaglandins*.

• **Dr. Galland recommends a diet rich in inflammation-fighting antioxidants—**eat lots of fruits, vegetables, nuts and seeds. He points out that antioxidant effects are greatest from food, noting that there are a mixed set of responses from antioxidant dietary supplements. In addition, Dr. Galland says that vegetables and fruits contain natural salicylates.

• **Eat fish three times a week.** Deepwater fish, such as wild salmon, mackerel and sardines, are rich sources of the anti-inflammatory omega-3 fatty acids. If you don't get enough of these fatty acids in your diet, Dr. Galland recommends fish oil supplements that supply up to 1,500 milligrams of DHA (one type of fatty acid) daily. It is also helpful to sprinkle a tablespoon of flaxseed on your cereal or salad every day.

• **Avoid foods that are high in saturated fat, trans fats and cholesterol,** such as red meat, french fries and other fast and processed foods. These types of foods increase your risk for inflammatory disease.

• **Maintain a healthy weight.** Dr. Galland says that obesity increases the inflammatory response in the body, which explains why it is associated with so many chronic inflammatory diseases.

• **Exercise is key.** Elevated CRP is associated with a two- to fivefold increase in the risk for heart attack. Studies show that moderate exercise dramatically decreases CRP levels.

• **In cases of cardiovascular disease,** Dr. Galland notes that the cholesterol-lowering drugs called statins may be helpful, though the risk associated with taking them must also be considered. Recently, scientists proposed that statins are effective against heart disease not only because they lower cholesterol, but because they have a significant anti-inflammatory effect. When plaque is inflamed, it is more likely to rupture and cause a heart attack.

• **See your health-care professional for a physical examination once a year.** If you are at risk for inflammatory disease because of health concerns (such as obesity, high blood pressure or diabetes), family history or negative lifestyle habits (such as heavy drinking or cigarette smoking), get tested for the inflammatory markers, such as CRP. Also, seek counseling to get yourself on a healthier path to wellness.

info Alzheimer's Association, *www.alz.org*.

American Cancer Society, *www.cancer.org*.

The American Heart Association (AHA), *www. americanheart.org*.

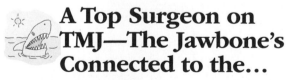

A Top Surgeon on TMJ—The Jawbone's Connected to the…

Michael G. Koslin, DMD, oral and maxillofacial surgeon and spokesperson, American Association of Oral and Maxillofacial Surgeons.

If you suffer from headache, neck, shoulder, back or facial pain, you may be one of the more than 10 million Americans who suffer from temporomandibular joint (TMJ) disorder. Although some symptoms of TMJ that involve the jaw and bite seem more obviously associated with this condition, we thought it might be helpful to connect the dots of other, less-obvious symptoms that may be associated as well. To do that, we called Michael G. Koslin, DMD, oral and maxillofacial surgeon and spokesperson for the American Association of Oral and Maxillofacial Surgeons.

Dr. Koslin first points out that the temporomandibular joint, otherwise known as the jaw joint, sits just in front of the ears and connects the mandible (the lower jaw) to the temporal bone of the skull with a small disk of cartilage in between. It is one of the busiest joints in the body, moving every time we speak, chew, swallow or yawn.

Dr. Koslin says that TMJ pain can be caused by two separate conditions—muscle spasms around the joint or a problem in the joint itself. The latter, he explains, is the true TMJ disorder. The pain TMJ causes can range from sharp and searing to dull and constant. However, Dr. Koslin reports that most commonly, complaints center on minor discomfort.

WHAT ARE THE CAUSES?

When the cause of TMJ is a muscle spasm around the joint, the symptoms include headache, ear pain and muscle tightening and tension. However, more severe symptoms can result when the problem is in the joint. These include painful jaw popping (not the routine clicks and pops that many people experience without discomfort), jaw locking and ear pain from nerves in the area. Another common symptom as well as a possible cause of TMJ is an irregular bite. A bad bite, says Dr. Koslin, puts pressure on the joint, irritating it and sometimes causing the cartilage to shift out of place.

TMJ can also result from injury to the jaw, ranging from such everyday situations as biting too hard on something, long-term grinding or clenching the teeth, and being bumped in the jaw…to major jaw injury caused by an accident of some kind. Stress can play a role in TMJ, primarily by causing muscle spasm.

WHO IS SUSCEPTIBLE?

For a long time, TMJ experts thought that women of childbearing age were particularly vulnerable to TMJ. Dr. Koslin says, though, that newer research is indicating that this is not quite true. Yes, more young women do have the muscle spasm–related TMJ, an indication, he feels, of this particularly stressful time in life. Joint-related TMJ, however, can set in anytime after the late teens, when the ligament tissue in the area becomes tougher and not as malleable. While the TMJ Association Web site (*www.tmj.org*) reports that 90% of people seeking TMJ disorder treatment are women during their childbearing years, Dr. Koslin estimates that in his practice 40% of TMJ patients are men.

HOW TO TREAT

Anyone who experiences jaw discomfort for more than a few weeks or months should go to his/her dentist for an evaluation. The good news, though, is that treatment is often not necessary. The first line of defense, says Dr. Koslin, is to change any habits you have that might be contributing to the problem, such as grinding your teeth, clenching them, chewing gum, biting on pencils and the like. That may be enough to stop the problem, and he recommends using simple pain and anti-inflammatory medication, such as aspirin, in the meantime. The next level would be to wear a plastic or rubber bite appliance at night to remove pressure from the joint. Physical therapy, including heat, ultrasound treatment and range-of-motion exercises, can help—but be careful to do exercises only with supervision because doing them improperly can make the condition worse.

SURGICAL OPTION

Occasionally, TMJ does not respond to standard treatment. Often this results because of a secondary condition that degenerates the jaw joint—such as arthritis. In this case, there are other measures available. Arthroscopic surgery allows an oral and maxillofacial surgeon to re-contour the cartilage, moving it into a more stable position.

Finally, in regard to our question about how much havoc this small joint can actually wreak, Dr. Koslin responds that TMJ is *not* responsible for aches and pains that are far removed from the jaw, and that if your symptoms are highly varied and your common sense tells you it's unlikely that they are related to your jaw joint, you should conclude that indeed, they are not.

New Hope for Chronic Sinusitis

Robert S. Ivker, DO, clinical instructor of otolaryngology at the University of Colorado School of Medicine, Denver, past president, American Holistic Medical Association and author of *Sinus Survival*. Tarcher/Putnam.

Andrew L. Rubman, ND, director, Southbury Clinic for Traditional Medicines, Southbury, Connecticut.

David A. Sherris, MD, chair of otolaryngology, SUNY, University at Buffalo School of Medicine, New York.

It can be incredibly annoying and uncomfortable to live with constant congestion and a runny nose…and then be perpetually asked if you have a cold. Yet, that's what happens to some 37 million Americans each year who suffer from chronic sinusitis. It is the number one respiratory chronic disease in this country, but unlike acute sinusitis, which goes away after a few weeks, the chronic variety is always present to some degree.

Treatment to date has not been particularly effective. This is primarily because doctors have focused on suppressing the symptoms (nasal and head congestion, post-nasal drip, etc.) rather than taking a broader look at the underlying cause(s). There is hope, however, for those who suffer.

FUNGUS'S FAULT

David A. Sherris, MD, chair of otolaryngology at the University at Buffalo, began exploring the possibility that the culprit in this disease is airborne fungi. After preliminary research done in the late 1990s, Dr. Sherris and his colleagues at the Mayo Clinic recently conducted a six-month double-blind study (neither participants nor investigators knew which group took drug versus placebo) of 24 patients with chronic sinusitis. At the study's end, 70% of the patients treated with Amphotericin-B, an antifungal spray, showed significant improvement. The placebo group showed no change.

We spoke with Dr. Sherris about his study. He said that the air is filled with millions of fungal spores. Although it is not a problem for most people, some are sensitive to the spores, resulting in an abnormally hyperimmune response.

The immune system's response gets rid of the fungus temporarily, but it also damages the person's sinuses, making them even more vulnerable to the fungal load that comes in with every breath. His earlier study revealed that 95% of the time chronic sinusitis was fungal-based, so the results of this study didn't surprise him.

Although use of Amphotericin-B for sinusitis is being reviewed by the FDA, the antifungal medication is used for systemic fungal infections in those who are immuno-suppressed as a result of chemotherapy and organ transplant, so doctors can prescribe it for off-label use. Since the late 1990s, Dr. Sherris has been studying this actively and has treated thousands of patients with antifungal sprays. Patients use them twice a day for three months or sometimes indefinitely. No safety issues have surfaced. He recommends that people have a thorough diagnostic workup first—an endoscopy of the nose and a sinus CT scan—to be sure that the primary problem is chronic sinusitis and not allergies or a deviated septum, which occurs when the midline of the nasal passage has shifted to one side.

THE HOLISTIC APPROACH

We also called Robert S. Ivker, DO, past president of the American Holistic Medical Association, to find out how he approaches treatment. Dr. Ivker said that he believes it is possible to cure chronic sinusitis with an integrative holistic medical treatment program that addresses the multiple causes of sinusitis. To achieve this result requires a two- to three-month commitment to making several lifestyle changes that will almost always result in at least a significant improvement, and often a cure, he says. In the most severe cases it also requires aggressive treatment of fungal sinusitis. Dr. Ivker says the primary causes of chronic sinusitis are air pollution, which brings on chronic inflammation of the mucous membranes…the overuse of antibiotics, which causes a weakening of the immune system and a yeast (fungus/candida) overgrowth… food allergy and sensitivities (especially to cow's milk and wheat products)…and emotional stress (especially repressed anger).

To conquer sinusitis, Dr. Ivker's approach has two primary goals—to heal the mucous membrane and to strengthen and restore balance.

HEALING THE MUCOUS MEMBRANE

• **Create optimum indoor air** that is clean, moist, warm and filled with oxygen and negative ions. (Negative ions attach to the positive ions of dust, mold, bacteria, viruses, animal dander, and other irritants, causing them to drop out of the air.)

This requires a negative ion generator that does not emit ozone…a warm mist humidifier in the bedroom (be sure to clean it weekly)…professional air duct and carpet cleaning (using natural products for the carpet)…and plants, for the oxygen they produce. Dr. Ivker likes spider plants, Boston fern and dracaena best.

• **To cleanse the sinuses,** Dr. Ivker instructs his patients to use a saline nasal spray to moisten dry and irritated membranes, such as Sinus Survival Botanical Nasal Spray (available at *www.sinussurvival.com*). Other brands of saline nasal sprays are also available at health food stores. Look for one that contains aloe vera and/or grapefruit-seed extract.

Dr. Ivker also suggests using a steam inhaler for 15 minutes two or three times a day, and more often during an attack. Following the steam, he advises nasal irrigation to flush out the infected or excessive mucus. He likes pulsating irrigation appliances, in particular the Hydro Pulse nasal irrigator or the Grossan nasal irrigator, which fits onto a standard Waterpik. SinuCleanse is less expensive and nearly as effective. When we checked with our medical expert, Andrew L. Rubman, ND, on his favorite brand, he suggested a saline and botanical formula, Alkalol, which is widely available. It's also helpful to drink more water to enhance mucus drainage—drink one-half ounce of water each day for every pound of body weight.

STRENGTHEN AND RESTORE BALANCE

• **To kill the fungus,** Dr. Ivker supports the use of antifungal sprays if necessary because he finds many patients suffer from fungus, specifically an overgrowth of *Candida* that he says weakens the immune system. To overcome this, he asks patients to change their diets, avoiding sugar and dairy products in particular, as well as wheat, vinegar and alcohol, and instead eat a diet of organic fruits and vegetables and protein, such as fish, antibiotic-free poultry, nuts and seeds.

In addition, for many of his patients he prescribes antifungal medication, such as Diflucan. He also has patients take a supplement that contains *Lactobacillus acidophilus* and *Bifidobacterium bifidus,* to repopulate healthy bacteria in the gut.

Best brands: HLC from Pharmax and Flor-Alive from Pure Essence Labs. Another effective supplement in destroying candida organisms is Candex, available at most health-food stores. Vitamins C, E, grape-seed extract, a multivitamin, fish oil and flaxseed oil are also often recommended.

One other element is critical to good sinus health—aerobic exercise. However, he says, get well first and then build up to a regular routine.

It's a demanding regimen, but he tells patients to try it for at least one month and their improvement will most likely make it easier to bear.

Pulmonary Embolism: Don't Let This Happen to You

K. Craig Kent, MD, chairman, department of surgery, University of Wisconsin School of Medicine and Public Health, Madison.

Before 39-year-old NBC correspondent David Bloom died as a result of a pulmonary embolism (PE) while covering the war in Iraq, many Americans didn't have a clue to what that was. It was frightening that this young, seemingly healthy, vibrant man died so suddenly.

What is even more unnerving is that public ignorance about PE puts many of us at risk. A report from the Centers for Disease Control and Prevention and the American Public Health Association revealed how little we know about this condition. More than half of us can't identify a single risk factor for PE… and virtually none of us has reviewed our risk for it with a doctor.

Frightening fact: PE is one of the leading causes of death in the US. Many of these deaths could be prevented if people just knew what to look for and what to do.

EMBOLISM DEFINED

To find out what we all need to know, we talked with K. Craig Kent, MD, chairman of the department of surgery at University of Wisconsin School of Medicine and Public Health, and former chief of vascular surgery at NewYork–Presbyterian Hospital in New York City. Dr. Kent explained that the umbrella term *venous thromboembolus* (VTE) describes two conditions—deep vein thrombosis (DVT) and PE.

DVT occurs when a thrombus, or a blood clot, forms in a large vein, almost always in a leg or the pelvis. There often are no symptoms, but when they do appear, they include swelling, pain, tenderness and redness, especially behind the knee or in the calf. DVT usually occurs in only one leg.

The body usually dissolves these and other clots when we don't need them. In some cases of DVT, however, a fragment of the clot breaks loose and makes its way to the lungs. If the fragment (which is known as an embolus once it breaks loose) lodges in a pulmonary artery or one of its branches, it blocks the artery and can cause death in as little as an hour.

WHAT TO LOOK FOR

The symptoms of PE can include shortness of breath…chest wall tenderness or chest pain that worsens with a deep breath…rapid pulse…sweating…and, understandably, a feeling of apprehension. Anyone experiencing these symptoms needs to get medical assistance immediately.

WHAT CAUSES DVT?

Several things can cause DVT, according to Dr. Kent…

●**When blood flows too slowly.** Blood flow can stagnate (called stasis) when you are immobile for long periods, which often happens when recovering from an illness or surgery.

●**When there is trauma.** Surgery is most often associated with DVT, in particular hip or knee replacement, although any surgery can set the stage for DVT.

●**When blood clots too easily.** Blood that clots too easily (a hypercoagulable state) can result from particular situations, including being pregnant or having cancer, which, when coupled with other risk factors, increases the risk of DVT. There have also been rare cases of DVT on long airplane flights—but Dr. Kent says this usually happens only to people who have a predisposition to clotting.

According to Dr. Kent, overclotting usually occurs because of a genetic condition (thrombophilia), which is typically caused by a gene mutation called *factor V Leiden*. About one in 20 healthy people have the mutation.

Other factors that contribute to risk for DVT include obesity, varicose veins, taking birth control pills or hormone replacement therapy and smoking. The most important indicator that you are at risk is if you previously had a clot or if anyone in your family has had clots.

ACTION!

Dr. Kent reports that there are several tests to diagnose the presence of DVT, including scans, ultrasound and checking blood pressure in the lower leg. When necessary, doctors treat DVT with an anticoagulant, such as *heparin* or *warfarin* (Coumadin), to keep more clots from forming.

The factor V Leiden mutation can be detected by a simple blood test, which may require anticoagulant treatment. If you think you might have the genetic risk factor, ask your doctor to test you, especially if you are considering complex surgery or a long continuous airplane flight.

To treat PE, doctors attempt to dissolve the clot and administer anticoagulants to prevent more clots from forming.

Clearly, though, since symptoms are rare, the best defense against DVT and PE is a good offense—prevent blood clots from occurring in the first place.

If you are having surgery, talk with your doctor about what measures the medical team will take to prevent clotting. Hip or knee replacement surgery, with its extremely high risk of DVT, requires presurgical treatment with an anticlotting medication. Post-surgical measures include compression stockings on the lower legs, and becoming mobile as quickly as possible to keep blood from pooling and possibly clotting.

Even though DVT is unlikely for most of us taking long flights, it is still a good idea for all passengers to wiggle their toes and to walk around a bit while in the air. Taking aspirin will *not* prevent DVT.

To decrease your risk of DVT even further, go for a brisk walk every day. Walking—as well as any other activity that exercises your lower legs—is an excellent way to protect yourself from DVT.

info Web MD, *www.webmd.com.*

Genetic Drift (Molecular Genetic Testing in Mainstream Medicine), *www.mostgene.org/gd/gdvol14b.htm.*

Older Adults Shouldn't Ignore Spinal Problems

Harry N. Herkowitz, MD, chairman of orthopaedic surgery and director, section of spine surgery, William Beaumont Hospital, Royal Oak, Michigan.

Many people ignore minor aches and pains. Well, that isn't always wise. Some things should not be ignored, because they're symptoms of a more dangerous condition.

Spinal stenosis is high on the list of diseases that cause great discomfort and that people do nothing about. Estimates are that some 400,000 Americans over the age of 60 have symptoms of spinal stenosis, and many of them don't even know what it is or that they have it.

SPINAL STENOSIS DEFINED

Spinal stenosis is a narrowing of the spinal canal caused by a number of factors, including osteoarthritis of the spine, spinal damage from a previous fall, being born with a narrow spinal canal, and wear and tear on the vertebrae and joints that can come with aging. Additionally, lifestyle issues, such as being overweight, lack of exercise, poor general health and smoking, can also cause stenosis.

The narrowing eventually starts to pinch the spinal cord and nerves, and the result is pain. Stenosis nearly always causes pain in the lumbar (lower part) of the spine, but it can create pain in the buttocks and legs as well. Pain generally kicks in as the person stands up and starts to move about. The legs often feel tired and cramped as well. As the disease progresses, pain will make walking and moving increasingly difficult—even standing up straight can be uncomfortable because an erect posture compresses the spinal canal.

DIAGNOSIS

Harry N. Herkowitz, MD, chairman of orthopaedic surgery and director of the section of spine surgery at William Beaumont Hospital in Royal Oak, Michigan, told us that stenosis is sometimes confused with other conditions, among them arthritis, diabetic neuropathy (nerve damage) and vascular claudication, which is pain from impaired circulation in the lower legs. Hence, getting a proper diagnosis is extremely important to ensure effective treatment. To diagnose spinal stenosis, the doctor usually requests magnetic resonance imaging (MRI), a computed axial tomography (CAT) scan or a myelogram (an X-ray taken after fluid is injected into the spinal canal).

TREATMENT

The first line of treatment, says Dr. Herkowitz, is short-term restriction of activity followed by physical therapy to strengthen the muscles in the back, along with an activity that does not cause discomfort, such as riding on a stationary bike. Additional treatment can include such anti-inflammatory agents as aspirin and ibuprofen, weight loss and the cessation of smoking.

Helpful: You can find relief by lying down and drawing your knees to your chest or by assuming the fetal position. Any position that can stretch out the spine reduces the compression on the nerves. Alternate applications of hot and cold compresses, called contrast therapy, may provide not only temporary relief, but reduce inflammation and slow the disease progress.

If exercise and anti-inflammatory medications are not effective, the next line of defense is an epidural— injections of cortisone into the epidural space in the spine. An epidural successfully relieves pain in about half of patients.

Not only does an epidural decrease inflammation, doctors believe it may also flush out some of the inflammatory proteins in the area. Dr. Herkowitz says that patients may need more than one injection and that it is acceptable to have up to three over a six-month period.

THE PROCEDURE

Getting an epidural isn't something you do in your local doctor's office. You must use a doctor who is qualified to administer epidurals, such as an anesthesiologist, radiologist, neurologist, physiatrist (a doctor who specializes in treating problems of the musculoskeletal system) or an orthopedic surgeon.

If you are taking aspirin or any other blood-thinning drugs, discuss this with your doctor ahead of time because you will probably need to stop taking them for a period around the time the epidural is performed to decrease the possibility of bleeding. Be sure that you are aware of the risks associated with this procedure.

While complications are rare, 2% to 3% of patients experience a bad headache. Other complications are much less likely—less than 1% of patients experience nerve injury, infection, meningitis or anaphylaxis. Most problems come from poor technique in administering the epidural.

LAST RESORT—SURGERY

The last alternative in the treatment process is a surgery known as *laminectomy*. The surgeon removes a portion of bone over the nerve root and also may trim part of any facet joints (small stabilizing joints between and behind the vertebrae) that are compressing the nerves. The goal is to give the spinal nerves more room. The surgery is successful for about 80% of patients, says Dr. Herkowitz.

While surgery can cure a specific area of stenosis, there is still about a 10% chance that the patient will develop stenosis in another area of the spine, which could ultimately require additional surgery. Risks include infection, a tear in the membrane that covers the spinal cord at the site of the surgery, bleeding, a blood clot in a leg vein, decreased intestinal function and neurologic deterioration, although these appear to be rare. The surgery should be performed by someone who is highly experienced in back surgery.

Although Dr. Herkowitz says there is nothing you can do to prevent spinal stenosis, there are many ways to treat it and to make yourself more comfortable. No matter what your age, you can and should seek treatment. Patients well into their 80s have benefited from laminectomies. "Getting old" should never be an excuse for not getting care.

Wrestling with Sleep: Conquering Restless Legs Syndrome

Claudia Trenkwalder, MD, professor of neurology at the University of Goettingen and medical director, Paracelsus-Elena Klinik, Germany.

Do you toss and turn at night? Have trouble relaxing your legs? Does your spouse complain that you accidentally kick him/her in your sleep?

If so, you may be suffering from restless legs syndrome (RLS), a movement disorder characterized by uncomfortable and sometimes painful sensations in the legs. People have described these feelings as pins and needles, prickling, twitching, tingling and crawling.

Symptoms are at their worst during periods of inactivity, especially at night, and are often accompanied by an uncontrollable, overwhelming urge to move the legs to provide at least temporary relief.

Although getting up, stretching or walking around the house can help, there is no cure for some chronic forms of RLS. However, a European study in the *Journal of Neurology, Neurosurgery & Psychiatry* noted that *ropinirole hydrochloride* (Requip)—a dopamine agonist drug used to control the tremors and shaking of Parkinson's disease—may help to diminish the symptoms of RLS.

Dopamine is a naturally occurring chemical in the brain. Like Parkinson's disease, some forms of RLS are linked to dopamine deficiency.

ABOUT THE STUDY

To learn more, we consulted lead researcher Claudia Trenkwalder, MD, of the University of Goettingen in Germany. Although treatment with Requip did not make RLS disappear completely in the 12-week study of 284 patients, she reports that significant improvements appeared within one week. These included "alleviating the symptoms of RLS, improving sleep quantity and adequacy, reducing sleep disturbance and daytime somnolence, and improving health-related quality of life." The main side effect was mild to moderate nausea, but only 5% of participants stopped taking medication due to nausea or vomiting.

This is good news for RLS sufferers (not to mention their significant others), who yearn for a good night's sleep and have found the condition persistent...and also welcome news since other interventions—such as massage and application of cold compresses—are ineffective.

SEE AN EXPERT

If you think that you may be suffering from this disorder, consult your health-care professional, who may refer you to a sleep clinic. Leg movements can vary from subtle to dramatic in RLS, and an expert in sleep disorders can help determine whether this syndrome lies at the root of your problem and if Requip or other non-pharmacologic therapies can help you.

info For more information, contact the Restless Legs Syndrome Foundation at *www.rls.org*.

Six Ways to Banish Bad Breath

Perry R. Klokkevold, DDS, MS, director, UCLA Postgraduate Periodontics and Implant Surgery Clinic, and associate professor, UCLA School of Dentistry, section of periodontics.

Margaret Stearn, MD, author of *Embarrassing Medical Problems: Everything You Always Wanted to Know But Were Afraid to Ask Your Doctor*. Hatherleigh.

Ray C. Wunderlich, Jr., MD, PhD, author of *Natural Alternatives to Antibiotics*. Good Health Guides.

Even the mighty can become meek when faced with an embarrassing problem like bad breath. Americans spend millions of dollars a year on breath-freshening products, attempting to mask the odor, rather than eliminate the cause.

Granted, that approach often works just fine. The bad breath that plagues nearly everyone after waking up may vanish after breakfast. (Water with lemon helps, too.) Breath mints or chewing gum may camouflage the problem before a business meeting.

Sometimes, however, the pungent aroma is more persistent. Interestingly, we may not even be aware of it—people often don't notice odors emanating from themselves.

Simple way to test yourself: Lick the inside of your wrist...wait four seconds...and then sniff where you licked. Or if you really want to get a good whiff, try scraping the back of your tongue with the side of a spoon and smell the scrapings.

Bad breath can be a sign of an underlying medical problem—respiratory disease, a gastrointestinal disorder, diabetes or other systemic conditions—but University of California, Los Angeles periodontal specialist Perry R. Klokkevold, DDS, MS, estimates that 80% to 90% of all cases originate in the mouth. What is the culprit? Gas-producing bacteria that thrive on food debris.

WET YOUR WHISTLE

Malodorous germs love dry mouths, so the key to sweetening your scent is to wet your whistle...

• **Drink more water.** Sounds obvious, but many people just don't drink enough water.

Other liquids, such as soda, coffee, tea, etc., are not a substitute for simple, plain water. Drink...drink...drink.

Note: Avoid drinking around mealtimes, when you want to increase stomach acid, not dilute it.

• **Keep the saliva flowing.** Part of saliva's function is to cleanse the mouth and remove particles of food.

To keep your saliva flowing: Chew. Chewing stimulates saliva production. Chewing parsley is particularly helpful.

• **Stay away from alcohol and alcohol-based mouthwashes.**

Best: Make your own mouthwash. Mix one ounce of tea tree oil, two teaspoons of hydrogen peroxide, one teaspoon of vitamin C powder and one pint of strong mint tea. Keep refrigerated, and shake before use.

• **Check your medications.** Ask your physician or dentist if any of your prescription or nonprescription medications—including certain antihistamines and antidepressants—decreases saliva production. If so, find out whether there are any good nondrying alternatives.

• **Stop smoking.** Another reason to quit—smoking reduces saliva flow.

Banishing bad breath requires good dental hygiene. Brush thoroughly…floss regularly…and scrape your tongue twice a day—after breakfast and before bed. Although you can try scraping with a toothbrush, preventive medicine expert Ray C. Wunderlich, Jr., MD, PhD, recommends using a plastic tongue scraper with a serrated edge. To scrape properly, start at the back of your tongue and sweep the scraper forward to the tip, rinsing it with water as debris accumulates. Be sure to rinse the scraper with a solution of 3% peroxide after each use.

If bad breath persists, your dentist or doctor may ask you to write down when it occurs, what medications you take and what you eat and drink. "Symptom diaries" are a superb doctor-patient tool to tackle other problems as well—including headaches, shortness of breath and flatulence.

info For more information, contact the American Dental Association at *www.ada.org*.

14

Coping with Arthritis and Pain

MSM...Should Stand For Miraculous

People who have been using a supplement called MSM claim it's nothing short of miraculous in alleviating arthritis pain. The sulfur in MSM (*methylsulfonylmethane*), an organic compound that can be found naturally in food sources, plays many roles in the human body. Key among those roles is helping to keep the body's tissues supple and flexible—which can alleviate arthritis pain.

WHY IT'S A MIRACLE WORKER

Sulfur as the source of MSM's reputation for being a miracle worker makes perfect sense when you consider that, for centuries, people have visited sulfur-rich hot springs to heal muscle aches and pains. Jacqueline Jacques, a former ND (naturopathic doctor), tells us that MSM has an important "structural role in maintaining connective tissues and joints" because sulfur is present in every cell of the human body. In a double-blind study of 50 men and women between the ages of 40 and 76, published in the journal *Osteoarthritis and Cartilage*, those who took 3 g (3,000 mg) of MSM twice daily for 12 weeks significantly reduced their pain and improved physical functioning without any major adverse effects.

MSM USAGE

Dr. Jacques said that MSM could also be helpful in fighting allergies, particularly those affecting the skin—again, because of its high sulfur content. Sulfur is important for phase II detoxification in the liver as well (processes called sulfation and glucoronidation), which is how the body eliminates many drugs, hormones and environmental toxins. By supporting detoxification, MSM helps the body to eliminate irritants that can cause allergic reactions.

Jacqueline Jacques, ND, is a former naturopathic doctor with more than a decade of experience in medical nutrition. Dr. Jacques is an expert on dietary supplements and frequently appears on television and radio. She is chief science officer for Catalina Lifesciences LLC, an Irvine, California, company that provides nutritional care to weight loss surgery patients.

233

Dr. Jacques says that there is research supporting the use of MSM at doses from 1,500 mg to 6,000 mg, but she believes higher doses may be tolerated as well, if advised and overseen by a knowledgeable physician. Typically she prescribes about 1,500 mg for joint maintenance and pain prevention, and higher doses for patients suffering with arthritis. As with any supplement, it is important to be sure your physician knows you are taking MSM and supervises your use.

HOW IT'S MADE

Because MSM is only found in small amounts in nature, commercial MSM is created in a laboratory, not extracted from plants. There are two methods for extracting and purifying MSM from natural sources—crystallization, which is less expensive but also less effective and less reliably pure...and distillation. Do not buy supplements that contain additives or fillers.

GREAT RESULTS

"I've seen incredible results with MSM," Dr. Jacques recounts. She tells us the story of one patient with a rare connective tissue disorder (eosinophilic fasciitis), whose tissues were so swollen that she couldn't bend her knees or fingers. After treatment with high doses of MSM, she came in for a visit. "She walked in and said 'you have to see what I can do!' For the first time in six months, she could bend her fingers."

 # Exercise Away Aches

Carol Krucoff, a registered yoga teacher, and Mitchell W. Krucoff, MD, a cardiologist, are coauthors of *Healing Moves: How to Cure, Relieve and Prevent Common Ailments with Exercise.* Healthy Learning. Visit their Web site at *www.healingmoves.com.*

When people have arthritis it often hurts to move, but inactivity can be crippling.

Whereas a generation or so ago, people with arthritis were sent to bed in an effort to "save their joints," Mitchell W. Krucoff, MD, coauthor of *Healing Moves: How to Cure, Relieve and Prevent Common Ailments with Exercise*

explains, scientific evidence now refutes that. "Study after study has shown that people with arthritis who exercise regularly report less pain and joint swelling, improved functioning and increased strength, endurance and flexibility—without harming their joints," he says.

EXERCISE EVALUATES MOOD

The psychological benefits are also dramatic. "The mind and body are not separate," adds coauthor and yoga instructor Carol Krucoff. "Exercisers experience less depression and anxiety, and greater feelings of control. When you can't function, it's very depressing. You can't walk stairs, or go places. And for seniors, the idea that they might fall down and not be able to get up is very frightening." Basic exercises give seniors a sense of control and the ability to do the functions of daily living. "They feel better about themselves and feel more capable," says Mrs. Krucoff.

USE THESE FOR ACHING JOINTS

This is all well and good, but it still hurts to exercise with achy joints. *So, what kinds of exercise do the Krucoffs recommend for arthritis sufferers?*

1. Range-of-motion exercises. These are exercises that help reduce stiffness and keep the joints flexible. Dr. Krucoff explains that range of motion simply means the normal distance your joints can move in all directions. *There are five primary movements he recommends...*

•Shoulders. Slow easy arm circles. Starting with your arms at your sides, bring them all the way up toward the ceiling and then as far behind the body as comfortable in a huge circle. Repeat several times.

•Hips. Lie on your back with knees bent, feet on the floor and arms down along your sides. Bring one knee to the chest and rotate the knee in an easy gentle circle. Repeat with other knee.

•Wrists. Make circles with your wrists, rotating hands in both directions.

•Ankles. Draw big circles in the air with your big toe in both clockwise and counterclockwise motion.

•Knee. Lie on your back and bring one knee to the chest. Straighten your leg, pointing your foot toward the ceiling and bend a few times. Repeat with the other leg.

2. Endurance exercise (aerobics). "Like anyone interested in good health, people with arthritis need to accumulate 30 minutes a day of cardio activity," Dr. Krucoff tells us. He also notes that for people with arthritis it's especially important to strengthen large muscles, such as those of the legs, allowing more gentle and consistent compression of the sore joints, which in turn stimulates the healing process in the cartilage. When choosing an exercise, it's important to pick something that doesn't exacerbate arthritis. *Here's what the Krucoffs suggest...*

•Walk on a flat, even surface.

Good choice: A school track, using good supportive shoes, or a mall or a sidewalk. Avoid bumpy fields or gravel roads.

•Water exercise. "For people who can't tolerate walking, water exercise is the gold standard," said Mrs. Krucoff. "When you're in the water, it supports the body so there's less stress on hips and spine and knees. The Arthritis Foundation runs classes at YMCAs called PACE classes— People with Arthritis Can Exercise. These classes are great because they keep you in warm water at chest level. And they take you through a good range of motion and aerobic conditioning."

3. Strengthening exercises. The idea of people with arthritis pumping iron is very new. "There are some very good studies showing that weight training for people with arthritis is very helpful," said Mrs. Krucoff, "particularly for those with rheumatoid arthritis."

When starting, it's best to begin with light weights or even no weights and work up from there. "Your goal is to work out with a weight you can lift at least 10 times without being too tired," said Mrs. Krucoff. "If you can't, it's too heavy."

•Chair extensions. Sit straight in a chair, knees bent 90 degrees, feet flat on floor. Then extend your leg straight out and bend it back down to starting position. "Do several of these extensions for each leg to strengthen the quadriceps," said Mrs. Krucoff. "When you can do eight to 12 repetitions, you can add light ankle weights."

•Toe raises. Work the calves by standing and raising your body up on your tiptoes and back down. Do eight to 10 repetitions.

•Chair squats. "These are probably the most useful exercises of all," said Mrs. Krucoff. "You sit in a chair and practice standing straight up and sitting back down again, using the leg muscles. It strengthens the legs and gives you confidence that you can perform a basic daily task."

START EXERCISING NOW

The number one cause of nursing home admissions is not heart disease or Alzheimer's disease or diabetes. "It's weak joints and muscles," said Dr. Krucoff. These people can't do the activities of daily life. They can't get up or down, can't go to the bathroom. "You can prevent these problems with a good exercise program," said Dr. Krucoff. "And the time to start is right now." (After you get approval from your treating physician, of course.)

Important: Be sure to review any exercise program with your physician.

Support for Arthritic Knees

Wayne Westcott, PhD, strength-training consultant, American Council on Exercise and Fitness, fitness research director, South Shore YMCA, Quincy, Massachusetts, and author of *Strength Training Past 50*. Human Kinetics.

Given the pain knee osteoarthritis (OA) can cause, patients are understandably reluctant to exercise the affected joint.

Many people even fear that building strength in the quadriceps (the muscles in the front of the thighs) can actually harm the knee joint, especially when osteoarthritis occurs in people with malaligned knees. But it's time to rethink that—as a recent report makes clear. The study evaluated how having stronger quads impacts the knee and its cartilage, and the results tell us that strong quads help—a lot.

STUDY ON QUADRICEPS

The 30-month study, conducted in part by the Mayo Clinic, in Rochester, Minnesota, followed 265 men and women, mean age of 67, who had symptomatic knee osteoarthritis. Researchers investigated how the strength of the quadriceps affected cartilage in the knee joint over time. The strength of the quadriceps was measured at the beginning of the study. Each person had an MRI of their knee at the beginning, middle and end of the study.

The results: Stronger quad muscles did not lead to an increased risk for cartilage loss in the knee joint, even in patients with malaligned knees. Furthermore, patients with stronger quads were less likely to have cartilage loss in the outer side of the knee joint behind the kneecap. In short, stronger quads, which help to stabilize the kneecap, help protect arthritic knees from getting worse.

STRENGTHENING STRATEGIES

We asked Massachusetts fitness expert Wayne Westcott, PhD, for advice on how people with OA could best improve their quads. He explains that strengthening the quads also improves the tendons and surrounding tissue of the knee and even the entire stretch of leg to hip.

According to Dr. Westcott, the best equipment for building quad strength is leg press equipment in which you push the weight away from you. Start slowly with abbreviated actions that do not cause pain. Find a weight that is light enough for you to comfortably do one to three sets of 10 repetitions. As you grow strong enough at the current level to move to the next, increase the weight by 5%—usually after at least several weeks of training with two or three workouts a week.

Caution: Avoid leg extension equipment (the kind that bring knees from a fully bent to a straight position and back) because this puts too much pressure on the knees.

Helpful: Other exercises include "half squats" …walking on a treadmill at an angle of 5 degrees or more…elliptical machines…and stationary cycle machines.

Note: Dr. Westcott recommends that a licensed physical therapist (PT) or certified occupational therapist (OT) at the gym or the local YMCA, guide you through a safe routine when you are first starting out. PTs and OTs are regulated by each state's licensing authority.

DAILY LIFE HELPS QUADS

Daily living activities also offer ways to improve the strength in your legs. In particular, plenty of walking improves general circulation and helps to keep legs strong. Stair climbing is also wonderful for quad strengthening.

Important: Always avoid any motion that brings your knee in front of your toes. The most frequent culprit is incorrect squatting. Most people go straight down so that the knee protrudes forward and the upper leg (thigh) and lower leg (calf) are touching.

Better: Hold shins straight toward the floor and lower hips into a squat so your "bottom" sticks out behind you like you are about to sit on a chair. Be careful to hold on to something for support until you are sure you can do this easily without losing your balance.

While these exercises will help, Dr. Westcott adds that "for people who are overweight, weight loss is a key factor in reducing the pain symptoms of osteoarthritis of the knee."

Happy Knees

Susan J. Bartlett, PhD, associate professor of medicine, division of rheumatology, Johns Hopkins University, Baltimore, specializes in weight management and weight loss effects on medical conditions.

Some believe that the knee is one of the most overworked, overstrained and under-appreciated parts of the human body. In our increasingly overweight world, that strain is becoming even greater.

Did you know that being overweight by just 10 pounds increases the force on the knee by 30 to 60 pounds with each step? Because of the wear and tear this causes the knee, combined with other gender-related factors, overweight women have nearly four times the risk of developing osteoarthritis (OA) in the knees, and overweight men have five times the risk as healthful-weight women and men. Once knees become arthritic, the pain makes ordinary activities difficult for some people and nearly impossible for others.

Susan J. Bartlett, PhD, associate professor of medicine, division of rheumatology at Johns Hopkins University in Baltimore, specializes in weight management and how weight loss affects medical conditions. She recently concluded a study of people who have mild to moderate OA in their knees, as diagnosed with X-rays, to determine how weight loss might affect knee pain from OA, and how much loss would be necessary to see a benefit.

Study participants met regularly over four months to explore nutrition, physical activity, behaviors and attitudes that promote healthier living. At the same time they embarked on a gradually increasing exercise program. By the end of the four months, all were walking for the equivalent of 30 minutes of walking daily—a total of 10,000 steps a day as tracked with a pedometer.

The final results were surprising: Participants—including even the most obese—improved their knee OA symptoms and pain by 50% after losing just 15 pounds. These results were based on self-reported answers to specific questions posed by validated standardized measures widely accepted in pain research—in this case the WOMAC (Western Ontario and McMaster Universities) Osteoarthritis Index. This is particularly impressive when compared with medications—the average improvement from drugs, including Vioxx when it was available, was only 20–30%.

A LITTLE WEIGHT LOSS CAN MEAN A LOT

When we called Dr. Bartlett about the study, she said that overweight people with arthritis and the doctors who care for them have long assumed only a substantial weight loss would help them. For example, the average woman in her study, age 58, was 5' 4" tall and weighed 200 pounds. Typically this woman thought she would have to get back to the 120 pounds she weighed 30 years before to start feeling better, and that seemed just too overwhelming. Learning that a modest loss could make such a difference was invigorating for everyone.

While a few of the study participants did not show any improvement from weight loss, says

Dr. Bartlett, this may have been because people with advanced knee OA have no cartilage left, have too much damage and need joint replacement at that point. Nonetheless, the study clearly indicates that there is an association between weight loss and happier knees.

Noninvasive Solutions To Knee Pain

Howard Hillstrom, PhD, director, the Leon Root, MD, Motion Analysis Lab, Hospital for Special Surgery, New York City.

Sufferers of arthritis in the knee (knee osteoarthritis, or OA) may find some uplifting news in the results of a recently released study. The study looked at whether full-length lateral-wedge shoes would diminish the joint pain and stiffness while improving the knee function of patients with medial compartment (bowlegged) knee OA.

The conclusion: After four weeks of wearing the insoles, study participants had significantly less pain, less stiffness and better function overall.

This study prompted us to call Howard Hillstrom, PhD, who is director of the Leon Root, MD, Motion Analysis Lab at the Hospital for Special Surgery in New York City, to learn more. He tells us there is a growing body of research that shows OA has a biomechanical involvement—meaning the structure of one's body (alignment) is related to the body's function (movement), which may, in some cases, even cause the disease. With medial knee OA (bowlegged alignment) there is an increase in pressure to the inner part of the knee called the medial compartment. Similarly, lateral knee OA (knock-kneed alignment) will place too much stress on the lateral compartment of the joint. As a result, the cartilage becomes overloaded and degraded, resulting in a knee that is quite sore. With specially designed shoe inserts, the extra weight load can be shifted and balanced over the entire joint, thus reducing pain and preserving what cartilage remains.

Dr. Hillstrom adds that specially designed knee braces can be lightweight, comfortable and helpful for knee OA.

BOW LEGS BEWARE

Biomechanical problems are common in people with bow legs, says Dr. Hillstrom. Leg length discrepancy can produce even more subtle biomechanical differences. In a study that involved 3,166 people in North Carolina (6.4% who had a leg length difference), researchers found that a leg length difference increased their risk for OA in both the knees and hips.

One way people notice this is because the legs on their pants hang differently, says Dr. Hillstrom. Knee OA patients may also feel pain while standing, walking or running. It is important to identify a possible body malalignment (bowlegged, knock-kneed, limb length discrepancy or excessive foot pronation where the arch tends to collapse) as early as possible in order to avoid problems down the road, says Dr. Hillstrom. If you suspect you have such a problem, perhaps because you are experiencing unexplained knee or hip pain, he advises seeing a health-care professional who is trained to detect and treat biomechanically related problems such as knee OA. These specialists include orthopedists, rheumatologists, physical therapists, podiatrists and orthotists.

SEE A PEDORTHIST
IF NECESSARY

Dr. Hillstrom also stresses the importance of proper footwear, especially for people with OA in their knees. Find footwear that is comfortable, naturally, but also look for shoes that come in a variety of widths, to be sure yours fit properly. They should be shaped to the natural contours of your foot with good cushioning to absorb mechanical shock. He adds that fashion may have to come second, in this case, but the payoff in greater body comfort will be well worth it. A pedorthist can provide excellent advice for footwear needs, says Dr. Hillstrom.

Knee braces, foot orthoses and shoe gear can be "off-the-shelf" or custom molded. Again, appropriate health-care specialists can help you decide which are appropriate for your condition. Custom-molded technology generally fits better, but costs more.

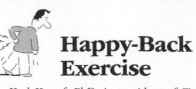

Happy-Back Exercise

Karl Knopf, PhD, is president of Fitness Educators of Older Adults Association (FEOAA) in Sunnyvale, California.

Eighty percent of Americans have some form of a back problem—leading to roughly $24 billion spent in medical costs each year directly related to low-back pain. Is it possible to exercise with back pain, and which exercises are gentle on the back? For options, we spoke with Karl Knopf, PhD, a leading authority on exercise for baby boomers and author of *Weights for 50+* and *Stretching for 50+* (both Ulysses).

POSTURE FIRST

Poor posture is a major contributor to back pain. Dr. Knopf believes that the first order of business for strengthening and rehabilitating the back are posture exercises, which can be practiced absolutely anywhere. "Stand upright with your weight evenly distributed over the balls of your feet and heels, with legs slightly bent. Then tilt your pelvis slightly forward so your tailbone is slightly tucked under your hips. Make the distance from your belly button to your sternum as far as possible by letting the chest rise and open, countering the "hunched over" effect. Your chin, sternum and belly button should be lined up from the front. From the side it should look like your earlobes are over your shoulders, which are over your hips." Practice that alignment whenever you are standing. When you sit, the alignment should be the same. Make sure you sit on the "sit bones" of the buttocks, not on the tailbone.

GUIDE WIRES FOR YOUR BACK

The back alone can't hold your body upright. "Think of standing a pencil upright on your desk balanced on the eraser," Dr. Knopf tells us. "You could make it stand—but it would take a lot of work and balance. How much more efficient to have guide wires? Well, the guide wires are the muscles that help keep the back aligned. These need strengthening to build a strong support system for the back.

The three basic "guide wire" muscle groups for the back are the abdominals, the gluteals (buttocks) and the perispinals (the muscles that run up and down the spine). "While many baby boomers are aware of the importance of training their abs, they often neglect the buttocks muscles, which are the other side of the guide wires. To strengthen the abs, back and glutes, *Dr. Knopf recommends the following exercises...*

1. Buttocks strengthener. Lie on your back, knees bent and feet flat on the floor. Tighten butt muscles and lift the butt off of the floor slowly. Hold for a few seconds, return. Do 10 repetitions.

2. Hamstring stretch. Lie on your back, feet straight out. Pull your right knee into the chest and hold it there for a few seconds. Then gently extend the leg toward the ceiling until you feel a stretch in the hamstrings (three muscles at the back of the thigh). Hold, return to start and repeat with the other leg.

3. Mad cat. Get on your hands and knees. Arch your back like a cat. Keep your neck in a relaxed neutral position. Hold for ten seconds, then release.

Note: Don't do this exercise if you have a ruptured disc.

OTHER EXERCISES THAT ARE GENTLE ON THE BACK

When choosing other exercises that are gentle on the back, Dr. Knopf recommends exercises that are done with the back supported and no "load" (or weight) on the spine.

Dr. Knopf has high praise for two specific forms of exercise. "The recumbent bike is my all-time favorite," he says. The recumbent bike, found in almost all gyms, is a bicycle (in either stationary or outdoor road versions) that allows you to sit as you would in a chair with

your back supported, instead of upright or hunched over the way traditional bicycles do. Dr. Knopf also loves water exercise. "Vertical water exercise allows you to work all muscle groups without putting any stress or strain on the back whatsoever."

As for strength-training exercises, again, Dr. Knopf recommends those in which the back is supported and that avoid putting any "load" on it. *His favorites...*

1. Seated chest press.

2. Lat pull downs to the front.

3. Sit-to-stands (see below).

Avoid: Military press...shoulder press... squats.

"You have to be careful with leg exercises," Dr. Knopf tells us. "If there's injury or pain, I'd prefer you do sit-to-stands. In this exercise, you sit on the edge of a chair, then stand up and sit down again. It's a "no load" version of the squat that works the front of the legs without putting any strain on the spine. You could work up to holding dumbbells in your hands to increase the resistance and build more muscle strength.

BACK PAIN CHRONIC? SEE A PHYSIATRIST

For anyone with chronic back pain who wants to exercise and eliminate pain, Dr. Knopf strongly suggests finding a physiatrist. "They are the most underused medical specialty I know of," he says. A physiatrist is a medical doctor who treats chronic pain and chronic conditions using a nonsurgical approach that often includes exercise. "They have no vested interest in doing surgery and are usually very open-minded to alternative interventions, such as chiropractic and acupuncture," said Dr. Knopf. "I've had back pain for years, and I always make the physiatrist the captain of my ship when it comes to back pain treatment."

15

Ease Allergy or Asthma Symptoms

Natural Remedies for Allergies and Asthma

Millions of Americans suffer from asthma and allergies, which are often triggered by such airborne substances as mold, dust mites or pollen. The immune system identifies these normally harmless substances as dangerous and releases inflammatory chemicals that can cause sneezing, wheezing, congestion and other symptoms.

The drugs used for these conditions—antihistamines, inhaled steroids, etc.—curtail symptoms but frequently cause side effects such as fatigue or anxiety.

Better approach: Studies have shown that many over-the-counter supplements act as natural antihistamines/anti-inflammatories that can reduce or prevent allergy or asthma flare-ups—with fewer side effects than drugs. Those who use nutritional supplements are often able to stop taking asthma and allergy drugs or signifi-

cantly reduce the dosages. You can take one or all of the supplements below daily, but always check with your doctor first.

QUERCETIN

Quercetin is a member of a class of nutrients known as bioflavonoids. It's a powerful anti-inflammatory that helps prevent the lungs, nasal passages and eyes from swelling after allergen exposure. It also inhibits the release of *histamine,* a chemical that triggers allergy and asthma flare-ups.

What is recommended to patients: 300 milligrams (mg) twice daily. If your symptoms are severe, increase the amount to 1,000 mg twice daily until symptoms abate. Then switch back to a maintenance dose of 300 mg twice a day. Quercetin works better for prevention than short-term treatment. It usually takes several weeks to become effective.

Richard N. Firshein, DO, medical director of the Firshein Center for Comprehensive Medicine, which specializes in treating allergies and asthma, New York City. An asthma sufferer himself, he is author of *The Nutraceutical Revolution* (Riverhead) and *Reversing Asthma* (Grand Central).

VITAMIN C

This potent antioxidant has a mild antihistamine effect.

What is recommended to patients: 500 to 1,000 mg daily. Vitamin C may cause diarrhea in some people. Divide the daily amount into two doses to reduce the risk of this side effect. Also, patients with a history of kidney stones should talk with their doctors before taking vitamin C supplements.

NETTLES

A traditional herbal remedy for allergies, nettles inhibit the body's production of inflammatory prostaglandins. In one study of 69 allergy patients, 57% had a significant improvement in their symptoms after taking nettles. Nettles work quickly, often within hours, and can be taken during flare-ups.

What is recommended to patients: 300 to 600 mg daily.

MAGNESIUM

This mineral is a natural bronchodilator that relaxes muscles in the airways and promotes better breathing. Supplementation with magnesium may be especially helpful if you're taking corticosteroids or other asthma drugs—they tend to reduce the amount of magnesium in the body.

What is recommended to patients: 200 to 600 mg daily.

ALLERGY TESTS

Your doctor may recommend skin or blood tests to determine if your allergies are caused by dust mites, mold, pollen, etc. Once you know what you're allergic to, you can take steps to minimize exposure.

Example: If you're allergic to dust mites, you can buy mattress and pillow casings that are impervious to allergens...and use a vacuum with a high-efficiency particulate air (HEPA) filter.

More from Richard N. Firshein...

New Ways to Treat Asthma—Naturally

Anyone who suffers from the wheezing, coughing and chest tightness caused by asthma knows all too well that conventional doctors typically treat these troublesome symptoms with prescription medication, such as steroids and bronchodilators (both available in inhalers and pills).

Problem: Long-term use of prescription drugs does nothing to solve the underlying causes of asthma (a disease of the lungs in which the airways become narrowed or blocked, resulting in breathing difficulties).

What's more, research shows that asthma medications can lead to side effects, including osteoporosis (from steroids) and anxiety and insomnia (from bronchodilators, which accelerate the asthma sufferer's heart rate).

Latest development: Exciting research confirms that asthma can be controlled with nondrug treatments, thereby reducing—or even eliminating—the need for medication.* *Here's how...*

NUTRITIONAL SUPPLEMENTS

•**Omega-3 fatty acids.** This component of dietary fat—found abundantly in cold-water fish, such as salmon, herring and mackerel, as well as in flaxseeds and walnuts—may act as a natural anti-inflammatory for asthma sufferers.

Scientific evidence: In a three-week study, researchers at Indiana University followed 16 adults who had exercise-induced asthma (narrowing of the airways during and after vigorous exercise). Participants were given either a daily placebo capsule or fish oil capsules containing two types of omega-3 fatty acids—*eicosapentaenoic acid* (EPA) and *docosahexaenoic acid* (DHA).

Researchers measured the participants' lung function and inflammation levels before, during and after the study. While taking fish oil capsules, the asthmatics had improved lung function, lower inflammation levels and reduced bronchodilator use. There was no improvement in those who took the placebo.

Self-defense: Take daily fish oil supplements, with a total of 1 gram (g) to 2 g of DHA and EPA. Benefits typically begin after a few months but may occur in as little as three weeks.

Caution: This dosage can produce blood-thinning effects. If you take daily aspirin or a blood thinner, such as *warfarin* (Coumadin), be sure to consult your doctor before trying fish oil supplements.

*Consult your doctor before trying any nondrug therapies for asthma.

•**Magnesium.** This mineral is considered a natural bronchodilator because it relaxes the muscles of the bronchial tubes that line the air passages.

Scientific evidence: In a two-month study, researchers in Brazil gave 37 asthmatic children and adolescents daily doses of either a placebo or 300 milligrams (mg) of magnesium. Those receiving magnesium had fewer bronchial spasms and asthma attacks, and used less asthma medication.

Self-defense: Take 250 to 500 mg of magnesium daily. Exceeding this dosage of magnesium can cause bloating, gas and diarrhea. Taking a calcium supplement (double the daily magnesium dose) can enhance absorption of both minerals. To ensure proper absorption of calcium, take no more than 500 mg of the mineral at a time.

•**Coenzyme Q10 (CoQ10).** This powerful antioxidant helps cells manufacture energy and also strengthens the cells of the lungs.

Scientific evidence: Researchers in Slovakia gave 41 adult asthmatics who took steroids either a placebo or a daily dose of 120 mg of CoQ10. After 16 weeks, the asthma patients who took CoQ10 used fewer steroids.

Self-defense: Taking 100 to 120 mg of CoQ10 daily may be helpful—whether or not you take steroids.

Important: If you use both medications and nutritional supplements to treat your asthma, take them at least one hour apart to enhance the absorption of both.

ANTIOXIDANT-RICH DIET

It is a widely accepted fact among health scientists that oxidative stress—the increase in cell-damaging free radicals caused by factors as varied as fried food, air pollution and stress—plays a role in more than 50 diseases, from arthritis to cancer. Now, most scientists have concluded that oxidative stress also affects asthma.

Scientific evidence: Researchers analyzed data from nearly 69,000 women and found that those with the highest intake of antioxidant-rich vegetables, such as carrots and leafy greens, had the lowest incidence of asthma.

Self-defense: Each day, eat a variety of antioxidant-rich foods, including fruits…leafy, dark green vegetables, such as spinach and kale…as well as carrots, any variety of winter squash and other colorful vegetables rich in carotenoids (a family of protective antioxidants that includes beta-carotene). Aim for five to six one-half-cup servings daily of these vegetables and fruits… and juices made from them.

BREATHING EXERCISES

Breathing exercises have been shown to reduce the need for bronchodilators in people with asthma. However, few physicians are aware of the benefits, so most patients are not encouraged to try breathing exercises.

Scientific evidence: When researchers taught 57 asthmatics breathing techniques, which they practiced twice daily for 30 weeks, their use of short-acting bronchodilators declined by 82%.

Self-defense: To strengthen the lungs, prevent an asthma attack or help stop an attack in progress, try breathing exercises.

What to do: While sitting, place one hand on your stomach, with the palm open. Use this hand to feel your abdomen rising and falling as you breathe. Use the thumb of the other hand to feel for the pulse point of the wrist that is on your stomach. Let yourself relax.

Next, synchronize your breathing with your heart rate. Breathe in through the nose, with the pulse…breathe out through the mouth, with the pulse. Blow out through pursed lips to create a mild resistance that improves the tone and function of the diaphragm, a muscle that plays a key role in breathing. Perform for 10 to 15 minutes, twice a day—or any time you're starting to have an asthma attack.

Caution: If you are experiencing a serious asthma attack, this breathing exercise may not be effective, and you may need to use medication. But in almost all other cases, this exercise can help regulate respiration.

ACUPUNCTURE

The National Institutes of Health recognizes acupuncture as a treatment for asthma. Thousands of years of anecdotal evidence from China also confirms that acupuncture works, perhaps by balancing fundamental but unseen energy flows that affect the body.

Self-defense: Try six to 10 initial acupuncture treatments, with additional treatments if needed.

Stop Springtime Allergies... No Drugs Needed!

Jamison Starbuck, ND, a naturopathic physician practicing in Missoula, Montana. She is a past president of the American Association of Naturopathic Physicians.

Many people assume that allergy drugs *cure* allergies. They don't. Allergy medications work by *suppressing* allergy symptoms. This, in turn, blocks the immune system's natural response.

When the drug wears off, the allergy symptoms typically return—often with a vengeance. The result? Increased allergy symptoms, dependence on medication and the possibility of a weakened immune system.

There are times when antihistamines make sense. For example, if you have an important event to attend, you'll want a few hours' relief from your sneezing, coughing and watery eyes. These drugs can rapidly reduce those symptoms for a few hours. For longer-term relief of symptoms, doctors often prescribe nasal steroids (cortisone-like drugs).

Taken in low doses, these drugs may not damage your overall health. Taken more often or in higher doses, however, these drugs may stress your immune system and perhaps even cause side effects, such as sleep disturbance or clouded thinking.

For long-term hay fever relief, natural medicine is a better alternative. With this type of treatment, your goal is to strengthen the immune system and soothe symptoms with medications that are nonsuppressive medications. *Here's a natural approach to fighting allergies...*

• **Take vitamin C and bioflavonoids.** A typical dose is 2,000 milligrams (mg) of vitamin C and 500 mg each of the bioflavonoids *quercetin* and *hesperidin*, taken twice daily with food. These supplements reduce inflammation and lower histamine levels in the blood.

Note: Do not expect them to act as quickly as Benadryl. You need to take them for at least two weeks before the anti-allergy effect kicks in.

Caution: High doses of vitamin C may cause diarrhea. If this occurs, reduce the dose.

• **Curb stress.** Studies show that allergy symptoms are much worse when a person is highly stressed. Stress aggravates the immune system, making it more likely to overreact to irritants, such as pollen. To prevent this, meditate for 15 minutes each day, do aerobic exercise early in the morning when the pollen count is low, take vacations regularly and talk out your emotional conflicts with a counselor if necessary.

• **Irrigate your nose.** To reduce your exposure to pollen, rinse the nasal passages twice daily. You can buy a nasal saline spray in drugstores or health-food stores. Or you can make your own by mixing one-quarter teaspoon of sea salt with one cup of warm water. Fill your cupped palm with the warm saltwater, close one nostril with your finger and gently inhale the water into the other nostril. Perform the same process on the other side. Tip your head back for 10 seconds, then gently blow your nose. Repeat on each nostril.

• **Use herbs.** Stinging nettle *(Urtica dioica)* and eyebright *(Euphrasia officinalis)* reduce acute allergy symptoms, such as burning eyes, runny nose and congestion. For quicker results, take these herbs in tincture form.

Typical dose: 30 drops of tincture of each herb in four ounces of water four times daily. Take 15 minutes before eating.

Better Ways to Beat Spring And Summer Allergies

Robert S. Ivker, DO, clinical instructor of otolaryngology at the University of Colorado School of Medicine in Denver. A cofounder and past president of the American Board of Holistic Medicine and the American Holistic Medical Association. He is author of Sinus Survival: The Holistic Medical Treatment for Allergies, Asthma, Bronchitis, Colds, and Sinusitis. *Tarcher.*

Pollen gets most of the blame for spring and summer allergies. What most people don't realize is that pollen is only the *trigger.*

Most hay fever and other allergy sufferers have mucous membranes that are chronically irritated. This—and a genetic predisposition to allergies—makes them hyperreactive to pollen, dust, animal dander, mold spores, etc.

Long-acting antihistamines, such as *loratadine* (Claritin) and *fexofenadine* (Allegra), and steroid nasal sprays, such as *fluticasone* (Flonase) and *mometasone* (Nasonex), have few side effects and can treat short-term (four- to six-week) flare-ups. But they're costly and don't correct the underlying problem.

Better: A holistic program that heals the mucous membranes. Once the irritation and inflammation are eliminated, most people can stop taking drugs or reduce the dosages. *Best approaches include...*

IMPROVE INDOOR AIR QUALITY

The average American spends 90% of his/her time indoors, so improving indoor air quality is the first step in preventing and treating allergies. *Here's how...*

• **Use a negative-ion generator.** These units work by emitting negatively charged ions that attract positively charged pollen particles. The charged particles then stick to walls or furniture instead of remaining airborne. As an alternative, use a high-efficiency particulate air (HEPA) filter. These units eliminate 99.7% of all allergens. Any brand of ion generator or HEPA filter is fine—as long as the model does not produce ozone, which irritates the mucous membranes. Use it in any room where you spend a lot of time.

Typical cost: Ion generator, $50 to $100... HEPA filter, $35 to $400.

• **Add moisture with a warm-mist humidifier.** Even in humid parts of the country, indoor humidity in the winter months can fall below 20%. The humidifiers sold in hardware and household-goods stores work well. Get a model that automatically turns on when humidity falls below the optimal range of 35% to 50%, and use it in your bedroom and office.

Good brands: Slant/Fin and Bionaire.

Typical cost: $50 to $150.

• **Install a high-grade furnace/air-conditioning filter.** The Filtrete model by 3M traps most particles, including pollen.

Typical cost: $19.

CORRECT FOOD ALLERGIES

Up to 11 million Americans are allergic to one or more foods—and most aren't aware of it. Food allergies can stimulate activity of *mast cells,* immune cells that produce hay fever symptoms, such as nasal congestion, watery eyes, etc.

Self-test: In the morning, take your pulse for one minute on an empty stomach. Then eat a food that you want to test, sit still for 20 minutes and check your pulse again. If it has increased by 15 to 20 beats per minute, you're probably sensitive to that food.

Patients who identify a food allergen in the self-test or who suffer from severe seasonal allergies should eliminate the suspected food and other common food allergens for three weeks to see if symptoms subside.

Most common food allergens: Dairy and wheat. Others include chocolate, corn, soy and tomatoes.

GET ENOUGH SLEEP

Insomnia, sleeping late on weekends and staying up late during the week, etc., can depress immunity and play a significant role in seasonal allergies.

Important: Set a regular bedtime and wake-up time to reattune your body to natural sleep rhythms. If you don't naturally wake up without an alarm clock, you probably need to go to bed earlier.

Also helpful: For occasional use, take 400 to 500 milligrams (mg) of magnesium and 1,000 mg of calcium within 45 minutes of your bedtime. These minerals will act as natural sedatives.

HERBS AND SUPPLEMENTS

Certain herbs and supplements have been shown to relieve allergy symptoms. In addition to a daily vitamin C supplement, consider taking all of the following supplements a week or two prior to the onset of your pollen allergy season (trees, April...grass, May...ragweed, August). Best choices...

• **Grapeseed extract is the most effective natural antihistamine.** In France, it's a popular choice for treating allergies. It contains *proanthocyanidin,* an antioxidant that helps reduce mucous membrane inflammation.

Typical dose: 100 to 200 mg three times daily between meals.

• **Nettles,** derived from the leaves, stems and roots of a perennial plant that grows throughout the US, are effective as a natural antihistamine. They can be taken during an allergy flare-up but are more effective as a preventive.

Typical dose: 300 mg three times daily with meals.

• **Quercetin, a bioflavonoid in many vegetables, is a powerful anti-inflammatory and antioxidant.** It can help reduce nasal congestion and it inhibits the effects of histamines, body chemicals that cause allergy symptoms.

Take a quercetin supplement that includes bromelain, a digestive enzyme that improves the body's ability to absorb quercetin.

Typical dose: 250 to 500 mg three times daily with meals.

WATCH YOUR EMOTIONS

The discomfort of seasonal allergies can trigger high levels of anxiety, fear and stress. These negative emotions increase the activity of mast cells and often exacerbate allergy symptoms.

Patients who suffer from troubling emotions should consider seeing a therapist or counselor.

Also helpful: Stress-relieving techniques include meditation and positive affirmations as well as visualization.

Best Way to Beat Seasonal Allergies? Boost Your Immune System

Gailen D. Marshall, Jr., MD, PhD, professor of medicine and pediatrics, and director, division of clinical immunology and allergy, University of Mississippi Medical Center, Jackson.

Andrew L. Rubman, ND, director, Southbury Clinic for Traditional Medicines, Southbury, Connecticut.

When it's that sneezing and wheezing time of year, you can look up the current pollen count at *www.pollen.com* and see how your area rates. Pollen counts can range from 0 to 12. Any reading above 8 is considered high.

South Florida recently had the lowest "achoo" factor—a mere 0.1. Should you pack up your bags and move?

Unfortunately, probably not. The American Academy of Allergy Asthma & Immunology says that seasonal allergies generally don't disappear when a person moves to a new area. Many of the same kinds of allergy-provoking plants—especially grasses—are found throughout the US. Allergies to plants found in the new location can develop within just one or two years.

A better way to minimize seasonal allergies is to strengthen your internal defense systems against inflammation and disease. Andrew L. Rubman, ND, a naturopathic physician and our medical expert, suggests a broad-spectrum antioxidant to help strengthen your immune system and decrease the sensitivity of cell membranes to allergens.

His favorite: Vita Biotic, which contains two core antioxidants—vitamins A and C—plus zinc, echinacea, garlic and other immune-boosting herbs. Take one tablet with each meal. Available at many health-food stores around the country or from Eclectic Institute (800-332-4372, *www.eclecticherb.com*).

Note: Although generally safe at this dose, always involve a practitioner formally trained in nutritional biochemistry, such as a naturopathic physician, in your care.

Dr. Rubman recommends a daily dose of vitamin E. Consult your doctor for the dose that's right for you.

Words of caution: Always consult your health-care adviser before starting a dietary supplement. Make sure that the supplement will not worsen an existing health condition or interact with anything else—prescription or over-the-counter—that you already are taking.

SNEEZE-PROOF YOUR DIET

Avoiding certain foods may also lessen pollen sensitivity. Top culprits include dairy and wheat products and corn derivatives, such as high-fructose corn syrup. This calorie-rich syrup is a "hidden sugar" used to sweeten many soft drinks and other beverages, baked goods, jams and jellies. Unfortunately, it is also linked to elevated levels of triglycerides—a risk factor for heart disease.

Surprisingly, fruit can be a problem as well. An apple a day may keep the doctor away—but not if your pollen allergy cross-reacts with a sensitivity to raw fruit. Cross-reaction occurs when the allergen in raw fruit is sufficiently similar to that in pollen, allowing the two to work in tandem to make an allergy attack worse. According to allergist/immunologist Gailen D. Marshall, Jr., MD, PhD, eating an apple when birch pollen is abundant may quickly lead to itchiness or swelling around the lips, mouth or throat. Ragweed pollen and watermelon are another ill-fated pair. If you notice a possible cross-reaction, keep a food diary—or simply stay away from the offending fruit at that time of year. You are unlikely to experience problems at other times.

HOMEMADE REMEDY

If you develop allergic symptoms—such as congestion, sneezing, runny nose or itching in the eyes, ears or throat—don't rush off to buy some heavily promoted allergy product. For one thing, *loratadine* (Claritin), *diphenhydramine* (Benadryl) and other antihistamines only work on histamine-related symptoms (e.g., runny nose, itchy eyes, sneezing). They will not help clear up nasal congestion.

Instead, try cleansing your nasal passages with warm saltwater drops. You can make your own solution by mixing one-half teaspoon of kosher or sea salt with eight ounces of distilled water in a sterile container (you can sterilize the glass jars by dipping them in boiling water). Pour the amount you will need into a small jar, and save the rest for future use. Sterilize a dropper with alcohol. After administering the drops, discard the extra solution in the small container.

It may sound like an unpleasant process, but Dr. Rubman promises it will wash away allergens and break up nasal congestion. That will reduce the severity of the allergic reaction.

As with so many health concerns, when it comes to allergies, an ounce of prevention is worth a pound of cure. Drugs come with their own problems. Antihistamines can cause chronic upper-respiratory disorders, rebound headaches and other health problems.

And how about allergic reactions to a drug that is often prescribed to fight allergies? People have even developed allergic reactions to *leukotriene modifiers*—a newer category of drug that includes *montelukast* (Singulair)—according to the FDA. It's no wonder prevention is the best defense.

info For more information, visit the Web site for the Allergy Prevention Center, *www.allergypreventioncenter.com.*

The American Academy of Allergy Asthma & Immunology, *www.aaaai.org.*

Search for "Singulair" on the United States Food and Drug Administration's database, *www.fda.gov/cder/drug.*

How Antibiotics May Cause Allergies And Asthma

Gary B. Huffnagle, PhD, professor and researcher, internal medicine, University of Michigan Medical School, Ann Arbor.

It's often been observed that the explosive increases in asthma and allergies we have seen over the past four decades have occurred in tandem with widespread increases in antibiotic use. Is there a link here? Yes, according to a recent study that examined the possible relationships between antibiotic use, bacterial changes in the gut and allergic response.

We spoke with Gary B. Huffnagle, PhD, professor and researcher in internal medicine at the University of Michigan Medical School in Ann Arbor where the study was conducted. Antibiotics weaken the natural bacteria in the gut and, in humans, can stimulate overgrowth of the yeast *Candida albicans*. Previous studies have shown that overgrowth of yeast adversely affects the body's mucosal immunity.

The result: A weakened immune system, vulnerable to allergies and asthma.

THE STUDY

In the University of Michigan study, mice were given antibiotics in their drinking water for five days to weaken their gut bacteria. They were then injected with candida yeast to mimic the response that antibiotics produce in humans. Finally, the mice's nasal passages were exposed to *aspergillus*, a mold spore that is a common allergy trigger in humans.

The mice that received antibiotics showed increased sensitivity to the mold spore in their respiratory systems, whereas the mice that did not receive antibiotics did not develop any of the sensitivities to mold.

The study reaffirms that what goes on in the gut can play an important role in regulating immune responses—even in the lungs, since they, too, secrete mucus. To take this concept one step further, if a problem in the lungs is found to originate at another site in the body, there should be little doubt that other chronic diseases can have their roots in places not previously explored.

Antibiotics, like so many drugs, do not work in isolated ways. Watch out for associated risks. We can only hope that one day our medical system will strike a balance between creating overall health and curing isolated symptoms of disease.

Surprising Food Dangers for Asthmatics

Thomas J. Fischer, MD, allergist in private practice and professor of clinical pediatrics, Cincinnati Children's Hospital Medical Center.

Christopher Portier, PhD, associate director for risk assessment, National Institute of Environmental Health Sciences, Research Triangle Park, North Carolina.

Andrew L. Rubman, ND, director, Southbury Clinic for Traditional Medicines, Southbury, Connecticut.

Are we endangering our health by using sulfites as preservatives in our food? Here's what we learned when we asked Christopher Portier, PhD, director of the environmental toxicology program at the National Institute of Environmental Health Sciences in Research Triangle Park, North Carolina, and Thomas J. Fischer, MD, an allergist and professor of clinical pediatrics at the Cincinnati Children's Hospital Medical Center.

SULFITE OVERVIEW

In 1986, when the salad-bar craze was in full swing, the FDA prohibited the use of sulfites as a preservative on fruits and vegetables sold or served raw to consumers. Currently, sulfites are used on dried fruits and vegetables to keep them crisp and from turning brown...on shrimp and lobster to prevent black spots (melanosis)...in wine and some juices to protect them from bacterial growth...and in many frozen products to bleach and preserve them. Sulfites are also used as a stabilizer in some drugs.

Although this may sound alarming for the vast majority of people, the presence of sulfites simply is not a problem. You may occasionally hear a rumor that sulfites are carcinogenic but, according to Dr. Portier, there has never been evidence indicating that they cause cancer.

However, this doesn't mean that sulfites are entirely off the hook as far as being problematic...especially if you are asthmatic.

ASTHMATICS BEWARE

For people who suffer from asthma, sulfites can be troublesome—and even occasionally dangerous, says Dr. Fischer.

In particular, steroid-dependent asthmatics are the most likely group to have trouble with sulfites. For these people, eating a sulfite-containing food may cause throat constriction and difficulty breathing. In very rare cases, he says, it has turned into an emergency situation. Though also rare, it may even occur in people who are not diagnosed as asthmatic.

Anyone with asthma—and today there are nearly 30 million such people in the US alone—should become familiar with the presence of sulfites and the problems they often cause.

KNOWLEDGE IS POWER

The first step is to become knowledgeable about which foods are likely to contain sulfites. The FDA now requires this information to appear on labels if sulfites appear in concentrations of 10 parts per million (ppm) or higher—a miniscule amount but meaningful for the sulfite-sensitive. Look for any words that end in "sulfite," or the words "sulfur dioxide."

Common foods that contain sulfites include frozen foods, baked goods (including tortillas and waffles), horseradish, pickles and relishes, and jams and jellies. Wine of any color almost always has sulfites—labeling of this is required in the US (if the added sulfites exceed 10 ppm), but even unlabeled bottles that you may consume abroad have sulfites as well. Beer and most distilled alcohols also have sulfites.

If more than 100 ppm: Sulfite-sensitive people should definitely avoid any foods with more than 100 ppm of sulfites, says Dr. Fischer. The biggest offenders are dried fruits (including raisins), nonfrozen lemon and lime juice, wine, molasses, sauerkraut juice and all grape juices and pickled cocktail onions.

When buying food that is not packaged—for instance, meats from a deli—you should ask the store manager if it contains sulfites. Restaurant managers may or may not be able to tell you if sulfites are in the food, but anyone eating out who is sensitive to sulfites always should avoid french fries, home fries and mashed potatoes because precut and dehydrated potatoes are treated with sulfites. Ask for a baked potato instead.

Use your common sense in determining which foods you should skip. If you have a reaction to a certain food, says Dr. Fischer, simply avoid it in the future. He adds that most people quickly learn which foods bother them and which don't.

CREATE A PLAN OF ACTION

Finally, Dr. Fischer urges everyone who has asthma or who has displayed sulfite sensitivity in the past to have a plan of action. Talk to your doctor—preferably an allergist or pulmonologist—and be prepared in knowing what you should do if a reaction occurs.

Ironically, some asthma medications contain sulfites. This is true, for instance, of *epinephrine* (often administered to allergy sufferers in the form of EpiPens), but there have never been any adverse effects reported with its use and it has saved lives in sulfite-sensitive asthmatic patients.

Even so, if you are extremely sulfite-sensitive, you should discuss the medications you take with your doctor. Our medical expert, Andrew L. Rubman, ND, suggests that you talk about taking daily doses of omega-3 fatty acids from cold-water fish and seed oils, such as evening primrose, borage and flax. These may dramatically reduce sensitivity and symptomatic severity of sulfite reactions.

As stress and environmental exposures cause the level and frequency of reactions to vary, always err on the side of safety. If you are sensitive, practice reasonable avoidance. Read the labels, ask the questions and stay safe.

Living with Pet Allergies

Annie B. Bond, author, *Better Basics for the Home* (Three Rivers) and founder and CEO of Green Chi Cafe, the Meeting Place for an Eco-Revolution, *www.greenchi cafe.com.*

Linda B. Ford, MD, past president, American Lung Association, and allergist, president and founder, Asthma and Allergy Center, Papillion, Nebraska.

No matter how hard you try, it may be impossible to keep your household free from every type of allergen. A study recently published in the *Journal of Allergy and Clinical Immunology* revealed that animal allergen exists in 100% of American homes. Furthermore, because clothing so easily transports the allergen, it is also in shopping malls, schools, cinemas, hotels and even hospitals.

Given that 40 million Americans suffer from nasal-related allergies, we spoke with allergist Linda B. Ford, MD, past president of the American Lung Association, about what people can do to protect themselves.

Dr. Ford explained that the severity of your symptoms are relative to how much you are exposed to. The more allergen you're around, the worse off you'll be. Some people with very bad allergies know to keep their home environment pet-free, but as this study made clear, it's impossible to avoid animal allergen completely.

Note: If you can't bear the idea of life without a pet, consider a male, black cat, a group that—for unknown reasons—has lower levels of allergen-producing dander. Because allergen is also found in cats' saliva and urine, give your pet a simple water bath at least once a week and keep a pristine litter box. Clumping litter is preferable. Always wear a facial mask when cleaning the box to prevent inhaling allergen that can become airborne. A good option for dog lovers who suffer from pet allergies is the Portuguese water dog.

CLEANING STRATEGIES

Even though it is impossible to free your home entirely of pet allergen, there are still ways you can keep them reasonably under control, says Annie B. Bond, author of *Better Basics for the Home* and founder and CEO of *www.greenchicafe.com*, a "site that speaks to the culture of green." High on your list should be several high-efficiency particulate arresting (HEPA) products—a HEPA vacuum, air purifier and air filters in your air conditioners and on your heating unit, if possible. HEPA products have been around for many years and are widely available.

Keep your pet outside as much as you can and above all, don't let Max or Toto into the bedroom of the allergy-prone family member. Bond also suggests cleaning surfaces with a high-quality soap, such as Dr. Bronner's Pure Castile Soap—look for the one with lavender oil in it, which acts as an antibacterial while it diffuses pet odors.

IMMUNOTHERAPY

For those people whose allergies are particularly persistent, immunotherapy, a regimen in which the patient is injected with gradually increasing amounts of the allergen with the idea that, over time, the immune system no longer responds to it, is an option. It has improved considerably in the last few years. Dr. Ford explains that today's high-potency standardized extracts are responsible for making this treatment much more successful than in the past. She recommends it for those who do not benefit from medical or avoidance strategies.

Immunotherapy shots are usually administered once a week for one year, with gradual reduction in frequency over the next three to five years until immunity is in place. The result for most patients is a decrease in allergy symptoms. Should you choose immunotherapy shots, make sure you ask your doctor about any impact it might have on your overall immune system.

16

Taking Care of Your Eyes and Teeth

Clearing Away Cataracts Naturally

More than half of people age 65 and over have some degree of cataract development. A cataract is a blurring of your natural lens, the part of the eye which focuses light and is responsible for sharp images. Cataracts generally develop slowly and vary in size, density and location. Their impact on sight is also gradual—for some people the first symptoms are needing more light to read by or having trouble seeing street signs. Cataracts also develop at different speeds in both eyes, so a person may not be aware of the severity of a faster-developing cataract because the other eye is clear enough to compensate for a time. However, left unchecked, cataracts' milky clouds can substantially obscure vision.

Eventually, the problem becomes so severe that many people undergo cataract surgery, an outpatient procedure in which the surgeon removes the clouded natural lens and then implants an artificial lens to take its place. Assuming that the surgery is successful, the result is clear vision—often virtually instantaneously—but with limitations. Because there is no way for the implanted lens to change shape to accommodate focusing at various distances the way a natural one does, doctors adjust implants to allow viewing at middle distance. This means that the patient will continue to need glasses for close and far vision.

HOLISTIC HELP

Although many doctors say that there is nothing you can do about cataract development, a few are taking a holistic approach. They claim that there are definite steps you can take that will make a difference. We spoke with one of these eye experts, E. Michael Geiger, OD, a New York City optometrist who specializes in the use of alternative medicine

E. Michael Geiger, OD, author, *Eye Care Naturally* (Safe Goods), and a New York City optometrist specializing in the use of alternative medicine to prevent and treat eye problems. *www.nutrasight.com*.

to prevent and treat eye problems. Dr. Geiger says that by controlling your environment and diet, and taking certain supplements, you can slow down the onset of cataracts at the very least, perhaps lessen their impact and, if you start early enough, prevent them entirely.

Dr. Geiger's first advice concerns the environment. Studies show that cataracts are more common among people who smoke and for those who live in sunnier climates and are subjected to greater UV-ray exposure. Because we absorb so many UV rays before the age of 18, it is important even for children to wear UV-protected sunglasses. Adults should wear sunglasses most of the time they are outside or invest in a broad-brimmed hat that will keep the rays from striking their eyes. As for smoking, the threat of cataracts is yet another entry on the long list of why you should not smoke.

WHAT TO EAT

On the food front, Dr. Geiger stresses the importance of vitamin C and other antioxidants for eye health. He advises his patients to eat all kinds of green vegetables, as well as carrots, onions, corn, citrus fruits, cantaloupe and apples. He also recommends garlic (it increases blood circulation, including to the eyes) and he has a tip for maximizing its nutrients—after slicing, wait five minutes before cooking to give it enough time to form a coat that seals in nutrients. Sea vegetables (including seaweed and other types you see in Japanese cuisine) are also good because they contain selenium and other minerals. Seeds, almonds and whole grains are helpful because of the vitamin E they contain.

WHAT TO AVOID

Foods to avoid include anything fried—the oil used is often hydrogenated and high temperatures and reuse can render it rancid. Hydrogenated, reused oil is damaging to the eyes. Also avoid foods barbecued over charcoal as well as smoked foods, which, Dr. Geiger says, have been associated with cataract development. Swordfish, which often has a high mercury content, has also been linked to cataracts.

SUPPLEMENTAL INFORMATION

Dr. Geiger is a strong supporter of taking supplements for eye health. In addition to a high-quality multivitamin, he advises taking specific antioxidants, including lutein, eyebright (available as an herbal supplement) quercetin, selenium and zinc, vitamins C and E and beta-carotene. He also suggests garlic as a supplement (one tablet a day) and coenzyme Q10 because it helps circulation. These should be prescribed by a naturopathic doctor or a natural eye-care physician.

It's not a difficult regimen to follow, but it is one that goes along with general health guidelines. If you have high blood-sugar levels or a family history of cataracts, be especially vigilant. People with diabetes are twice as likely to develop them.

What to Do If You Get Cataracts

E. Michael Geiger, OD, author, *Eye Care Naturally* (Safe Goods), and a New York City optometrist specializing in the use of alternative medicine to prevent and treat eye problems. *www.nutrasight.com.*

Neil F. Martin, MD, FACS, clinical assistant professor of ophthalmology, Georgetown University Medical Center in Washington, DC, and surgeon, Washington Eye Physicians & Surgeons, Chevy Chase, Maryland.

Thanks to recent research, cataracts are no longer as inevitable as death and taxes. To learn more, we spoke with New York City optometrist E. Michael Geiger, OD, author of *Eye Care Naturally.*

KEEPING CLEAR

Dr. Geiger's first line of defense in avoiding the cloudy lenses of cataracts is to eat right. Antioxidants, especially vitamins C and E, protect against cataracts. They can also prevent newly developed cataracts from getting worse—and sometimes even reverse them.

• **Champion vitamin C sources.** Citrus fruits …kiwis…tomatoes. Dr. Geiger recommends people get 500 milligrams each day.

• **Champion vitamin E sources.** Nuts, vegetable oils and leafy green vegetables are excellent sources—but it is difficult to get enough vitamin E from food alone. Consult your health-care provider about taking a 400 international unit (IU) supplement daily.

Dr. Geiger also suggests the dietary supplement Healthy Eyes, which contains key vitamins, minerals and other nutrients. Manufactured by DaVinci Laboratories of Vermont, it is available only through licensed health professionals.

Foods to avoid: Certain foods can increase cataract risk. Avoid fried or smoked foods…foods cooked on charcoal barbecues…swordfish, king mackerel and other fish that have high mercury content.

Dr. Geiger says it is also important to watch your waistline. According to a Harvard Medical School study published in *The American Journal of Clinical Nutrition*, men with excess abdominal fat—as measured by the waist size relative to the hips—are more likely to have cataracts than people with skinnier waistlines.

Also at increased risk: People with a high body mass index (BMI)—a measure of body fat based on weight and height. To calculate your BMI, go to the National Institutes of Health's Web site *(http://nhlbisupport.com/bmi).*

Cataracts are associated with obesity, diabetes and smoking—another powerful reason to eat healthfully, exercise regularly and stop smoking (or never start!).

Wearing sunglasses to protect the health of your eyes is also critical, especially when around water or snow. This is particularly important for children under age 18—but your eyes will thank you at any age. If you use eyeglasses, consider having your prescription lenses made with ultraviolet-blocking glass. Many people prefer these to wearing clip-ons. Polarized lenses help against glare but do not affect the health of the eye once cataracts have been detected.

ONCE DETECTED

Despite your best efforts, cataracts may still develop. If they show up on an eye exam, Neil F. Martin, MD, FACS, clinical assistant professor of ophthalmology at Georgetown University Medical Center in Washington, DC, says that there is no need to panic. He notes that some cataracts stay small and interfere very little with vision. Various optical aids—a new eyeglass prescription, anti-glare sunglasses, magnifying glasses, etc.—may help people who are experiencing such symptoms as blurred vision or excessive glare. But if cataracts interfere with everyday activities, surgery may be the best—and the only—option. Cataracts will not go away on their own or with drugs.

Cataract surgery involves the removal of the clouded lens and insertion of an artificial, intraocular lens. Once upon a time, a lengthy hospital stay was required. Today, most cataract operations take less than one hour and are performed on an outpatient basis. According to the NIH Web site, cataract surgery is one of the most common surgeries performed in the US each year. *Other important details…*

• **The small incision is "self-sealing" and usually requires no stitches.**

• **Most patients return to their normal activities within a day or two.**

• **Complete healing takes approximately eight weeks.** If a patient needs cataracts removed from both eyes, the surgeon usually does one eye at a time, waiting for one eye to heal before doing the other.

SURGERY RISKS

While cataract surgery is one of the most common and successful procedures, as Dr. Martin observes, no surgery is truly risk free. Possible risks include infection, bleeding and inflammation—which all can be treated successfully if medical attention is sought promptly. Very rarely, retinal detachment occurs after surgery. If you experience excessive pain, vision loss or nausea, report these symptoms to your eye surgeon immediately.

Sometimes an "after-cataract"—a clouding of the tissue that encloses the artificial lens—develops months, or even years, after surgery. Lasers are used to treat after-cataracts in a painless, outpatient procedure.

More than 1.5 million cataract operations are performed in the US each year, with about a 95% success rate. Nearly all patients see better after the surgery than they did before—and often better than before any evidence of cataracts showed up.

Reason: Thanks to new surgery techniques and new types of lenses, cataract surgery can alleviate certain other vision problems, too—including presbyopia, the diminution of the ability to focus on near objects that becomes noticeable when people are in their 40s.

Foods for Better Sight

Lylas G. Mogk, MD, founding director, Visual Rehabilitation and Research Center, Henry Ford Medical Center, Grosse Pointe Park, Michigan, and coauthor, *Macular Degeneration: The Complete Guide to Saving and Maximizing Your Sight.* Ballantine Books.

Andrew L. Rubman, ND, director, Southbury Clinic for Traditional Medicines, Southbury, Connecticut.

Age-related macular degeneration (AMD) is the number one cause of blindness in older adults, affecting millions of people in this country alone. It ultimately destroys the vision field in the center of the eye, making driving, reading and other normal life functions virtually impossible.

Although today there are rehabilitation programs available in which patients can learn to adapt peripheral vision for regaining life functions, there is no known cure for AMD. Consequently, any news about how to avoid it is especially helpful.

And there is good news from a study done by Harvard-based researcher Eunyoung Cho, ScD. Dr. Cho analyzed the data from the Brigham and Women's Hospital long-range Nurses' Health Study that followed 118,428 men and women for up to 18 years. In her analysis of the data, Dr. Cho found that people who ate three or more servings of fruit a day had a 36% decreased risk of developing AMD.

HOW FRUIT HELPS

We called Lylas G. Mogk, MD, founding director of the Visual Rehabilitation and Research Center at the Henry Ford Medical Center in Grosse Pointe Park, Michigan, to discuss the reasons that fruit and good eyesight go together.

Dr. Mogk explains that many experts believe that free radicals found in the environment and from the sun may be the cause of AMD, so the idea of protection from a diet rich in antioxidant-containing fruits makes sense. Furthermore, a number of past studies have shown that antioxidants in foods and supplements are generally protective.

Dr. Mogk has additional recommendations to help prevent AMD—especially important for fair-skinned, light-eyed people who are at the greatest risk. *Besides consuming plenty of fruit, she says you should...*

•**Increase omega-3 intake** (fish, flaxseed oil and supplements) and decrease intake of omega-6s (vegetable oils, often found in packaged foods).

Note: The body does need a proper balance of omega-3s and omega-6s. According to our medical expert, Andrew L. Rubman, ND, processed foods carry an abundance of omega-6s, but the processing often damages them to the degree that it is more reliable to take a supplement that contains both omega-3s and high-quality omega-6s. People who consume an abundance of fresh food may need only an omega-3 supplement.

High-quality capsules of both varieties of omegas can be purchased from Nordic Naturals (call 800-662-2544 or visit *www.nordicnaturals.com*)...or your health-care provider can provide you with Pharmax products. Many adequate forms are available from other retail providers.

•**Eat lots of dark green, leafy vegetables,** the darker the better (kale is at the top of the list).

•**Wear UV-protected sunglasses,** but be sure the lenses are amber-orange.

Reason: Amber-orange lenses protect eyes from the blue end of the light spectrum—a risk for AMD.

•**If you smoke, give it up.** Dr. Mogk says that smoking has been proven to be associated with AMD. It's one more addition to the long list of reasons why people should not smoke.

Sunglasses: 100% UV Protection Isn't Enough

Yasmin S. Bradfield, MD, assistant professor, department of ophthalmology and visual sciences, University of Wisconsin, Madison, and pediatric ophthalmologist.

Andrew L. Rubman, ND, director, Southbury Clinic for Traditional Medicines, Southbury, Connecticut.

While sunglasses have long set fashion trends, style is actually low on the list of reasons to wear them. Just as excessive exposure to the sun's UV rays can harm your skin, it can also cause trouble for your eyes.

Yasmin S. Bradfield, MD, is assistant professor of ophthalmology and visual sciences at the University of Wisconsin, Madison, and a pediatric ophthalmologist. We spoke with her about the importance of sun protection for your eyes.

Dr. Bradfield said that while the data linking cataracts and macular degeneration with UVA and UVB light are not conclusive, experts in the visual field believe that these rays are definitely a factor. Furthermore, extreme exposure, such as skiing without protection on a sunny day, can trigger a type of short-lived eye "sunburn" known as *photokeratitis*, or snow blindness. Consequently, the experts recommend *always* wearing the right sunglasses when you are outside.

Our medical expert, Andrew L. Rubman, ND, has one small deviation from this rule: He recommends getting 10 to 15 minutes a day of unfiltered sunlight to produce enough vitamin D, which helps to keep bones and teeth strong and helps the pineal gland, a member of the endocrine system located in the head, produce adequate levels of melatonin for the prevention of seasonal affective disorder (SAD). The best time for this sun exposure is in the morning.

THE RIGHT GLASSES

Once you have had your daily dose of sunlight, the right sunglasses to protect your eyes are those that are polarized and offer 100% UV protection. Dr. Bradfield says that this guarantees protection from both types of UV rays. Polarized lenses protect your eyes from extraneous light, which is light that is reflected off surfaces, such as the hood of a car or a lake. However, keep in mind that polarized lenses can also reduce visibility of some electronic screens, including, perhaps, those on your car's dashboard.

IMPORTANT AT EVERY AGE

Children also need to protect their eyes from the sun, especially kids who demonstrate that they are light sensitive by squinting frequently or covering their eyes in bright light. Light sensitivity is more prevalent in light-eyed children because, says Dr. Bradfield, lighter eyes have less pigment in the layer of the eye behind the retina (the choroid) that absorbs UV light.

Children who are extremely light sensitive should see a pediatric ophthalmologist for a complete evaluation. Their sensitivity could indicate glaucoma, which even very young children can develop—especially if it runs in the family. In some cases, further steps may be necessary to prevent the disease from causing blindness.

Dr. Bradfield doesn't worry about polarized lenses for children, but she says that the sunglasses they wear should provide complete UV protection. Because many young children (and some grown-ups) don't like wearing sunglasses, she says broad-brimmed hats are also an effective way to protect your eyes.

Best Ways to Heal Dry Eyes

Stefano Barabino, MD, research fellow, ophthalmology, Harvard University, Cambridge, Massachusetts.
Andrew L. Rubman, ND, director, Southbury Clinic for Traditional Medicines, Southbury, Connecticut.

We tell our children to dry their eyes after they have been crying, but for more than 10 million Americans—mostly women—dry eyes are the problem that is causing itchiness and constant pain. If left untreated, dry eye syndrome (technically called *keratoconjunctivitis sicca*) can cause scarring of the cornea and even lead to blindness.

ABOUT YOUR TEARS

Healthy tears are made up of three layers: The outer lipid layer prevents evaporation…the second provides antibodies, salinity and acidity to the cornea…and the inner layer contains mucus that coats the cornea (the better for sticking).

Although aging eye glands are the most frequent culprits in dry eye syndrome, it can also result from several chronic diseases and autoimmune disorders that affect tear production, including rheumatoid arthritis, lupus and Sjögren's syndrome, as well as some allergies.

Dry eyes can also be a side effect of laser surgery, a procedure that involves cutting the nerve of the cornea, which disrupts tear production. Additionally, certain medications, including diuretics, beta-blockers, antihistamines, antianxiety and antidepression drugs, can cause dry eye. (Once you stop taking the medication, dry eye problems usually go away.)

RESEARCH HORIZON

Although dry eye syndrome is largely incurable, there is movement on the research and treatment front. We talked with ophthalmologist Stefano Barabino, MD, who is a specialist in dry eye and currently on a research fellowship at Harvard University. He explains that there is exciting new research that is revealing more precisely what the syndrome is. The long-held belief about dry eye is that one simply does not have enough tears or that they evaporate too quickly. Now, though, it appears that the syndrome frequently involves inflammation as well, and that it affects both the tear glands and the surface of the eyeball. Therefore, continues Dr. Barabino, current treatment research is focused on therapies that work to diminish inflammation, which in turn leads to an improvement in symptoms.

TREATMENT OPTIONS

●**Inflammation.** Before discussing the treatment options, Dr. Barabino stresses that anyone with dry eye must first go to an ophthalmologist to determine what is causing the problem. Treatment methodology is determined by the underlying cause.

The drug *cyclosporine* (Restasis), is designed specifically to treat inflammation, and it seems to help many of these patients. A simpler approach is one that Dr. Barabino and his colleagues tried in Italy. They gave supplements of the anti-inflammatory essential fatty acid omega-6 to patients who had inflammation. (Although they used omega-6 alone, he suggests that Americans take a balanced combination of omega-3 and omega-6 because of the common dietary imbalance here where omega-6 vastly outnumbers omega-3.)

Our medical expert, Andrew L. Rubman, ND, gives another important piece of advice on how to help reduce inflammation, and that is to improve your immune function. This is accomplished by taking an antioxidant supplement and an additional dose of selenium. Selenium, once plentiful in the American diet, has been lost due to modern fertilization and farming techniques. Dr. Rubman recommends 80 to 100 micrograms of selenium a day, which you can get as part of a general supplement. Check the labels.

●**Eye infection.** Patients with an infection of the eyelid glands, called *meibomianitis,* can use antibiotic drops. This requires cleaning the gland daily to remove the lipid buildup. Over time, the antibiotic generally improves the patient's condition, but Dr. Barabino stresses that these patients remain prone to recurrence. Patients who have insufficient tear production have the option of plugging the eye ducts that normally drain tears. Successful for about 90% of patients, the plugs can remain in place indefinitely—but this is not advisable for patients with considerable eye inflammation.

WHAT YOU CAN DO

As a general guideline, Dr. Barabino advises relieving discomfort with frequent use of artificial tears (avoid the drops that reduce redness—they may further dry out your eyes), keeping humidifiers going in your home and avoiding smoke, dust, pollen and the like. Certain activities, including using a computer, watching TV, driving and reading, tend to reduce blinking. This aggravates dry eye even more, so remind yourself to blink regularly in these situations.

For severe cases, your eye doctor can give you a special prescription for "moisture chamber" goggles. Similar to ski goggles, they wrap around completely, protecting your eyes from outside forces, such as the wind and allergens, and they keep natural moisture in. Although they won't make a fashion statement, anyone who wears them will value the comfort that they provide.

Brush Up On Health

Robert Bonow, MD, past president of the American Heart Association, Dallas, Goldberg Distinguished Professor of Medicine at Northwestern University Feinberg School of Medicine and chief of the division of cardiology, Northwestern Memorial Hospital, Chicago.

Dentists have always encouraged us to brush and floss for strong teeth and a pretty smile. Now research linking gum disease with hardening of the arteries suggests that good dental hygiene may do more than just protect your teeth and gums—it may also prolong your life.

RECENT RESEARCH

In a University of Minnesota study of more than 711 people with no history of heart disease, researchers found a direct relationship between missing teeth (an indicator of serious gum disease) and arteriosclerosis—plaque buildup in their carotid (neck) arteries. What's more, the American Academy of Periodontology recently reported that people with periodontal disease—a chronic infection of the gums—are nearly two times as likely to have a fatal heart attack as those with healthy gums.

THE INFLAMMATION CONNECTION

What's the connection? Inflammation, says Robert Bonow, MD, past president of the American Heart Association in Dallas, Goldberg Distinguished Professor of Medicine at Northwestern University Feinberg School of Medicine and chief of the division of cardiology at Northwestern Memorial Hospital in Chicago. "Anything that causes low-grade inflammation, such as chronic gum disease, may accelerate arteriosclerosis," he says. While more research is needed, a leading theory is that enzymes and other debris thrown off by bacteria associated with dental plaque—a marker of gum disease—can enter the bloodstream through inflamed gums and then produce compounds that make blood platelets stickier and more likely to clot, contributing to hardening arteries, heart attack and stroke.

The good news is that this is a risk factor you can control. "It's a good idea to take care of your teeth anyway. And if it helps your heart, too, all the better," says Dr. Bonow.

BRUSH UP ON ORAL HEALTH

To help keep your heart (and your teeth) healthy, practice good dental hygiene daily. *The following steps can help...*

•**Brush, floss and rinse.** The earliest, most mild form of periodontal disease is gingivitis—red, swollen gums that bleed easily. Gingivitis is usually caused by inadequate dental care and is reversible. Since gingivitis begins with plaque (the sticky, colorless film that forms on teeth), your first line of defense is brushing twice a day, flossing once a day and using an antibacterial/antifungal mouthwash like Listerine as directed.

•**Share your medical information.** Certain medications, such as blood pressure pills and oral contraceptives, can increase your risk for periodontal disease. Share all drug information with your dentist.

•**Go to a pro.** Have your teeth professionally cleaned twice a year. People with heart disease should have a professional cleaning every three months.

•**Butt out.** Smoking or chewing tobacco increases your risk for both periodontal and heart diseases. Ask your doctor about ways to quit.

•**Know the warning signs.** It is possible to have periodontal disease without any symptoms, so visit your dentist regularly. But you should be aware of the warning signs of gum disease. *According to the American Dental Association, if you have any of the following symptoms, make an appointment with your dentist...*

•Gums that bleed easily.

•Red, swollen, tender gums.

•Gums that have pulled away from any of your teeth.

•Persistent bad breath or a bad taste in your mouth.

•Permanent teeth that are loose or separating from your gums.

•Any change in the way your teeth meet when you bite.

•Any change in the fit of partial dentures.

For your overall health, brush up—don't brush off—your teeth.

Sleep Your Way to Healthy Teeth

Andrew L. Rubman, ND, director, Southbury Clinic for Traditional Medicines, Southbury, Connecticut.

Allen D. Samuelson, DDS, practices general dentistry in Chapel Hill, North Carolina. He is a clinical associate professor and director, department of dental ecology, School of Dentistry, University of North Carolina at Chapel Hill.

Nobody likes going to the dentist, and some people fail to seek the care that they vitally need due to nervousness or fear. The good news is that there is an alternative—sedation dentistry. Treatment takes place after you have taken medication that makes you calm and relaxed.

To learn more about this approach, we contacted Allen Samuelson, DDS, clinical associate professor in the School of Dentistry at the University of North Carolina at Chapel Hill. He told us that while it is most often used with adults and children who are especially fearful of dental treatment, virtually anyone can opt for sedation dentistry. People with busy schedules may want to get extended treatments over with in a single sedated visit rather than multiple appointments. Sedation can be beneficial if you have high blood pressure or other heart-related issues, because heart rate, pulse and blood pressure rise when you are nervous.

DIFFERENT TYPES OF SEDATION

According to Dr. Samuelson, there are three types of sedation, although in sedation dentistry, usually only the first type—conscious sedation—is used.

• **Conscious sedation** is most commonly administered by mouth or inhalation. When under conscious sedation, all protective reflexes (swallowing, coughing, etc.) are preserved, and a person is aroused relatively easily after the procedure by voice or other external stimulation.

• **Deep sedation** is when the protective reflexes are blunted and their function is unpredictable. Basic coughing and swallowing may or may not be present. A person cannot be aroused easily by voice or other external stimuli.

• **General anesthesia** is where all protective reflexes are absent. In this state, a person is unable to maintain an effective airway, and coughing and swallowing reflexes are no longer present.

Sedation dentistry usually implies conscious sedation only, explains Dr. Samuelson. This technique controls fear and anxiety, and is typically administered along with a local anesthetic to relieve pain. It can be used for most procedures (fillings, extractions, root canals, etc.).

Deep sedation and general anesthesia are reserved for the more complicated dental procedures, such as extensive jaw surgery. These anesthetics are administered intravenously or via inhalation.

BENEFITS OF SEDATION DENTISTRY

According to Dr. Samuelson, sedation dentistry is generally used...

• **To control anxiety,** fear or phobias about visiting the dentist.

• **To alleviate fear-induced cardiac symptoms,** (such as angina or hypertension).

• **When local anesthetics are not recommended** (for example, with bleeding disorders, such as hemophilia).

• **In cognitively impaired patients** (sedation may reduce the combativeness of people with dementia).

• **To diminish a person's movement** (so that the dentist can perform more precise procedures).

SAFETY CONCERNS

Conscious sedation is normally very safe, says Dr. Samuelson. Of course, special care must be taken with very young children, older people and those with serious health conditions, such as advanced cancer or AIDS. Whatever your age and health status, make sure that your dentist always performs a thorough review of your medical history prior to conscious sedation or any other procedure involving anesthetics.

The safety concerns include over-sedation and loss of airway, which in extreme cases can result in loss of oxygen, disability or even death. Dr. Samuelson adds that depending on the agent used, reversal drugs can be administered if a person is over-sedated.

CHOOSING A DENTIST

If you think sedation dentistry may be right for you, it's even more important than usual to choose the right dentist. Before undergoing treatment, ask about a dentist's education and experience—if he/she has done a residency in dental anesthesiology, how much training and clinical experience he has in sedation dentistry, and when and where he received it. Dr. Samuelson notes that some dentists have postgraduate training as general practice residents in hospitals and obtain sedation training in this way.

Because they demand considerably more extensive skill and experience, deep sedation and general anesthesia (in contrast to sedation dentistry or conscious sedation) are performed only by well-trained oral surgeons or anesthesiologists in very safe and controlled environments. According to the American Dental Association (ADA), these techniques are beyond the scope of predoctoral and continuing education programs, and they require specific advanced education, such as completion of an ADA accredited postdoctoral training program.

With conscious sedation, people who experience fear and anxiety about going to the dentist can feel more comfortable about seeking care. Still, concludes Dr. Samuelson, the ultimate goal should be to wean yourself from sedation and instead establish a trusting relationship with your dentist. Relaxation techniques, such as meditation and yoga, may also be helpful.

NATURAL HELPERS

Our medical expert, Andrew L. Rubman, ND, adds that there are natural interventions that can be used to decrease the side effects experienced during recovery from anesthesia, such as headaches, nausea and mental and physical confusion. Often, supplementation with a multiple-B vitamin and a well-absorbed vitamin B-12 can help speed recovery from anesthesia. Additionally, the Bs may lessen the fear experienced in anticipation of the procedure due to their mood-modulation ability. These natural medications should be taken for at least three days before the procedure and prescribed and monitored by a consulting naturopathic physician.

info For more information, contact the American Dental Association at *www.ada.org*.

How to Get a Whiter, Brighter Smile

Edward J. Swift, Jr., DMD, professor and chair, department of operative dentistry, University of North Carolina at Chapel Hill.

A dazzling smile packed with pearly whites seems within reach, thanks to the array of tooth-whitening products available in drugstores and dentists' offices.

Which one is right for you? Are these products safe? Are they effective?

According to Edward J. Swift, Jr., DMD, professor and chair of the department of operative dentistry at the University of North Carolina at Chapel Hill, tooth-whitening products are generally easy to use, and most are safe and effective. The one you choose should depend on how much whitening you need.

When you have darkly stained teeth, dentist-supervised products are best, recommends Dr. Swift. If you just need to lighten teeth a little, it's fine to use an over-the-counter (OTC) product. He also sometimes suggests that patients use OTC whitening products as follow-ups to whitening by the dentist.

WHITENING OPTIONS

There are three basic alternatives for basic whitening: Strips available OTC or from your dentist...custom-fitted trays available from the dentist...and in-office whitening.

As a rule, it's safer to get whitening products from your dentist than to purchase them OTC at your local drugstore, says Dr. Swift. He says that products from the dentist contain higher percentages of peroxide and produce faster and more dramatic whitening results. Some people who use at-home bleaching products fail to read all the directions and then end up with spotted teeth.

Helpful: Be sure to "trace the strip" into the spaces between the teeth so that you don't get a "picket fence" effect.

The thin, flexible strips are coated with a tooth-whitening gel that contains peroxide, and they conform to the shape of your teeth. By keeping the whitening gel on your teeth for 30 minutes a day for seven days, the strips attack stain buildup below tooth enamel to visually whiten the teeth. When you want to speed up the process, you can use two strips back-to-back for 30 minutes each, or use a second box of whitening strips after the first.

There is substantial research indicating that OTC tooth-whitening strips are safe and effective. However, Dr. Swift has some concerns about the newer paint-on products that apply whitening material to teeth much like polish on nails. Because they are so new, he advises waiting—until these products are more thoroughly researched.

In contrast to the strips, Dr. Swift says that custom-fitted trays hold the whitening material in place and fit very well. However, both are safe and effective tooth-whitening options. You simply have to ask yourself if you are more comfortable with strips that you put on once or twice a day, or custom-fitted trays that you apply at night.

SEE A PROFESSIONAL

Another option is to have your teeth professionally whitened in the dentist's office. Products used in the office have higher concentrations of peroxide, ranging from 15% to 35%. These are sometimes used with a special light, which is said to accelerate the whitening process. Before the whitening material or light is applied, the gums are protected with a rubber dam or gel. The process lasts about an hour. A higher concentration of peroxide means that whitening is faster and more effective—and it's also safer because it is applied under your trained dentist's care. However, it is also considerably more expensive.

WHAT TO WATCH OUT FOR

Although tooth-whitening products generally receive your dentist's approval, there are a few points to keep in mind before you decide to move ahead...

•**No product will bleach your fillings or crowns,** warns Dr. Swift. Whitening products only help to whiten natural teeth. They do not whiten veneers, crowns, caps, fillings or dentures. They should also not be used if you wear any kind of braces.

•**A controversial factor is using bright lights in tooth whitening.** No one has ever shown that these lights, used during in-office procedures, do anything, says Dr. Swift. Until research proves otherwise, he tends to discourage his patients from seeking out this option. Whitening products using lasers are currently not on the American Dental Association's (ADA) list of accepted products.

•**Most dentists once believed that people whose teeth were stained gray, yellow or brown** from the use of the antibiotic tetracycline were just stuck with them. Now, the dental bleaches can make some headway against tetracycline staining, says Dr. Swift. However, it requires time and patience and, generally, daily use for six to nine months. This can become expensive.

•**Many people experience some degree of tooth sensitivity** or gum irritation when using whitening products. In most cases, this is mild and transient, says Dr. Swift, but if it becomes troublesome, stop using the product and be sure to consult your dentist.

•**As for tooth-whitening toothpastes,** according to the ADA, whitening toothpastes in the ADA seal of acceptance program have special chemical or polishing agents that provide additional stain removal. Unlike bleaches, these products do not alter the intrinsic color of teeth.

•**According to the ADA, you may want to speak with your dentist if any side effects become bothersome.** For example, teeth can become sensitive during the period you are using the bleaching solution. In many cases, this sensitivity is temporary and should lessen once the treatment is finished.

Some people also experience soft-tissue irritation—either from a tray that does not fit properly or from solution that may come in contact with the tissue.

Info For more information, contact the American Dental Association at *www.ada.org*.

Latest News on Tooth Whiteners And Oral Cancer

Van B. Haywood, DMD, professor, department of oral rehabilitation, School of Dentistry at the Medical College of Georgia, Augusta.

Tooth whiteners have become increasingly popular in recent years, tripling in use since 2001. Yet a study of 19 oral cancer patients at Georgetown University Hospital in Washington, DC, has raised questions about their safety, pointing to a possible link between tooth whiteners and oral cancer. Cause for alarm? Or alarmist?

Given the very small size of the study and the uncertainty of the connection, Van B. Haywood, DMD, a professor in the department of oral rehabilitation at the School of Dentistry at the Medical College of Georgia in Augusta, believes that it is alarmist.

ABOUT THE STUDY

A team of Georgetown head and neck surgeons conducted a retrospective study of 19 people of all ages with oral cancers. These abnormal growths typically occur in individuals over age 45 after years of smoking or drinking—but researchers discovered that six out of the 19 patients developed oral cancer before age 40. Two of these had used tooth-whitening products, did not smoke or drink more heavily than the others and had more advanced cancer.

The theorized culprit is the hydrogen peroxide used in the tooth-whitening kits, both the over-the-counter kits and those offered by dentists. Hydrogen peroxide has caused cancer in rodent studies. Ideally, the whitening gel that contains the peroxide comes into contact only with tooth enamel, not the soft tissue in the mouth. Researchers theorize that hydrogen peroxide may leak from the trays that hold the whitening material in place, triggering an inflammatory response in soft tissue and the release of free radical compounds that are implicated in cancer. Trays that are custom-fitted by a dentist most likely fit better and are thus less likely to leak.

NO DISCERNIBLE LINK

The limitations of the study: It was very small, it did not compare cancer patients with controls and, because it was presented at a conference, it did not undergo the rigorous peer review demanded of a journal article. The researchers themselves acknowledge that further study is needed to establish any conclusive link.

In the meantime, the American Dental Association has investigated the question of hydrogen peroxide and oral cancer risk and found no cause for concern. Although some peroxides are potential carcinogens, they do not include those used at relatively low concentrations in the tooth-whitening kits, according to Dr. Haywood. Moreover, toothpastes that contain peroxide (such as Mentadent) are considered safe for lifetime use by the US Food and Drug Administration (FDA).

Of course, there are proper safety precautions to take with any dental intervention. Before using a tooth-whitening product, always consult your dentist. While the custom-fitted trays that hold the whitening material in place generally fit well, stop using the product and speak to your dentist if you are having any problems with leakage, tooth sensitivity or gum irritation.

info For more information, contact the American Dental Association at *www.ada.org*.

17

Protect Your Skin And Hair

Surprising Soothers for Sunburn

When it's summertime, most people like to soak up some rays. The problem is that we occasionally get carried away and soak up one ray too many, ending up with a painful sunburn.

According to Jamison Starbuck, ND, a naturopathic physician in family practice in Missoula, Montana and a past president of The American Association of Naturopathic Physicians, your best bet is to avoid getting a sunburn in the first place.

Helpful: Spend less time in the direct rays and more time in the shade. If you're heading out at midday, be sure to cover up with a hat and shirt. Light-colored clothing is best, since it reflects the sun most effectively.

Dr. Starbuck is not a fan of sunscreen, and says if you must use it, to do so in limited amounts. In addition to containing powerful chemicals, she notes that sunscreen blocks the absorption of vitamin D—a vital nutrient that many Americans don't have enough of.

TAMING A SUNBURN

If, despite your best efforts, you still end up getting burned, don't despair. *Dr. Starbuck recommends the following…*

• **Calendula** (made from marigolds) is one of her favorite sunburn remedies. Naturally anti-inflammatory and antimicrobial, calendula softens and heals burned, dry and itchy skin, and generates new skin cells. High-quality calendula is available in gels and salves from top providers, such as Herb Pharm and Eclectic Institute. Apply locally as needed.

• **Aloe.** Dr. Starbuck also highly recommends aloe vera gel. Aloe is so effective in relieving pain and inflammation that researchers are investigating its use in treating radiation burns

Jamison Starbuck, ND, a naturopathic physician in family practice and a guest lecturer at the University of Montana, both in Missoula. She is a past president of The American Association of Naturopathic Physicians.

associated with cancer therapy. To make your own sunburn salve from an aloe plant, snip off a two-inch leaf end, slit it open and lightly apply the soothing gel to burned skin. Fresh aloe is best since its healing properties degrade within hours, but if fresh is not available, aloe gel from the health-food store is a good alternative.

When should you use calendula versus aloe? Aloe gel is best when applied as soon as possible after the burn…while calendula is best for healing previously burned tissue that may be discolored or scarred.

- **Warm shower.** To draw out the heat of a sunburn, Dr. Starbuck suggests a warm shower or bath. The warm water stimulates circulation to the tissue while hydrating it. This stimulates the natural healing process and lessens the perceived feeling of heat.

- **Cool vinegar.** Dr. Starbuck notes that some people find cool vinegar compresses helpful.

- **Aspirin.** If the discomfort gets really bad, Dr. Starbuck prefers aspirin to ibuprofen and acetaminophen because it is more natural and less distressing to the kidneys and liver.

Beware the signs of sun poisoning. If you experience signs of a severe sunburn, such as blistering, chills, fever or a rash, see your health-care provider.

The sun provides many health benefits. Like so many other things in life, moderation is key. In excess, the benefits are overcome by the dangers.

Spots, Tags, Bumps. Are They Skin Cancer?

Barney J. Kenet, MD, dermatologist, New York-Presbyterian Hospital–Weill Cornell Medical Center, New York City, author of *Saving Your Skin* (Four Walls Eight Windows) and cofounder of the American Melanoma Foundation.

As we grow older, various lumps, bumps and spots (skin tags, wartlike growths, brown or black raised spots) come to mar the flawless skin of our youth. Dermatologists sometimes refer to these as the "barnacles of aging." The million-dollar question

that everybody asks is, "When is a bump just a bump—and when is it a sign of skin cancer?"

THREE TYPES OF SKIN CANCER

Skin cancer is the most common type of cancer in the US, with more than one million new cases diagnosed each year, observes Barney J. Kenet, MD, a New York City dermatologist who specializes in skin cancer and is the author of *Saving Your Skin*.

Of the new cases each year…

- **80% are basal cell carcinoma.**
- **16% are squamous cell carcinoma.**
- **4% are melanoma.**

Basal cell and squamous cell carcinomas have a cure rate of more than 95%. However, melanoma is a different story. This deadly cancer can spread quickly to organs, such as the liver and lungs, and it accounts for more than three out of four deaths from all skin cancers.

Because even melanoma can be completely cured with early diagnosis and treatment, it's essential to learn the warning signs of skin cancer.

BASAL CELL CARCINOMA

This most common form of skin cancer first appears as small and occasionally discolored, fleshy nodules or bumps on frequently sun-exposed areas of the body, such as the hands, head or neck. If the lesions occur on the trunk, they are generally flat instead of raised. Slow-growing basal cell carcinomas may take as long as months or even years to reach a diameter of half an inch. Yet this does not mean you should ignore them. Left untreated, they may bleed and crust over again and again, and after years, a neglected lesion can eventually penetrate the bone beneath.

SQUAMOUS CELL CARCINOMA

The second most common skin cancer may first appear as a pink, tan or brown bump or patch on a sun-exposed area of the skin, or it can develop out of an *actinic keratosis* (a precancerous condition of rough red or brown scaly patches). Squamous cell tumors are also relatively slow to spread—however, they do grow more quickly than basal cell carcinomas.

This cancer is sometimes difficult to detect in its early stages. At first, squamous cell carcinomas are firm to the touch. As they begin to grow, the tumors form a central crust, which becomes ulcerated and results in the surrounding skin becoming red and inflamed.

Both basal cell and squamous cell cancers most often occur in fair-skinned people who do not tan easily.

MELANOMA

Melanoma is more common in fair-skinned people. However, it shows up more frequently than basal and squamous cell carcinomas in people of color. This virulent disease is on the rise, affecting a greater number of people every year. Those who have a large number of freckles and moles—especially unusual-looking moles that have uneven textures, margins or coloration that change suddenly in sensitivity, appearance or size—are at the highest risk. Unlike basal and squamous cell cancers, melanoma most commonly occurs on parts of the body that are less frequently exposed to the sun, including the back, trunk, arms and legs.

According to the American Academy of Dermatology, you should see your dermatologist immediately if you see any of the following changes in a mole or pigmented area (the A-B-C-Ds of melanoma)…

• **Asymmetry,** when one-half of the mole does not match the other.

• **Border irregularity,** when edges are either ragged or notched.

• **Color varied from one area to another** in shades of brown, tan or black, or sometimes red, blue or white.

• **Diameter of greater than 6 millimeters** (the size of the top of a pencil eraser).

SIGNS AND SYMPTOMS OF SKIN CANCER

Skin cancers do not all look the same. Some are raised, others are flat…some bumps look pale, others are colored.

Warning signs include…

• **A new growth on the skin that does not heal.**

• **Any change in the size or color of a mole or other pigmented spot.**

• **Scaliness, oozing, bleeding or change in the appearance of a bump or nodule.**

• **Tenderness, itchiness or pain in a growth on the skin.**

VIGILANCE PAYS

Now that you know what to look for, conduct a thorough skin self-exam once a month. Using a full-length as well as a handheld mirror, search for any new blemishes or alterations in existing growths. If you detect something suspicious, see your doctor. Remember to look in places that are not usually exposed to the sun, such as in between toes and the soles of feet.

If you're age 40 or older, also visit a dermatologist once a year for a full skin exam, in which you will be checked from head to toe. Between ages 20 and 40, have your skin examined every three years. Although it is rare, Dr. Kenet says that every once in a while a seemingly benign skin growth, such as a freckle, turns out to be an indication of skin cancer. Only your dermatologist can make this evaluation.

Basic rule: Early detection and treatment are the secrets to a complete cure.

info American Academy of Dermatology, *www.aad.org.*

American Melanoma Foundation, *www.melanomafoundation.org.*

National Cancer Institute, *www.cancer.gov.*

New! Topical Cream Treats Skin Cancer

Nelson Lee Novick, MD, FACP, FAAD, clinical professor of dermatology at Mount Sinai School of Medicine in New York City, and author of *You Can Look Younger at Any Age.* Henry Holt.

People who have basal cell carcinoma—the most common form of skin cancer—now have an alternative to getting surgery. In 2004, the US Food and Drug Administration (FDA) announced the approval of *imiquimod* (Aldara) topical cream for the treatment of certain superficial basal cell skin cancers on the body, neck, arms and legs.

To learn more about this alternative, we consulted Nelson Lee Novick, MD, FACP, FAAD,

263

clinical professor of dermatology at Mount Sinai School of Medicine in New York City.

He told us that while using a cream sounds great, it is not quite as simple as one would hope. In contrast to a 10-minute in-office minor surgical procedure for most superficial basal cell skin cancers, Aldara cream must be applied a minimum of three to five times weekly for as long as 12 to 16 weeks to come close to a similar cure rate, and resulting skin irritation can take longer to heal.

ABOUT THE RESEARCH

According to Dr. Novick, imiquimod was originally approved to treat genital warts, and is in a class of drugs known as *topical immunomodulators* (TIMs). It works by stimulating the local production of immune system chemicals, one of which is *interferon*, which in turn stimulate the immune system to attack the tumor and lead to its destruction.

The safety and effectiveness of Aldara cream in treating basal cell carcinoma were established in studies funded by its manufacturer, Graceway Pharmaceuticals in Bristol, Tennessee (*www.gracewaypharma.com*).

Researchers found that...

• **In two double-blind controlled studies of 364 people,** 75% had no evidence of skin cancer 12 weeks after completing treatment.

• **In a separate long-term study of 182 patients,** 79% had no evidence of superficial basal cell carcinoma two years after they had finished treatment.

The downside? Local skin reactions are common with Aldara cream. Most people experience redness, swelling, a sore or blister, peeling, itching or burning at the treatment site. The cream may also aggravate inflammatory skin conditions, and sun exposure (including sunlamps and tanning beds) should be avoided during use to prevent heightened sunburn susceptibility. Do not apply to the head, face or anogenital area.

SURGERY OR CREAM?

Dr. Novick observes that he would personally prefer the shorter two-week healing time of a minor surgical procedure to the protracted treatment and skin irritation associated with the cream. But while Aldara is not for everyone, it represents another option for those who refuse surgery or for people in whom even minor surgery is not recommended because of other medical conditions.

Aldara cream may also prove useful as an adjunct to surgery, to increase the odds of a complete cure and to reduce the chances of skin cancer recurrence. It is available by prescription only. However, it is not recommended for people who are immunocompromised because its safety for this group has not been established yet. It is also not recommended until the skin is completely healed from any previous drug or surgical treatment. Aldara cream has the potential to exacerbate inflammatory conditions of the skin.

A Not-So-Sunny Side of Sunblock

Joseph Mercola, DO, an osteopathic physician and editor of the health newsletter Mercola.com.

Andrew L. Rubman, ND, director, Southbury Clinic for Traditional Medicines, Southbury, Connecticut.

Given that just about everyone advises slathering on sunscreen before heading out to enjoy the summer sun, it's surprising to hear someone say that sunscreen is bad. But that's exactly what Joseph Mercola, DO, tells readers of his health newsletter titled Mercola.com. *We gave Dr. Mercola a call to find out his reasons for his unpopular stand...*

Sunscreens largely block UVB rays through the use of powerful chemicals, such as *octyl methoxycinnamate* (OMC) and *titanium dioxide*. These chemicals are much too powerful to be healthy for you, says Dr. Mercola. Although there are no definitive studies yet to prove this, he says it is common sense to be concerned about these topical chemicals that are absorbed by your skin in much the same way medicated skin patches are absorbed.

Furthermore, Dr. Mercola is against sunscreen because we need sunshine on our skin. Vitamin D from sunshine enables us to absorb calcium. Dr. Mercola says that vitamin D is also an anti-cancer vitamin, especially for colon, breast and prostate cancers, because it helps prevent abnormal cell proliferation. And the best place to get vitamin D is from the sun.

SUN SAFETY

Even so, Dr. Mercola has important advice for handling the sun. One type of ultraviolet light, UVA, is what causes melanoma, the most dangerous of all skin cancers. Instead of worrying about sunscreen, which cannot block most UVA, Dr. Mercola suggests you be sure you are getting enough omega-3 oils.

Several studies demonstrate a link between melanoma and lack of omega-3 oils. One, from Australia, showed a 40% drop in melanoma rates among people who regularly ate fish with omega-3 oils (good sources are wild salmon, mackerel and sardines).

Best bets: Iceland Health (*www.iceland health.com*), which comes in soft gels...and Carlson (*www.carlsonlabs.com*), which also comes in soft gels. One teaspoon or one soft gel a day does the trick.

Dr. Mercola also suggests careful exposure to the sun and to always avoid getting sunburned. Start your sun exposure for a few minutes each day, early in the season and early or late in the day, to build up tolerance. Throughout the warm-weather season, continue to avoid direct exposure from 10 am to 4 pm, wear a broad-brimmed hat to protect your face as well as long sleeves to cover your arms.

If you're at the pool or beach, be sure to sit in the shade.

If you're stuck in the sun for a prolonged period of time and can't go for cover, our medical expert, Andrew L. Rubman, ND, says "sunscreen beats sun damage," so use an SPF-40 or better to protect yourself.

Most important: Become aware of when your skin starts to feel even a tiny bit uncomfortable or warm. That's your cue that damage is starting and it's time for shade.

Doctors' Top Ideas For Skin Care

Annie B. Bond, founder and CEO of Green Chi Cafe, *www.greenchicafe.com*, and author of *Clean & Green*. Ceres.

Nick Lowe, MD, consultant dermatologist, University College, and director, Cranley Clinic, both in London. He is also clinical professor of dermatology, UCLA School of Medicine, Los Angeles.

Andrew L. Rubman, ND, director, Southbury Clinic for Traditional Medicines, Southbury, Connecticut.

Michael Traub, ND, past president of the American Association of Naturopathic Physicians, and naturopathic physician in private practice, Kailua Kona, Hawaii.

Flaking, scaling and itching are especially common skin problems in the winter months, when humidity is low. But as we grow older, many of us suffer from dry skin year-round. To learn how to help prevent this condition and to keep skin soft and supple, we spoke with Nick Lowe, MD, consultant dermatologist at the Cranley Clinic in London and clinical professor of dermatology at the UCLA School of Medicine in Los Angeles.

A DERMATOLOGIST'S POINT OF VIEW

Dry skin is the result of a defect in the barrier of the outer or top layer of skin, says Dr. Lowe. Factors such as genetics, overuse of soaps and detergents, aging and a dry environment can all damage this vital skin barrier.

Left untreated, dry skin can lead to more serious dermatitis or eczema (inflammatory skin conditions). *Fortunately, a number of simple strategies can help prevent or relieve dry skin...*

●**Throw out the harsh soaps and detergents,** advises Dr. Lowe, and use moisturizing soaps and body washes. Soaps are drying when they do not contain moisturizers.

●**It's best to avoid long, hot baths when you have dry skin.** These might feel good at the time, but soaking in hot water removes natural oils from the skin, and usually leaves you feeling dry and itchy. Instead, Dr. Lowe suggests short (five- to 10-minute) lukewarm showers.

●**Always apply moisturizer after bathing,** showering or washing your hands. For the best results, Dr. Lowe suggests a cream, lotion or ointment on skin when it is still moist. Damp skin is best able to absorb and hold moisture.

265

• **If you have dry or sensitive skin,** he says to avoid moisturizers that contain fragrances. These can irritate skin.

• **Don't forget the sunscreen.** Use it every day, year-round, advises Dr. Lowe. He warns that sunburn damages the skin barrier. For best results, he recommends a separate moisturizer and a dedicated sunscreen (one that is labeled and marketed as a sunscreen, as opposed to a sunscreen that is only an added ingredient to a moisturizer).

Also: Avoid the peak hours of sunshine—10 am to 4 pm—when UV rays are most harmful. It is helpful to wear a hat and buy clothing with UV protection for the times you must be in direct sunlight.

• **If you develop severe dry skin** that does not respond to simple self-care, make an appointment to see your dermatologist.

THE NATUROPATHIC PERSPECTIVE

To improve dry skin, naturopathic doctors take an inside-out philosophy, favoring supplements such as omega-3 fatty acids, selenium and antioxidant vitamins and minerals. Good dietary sources of omega-3s include deepwater fish (such as wild salmon, mackerel and sardines), nuts, seeds and avocados.

Most of us don't get enough omega-3 fatty acids through our diets alone. Michael Traub, ND, past president of the American Association of Naturopathic Physicians and currently in private practice in Kailua Kona, Hawaii, recommends four capsules daily of a high-quality fish oil. He also says that it is essential to stay hydrated by drinking plenty of water, and suggests using a moisturizing cream (rather than a lotion) within three minutes after showering or bathing.

MOISTURIZER FAVORITES

Which moisturizer to go with? Many people prefer *squalane*, an ingredient in a number of high-end cosmetics that can also be purchased in its pure form and applied regularly with great results. Our medical expert, Andrew L. Rubman, ND, recommends the Mayumi brand from Japan, which is widely available in the United States and abroad.

One favorite moisturizer of Annie B. Bond, former executive producer of the on-line environmental network, Care2, is naturally hydrating aloe vera gel. She applies the gel straight to her skin or, to make it even more lubricating, adds pure vegetable glycerin (add about one-quarter of the amount of aloe used). Check out Bond's recipes for Satiny Skin Cream and Emollient Honey Bath—on Care2.com's Web site at *www.care2.com*.

Whatever skin you're in, keep in mind that this is your body's largest organ and may be the first to reflect your dietary indiscretions and nutritional deficiencies. As always, good health comes from the inside out.

info For more information, visit the American Academy of Dermatology's Web site at *www.aad.org*.

Stopping the Itch of Eczema

Amy Paller, MD, professor and chair, department of dermatology, professor of pediatrics at the Feinberg School of Medicine, Northwestern University, Chicago.

Andrew L. Rubman, ND, director, Southbury Clinic for Traditional Medicines, Southbury, Connecticut.

Jamison Starbuck, ND, a naturopathic physician practicing in Missoula, Montana. She is a past president of The American Association of Naturopathic Physicians (AANP). *www.naturopathic.org*.

Fifteen million Americans of all ages battle eczema, a chronic, itchy skin disease that typically appears on the insides of the elbows, the backs of the knees, the wrists and the face. The red, dry and scaly patches may be unsightly and uncomfortable, but eczema is not contagious.

WHAT CAUSES ECZEMA?

Eczema is an allergic disease. It often affects people who suffer from asthma and hay fever or who have family members who do. It also tends to run in families. Amy Paller, MD, chair of the dermatology department, and professor of dermatology and pediatrics at the Feinberg School of Medicine at Northwestern University in Chicago, says recent research suggests that people who have eczema have localized skin immune system problems.

When the immune system is "activated" by an agent it perceives to be foreign, the result, for those who are genetically predisposed to the disease, can be an outbreak of eczema.

WHAT PULLS THE TRIGGER?

According to Dr. Paller, eczema outbreaks may be triggered by any of the common "allergy" foods, such as dairy products, eggs, soy, wheat or peanuts. But figuring out if there is an allergen at fault can be very difficult. In infants, cow's milk may be an allergen. Certain environmental factors can cause outbreaks, too. Wool clothing, dust, animal dander, detergents and fragrances are typical environmental triggers. Stress is also an all-too-common trigger.

In women, eczema outbreaks can also result from changes in estrogen levels prior to menstruation, according to Dr. Jamison Starbuck, a naturopathic physician in Missoula, Montana, who herself has had eczema. Hormonal shifts can not only cause an eczema outbreak, she says, but can aggravate an existing one.

How can you combat this irritating ailment?

DETERMINE YOUR TRIGGERS

To manage eczema, you must first determine what your personal triggers are and then avoid them for a few weeks. Although Dr. Starbuck agrees that the "allergy foods" listed above can trigger eczema, she believes that there are what she calls the "big three" allergy foods, which are also often involved in eczema outbreaks. These include coffee…sugar…and chocolate. She reports that in her experience, simply avoiding the "big three" can be successful in eliminating symptoms.

Be alert as to when outbreaks occur. Did you experience an outbreak after playing with the neighbor's dog? Animal dander may be a trigger for you. After spending the afternoon in the park? Ragweed or other grasses could be the cause. After wearing a new sweater? You may be allergic to wool. Be particularly aware of reactions following stressful events.

SYMPTOM RELIEF:
HOW TO STOP THAT ITCH

Corticosteroid creams and ointments still remain the treatment of choice for eczema. In general they are effective and rarely cause any side effects when used appropriately and under a doctor's care. In the last few years, a new class of medications known as calcineurin inhibitors have offered an alternative to topical corticosteroids.

Calcineurin inhibitors, also used topically, may be safer than steroids, according to Dr. Paller, because they don't have most of the steroid side effects, such as thinning of the skin, and they can be safely applied around the eyes. They do, nevertheless, have their own share of side effects, including skin burning, itching and erythema (abnormal redness of the skin). Calcineurin inhibitors, however, are still relatively new, and Dr. Paller stresses that safety over decades of usage is still unknown.

SKIN SOOTHERS

As a first line of defense, Dr. Starbuck recommends natural lotions containing vitamin E, vitamin A or comfrey. She says they can soothe and calm the skin. Lotions containing calendula are helpful for some people, but others may find calendula irritating.

Bathing and moisturizing every day is essential for eczema sufferers. Bathe in lukewarm water, using a mild, nonirritating soap or no soap at all. Avoid antibacterial soaps, as they are particularly harsh. Dr. Starbuck uses a pure cucumber soap, but any vegetable-based soap is fine, she says. After a short bath, it is critical to liberally apply moisturizer on damp skin within a few minutes after coming out of the bath—to seal in the hydration provided by the bath itself. Avoid lotions that contain lanolin (which is made from wool).

SUPPLEMENT WELL

Our medical expert, Andrew L. Rubman, ND, adds that selenium supplementation—a mineral which is deficient in most American soils—is a good form of intervention for eczema.

A HEALTHY LIFESTYLE

Dr. Starbuck prescribes the following regimen to her patients with eczema. She has used it in treating her own eczema successfully for 20 years.

•**Recommendations for diet and nutrition.** Include at least two fruits and three vegetables a day in your diet (more is better)…avoid fried foods…use olive or canola oils to cook with and on salads…and avoid wheat. Lean meat is OK. Drink dandelion tea—it helps the liver process fats, which is good for the skin.

It's also important to drink plenty of water as well as supplement daily (with your physician's approval). Include 2,000 milligrams (mg) of vitamin C…at least 1,500 mg of bioflavonoids… 200 mg of vitamin E…45 mg of zinc. In addition, take omega-3 oil at 2,000 mg…or 500 mg borage…or 1,500 mg evening primrose oil.

• **Manage stress.** Try meditation, yoga, prayer, exercise or a combination that makes sense to you. Dr. Starbuck recommends the homeopathic Bach Flower Rescue Remedy for immediate relief in very stressful situations (*www.bachflower. com*). Rescue Remedy comes in liquid form with an eyedropper. The recommended dose is a few drops under the tongue. Bach Flower Remedies are available at most health-food stores.

How to Banish Blisters

Howard Palamarchuk, DPM, director of sports medicine, Temple University School of Podiatric Medicine, Philadelphia, and an attending podiatrist for the Boston Marathon.

D on't you just hate it when you buy a new pair of shoes or sneakers and on the first day of wearing them you come home with a painful blister?

While blisters are seemingly benign, they are no laughing matter. Caused by friction and burns, these raised areas of skin filled with a watery fluid are breeding grounds for infection—especially if you have diabetes or other circulatory problems.

To find out how to prevent and treat blisters, we spoke with Howard Palamarchuk, DPM, director of sports medicine at Temple University School of Podiatric Medicine in Philadelphia and an attending podiatrist for the Boston Marathon.

AN OUNCE OF PREVENTION

Dr. Palamarchuk emphasizes that proper protection is essential for preventing blisters. *This is what he recommends…*

• **To protect an area on your hands or feet from rubbing and friction,** wear gloves, padded socks, well-fitting shoes or a bandage.

• **Choose the proper shoes for whatever activity you engage in.** You can walk in running shoes, but you should not run in walking shoes, cautions Dr. Palamarchuk. Running shoes are more stable and have better cushioning.

• **Shop for shoes late in the afternoon,** when your feet are larger, and try them on with the type of socks that you normally wear.

HOW TO TREAT BLISTERS

Without proper care, infection is a possibility for anyone (even if he/she doesn't have diabetes). To prevent infection, blisters require proper care. Your best bet? If a blister is not too painful, simply leave it intact, and cover with a small bandage. Do not pop blisters. An unbroken blister is a natural deterrent to bacteria and infection. Once it is open, the risk for infection begins.

If the blister is painful, it may be necessary to drain it. *To do this…*

• **Wash your hands.**

• **Gently wash the blister and swab it with rubbing alcohol.**

• **Sterilize a clean, sharp needle with rubbing alcohol**—or better yet, Dr. Palamarchuk recommends a sterile lancet that you can purchase in the drugstore—and use it to puncture the blister.

• **Allow the fluid to drain** while *leaving the overlying skin in place.*

• **Apply an antiseptic cream or ointment** and cover the blister with a proper bandage. Never cover with moleskin or plain adhesive tape—when you remove them, you can tear off the top of the blister accidentally.

BLISTERS AND DIABETES

If you have diabetes, never attempt to treat a blister yourself. Inspect your feet every day, and if you detect even a minor injury, such as a small blister, see your health-care provider. Blisters are slower to heal when you have diabetes, and infection can spread more quickly. Do not be embarrassed to see a professional for such a "small" thing. Treated improperly, it can become a very big problem—an infection can lead to ulceration and even amputation.

Warts Begone! A Gentle Solution

Kenneth H. Haller, DO, Central Indiana Orthopedics, Muncie, Indiana, specializing in sports medicine.

Eric Yarnell, ND, is president of the Botanical Medicine Academy in Seattle and is a core faculty member at Bastyr University in Kenmore, Washington. He is coauthor of *Clinical Botanical Medicine.* Mary Ann Liebert.

People have gone to all sorts of extreme measures to remove unsightly, embarrassing and stubborn warts. Conventional treatment includes burning or freezing them, but they often grow back because the treatments generally don't fully destroy the warts' roots. Now, researchers from the University of Lund in Sweden have discovered a gentle solution—mother's milk.

According to the results of a study published in the *New England Journal of Medicine*, a protein present in human breast milk can eliminate warts. Treatment with a cream containing the protein complex *alpha-lactalbumin–oleic acid* (which contains a protein found in breast milk) eventually eliminated warts completely in all those who received it.

THE STUDY

Forty patients with common skin warts that had previously resisted the conventional wart-removal methods received daily topical treatments of the breast milk protein complex or a placebo. After three weeks, *most* of the warts in *all* of the patients in the breast milk group decreased in size by 75% or more, while only a *few* of the warts in *some* of the placebo group patients decreased by 15%.

The placebo group was given the breast milk protein complex treatment after the initial phase of the trial, and their response was equally impressive—an 82% reduction in wart size. In a follow-up study conducted two years later, *all* lesions were completely gone in 38 of 40 patients, with no adverse reactions reported.

WHY WAS TREATMENT SO EFFECTIVE?

Warts are benign tumors. The protein in breast milk has considerable tumor-killing abilities, explain the researchers, with the ability to selectively target *only tumor cells* and kill them, while leaving healthy cells unaffected. The breast milk study was undertaken to prove this very principle—alpha-lactalbumin kills transformed cells but bypasses healthy ones. Study authors note that although their findings are preliminary, the treatment may be promising in cancer therapies. There were no differences in treatment outcomes between immunosuppressed patients and those with competent immune systems.

STRATEGIES FOR TODAY

Warts are noncancerous growths caused by the human papillomavirus (HPV). "The biggest challenge in wart treatment is getting the body's immune system to recognize the wart virus as a foreign invader so that the natural immune response will kick in and fight it," says sports medicine specialist Kenneth H. Haller, DO.

Dr. Haller injected warts with *Candida* (yeast) antigen, and roughly 84% of patients in his study experienced significant wart diminishment after two injections, which were given one month apart. At a six-month follow-up, none of the warts cleared by candida antigen treatment had returned.

The antigen was injected directly into individual warts. One interesting result was that those patients with multiple warts experienced a 40% reduction in locations other than the injection site. "Maybe not all of them would disappear, but we saw beneficial results in those warts that were not directly treated," says Dr. Haller. He cites one amazing case in which a young boy with more than 100 warts on his body experienced complete clearing after two injections into a single wart on his hand.

Candida antigen injections offer several advantages over other more traditional wart treatments. There are no known significant side effects—such as wounds that result from cutting, burning or freezing techniques—and it is inexpensive and easy to administer. Today, Dr. Haller's treatment is widely available, and most dermatologists as well as many general practitioners are able to provide candida antigen injections.

HERBAL OPTIONS

Eric Yarnell, ND, RH, a core faculty member of botanical medicine at Bastyr University in Kenmore, Washington, says that, in his experience, any irritation applied to the area of the wart regularly and consistently (sometimes for weeks or months) will eventually cause the immune system to "wake up" and kill the HPV. He thinks this helps explain the old wives' tale about rubbing warts with such objects as potatoes and pennies.

"Sometimes, I simply advise people to rub the wart every day with their finger and employ some power of suggestion, such as by thinking *Wart, go away*," he says. Typically, Dr. Yarnell will also supplement these suggestions with immune-modulating herbs, such as a combination of schisandra, *Eleutherococcus senticosus* (eleuthero) and, the most common, *Aralia californica* (California spikenard). This last one, along with eleuthero, is in the same family as ginseng.

Don't use these herbs without the supervision of a licensed naturopathic physician, as they can create inappropriate levels of inflammation or immune stimulation.

Dr. Yarnell says that he also tends to use either tincture of *Chelidonium majus* (greater celandine) or dandelion. "I believe that the fresh sap from either plant is more effective than the tinctures," he says.

Whatever treatment strategy you choose, it is important to know that there are far better options today than those previously available.

Easing the Poison Ivy Itch

The late William L. Epstein, MD, professor emeritus of dermatology, University of California, San Francisco.
Andrew L. Rubman, ND, director, Southbury Clinic for Traditional Medicines, Southbury, Connecticut.
Jamison Starbuck, ND, a naturopathic physician practicing in Missoula, Montana. She is a past president of The American Association of Naturopathic Physicians (AANP).

If you love to garden but are very sensitive to poison ivy, what can you do to avoid this outdoor nuisance?

PREVENTION IS THE BEST REMEDY

According to the late William L. Epstein, MD, professor emeritus of dermatology at the University of California, San Francisco, it is easier to prevent poison ivy than to cure it.

First off, be an herbologist. Be aware that it's the oil in poison ivy plants—*urushiol*—that causes the rash. *You can develop the rash in several ways…*

• **Touching the plant.**

• **Touching something that the oil has touched** (such as clothing, sports equipment or your dog).

• **Coming in contact with particles in the air that touch your skin** (which is why you should never try to get rid of poison ivy by burning it).

To prevent poison ivy, Dr. Epstein gave the following advice…

• **Leaves of three, let them be.** Learn to recognize three-leaved, low-to-the-ground poison ivy plants, and avoid them. Teach your children to avoid them, too.

Three-leaved poison oak also grows as a low plant or bush. Its leaves resemble oak leaves. Poison sumac bushes or trees are most common in wet, marshy areas. Each leaf has seven to 13 shiny, smooth-edged leaflets.

• **If you can't avoid contact, take steps to protect yourself** by wearing long pants, socks and a long-sleeved shirt.

A special technique developed by Dr. Epstein for members of the USDA Forest Service is to spray arms and legs with deodorant. An additive in the spray prevents the oil from entering the skin.

A product called Ivy Block is based on this same deodorant-barrier concept, so applying either to your skin should provide protection that can last up to 24 hours.

• **As soon as possible following exposure, wash off urushiol with soap and water.** According to Dr. Epstein, you don't have to buy anything special to wash it off—just wash as quickly as you can after contact.

Best: Try to catch contact within 15 minutes or less. Our medical expert, Andrew L. Rubman, ND, advises that good old-fashioned lye soap is especially effective.

• **Keep in mind that urushiol remains active for a long time.** Make sure to wash any clothing that has come into contact with the oil, such as gardening gloves, as well as any camping, fishing or sporting gear, since lingering oil can still cause a reaction weeks or months later. And, poison ivy doesn't die in winter, so you still have to be cautious while you're around it.

TREATMENTS

Once exposure occurs, a rash will develop in one to two days. At this point, the focus is on relieving symptoms, calming inflammation, preventing infection and helping blisters heal.

Dr. Epstein advises…

• **Learn to recognize the early warning signs of a poison ivy rash.** Six to 12 hours after exposure, you will develop what looks like little insect bites. At this point, Dr. Epstein recommends prompt preemptive action. Apply a prescription topical corticosteroid medication, such as Temovate. After applying, let the skin air dry. Do not cover with a bandage or Band-Aid.

• **Over-the-counter (OTC) treatment options include calamine lotion and low-dose hydrocortisone cream.** But when it comes to poison ivy, Dr. Epstein says that topical OTC medications generally don't work very well. *Prescription* prednisone is the standard treatment that is used for serious cases.

• **OTC oral antihistamines,** such as *Chlorpheniramine* (Chlor-Trimeton) and *diphenhydramine* (Benadryl), help control itching.

• **Take cool showers and lukewarm baths to relieve the itch.** Adding oatmeal and baking soda to baths can help dry up any oozing blisters. Ice and cool compresses can also be soothing.

• **Severe cases in very sensitive people,** as when the rash is all over the body or on the face, call for more serious interventions, such as prescription oral corticosteroids or a corticosteroid injection. Antibiotics are required if a secondary infection develops.

THE NATUROPATHIC POINT OF VIEW

Of course, corticosteroids have numerous side effects (from increased appetite and weight gain to decreased ability to fight infection and poor wound healing), so you don't want to use them unless absolutely necessary. To learn about natural treatment alternatives, we also spoke with Jamison Starbuck, ND, a naturopathic physician in family practice in Missoula, Montana.

Dr. Starbuck recommends…

• **Take one of two homeopathic remedies—** homeopathic poison ivy (*Rhus tox*) or sulphur as soon as possible after exposure. Rhus tox should not be taken by people who are extremely sensitive to poison ivy.

• **An immediate application of calendula salve after exposure** can help prevent a rash from developing. If a rash appears, topical *calendula succus* in a spray form is soothing and helps relieve the itch.

• **Stimulate the body's own cortisone system to fight off an attack of poison ivy.** To that end, Dr. Starbuck recommends large doses of a vitamin C supplement, up to 3,000 milligrams (mg) per day.

Dr. Rubman suggests a high-potency multi-B complex, typically 100 or 150 mg, two or three capsules a day. Reduce your dosage of vitamin C if diarrhea develops.

The bottom line? Take measures to protect yourself whenever you go camping or hiking in the woods. If you are exposed to poison ivy, take prompt action. It's a nasty rash, but there are plenty of remedies out there to beat it.

Selenium—The Dandruff Deterrent

Andrew L. Rubman, ND, director, Southbury Clinic for Traditional Medicines, Southbury, Connecticut.

Dandruff is an equal opportunity offender for the 97% of us who will suffer an embarrassing bout of falling flakes at least once in our lives.

To a certain extent, flakes are normal. Your skin sheds dead cells every day, replacing itself entirely about every 24 days.

In most people, this renewal process is orderly and mostly imperceptible. But when the scaly, dead skin cells of the scalp in particular slough off in mass quantities, clumping together and becoming noticeable, it's known as dandruff.

Everything from indoor heating to the excessive use of hair-care products can trigger an outbreak, but often, experts say, these external skin eruptions are an inside job caused by the overgrowth of fungus and yeast. If people can strengthen the underlying tissue to be more resistant to external triggers, they can limit outbreaks. Since these organisms can live in the deeper recesses of the skin itself, external treatments are not very effective on their own.

MORE THAN SKIN DEEP

"One of the first things people reach for to take care of their dandruff is a dandruff shampoo, such as Selsun Blue," notes our medical expert, Andrew L. Rubman, ND. "What makes Selsun Blue effective? Selenium sulfide. Selenium is a trace mineral that is excreted through the skin and the nails, helping to create a healthy skin mantle. Without it, yeasts like *candida albicans* can infect the skin and create the waxy buildup that causes dead cell clumping and dandruff flakes. While you can help fight dandruff by applying selenium topically, *curing* the problem requires more of this mineral internally, too."

THE SELENIUM SOLUTION

In theory, we should all get enough selenium from our diets, but modern farming practices have stripped the soil of this essential ingredient in various parts of the country. If you suffer from dandruff, try supplementing with selenium.

"The best bioavailable selenium source is liquid drops called Aqua Sel, made by T.E. Neesby in Fresno, California [*www.wellnessworks. net*]. Each drop contains about 95 micrograms of selenium," says Dr. Rubman. "I recommend about four drops a day, or about 400 mcg."

You should see results within 10 days to two weeks. "The skin should be substantially better, if not cured within a month," says Dr. Rubman. "Then, maintain your healthy scalp by taking about 12 drops a week—that is, three drops, four days a week."

Helpful: You can accelerate the healing process by buying a second bottle of selenium drops and pouring it into your favorite shampoo, so you get a topical treatment, too.

How to Fight Hair Loss

Andrew L. Rubman, ND, director, Southbury Clinic for Traditional Medicines, Southbury, Connecticut.

There have been many reports over the years about both medicinal and surgical ways to treat hair loss. For the most part, though, these strategies address the problem after "the horse is out of the barn," or in this case, the hair is off the head.

Is there something people can do sooner to prevent hair from falling out before they have a problem?

Although no major studies have been done in this area, our medical expert, Andrew L. Rubman, ND, told us that indeed, there are natural alternatives people have been using for years—and some of them may surprise you.

PROTEIN AT THE ROOT

Dr. Rubman explains that the body must have protein for a host of important reasons, including healthy hair. Consequently, you want to be sure that you get plenty of protein and that your body is able to absorb it efficiently.

For your body to digest protein sufficiently—to get it from your stomach to your liver where it can be put to work—requires the presence of adequate stomach acid *during* a meal.

To achieve this, he advises taking a digestive enzyme before each meal. He recommends Panplex 2-Phase (made by Tyler) or DuoZyme (by Karuna), both available at *www.nutrition surplus.com.*

Note: If you are taking antacids to decrease stomach acid and acid reflux, you may be impeding the digestion of proteins.

Also: If you are taking antacids under medical supervision, check with your doctor before changing your protocol.

GO GREEN

One type of protein is particularly important to keep hair healthy and in the scalp where it belongs, says Dr. Rubman. This group, the crucifers, which contains foods such as broccoli and Brussels sprouts, is "built" with sulfur, although it is difficult to ingest adequate amounts for these purposes.

To ensure that you are getting enough sulfur, Dr. Rubman recommends taking one to two grams of methylsulfonylmethane (MSM) daily with a meal. You'll know you've achieved the right amount, he says, if your bowel movements take on a sulfurous (or deviled egg) odor.

Bonus: Sulfur not only promotes healthy hair, it also improves skin and nails.

DHT DEFENSE

Finally, we wondered if there was any way to decrease the damage caused by DHT, the hormone converted from testosterone that triggers hair loss in sensitive people. Dr. Rubman explains that the best way to combat DHT—which has a fat component—is to help the body transport it out. You can do this by taking a fat-binding substance called *glucomannan*, available at health-food stores. Take one capsule a day, one-half hour before a meal.

Bonus: Dr. Rubman says that glucomannan will also promote healthy skin as well as regularity. For this particular supplement, he likes the Nature's Way brand.

18

A Healthy Digestive System

Lowering Stomach Acid May Make Problems Worse

 **T**urning on the television or reading the newspaper is becoming an exercise in anxiety. It's either some natural disaster or dire predictions about the economy. All this stress is sending lots of us to our medicine chests to calm our nervous stomachs. And what do we usually reach for? That old standby—an over-the-counter (OTC) antacid.

Advertising claims might lead you to believe that any OTC antacid, such as Tums, Rolaids and Maalox or acid blocker such as Pepcid and Prilosec, is harmless enough. Little did you know that taking these drugs may make your stomach problems worse.

STOMACH ACID: "A GOOD THING"

You may be surprised to learn that our medical expert, Andrew L. Rubman, ND, describes stomach acid as a good thing. Proper digestion takes place as a series of functions, some of which depend on the presence of adequate stomach acid while you are eating.

Taking an OTC antacid, acid blocker or even worse, the "more effective" prescription variety, you're cutting down or even eliminating the acid you need at mealtimes. Without it, your stomach can't adequately break down food into its nutrient components. What's more, inadequate digestion of proteins encourages the liver to increase production of LDL cholesterol—the kind that does the most damage to your body.

A common result of taking acid-lowering drugs on a regular basis is an increase in cholesterol, which is then often treated with yet another drug to lower cholesterol levels—a roller-coaster ride you don't want to be on.

GO WITH THE FLOW

If you stop taking antacids as a favor to your liver, what do you do about your sour stomach?

"Prevent it in the first place," says Dr. Rubman. Make sure you have adequate acid in your

Andrew L. Rubman, ND, director, Southbury Clinic for Traditional Medicines, Southbury, Connecticut.

274

stomach during mealtimes, when you need it, and less stomach acid when you don't. "What we call excess stomach acid," he says, "is what should be called inappropriate stomach acid."

To make sure your stomach has sufficient acid at mealtimes, Dr. Rubman advises against "grazing"—snacking on food—throughout the day. Snacking signals the stomach to pump acid rather than saving it for mealtimes.

In addition…

• **Always chew your food thoroughly.** Introducing saliva into the food as you chew will get the digestion process off to a good start.

• **Don't drink very much liquid while eating a meal.** Dr. Rubman says that more than a few sips of fluid will dilute the acid in the stomach. Also try to limit fluids for 30 minutes before you eat and for an hour afterward.

His general rule: One fluid ounce of water for every two ounces by weight of solid food.

To avoid acid overproduction, Dr. Rubman also advises a few changes in eating habits…

• **Don't overeat.** Leave that extra little bit of room for dessert, and then skip it.

• **Eliminate foods that have refined sugars, such as desserts, from your diet.** Sugars tend to destabilize the stomach, decreasing efficiency of digestion and nutritional value as well as creating gas.

• **Avoid caffeine and fried foods.** Caffeine slows starch digestion and may impair acid production during meals. Fried foods create gastrointestinal inflammation and can also speed the aging process.

BETWEEN-MEAL DEFENSES

If you still suffer from a sour stomach between meals, put something in it that will quiet it without triggering more acid production. Dr. Rubman has several suggestions…

"A time-tested remedy, believe it or not, is sauerkraut," he says. In Europe, you can even buy sauerkraut juice for just this purpose. Five or 10 minutes after consuming sauerkraut, your stomach will relax and you'll feel great. It sounds weird, but the enzymes released during the fermentation of cabbage as it turns into sauerkraut help break down as well as neutralize the inflammatory components of a sour stomach.

HERBAL REMEDIES

Should sauerkraut not be for you, there are some herbal products that can soothe and normalize the stomach without suppressing acid production. Dr. Rubman recommends gentian, an herb that comes in tinctures, capsules and fluid extracts. "Usually using eight to 10 drops in a little bit of water will do the job," he says. Use this as needed rather than prophylactically.

Glyconda, a traditional herbal combination that includes turkey rhubarb root, cinnamon and goldenseal, is another old-fashioned remedy, one that grandmothers in Italy have been giving their families for years. Dissolve 10 to 20 drops in two ounces of warm tea or water, and drink before a meal.

Other products that address the problem…

• **Gastri-Gest,** a combination of plant-derived enzymes taken as needed as an antacid substitute in capsule form. Available from Priority One (800-443-2039).

• **Compound Herbal Elixer,** a botanical mixture that can be used as needed as a "tummy tonic." Available from Eclectic Institute (800-332-4372, *www.eclecticherb.com*).

Both of these products are also available at quality health-food stores.

WHEN PROBLEMS AREN'T RESOLVED

Occasionally, a more severe stomach problem causes between-meal acid production. "This occurs when something in the stomach lining stimulates it in the same way that food does," says Dr. Rubman. Typically, the cause is a yeast organism or something similar. Often, the culprit is the same creature, candida found in vaginal or oral thrush. You can avoid it by following the above steps to maintain adequate stomach acid levels during meals.

Caution: Anyone with gastritis that persists for more than 10 days or recurs more than once a month should be tested for the bacterium Helicobacter pylori.

It might also be an ulcer, which would require special treatment. "Having a gastric or duodenal ulcer is one of the few problems that calls for prescription drugs to suppress stomach-acid production while the lesion heals properly," says Dr. Rubman.

If your problem does not respond to the natural remedies suggested above within a few days, see your health-care provider to rule out a more serious condition.

When it comes to acid indigestion, don't let the cure be worse than the disease. Healthy eating habits and a strategy to work with the body's natural digestive function will go a long way in calming that grumbling pain.

Acid Reflux Drugs: More Harm Than Good

Chris D. Meletis, ND, executive director, the Institute for Healthy Aging (*www.theiha.org*). He is author of several books, including *Better Sex Naturally* (Harper Resource), *Complete Guide to Safe Herbs* (DK Publishing) and *Instant Guide to Drug–Herb Interactions* (DK Publishing).

The first time it happens, you may think you're having a heart attack or that you're choking—or both. Or you might have a feeling of being overly full. Perhaps you even find it difficult to swallow. It turns out it is acid reflux, a common problem with a number of uncomfortable symptoms.

For some people, what starts as an occasional episode progresses to a chronic condition known as *gastroesophageal reflux disease* (GERD), but for many people, it is simply an unpleasant now-and-then part of life. Indeed, estimates are that 40% of Americans have acid reflux at least once a month. Although it often accompanies aging, acid reflux is by no means only an age-related problem.

The persistent deluge of TV ads for acid reflux medication would have you believe that drugs are the answer. However, other than to treat ulcers, these drugs are mostly unnecessary and even harmful.

For advice on the natural approach to easing acid reflux, we called Chris D. Meletis, ND, executive director of the Institute for Healthy Aging and author of several books on natural health.

WHAT'S GOING ON?

Dr. Meletis says that the reason acid reflux is so often a problem with age is because when your body reaches age 50, it produces a greater volume of acid, but it is weaker and less effective. Additionally, the production of digestive enzymes by the pancreas goes down and, for people who have had their gallbladders removed, there is considerably less bile to aid digestion. It's not a rosy picture—instead of a reasonable amount of efficient stomach acid, there is a large volume of weak acid without strong digestive partners to assist it.

In addition to the digestive mayhem is the weakening or relaxation of the lower esophageal sphincter (LES), an event that is especially frequent among the over-50 crowd. This is the flap that opens to receive what you've swallowed and shuts to keep it down. If the LES relaxes or weakens, the door is open, and when there is a large volume of food and diluted digestive acid present in the stomach, an acid reflux episode follows. Dr. Meletis compares it with a coffeepot, filled up and percolating nicely—but this "coffeepot" is your stomach pulsing diluted acid into your esophagus. Dr. Meletis adds that the LES sometimes relaxes suddenly, particularly in response to large amounts of high protein, which explains why you might occasionally experience a startling rush of pressure in the chest when you are eating.

PREVENTION OPTIONS

Even given the bodily changes that impact digestion, we are often our own worst enemies when it comes to acid reflux. *Some simple lifestyle changes can help…*

• **Lose weight if necessary.** Being overweight adds pressure to the area and is highly associated with acid reflux.

• **Don't eat before bed.** Since gravity helps keep stomach contents moving downward, you'll sleep better if your stomach is nearly empty. Don't eat or drink (except a bit of water) for several hours before bedtime and avoid large evening meals, says Dr. Meletis.

• **Sleep at an angle.** Prop up the head of your bed or sleep with enough pillows so that you can angle your torso.

• **Avoid trigger foods.** You may already be avoiding certain foods that you notice trigger unpleasant reactions, but there are some—chocolate, mint of any sort and caffeine—you should definitely shun because they cause the LES to relax. (Ironically, for those people who have normal digestion, mint is helpful because it increases acid production.)

• **Minimize fluids at mealtime** to prevent further diluting stomach acids that you now need to digest your food.

• **Don't overeat.** Pressure in your stomach from large meals puts pressure on the LES.

• **Chew your food thoroughly to give it an early assist in digestion.** Dr. Meletis says that being stressed or eating in a rush is often to blame, especially if you get a sudden feeling of a lump in your chest and have trouble swallowing. Should that happen, sit quietly, take a few sips of liquid if you can and squirm around in a snakelike fashion. Moving slightly to the right and left will help stomach contents head downward again.

TREATMENT OPTIONS

For immediate relief, Dr. Meletis recommends deglycerized licorice (DGL). It coats the stomach lining with mucus and has been shown to work as well as acid blockers for instant relief. DGL is available at natural-food stores and does not affect blood pressure, as does regular natural licorice.

For long-term correction, he advises plant-based digestive enzymes, such as Prevail's Vitase Digestion Formula or Rational Alternatives' Super Assimilate.

The rule of thumb with enzymes is to go low and start slow—take several pills with larger meals (lunch and dinner as a rule) and see how you do.

Our medical expert, Andrew L. Rubman, ND, adds that digestive enzymes with meals, fresh fruit and vegetable juices and, believe it or not, sauerkraut, are some other options to improve digestion and ease discomfort.

Speak to your health care professional about the best course of action for you.

Slow and Steady Eases Acid Reflux

Chris D. Meletis, ND, executive director, the Institute for Healthy Aging (*www.theiha.org*). He is author of several books, including *Better Sex Naturally* (Harper Resource), *Complete Guide to Safe Herbs* (DK Publishing) and *Instant Guide to Drug–Herb Interactions* (DK Publishing).

Jana Klauer, MD, former research fellow, New York Obesity Research Center, St. Luke's–Roosevelt Hospital Center, New York City. She is also a weight-reduction physician in private practice in New York City.

Recently, there have been several studies that have shown that careful chewing can reduce acid reflux and even help you lose those unwanted pounds.

THE NEW RESEARCH

Acid reflux is an uncomfortable condition in which food and stomach acid pulse back into the lower esophagus through the lower esophageal sphincter (LES).

When the subjects in several studies slowed their eating—taking 30 minutes to consume an average-sized meal versus downing it in five minutes—they reduced acid reflux episodes by nearly one-third. The researchers speculated that the likely reason for the improvement was that subjects had less food in their esophagus at any given time. This reduced pressure on the LES as well as distention of the stomach—both helpful when it comes to curbing acid reflux.

MORE INSIGHT

To find out more, we interviewed Chris D. Meletis, ND, executive director of the Institute for Healthy Aging. Dr. Meletis says that he enthusiastically endorses the concept of small bites and ample chewing. In fact, he suggests chewing 15 to 20 times per bite as part of a general approach to reducing acid reflux.

Thorough chewing starts to break down food before it reaches your stomach, making it easier for stomach acids and digestive enzymes to finish up the job. In addition, focusing on eating in this manner may relax you mentally, thereby reducing stress that can exacerbate reflux.

OTHER BENEFITS OF SLOWING DOWN

Chewing slowly may be helpful as a weight-reduction strategy as well. This was confirmed recently in a North American Association for the Study of Obesity report on a study in which 28 overweight subjects all ate less when they slowed their eating of a typical meal. Although this does not prove that chewing more will cause weight loss, it is suggested evidence.

Dr. Jana Klauer, a weight-reduction physician in New York City, tells us that slower eating definitely helps people lose weight. The reason for this, she says, is that the stomach and small intestine signal the brain when the body has been fed and doesn't need more. But it takes about 15 minutes for the message to arrive. Slow eaters are able to receive and then act on this message. Rapid eaters typically don't get the signal in time and overeat.

To correct the speedy-eating habit, Dr. Klauer advises turning mealtime into more of a ceremony. Sit at the table instead of eating on the go, and avoid finger foods in favor of eating with utensils. Savor the color, texture, smell and taste of your foods—remember, you are nourishing your body and honoring it in the process.

Can Acid-Blockers Contribute to Respiratory Infections?

Andrew L. Rubman, ND, director, Southbury Clinic for Traditional Medicines, Southbury, Connecticut.

Acid reducers, such as Prilosec and Nexium, taken to suppress stomach acid and control heartburn and acid reflux, are among the best-selling medicines in the United States.

However, a recent Dutch study questions the safety of these drugs, suggesting that they may raise the risk for pneumonia.

Although the risk is small, so many people take them that a large number might be affected.

Link: Stomach acid not only plays a valuable role in the digestive process, it also kills bacteria and viruses such as those that cause pneumonia and influenza.

According to our medical expert, Andrew L. Rubman, ND, one also has to ask whether acid-suppressing drugs similarly cause increased vulnerability to the common cold. In his view, there is no such thing as "excess stomach acid." Dr. Rubman believes that there are safer ways to control heartburn and reflux, and suppressing stomach acid is not the answer.

ABOUT THE STUDY

Researchers in the Netherlands examined the medical records of 364,683 individuals, in whom 5,551 cases of pneumonia were diagnosed. They found that those who used proton pump inhibitors, or PPIs (such as Prilosec, Nexium and Prevacid), were almost twice as likely to risk developing pneumonia than the former users.

These drugs work by inhibiting the chemical pump necessary for stomach cells to make acid. People who took another class of acid-suppressing drugs known as H2 receptor antagonists, including Tagamet, Pepcid and Zantac, also faced a higher risk, although to a lesser degree.

Older people and those who have chronic lung conditions were especially vulnerable, and researchers recommended that these groups use acid-suppressing drugs only when necessary and at the lowest possible dose.

WHAT YOU CAN DO

According to Dr. Rubman, the use of acid-suppressing drugs on a short-term basis for two to three weeks is fine for stomach ulcers or acute gastritis. *However, on a day-to-day basis he advises that you instead follow a natural approach to achieve efficient digestion…*

- **Eat slowly and take more time** to chew your food thoroughly.

- **Do not drink fluids with meals.** In the absence of fluids, saliva does not get diluted and contributes to more efficient digestion of food.

- **Do not lie down immediately after meals**—wait at least an hour.

- **Do not eat late at night.**

- **Identify and avoid the foods that contribute to your heartburn.** Common offenders include fried foods, fatty foods, spicy dishes, coffee, alcohol and chocolate.

- **Stop smoking.**

- **If you are overweight,** make an effort to shed pounds.

If despite these measures you experience heartburn and reflux, Dr. Rubman recommends that you see a naturopathic physician. He/she can prescribe a digestive enzyme to take with meals, which will calm your stomach without also suppressing beneficial, germ-fighting stomach acid.

As for the risk of getting pneumonia—the healthier your entire body, the better able you will be to fight it.

A Treatment That May Cure Ulcers

Barry Marshall, MD, The Helicobacter Foundation, *www.helico.com*.

Steven R. Peikin, MD, professor of medicine and head, division of gastroenterology and liver diseases, Robert Wood Johnson Medical School, Cooper University Hospital, Camden, New Jersey, and author of *Gastrointestinal Health*. HarperCollins.

Andrew L. Rubman, ND, director, Southbury Clinic for Traditional Medicines, Southbury, Connecticut.

Imagine a scenario in which a patient comes down with burning discomfort in the area between his navel and lower breastbone. His doctor gives him a breath test. A short time later, the diagnosis is in—active infection with a bacteria called *Helicobacter pylori* (H. pylori) …and a possible ulcer.

Quite a difference from a few years back, when Dr. Barry Marshall, an enterprising young physician from Australia, was repeatedly laughed off the stage at medical meetings after claiming that H. pylori, and not stress or spicy foods, caused most cases of peptic ulcers.

Dr. Marshall's persistence paid off—he was proven right—and the mainstream medical community finally came around.

STEALTH FIGHTERS

These corkscrew-shaped bacteria burrow into the mucosal lining that protects the digestive tract, evading the immune system and sending out toxins that can neutralize stomach acids and cause damage. The result may be craterlike sores (ulcers), the chronic inflammation of gastritis and even stomach cancer.

To learn more about these hardy bugs, we spoke with Steven R. Peikin, MD, professor of medicine and head of the division of gastroenterology and liver diseases at Robert Wood Johnson Medical School, Cooper University Hospital in Camden, New Jersey.

Dr. Peikin says that most people who are infected with H. pylori don't even know they have it because they have no symptoms. And he's referring to a lot of people—up to half of all Americans age 60 and older probably contracted the bug as children, he notes.

Improved hygiene in recent decades, however, means that fewer kids become infected today. Why?

It is believed that the primary path to infection for this organism is from sewage to food. Thus, in countries where people buy meat that hangs in open markets, H. pylori is quite common.

Dr. Peikin notes that many people are chronically infected and are at an increased risk of ulcers or stomach cancer. Genes, virulent strains of the bug and possibly immune-system disturbances may allow H. pylori to flourish and produce symptoms.

A MIXED BAG

Based on studies of those infected, Dr. Peikin says that 10% to 15% may develop an ulcer in their lifetime. However, fewer than one in 100 get cancer.

Studies have linked H. pylori to other maladies as well. Some, like bad breath, chronic hives or Raynaud's disease (cold, numb fingertips), can make life difficult. Others, like pancreatic cancer or heart disease, can kill you.

The good news is that, as with many bacterial infections, H. pylori infection may be cured with a two-week course of antibiotics. Usually two are prescribed together, *clarithromycin* and *amoxicillin,* in conjunction with a bismuth, such as Pepto-Bismol.

Some doctors may prescribe an acid-suppressing medication, such as Prevacid, Prilosec or Nexium.

With this three-pronged treatment—the two antibiotics and Prevacid or another acid-suppressing medication—studies have shown that less than 3% of people infected with H. pylori have recurrences of ulcers, compared with 90% of those who received no treatment.

According to our medical expert, Andrew L. Rubman, ND, recent studies have questioned the use of Prevacid, and he favors a triple therapy that consists of an antibiotic, an antiparasitic and a bismuth.

SHOULD YOU BE SCREENED?

In most instances, your doctor can quickly and accurately check for the H. pylori infection through a simple breath, blood or stool test. Some cases require an *endoscopy* in which a tube is inserted down the esophagus to view it and the stomach and small bowel.

But because the bug is so widespread, it's not practical to test everyone. *Dr. Peikin advises testing if...*

• **You have symptoms of an ulcer,** such as pain in the middle to upper abdomen.

• **You've had stomach cancer.**

Reason: Eradicating the bug may help decrease the chance that the cancer will return.

• **A relative had stomach cancer.**

Reason: You may be genetically predisposed to the disease if your mother, father, brother or sister had it.

• **You're taking an NSAID pain reliever** for arthritis or another condition.

Reason: Taking aspirin, *ibuprofen* or other NSAIDs raises your ulcer risk, particularly if you carry H. pylori, and may make you more vulnerable to catching the bug if exposed.

• **You're from an area of the world where infection rates are very high,** such as Asia or Eastern Europe.

• **You suffer chronically from any of the maladies that have been linked to H. pylori,** such as bad breath, migraines, Raynaud's disease or chronic hives.

SUGGESTED TREATMENT

Dr. Peikin believes that H. pylori should *always* be treated with drugs if detected.

Some doctors, he says, adopt a "don't test, don't tell" policy because they worry that eradicating the bug may actually increase levels of stomach acid and worsen symptoms of heartburn and acid reflux for a while. But, he counters, "The World Health Organization has declared that H. pylori is a Class I carcinogen. You don't know which person will get a bleeding ulcer or gastric cancer."

ADDITIONAL REMEDIES

Although a short course of antibiotics and Pepto-Bismol is your best bet for eliminating H. pylori, nutritionally oriented physicians sometimes recommend additional measures in the battle against the bug.

• **Get extra vitamin C.**

Reason: H. pylori may impair the body's ability to absorb this vitamin. Remember to take it between meals, when it won't quench mid-meal stomach acid.

• **Fight back with foods.**

Reason: Broccoli and broccoli sprouts contain *sulforaphane,* a substance that in lab tests is lethal to H. pylori—even drug-resistant strains. Celery, onions, apples, red wine and green and black teas contain compounds called flavonoids, which may also inhibit growth of the bug.

• **Drink cranberry juice.**

Reason: It may help prevent H. pylori from penetrating the lining of the gut. It works by making the lining more slippery...so the bugs just can't hang on.

• **Avoid coffee and any kind of soda.**

Reason: Whether caffeinated or not, these beverages can rev up stomach acid production between meals and increase irritation and susceptibility to H. pylori.

If you're being treated for H. pylori...

• **Let stomach acids work for you.** If you're on an acid suppressor to fight the bug, you may want to avoid "grazing" on food throughout the day. Doing so can dilute your supply of digestion-promoting stomach acids.

Also: Chew food thoroughly to help release nutrients, and avoid drinking too many fluids with meals—they dilute acid further.

If treated properly, this little belly bug can be a thing of your past. If left untreated, it can wreak havoc on your system far beyond a few aches and pains.

info Centers for Disease Control and Prevention, "*Helicobacter pylori* and Peptic Ulcer Disease," *www.cdc.gov/ulcer.*

National Digestive Diseases Information Clearinghouse (NDDIC), National Institutes of Health, *www.digestive.niddk.nih.gov.*

Five Easy Ways To Stop IBS

Christine Frissora-Rodeo, MD, gastroenterologist, New York–Presbyterian Hospital/Weill Medical College of Cornell University, New York City.

Andrew L. Rubman, ND, director, Southbury Clinic for Traditional Medicines, Southbury, Connecticut.

Millions of men and women in the US and the United Kingdom are prisoners of their own intestines, suffering from irritable bowel syndrome (IBS).

Surprisingly, most IBS sufferers don't bother to seek treatment for the condition. Why? Because many people don't realize that IBS is a real disorder, not just "bad digestion"…and that its symptoms can often be treated.

KNOW THE SIGNS

IBS causes misery for those who suffer from it. Most have chronic diarrhea, while the rest are chronically constipated. A few IBS sufferers alternate between the two conditions. Most of them experience abdominal pain, bloating and gas.

Fortunately, even severe IBS doesn't cause serious damage. However, the symptoms can be so disruptive that they force some people to curtail their social and professional lives. Sometimes the condition is so difficult to control that sufferers are afraid to leave their own homes in case they experience an attack.

IT'S PHYSICAL…IT'S MENTAL…IT'S BOTH

Medical professionals generally agree that IBS has both a physiological and a psychological element to it. Here is some insight into the physical causes of IBS and the treatments currently available. (*See "Stopping the Stress…" on page 282 for the psychological causes of IBS.*)

No one has been able to pinpoint the exact cause of IBS, but several interesting associations recently have come to light, according to IBS specialist Christine Frissora, MD, gastroenterologist at NewYork–Presbyterian Hospital/Weill Medical College of Cornell University in New York City.

Dr. Frissora explains that IBS is a chemical imbalance in the enteric nervous system (ENS). The ENS is a second nervous system, present in all vertebrates, which manages the digestive system. This imbalance causes the ENS to fail to communicate with the central nervous system, causing a breakdown in normal bowel function.

It appears that up to 30% of IBS cases are triggered by a specific event—a course of antibiotics…a severe gastrointestinal infection, such as food poisoning…or a traumatic event, such as a physical assault. Hormones, including birth control pills and hormone replacement therapy, can also trigger long-term IBS.

BREAKING THE CYCLE

Lifestyle changes can make a dramatic difference for those who have IBS. *Dr. Frissora advises the following for all types of IBS…*

• **Follow a careful diet plan.** Avoid fast foods and other high-fat temptations…carbonated beverages…and drinks sweetened with *sorbitol* or *fructose* (check labels).

• **Give up alcohol and foods made with high-fructose corn syrup.** These make symptoms worse.

• **Don't chew gum.** It introduces excess air into your system and exacerbates symptoms.

• **Exercise regularly.**

• **If you smoke, quit.**

• **Speak to your gynecologist** if you suspect that birth control pills or hormone therapy is a factor.

Everyone with IBS should be sure to get sufficient fiber in their diets—but not all fiber is good fiber. The crude insoluble fiber passes through the digestive system largely intact. Eating this type of fiber only adds to the misery of IBS. The biggest offenders are bran, bell peppers and eggplant skin.

Instead, choose soluble fiber, found in oatmeal, most fruits, barley, beans and legumes. Psyllium, found in some cereal products, some supplements and in bulk fiber laxatives, is also a good choice.

IBS patients with constipation often find that supplements containing magnesium are helpful because magnesium loosens the stool. These patients also should avoid wheat and dairy products, which aggravate symptoms.

info Learn more at the Web site for the National Institutes of Health Office of Dietary Supplements, *http://dietary-supplements.info.nih.gov.*

International Foundation for Functional Gastrointestinal Disorders, *www.aboutibs.org.*

National Institute of Diabetes and Digestive and Kidney Diseases, *www.niddk.nih.gov.*

IBS Symptom Checklist— Do You Have It?

Nicholas Talley, MD, professor of medicine in the division of gastroenterology, Mayo Clinic College of Medicine, Rochester, Minnesota. He is the author of *Conquering Irritable Bowel Syndrome.* BC Decker.

How do you know if you have IBS? Ask yourself the following questions, and if you answer "yes" to the first question, as well as any of the other three questions, you may have IBS.

1. Have you experienced abdominal pain or discomfort once a week—or more—in at least three of the last 12 months?

2. Does your discomfort or pain often dissipate after you have had a bowel movement?

3. Is your abdominal pain or discomfort often accompanied by a change in the frequency or consistency of your bowel movements?

4. Have you often experienced any of the following symptoms over the past year?

• Change in frequency or consistency of your stools.

• Straining or urgency during your bowel movements.

• Feeling like you can't completely empty your bowels.

• Mucus-coated stools.

• Abdominal bloating, fullness or swelling.

Best: See your doctor to discuss the right diagnosis and treatment for you.

Stopping the Stress That Causes IBS

Lucinda Bassett, founder and CEO of Midwest Center for Stress and Anxiety, 866-955-6027, *www.stresscenter. com,* and author of *From Panic to Power.* Collins.

Andrew L. Rubman, ND, director, Southbury Clinic for Traditional Medicines, Southbury, Connecticut.

Irritable bowel syndrome (IBS) isn't dangerous, but its symptoms—abdominal pain, bloating and constipation or diarrhea—can be agonizing.

Though the causes of IBS are still unknown, we have learned a few things about what can trigger episodes.

Unpleasant as IBS is, it can be comforting to know that it is not life threatening. Be sure to have a thorough physical exam to rule out other more serious medical conditions. (*See "Five Easy Ways..." on page 281 for a discussion on the physical causes of IBS.*)

High on the list of IBS triggers is stress. Stress can trigger an episode of IBS and IBS symptoms can, in turn, increase stress. It can become a vicious cycle.

EASING THE STRESS

To learn more about stress and how to control it, we called Lucinda Bassett, founder and CEO of Midwest Center for Stress and Anxiety. She herself suffers from IBS and knows how stress can exacerbate her symptoms.

Ms. Bassett offers several suggestions for reducing stress...

•**Talk back.** Learn to underreact, says Ms. Bassett. When you sense that an episode may be imminent, tell yourself that you are fine…and that an episode is no big deal. The brain will forward these calming messages to your digestive system and help it relax.

•**Calm yourself.** Lie in a comfortable place, and breathe deeply using your diaphragm (just below your breastbone). Breathe in through your nose and out through your mouth. Take 12 full breaths per minute for three to five minutes. This technique is a variation of the yoga breath meditation called *pranayama*.

Also: Other yoga postures, breathing exercises and meditation may help. The key is to find calming techniques that work for you, such as listening to music, taking a warm bath, etc.

•**Keep medication close by.** Those who suffer from the diarrhea variant of IBS should carry one-half of an Imodium A-D tablet at all times. Ms. Bassett explains that the drug is fast-acting for diarrhea, and that the comfort of having it at hand is generally enough to halt the onset of an episode.

LIVE HEALTHY

Both Ms. Bassett and our medical expert, Andrew L. Rubman, ND, underscore the importance of a healthy lifestyle…

•**Watch what you eat.** IBS episodes can be triggered by certain foods, though these triggers vary from person to person. Common ones include caffeine, dairy, protein, wheat and sugar.

•**Exercise regularly.** Dr. Rubman advises walking for at least 15 to 20 minutes every day, briskly enough so that you push yourself somewhat.

•**Maintain structure.** Dr. Rubman also recommends establishing a schedule that works for you. Find out through experimentation how much sleep you need each night and when it is best to eat your meals. Once you establish what is best for you, make it a stable part of your life.

•**Get your vitamins.** To ensure proper digestive activity, Dr. Rubman suggests a daily B-12 supplement. Look for a tablet that dissolves in your mouth and that contains 800 micrograms to 1 milligram of either *hydroxyco-*

balamin or *methylcobalamin,* both of which can pass through the lining of the mouth into the bloodstream.

Note: Supplements containing *cyanocobalamin* can't pass through the mouth lining and so are not recommended.

info Visit the International Foundation for Functional Gastrointestinal Disorders' Web site at, *www.aboutibs.org.*

Natural Cure for Constipation

Jamison Starbuck, ND, a naturopathic physician in family practice and a guest lecturer at the University of Montana, both in Missoula. She is a past president of The American Association of Naturopathic Physicians (AANP).

So-called herbal "bowel cleansers" are touted as a healthy and effective treatment for chronic constipation.

In my clinical experience, this claim simply is not true. Bowel-cleansing formulas typically contain strong laxative herbs, such as aloe resin (sometimes listed as "aloe leaf"), buckthorn, cascara, rhubarb and senna. While these herbs can increase *peristalsis,* the wavelike movement of the bowel that facilitates elimination of stool, but they also irritate the gut wall.

Like any good laxative, these herbs will promote a bowel movement, but repeated or large doses of them can also create cramping, diarrhea and blood in the stool.

I define constipation as having less than one bowel movement per day. Common causes of constipation include irregular bowel habits (ignoring the urge to go or not allowing enough time)…inadequate fiber or water…lack of exercise…and poor digestive function (due to low secretion of digestive enzymes).

Certain medications including tricyclic antidepressants, some blood pressure drugs, antacids and opiate pain relievers (such as codeine) can cause constipation. Unless your constipation is temporary (caused, for example, by the use of opiate medication following surgery), avoid strong laxatives—even if they are natural or herbal products. The bowel becomes reliant on laxatives, which can worsen your constipation and create inflammation and irritation in your intestinal tract.

Rather than seeking a temporary solution, people who are constipated should slowly retrain their bowels to work correctly. This process usually takes about four weeks. *Here's how…*

1. Eat fiber. Fiber helps retain water in the colon, which promotes softer and larger stool. While a healthy, toned bowel will respond to a moderate amount of fiber, a bowel that has become slack and weak (due to the effects of insufficient fiber) will need much more fiber.

Helpful: Start with five half-cup servings of vegetables and four half-cup servings of fruit per day.

Also: Have at least one cup daily of a whole grain, such as brown rice, oatmeal, quinoa, millet or a fortified cereal.

2. Exercise. Physical activity improves peristalsis. Get at least 20 minutes each day. My favorite exercises are yoga and aerobic activity, such as brisk walking, cycling or swimming.

3. Drink lemon water. To expand stool size and encourage elimination, drink 64 ounces of water daily. Twice a day, before meals, drink 16 ounces of water that contains the juice from half a fresh lemon (bottled lemon juice also can be used, but it is not as healthful). Lemon water encourages the secretion of bile, a digestive fluid that acts as a laxative.

4. Use small doses of herbs. A tea made with equal parts dandelion, yellow dock, burdock and licorice root has a mild laxative effect.

What to do: Mix one-half ounce of each dried herb. Use two teaspoons of the mix per eight ounces of water, simmer for eight minutes, strain and drink. Start with one cup four times daily during the first week of bowel retraining. Reduce by one cup per week until you are able to eliminate regularly without the tea.

The "Four Rs" Strategy to Relieve Constipation

Robert Rountree, MD, family practitioner, Boulder Wellcare, Boulder, Colorado, professional member of the American Herbalists Guild and author of several books on integrative medicine.

Constipation is disaster. This is what a user said in a commercial for Dulcolax laxatives that ran several years ago. How right she was.

It is the cause of some 2.5 million visits to the doctor and nearly 100,000 hospitalizations a year in this country alone. More important, according to Robert Rountree, MD, family practitioner, professional member of the American Herbalists Guild and the author of several books on integrative medicine, is the fact that chronic constipation can have long-term health consequences including autoimmune disorders, such as rheumatoid arthritis, and even colon cancer.

Constipation occurs when food is not fully digested and ends up staying in the gut longer than it is supposed to. Ideally, food should stay in the gut just long enough for the intestines to extract its nutrients and then it should get out, he says. If it lingers, as it does with chronic constipation, it can be truly disabling.

WHAT'S NORMAL?

Dr. Rountree defines constipation as not having at least one bowel movement each day, and he considers it chronic if the situation continues for several weeks. While some people consider it normal to have only one or two bowel movements a week, Dr. Rountree notes that though there may not be any symptoms associated with this situation, it can still predispose a person to chronic toxicity and systemic disease.

TAKING ACTION

For Dr. Rountree's patients, the first step in treatment of constipation includes a physical examination and a particularly sophisticated stool analysis called a "comprehensive digestive stool analysis." This type of analysis is important because it reveals what he calls the "internal milieu." According to Dr. Rountree, we all have about three pounds of bacteria in the gut that processes food, extracts nutrients, keeps the gut clean and helps us fight infections. A good stool analysis shows the levels of both the good and the bad bacteria and how they balance each other. It also determines whether there are indicators of such serious problems as inflammatory bowel disease, allergies or cancer. For most people, though, constipation results from a gut that has become sluggish and unhealthy from poor exercise and dietary habits.

REPAIR STRATEGY

To turn an unhealthy gut around, Dr. Rountree practices what is called the "Four R Program," which was developed by the Institute of Functional Medicine (IFM) in Gig Harbor, Washington, under the direction of Jeffrey S. Bland, PhD. This testing process takes a number of months and should *always* be guided by a trained physician. IFM seminars provide the best guidelines for physicians.

The Four Rs are part of an integrated strategy for re-creating health in the digestive tract. For clarity, they are presented here in a stepwise fashion, but in actual practice, they can be addressed simultaneously or as individual components. *Consider the following…*

Remove: The first step is to remove the bad bugs, which may include bacteria, yeasts and parasites. To do this, Dr. Rountree uses natural antibiotics, including oregano, garlic and olive-leaf extracts or berberine, an extract found in goldenseal and other medicinal plants. Choice of antibiotics depends upon the results of the stool test. This phase usually lasts somewhere between two weeks and one month, but may sometimes require extended treatment. In severe cases, prescription antibiotics or antifungal agents may be necessary.

Repair: The repair phase is necessary because in an unhealthy gut, the mucosal lining can erode. When this happens, microscopic molecules from food can leak into your bloodstream, which might lead to autoimmune diseases. Some of the best nutrients for repairing the lining of the gut include L-glutamine, a type of amino acid that is found in cabbage juice, aloe vera gel, deglycyrrhizinated licorice root extract and arabinogalactan, a starchy substance derived from the inner bark of Western larch

trees. The repair phase typically takes one to two months.

Replace: The replace phase involves restoring what is often undersupplied or missing in the gut—hydrochloric acid (HCL) and the digestive enzymes. Dr. Rountree often prescribes betaine HCL with pepsin with or without an herbal bitter called gentian root. In addition, digestive enzymes—either pancreatic enzymes (from animals) or plant- or fungus-based enzymes—may be prescribed. Both of these help your stomach more effectively digest the food in it and thereby improve the remainder of the digestive process. This phase of the treatment should last for at least one month …however, some individuals may need to continue replacing enzymes or HCL indefinitely. According to Dr. Rountree, for people who need them, there are no harmful consequences of using these supplements long-term.

Reinoculate: This phase involves restoring the impaired or destroyed healthy bacteria that has been "run out of town" by the bad bacteria—in much the same way that weeds take over your lawn. A combination supplement often containing medically potent strains of *Lactobacillus acidophilus* and *Bifidobacteria* may be prescribed.

Note: Many commercially available strains of these "probiotics" are too weak to be of value. A good-quality product should guarantee that it provides between five billion and 15 billion live organisms in a daily dose. To achieve the best results, one can start with 15 billion Lactobacillus plus 15 billion Bifidobacteria per day for the first three months, then decrease the dose five or 10 billion of each bacteria per day for another six months.

MAINTENANCE

Once a healthy balance is achieved, you'll want to keep it that way. Dr. Rountree points out that most people do not eat enough fiber—most require a minimum of 15 grams (g) a day, although some chronically constipated people may need as much as 60 g. It is very important to drink an adequate amount of water or the fiber could exacerbate constipation. Usually, six full glasses of water a day for the typical adult will prevent the fiber from caking and keep your system flushed out. Dr. Rountree explains that having to urinate frequently is often a healthy sign associated with this therapy. A diet rich in fruits and vegetables only provides a minimal amount of fiber, so it is usually necessary to add additional sources, such as flax meal, unsweetened psyllium seed husks or wheat bran. High-fiber foods, such as figs and prunes, should also be included on a regular basis. In addition, a nutritional supplement containing 2 to 10 g of vitamin C and 300 to 800 milligrams of magnesium can help keep bowel movements regular—ask your doctor what is right for you.

For occasional bouts of constipation in an otherwise healthy gut, Dr. Rountree often prescribes a Chinese herbal formula called BoweLax (Vita Pharmica, 888-686-3683, *www.vitaphar mica.com*). With a fully functional gut, you will feel and even look better, and have more energy to enjoy life.

New Test That's Better Than a Colonoscopy

Robert E. Carroll, MD, gastroenterologist and associate professor of medicine, University of Illinois at Chicago.

The "gold standard" for colon cancer screening has been colonoscopy, which allows doctors to detect and remove growths *before* they become malignant. *But now there's something even better…*

MAGNIFICATION ENDOSCOPY

According to Robert E. Carroll, MD, a gastroenterologist and assistant professor of medicine at the Chicago campus of the University of Illinois, a new type of colonoscopy reaps even greater rewards. *Magnification endoscopy* requires the same cleansing process beforehand—patients must drink an enormous amount of fluid—and also takes the same amount of time (about an hour.) The difference? As the name suggests, the technology magnifies the image some 70 times, allowing a trained eye to detect microscopic, non-cancerous lesions

that would not be visible during the standard procedure. The doctor looks at the entire lining of the colon under magnification.

These lesions foretell the future. Few to none of them suggests low colon cancer risk—which is news that anyone can cheer about, especially people with a family history of the disease. Although the presence of these lesions suggests increased risk, Dr. Carroll says that patients can take steps to improve the odds. *Among the things they can do…*

- **Increase screening frequency.**
- **Stop smoking.**
- **Eat more fiber.**
- **Eat less fat.**
- **Drink fewer alcoholic beverages.**

Currently, only about one dozen facilities worldwide—including the University of Illinois at Chicago, the Mayo Clinic and the University of Washington—perform magnification endoscopy. It poses no additional risks above those associated with standard colonoscopy.

Dr. Carroll states that it is important to be screened for colon cancer, even if magnification endoscopy is not available.

Virtual Colonoscopy Finds Problem Polyps In Just 10 Minutes

Michael Macari, MD, associate professor of radiology, NYU Medical Center, New York City.

Even though most of us know that the most effective way to screen for colon cancer is to undergo a colonoscopy, it is shocking to see how many people don't bother to have the test. Nearly half of those over age 50—the age at which routine screening should begin—avoid ever having the procedure.

There have been numerous reports in the news about an innovative 10-minute technique called *virtual colonoscopy,* which uses computed tomography, or CT scan, to take hundreds of three-dimensional X-ray pictures of the bowel wall while you remain awake and alert, free of sedation or anesthesia. To find out more about this test, we spoke with Michael Macari, MD, associate professor of radiology at NYU Medical Center in New York City.

A VIABLE OPTION

"Virtual colonoscopy is probably not quite as good as conventional colonoscopy, all things considered," Dr. Macari states, "but it's definitely a viable option." It finds about 90% of larger polyps (10 millimeters or more in size)—the bud-like growths in the lining of the gut that can turn cancerous—which is similar to the rate achieved with the conventional technique.

It's not as good at finding smaller polyps, Dr. Macari says, but these small polyps do not pose a cancer risk until they grow larger over many years, at which point they would likely be caught during subsequent five-year follow-up exams.

According to Dr. Macari, certain types of patients are especially likely to benefit from virtual colonoscopy…

• **Anyone who, for a variety of reasons, refuses to have the conventional test.**

• **People who have an incomplete traditional colonoscopy** because their doctor cannot advance the scope past an obstruction in the gut.

• **People who are very sick** and cannot endure the conventional procedure or sedation.

• **People at high risk for bleeding** because they are on blood-thinners such as *warfarin* (Coumadin) or have other problems with clotting. About one in 1,000 people who have conventional colonoscopy suffer from perforation of the bowel wall and subsequent bleeding. This risk is eliminated with the virtual technique.

In some states, you need a doctor's referral to have a virtual colonoscopy. It's about half the cost of a conventional test, but because its benefits have not been proven in larger studies, it is not yet widely covered by insurance. A virtual colonoscopy can cost from $500 to $1,000, compared with the conventional technique, which usually costs from $700 to $2,000.

There are some additional caveats to the virtual approach…

• **You will still need to fast and empty the bowel with the dreaded "prep" the night before.** Researchers are, however, perfecting a "prep"-less method.

• **Gas is pumped into the gut during the procedure,** so you'll likely experience some cramping.

• **If a polyp is found,** which happens about 5% of the time, you'll need to have a conventional colonoscopy so that it can be removed.

• **Finally, as with any X-ray procedure, you're getting an extra dose of radiation,** which can increase your lifetime cancer risk.

"If you're over age 50 and not having any children, the radiation risk is almost negligible," says Dr. Macari, who performs three to five virtual colonoscopies a day using a high-contrast gas, such as xenon, and low doses of radiation. If you do opt for the virtual route, he advises, check to make sure the center uses the low-dose radiation approach.

info National Institutes of Health, National Cancer Institute, Colorectal Cancer Screening, *www.nci.nih.gov.*

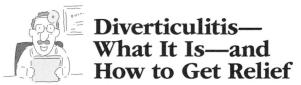

Diverticulitis— What It Is—and How to Get Relief

Judith Mabel, RD, PhD, nutritionist in private practice in Brookline, Massachusetts.

Felice Schnoll-Sussman, MD, assistant attending gastroenterologist, Jay Monahan Center for Gastrointestinal Health, New York–Presbyterian Hospital, New York City.

It's classified as a disease, but it causes very few symptoms. Although it is common as people age—half of people older than age 60 have it, and the numbers climb from there—most people with it don't know they have it. When small pouches or saclike protrusions develop in the colon wall, it is called *diverticulosis.*

Were it not for the fact that complications sometimes occur, it's unlikely that anyone—patients or doctors—would pay much attention to it. But because complications can develop—

and they can be serious—it's wise to be aware of this disease.

Diverticulosis was virtually nonexistent 100 years ago when people filled their plates with whole-grain breads and other fiber-rich foods. Once refined flour entered the picture, though, diverticulosis followed suit, leading to the obvious theory that it directly relates to not having enough fiber in the diet.

Felice Schnoll-Sussman, MD, assistant attending gastroenterologist at the Jay Monahan Center for Gastrointestinal Health at NewYork–Presbyterian Hospital, says that because there are so few overt symptoms of diverticulosis—generally not more than occasional abdominal crampiness, if that—discovery of the condition is almost always through a diagnostic exam, such as a colonoscopy, being administered for other reasons. *However, two principal complications of diverticulosis can develop...*

• **Diverticulitis.** This occurs when the diverticula—the saclike pouches that define diverticulosis—become inflamed. This happens in about 10% to 25% of people with diverticulosis.

• **Bleeding from a pouch.** About 10% to 15% of people with diverticulosis will develop bleeding.

DIVERTICULITIS

Most people who go on to have this condition experience what's called "simple" diverticulitis—a localized infection that develops in the diverticula and causes pain, usually in the lower left abdomen (the site of the sigmoid colon), and accompanied by fever. A short course of antibiotics is usually all that is needed to treat such an attack.

If symptoms are more severe, including chills and an inability to keep food down, the patient may have to go on a short-term liquid or soft diet to rest the colon or, in some cases, a fast, which would require hospitalization for intravenous feeding.

About one-third of the people who have a diverticulitis attack have a simple one such as this and never have another one, says Dr. Schnoll-Sussman.

Another one-third will continue to have minor crampy spasms now and then but nothing more than that.

The last one-third will have a second major attack, and that is when real trouble can set in. The colon sometimes becomes truly diseased, leading some patients to opt for surgery to have the diseased section of the colon removed.

Those who suffer from recurrent diverticulitis are also vulnerable to secondary complications, such as abscesses, so diverticulitis attacks need to be respected and treated carefully.

BLEEDING

The second more common complication of diverticulosis is bleeding and it is generally more terrifying than it is dangerous. A large gush of bright red blood emerges from the rectum or appears in the stool, causing no pain at all but obviously great anxiety.

Interestingly, says Dr. Schnoll-Sussman, this almost always concludes the episode.

The reason: It is the rupturing of a small artery in a single pouch that causes the bleeding —the artery bursts, it bleeds and it's over. Only occasionally (about 5% of the time), the bleeding is great enough that the patient must be hospitalized for a transfusion.

Caution: Even though for most patients such an episode is not life threatening, *any* rectal bleeding should prompt an immediate call to the doctor, says Dr. Schnoll-Sussman, because it could signal a serious colon problem, such as cancer.

SELF-HELP

For many years, doctors urged patients with diverticulitis to avoid consuming anything that had seeds, such as cucumbers, tomatoes, nuts, corn and popcorn, for fear these would lodge in diverticula and cause inflammation. Dr. Schnoll-Sussman says that there are no data to substantiate the theory and many doctors no longer subscribe to it.

However, if you develop abdominal discomfort after consuming certain foods, she says it makes sense to avoid them in the future. She does prescribe a high-fiber diet and recommends taking a fiber supplement, such as Citrucel, daily.

Note: Be careful when selecting fiber supplements. There are many products on the market and some of them contain a lot of sugar, which may feed the bacteria responsible for the inflammation.

Taking fiber supplements helps bulk up the stool while at the same time keeping it soft and easier to pass.

To help increase the fiber in your diet, nutritionist Judith Mabel, RD, PhD, suggests consuming flaxseed and flax meal, in addition to lots of fruits, vegetables and whole-grain products. You can grind flaxseed in a coffee grinder and toss it on salad, into your morning cereal or in a shake for added taste, says Dr. Mabel.

Also: To soothe any gastrointestinal problem, including diverticulosis, Dr. Mabel advises aloe juice, licorice tea or the herb deglycerized licorice.

Take Calcium to Lower Your Risk of Colon Cancer

Eunyoung Cho, ScD, assistant professor of medicine, Harvard Medical School, and associate epidemiologist, Brigham and Women's Hospital, both in Boston.

Andrew L. Rubman, ND, director, Southbury Clinic for Traditional Medicines, Southbury, Connecticut.

If strong, healthy teeth and bones aren't reason enough to be certain you get enough calcium in your diet, now there's another one—it can lower your risk for colon cancer.

THE RESEARCH

In a review of 10 studies that involved more than 500,000 people from five countries, Eunyoung Cho, ScD, and researchers at Brigham and Women's Hospital in Boston recently found that higher milk consumption reduces the risk for colon cancer.

Findings indicated a 12% drop in colon cancer risk for those people who drank at least two eight-ounce glasses of milk daily, which provided them with approximately 600 milligrams (mg) of calcium. Higher amounts of calcium could lower risks further, but the research showed no significant decreases in risk at levels above 1,000 mg a day.

Although milk consumption clearly had the highest association with a lowered risk, the study also focused on other dairy products as the calcium source.

If you do not want to drink milk or eat dairy products, you can still get your calcium from other dietary sources that may protect you from colon cancer.

NONDAIRY OPTIONS

Happily, there are many nondairy calcium sources available. Soy milk, almond milk and rice milk are all good substitutes for cow's milk, says Dr. Cho, if they are calcium fortified. And calcium-fortified orange juice is another good option.

According to our medical expert, Andrew L. Rubman, ND, if you are not overly "dairy sensitive," you can enjoy sheep's or goat's milk, yogurt and cheeses.

It might surprise you to learn that most people who have a problem with dairy react to the protein, not the lactose. Lactose intolerance is an uncommon problem, Dr. Rubman says, yet dairy sensitivity exists in some form in about 75% of the human population.

EAT YOUR CALCIUM

If you do not want to drink your calcium, other nondairy dietary sources include tofu, legumes and dark green, leafy vegetables, such as broccoli, kale and collard greens.

Note: Be sure your tofu has been processed in calcium (check the label to see if it contains calcium sulfate to be certain).

Taking daily calcium supplements in pill or powder form is, of course, another option. The best supplements include magnesium, which will help the calcium absorption. The supplement should have a two-to-one ratio of calcium to magnesium and should be taken in increments of 500 mg or less several times per day rather than all at once.

Milk drinker or not, it is easy to get the 1,000 to 1,300 mg of calcium you need a day to help keep your bones—and your colon—healthy.

Dr. Cho's comment about alcohol and colon cancer are on the next page.

More from Eunyoung Cho...

Alcohol Increases Risk of Colon Cancer by 40%

Alcohol's role in health intrigues many medical researchers. One or two drinks a day appears to be good for your heart. Yet alcoholism's negative impact on individuals and society is well-known. Through the years, there have been numerous studies attempting to understand the real impact of alcohol on our health. A recent report finds a link between alcohol consumption and colorectal cancer... and the news is not good.

Eunyoung Cho, ScD, an assistant professor of medicine at Harvard Medical School and associate epidemiologist at Brigham and Women's Hospital in Boston, gathered information from eight studies that followed subjects for up to 16 years in North America and Europe. From this, she developed a database to evaluate certain behaviors and health risk factors. Dr. Cho found that drinking two alcoholic beverages a day was only slightly associated with an increased risk for colorectal cancer, but people who drank more than three alcoholic beverages a day had a 40% higher risk compared with people who did not drink alcohol at all. This was true for both men and women in the study and for all types of alcohol. The findings are especially significant, since cancer deaths due to colorectal cancer are second only to those due to lung cancer.

We talked with Dr. Cho to discuss her findings. Because it is not unusual for heavy drinkers to also have a poor diet, we inquired about the people in her database. Dr. Cho responded that she made adjustments for dietary habits in determining results of the study, as well as for smoking, age and any other factors that had been identified as potentially impacting the findings.

According to Dr. Cho, there are several theories about why alcohol is associated with colorectal cancer, but many researchers think it is due to something called *acetaldehyde,* which is produced in the colon. The liver converts the ethyl alcohol to acetaldehyde, which is then further converted into harmless acetic acid. But if there is too much acetaldehyde, it can spill out into the bloodstream. Acetaldehyde is *not* harmless. In fact, it is more toxic than alcohol and is responsible for the unpleasant effects of hangovers, says Dr. Cho—*and* it is a known carcinogen.

While this study can't answer all existing questions about alcohol and health, it is an important building block in better understanding the many dangers of excess...and the importance of moderation in all areas.

Cheers! Women Benefit More from Moderate Drinking Than Men

Carla A. Green, PhD, MPH, research associate professor, Oregon Health & Science University and senior investigator, Kaiser Permanente Center for Health Research, both in Portland, Oregon.

Lower tolerance isn't the only difference between men and women when it comes to alcohol. A recent study published in the journal *Alcoholism: Clinical and Experimental Research* points to some other interesting sex-specific consequences of drinking.

RESEARCH RESULTS

The negative impact: On one hand, the research shows that women are more sensitive to alcohol's negative effects—women report worse physical and mental health functioning than men after drinking the same amount. "That's because women have lower ratios of water to fat," explains lead author Carla A. Green, PhD, MPH, of Oregon Health & Science University in Portland. "Alcohol is dissolved in body water. Because women have less (and usually weigh less), they end up with a higher blood alcohol concentration." This means that women not only tend to get intoxicated faster, they also suffer greater incidence of high blood pressure, liver disease, breast cancer and behavioral problems.

THE SURPRISING UPSIDE

On the other hand, and what surprised the researchers most of all, was that women were also more sensitive to alcohol's positive effects. Among the 2,600 women and 3,069 men surveyed, women who drank at light to moderate levels (one to two drinks two or three times weekly) reported better physical health and functioning than men with similar drinking habits. "They seem to have reduced coronary heart disease, reduced incidence of type 2 diabetes and increased sense of well-being," says Dr. Green. "These benefits were proportionately smaller among men." Moderate-drinking women also reported better health than women who drank more heavily and women who didn't drink at all.

WHY THE DIFFERENCE?

The reasons are still not well understood, according to Dr. Green, but differences in alcohol metabolism and body composition are one possible explanation.

The other possible explanation simply involves number-crunching. "Because we don't have causal evidence, it's possible that when women are in bad health, they're more likely to quit drinking and end up in the abstainer group," Dr. Green says, which would boost the health statistics of the moderate women drinkers by default.

Research does show that women are more willing to change their drinking patterns in response to news about their health.

Either way, Dr. Green is clear on the finding that "women are more sensitive to the negative effects of alcohol and *may* be more sensitive to the positive." She wouldn't recommend that women start drinking if they do not already—because of the health risks associated with it—but if they're going to imbibe, it should be no more than one drink per day. (For men, the limit should be two drinks per day.) The US Department of Agriculture and the National Institute on Alcohol Abuse and Alcoholism define a drink as a 12-ounce bottle of beer (less than one pint), a five-ounce glass of wine or 1.5 ounces of 80-proof distilled spirits.

The bottom line? Everything in moderation—and don't always trust the numbers in a study.

Don't Be Shy About Bladder Syndrome

Steven D. Soifer, PhD, MSW, associate professor of social work, University of Maryland, Baltimore; past president, International Paruresis Association, Baltimore and coauthor of *Shy Bladder Syndrome: Your Step-By-Step Guide to Overcoming Paruresis*. New Harbinger.

Several years ago, Tom Smith was fired from his job at Caterpillar, Inc., because he was unable to urinate for a drug test. Tom Smith suffers from shy bladder syndrome (*paruresis*), a condition characterized by trouble using a bathroom away from home. Now he's fighting back. He passed an "independent hair" drug test that he paid for himself (which is more accurate than the urine drug test), and is suing Caterpillar, contending that it violated the Americans with Disabilities Act.

THE SECRET PHOBIA

Roughly 7% of the American population—17 million men, women and children—have paruresis, which is recognized as a social phobia by the American Psychiatric Association. These individuals suffer mostly in silence, hiding their disorder from friends and family members.

People with shy bladder syndrome find it difficult or even impossible to urinate in the presence of others. Visiting a public restroom at a movie theater or baseball game can be a nightmare. Some even experience difficulties at the private homes of friends or in their own home when guests visit.

The good news is that those with paruresis need not suffer in silence. According to Steven Soifer, PhD, MSW, associate professor of social work at the University of Maryland in Baltimore and past president of the International Paruresis Association in Baltimore, paruresis is nothing to be ashamed of, and there are steps you can take to overcome this condition.

THE ROOT OF SHY BLADDER SYNDROME

When you look at the social pressures surrounding using a public restroom, the impact of paruresis becomes very clear...

For men: There is virtually no privacy in public restrooms. Urinals create anxiety for some men, says Dr. Soifer.

For women: The cultural pattern of women going to the bathroom in groups can cause problems for females with paruresis. Dr. Soifer says that some women become agoraphobic or housebound because they are so fearful about being pressured to use a public restroom in the company of colleagues or friends.

For children: Children can develop shy bladder syndrome in public schools, where cleanliness is an issue, stalls often lack doors or locks and there may be bullying or intimidation.

COPING WITH PARURESIS

How do people cope with shy bladder syndrome? They urinate as much as possible before leaving home…drink few fluids when out…and avoid lengthy social or business commitments. Not surprisingly, this can be very disruptive to one's family, social and professional life.

The first step is to see your health-care provider to rule out underlying medical conditions. For example, older men often have prostate problems and consequently, difficulties with urination. Generally speaking, if you have no problem going to the bathroom at home alone but have difficulty using public restrooms, chances are you have shy bladder syndrome. Dr. Soifer says that researchers are only now beginning to explore possible physical causes, and he would not be surprised to discover that there is a physiological reason for shy bladder syndrome, since most people with this problem suffer from no other psychological disorder.

Treatment can take place on an individual basis or in workshops. Dr. Soifer recommends either a weekend workshop or eight to 12 sessions of therapy.

BEHAVIORAL EXPOSURE THERAPY

With behavioral exposure therapy, Dr. Soifer notes that there is an 80% to 90% success rate in conquering paruresis. In a series of gradual exposure exercises, a person slowly learns to urinate in increasingly challenging locations.

Note: It helps to jump-start this process by drinking plenty of fluids, so the urge to urinate will be strong.

Many participants find workshops to be a phenomenally liberating experience, observes Dr. Soifer.

He says that just attending one is often half the battle. He has seen grown men cry with relief when they realize that other people also suffer from this condition and that there is something they can do about it.

Of course, not everyone is helped by behavioral exposure therapy. Dr. Soifer notes that some people have coexisting conditions, such as depression or other phobias, and must often get control of these problems in order to overcome shy bladder syndrome.

In a South African study, 25% of those with shy bladder syndrome also had a generalized social phobia—but 75% had no other problems.

The bottom line? You don't have to suffer in silence. If you have shy bladder syndrome, help is available.

info To learn more about therapists, workshops, support groups and self-treatment, contact the International Paruresis Association at *www.paruresis.org*.

19

How to Prevent Heart Disease and Stroke

Natural Ways to Cure Heart Disease

If you've just had a cardiac event or been diagnosed with some type of heart disease, you may be wondering what you can do to make yourself better.

We interviewed a leading naturopathic doctor (ND), Bobbi Lutack, at Bastyr University in Kenmore, Washington, to get her recommendations on how to heal yourself back to health without resorting to conventional medicine and drugs.

Dr. Lutack observes that while conventional medicine focuses on treatments—such as bypass, stents, angioplasty and prescription drugs—which primarily reduce symptoms, NDs focus on creating a healthy cardiovascular system through diet, exercise, stress management and supplements.

IS THE CURE WORSE THAN THE DISEASE?

When people walk into Dr. Lutack's office after a heart attack, they are often uncertain and depressed. Can they exercise again? Is it safe to have sex? She stresses that individuals with any type of heart disease need to speak candidly with physicians about their questions and their concerns.

She spends one hour with each patient at the first appointment, attempting to gain a full understanding of the patient's physical and emotional state, and coming up with a game plan for treatment.

According to Dr. Lutack, once the issue becomes one of "cure" rather than prevention, the approach should be more aggressive and proactive. Still, in natural medicine, the first question is always, *Is the cure worse than the disease itself?*

Take cholesterol, for example. The greater the family history of heart disease and the higher a person's cholesterol, the more aggressive Dr. Lutack is in taking measures to lower it. Yet, this does not mean that she automatically prescribes cholesterol-lowering statin drugs, which have been associated with harmful side

Bobbi Lutack, ND, adjunct faculty member, Bastyr University, Kenmore, Washington.

effects such as muscle pain, abdominal discomfort and damage to the liver.

Instead, Dr. Lutack begins with close attention to diet and exercise. For many people, this is all that is necessary to get cholesterol under control. If this fails to do the trick, she has an arsenal of dietary supplements at her disposal.

If, after all this, cholesterol is still high, only then will she prescribe a low-dose statin, along with the herb milk thistle to lessen the possibility of liver damage.

Dr. Lutack adds that we now need to look beyond the common fixation with cholesterol and examine other risk factors for heart disease, especially the inflammation marker *C-reactive protein* (CRP).

Today, more and more physicians recognize that inflammation plays a key role in heart disease, and treatment also entails keeping these markers—and thus inflammation—at normal levels in the body.

THE NATUROPATHIC WAY

Naturopathic physicians see patients not as passive but primary, active participants in maintaining health. *Dr. Lutack's recommendations for getting your heart back on the right track include…*

• **Follow a healthy diet.** Dr. Lutack thinks of food as medicine. She recommends plenty of fresh fruits and vegetables, cold-water fish, such as salmon and mackerel (rich sources of heart-healthy essential fatty acids), flaxseed rather than artery-clogging saturated oils and organic, hormone-free turkey, chicken and lean beef in moderation.

Foods such as oats, apples and bran can help lower cholesterol, and the US Food and Drug Administration (FDA) recommends soy (such as tofu, edamame and soy milk) to reduce the risk for heart disease.

Note: Junk food contributes to high cholesterol, inflammation and uneven insulin levels in the body (risk factors for heart disease), so go easy on the fried and fatty foods, sugar, white bread and pasta.

• **Get moving.** If you're uncertain about which level of exercise is safe for you, the first step is to get a stress test. This generally entails walking on a treadmill while your doctor monitors your heart.

Afterward, you can get started on a regular program of aerobic exercise, such as walking, swimming or biking. You may want to join a cardiac rehabilitation program at a local gym or YMCA, where you will be set up with a heart monitor that will tell you exactly what level of exercise is appropriate. Ask your doctor to refer you—the program usually is covered by insurance.

• **Get a handle on stress.** To relieve stress, which is harmful to your whole body including your heart, Dr. Lutack recommends a variety of techniques, including acupuncture and traditional Chinese medicine, homeopathy, meditation, yoga and counseling. Go with whatever works best for you.

She notes that stress is all about perception and warns that a pill just puts a bandage on the problem. Other approaches, such as meditation, allow you to look inward and examine your life. Often your life doesn't change at all, but a shift in attitude allows you to view people and situations in a new and more positive light.

• **Take dietary supplements.** Given the many side effects of prescription drugs and also the obvious risks of invasive procedures, it's important to consider the many natural alternatives that are available to help you cope with heart disease. *These include the following dietary supplements…*

• Carlson's Cod Liver Oil. According to Dr. Lutack, this old-fashioned remedy reduces blood coagulation similarly to how *ibuprofen* works, but with fewer side effects. It also lowers C-reactive protein levels.

• Coenzyme Q10, a chemical made naturally in the body that grows scarcer as we experience stress, smoke or grow older. This supplement produces energy and acts as an antioxidant to scoop up cell-damaging free radicals that lead to inflammation, plaque buildup and blood clots.

• Guggulipid, an ancient Ayurvedic remedy made from a resin extract from the guggul tree. Used for centuries in India, this supplement reduces cholesterol and inflammation, acts as an antioxidant and reduces platelet aggregation to make blood thinner.

• Red yeast rice (*monascus purpureus*) is a traditional element of Asian cuisine made from fermenting red yeast on rice. This supplement contains a natural form of *lovastatin,* the active ingredient in the statin drug Mevacor. Less expensive and with fewer side effects than statins, Dr. Lutack recommends red yeast rice to lower total cholesterol, LDL ("bad") cholesterol and harmful blood lipids called triglycerides.

It also may reduce elevated C-reactive protein levels.

•Folic acid, B-6, B-12 and hydrochloric acid to lower homocysteine. Dr. Lutack observes that most medical doctors prescribe only folic acid to control elevated homocysteine, but the others are necessary to help your body absorb the folic acid more efficiently.

A WORD OF CAUTION

Although you can purchase dietary supplements on the Internet or from quality health-food stores, Dr. Lutack strongly recommends consulting an ND.

Dosages and combinations vary according to each person's condition, and many dietary supplements must be used with caution (if at all) with prescription drugs.

In addition, you will need regular blood tests to determine whether supplements are successful in bringing risk factors within target range.

info For more information, visit the American Heart Association's Web site at *www.americanheart.org.*

The National Center for Complementary and Alternative Medicine at *http://nccam.nih.gov.*

The US Food and Drug Administration at *www.fda.gov.*

Exercise Keeps "Old" Hearts Young

Dean Palmer, MS, senior research associate in exercise physiology, affiliated with the University of Texas Southwestern Medical Center, Dallas.

Some years ago, aerobic training became the rage because it was known to enhance heart health. Also called *endurance training,* aerobic activity gets the heart rate up and sustains it for a period of time, whether by walking, jogging, cycling or swimming. It took a study from the University of Texas Southwestern Medical Center in Dallas to demonstrate just how beneficial aerobic activity can be. The study shows that prolonged, consistent endurance training prevents stiffening of the heart walls, a problem that often accompanies aging and leads to a condition called *diastolic heart failure.*

Diastolic heart failure occurs when the heart can't get enough blood into the left ventricle, because the heart walls have become too stiff to expand sufficiently. It is the reason that 40% of heart patients over age 65 are in the hospital, and aging has generally been considered the cause of it. However, according to Benjamin Levine, MD, the study's senior author, the study found that lifelong exercise completely prevented heart stiffening among participants.

RESEARCH RESULTS

In this study, three groups of men and women were tested: 12 healthy but sedentary older adults, average age, 70...12 Master's athletes (older athletes who compete at high levels in various sports), average age, 68...and 14 healthy but sedentary young people, average age, 29.

The first result wasn't a surprise: The older sedentary participants' hearts were 50% stiffer than those of the Master's athletes.

The second result, though, was totally unexpected: The hearts of the older Master's athletes were indistinguishable from those in the young group.

To determine if starting exercise later in life is too late, researchers put the older sedentary group into a training regimen. We spoke with Dean Palmer, MS, senior research associate in exercise physiology, who designed and led the group's training. At first, the group exercised moderately, three days a week, and gradually increased the workload. At six months, the program incorporated once-a-week interval training—eight cycles of 30 seconds at high intensity followed by 90 seconds of lowered effort. (For example, 30 seconds of jogging with a return to brisk walking.) By the time the group completed its yearlong program, participants were exercising six days a week for 60 minutes, with an additional six or seven minutes of warm up and cool down.

The result? Palmer says that their hearts showed some improvement, enough to demonstrate that the training has a real effect. So the question remains—how much training would it take to effect greater heart flexibility and strength? Some participants have continued to train and at the end of the second year will be tested for impact on their hearts.

Although earlier is clearly better, the study does show that it's never too late to start heart-friendly exercise. Palmer recommends doing an endurance activity just about every day for 20 to 30 minutes. A reasonable level is okay so long as you get your heart rate up and keep it there. He suggests exercising with a heart-rate monitor—it will tell you if you're at the right level for you and, he says, motivate you to kick it up a notch on lazy days. Whatever activity you choose, it's keeping with the program—even when it rains or if you don't feel like it—that will make a difference in your heart's health.

The Four Greatest Risk Factors for Heart Disease

Philip Greenland, MD, professor of medicine, and senior associate dean for clinical and translational research, Northwestern University, Feinberg School of Medicine, Chicago.

Time to snuff the cigarettes, eat your veggies, see your doctor and start exercising. Two large population studies recently confirmed that the vast majority of people who have heart attacks or other types of plaque-related heart disease already have at least one of four well-established risk factors—cigarette smoking, diabetes, high blood pressure (140/90 or higher) or high cholesterol (240 mg/dL or higher).

In the first study, researchers looked at data from three other studies that investigated the heart and general health history of 386,915 men and women. They found that between 87% and 100% of people who had a fatal heart attack had at least one of these major risk factors. Among those who had nonfatal heart attacks, about 90% had at least one risk factor.

The second study, which included 122,450 men and women, found that 85% of women and 81% of men with heart disease also had at least one of the four main risk factors.

This landmark research debunks a commonly held theory that these major risk factors account for only about half of all heart attacks. "These findings reemphasize the importance of the well-known risk factors for heart disease," says study researcher Philip G. Greenland, MD, senior associate dean for clinical and translational research, Northwestern University's Feinberg School of Medicine in Chicago. "Once these risk factors are present, heart disease is harder to avoid."

The good news is that all of these risks can be modified with healthy lifestyle changes and, in some cases, a bit of noninvasive medical intervention. "These are all medical problems that we can treat and, therefore, significantly lower heart disease risk," Dr. Greenland says.

Of all the risk factors, smoking may be the worst. According to the heart disease study, cigarette smokers suffered symptoms of heart disease nearly a full decade earlier than those with other risk factors.

STEPS TO SUCCESS

While none of this is new, it bears repeating. To keep your heart healthy and disease-free…

•**Stop smoking.** There are now more ways than ever to quit. Talk to your doctor about the best methods for you.

•**Get moving.** Exercise—even moderate activity, such as walking—improves cholesterol levels and HDL ("good") cholesterol and LDL ("bad") cholesterol balance, and helps lower blood pressure. Aim to accumulate at least 60 minutes of activity, such as walking, gardening and housework, as well as recreational activity, such as swimming, cycling or playing sports, on most days of the week.

• **Eat a balanced whole-foods diet.** Focus on fresh fruits, vegetables and whole grains, which are all naturally good for your heart. Also eat a diet containing proper levels of the three fat classes—saturated, monounsaturated and polyunsaturated—to help keep the heart healthy. Remember, eating too little of the right fats (such as those found in nuts, seafood and lean beef without added hormones) puts you at risk, too. Focus on these heart-healthy foods.

• **Talk to your doctor.** If your cholesterol or blood pressure remains stubbornly elevated, talk to your health-care provider about the best medical therapies and natural interventions to bring your numbers back to a safe range.

Get Your Doctor to Take Your Blood Pressure the Right Way

Sheldon G. Sheps, MD, emeritus professor of medicine and former chair of the hypertension division, department of medicine, Mayo Clinic, Rochester, Minnesota.

At your last examination, did your doctor measure your blood pressure levels just once—and quickly, too? You may be seeing some changes during your next visit. The manner in which most doctors take blood pressure has come under fire in an article published in the *American Journal of Hypertension.*

According to Sheldon G. Sheps, MD, emeritus professor of medicine and former chair of the hypertension division in the department of medicine at the Mayo Clinic in Rochester, Minnesota, there are a number of concerns about the way measurements are currently made. Doctors often are overwhelmingly busy, with little time to follow the recommendations outlined in the National Institutes of Health's "Seventh Report of the Joint National Committee on Prevention, Detection, Evaluation and Treatment of High Blood Pressure." These recommendations include, among others, taking measurements several times and allowing for periods of patient rest before and in between in order to gather comparable readings that can be tracked over time.

Furthermore, doctors often round numbers, which may seem incidental, unless your systolic pressure is consistently around 142 or 143—even though that's only a few points above 140—in which case it is cause for worry.

BETTER WAYS

Dr. Sheps says that he promotes several approaches to eliminate these problems.

Automated devices now exist that take pressure at intervals of a few minutes. The doctor can leave a patient sitting quietly in a room attached to such a device, and can return after multiple readings are completed.

A second solution is to have someone who is specially trained take the time to do the measurements that meet the "Seventh Report" recommendations. Using a nurse or technician should also reduce the white-coat phenomenon, the situation in which a person's pressure rises in response to being with a medical doctor—a problem that affects at least 15% of patients.

A detailed set of new recommendations for the proper procedures for taking blood pressure has recently been released.

THE RIGHT READING

In the meanwhile, levels for most people—no matter what their age—should be less than 140/90…and for those with diabetes or chronic kidney disease, levels should not be less than 130/80. If your blood pressure is on the high side, talk to your doctor about more thorough monitoring of your levels.

Cholesterol Breakthrough: Lower Than Low Is Best

Bruce D. Charash, MD, chief, cardiac care unit, Lenox Hill Hospital and clinical associate professor, department of medicine, Columbia University, both in New York City.

Andrew L. Rubman, ND, director, Southbury Clinic for Traditional Medicines, Southbury, Connecticut.

Was your cholesterol at a healthy level at your last checkup? You may have thought so at the time, but according to a recent study conducted at Harvard Medical School, it may be time to take another look.

LOWER YOUR LDL

Results of the study comparing *atorvastatin* (Lipitor) and *pravastatin* (Pravachol), two rival cholesterol-lowering drugs, were announced at a meeting of the American College of Cardiology. The key finding demonstrated that lowering your levels of LDL (the so-called "bad" cholesterol) significantly below commonly recommended levels—130 mg/dL (milligrams per deciliter of blood)—could substantially decrease heart attack risk.

According to Bruce D. Charash, MD, chief of the cardiac care unit at Lenox Hill Hospital and clinical associate professor at Columbia University, both in New York City, everyone should have an LDL below 160 (70 is optimal)…people at moderate to high risk (if they are smokers, have hypertension or a family history of heart disease) should be below 130…and those who have had a heart attack or who have heart disease or diabetes should be below 100. Everyone should have an HDL of 40 mg/dL or higher.

The primary outcome of the study, explains Dr. Charash, indicates that it is very important to lower your levels of LDL.

ABOUT THE STUDY

The two-year study involved 4,162 people who had experienced a sudden attack of chest pain due to heart disease. Half were randomly assigned to receive 80mg of Lipitor daily, and the other half were given 40mg of Pravachol daily. The study was funded by Bristol-Myers Squibb, the maker of Pravachol, in hopes of proving that its statin was just as effective as Lipitor, the best-selling drug in the world.

To just about everyone's surprise, results of the study showed that aggressive treatment with large doses of Lipitor had significantly more impact on cholesterol reduction and prevention of heart attack and death in people already at risk. Further studies are necessary to see if aggressive cholesterol-lowering strategies are necessary in those without other risk factors for heart disease. Benefits appeared within 30 days from the onset of treatment and were most significant in recent cardiac patients.

The death rate from cardiovascular disease in study participants was 30% lower among those taking Lipitor compared with those taking Pravachol. Since the study was conducted, the maximum recommended dose of Pravachol has been increased from 40 mg to 80 mg. It is possible that this higher dose of Pravachol would be as effective as the 80 mg of Lipitor used in the study.

Although previous standards indicate that those who have had heart attacks should lower their LDL levels to below 100 mg/dL, the Harvard study showed significant benefits in those with cholesterol as low as 62.

This suggests that giving current heart disease patients higher doses of statins can further reduce their risk of having a heart attack. It also supports the notion that prescribing a cholesterol-lowering medication for healthy individuals previously assumed to have safe levels of LDL cholesterol (below 130) may lead to significant health benefits. But again, since there was no control group in the study, this is not certain. Further research is necessary to determine whether people with "normal" cholesterol levels should take statins.

SIDE EFFECTS

We all have heard about the risks of statins. According to Dr. Charash, a significant minority of people taking statins experience side effects. The most frequent are upset stomach, constipation, gas, cramps and fatigue. Potentially more serious side effects include liver damage and muscle breakdown or weakness. To monitor liver function, your health-care professional should give you regular blood tests when you are taking a statin. Inform your health-care provider at once about any unusual muscle pain or weakness.

ALTERNATIVES TO DRUG THERAPY

Dr. Charash stresses that diet and exercise are the first weapons against high cholesterol. Our medical expert, Andrew L. Rubman, ND, advises including plenty of soy in one's diet (such as tofu, tempeh, miso and edamame) and using natural fiber.

Fiber helps to bind excess cholesterol passing out of the liver into the gut and delivers it out of the body. His preferred fiber alternative is the Japanese plant konjac. The powdered root of the plant is available in capsule form under the herbal name glucomannan. Take one or two capsules before lunch or dinner with a large glass of water.

Dr. Rubman notes that not only does this avoid the possibly serious side effects of statins, it is also far more economical. A month's supply of glucomannan is much less expensive than a month's supply of statins.

NEW INSIGHTS

Consistent with the study's findings is an emerging theory about heart disease that involves inflammation and the ability of statins to reduce it.

The accepted view had been that fatty deposits called plaques build up in arteries and eventually clog them—just as everyday sludge can build up and clog your home's water pipes. When the artery opening becomes so blocked that no blood can pass through, the person has a heart attack.

The current thinking is that areas of plaque become increasingly unstable, eventually breaking free and causing a blood clot to form. This is what blocks blood flow and causes a heart attack.

In most cases, the unstable plaque does not obstruct any artery and produces no symptoms (such as chest pain) before rupturing. However, statins might help head it all off at the pass since they also have an effect on clotting factors in the blood and lower the risk for clot formation.

Dr. Charash explains that statins have powerful anti-inflammatory properties. This is significant because when plaque is inflamed, it is more likely to rupture…and when healthy arteries are inflamed, they are more likely to develop plaque in the first place.

THE CHOLESTEROL DEBATE CONTINUES

Although LDL is commonly called "bad" cholesterol, it also performs a number of essential functions in the body. Cholesterol makes up cell walls, carries waste from the liver, improves adrenal function and preserves youth and sexual function. Dr. Rubman warns that contrary to all this new medical thinking, it may be possible to lower cholesterol levels too much, and risk decreased sexual function, compromised immune function and accelerated aging.

No doubt, these latest research findings will lead to additional research and possibly more aggressive national standards for lowering cholesterol. Speak with your medical professional about what is right for you.

info Contact the American Heart Association at *www.americanheart.org* or the National Heart, Lung, and Blood Institute at *www.nhlbi.nih.gov* for more information.

"Good" Cholesterol Doesn't Outweigh The Bad

Leo Galland, MD, director, Foundation for Integrated Medicine, New York City. He is author of *The Fat Resistance Diet*. Broadway. Dr. Galland is a recipient of the Linus Pauling award. *www.fatresistancediet.com*.

Andrew L. Rubman, ND, director, Southbury Clinic for Traditional Medicines, Southbury, Connecticut.

While it is comforting to feel that current medical thinking is based on scientific fact—the real fact is that it is just the latest information available. A case in point is the upheaval surrounding the role of cholesterol as a risk factor for heart disease. For a long time now, medical science has talked about the virtues of having low total cholesterol and, more importantly, having a proper ratio of HDL ("good" cholesterol) to LDL ("bad" cholesterol). Now the news is that extremely low LDLs make a big difference and, more significantly, that "inflammation" may be an even larger indicator of risk than cholesterol levels.

A recent Lipitor study found very low LDL cholesterol to be good, but some people are now confused about the relative importance of raising HDL cholesterol.

To know more about the current thinking, we interviewed Leo Galland, MD, director of the Foundation for Integrated Medicine in New York City. There is good reason that we are all very confused. According to Dr. Galland, the question of the importance of LDL vs. HDL cholesterol is not an either-or proposition. LDL levels are very significant, but HDL levels continue to be an important independent risk factor for heart disease, along with other factors.

THEN AND NOW

In recent years, experts believed that a high HDL offset a high LDL, and that it was the ratio of HDL to LDL that was most significant.

More recently, a study showed that very low levels of LDL (as low as 62) offer significant protection not only against plaque growth in the arteries but also against heart attack. This finding suggests that treating elevated LDL is of paramount importance, whether or not HDL is high. Our medical expert, Andrew L. Rubman, ND, reminds us, however, that this was not a properly "controlled" study—it only looked at the impact of two statin drugs on LDL reduction in people who already had a history of heart conditions. There was no control without heart disease, nor did the study look at the role of HDL or plaque and coronary-artery narrowing.

HDL AND HEART DISEASE

While there is increasing doubt that high HDL can completely counteract high LDL, there is no question that a low HDL increases the risk for atherosclerosis (accumulation of fatty deposits on artery walls) and cardiovascular disease. *Particularly dangerous combinations are…*
- **Low HDL and elevated triglycerides (fat-carrying particles).**
- **High LDL and low HDL.**

What can you do to boost low levels of HDL? Primarily, exercise and control your weight, says Dr. Galland. Smokers who quit can raise their HDL by up to 20%. For those with no history of alcoholism or alcoholic liver disease, many researchers recommend a glass of red wine each day for women (two for men).

LOOKING BEYOND CHOLESTEROL—HEART DISEASE IS MULTIFACETED

No single factor, such as high LDL, causes heart disease. Nor does any one factor, such as high HDL, prevent you from developing it.

Since only half of all people who have heart attacks have high LDL cholesterol, you have to look at the entire picture—family history, blood pressure, weight, level of exercise, diet, smoking status and coexisting conditions, particularly diabetes.

Other important factors to consider are C-reactive protein (CRP), homocysteine and insulin resistance.
- **CRP is a protein produced in the liver and is a significant marker for inflammation, which is increasingly seen as playing a major role in heart disease.** CRP can be measured with a standard blood test available through any clinical laboratory and should be included when screening for heart disease.

Note: CRP testing is currently recommended for those with heart disease or known risk factors for heart disease.
- **Elevated homocysteine is also associated with a higher risk for coronary-artery disease.** Evidence suggests that a buildup of this amino acid damages the inner lining of arteries, promotes blood clots and encourages atherosclerosis. Homocysteine is also tested in panels for cardiac-risk assessment.
- **Insulin resistance.** Insulin is a hormone that normally helps your body metabolize sugar. However, sometimes tissues in the body stop responding to insulin, as is true in most people with type 2 diabetes. Some people whose blood sugar levels are elevated but not high enough to be diagnosed with diabetes have insulin resistance. Their ability to control blood sugar is dampened. A recent study showed insulin resistance to be a more significant risk factor for heart attack than either HDL cholesterol or triglycerides.

HOW TO LOWER YOUR RISK

The more you educate yourself and learn about heart disease and its causes, the more steps you can take to lower your risk. *Heart-protective strategies include…*
- **Get moving.** Regular exercise can help you raise HDL and lower LDL, triglycerides and CRP.

• **Maintain a healthy weight.** Being overweight causes HDL to fall and LDL and CRP to rise.

Dr. Galland recommends a diet that's rich in natural disease-fighting antioxidants, which can be found in fruits, vegetables, nuts and seeds.

Also, avoid foods that are high in saturated fat, trans fats and cholesterol, such as higher-fat beef products, fried foods, processed foods and full-fat dairy products. These raise your bad LDL cholesterol, and trans fats can also lower your good HDL.

Generally, Dr. Galland does not recommend treating low HDL levels with drugs. However, if you also have high LDL and high triglycerides, and diet and exercise are not sufficiently controlling them, then statins may be an appropriate choice. Watch out for any side effects, such as changes in liver function (as measured by your health-care professional with regular blood tests). Muscle weakness can be a problem, too.

According to Dr. Galland, potentially helpful supplements include folic acid (your best bet for lowering high homocysteine levels), fish oils, chromium, magnesium, green tea flavonoids and red yeast rice.

A word of caution about red yeast rice: It acts as a natural statin, so you should be on the lookout for side effects just as with statin drugs.

The bottom line? The cholesterol question will take years to sort itself out conclusively. However, what you can do to reduce your risk factors has remained consistent—make smart lifestyle choices. Adhering to a healthy diet, exercising regularly and quitting smoking can significantly improve your odds.

If these prove insufficient and your health-care provider prescribes statins, be sure that you weigh the consequences of the decision. Statins have been associated with serious side effects, including birth defects. They are specifically not recommended for pregnant or breast-feeding women.

info For more information on heart health, contact the American Heart Association at *www.americanheart.org*.

Are Ulcer Meds as Effective as Statins?

David A. Peura, MD, professor of internal medicine and associate chief of gastroenterology and hepatology, University of Virginia Health System, Charlottesville, Virginia.
Andrew L. Rubman, ND, director, Southbury Clinic for Traditional Medicines, Southbury, Connecticut.

Most people would assume that cholesterol levels and *Helicobacter pylori*—the bacterium also known as H. pylori, which often causes ulcers—have no relationship. But a doctor in Austria thought they might. Hubert Scharnagl, PhD, of the University of Graz, noticed that chronic H. pylori infection tended to coincide with low HDL (the "good" cholesterol) levels. He ran a study and did, indeed, find a connection.

Dr. Scharnagl and his colleagues looked at 87 patients who were being treated with anti-H. pylori medications for intestinal ulcers to assess any changes in the patients' cholesterol levels. They discovered that after eradication of H. pylori, the patients had more total cholesterol overall, but significantly more HDL. Indeed, it overshadowed the much smaller increase of LDL. The research team concluded that the increase was at least as strong as that reported for patients who were taking a statin drug to increase the relative proportion of their HDL.

Our medical expert, Andrew L. Rubman, ND, explains that the combination of H. pylori infection and medications that lower stomach acid interferes with normal digestion, especially of protein. But the liver must have protein available to create both HDL and LDL, especially HDL. When the digestive system is doing its job without interference, it is better able to pass the fractionated protein materials, which are amino acids, through to the liver. Once the liver has the protein-derived amino acids it needs, it produces more HDL and more LDL cholesterol. Without enough protein, the liver produces the "easier to make" LDL.

However, David A. Peura, MD, professor of internal medicine and associate chief of gastroenterology and hepatology at the University of Virginia Health System in Charlottesville, Virginia, adds that we need much more research to confirm the findings of the Austrian study. It was a small study in scope and there is no way to know yet if the relationship it found is clinically significant. Dr. Peura adds, though, that anyone with a history of ulcers, whether experiencing cholesterol problems or not, should consult a doctor about treatment for H. pylori. By treating H. pylori promptly, you can avoid possible long-term impact of the bacterium on your cholesterol levels.

Natural Way to a Healthy Heart

Allan Magaziner, DO, director of the Magaziner Center for Wellness in Cherry Hill, New Jersey. *www.dr magaziner.com.*

Cardiovascular disease will kill one million Americans this year—despite billions of dollars spent trying to stop it. Prescription costs for cholesterol-lowering drugs have skyrocketed. We pay $10 billion a year for blood pressure drugs, yet these drugs don't work adequately for many patients.

Good news: Research shows that certain foods and supplements can help lower your total cholesterol and blood pressure without most of the side effects—and expense—of prescription pharmaceuticals.*

FOOD

By now, most people know that the omega-3 essential fatty acids (EFAs) found in cold-water fish make this one of the most heart-healthy foods. That's why I tell my patients to eat low-mercury, cold-water fish, such as halibut, three times a week.

My other favorite cardio-friendly foods…

• **Oat and rice bran.** All whole grains contain cholesterol-lowering soluble and insoluble fiber. But oat and rice bran contain the most

*People taking medication for heart disease can also follow these recommendations, to lower their dosages or stop taking the drugs altogether. Consult your physician.

soluble fiber, which has the greatest cholesterol-lowering effects.

Smart idea: Eat three one-half cup servings of oat or rice bran per week.

• **Sterol-enriched spreads.** Plant sterols are compounds that block the body's absorption of cholesterol.

Best source: Plant sterols are found in vegetable oils, nuts, whole grains, vegetables and fruits. Because it's difficult to get sufficient quantities, your best bet is to consume food products, such as sterol-enriched spreads and orange juice.

Smart idea: Get 2 grams (g) to 3 g of plant sterols daily. One tablespoon of Take Control or Benecol spread contains 1.7 g…eight ounces of Minute Maid Premium Heart Wise orange juice contains 1 g.

• **Nuts.** In addition to plant sterols, nuts offer a healthy mix of monounsaturated fats, fiber and polyphenols, compounds that help block the oxidation of LDL cholesterol—a process that slows or prevents arterial plaque buildup.

Smart idea: Eat a handful of one or a combination of these nuts daily. Just don't go nuts —they are high in calories.

• **Potassium-rich foods.** Potassium works in combination with magnesium to balance sodium in the body and lower blood pressure. If you're taking a diuretic for high blood pressure, you may be excreting potassium via your urine and should be extra vigilant about eating a diet that is rich in potassium.

Best sources: Bananas, oranges, tomatoes and dried apricots.

Smart idea: Eat at least one serving per day of a potassium-rich food.

SUPPLEMENTS

For general heart health, I tell my patients to take the following supplements daily—a good multivitamin/mineral, such as one made by Solgar or Twinlab, *plus* a 1,000-milligram (mg) vitamin C supplement…200-international unit (IU) vitamin E supplement…a 50-mg B-complex vitamin…and an omega-3 supplement that contains at least 360 mg of *eicosapentaenoic acid*

(EPA) and 240 mg of *docosahexaenoic acid* (DHA).

To lower blood pressure and regulate heart rhythm, I suggest a combination supplement of calcium (1,200 mg) and magnesium (600 mg), plus 400 IU of vitamin D in addition to the multivitamin.

If you have heart disease, ask your doctor about also trying…*

•**Arginine (3,000 mg daily).** Also called L-arginine, this amino acid triggers the production of nitric oxide, a naturally occurring substance that lowers blood pressure.

Who should consider taking it: Anyone with hypertension, angina, peripheral artery disease, high cholesterol or systemic inflammation (a major risk factor for cardiovascular disease confirmed with a blood test for C-reactive protein).

Helpful: Don't take arginine two hours before or after consuming protein (meat, fish, etc.). The amino acids in the food will block absorption of the supplement. Take arginine with a carbohydrate, such as bread, pasta or fruit. If it doesn't cause gastrointestinal upset, take arginine on an empty stomach.

•**Coenzyme Q10 (100 mg to 300 mg daily).** This fat-soluble compound is abundant in heart muscle, where it helps provide the heart with the oxygen and energy it needs to beat properly. Insufficient CoQ10 can lead to congestive heart failure or arrhythmia.

Cholesterol-lowering statin drugs block CoQ10 production—which may explain the muscle aches and fatigue many patients experience while taking these medications.

Who should consider taking it: Anyone who is taking a statin or is diagnosed with hypertension, high cholesterol, angina, congestive heart failure or systemic inflammation…or is over age 60 (CoQ10 levels naturally decline with age).

*Consult your physician before starting these supplements, particularly if you are pregnant, nursing, have liver or kidney disease or are taking prescription medications.

Stay Warm and Lower Your Risk of Heart Attack

Samuel J. Mann, MD, hypertension specialist and associate professor of clinical medicine, NewYork–Presbyterian Hospital/Weill Medical College of Cornell University, New York City, and author of *Healing Hypertension: A Revolutionary New Approach*. Wiley.

I f you suffer from cardiovascular problems, bundle up this winter. A recent study warns that low temperatures and sudden cold snaps can bring on heart attacks in people with high blood pressure.

HEART PATIENTS VULNERABLE

At the University of Dijon in France, a two-year study was conducted involving more than 700 people with heart attacks admitted to area hospitals. When matched with the weather conditions, researchers found that in those with hypertension (defined as having blood pressure higher than 140/90), heart attacks were more frequent when the temperature dropped below 25° F. This effect was not observed in the 50% of people in the study with normal blood pressure. Additionally, sudden day-to-day changes in temperature posed an especially serious danger. A drop of five degrees or more in a single day was associated with a more than 60% increase in heart attack risk in people with hypertension.

We contacted Samuel J. Mann, MD, hypertension specialist at NewYork–Presbyterian Hospital/Weill Medical College of Cornell University, to get his thoughts on the study. He told us that blood pressure is a little higher in the winter than in the summer, but this should not have a huge impact.

More broadly, researchers don't know the exact reason for increased health risks with low temperatures, but there are several theories…

•**Cold weather makes blood vessels constrict,** which makes it more difficult for blood to pass through them.

•**The cold makes blood thicker and stickier,** which makes it more apt to clot.

•**Cholesterol rises during cold weather.**

•**Colds and flu may lead to inflammation and contribute to heart-attack risk.**

BUTTON UP YOUR OVERCOAT

No matter what the theory is behind it, the facts are still the facts. If you suffer from cardiovascular problems, exercise good common sense this winter…

•**Avoid any unnecessary trips out into the cold.**

•**When you go outside,** wear a warm hat and layered clothing.

•**Make sure your home is sufficiently warm.** This is especially important for older people, who have more temperature-related health concerns.

•**If you suffer from heart problems,** see your health-care provider and carefully follow his/her recommendations.

New Discovery Better Than Stents?

Norman J. Marcus, MD, founder, Norman Marcus Pain Institute, New York City, past president, American Academy of Pain Medicine, Glenview, Illinois, and coauthor of *Freedom from Pain.* Fireside.

The world of cardiovascular disease was recently rocked with results from several studies, one of which showed that using stents to resolve vascular blockages may not prevent future coronary events. Given this news and the risks involved with surgery, an exciting noninvasive alternative for those with coronary artery disease—enhanced external counterpulsation (EECP)—is now a significant alternative.

In EECP, developed at Harvard in the 1950s and later refined in China, pressure cuffs on the legs are inflated, compressing the blood vessels and forcing blood back to the heart. It enhances circulation through the coronary arteries and thus improves heart function.

This noninvasive treatment, which is performed over a series of weeks and provides physiological impact similar to some aerobic exercises but without any effort from the patient—is most commonly used to relieve angina pectoris, a tightness or heaviness in the chest that develops when the heart is not receiving enough blood. Angina, a painful symptom of heart disease, is most often caused by atherosclerosis.

A PAIN EXPERT'S VIEW

To learn more about EECP treatment, we spoke with Norman J. Marcus, MD, founder of the Norman Marcus Pain Institute in New York City. He said that there are about 1,500 EECP machines worldwide, with most of them in this country—including one at his pain institute.

Physicians at the Mayo Clinic's Division of Cardiovascular Diseases published a review of EECP in the *Journal of the American College of Cardiology.* It concluded that EECP is a valuable treatment option in angina patients. Even though some skepticism remains about this treatment, EECP has been approved by the US Food and Drug Administration (FDA) and is covered by Medicare, but only for the treatment of coronary artery disease with angina. Multiple studies document its safety and effectiveness. Dr. Marcus reports that there have been more than 186,000 courses of EECP treatments in the US.

HOW IT WORKS

Increasing the amount of arterial and venous blood that is returned to the heart gently opens blocked vessels and stimulates receptors in the lining of heart arteries. They, in turn, signal the body that more blood is now available. The body responds by lowering levels of the hormone angiotensin, which raise blood pressure, thereby potentially lowering blood pressure and stimulating hormones that encourage the formation of new blood vessels in the heart. During treatment, the patient is attached to an electrocardiographic monitor. Three sets of fabric cuffs—like the one used to measure blood pressure—are placed on the calves, thighs and buttocks. The EECP system pumps when the heart is resting and releases pressure when the heart contracts.

The most important thing about EECP, says Dr. Marcus, is that you're not only unblocking arteries, you're also generating new blood-vessel growth in the heart. Over time, these new blood vessels form a natural bypass around blockages. As new pathways increase blood flow to the heart, improved circulation relieves and perhaps even eliminates the symptoms of angina pectoris. This means that you may be able to be more active, walk greater distances, climb stairs and exercise without suffering angina attacks. Quality of life increases and the need for medication decreases. Most important, there have been no deaths reported with the use of EECP.

IMPLEMENTING TREATMENT

The duration of treatment depends on factors such as a person's condition, his/her tolerance of EECP and the exact nature of the condition being treated. For coronary artery disease, 35 hours of EECP are normally required. Treatment typically takes place for one hour a day, five days a week, for seven weeks. Some people choose two hours of treatment at a time, which can shorten the regimen to three weeks.

THE OUTLOOK OF ECP

With growing physician and patient awareness, the availability and use of EECP is on the rise. You may be particularly interested in exploring this option if you are a possible candidate for heart surgery.

Studies have shown that EECP is effective in treating acute heart attack and congestive heart failure. Its future use may not be limited to heart problems alone. This treatment not only improves circulation through coronary vessels, it also increases blood flow to every part of the body, so it potentially could treat other diseases in which impaired circulation plays a role. Dr. Marcus found that in China, EECP is already prescribed for a number of other conditions—stroke recovery, blindness caused by lack of blood supply to the optic nerve and vascular dementia.

While EECP is somewhat "out of the box" relative to conventional cardiac treatments, its value continues to be demonstrated.

Cough to Save Your Life

Bruce D. Charash, MD, chief, cardiac care unit, Lenox Hill Hospital and clinical associate professor, department of Medicine, Columbia University, both in New York City.

It's been the stuff of urban legend for eons: Coughing during a heart attack may save your life. Surprisingly, recent research appears to lend some credibility to this claim. The study, presented at a meeting of the European Society of Cardiology, involved 115 people who had previously fainted or nearly fainted because of heart problems. These individuals used the cough in 365 instances in which they thought they were going to faint. Symptoms disappeared in 292 cases. The theory is that coughing vigorously when the heart begins to fail can keep a person conscious long enough to call for help.

So is it true or isn't it? To get to the "heart" of the matter, we talked with Bruce D. Charash, MD, chief of the cardiac care unit at Lenox Hill Hospital and clinical associate professor at Columbia University, both in New York City.

THE THEORY

In three out of four heart attacks, a person is at home, often alone. Circulation ceases, the person faints, brain damage rapidly occurs, followed by death.

Cardiopulmonary resuscitation (CPR) can keep the heart and brain going for approximately six to 10 minutes, which is hopefully long enough for an ambulance to arrive.

"COUGH CPR"

According to the study, if you experience sudden symptoms, such as dizziness, lightheadedness or shortness of breath, and CPR is not available or you are alone, the idea is to lie down and cough vigorously to stimulate electrical activity in the heart and keep it going. The coughing acts as a kind of do-it-yourself CPR. A typical adult should lie down...cough about once every second... stop every five coughs...and take two slow, deep breaths...until he/she can cough for 10 to 30 coughs.

THE REALITY

Dr. Charash makes several important points about cough CPR...

●**Often, there is no warning of a heart attack.** For the lucky people who experience lifesaving warning signs, such as dizziness or light-headedness, by all means lie down and cough. (It doesn't work unless you're lying down.) But first call 911.

●**It's true that when you cough, you press down on the heart and force blood out of it.** In fact, when patients undergo angiography to check for blockages in arteries, the heart slows down and cardiac arrest symptoms sometimes develop. In these cases, Dr. Charash instructs patients to cough vigorously to keep their circulation going.

The greatest difference is that medical tests take place in a controlled environment. If you suddenly feel dizzy and faint, you have only seconds to remind yourself to cough in order to try to maintain consciousness. Moreover, feeling faint can be due to many different causes and, in most cases, has nothing to do with a heart attack.

How long can you keep going with cough CPR? It's probably only buying you seconds, says Dr. Charash. On the other hand, if it gives people a sense that they can protect themselves, it's a good thing.

Important: Either way, be sure to call 911 first.

LOOK HERE!

New Risk Factors Found for Heart Disease and Stroke

Ralph L. Sacco, MD, MS, chairman of neurology, Miller School of Medicine, University of Miami, Florida and adjunct professor of neurology, Columbia University—where he established the pioneering Northern Manhattan Stroke Study.

Doctors have discovered a whole new way to identify risk for heart disease and stroke. Rather than looking at individual risk factors, they have identified five core measures that, when viewed as a group, act as a significant indicator of future risk. If you experience at least three of the five problems, you have "metabolic syndrome."

Components of this syndrome are elevated blood pressure, large waist circumference, elevated triglycerides, low HDL (the "good" cholesterol) levels and elevated blood sugar.

In a sense, metabolic syndrome is having a little bit wrong with a number of things. For example, a fasting blood sugar level that's greater than 110 mg/dL is a syndrome risk factor, but a diabetes diagnosis requires a level of 126 mg/dL or higher. To be a syndrome risk factor, high blood pressure is 130 over 85 or higher...for a diagnosis of high blood pressure, the reading must be 140 over 90 or higher.

New research has shown that metabolic syndrome—formerly called "syndrome X"—is a significant risk for heart disease and stroke.

Research from the Framingham Heart Study at Boston University School of Medicine showed that women who have the syndrome more than double their risk for stroke, and men with it have a 78% greater risk for stroke compared with those who do not have the syndrome. The researchers recently presented their findings at the American Stroke Association's International Stroke Conference in New Orleans.

We asked Ralph L. Sacco, MD, MS, chairman of neurology at University of Miami's Miller School of Medicine and a pioneer of Columbia University's Northern Manhattan Stroke Study, about the implications of this study. He explained that no one is yet exactly sure why having the syndrome increases heart disease and stroke risk.

Dr. Sacco feels, however, that this research may hold the key to future treatment. Although a person with the syndrome has lower individual measures for disease, having them clustered in a group like this might warrant starting aggressive treatment earlier.

For the moment, Dr. Sacco points out that it is never too late for people to focus on prevention by eating a healthy diet, exercising and keeping their weight in the correct range. If that doesn't prevent metabolic syndrome, he says, talk to your doctor about possible medications that will help keep the measures down.

How You Can Dramatically Decrease Your Risk for a Heart Attack and Stroke

Michael D. Ozner, MD, medical director of Wellness & Prevention at Baptist Health South Florida and past chairman of the American Heart Association of Miami. He is author of *The Miami Mediterranean Diet.* Cambridge House.

For years, doctors have performed routine cholesterol tests to help identify people who are at risk for a heart attack or stroke.

Problem: Traditional cholesterol tests that provide basic readings—such as total cholesterol, HDL "good" cholesterol and LDL "bad" cholesterol levels—identify only 40% of people at risk for cardiovascular disease.

Each year, about 869,000 Americans die of heart attack or sudden cardiac death (abrupt loss of heart function). Unfortunately, for the majority of people, heart attack or sudden cardiac death is the initial symptom of heart disease. A test that more accurately predicts heart disease risks could prevent many of these deaths.

New approach: Expanded lipid testing identifies up to 90% of patients at risk for heart disease, according to researchers at Duke University.

LDL ALONE IS NOT ENOUGH

LDL is the form of cholesterol most closely linked to cardiovascular disease. Yet the long-running Framingham Heart Study has reported that 80% of patients who suffered a heart attack had similar LDL levels to those who did not have a heart attack.

Reason: Risk is determined not only by the level of LDL cholesterol measured in a blood test, but also by the size of the LDL particles.

Example: Two patients could both have normal LDL readings of 98 mg/dL. The patient with a higher percentage of small LDL particles is more likely to have a heart attack or stroke than the patient with more of the large LDL particles.

LDL SUBCLASSES

Expanded lipid testing includes a variety of LDL subclasses.

Most important…

• **Lp(a) is a very small, dense form of LDL.** Lp(a) particles readily penetrate the *endothelium* (the artery lining) and enter the artery wall itself, causing deadly inflammation and atherosclerosis (fatty buildup in the arteries). In fact, patients with elevated Lp(a) are up to *10 times* more likely to have a heart attack than those with lower levels.

Treatment: Initial treatment for patients with elevated Lp(a) focuses on lowering their LDL levels, then addressing Lp(a) levels. Niacin (vitamin B-3) can lower LDL and Lp(a) levels and increase HDL. Patients with high Lp(a) also may need to take the triglyceride-lowering drug *fenofibrate* (Tricor), which can help reduce Lp(a) levels.

• **IDL stands for intermediate-density lipoprotein (a type of protein combined with lipids).** It's a midsized particle that's more likely to cause atherosclerosis than an equal amount of LDL.

Treatment: A cholesterol-lowering statin drug, such as *atorvastatin* (Lipitor) or *simvastatin* (Zocor), used in combination with niacin.

• **Size pattern.** Pattern A means that a patient has a high percentage of large particles, which are desirable. Pattern B indicates a higher percentage of dangerous small particles. A patient with Pattern B is up to *six times* more likely to suffer a heart attack than a patient with Pattern A.

Treatment: Usually a statin drug, combined with niacin and/or fenofibrate.

• **Total number of particles.** The higher the number of LDL particles, the higher the risk for cardiovascular disease. That's because a greater amount increases the likelihood that particles will penetrate the endothelium and travel to the artery wall.

Treatment: Typically, a statin drug.

HDL SUBCLASSES

The HDL form of cholesterol is protective because it helps to remove LDL from arterial walls. Like LDL, it can be subdivided into different particle sizes. *Most important…*

●**HDL-2.** These are the larger HDL particles. They transport LDL out of the arterial wall and into the liver for disposal. They also have anti-oxidant/anti-inflammatory effects.

Treatment: Niacin increases total HDL as well as HDL-2.

●**HDL-3.** Like HDL-2, these particles lower LDL and can help prevent the dangerous oxidation of cholesterol that's already present in artery walls. However, HDL-3 is smaller than HDL-2 and may not be quite as protective.

Treatment: Niacin helps to increase the size of HDL particles, changing them from HDL-3 to HDL-2 particles.

ARE THESE TESTS FOR YOU?

All patients with cardiovascular risk factors, such as hypertension…diabetes…family history of heart attack or stroke…or smoking should ask their doctors about getting expanded lipid testing. This testing is not necessary for people with no known risk factors for cardiovascular disease, but it could help uncover hidden risks in such individuals.

Expanded lipid testing costs about the same as the older cholesterol tests and may be covered by insurance, depending on the patient's medical history. Even if it's not covered, this type of testing, which costs about $100, on average, is far less expensive than the cost of being treated for a heart attack or stroke.

New Ways to Stop Stroke Damage

Gregory Albers, MD, professor of neurology and neurological sciences and director of the Stanford University Stroke Center in Palo Alto, California.

Andrew L. Rubman, ND, director, Southbury Clinic for Traditional Medicines, Southbury, Connecticut.

James F. Toole, MD, the Walter C. Teagle professor of neurology and director of the Cerebrovascular Research Center, Wake Forest University Baptist Medical Center, Winston-Salem, North Carolina. Dr. Toole is past president of the International Stroke Society.

This year, more than 750,000 Americans will suffer a stroke and, potentially, its debilitating effects. The good news is that intense research efforts are identifying new methods to minimize the damage caused by stroke, increase the chances for rehabilitation after a stroke and identify ways to avoid one in the first place.

To learn more, we interviewed James F. Toole, MD, and Gregory Albers, MD. Dr. Toole is past president of the International Stroke Society as well as the Walter C. Teagle professor of neurology and director of the Cerebrovascular Research Center at Wake Forest University Baptist Medical Center in Winston-Salem, North Carolina. Dr. Albers is professor of neurology and neurological sciences and director of the Stanford University Stroke Center.

EARLY INTERVENTION IS KEY

The first line of defense in minimizing stroke damage is getting rapid treatment. If the stroke is "caught" within three hours, the chances of success are far greater than when the delay is longer. Unfortunately, according to the National Stroke Association, most people go to the emergency room 24 hours or more after a stroke.

RECOGNIZE THE WARNING SIGNS

The warning signs include…

●**Sudden numbness or weakness of the face,** arm or leg, especially when it occurs on one side of the body.

●**Sudden confusion, slurred speech.**

●**Sudden trouble seeing in one eye or both eyes.**

●**Sudden trouble walking, dizziness or loss of balance or coordination.**

●**Sudden and severe headache with no known cause.**

If you think you're having a stroke, call 911 or ask someone to take you to the nearest emergency room (ER) or stroke center *fast,* advises Dr. Toole.

There may be false alarms—but go to the ER anyway and get a full workup. Once there, Dr. Albers says that a magnetic resonance imaging (MRI) technique known as *diffusion weighted imaging* (DWI) can help inform and guide the treatment of acute stroke patients by pinpointing oxygen-starved areas in their brains. DWI is particularly effective in distinguishing recent stroke damage from chronic changes due to a previous stroke.

In studies conducted at Stanford University Stroke Center, almost half of the extra sensitive DWI scans detected damage that was undetectable by conventional methods, and in some cases, radically changed the course of treatment for patients. With better diagnosis, treatment will be more effective.

EFFECTIVE TREATMENTS
FOR ACUTE STROKE

Perhaps one of the best interventions in stroke treatment is the drug *alteplase* (Activase) also known as a tissue plasminogen activator (tPA). It is widely available at hospitals across the country. It was approved by the FDA in 1996 and is the only FDA-approved drug for the treatment of acute stroke.

This drug works by dissolving a clot and restoring blood flow to stroke-damaged tissue. However, it is only for ischemic (not hemorrhagic) strokes.

Ischemic strokes occur when a clot or particle clogs a blood vessel, thereby cutting off the blood supply to a part of the brain. They account for 80% or more of all strokes, so tPA has broad application.

Research has found that tPA can increase the odds of recovery by 33% when administered within three hours of the onset of symptoms. After the three-hour window of opportunity passes, the risks for further damage (including potentially fatal bleeding into the brain) outweigh the benefits of treatment.

In another treatment, doctors thread a catheter through an artery to the brain, and then use a tiny corkscrew-like instrument called the MERCI (*mechanical embolus removal in cerebral ischemia*) Retriever to pull a clot out. Dr. Albers says that this approach looks very promising. It is approved by the FDA and has been successfully used up to eight hours after a stroke.

TREATMENTS IN RESEARCH STAGES

While tPA represents a major advance, because of such factors as time delays and the risk for bleeding, the fact is that fewer than 5% of stroke victims ever receive this drug. *Thus, scientists continue to investigate other avenues of acute stroke treatment, including…*

- **Combining tPA and ultrasound.** At a recent meeting of the American Stroke Association, researchers from the University of Texas at Houston Medical School reported that the combination of ultrasound and tPA was more effective than tPA alone in restoring blood flow to the brain.

- **Bat saliva.** At the stroke conference, international researchers reported that a genetically engineered version of an enzyme in bat saliva, which prevents clotting, could be administered up to nine hours after a stroke, and with less risk for hemorrhage than tPA.

- **Brain-cooling therapy.** At research facilities, including the Stanford University Stroke Center, doctors are experimenting with different ways to cool the brain in order to prevent stroke damage. Researchers theorize that cold temperatures may preserve and protect brain cells when their oxygen is cut off.

THE EUROPEAN WAY

Our medical expert, Andrew L. Rubman, ND, adds *L-carnitine* to the list of cutting-edge stroke treatments. While virtually unknown in the US, this amino acid is routinely administered in the ER of most hospitals in Western Europe upon admission for stroke.

Adequate levels of this nutrient allow the brain to use one-third the oxygen that it would normally burn by allowing fats to be used instead of glucose for fuel. This helps injured tissue survive.

Individuals who are prone to strokes or who have high risk for stroke can take L-carnitine prophylactically. Typically, 350-milligram capsules taken twice daily are prescribed.

L-carnitine appears to be safe. However, it may interact with other medicines, so it is important to discuss this and all other patient-initiated interventions with your primary care physician. Always err on the side of safety.

ADVANCES IN REHABILITATION

Once a person has survived a stroke, he or she faces a whole new set of challenges. Nine out of 10 stroke survivors experience some level (from slight to extreme) of disability that could be physical and/or mental.

For years, conventional wisdom held that after the initial six-month recovery period, there was nothing further that doctors could do to help people with stroke-related disabilities. Not any more. New advances in imaging and rehabilitation have revealed that the brain can compensate for function lost as a result of a stroke.

Practically speaking, this means that a person may be able to relearn life's basic skills—such as walking and speaking—in much the same way he or she would normally learn any new skill, such as playing the piano or violin.

The new thinking goes like this: When cells in an area of the brain responsible for a certain function die as a result of a stroke, a person becomes unable to perform that function. But if a person retains at least 10% of the nerve cells in the stroke-damaged area, the brain may be able to recruit nearby neurons to replace the role of killed cells. Dr. Toole notes that a similar approach was taken with actor Christopher Reeve, who severed his spine in a horseback-riding accident.

This rewiring of the brain and restoration of function sometimes occurs automatically, but scientists have learned that the process can be helped along by therapy.

At stroke research centers around the country, doctors are experimenting with a variety of machines that stimulate stroke-damaged areas of the brain.

Currently, several studies sponsored by the National Institute of Neurological Disorders and Stroke (NINDS) are testing the use of transcranial magnetic stimulation (TMS) in stroke rehabilitation. TMS is performed using a small coil that is held outside the head over that part of the brain that requires stimulation. A small magnetic current is delivered to an area of the brain to increase brain plasticity (the ability to adapt to deficits and injury) and speed recovery of function after a stroke.

Yet another experimental approach toward long-term rehabilitation is the use of Botox injections to counter muscles' vulnerability to spasm. Dr. Albers says that this approach can be useful for some patients.

Note: Visit the NINDS Web site at *www.ninds. nih.gov* to learn more about NINDS-sponsored stroke clinical trials, and to find the location of stroke research centers around the country.

PREVENTION IS KEY

Dr. Toole cautions that we should not lose sight of the fact that most strokes can be prevented in the first place by controlling risk factors.

There are many healthy steps you can take toward stroke prevention…

•**Get checked for stroke risk factors,** such as high blood pressure, elevated homocysteine or C-reactive protein (CRP), elevated cholesterol levels, diabetes and carotid artery stenosis (a narrowing in one or both of the carotid arteries in the neck, which supply blood to the brain).

If you have any of these risk factors, seek treatment to get them under control.

•**Do not ignore a transient ischemic attack (TIA), or ministroke.** This starts out like a stroke—the warning signs are the same—but unlike most strokes, you are not left with an obvious disability. It lasts from a few minutes to an hour. *All* stroke symptoms signal an emergency and demand immediate medical care. Moreover, one-third of people who have a TIA go on to have a more serious and debilitating acute stroke.

•**See your health-care professional for regular medical checkups.** Timing of exams is individual and should be based on your risk factors and age.

•**Don't smoke or engage in heavy alcohol use.** Drink no more than one alcoholic beverage per day for women, two for men.

•**Avoid foods that are high in cholesterol** and the "bad fats," such as saturated fats and trans fats.

•**Enjoy regular exercise.** Walking 20 minutes to 30 minutes a day, four times a week, is beneficial. If you can gradually increase this, so much the better.

•**Decrease your stress level** or learn ways to manage stress, including meditation, yoga, tai chi, etc.

info For more information, contact the American Stroke Association at *www.strokeasso ciation.org*…the National Institute of Neurological Disorders and Stroke at *www.ninds.nih. gov*…and the National Stroke Association at *www.stroke.org*.

Two Simple Tests That Could Save Your Life

James F. Toole, MD, the Walter C. Teagle professor of neurology and director of the Cerebrovascular Research Center, Wake Forest University Baptist Medical Center, Winston-Salem, North Carolina. Dr. Toole is past president of the International Stroke Society.

With stroke and stroke deaths on the rise, and stroke being the leading cause of disability in the US, it is important to know that there are two very simple diagnostic tests to detect artery blockages that can lead to stroke.

The bad news: Neither test is routinely offered by physicians and insurance may not cover them. To learn more, we interviewed James F. Toole, MD, the Walter C. Teagle professor of neurology and director of the Cerebrovascular Research Center at Wake Forest University Baptist Medical Center in Winston-Salem, North Carolina, and past president of the International Stroke Society.

He told us that once you have a stroke, the damage is done. Prevention is especially important for people at high risk—those who have a family history of stroke, suffer from high blood pressure or diabetes, or smoke.

THE TWO TESTS—CAROTID ULTRASOUND AND ANKLE-BRACHIAL TEST

• **Carotid ultrasound.** Blockage of the carotid arteries, located on each side of your neck, is a common cause of stroke, and those with severe blockages face an especially high risk. At your next physical exam, Dr. Toole strongly advises that you ask your physician to use a stethoscope to listen to the two arteries. These vital arteries supply blood to the brain. If there is a bruit (an indication of a blockage), be sure to schedule a simple, noninvasive imaging test called a *carotid ultrasound.*

A carotid ultrasound can detect carotid artery stenosis (or narrowing). It is atherosclerosis—a blood vessel disease in which fatty deposits called plaque build up in arteries—that typically causes arteries to narrow, thicken, harden and decrease blood flow. When plaque or clots block the blood flow to the brain, a stroke occurs and brain tissue dies.

Whether or not your physician detects a bruit in a carotid artery, Dr. Toole recommends carotid ultrasound screening for everyone age 60 and older. There is no standard recommendation for how often one should be screened. Consult with your doctor. He adds that people should consider getting a baseline test in their 50s…those with diabetes should think about screening in their 30s…and people with high blood pressure should consider it in their 40s. For the sake of accuracy, it is best to get these imaging tests evaluated at a lab with an experienced technician. Given that this test is totally dependent on the quality of the data collection, it is crucial that the work is done at an experienced lab. Talk to your doctor about the "best place in town."

Fortunately, carotid artery stenosis is a very treatable condition. The key is to catch it in time. If a carotid ultrasound reveals a partial blockage, plaque accumulation can generally be controlled through improved diet or drug therapy, as well as proper management of high blood pressure, cholesterol levels and diabetes. More serious blockages require surgery to remove the plaque that is narrowing a carotid artery (carotid endarterectomy) or placement of a stent in the artery to widen it.

• **Ankle-brachial test.** Another useful test measures the accumulation of fatty plaque throughout the arteries in the body. In this assessment, blood pressure readings are taken at arteries in the ankle and at the brachial artery in the upper arm. A normal ankle-brachial index (ABI) reading is 1. This means that blood pressure at the ankle is the same as that in the arm, and there is no significant narrowing or blockage of blood flow. If the arteries between the heart and the ankle are partially blocked, the pressure at the ankle will be less than the pressure at the arm. An ABI of 0.9 is abnormal, and an ABI of 0.6 or less constitutes high risk of stroke.

While the ABI is primarily used to diagnose peripheral arterial disease of the legs, plaque buildup in one area of the body is a sign of plaque buildup elsewhere. This test is recommended for those age 60 and older, and for younger people who have stroke risk factors.

If an ABI indicates a partial blockage, the first line of defense—as with carotid ultrasound—is medication, better diet and optimum management of underlying risk factors. If further testing reveals blockages that do not respond to nonsurgical treatment, surgical intervention may be required. Depending on the location of the blockage, surgery could involve plaque removal or placement of a stent.

STROKE PREVENTION
IS KEY

Once you identify and treat their causes, most strokes can be prevented, says Dr. Toole.

Be proactive about your health: Ask your physician about these tests, particularly if there is a history of stroke in your family, or if you smoke or have high blood pressure or diabetes. If your insurance doesn't cover them, consider paying for the tests out of your own pocket. A carotid ultrasound can cost up to several hundred dollars, and an ABI test runs anywhere from $50 into the hundreds of dollars.

Although there is a lot that your physician can do to prevent stroke, keep in mind that there are also many simple steps that you can take to enhance your cardiovascular health—don't smoke, avoid foods high in saturated fat and cholesterol, get regular exercise, maintain a healthy weight, find ways to cope with stress and manage underlying medical problems such as high blood pressure and diabetes.

Now that we have made significant progress against heart disease, Dr. Toole emphasizes that it is time to focus on preventing stroke.

info For more stroke prevention information, contact the American Stroke Association at *www.strokeassociation.org.*

20

Managing Your Diabetes

A Monster of a Diabetes Drug

What in the world does a poisonous lizard have to do with diabetes? More than you might think.

Gila monsters—one of the only two known venomous lizards in the world—produce a hormone in their saliva that has been a useful tool in the development of a new drug for the management of type 2 diabetes. Researchers isolated this hormone and created a new synthetic medication based on it called *exenatide injection* (Byetta). But like all medications, it has its pros and cons.

THE PROS

"The drug Byetta works similarly to a naturally produced substance in the body called GLP-1 —glucagon-like peptide," David M. Nathan, MD, from Massachusetts General Hospital and Harvard Medical School (both in Boston), says. "GLP-1 increases insulin secretion and was

discovered in the 1980s as a possible new way to help type 2 diabetics secrete more insulin. But the problem with GLP-1 was that they were degraded in the body so quickly that you had to give them intravenously."

HOW IT WORKS

Enter the gila monster. A hormone in the saliva of the gila monster was found to have a similar structure to GLP-1, and by producing a synthetic form of the hormone, researchers developed Byetta. "Byetta has a high degree of similarity to GLP-1," Dr. Nathan notes. "It increases insulin production and secretion."

A person with type 2 diabetes has the ability to make insulin—but it isn't enough to lower blood sugar effectively because the cells are resistant to it.

David M. Nathan, MD, director of the General Clinical Research Center and of the Diabetes Center at Massachusetts General Hospital, and a professor of medicine at Harvard Medical School, both in Boston. He is also chairman of the Diabetes Prevention Program, a National Institutes of Health sponsored multicenter trial to prevent type 2 diabetes.

Doctors go about treating this with two main strategies. The first is to increase insulin secretion or to give insulin by injection to meet the higher demands, and the second is to lower the resistance of the cells so that the amount of insulin produced is enough to get the job of lowering blood sugar accomplished.

These two strategies are not mutually exclusive. Some diabetic medications help lower glucose produced by the liver and reduce insulin resistance—*metformin* (Glucophage)—while others, a class called *sulfonylureas*, which includes Glucotrol and Micronase, help the body release more insulin. Byetta is in the latter category, stimulating insulin production and secretion. Byetta also appears to slow stomach contractions, delaying the absorption of food, which also helps to lower blood sugar levels.

THE CONS

"The problem is that you have to inject it twice a day and people are squeamish about that," Dr. Nathan says. "And compared with insulin, it's less effective at lowering blood sugar." Nonetheless, Byetta also modestly lowers weight, typically about five to eight pounds over six months, which is a big plus for a lot of people. "This is the opposite effect of insulin," Dr. Nathan points out, which usually increases weight.

The other problem with Byetta is nausea, diarrhea and vomiting. "About 40% of people experience nausea or diarrhea," Dr. Nathan explains. Byetta comes in only two doses—high and low. "The high dose is associated with greater weight loss," but it's also associated with more stomach upset.

THE WHOLE PICTURE

"As an injectable drug we have to be careful not to confuse Byetta with insulin, which is far more effective at lowering blood sugar," Dr. Nathan concludes. "But there may be a population of patients for whom Byetta—or a combination of Byetta and other medications—is useful."

Keep Diabetes at Bay

Michael Hirt, MD, medical director, the Center for Integrative Medicine, Encino-Tarzana Regional Medical Center, California and associate clinical professor, University of California, Los Angeles (UCLA). *www.drhirt.com.*

There are some illnesses that it seems you just "can't help." Then there are some that can be helped but require commitment on the part of the sufferer. Such is the case for the nearly 24 million Americans who have diabetes. Then there's the 54 million who have pre-diabetes, in which a person has elevated glucose levels but is not yet classified as type 2 diabetic.

Much to the frustration of doctors, many people dismiss the impact of diabetes because some of its risks—including kidney failure, blindness, amputation and death—can be felt in the long term, but not right away.

While diabetes is definitely no fun to live with, it is often very manageable. There are a number of medications for diabetes, and many patients have progressed to the point that they must take them, but there are also vitamins and other supplements that address the particular problems. We reviewed the protocol for these with Michael Hirt, MD, who is medical director of the Center for Integrative Medicine at Encino-Tarzana Regional Medical Center, California.

FREE RADICAL ATTACK

The main issue for people with diabetes is that high blood sugar levels cause dysregulated oxidative reactions in the body. This process can accelerate internal aging, resulting in such things as more rapidly hardening arteries and increased cardiovascular disease risk. To combat the free radicals contributing to this oxidation, it is necessary to take more antioxidants than diet alone commonly provides.

Dr. Hirt recommends 1,000 milligrams (mg) a day of vitamin C (the long-acting one that lingers in the system) also known as Ester-C... and 200 mg to 300 mg a day of alpha-lipoic acid. This little known antioxidant is one of the most powerful, in part because it is the only one that can deactivate free radicals in both fat and water, giving much more bang for the buck. Studies show that alpha-lipoic acid has beneficial effects on the long-term nerve damage that often occurs in diabetes. Research also suggests that it helps improve insulin sensitivity.

EAT AND DRINK WISELY

A surprising aid to helping stabilize blood sugar is undoubtedly in your kitchen already—cinnamon. Dr. Hirt reports that researchers discovered this while testing people with diabetes to see how common foods affected their blood sugar levels. For some reason, patients' sugar levels didn't rise as anticipated when they ate apple pie. Ultimately, the researchers found that it was the cinnamon in the pie that helped prevent a rise. He recommends having one-half to one teaspoon a day, sprinkled over cereal, yogurt, fruit or other food or beverages.

Also: Tea made from an herb called *Gymnema silvestre* seems to lower blood sugar and help pancreas cells work more efficiently.

MANAGING WEIGHT

An ongoing problem for diabetics is weight. One reason, of course, is that excess weight is a risk factor for developing the disease. In fact, 80% of people with diabetes are overweight. But as a double whammy, insulin—used to treat diabetes—can cause weight gain. Dr. Hirt says that he hasn't seen anything surefire to address this problem, but chromium picolinate may help. Being deficient in chromium, a trace element, can cause insulin resistance and increase blood glucose.

According to the USDA Human Nutrition Research Center, diabetics who are chromium deficient significantly reduce fasting blood glucose levels by taking chromium picolinate. There are actually other more efficient delivery systems for chromium than the picolinate salt used in research. Consult your naturopathic physician or pharmacologist for other options for you.

Important: Discuss every medicine you take or are considering with your physician. Doctors must have an overview in general, and with diabetes, it is especially critical.

The reason: One substance might offset or enhance the effectiveness of another. At the very least, your doctor may want to alter the dosages of your medication or supplementation. Diabetics should also avoid taking unprescribed

glucosamine, a popular supplement used as a remedy for osteoarthritis. According to a report from the National Institutes of Health National Center for Complementary and Alternative Medicine glucosamine can make insulin resistance worse.

Dr. Hirt also strongly urges those with diabetes to make any necessary changes in lifestyle to bring about better health. He explains that diabetes is a disease of poor nutrition and lack of exercise—both situations that people have the power to turn around. Eat well, exercise regularly, take your multivitamin once a day in addition to the other supplements you need and, he says, you should be able to greatly improve or even eliminate adult-onset, or type 2 diabetes.

Free Radical That Protects Against Diabetes

Xingen Lei, PhD, professor, department of animal science, College of Agriculture and Life Sciences, Cornell University, Ithaca, New York.

Even the most obvious issues are never black and white. So it is in the case of oxidants and their effect on the body. Oxidants, also called free radicals, are single-electron molecules that attach themselves to healthy cells, causing many different kinds of health problems. How many times have we heard about the benefits of eating a diet rich in antioxidants to fight the damage caused by free radicals?

Now there's a study indicating that oxidants may have a constructive purpose after all. One oxidant, in particular, seems to regulate insulin sensitivity, which in turn helps protect against developing type 2 diabetes.

THE STUDY

Researchers at Cornell University bred mutant mice to overproduce a naturally occurring enzyme called *glutathione peroxidase* (GPx). The important thing about GPx is that it contains a great deal of the trace mineral selenium, an antioxidant. In fact, GPx uses about 60% of the body's selenium supply. The mutant mice produced as much as three times the normal amount of GPx in various tissues.

315

Result: The mice became fat, developed high blood sugar and insulin levels and became insulin resistant—the direct route to developing diabetes—all apparently because they had an overabundance of an *antioxidant.*

We discussed this surprising finding with one of the study's authors, nutritional biochemist Xingen Lei, PhD, associate professor of animal science at Cornell University's College of Agriculture and Life Sciences. He explains that there are several enzymes that, if not blocked, turn off the insulin regulatory system. The substance that stops these enzymes from doing their damage is the oxidant hydrogen peroxide. That is all fine unless an abundance of selenium-containing GPx enters the picture. When it does, it destroys *hydrogen peroxide.* In other words, the theory goes, it kills the messenger. And in this case, the messenger would have prevented setting the stage for diabetes.

A SECOND STUDY

This theory concerning GPx and prediabetes was reinforced by a second, seemingly unrelated, study of pregnant women. Conducted at the University of Medicine and Dentistry of New Jersey, the study followed 408 women who were having normal pregnancies. It's usual in pregnancy for insulin resistance to develop, and the study found that the GPx rose along with it. The women who had higher levels of GPx, however, went on to develop more severe gestational diabetes. (Fatty diets also played a role. The study showed that the women who ate high-fat diets were particularly susceptible to gestational diabetes. Dr. Lei explained that fat induces overexpression of the enzyme activity that blocks insulin regulation.)

NOW WHAT SHOULD YOU DO?

What are we to make of this seeming conflict? A multitude of studies have established that antioxidants are invaluable in protecting health. Now, in spite of this plethora of evidence in their favor, are we to reconsider antioxidants?

This isn't the first study to point to an antioxidant as potentially unhealthy and perhaps even dangerous. There have been reports of problems that developed after beta-carotene supplementation resulted in a link to lung cancer, and there's also been a new study that links antioxidants to overproduction of LDL ("bad") cholesterol.

Dr. Lei is quick to say that he isn't against antioxidants. Obviously, antioxidants provide a great deal of protection in the human body. But, once again, too much of a good thing can go awry. It appears that at least some oxidants have a signaling role in the body, and we need them to serve that purpose. His concern is that people will be tempted to take a heavy load of antioxidants in supplemental form, thinking their health will benefit from it. Doing so, he says, may put them unknowingly at risk.

Dr. Lei strongly advises approaching antioxidant supplementation carefully because, as he says, the body appears to need balance. Not surprisingly, Dr. Lei adds that we need more research in this important area.

info To find a physician with specific clinical training in nutritional biochemistry, visit the American Association of Naturopathic Physicians at *www.naturopathic.org.*

More Coffee, Less Diabetes

Rob M. van Dam, PhD, assistant professor of medicine, Harvard Medical School, Boston.

Recently, coffee has been linked to a reduced risk for liver cancer. There is more good news for latte lovers from researchers at the Harvard School of Public Health (HSPH)—they found that people who drink coffee on a regular basis experience a substantially lower risk for type 2 diabetes.

These findings appeared in the *Journal of the American Medical Association* (JAMA).

ABOUT THE STUDY

In a retrospective review of nine studies of coffee consumption and type 2 diabetes risk, Harvard researcher Rob M. van Dam, PhD, and his colleagues in Boston looked at 193,473 regular coffee drinkers who experienced 8,394 cases of type 2 diabetes. They excluded studies that involved type 1 diabetes, animals or short-term exposure to coffee or caffeine.

Next, researchers calculated the relative risk of type 2 diabetes in relation to how many daily cups of coffee the participants consumed. *It turned out that the more coffee, the better...*

•**The risk for diabetes was lowest in people who consumed the most coffee each day (six or more cups).**

•**Those who drank four to six cups daily also faced a lower risk for diabetes** (about 30% reduction in risk) as compared with people drinking little or no coffee.

These numbers did not differ significantly according to sex, obesity or geographic region (which in this case meant the US and Europe). However, Dr. van Dam adds that the results were rather diverse in the lowest consumption category. He would not be surprised if future studies that are able to measure coffee consumption more precisely find a lower diabetes incidence for any amount of coffee.

MORE COFFEE, LESS DIABETES

These findings serve to underscore the results of an earlier HSPH study in 2004. It found those who drank more than six cups of coffee a day reduced their risk of type 2 diabetes by more than 50% for men and for women 30% compared to non-coffee drinkers. This beneficial effect was observed independent of lifestyle choices such as smoking, exercise and obesity.

Scientists don't know exactly how coffee cuts diabetes risk. Paradoxically, caffeine reduces insulin sensitivity and raises blood sugar in the short term—both no-nos for diabetes. However, Dr. van Dam emphasizes that coffee is a complex beverage that contains numerous chemical compounds and minerals, which may have both helpful and harmful impacts on the body. Components other than caffeine—such as the antioxidants chlorogenic acid and magnesium—actually improve sensitivity to insulin and thus help lower diabetes risk. In animal studies, trigonelline and lignans, also found in coffee, improved glucose levels. Dr. van Dam adds that additional studies on effects of coffee components in humans are clearly needed.

WHAT ABOUT DECAF?

For those of us who prefer decaf, coffee still packs some protection against type 2 diabetes.

Although the effect appears to be more modest, some of this discrepancy may be attributed to study limitations. Decaffeinated coffee consumption was substantially lower than caffeinated coffee consumption, and this may have affected the estimates, explains Dr. van Dam. He points out that it is easier to detect larger contrasts in consumption than smaller differences. In addition, one can expect some misclassification when you ask for the amount of coffee people consume (change over time, differences in strength and cup size, etc.).

Dr. van Dam notes that in a recently published study on coffee consumption and C-peptide concentrations (a marker for insulin resistance), the association was actually similar for decaffeinated and caffeinated coffee consumption. He adds that it is currently unclear whether caffeine has detrimental effects on insulin sensitivity over the long term, because only short-term studies have been conducted. Nor is it clear if non-coffee sources of caffeine would have similar effects.

THE JOLT OF JAVA

Other trials have already lined up in coffee's favor, demonstrating that it can lower the risk of liver problems, gallstones, colon cancer and Parkinson's disease. Of course, there's also a downside to coffee (which pregnant women, children and people with colitis, hepatitis and other dietary challenges should not drink), such as jitteriness, insomnia and a rapid heartbeat. (Coffee stimulates liver function, which in healthy people is fine in moderation, but those with active liver disease may have symptoms worsen when they consume coffee.)

Promising as it seems, Dr. van Dam and his colleagues do not go so far as to recommend drinking coffee to prevent type 2 diabetes. They emphasize that while coffee consumption may contribute to the reduction of risk for diabetes, it cannot replace the myriad health benefits of diet, exercise and weight management.

Many people stop drinking coffee because they think this is good for their health. Now coffee drinkers can take comfort in knowing that their daily jolt of java not only gets them up and moving, it also provides a health benefit.

Full-Body Management For Diabetes

Mark H. Schutta, MD, medical director, Penn Rodebaugh Diabetes Center, University of Pennsylvania Health System, Philadelphia.

In study after study we learn more about how chronic diseases overlap and how one can lead to another. This is especially true of diabetes, which for many people is followed by kidney or cardiovascular disease and often other problems. While adequate control of diabetes requires careful monitoring of blood glucose levels to keep them as close to normal as possible, a new study indicates that the amount of fat people have in their cells may also be a key factor in preventing diseases related to diabetes.

FAT KILLS CELLS

One of the critical elements in scientific research of disease is the concept of cell death (apoptosis). All cells die but not all die as planned. This is especially evident in cancer cells.

Scientists at Washington University School of Medicine in St. Louis investigated the role excess fat might have in the process of cell death. They discovered through studying culture tissues and rodents that cells can become overloaded with saturated fat, resulting in an overproduction of the protein EF1A-1. This protein is abundant in the body and necessary for a number of cellular activities including protein synthesis and maintaining the cell's internal support structure.

However, when EF1A-1 increases substantially, as it does in the presence of excess cellular fat, it appears to turn on the cells and cause them to die. *The theory that has emerged from these studies is this...*

If insulin-producing cells in the pancreas are jammed with too much saturated fat (and so too much EF1A-1), these vital pancreatic cells end up dying. This likely contributes to the development of diabetes. Additionally, this study suggests that the same pattern of cell death takes place in cardiac muscle cells when they have a concentration of saturated fat, and this might well contribute to the association of diabetes and cardiac disease.

NEED MORE RESEARCH

We called endocrinologist Mark H. Schutta, MD, medical director of the Penn Rodebaugh Diabetes Center at the University of Pennsylvania Health System in Philadelphia, to discuss the studies. He describes the information as interesting, but adds that until we have additional research, the theory of saturated-fat-induced protein causing apoptosis remains speculative.

Of course, just because there is more research to be done doesn't mean it isn't a warning worthy of heeding. Dr. Schutta observes how this study underscores once again the ill effects of obesity and the dangers of the typical American diet. The study team used the saturated fatty acid palmitate in the research—the major component of palm oil and one of the most common saturated fats in processed foods.

Among his patients, Dr. Schutta says there are some who are genetically predisposed to insulin problems, but there are many others whose diets are a strong contributory factor. He estimates that although his entire patient group receives extensive information about weight loss and a healthful lifestyle, only 10% to 20% of patients actually go on to make these changes.

FEWER POUNDS, SO MANY BENEFITS

Admittedly, losing weight is especially difficult for people with diabetes. The disease itself predisposes people to excess weight because diabetes makes it more difficult to metabolize fats efficiently. Nevertheless, it is of the utmost importance for people with diabetes and those who have become insulin resistant to lose weight. Weighing less improves metabolism of fats, insulin sensitivity and can even lower blood pressure. Being lighter also increases energy, which in turn makes exercising easier.

Interestingly, it doesn't take a lot of weight loss to improve health among people with diabetes. Dr. Schutta says that his patients assume when he tells them they need to lose weight that he is recommending they get back to what they weighed in their youth. But in fact, this isn't so. A weight loss of just 5% to 7% of a person's current weight is all that is necessary to make a substantial difference. This holds true for both those considered obese, with a body mass index (BMI) of 30 or above, and those with the all-too-typical extra 10 pounds to lose. This doesn't require any kind of dramatic dieting—just a healthful approach that includes protein, fruits (though no fruit juice because of its high sugar content), vegetables and whole grains—and getting rid of those saturated fats.

Cholesterol Care For Diabetics

Jay S. Cohen, MD, author of *What You Must Know about Statin Drugs and Their Natural Alternatives*. Square One.

People with type 2 diabetes sometimes feel like they are between a rock and a hard place. They are at high risk for cardiovascular disease—four times more likely to develop it than people without diabetes—and 65% of people with diabetes will eventually suffer a stroke or heart attack. Many might be tempted to take statins such as *atorvastatin* (Lipitor) to reduce their cholesterol levels. However, because statins can impair liver function, a risk that diabetes also creates, doctors are concerned about the safety of statins for diabetics. A recent large study seems to show that the risk may be worth taking if you have diabetes.

ABOUT THE STUDY

The study, which took place in the UK and Ireland in collaboration with Pfizer, was called the Collaborative Atorvastatin Diabetes Study (CARDS). It included more than 2,800 people with type 2 diabetes who were separated into two groups—one took a statin, in this case Lipitor by Pfizer, and the other took a placebo. The statin group had a 37% reduction in major cardiovascular events compared with those who took the placebo. Furthermore, the statin group's overall mortality rate was 27% lower than the placebo group. The study was stopped nearly two years earlier than planned because of the significant benefits to diabetic patients on the statin. The American Diabetes Association recommended that even for those with reduced low-density lipoprotein (LDL) levels (the "bad"

cholesterol), all adults with type 2 diabetes should be considered for statin therapy.

Some medical professionals, however, are deeply disturbed by the current broad use of statins because all statins have side effects. Some are relatively minor, such as mild diarrhea or constipation, but some are much more serious. As mentioned earlier, statins can damage liver function—in fact, all people taking statins need to have regular liver enzyme checks, and people with diabetes must discuss their liver function before starting statins to be sure they are candidates for the drugs. Statins can cause muscle problems including statin myopathy, which if it becomes severe can lead to impaired kidney function. There is also considerable anecdotal evidence that statins can cause memory problems sometimes so severe they are perceived as Alzheimer's disease.

EXPERT OPINION

We called Jay S. Cohen, MD, a nationally recognized expert on medications and side effects. Dr. Cohen is definitely not "anti-statins." They are good drugs, he says, when prescribed correctly and for the right people, and because they are at high risk of cardiovascular disease, most people with type 2 diabetes are right to be taking them. But Dr. Cohen has strong reservations about how doctors are prescribing statins, to this population or others. He explains that many doctors today are routinely prescribing high doses of the most potent statins on the market—*atorvastatin* (Lipitor), *rosuvastatin* (Crestor) and *simvastatin* (Zocor)—without careful consideration of individual patients' needs. This problem results at least in part from the pressure our current medical system puts on doctors to rush patients in and out. To counterbalance this trend, patients must be prepared to take a stand and demand what Dr. Cohen calls a start-low, go-slow approach.

AIM FOR FEWER SIDE EFFECTS

First, review your risk factors, such as family history, diabetes and high blood pressure with your doctor, and ask how much you actually need to lower your LDL level. Most people with a so-called cholesterol problem are only mildly elevated and simply do not need high doses of powerful drugs. People who have no or few risk factors for cardiovascular disease and who have only mildly or moderately elevated LDL levels for whom diet and nutritional supplements have been ineffective should start with low doses of less powerful drugs from the earlier generation of statins. These include *pravastatin* (Pravachol), *lovastatin* (Mevacor) and *fluvastatin* (Lescol), any of which may well do the job and have fewer side effects. Even patients who are at high risk and need the new generation of statins should still inquire about starting low and going slow, raising dosage levels only if it becomes clear that lower dosages are not working.

Dr. Cohen goes on to say that lifestyle changes—regular exercise, normal weight, a balanced diet full of healthful foods, not smoking and the like—are enough for many people to bring LDL levels under control (generally considered as under 130 mg/dL). Some natural supplements also have a proven track record of helping control LDLs and cardiovascular risk. He recommends fish oil in particular because of the omega-3 essential fatty acids it contains. Our medical expert, Andrew L. Rubman, ND, advises taking 1,000 milligrams (mg) a day of a fish oil that combines omega-3 EPA and DHA. He likes fish oils from Pharmax and Nordic Naturals.) There are other natural products as well, including niacin and plant sterols that might help. Work with a medical professional knowledgeable about supplements to explore what is most effective for you. Everyone on statins, though, must take supplements of coenzyme Q10 (CoQ10), a powerful antioxidant, because statins destroy CoQ10 in the body. Dr. Cohen recommends taking 45 mg to 90 mg of softgel CoQ10 daily and more for people with cardiovascular disease.

REVIEW ALL FACTORS

Remember that statins do not remove the risk of heart attack and stroke—they *reduce* it. Dr. Cohen cautions everyone, including those whose LDL levels have plummeted because of statin therapy, that LDL levels are just one component of cardiac risk. Other factors, such as a low HDL level, high C-reactive protein level or other factors—triglycerides, homocysteine, lipoprotein A, etc.—may be just as important. Maintaining a healthful lifestyle (nutritious diet,

normal weight, moderate exercise) is as important as any medication in preventing heart disease and stroke.

The Colon Cancer Connection

Donald Garrow, MD, MSc, clinical instructor, Medical University of South Carolina, Charleston.

Diabetes for many people is much more than one disease. Having diabetes increases risk for heart disease, stroke, kidney failure and eye problems, among others. Now a new study has confirmed yet another increased risk—colon cancer. The study, from the Medical University of South Carolina, in Charleston, collected data from the National Health Interview Survey (an ongoing in-person collection of data on a wide variety of health-related matters) on more than 226,000 Americans. In analyzing the data from the 5.9% of respondents who had diabetes (mainly type 2 diabetes—which is approximately reflective of the national incidence of diabetes), the study researchers discovered that they were 1.4 times more likely to develop colon cancer than people without diabetes. This was after the study team compensated for known colon cancer risk factors including age, gender, tobacco use and exercise.

STUDY DETAILS

We called lead author of the study, Donald Garrow, MD, MSc, a clinical instructor at the university, to find out more about this recently discovered risk. The increase in risk, he says, pertains to people who have type 2 diabetes rather than type 1. Type 1 diabetics do not produce any insulin, unlike the situation affecting those with type 2 diabetes, in which the body pumps out plenty of insulin but can't use it efficiently, resulting in soaring blood sugar levels. Dr. Garrow speculates that the increased cancer risk might have to do with how high levels of insulin in the blood—as happens with type 2 diabetes—affect cells in the mucosal lining of the colon. These cells contain insulin-like receptors, and lab experiments have shown that when high levels of insulin attach themselves to the receptors, the cells develop into cancer.

This study is clearly a cautionary message for everyone with type 2 diabetes to be especially careful about having colon cancer screenings. While there are several types of screening available, for this group of people Dr. Garrow recommends colonoscopy, in which the colon is viewed directly, because it has been shown repeatedly to be the most effective screener for colon cancer. He is currently evaluating data to determine if age has a role in the increased cancer risk. In the meantime, he supports the standard recommendation of starting at age 50.

The study team also plans to evaluate if spiking insulin and blood sugar levels impact risk. We should know this soon, Dr. Garrow says, but it just makes good sense for all people with diabetes to tightly control their blood sugar and to eat the healthiest diet possible. In addition to perhaps helping lower their colon cancer risk, this approach likely offers better protection from all those other diseases as well.

Diabetes Seeping Into Our Systems

Duk-Hee Lee, MD, PhD, associate professor in the department of preventive medicine, Health Promotion Research Center, School of Medicine, Kyungpook National University in South Korea. She is a medical doctor and epidemiologist who has written extensively about the relationship between persistent organic pollutants (POPs) and diabetes.

Rick Relyea, PhD, professor of ecology and director, Pymatuning Laboratory of Ecology, University of Pittsburgh, Pennsylvania.

The following almost reads like a detective story and sets the stage for what's to come…

Several years ago a story came out about the population of gray tree frogs being decimated by the use of a common pesticide, *carbaryl*. But the makers of carbaryl insisted it wasn't harming the frogs. They had numerous studies showing that if you take the little creatures and put them in a lab setting and expose them to the pesticide, nothing happens. Still, the tree frogs were dying. And the environmentalists were positive it had something to do with their continued exposure to this pesticide.

FROGS RELEVANT TO DIABETES?

Rick Relyea, PhD, an ecologist from the University of Pittsburgh, in Pennsylvania, discovered that carbaryl was less harmful to frogs in the unnaturally tranquil setting of the lab (at least it was less likely to kill them). But most tree frogs don't live in a lab, and in the wild there are constant dangers from predators. When tree frog tadpoles were exposed to a predator, the predator emitted a chemical cue. This resulted in a stress response in the gray tree frog—just like we get when we're caught in traffic or miss a deadline. Expose a stressed frog to the pesticide and you've got a dead frog. The combination of the two—physiological stress and a low-level pesticide, neither of which has a significant impact on survival alone—was lethal for a majority of the gray tree frog tadpoles.

"In other species such as bullfrog tadpoles, carbaryl became up to 46 times more deadly with the addition of predator cues. This phenomenon has since been observed with both insecticides and herbicides, suggesting that it may be a common phenomenon," says Dr. Relyea.

The take-home point is that elements in the environment often interact with elements of our own physiology to cause serious problems. New research is emerging that suggests we may be seeing exactly the same phenomenon with diabetes.

AN INTERESTING TRAIL OF BREADCRUMBS

We've long known that obesity is a major risk factor for diabetes. But now it appears that exposure to pollutants can seriously aggravate the risk, and—in combination with obesity—may be associated with the increased risk of becoming diabetic. A recent study in the journal *Diabetes Care* looked at the connection between six persistent organic pollutants (known as POPs) and diabetes. What they found was dramatic.

The prevalence of diabetes increased by 14- to 38-fold as the concentrations of the sum of the six POPs increased, irrespective of participants' weight, says lead researcher Duk-Hee Lee, MD, PhD, associate professor at the School of Medicine, Kyungpook National University in South Korea. Her team divided the 2,016 subjects into groups comparing five levels of pollutants. Group 1 had the lowest levels and group 5 had the highest levels. Compared with group 1 (which had a 0.4% incidence of diabetes), group 2 had a 6.7% incidence of diabetes, while group 5 had an astonishing 25.6% incidence of the disease (groups 3 and 4 ranged in between). Dr. Lee notes that while obesity remains a risk factor for type 2 diabetes, the obese and overweight people with very low concentrations of POPs had a much lower incidence of diabetes. Could obesity and pollutants interact to cause diabetes in much the way that the pesticide and stress interacted to cause the death of frogs?

WHAT IT ALL MEANS

"It's our hypothesis that obesity might be only weakly associated with diabetes among people with very low serum concentrations of POPs," Dr. Lee says. She explains that while her research concentrated on only six specific pollutants out of about 50 POPs identified in the National Health and Examination Survey, there was a striking connection between the blood concentrations of these six toxins and the prevalence of diabetes. This is not the first time that such a connection has been demonstrated. Earlier research from Sweden also found that exposure to POPs may contribute to the development of type 2 diabetes. And earlier research also demonstrated that exposure to at least one toxin—a dioxin called *TCDD*—increases the risk of diabetes and insulin resistance. It's believed that these toxins may interfere with glucose metabolism.

POPS ARE EVERYWHERE

POPs include certain chemical byproducts, PCBs and certain insecticides that have been linked to cancer, neurobehavioral impairment, endocrine problems and reproductive disorders. Previous researchers looked at special popula-

tions that are occupationally or accidentally exposed to high levels of these pollutants—for example, Vietnam veterans. (The US Department of Veterans Affairs includes type 2 diabetes in its list of presumptive diseases associated with exposure to the dioxin-containing Agent Orange.) But Dr. Lee's study is the first to examine the cumulative effect of most commonly detected POPs among a random low-level exposure in the general population. The six toxins in the study are found in the environment, and move through the air and water to accumulate in the environment.

Dr. Lee points out that pollutants by themselves do not necessarily cause diabetes, and expresses caution about jumping to strong conclusions based on one or two studies. "Plenty of people have exposure to these pollutants and don't get diabetes," she explains. "But the strong connection between high levels and increased incidence is very hard to ignore, as is the fact that there are such low levels of diabetes among those with low levels of exposure, even among the overweight and obese." Could genes be a factor? "It's prudent to act as if everyone is at risk, regardless of genetic makeup," she advises.

How do we get exposed to these chemicals in the first place? "Exposure to POPs comes mostly from fatty animal food consumption," Dr. Lee tells us.

When asked what protective measures people might take, Dr. Lee answers concisely: "A low intake of animal foods and a higher intake of plant foods may be beneficial. And, aside from trying to avoid POPs, preventing obesity is still very important because the toxicity of POPs appeared to synergistically

21

Better Cancer Care

All Natural, Genuine, Cancer Helper

We are always on the lookout for new, interesting information on alternative or integrative treatments for health conditions, but something that sounds too good to be true can be a scam.

That's why, when a groundbreaking report appeared in the highly respected newsletter *Alternatives* about a relatively new adjunct treatment for cancer called Avemar, we decided to thoroughly investigate.

BACKGROUND ON AVEMAR

First, a bit of background. A defining characteristic of cancer is its uncontrolled metabolism and rampant cell division. Cancer cells really have only one function—proliferation. In the 1950s, a Nobel Prize-winning Hungarian scientist (named Albert Szent-Györgyi) made great strides in cancer research by examining how naturally occurring compounds could help control metabolism in cells, which in turn controls cell profileration.

Another Hungarian doctor built on Szent-Györgyi's work in the 1990s by showing that fermented wheat germ extract could achieve this effect. Avemar is a fermented wheat germ product.

AVEMAR'S EFFECTIVENESS

Avemar appears to have extraordinary abilities against cancer cells. "The pedigree on this stuff is pretty impressive," says our medical expert, Andrew L. Rubman, ND. "Currently there are more than 18 published studies in peer-reviewed journals, nearly all of them showing positive results. Research at the University of California, Los Angeles (UCLA) has demonstrated that Avemar reduces glucose flow into cancer cells, which inhibits their ability to reproduce."

Although no one is saying Avemar is a cure for cancer, it has been used as an adjunct to

Andrew L. Rubman, ND, director, Southbury Clinic for Traditional Medicines, Southbury, Connecticut.

323

conventional therapies. It seems to be especially effective at reducing metastasis, or the spreading of the cancer to other sites throughout the body. "It seems that Avemar boosts immune system function sufficiently to allow the natural process of the body routinely killing cells to succeed much more effectively, " Dr. Rubman says. "It's conceivable that its ability to boost the immune system is the reason it is so effective at reducing the spread of cancer."

WHO SHOULD USE IT

Avemar is now being tested on patients with autoimmune conditions.

In Hungary, Avemar is an over-the-counter dietary supplement that is used by cancer patients in conjunction with other drugs. "In one pilot study in Budapest," Dr. Rubman notes, "a group of patients with advanced colorectal cancer were given Avemar and had no disease progression over nine months." And David Williams, MD, editor of *Alternatives*, has been quoted as saying, "There's absolutely no reason that Avemar shouldn't be used with every single cancer patient—particularly in those with severely impaired immune systems and those who are undergoing conventional therapies."

AVAILABILITY

Avemar isn't cheap, but its benefits seem substantial. It's available in this country under the name of Ave, and contains Avemar. It's sold through the Harmony Company, P.O. Box 93, Northvale, New Jersey 07447, at 800-521-0543 or on the Web at *www.theharmonyco.com*. It comes in packets and is taken as a drink once per day or as prescribed by your oncology team. Of course, don't take Avemar without your doctor's consent.

With such great immune-boosting benefits, can non-cancer patients benefit from Avemar, or even just plain wheat germ? Dr. Rubman says that eating wheat germ as a general immune booster can be good for many. As for taking Avemar prophylactically, if your health-care adviser believes that your immune system could stand improved function, Avemar may be a reasonable choice.

Stopping Cancer Before It Grows

John J. Laterra, MD, PhD, research scientist, Kennedy Krieger Institute, Baltimore.

As therapy for many forms of cancer moves steadily forward, treatment for malignant gliomas, the most common primary brain tumor, has remained stubbornly complex and challenging. Standard therapy for cancerous gliomas includes one or all of the following, depending on tumor type—surgery, radiation and chemotherapy—and has a dismaying lack of success and can cause considerable brain damage, especially in children whose brains are particularly sensitive to these conventional therapies. Recently, though, news came of promising research that could profoundly affect treatment not only for gliomas but also for some more common cancers including breast, prostate and colon cancer.

ADAPTING CURRENT TECHNOLOGY FOR NEW USES

Monoclonal antibody (mAb) therapy for cancer involves administering a type of antibody that targets a specific growth factor protein responsible for stimulating certain kinds of cancer. The therapy is in use today to address a number of cancers including breast cancer. Doctors at Kennedy Krieger Institute in Baltimore and Galaxy Biotech, LLC, in Mountain View, California, tested a new form of mAb— mAb L2G7. Researchers found mAb to be effective against hepatocyte growth factor protein (HGF), a trouble-making protein in gliomas.

Using live mice, the researchers administered L2G7 into the circulation and found that it induced tumor regression and dramatically increased survival. The animals in the control group receiving a similar but inactive type of mAb died within 41 days of starting the experiment…those treated with mAb L2G7 survived through day 70 with 80% of them remaining alive at day 90. To further test L2G7, researchers had waited to treat one group of mice until their tumors were advanced. Just three doses of

L2G7 shrunk the large tumors to less than half their pre-treatment size.

Note: In pilot studies of this type, it is standard to monitor results at 90 days. If successful, the next step is then more expensive longitudinal studies. The difference in results between the control group and the test groups is very significant in this test and shows great promise for the future.

MORE RESEARCH NEEDED

We talked with the study's coauthor John J. Laterra, MD, PhD, a research scientist at Baltimore's Kennedy Krieger Institute, about this exciting development. Dr. Laterra says that in addition to attacking gliomas, mAb L2G7 will likely be useful to treat some breast, prostate and colon cancers because they, too, have the cancer-stimulating HGF protein. Furthermore, because HGF protects tumor cells in these cancers, adding L2G7 should enhance standard chemotherapy and radiation therapy as well.

While the side-effect profile of L2G7 in patients is not yet known, it is expected to be well tolerated. Even if not completely side-effect free, it is anticipated that L2G7 will be a significantly better treatment for these cancer patients whether used alone or in conjunction with chemo or radiation.

Results of human trials will determine if findings in mice hold up for people and provide answers to such questions as appropriate dosage and delivery methods.

Shedding Light on Blood Irradiation

Timothy C. Birdsall, ND, vice president, integrative medicine, Cancer Treatment Centers of America, Zion, Illinois.

Barrie R. Cassileth, PhD, Laurance S. Rockefeller Chair in Integrative Medicine, chief, integrative medicine service, Memorial Sloan-Kettering Cancer Center, New York City.

A technology that could potentially be an effective alternative treatment for cancer recently came to our attention. It is called photoluminescence therapy, also known as ultraviolet blood irradiation.

WHAT IS PHOTOLUMINESCENCE?

Photoluminescence was first performed in the late 1920s. The basic procedure is similar today to what it was back then. Essentially, doctors withdraw a small sample of blood from a patient (the amount of blood is based on the weight of the individual), mix the blood with an anticoagulant and then expose the blood to ultraviolet light (a known way to kill viruses and bacteria). The blood, which is kept in an airtight container throughout the procedure, is then reinjected into the patient.

Early treatments were seen as a way to treat bacterial infections. (The first known use of photoluminescence was to treat a patient with a blood-borne bacterial infection—the infection reportedly cleared up within 24 hours.) Of course, the first antibiotic was being discovered at about the same time (penicillin was discovered in 1928), and, once further developed, those antibiotics quickly overtook photoluminescence as the treatment of choice. At that point, it seems that photoluminescence fell out of favor. The technology received little further scientific investigation.

CANCER READY?

So what about photoluminescence as a cancer treatment? Though there seem to be plenty of claims that photoluminescence is a viable treatment for cancer, our research turned up little to support the assertions.

One exception: In New Haven, Connecticut, Yale School of Medicine researchers have used UV exposure as part of an experimental treatment called *transimmunization* for a certain type of lymphoma. This treatment is still being studied—and many photoluminescence-promoting Web sites mention this research as proof that photoluminescence works. However, transimmunization relies on UV light to activate a drug known as 8-MOP (which the patient has ingested) in a relatively complicated and time-consuming process—not the simple withdrawal and reinjection of the typical photoluminescence procedure. What's more, as mentioned above, transimmunization is noted as a potential treatment for cutaneous T-cell lymphoma, a relatively rare type of non-Hodgkin's lymphoma, and possibly other types of cancer.

A LACK OF EVIDENCE

Since we weren't having much luck finding solid photoluminescence research, we called some cancer experts to try to finally get some answers.

What we found: We were already on the right track.

"As a general rule, I'd say there's inadequate data to say that [photoluminescence] is an effective treatment for cancer," says Timothy C. Birdsall, ND, vice president of integrative medicine for Cancer Treatment Centers of America in Zion, Illinois. "Almost all of the data that was generated in the '30s and '40s really has to do with treating infectious processes, and it does appear that that approach would be very effective in that case." But, Dr. Birdsall adds, photoluminescence is invasive—blood has to be withdrawn and reinjected—plus it's not readily available, which means it has little chance of challenging the ease of taking an antibiotic pill three times a day.

According to Dr. Birdsall, the problem with photoluminescence as a cancer treatment is that, while the treatment can potentially boost the immune system, that boost would primarily be useful in a fight against bacteria and viruses, and wouldn't do much to fight cancer. Plus, it hasn't been studied in a clinical setting to see what, if any, kind of benefit it has.

"There's no such thing as a simple one-size-fits-all cure for cancer," Dr. Birdsall says, "and I get really concerned and more than a little suspicious when proponents of a particular therapy imply that it's the end-all, be-all therapy for all cancers."

Barrie R. Cassileth, PhD, chief of the integrative medicine service at the Memorial Sloan-Kettering Cancer Center in New York City, is even more skeptical. "These approaches spring up rather constantly, and there's just no data behind them," she says. "You can do a Google search on 'alternative' and 'cancer'—there are probably around 36 million hits these days—and you look at many of them and they're just selling absolute garbage. Patients need to be very vigilant."

OTHER OPTIONS

Of course, this shouldn't stop cancer patients from exploring their treatment options. Both Dr.

Birdsall and Dr. Cassileth made recommendations in this regard.

One such recommendation from Dr. Cassileth is clinical trials. "There are exciting new therapies that come along about every month," she says, "and some exciting advances that would have an infinitely better chance of doing something positive for the world, if not for that particular individual." Of course, clinical trials can be risky since the treatments are experimental, which means that information is not available regarding both effectiveness and risk.

Another approach mentioned by Dr. Birdsall is called integrative oncology, which "utilizes the best of conventional treatment alongside intensive nutritional support, mind/body medicine, exercise and rehab, and intensive naturopathic remedies to enhance the effectiveness of the conventional treatment, reduce side effects and boost immune function."

"This requires a team approach to cancer care," warns Dr. Birdsall, "so that one therapy doesn't interfere with the efficacy of another therapy." Unfortunately, to be successful, it also requires an oncologist who is open to integrated treatments.

It seems like bad news concerning photoluminescence as a cancer treatment option, but luckily there are other possible avenues of help.

info For more on clinical trials, visit the National Cancer Institute's information page at *www.cancer.gov.*

Non-Hodgkin's Lymphoma Prevention

Linda E. Kelemen, MSc, ScD, adjunct assistant professor, department of medical genetics, University of Calgary, Alberta.

As if you needed one more reason to load up your plate with healthful veggies, a recent study indicates that a higher vegetable intake may lower the risk for non-Hodgkin's lymphoma (NHL). According to lead researcher Linda E. Kelemen, MSc, ScD, former assistant professor of epidemiology at the Mayo Clinic College of Medicine in Rochester, Minnesota, disease-fighting antioxidants in foods such as broccoli and Brussels sprouts may have a protective effect against this dangerous lymphatic system cancer that has recently afflicted an estimated 66,120 Americans with a positive diagnosis in a single year.

ABOUT THE STUDY

To determine the association between antioxidants in vegetables and fruits and the risk of developing this type of lymphoma, Dr. Kelemen and her colleagues examined the diets of more than 800 American adults with and without NHL. Normal, everyday living can create excess free radicals or oxidants that damage cells and may lead to cancer, explains Dr. Kelemen. She compares it with the development of rust on an unprotected car. Fortunately, eating antioxidant-packed vegetables and fruits protect against damage to cells—just like rust-proofing protects your car. *In the study, researchers found that...*

●**People who ate the most vegetables a week** (20 or more servings) had a 42% lower risk for non-Hodgkin's lymphoma than those who ate the fewest (eight or less servings).

●**Leafy greens such as spinach and green salad and cruciferous vegetables** (Brussels sprouts, broccoli, cauliflower, etc.) provided the greatest protection.

●**Two nutrients in particular, lutein and zeaxanthin** (high in leafy greens, spinach and broccoli), were singled out for their potent antioxidant action.

●**The mineral zinc** (common in certain nuts and seeds) also demonstrated a protective effect against NHL.

While researchers did not uncover any strong link between fruit intake and non-Hodgkin's lymphoma risk, Dr. Kelemen points out that the benefits of eating whole fruits to reduce the risk of other diseases is well known.

These findings were published in the *American Journal of Clinical Nutrition.*

EAT YOUR GREENS

When Dr. Kelemen was asked about dietary supplements, she responded that supplements do not contain the more than 100 antioxidants and phytochemicals found in fresh vegetables and fruit. If needed, they could be taken as an addition to—not as a replacement for—a healthy diet.

Too Much Bread Can Be Bad for the Kidneys

Francesca Bravi, ScD, an epidemiologist and researcher at the Mario Negri Institute for Pharmacological Research in Milan, Italy. Dr. Bravi has published numerous research papers on the relation between cancer and diet.

In 1981, epidemiologists estimated that "dietary factors" accounted for 35% of cancer deaths in the United States—roughly the same amount attributed to smoking at the time. In recent years, similar conclusions on diet and cancer have been reached by experts at the National Cancer Institute and the World Health Organization.

A recent study from Italy adds another piece of data on the rapidly accumulating pile of evidence linking dietary choices with cancer risk. Researchers examined the food records of 2,301 Italians to see if they could uncover associations between certain foods and kidney cancer.

What they found was shocking: High bread consumption significantly raises the risk of renal cell carcinoma (kidney cancer).

"The association with bread consumption—which in Italy is mainly refined—may be due to the high glycemic index of refined cereals," Francesca Bravi, ScD, from the Mario Negri Institute for Pharmacological Research in Milan, Italy, and lead researcher on the study, says.

Note: In terms of this research, refined cereals mean pasta, rice and bread—not breakfast cereals. The glycemic index is a measure of how quickly blood sugar is raised after eating a food. When blood sugar is high, the body compensates by secreting a higher level of the hormone insulin, excess amounts of which may cause many problems. "It's possible that refined cereals may have affected the process of carcinogenesis by influencing the levels of insulin-like growth factors." Pasta and rice—other cereals that are known for having a high glycemic impact—also showed a relationship to kidney cancer, though not as strong a relationship as bread did. "The highest quintile of bread eaters were consuming about 28 portions a week," Dr. Bravi explains. "At approximately four slices a day, these people had about twice the risk of getting renal cancer."

EAT YOUR FRUITS AND VEGGIES

While renal cell carcinoma accounts for only 2% of all cancers in adults, it's hardly the only cancer associated with diet…in particular, colon cancer has been shown in previous studies to have a major connection to diet. The Italian researchers also noted that vegetables had the strongest inverse association with the development of kidney cancer—the more vegetables you eat, the less risk of getting the disease. That correlation should come as no surprise to anyone. More than 200 studies have looked at the relation between diets high in fruits and vegetables, and the overwhelming bulk of them have found that eating plenty of them significantly lowers your chance of getting cancer.

There's a popular quote that is often repeated: "The whiter the bread, the quicker you're dead." It may possibly be true.

Indoor Lifestyle Linked to Cancer Risk

Krispin Sullivan, CN, a Petaluma, California-based clinical nutritionist. She spent more than six years working with clients and researching the literature on vitamin D and is the author of *Naked at Noon: Understanding the Importance of Sunlight and Vitamin D.* Basic Health.

Andrew L. Rubman, ND, director, Southbury Clinic for Traditional Medicines, Southbury, Connecticut.

Sometimes it seems the more we learn, the more confused we get about the pros and cons of sun exposure.

Case in point: Everyone "knows" you should avoid midday sun and always wear potent sunscreen. Or not? In fact, numerous health experts are worried that we have turned into a nation (if not a world) of people suffering from vitamin D deficiency—yes, the sunshine vitamin. And that's a serious issue because studies are emerging at

a rapid rate that associate insufficient vitamin D with increased risk for many diseases.

The department of family and preventive medicine at the University of California, San Diego, published a study that showed a striking link between vitamin D deficiency and higher rates of cancer, specifically prostate, colon, breast and ovarian cancer.

Another study from the Tufts-New England Medical Center in Boston, based on the long-term Nurses' Health Study (from Harvard in Boston), demonstrated that insufficient amounts of vitamin D and calcium may heighten the risk for type 2 diabetes. It also pointed out other studies that linked insufficient vitamin D to insulin resistance.

To find out more about this complex vitamin, we called nutritionist and writer Krispin Sullivan, CN, who has spent several years researching the literature on vitamin D, teaching clients how to get vitamin D safely, and has written a book about sunlight and vitamin D.

THE CHEMISTRY OF VITAMIN D

Sullivan says that the vitamin D we make from sunlight or get from food and supplements is actually a prohormone from which our bodies produce *calcitriol,* the active form of vitamin D. The hormone calcitriol is one of the controllers of calcium in our bodies, which is why vitamin D is associated with rickets and osteoporosis. Recent research suggests this metabolite of vitamin D has other profound effects within our cells, regulating numerous cellular body functions, in processes in our skin, hair, muscles, bones and glands.

Getting enough vitamin D is vital for good health—but there's a catch. Too much vitamin D is dangerous as well. Excess may cause bone loss, soft tissue calcification and other serious problems.

Deficiencies in children and adults can impair normal bone growth or strength (rickets, osteomalacia and osteoporosis). It is also associated with poor development or a decline in health of the jaw and teeth. In fact, getting enough vitamin D and calcium may prevent cavities and periodontal disease in young and old. Low levels of vitamin D are associated with many autoimmune diseases, obesity and many types of cancer, including breast and prostate.

Getting enough vitamin D in later years has been shown to reduce fractures, maintain muscle mass, keep the immune system strong and improve memory and mood.

THE BEST SUN

The best and safest way to get vitamin D is through carefully regulated exposure to the sun, specifically to UVB rays, the rays of light that stimulate production of vitamin D in our skin. However, excess exposure to ultraviolet light, UVB or UVA is harmful. *Safe and effective sun exposure depends on the following factors...*

●**Location.** UVB decreases as latitude increases. Latitudes below 30 degrees (closer to the equator) have stronger UVB rays most of the day and most of the year.

Example: Miami is 25 degrees North latitude, providing UVB most of the day and most of the year...New York is 40 degrees North latitude, with little UVB much of the day and year. Altitude also matters. The higher the altitude, the higher the intensity of UVB rays.

●**Time of year.** Vitamin D production in the skin requires the presence of sufficient UVB-containing sunlight. In most northern latitudes in the US, that's typically from late April or May until mid-August. Only Florida and some parts of Texas and Arizona, and some locations at higher altitudes have significant, nearly year-round, UVB.

Note: To make sunning for vitamin D worthwhile, the UV index really needs to reach 8 to 10. Lower UV index ratings require more exposure.

●**Time of day.** In most of the US the sun provides UVB primarily between the hours of 10:00 am and 2:00 pm, precisely the time most people are inside working or avoiding the sun for fear of sun damage. Yet this is when Sullivan recommends people be in the sun.

●**The amount of time exposed**—very fair-skinned people may need as little as five minutes (front and back), four or more times a week, without sunscreen. Melanin, the coloring agent in our skin, protects against UVB damage, but also increases the time needed to make vitamin D, so those with very dark skin or with suntans need more exposure to UVB to make adequate vitamin D (as much as 90 to 120 minutes a day),

according to Sullivan. This could be nearly impossible for many busy people.

Important: How much is too much? If your skin turns pink, you've stayed too long.

●**The amount of skin exposed.** There is a substance in the skin, called pre-D, that is converted by UVB into cholecalciferol. The amount of pre-D is limited and genetically variable such that only so much vitamin D will be produced in any given skin area within a day. The more skin exposed, the more vitamin D produced. This means exposing small patches of skin for longer periods won't produce more vitamin D. Excess UV exposure, staying longer than you need to make your daily vitamin D, may actually begin degrading vitamin D that has already been produced. Sullivan advises exposing as much skin as possible, especially the back.

●**Vitamin A.** It is also important for vitamin D to be in balance with vitamin A (which, like vitamin D, is converted into an active messenger, regulating cell functions), since the two work together in the body. Sunlight exposure depletes levels of vitamin A in the skin, a nutrient important for skin health and repair, so if you decide to sun it is especially important to get adequate vitamin A in your diet—in effect, sunning increases your need for vitamin A.

Try: Sullivan advises eating liver—preferably beef, buffalo or venison liver—once a week to assure adequate vitamin A intake, but supplements can do the trick. According to our medical expert, Andrew L. Rubman, ND, typically, the 10,000 international units (IU) of Vitamin A found in certain fish oil supplements will provide an adequate daily intake, if combined with sun exposure.

HOW MUCH VITAMIN D IS ENOUGH?

Ideally a person will get enough summer sun to meet vitamin D needs throughout the rest of the year simply by spending regular active time outdoors. Of course, in our decreasingly active society that spends an increasing amount of time in front of the computer or television, this is not the case for many. And, in reality, it is virtually impossible for most people to get enough vitamin D naturally.

Getting adequate levels of vitamin D is a particularly complex issue. The only food source with significant levels of vitamin D is the fat of fatty cold water fish, and there is considerable disagreement among health professionals about how much vitamin D is safe—whether from supplements, food, the sun or in combination.

The Dietary Reference Intakes (DRI) for vitamin D is 200 IU for people under age 50…400 IU for ages 51 to 70…and 600 IU for those over age 70. According to Sullivan's review of the literature, a number of medical professionals are now advocating a routine daily intake of 1,000 IUs of vitamin D for everyone except infants.

If supplementation is appropriate, there are several considerations…

•**How much is right?** The highest safe amount (upper limit of safety, or UL, from the DRI group) is currently considered to be 2,000 IU a day.

Caution: Sullivan firmly disagrees with the higher figure for most people. Vitamin D stores in fat and builds up over time. An initial high dose may be quite safe for many months, even a year or longer, but then rapidly increases blood levels of vitamin D to levels that may contribute to deposition of calcium in soft tissues, bone loss or heart disease. These changes may take place even when blood levels of calcium remain within normal range.

Best: Sullivan believes a safer dose would be between 800 and 1,200 IU daily.

•**Regular testing.** Tracking levels of 25(OH)D (25-hydroxy vitamin D) should occur on a regular basis over a long period of time. The safest bet is to work with a trained, licensed healthcare professional willing to monitor vitamin D and only supplement vitamin D under his/her watchful eye. The challenge is that vitamin D levels move up and down slowly, over time, and it takes having vitamin D levels tested every three or four months for a clear pattern to eventually emerge and give you information about whether your sun exposure or supplementation is producing the vitamin D level you need.

Note: Insurance may cover the cost of the first test, but will probably not cover subsequent tests.

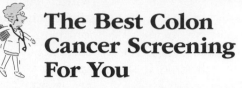

The Best Colon Cancer Screening For You

Thomas F. Imperiale, MD, professor, department of medicine, Indiana University School of Medicine, and research scientist, Regenstrief Institute, both in Indianapolis.

It's a simple truth. When it comes to any type of cancer, early detection can save lives.

Although colon cancer screening rates are on the rise, some sources estimate that nearly 41 million Americans age 50 (when screenings should generally start) and older have not been screened appropriately. That's a shame, because not only is colon cancer the third leading cause of cancer death in the US, it's also very easy to screen for and highly treatable.

Important: The disease is curable more than 90% of the time if caught in its early stages. About one in fifteen people develop colon cancer—a statistic which could drop dramatically if only more people would get screened.

NO PLEASANT OPTION

The problem is, of course, that screenings for colon cancer aren't exactly pleasant. Noninvasive screenings, such as the fecal occult blood test (FOBT), the immunochemical fecal occult blood test (I-FOBT, also called FIT) and the stool DNA test require that you collect a feces sample of varying sizes depending on the test. With the invasive screenings (either colonoscopy, which examines the entire colon, or sigmoidoscopy, to examine the last segment of the large intestine), a flexible tube containing a light, a small camera-like device and a means to remove lesions is inserted in your rectum so the doctor can visually examine the tissues of the colon and take biopsies or remove any precancerous polyps. Typically, these procedures require unpleasant preparation, including a restricted diet and laxatives, in addition to sedation during the procedure (for colonoscopy).

A relatively new option—"virtual colonoscopy"—is noninvasive, but still requires the unpleasant cleansing preparation. Plus, reports vary on the efficacy of the test itself, not to mention that if there are any findings at all, you will need to undergo a colonoscopy anyway. And finally, another option—the double contrast barium enema—enables visual examination of the entire colon with a series of x-ray images. This, too, requires an enema beforehand, and the test could potentially miss smaller polyps.

WHICH IS "BEST"?

The colonoscopy remains the gold standard. According to Thomas F. Imperiale, MD, professor of medicine at the Indiana University School of Medicine in Indianapolis, of the available noninvasive tests, the I-FOBT is likely the best option for most people who are not considered at high risk for colon cancer. This is because of its specificity (the test measures antibodies to human blood in the stool, not the presence of blood itself, so it isn't thrown off by red meat or tricky foods), as well as its simplicity.

As many as 25% of colon cancers are thought to have a genetic basis, so genetic counseling (available at most major cancer centers) might be an option to consider if you have a family history of the disease. People with a higher than average risk of colon cancer should begin screening earlier than age 50 (discuss this with your doctor) or have more frequent screenings. *Here is a list of factors that put you at higher risk for colon cancer...*

•**Personal history of colorectal cancer or adenomatous polyps** (which means you have had a colonoscopy at least once before).

•**Personal history of chronic inflammatory bowel disease.**

•**Strong family history of colorectal cancer or polyps** (first-degree relative, which probably means a parent, sibling or child younger than age 60, or in two first-degree relatives at any age).

•**A known family history of hereditary colorectal cancer syndromes.**

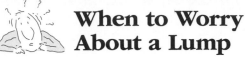

When to Worry About a Lump

Ellen Warner, MD, MSc, medical oncologist, Toronto Sunnybrook Regional Cancer Centre, Canada.

C hildhood is full of lumps and bumps as kids jump, climb, leap—and, yes, fall. But as people grow up and slow down, lumps and bumps become more unusual so any appearance of one can be cause for alarm. Why that peculiar lump on my arm? Why do the glands in my throat seem bigger today? What's the bump on the back of my neck? In truth, lumps and bumps are almost never anything to worry about. But that said, some are definite cause for concern and should prompt a call to the doctor because certain lumps and bumps might signal one of several types of cancer. How do you know what's what? When to worry and when to ignore it and wait for it to go away?

LYMPH NODES ARE KEY

Ellen Warner, MD, who is a medical oncologist at the Toronto Sunnybrook Regional Cancer Centre in Canada, says the type of lump, bump or swelling that is the most common cause for concern has to do with lymph nodes. These nodes exist throughout the body and in numerous locations—the head and neck, under the arms, in the chest and abdomen, in the groin area and in the legs.

They also appear in approximately the same place on either side of the body. Lymph nodes are part of the body's immune system and swell in response to any type of infection and inflammation as part of their role in helping to fight it off or resolve it.

However, if a node swells and stays swollen on just one side or in several lymph nodes, and if there is seemingly no reason, such as a sore throat or other recent illness, Dr. Warner cautions that it must be checked out. Cancer of the lymph nodes (as opposed to cancer that metastasizes to nodes from another location) can be one of two types—Hodgkin's or non-Hodgkin's lymphoma. Dr. Warner explains that the difference between the two mostly has to do with cellular structure that shows up under the microscope.

They also have different survival rates. Hodgkin's is the more curable of the two with an 85% survival rate while the non-Hodgkin's rate is 60% after five years. However, both types are rare, especially Hodgkin's. Annually, an estimated 8,220 Americans are diagnosed with Hodgkin's lymphoma as opposed to more than 66,000 cases of non-Hodgkin's lymphoma diagnosed. Hodgkin's tends to be more common between ages 15 and 34 and at age 60 and over, though non-Hodgkin's is more common in older adults, 50 plus, and people who have compromised immune systems.

What to watch for: A considerable (not slight) swelling in a lymph node that may or may not be tender or possibly painful on one side, or in several lymph nodes, especially in the neck, and less commonly in the armpits or groin, when there has been no recent illness. Usually the swelling is under the chin, along the side of the neck. While there is no way to detect internal swelling of lymph nodes, there are symptoms such as itching, fatigue, coughing, fever, night sweats, weight loss and chest or abdominal pain, says Dr. Warner.

CANCEROUS BUMPS

Another frightening but even less common cause of dangerous lumps and bumps is cancer of connective tissue, a form of sarcoma called soft-tissue sarcoma. Fortunately, this type of cancer is extremely rare, accounting for less than 1% of malignancies diagnosed in this country each year. However, it can appear in numerous places in the body and is subclassified according to which soft tissue it develops. Do not confuse soft tissue sarcoma with fatty nodules called lipomas, which are benign. These are extremely common, usually appearing just under the skin in the arms, legs and trunk of the body.

Dr. Warner says lipomas are generally round and smooth with what she calls a roly-poly feel to them...they grow slowly and can become quite large, even several inches in diameter, and they are not malignant. Soft tissue sarcomas, on the other hand are almost always malignant and the tumor can grow quickly, most often appear-

ing on the limb. But, it can show up on the abdomen or in other parts of the body as well, including the head, neck and trunk.

What to watch for: A sudden swelling that may or may not be tender or painful, beneath the surface of the skin, usually over a fairly large and diffuse area and a lump that does not have distinct borders. Do not hesitate to see a doctor immediately since the survival rate for soft tissue sarcoma that is diagnosed while the tumor is still small and shallow is over 80%.

CANCER PATIENTS PAY ATTENTION

Finally, Dr. Warner says that anyone who already has cancer should be alert for any lump or bump that appears elsewhere on the body seemingly unrelated to the primary site. As is true with any mysterious lump or bump—one that cannot be explained for ordinary, everyday reasons such as a recent infection or fall—go to the doctor and insist on getting it checked, especially if it seems to grow quickly or change character, or becomes itchy.

No need to panic. Just be aware of your body and its changes. Careful observation can make a big difference in the long run.

Soothing the Side Effects of Chemotherapy

Matthew D. Bauer, LAc, has practiced acupuncture for more than 20 years. He is a regular contributing columnist to *Acupuncture Today*, and formerly served on the executive committee of the California Acupuncture Association. His practice is in La Verne, California.

Nausea and vomiting are two of the most dreaded side effects of chemotherapy. Considering that the cure can sometimes feel worse than the cancer it is meant to treat, some patients even elect to discontinue treatment. Although recent advances in antinausea and antivomiting medications have helped many cancer patients, the search for additional and more natural methods of relief for these hard-to-tolerate side effects continues. One recently studied method is acupuncture.

STUDY PINPOINTS WHAT WORKS

Can acupuncture reduce chemotherapy-induced nausea and vomiting? The Chinese healing method has been successfully used to treat a wide variety of ailments, including temporomandibular joint disorder (TMJ), drug addictions, alcoholism, allergies and back pain. It works by stimulating prescribed anatomical sites on the body.

In a review of 11 studies of acupuncture and its effects on chemotherapy-induced nausea or vomiting, the Cochrane Collaboration, an international organization that evaluates medical research, found a mixed bag of results, depending upon which acupuncture method was used and for which side effect.

A REVIEW OF THE FINDINGS

Electro-acupuncture (in which a small electrical current is passed through the needle) was effective in reducing vomiting during the first 24 hours after chemotherapy.

Traditional manual acupuncture using needles was not shown to be significantly effective for acute vomiting or nausea severity (within 24 hours of treatment).

Based on similar principles, but using (highly trained) fingertip pressure on acupuncture points, "acupressure" was looked at as well. This method showed no benefit for vomiting, but did reduce acute nausea—although it was ineffective for delayed nausea (after 24 hours of treatment).

It is unclear why electro-acupuncture reduced acute vomiting while needles-only acupuncture did not, or why one method was successful with nausea while another was successful for vomiting. Of note is that all participants in all the trials reviewed were taking antivomiting drugs, so additional research is needed to determine whether acupuncture alone is effective, or whether it should be considered an effective adjunct to medications.

EXPERT OPINION

Surprised by these findings, we asked acupuncturist Matthew D. Bauer, LAc, a former member of the Board of Directors for the California Acupuncture Association and a practicing acupuncturist in La Verne, California, with more than 20 years experience, about these findings. In his view, it's hard to standardize this sort of study enough to make the findings meaningful. "So much depends on the practitioner's skill in placing needles at just the right angle in just the right place," he said. "In looking at this many trials, you're obviously dealing with many practitioners at varying levels of skill and experience, which, of course affects outcomes."

Acupuncture, he says, can be helpful in many ways for people undergoing treatment for cancer. It's worth a try since there's little risk and much potential benefit. It's important to work with a seasoned practitioner who has experience with oncology patients. And, of course, all cancer patients should check with their doctors before adding acupuncture or any other treatment to their cancer protocols.

Index

Beets, liver function and, 23
Behavioral exposure therapy, 292
Belladonna, 5
Benign paroxysmal positional vertigo (BPPV), 119–20
Beta-carotene, risks associated with, 130–31, 132
Betaglucans, 109
Bifidobacteria, 285
Bifidobacterium bifidus, 227
Bioflavonoids, 72, 243
Bisphosphonates, side effects of, 170
Bitter orange, safety concerns, 138
Black cohosh, hormone regulation by, 115
Bladder, shy, 291–92
Bladder cancer, dogs' smelling of, 211
Blisters, banishing, 268
Blood clots
   natto for prevention of, 30–31
   tomato juice for prevention of, 37
Blood irradiation, 325–26
Blood pressure. *See also* Hypertension
   Alzheimer's disease and, 208
   pet effects on, 210
   proper measurement of, 297
Bone health. *See also* Osteoporosis
   fluoride-related problems, 201
   fruits and vegetables for, 21–22
   green tea for, 33
Botox for stroke patients, 310
Botulism, infant, 34
Brain
   exercise and, 35, 65–66
   new ways to fuel, 34–35
Brain-cooling therapy, 309
Bread, kidney cancer and, 327–28
Breakfast, importance of, 42, 69
Breast calcification, 73
Breast cancer
   broccoli vs., 20, 21
   exercise and risk reduction, 62
   green tea protection, 33
   L2G7 for, 324, 325
   soy and, 31
   vitamin D deficiency and, 328
Breathing exercises
   for asthma, 89–90, 242
   for back pain relief, 126
Broccoli, cancer-fighting properties, 20–21
Bromelain, wound healing and, 181
Bruises, arnica for, 15, 72
Buckwheat, 51
Burns, cantharis for, 15
Buteyko Breathing Method, 89–90
Byetta, pros and cons of, 313–14

C

Cabbage juice, for stomach ulcers, 23
Caffeine
   diuretic properties disputed, 200
   pros and cons of, 59–60
Calcification, how to fight, 73–74
Calcitriol, 43
Calcium
   age and, 128, 129
   caffeine and, 59–60
   colon cancer risk reduced with, 289

interactions with drugs, 154–55
   recommended dosage, 170
   weight loss and, 43–44
Calendula
   for poison ivy, 271
   for sunburn, 261
Cancer, 323–33. *See also* Bladder cancer;
   Breast cancer; Colon cancer; Cutaneous
   T-cell lymphoma; Hodgkin's lymphoma;
   Kidney cancer; Lung cancer; Non-
   Hodgkin's lymphoma; Oral cancer;
   Prostate cancer; Skin cancer
   air fresheners as cause of, 187–88
   aromatherapy in treatment of, 8–10
   Avemar for, 323–24
   broccoli vs., 20–21
   dogs' smelling of, 211–12
   fruits and vegetables for fighting,
      19–20, 326–27, 328
   green tea protection, 33
   indoor lifestyle linked to risk, 328–30
   inflammation and, 223
   L2G7 for, 324–25
   photoluminescence therapy for, 325–26
   soothing chemotherapy side effects,
      332–33
   vitamins and, 131–32
   worrisome lumps, 331–32
CankerMelts, 13–14
Canker sores, 13–14
Cantharis, for burns, 15
Carb-conscious diet, 48–49
Carbohydrates. *See also*
   Low-carbohydrate diets
   chromium cuts cravings for, 136
   sleep and, 92–93
Carnitine. *See* L-carnitine
Carotid ultrasound, 311
Cataracts
   clearing away naturally, 250–51
   management of, 251–52
Catechin, 32–33
Cavities, green tea for prevention, 33
Celecoxib (Celebrex), risks associated
   with, 167
Cell death, fat and, 318
Cereals, evaluating, 28–29
Chakras, 122–24
Chamomile tea for allergy relief, 6
Chaparral, safety concerns, 138
Chapped lips, soothing, 193–94
Chemotherapy, soothing the side effects
   of, 332–33
Cherry tomatoes for constipation relief, 24
Chocolate, health benefits questioned, 32
Cholesterol. *See also* High-density
   lipoprotein; Low-density lipoprotein;
   Statins
   Alzheimer's disease and, 208
   antioxidants and rise in, 196–97
   diabetes and, 319–20
   glucomannan for reducing, 144
   H. pylori infections and, 301–2
   heart disease and, 296, 297
   lower levels are best, 298–99
   new tests for, 307–8
   ratio of good to bad, 299–300

Chromium
   carb cravings cut by, 136
   diabetes control and, 36, 136, 315
   for energy, 135
Cinnamon, blood sugar managed with, 315
Ciprofloxacin, interactions with calcium,
   154
Clarithromycin for ulcers, 279
Cleaning, correlation with sickness, 205–7
Clinical trials, 150–51
Cocoa
   coughs quieted by, 202–3
   health benefits of, 32
Cod liver oil, 294
Coenzyme Q10
   age and, 129
   for asthma relief, 242
   in diabetes management, 320
   for fibromyalgia relief, 218
   for the heart, 294, 303
Coffee, diabetes risk reduction and,
   316–17. *See also* Caffeine
Colds
   echinacea for, 3–4, 142–43
   green tea for, 33
Cold sores
   oregano for, 111
   tea tree oil for, 112
Coliform bacteria, 194
Colon cancer
   alcohol and increased risk of, 290
   apples vs., 19
   the best screening for, 330–31
   broccoli vs., 21
   calcium for reduced risk, 289
   diabetes and, 320–21
   diet and, 328
   inflammation and, 223
   L2G7 for, 324, 325
   vitamin D deficiency and, 328
Colonoscopy, 157
   new test superior to, 286
   virtual, 286–87, 331
Comfrey, safety concerns, 138–39
Common fennel, growing, 141
Compound Herbal Elixer, 275
Constipation
   cherry tomatoes for relief of, 24
   defined, 283, 284
   four Rs strategy for relief of, 284–86
   glucomannan for relief of, 144
   natural cure for, 283–84
Copper, wound healing and, 72, 180
Cordyceps (*Cordyceps sinensis*), 109
Coronary arteries, calcification of, 73, 74
Corticosteroids, interactions with
   calcium, 155
Coughs/coughing
   cocoa for, 202–3
   during heart attacks, 305–6
Country living, weight gain and, 212
Cranberry juice, *H. pylori* controlled
   with, 280
Craniosacral therapy (CST), 100–102
C-reactive protein (CRP), 41, 223, 294,
   295, 300
Cuprum metallicum for back pain, 126

Curcumin, 27
Curry, for memory, 27
Custom prescriptions, 160–61
Cutaneous T-cell lymphoma,
  photoluminescence therapy for, 325–26
Cuts, tea tree oil for, 112
Cytokines, 223

D

Dairy products, health problems caused
  by, 45–46
Damiana, danger of, 115
Dandruff
  selenium for, 271–72
  tea tree oil for, 112
Decongestant snack (recipe), 6
Deep breathing for back pain relief, 126
Deep vein thrombosis (DVT), 37, 228–29
Deglycerized licorice (DGL), 277
Dehydration, preventing, 69–70
Depression
  St. John's wort for, 7–8, 155
  SAMe for, 85–86
  seasonal, 83–85
Dermatologists, ideas on skin care,
  265–66
Detox diets, 91
DHA. *See* Docosahexaenoic acid
DHT, defense against, 273
Diabetes
  ABCs of prevention, 36
  blisters and, 268
  Byetta for, 313–14
  cholesterol care and, 319–20
  chromium and, 36, 136, 315
  coffee and reduced risk of, 316–17
  colon cancer and, 320–21
  dangers of, 35–36
  drug interactions and, 155
  full-body management for, 318–19
  glutathione peroxidase and, 315–16
  keeping it at bay, 314–15
  magnesium for risk reduction, 36–37
  persistent organic pollutants and, 321–22
Diastolic heart failure, 295
Diet(s). *See also* Food(s); Nutrition;
  Weight loss
  adrenal fatigue and, 221–22
  for allergy control, 245–46
  calorie-restricted for longevity, 41
  for cancer protection, 328
  conquering illness with, 45–46
  eczema relief and, 267–68
  fatigue and, 215
  for heart health, 294, 297, 302
  Mediterranean, 38–39
  the only one that works, 40–41
Dietary supplements
  for adrenal fatigue relief, 222
  age and, 127–29
  for allergy relief, 244–45
  for asthma relief, 241–42
  cataract prevention and, 251
  fatigue diminished by, 215
  for fibromyalgia relief, 218
  for heart health, 294, 302–3
  interactions with drugs, 154–55

for mood elevation, 7
  unsafe, 137–38
Diet drinks, obesity and, 58–59
Diffusion weighted imaging (DWI), 308–9
Digestion
  green tea for, 33
  whole grains and, 50
Digestive system, maintaining healthy,
  274–92
Dilantin (phenytoin), 147, 148
Diverticulitis, 287–89
Dizziness, steps to stop, 119–20
Docosahexaenoic acid (DHA), 10, 128,
  224, 241, 303
Doctors
  age as criteria for selecting, 184–86
  drug advertising to, 153
  drug company solicitation of, 152,
    173–74
Dogs, cancer smelled by, 211–12
Dong quai, 115
Drug(s), 147–67. *See also* Generic drugs;
  Over-the-counter drugs; Prescription
  drugs
  advertising of, 152–54
  clinical trials, 150–51
  cost of brand-name, 147–48
  dangers of painkillers, 166–67
  epidemic of overmedication, 158–60
  false bargains, 149–50
  interactions with foods and
    supplements, 154–55
  interactions with other medications,
    155–56, 165–66
  for osteoporosis, overuse of, 169–71
Drug companies
  doctors solicited by, 152, 173–74
  link between insurance companies
    and, 151–52
Drugstore medical clinics, 177–79
Dry eyes, best ways to heal, 254–55

E

Eastern medicine, 122–24
Echinacea
  for colds, 3–4, 142–43
  for flu symptom relief, 4
  for hospital patients, 182
Eczema, stopping the itch of, 266–68
EF1A-1, 318
Eicosapentaenoic acid (EPA), 10, 128,
  241, 303
Electro-acupuncture, 333
Eleuthero (*Eleutherococcus senticosus*), 8
Emergency room care, 175–76
Energy boosters
  aromatherapy, 118
  chromium, 135
Enhanced external counterpulsation
  (EECP), 304–5
Enoki (*Flammulina velutipes*), 110
EPA. *See* Eicosapentaenoic acid
Epicatechin, 32
Epigallocatechin gallate (EGCG), 32
Epinephrine, sulfites in, 248
Epley maneuver, 119–20
Epsom salts

for back pain relief, 126
  uses for, 113
Erectile dysfunction, ginkgo for, 115
Erythromycin, interactions with other
  drugs, 165–66
Escherichia coli
  in airplane water, 194
  on foreign fruits, 26
  urinary tract infections and, 12
Eucalyptus oil
  in aromatherapy for cancer patients, 9
  for winter discomfort, 15–16
Exercise
  adrenal fatigue and, 222
  arthritis pain reduced by, 234–35
  for back pain relief, 238–39
  benefits of, 62–63
  benefits of moderate, 41
  for bone health, 170
  for brain function, 35, 65–66
  fatigue diminished by, 215
  for fibromyalgia relief, 218
  for heart health, 294, 295–97
  for inflammation control, 224
  for neck pain relief, 93–94
  weight loss and, 42, 43, 45
  for winter blues, 82, 83
Exercise ball, sitting on, 65
Eyebright (*Euphrasia officinalis*) for
  allergy relief, 6, 243
Eyesight, foods for better, 253

F

Facial mask, Epsom salts in, 113
Facial yoga, 103–5
Factor V Leiden mutation, 228
Fasting, for body and soul, 90–91
Fat(s). *See also* Low-fat diets
  cell death and, 318
  friendly, 51–52
  for health, 31
  for the heart, 297
Fatigue
  adrenal, 220–22
  sinusitis linked with, 219–20
  ten ways to fight, 214–15
Fennel, common, 141
Fenofibrate (Tricor), 307
Fever, managing, 5
Fiber, 25, 284, 285–86, 288–89
Fibromyalgia
  mystery of, 216–17
  natural relief for, 217–19
  sinusitis linked with, 219–20
First aid, homeopathic, 14–15
Fish oil. *See also* Omega-3 fatty acids
  choosing a supplement, 10–11
  for diabetes management, 320
  for fibromyalgia relief, 218
  for inflammation control, 224
  post-heart attack administration, 10–11
Flavonoids, 180
Flavonols, 32
Flu
  gelsemium for, 5, 15
  natural virus killers for, 4–5
Fluoride, pros and cons of, 200–202

Vinegar
  health-promoting properties of, 24
  for sunburn, 262
Vioxx (rofecoxib), risks associated with,
  166, 167, 172
Virtual colonoscopy, 286–87, 331
Vita Biotic, 245
Vitamin(s)
  Alzheimer's disease risk reduction,
    134–35
  heart disease and, 131–32
Vitamin A
  for flu symptom relief, 4–5
  vitamin D balance with, 330
  wound healing and, 180
Vitamin B (complex). See B-complex
  vitamins
Vitamin B-3. See Niacin
Vitamin B-6, properties and uses of, 130
Vitamin B-12, properties and uses of,
  130
Vitamin C
  age and, 127
  for allergy relief, 6, 241, 243
  Alzheimer's disease risk reduction,
    134–35
  arthritis risk reduction, 22
  for asthma relief, 241
  in bananas, 24
  cataract prevention and, 251
  deficiency in low-carb diets, 133–34
  for flu symptom relief, 4
  H. pylori infections and, 280
  heart disease and, 132
  for hospital patients, 182
  importance of, 132–33
  recommended dosage, 133
  wound healing and, 72, 180

Vitamin D, 188
  age and, 129
  best sources of, 137
  cancer risk linked to deficiency,
    328–30
  recommended dosage, 170
  sunscreen blockage of, 264–65
Vitamin E
  age and, 128
  Alzheimer's disease risk reduction,
    134–35
  cataract prevention and, 251
  cholesterol level raised by, 196–97
  heart disease and, 132
  in nuts, 27
  wound healing and, 180
Vitamin K, 74
Volunteering, health benefits of, 87–88

W

Walking
  for back pain relief, 126
  with a buddy, 54
  10,000 Steps Program, 212
Warts, removing, 269–70
Water
  on airplanes, avoiding, 194
  calorie burning rate and, 69
  eight-glass rule disputed, 199–200
Water retention, horseradish for, 23
Weight gain, country living and, 212
Weight loss. See also Diet(s); Obesity
  aromatherapy for, 117
  diabetes and, 318–19
  milk for, 43–44
  osteoarthritis relieved by, 236–37
  quick fixes for, 44–45

secrets to lasting, 42–43
  sleep and, 45, 67, 68–69
Wheat
  alternatives to, 50–51
  health problems caused by, 45, 46
Whole grains
  benefits of, 49–50
  non-wheat, 50–51
Winter blues/doldrums
  beating, 82–83
  causes and treatments, 83–84
Worry, avoiding, 80–81
Wound healing
  honey for, 16–17
  from the inside out, 71–72
  oregano for, 111–12
  post-surgery, 180–81

X

Xanthine oxidase (XO), 205
Xenical, 44

Y

Yoga
  facial, 103–5
  Pilates compared with, 64
  for stress reduction, 78
Yohimbe, safety concerns, 138

Z

Zeaxanthin, 327
Zinc
  non-Hodgkin's lymphoma and, 327
  wound healing and, 72, 180
Zocor. See Simvastatin